PSYCHOLOGY FOR LAWYERS

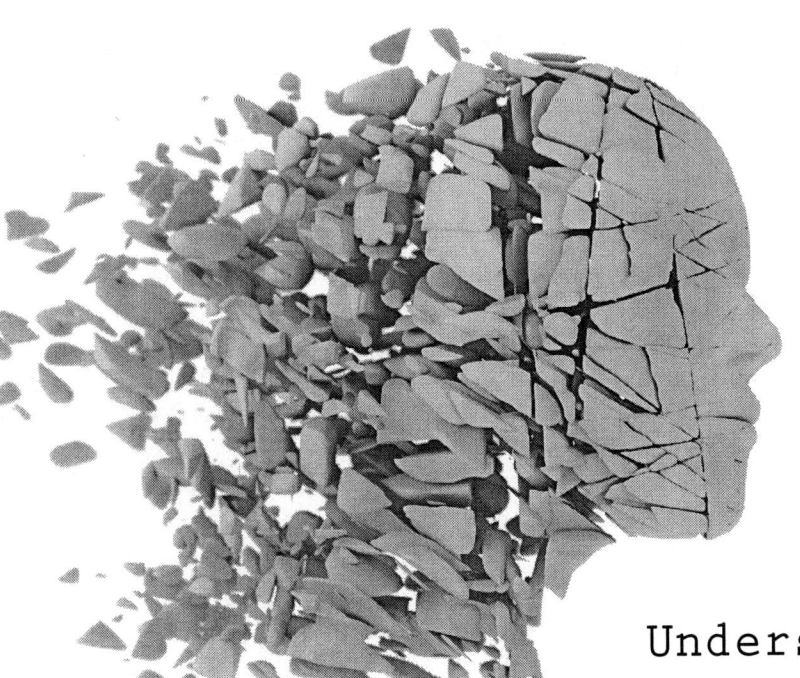

Understanding the Human Factors in Negotiation, Litigation, and Decision Making

JENNIFER K. ROBBENNOLT | JEAN R. STERNLIGHT

Cover design Andrea Siegert/ABA Publishing.

The materials contained herein represent the opinions and views of the authors and/or the editors, and should not be construed to be the views or opinions of the law firms or companies with whom such persons are in partnership with, associated with, or employed by ABA Publishing or the Dispute Resolution Section, unless adopted pursuant to the bylaws of the Association.

Nothing contained in this book is to be considered as the rendering of legal advice, either generally or in connection with any specific issue or case. Readers are responsible for obtaining advice from their own lawyers or other professionals. This book and any forms and agreements herein are intended for educational and informational purposes only.

© 2012 American Bar Association. All rights reserved.

No part of this publication may be reproduced, stored in a retrieval system, or transmitted in any form or by any means, electronic, mechanical, photocopying, recording, or otherwise, without the prior written permission of the publisher. For permission, contact the ABA Copyrights and Contracts Department at copyright@americanbar.org or via fax at 312-988-6030, or complete the online form at http://www.americanbar.org/utility/reprint.html.

Printed in the United States of America.

16 15 14 13   5 4 3 2

Library of Congress Cataloging-in-Publication Data

Psychology for lawyers / by Jennifer K. Robbennolt and Jean R. Sternlight.—1st ed.
  p. cm.
 Includes bibliographical references and index.
 ISBN 978-1-61438-354-3 (print : alk. paper)
1. Law—Psychological aspects. 2. Practice of law—United States. 3. Lawyers—United States. 4. Trial practice—United States. I. Robbennolt, Jennifer K. II. Sternlight, Jean R.
 K346.P799 2012
   150.2'434—dc23

                                                                2012022739

Discounts are available for books ordered in bulk. Special consideration is given to state bars, CLE programs, and other bar-related organizations. Inquire at Book Publishing, ABA Publishing, American Bar Association, 321 North Clark Street, Chicago, Illinois 60654-7598.

www.ShopABA.org

Dedication

We dedicate this book to our partners and our children. Their love and support helped us complete this immensely challenging and rewarding project. Interacting with them also provided us with many opportunities to explore the insights of psychology. Thank you to: Grant, Sylvia, Dale, Jake, Samuel, and Benjamin.

—J.K.R. & J.R.S.

Contents

Acknowledgments xiii
About the Authors xv

Introduction   1

Chapter 1
Perceiving and Understanding the World   7

The Limits of Attention 8
Observation and Interpretation 11
    Priming and Concept Accessibility 11
    Schemas, Scripts, and Stereotypes 12
    Confirmation Bias and Biased Assimilation 14
Causal Attribution and Judgments of Responsibility 17
Naïve Realism, False Consensus, and the Illusion
    of Asymmetric Insight 21
Perspective Taking 25
For Further Reading: Perception and Construal 27

Chapter 2
Memory   29

The Workings of Memory 30
Misperceptions of Memory 38
Elicitation of Memories 39
Accurate Versus Inaccurate Memories 42
For Further Reading: Memory 43

Chapter 3
Emotion 45

Perceiving and Understanding Emotions 48
    General Effects of Mood 50
    Emotions and Appraisal 52
Managing Emotions 57
Using Emotions 61
    Emotions as a Source of Information 62
    Emotions as a Source of Motivation 62
    Emotions as a Facilitator of Thought 62
    Display of Emotions 63
For Further Reading: Emotion 66

Chapter 4
Judgment Shortcuts 67

Positive Illusions 68
Anchoring 71
Availability and Representativeness 72
    Availability 72
    Representativeness 73
Affect Heuristic 75
Hindsight Bias 75
Debiasing 77
For Further Reading: Judgment Shortcuts 83

Chapter 5
Decision Making 85

Decision-Making Strategies 85
Information Gathering 87
Evaluation of Options 88
    Framing 88
    Contrast and Compromise 92
    Inaction Inertia 94
    Choice and Time 95
    Reactive Devaluation 96
Emotions and Decision Making 97
    Affective Forecasting 97
    Decision Regret 99
Not Deciding 100

Structuring Decision Making................................102
    Reason Giving..103
    Preferred Decision-Making Approaches...................104
    Selection Versus Rejection.............................105
    Joint Versus Separate Evaluation.......................106
    Deadlines..108
Group Decision Making......................................108
Implementation of Decisions................................111
For Further Reading: Decision Making.......................112

Chapter 6
Persuasion and Social Influence   115

Two Paths to Persuasion....................................116
    Source Credibility.....................................118
    Message Characteristics................................120
Influence Tactics..126
    The Psychology We've Already Discussed.................126
    Reciprocity..127
    Scarcity...129
    Consistency and Commitment.............................129
    Liking...130
    Social Proof...131
    Obedience to Authority.................................134
    Channel Factors and Tension Systems....................136
Resistance...138
For Further Reading: Persuasion and Influence..............140

Chapter 7
Interpersonal Communication   141

The Complexities of Human Communication....................142
    Perspective Taking in Communication....................143
    Conversational Norms...................................144
    Nonverbal Communication................................145
    Communication Mediums..................................148
    Culture and Communication..............................151
    Lying..153
Development of Effective Communication.....................157
    Building Trust...158
    Establishing Rapport...................................159
    Listening..161

Avoiding Talking Like a Lawyer 163
   Facilitating Disclosure 165
   Conveying Information 166
For Further Reading: Communication 169

Chapter 8
Justice   171

Distributive Justice 172
Procedural Justice 176
Reestablishment of Justice 180
   Retribution 181
   Restoration of Justice 182
For Further Reading: Justice 184

Chapter 9
Interviewing Clients and Witnesses   187

Preparing for the Client Interview 188
   Gathering Pre-Interview Information 188
   Setting the Stage 189
Conducting the Interview 190
   Establishing a Good Relationship with the Interviewee 190
   Recognizing Differences 191
   Questioning and Listening 193
   Addressing Emotions 194
   Questioning 198
   Confirming Accuracy 207
Remembering the Interview 209
For Further Reading: Interviewing 210

Chapter 10
Counseling Clients   211

Broadening the Focus of the Consultation 211
   The Quest for Information 213
   The Quest for Justice 215
   The Quest for Reform 217
   The Quest for Other Nonmonetary Outcomes 219
   The Quest for Litigation 221
Challenging Preconceptions 222

Assessing the Likelihood of Success 224
    Dealing with Positive Illusions 224
    Dealing with Availability and Anchoring 229
    Dealing with Hindsight Bias 231
    Dealing with the Representativeness Heuristic:
        The Gambler's Fallacy 231
Choosing Among Alternatives 232
    The Decision-Making Process 232
    Tendency to Gather Irrelevant Information 233
    Presenting Options 235
    Sunk Costs 238
    Comparison of Options 239
    Decisions for the Future 241
Dealing with Strong Emotions 244
Using Persuasion Effectively 247
For Further Reading: Client Counseling 251

Chapter 11
Negotiating and Mediating   253

A Psychologically Expanded Model of Negotiation 254
Constructing Initial Proposals 256
    Assessing What the Client Wants 256
    Assessing What the Other Side Wants 260
    Devising a Proposal 264
    Presenting Proposals 270
The Dynamics of Negotiation 275
    Building Relationships 275
    Interpreting Counterparts' Behavior 276
    Conveying Information 278
    Presenting Options 280
    Persuading and Eliciting Concessions 281
    Dealing with Emotion 285
Responding to a Counterpart's Proposal 287
    Conveying Offer to Client 287
    Evaluating the Offer 288
Mediation 295
    Psychological Opportunities Offered by Mediation 295
    Psychological Challenges Posed by Mediation 300
    Mediation as a Benefit for Clients 301
For Further Reading: Negotiation and Mediation 305

Chapter 12
Discovery and Due Diligence   307

Deciding What Information to Seek 308
Dealing with Written Requests for Information 310
    Preparing Interrogatories and Document Requests 310
    Responding to Interrogatories and Document Requests 311
Conducting and Defending Depositions 314
    Conducting the Deposition 315
    Preparing the Witness for Deposition 333
    Defending the Deposition 346
    Debriefing the Client 347
    Dealing with Videotaped Depositions 348
Reviewing Information Obtained through Discovery
    and Due Diligence 349
For Further Reading: Discovery and Due Diligence 352

Chapter 13
Writing   353

General Psychological Guidance for Writers 354
    Clarity and Accessibility 354
    Audience Perspective: In the Reader's Shoes 358
Briefs 359
    Credibility 360
    A Good Story 361
    Using Facts 364
    Early Sections of the Brief 367
    Describing Alternatives 368
    Order of Arguments 369
    Word Choice 370
Complaints 371
    Stories and Facts 371
    Word Choice 373
    Credibility 374
Letters 374
    Letters to Clients 374
    Letters to Others 378
Contracts 379
    Framing, Status Quo Bias, and Anchoring 380
    Promotion of Positive Relationships 381
For Further Reading: Writing 383

Chapter 14
Ethics — 385

- Bounded Ethicality 387
  - Ethical Blind Spots 387
  - Slippery Slopes and Boiling Frogs 389
  - Ethical Fading 390
- Ethics in Law Practice 393
  - Ethical Rules and Standards 393
  - The Agency Relationship 395
  - The Challenges of the Adversarial System 400
  - The Tolls of Law Practice 403
  - Lawyers in Groups 404
  - Responses to Others' Ethicality 407
- Inability to Recognize and Learn from Ethical Failures 409
- Solutions 411
  - Be Aware 411
  - Make Ethics Salient 411
  - Be Critical 412
  - Plan Ahead 413
  - Counsel Clients on Ethics 414
- For Further Reading: Ethics 416

Chapter 15
On Being Productive, Successful, and Happy — 417

- Attorney Productivity and Success 417
  - Time Management 417
  - Mistakes 425
  - Explanatory Style: Lawyers and Pessimism 428
  - The Choke: Keeping Cool Under Pressure 430
  - Collaboration 432
- Attorney Happiness and Well-Being 444
  - Lawyer Satisfaction 445
  - Improving Well-Being 447
  - But Not Too Happy 457
- Final Thoughts 459
- For Further Reading: On Being Productive,
  Successful, and Happy 460

Endnotes 461
Index 577

Acknowledgments

We have spent seven years writing this book. During that period we received invaluable assistance from many people and organizations.

The editors and staff at ABA Publishing were extremely helpful and supportive. We particularly thank Rick Paskiet for his patience, encouragement, and good sense.

Our research assistants were fabulous. They demonstrated true grit in tracking down studies and sources and helping us with the many endnotes. At the University of Illinois these included: Jessica Bregant, Bill Pipal, Matt Taksin, and Marcy Zora. At UNLV these included: Stephanie Buntin, David Schell Davis, Kenton Eichacker, Kim DelMonico, Michael Hammer, Jennifer Kopecko, Patrick McDonnell, Amy Ma, Koa Perlac, Felicia Quinlan, Will Thompson, Kathleen Wilde, Hetty Wong, and Jamie Zimmerman.

Our colleagues, both within and without our own institutions were incredibly generous. They helped us tremendously by reading and commenting on drafts and by supplying us with additional materials. We particularly thank Dan Bowling, Linda Edwards, Neal Feigenson, Michael Gutentag, Chris Guthrie, Lynne Henderson, Ellen Kordik, Sylvia Lazos, Ann McGinley, Jenny Pahre, Terry Pollman, Nancy Rapoport, Peter Reilly, Arden Rowell, Keith Rowley, Donna Shestowsky, Jeffrey Stempel, Dennis Stolle, Christina Studebaker, Nina Tarr, Tom Ulen, Ellen Waldman, Nancy Welsh, and Maureen Weston.

Students in the Spring 2011 Psychology and Lawyering class at UNLV provided us with valuable feedback on an early version of the book. Students in the Spring 2011 Professional Responsibility and the Fall 2011 Behavioral Law and Economics classes at the University of Illinois gave us very insightful comments on individual chapters. Thank you to all of you.

The deans, librarians, and support staff at University of Illinois College of Law and University of Nevada Las Vegas Boyd School of Law were generous, helpful, and hardworking. At the University of Illinois we particularly thank Tina Lamb and Nicholas Stark. At UNLV we particularly thank Jennifer Gross, Jeannie Price, and Sandra Rodriguez.

Editor extraordinaire Judy Sternlight provided us insider advice and good counsel throughout this process.

Grant Robbennolt tirelessly offered feedback and excellent editorial suggestions.

About the Authors

Jennifer K. Robbennolt is professor of law and psychology at the University of Illinois. A lawyer and Ph.D. social psychologist, Dr. Robbennolt has won numerous awards for both her teaching and writing and is well known for her integration of psychology into the study of law and legal institutions.

Jean R. Sternlight is the Michael and Sonja Saltman Professor and Director of the Saltman Center for Conflict Resolution at the University of Nevada Las Vegas Boyd School of Law. Prior to entering academia she clerked for a federal district court judge and practiced law for eight years in Philadelphia.

Introduction

> How long we shall continue to blunder along without the aid of unpartisan and authoritative scientific assistance in the administration of justice, no one knows; but all fair persons not conventionalized by provincial legal habits of mind ought, I should think, unite to effect some some such advance.
> —Judge Learned Hand[1]

Most lawyers would benefit greatly from knowing more about psychology, that is, the science of how people think, feel, and behave.[2] After all, the typical lawyer spends much of his time interacting with people: clients, other lawyers, staff, witnesses, mediators, arbitrators, insurers, experts, judges, and jurors.

Lawyers who can harness the insights of psychology will be more effective interviewers and counselors, engage in more successful negotiations, conduct more efficient and useful discovery, more effectively persuade judges and others through their written words, better identify and avoid ethical problems, and even be more productive and happier.

> [W]hat we learn from experience is that men never learn from experience.
> —George Bernard Shaw[3]

Lawyers, however, typically thrive or falter in navigating the psychological aspects of their work using either skills they possessed before law school or skills they acquire on the job. Law school courses do not usually focus on the part of the job that involves understanding human psychology. And while many lawyers pick up some psychology through on-the-job experience and intuitively understand its value, one thing that psychology teaches us is that we tend to overestimate our ability to learn from experience.[4] Thus, even the best lawyers

> We all believe that we are capable of seeing what's in front of us, of accurately remembering important events from our past, of understanding the limits of our knowledge, of properly determining cause and effect. But these intuitive beliefs are often mistaken ones that mask critically important limitations on our cognitive abilities.
> —Christopher Chabris & Daniel Simons[6]

tend to have little systematic grounding in much of the psychological research that could be useful to their work.

Instead of relying on a nuanced understanding of scientific psychology, lawyers, like most people, typically rely on intuition and lay theories of psychology. While some of these lay theories work reasonably well much of the time, we will see that they can also lead lawyers astray.[5] Just as our visual capacities often serve us quite well but fail us when we fall prey to optical illusions, so, too, may our psychological intuitions let us down. Indeed, much of what we will discuss in this book will not be obvious—even to an experienced legal practitioner. And some of the ideas we present will even be counterintuitive.

Given the central importance of human psychology to the practice of law, we believe that all lawyers can benefit from a more complete scientific understanding of human thinking and interaction and from detailed discussion of how to apply those insights in practice. We focus in particular on empirical research, drawn primarily from social and cognitive psychology, that has explored how people think, feel, and behave.

❖ ❖ ❖ ❖ ❖
Psychological Science Versus Trial and Error

How do lawyers come to believe that certain techniques are successful and others are not? How does the acquisition of practice knowledge among lawyers compare with the acquisition of knowledge in comparable fields? How do lawyers come to know—or to think they know—what works and what does not in the practice of law? The two basic sources are advice from others and personal experience based on (forgive the expression) trial and error. If we ask how those from whom the advice is received know, we realize that the first of those categories is nothing more than the second one in disguise. Trial and error is not without value. But it progresses at a glacial pace and sometimes can be deceptive.[7]

In contrast to intuition and trial and error, psychological science capitalizes on the systematic study of human behavior, that is, using empirical methods to test hypotheses about the effects of particular practices and to compare one strategy or technique to another.

Introduction

The first part of the book offers a crash course in those aspects of psychology that we think will be the most useful to practicing attorneys. Thus, we begin in chapter 1 by examining how attention and construal influence our perceptions of the world. Chapter 2 considers the science of memory. Chapter 3 examines a number of ways in which emotions influence thinking and behavior. Chapters 4 and 5 explore the psychology of judgment and decision making, examining the ways in which cognitive heuristics, or rules of thumb, influence judgment and the ways in which people grapple with and make decisions. Chapter 6 studies the psychology of how people persuade and influence each other. Chapter 7 reviews the complexities of verbal and nonverbal communication—including lying—and offers a range of strategies for facilitating good communication. Finally, in chapter 8, we consider research on the psychology of justice.

> The real purpose of [the] scientific method is to make sure Nature hasn't misled you into thinking you know something that you actually don't.
> —Robert Pirsig[8]

Throughout this discussion we recognize that each of us exists within one or more cultural environments that provide us with a set of lenses through which we see the world. These lenses do not dictate or inevitably determine our behavior: there is much overlap in perspective across cultures, much variation within cultures, and many differences in the extent to which individuals identify with a particular culture. But culture does shape our perceptions and intuitive responses, our values and beliefs, our assumptions, our memories, and our typical behaviors and practices.[9] Accordingly, throughout the book we describe the ways in which culture moderates the psychological phenomena we describe, noting the extent to which the ways of thinking we describe are or are not common to people from different cultural backgrounds.

Of course, we cannot hope to cover all aspects of psychology or even all the nuances of the areas that we do review. Rather than attempt comprehensive coverage of the vast field of psychology, we instead concentrate on those aspects of the research that we think will be the most helpful to the everyday practice of law. In addition, we focus less on the psychology of special populations (such as children or people with mental illnesses) in favor of a closer examination of the findings from psychological research about how ordinary adults think, decide, and behave.[10]

The second part of the book applies the insights of the research to tasks that lawyers face on a regular basis. Specifically, we look at how psychology can help lawyers do a better job of interviewing (chapter 9) and counseling their clients (chapter 10). Next, we examine how knowledge of psychology can help lawyers be more effective as negotiators and in mediation (chapter 11); conduct better written and oral discovery and due diligence (chapter 12); and write more effective letters, briefs, and transactional documents (chapter 13). In chapter 14, we examine the insights of psychological research for understanding and preventing ethical lapses. Finally, in chapter 15, we consider the implications of psychology for lawyers' productivity and personal well-being. In making these applications, we recognize that psychology is not the only consideration in every dilemma and that different aspects of psychology will occasionally lead in multiple directions. Nonetheless, we believe that practitioners can draw a great deal of practical guidance from psychology as they carry out the full range of lawyering tasks.

We focus here on the myriad tasks on which lawyers spend most of their time: interviewing and counseling, negotiating, conducting discovery, and writing. The possibility of trial or other adjudicative action lies in the background of much of this work. In that sense, much of what we discuss here is directly relevant to trial practice. Nonetheless, we do not explicitly cover the vast quantities of psychological research on trials and jury decision making both because so few cases actually go to trial and because many books and articles already examine the psychology of how juries make decisions and use psychology to guide lawyers on how to conduct themselves at trial.[11]

A Note on Audience

The primary goal of this book is to expose lawyers and law students to how some of the key insights offered by the field of psychology can improve the practice of law. We expect lawyers will see many ways to apply psychology to help them understand others with whom they work.

We also hope that attorneys and students who read this book will gain insights about themselves. Interestingly, gaining insights about oneself may prove more challenging than gaining insights about others. Introspection can only take us so far in understanding ourselves, our perceptions and judgments, our motives, and our behavior and can lead to predictable misapprehensions. Indeed, the *introspection illusion* refers to a tendency to place undue confidence in the value of introspection for gaining insight into ourselves. In addition, psychological research has found that it is typically easier to recognize some of the psychological phenomena described here in others than in ourselves—evidence of a *bias blind spot*.[12] We tend to think that we are more logical and objective (see chapter 1), less self-interested (see chapter 1), less influenced by intuition (see chapters 4 and 5), less persuadable (see chapter 6), better able to read other's emotions and to communicate (or mask) our own emotions (see chapter 3), and more ethical (see chapter 14) than are others. Thus, we encourage readers to give particular attention to the ways in which the phenomena we explore describe their own psychology.

We also hope that the work reviewed here will be of interest to psychological researchers. Indeed, we hope to inspire psychological researchers to more carefully study the myriad interactions and decisions that take place in the course of legal representation. We have grounded our discussion in a relatively robust set of empirical findings. Where there are studies expressly examining the relevant phenomena in

> ✦ ✦ ✦ ✦ ✦
> ### What Makes a Good Lawyer?
>
> Law professor Marjorie Schultz and psychologist Sheldon Zedek conducted extensive empirical research designed to identify the skills possessed by effective lawyers. It is striking to note the extent to which psychological research can inform each of the skills identified.
>
> Intellect and Cognition
> *Analysis and Reasoning • Creativity/Innovation • Problem Solving • Practical Judgment*
>
> Research and Information Gathering
> *Researching the Law • Fact Finding • Questioning and Interviewing*
>
> Communications
> *Influencing and Advocating • Writing • Speaking • Listening*
>
> Planning and Organizing
> *Strategic Planning • Organizing and Managing Own Work • Organizing and Managing Others (Staff/Colleagues)*
>
> Conflict Resolution
> *Negotiation Skills • Ability to See the World Through the Eyes of Others*
>
> Client and Business Relations: Entrepreneurship
> *Networking and Business Development • Providing Advice and Counsel and Building Relationships with Clients*
>
> Working with Others
> *Developing Relationships Within the Legal Profession • Evaluation, Development, and Mentoring*
>
> Character
> *Passion and Engagement • Diligence • Integrity/Honesty • Stress Management • Community Involvement and Service • Self-Development*[13]

legal settings, we have drawn on such studies directly. In other instances, we describe research that has been conducted in other settings and how it might apply to the practice of law. We hope that our discussion will stimulate researchers in psychology and law to examine these areas in greater depth, exploring the nuances and boundaries of how these phenomena operate in the rich setting of legal practice.

It has been said that "neither LAW nor HUMAN NATURE is an exact science,"[14] and surely many lawyers would agree. Nonetheless, the science of psychology has much to contribute to the art of legal practice and to the craft of working with clients, opposing counsel, staff, witnesses, mediators, judges, and others. While we cannot provide an exact recipe for success, we hope that by highlighting the importance of psychological science and some of the critical insights offered by that field, we provide some useful tools for improving the ways in which lawyers are able to successfully represent their clients.

Perceiving and Understanding the World   1

> We may try to see things as objectively as we please. Nonetheless, we can never see them with any eyes except our own.
> —*Supreme Court Justice Benjamin N. Cardozo*[1]

Some of us tend to think of people as akin to seismographs, constantly and accurately recording sensory information from the world around them as it occurs. However, decades of psychological research reveal that "[t]he perceiver . . . is not simply a dutiful clerk who passively registers information. Rather, the perceiver is an active interpreter, one who resolves ambiguities, makes educated guesses about events that cannot be observed directly, and forms inferences about associations and causal relations."[2] In the process of observing and constructing an understanding of the events and information to which we are exposed, we make assumptions and inferences, fill in gaps, impose patterns, change our perceptions (or not) in response to new information, and otherwise engage in interpretations that may differ from others' experiences of the same events.

These vagaries of perception and interpretation have important implications for the ways in which attorneys grapple with their clients' understandings of what they have experienced. Recognition of this active perception and construal process is useful for understanding the perceptions of witnesses, opposing parties and counsel, judges and jurors, and other actors in the legal system. Similarly, understanding how these processes affect attorneys' own perceptions can help attorneys to tread carefully in seeking to build a picture of their client and the case or transaction at issue.

The Limits of Attention

Imagine being asked to watch two teams of three basketball players pass basketballs and trying to keep track of the passes made by one team. While engaged in this task, would you notice a person in a gorilla costume walk through the game? What if, instead of observing basketball, you were engaged in a conversation with a stranger, for example, someone you had stopped and asked for directions? If your conversation was interrupted—perhaps by two people carrying a door who passed between you and your guide—would you notice that you were talking to a different person when the conversation resumed? You probably think that you would notice such intrusions. However, as implausible as it may seem, when people are put in exactly these situations, nearly half fail to notice the unexpected appearance of the gorilla and more than half fail to notice that their conversation partner has been replaced![3] In another recent study, researchers created a video in which one supermarket shopper walked behind a stack of boxes while another shopper emerged from behind the boxes; the second shopper then shoplifted a bottle of wine. Nearly two-thirds of people viewing the videotape failed to notice that a different person had appeared from behind the boxes, and those who did not notice the change commonly misidentified the first (innocent) shopper as the shoplifter.[4]

These are just a few examples of the limits on people's ability to attend to stimuli. Psychologists call such failures to notice objects or substantial changes in objects *inattentional blindness* and *change blindness,* respectively. Interestingly, just as you may have done, people tend to incorrectly predict that they will be able to detect such changes—in one study, 90% of participants predicted that they would have seen the gorilla[5]—a phenomenon known to psychologists as *inattentional blindness blindness* or *change blindness blindness.*

Once we stop and think about it, perhaps it should not be so surprising that we cannot attend to everything that we encounter. Our senses are constantly bombarded with an amazing array of information: sounds, sights, physical sensations, odors, and tastes. It would be virtually impossible to pay attention—let alone close attention—to all of the stimuli to which we are exposed. Accordingly, we attend to only a fraction of the possible features of the environment at any given moment. Features of both the stimuli themselves (for example, intensity, suddenness, unexpectedness, or movement) and the perceiver (for example, expectations or distractions) can influence what it is that gets noticed. But because "we vividly experience some aspects of our world, particularly those that are the focus of our attention," we mistakenly believe that we "process *all* of the detailed information around us."[7]

> "Looking isn't the same as seeing. You have to focus attention on something in order to become aware of it."
> —Daniel Simons[6]

> ✦ ✦ ✦ ✦ ✦
> ### Inattentional Blindness and the Case of Kenny Conley
>
> Consider how these limits on attention and our failure to recognize them might play out in the real world:
>
>> At 2:00 in the morning on 25 January 1995, Boston police officer Kenny Conley was chasing a shooting suspect who climbed over a chain-link fence. An undercover officer named Michael Cox had arrived on the scene moments earlier, but other officers had mistaken him for a suspect, assaulted him from behind, and brutally beat him. Conley chased the suspect over the fence and apprehended him some time later. In later testimony, Conley said that he ran right past the place where Cox was under attack, but he claimed not to have seen the incident. The investigators, prosecutors, and jurors in the case all assumed that because Conley could have seen the beating, Conley must have seen the beating, and therefore must have been lying to protect his comrades. Conley was convicted of perjury and obstruction of justice and was sentenced to thirty-four months in jail.[8]
>
> To investigate whether it was possible that Conley simply did not notice the beating, researchers asked study participants to jog after a male confederate for four hundred meters "at night in an area lit by streetlamps." To keep the participants' focus on their target, researchers asked the participants to count the number of times the male touched his head, which he did nine times. Part way through the run, participants passed a staged fight in which two men "shouted, grunted, and coughed" while they pretended to beat up a third man. Consistent with the phenomenon of inattentional blindness, only 35% of participants noticed the fight.

Even when we think we are looking carefully, there are limits to what we see. Consider radiologists, who are trained to spot abnormalities in medical scans such as X-rays and MRIs. When reading an image, radiologists "can't take in everything in the image, so they focus their attention on the critical aspects of the image, just as the subjects in the gorilla study focused on counting the passes of one team of players."[9] Because their attentional capacity is limited, there is a tendency to miss features of the scan that are unexpected. Thus, a radiologist looking for a broken bone tends to be less likely to see a tumor. Similarly, the rarer and, therefore, more unexpected, a particular abnormality is, the less likely it is to be detected.[10] In addition,

> **Multitasking: A polite way of telling someone you haven't heard a word they said.**
> —urbandictionary.com[11]

the radiologist is more likely to miss a particular abnormality in a scan when it is accompanied by an additional anomaly than when it is the only anomaly on the scan—a phenomenon known as *satisfaction of search*. The likelihood of detecting the target anomaly is decreased by the presence of a second anomaly even if the two anomalies are from the same category; for example, the presence of one tumor makes it less likely that another tumor will be detected.[12]

These limits on attention also demonstrate how difficult it is to attend to and take in information from multiple sources simultaneously—a problem of divided attention. Indeed, when people attempt to pay attention to multiple things or to engage in multiple tasks at the same time, performance often suffers. This is an important realization for busy attorneys who must constantly manage multiple projects and deal with numerous interruptions.[13] While we might think that we are effective multitaskers, it turns out that multitasking is not efficient.

Try the following exercise: Time how long it takes you to write down two lines of text on a piece of paper. On the first line, write this sentence: "Multitasking is not efficient." On the second line, write the numbers 1 through 26, one for each letter in the sentence on line 1. However, as you write, alternative between the two lines. Thus, after you write the letter *M* on the first line, you should write the number *1* on the second line; after you write the letter *u* on the first line, you should write the number *2* on the second line; and so on. Now, time yourself again. This time, however, simply write the sentence on the first line and then write the series of numbers on the next line.[14]

When we attempt to do more than one task at the same time, our brain has to switch its attention back and forth between the tasks.[15] And it turns out that there are costs to this task switching. Each time we turn our attention from one task to another—say, turning attention away from the motion being drafted to focus on answering the ringing phone or to look at e-mail or text messages—we are required to mentally change gears, calling to mind a new set of facts, relevant goals, decision rules, prior work, and a range of appropriate responses. Similarly, it may be difficult to leave behind the thoughts that were relevant to the prior task. And then when switching back to a prior task, we have to regain our train of thought and may even have to retrace our steps. Such mental reconfiguring takes time. Thus, people tend to process more slowly and to make more errors when switching between tasks than they do when they are able to perform one task at a time.[16]

Interestingly, recent research has shown that people who report that they engage in a high degree of multitasking were actually more easily distracted by irrelevant stimuli and less efficient in switching tasks than people who multitasked less.[17]

Observation and Interpretation

While many things escape our conscious awareness, many other things do capture our attention. It turns out that what we pay attention to and how we understand what we perceive are not determined at random. Rather, preexisting patterns of thinking direct our attention in predictable ways and color our interpretations of those stimuli to which we do attend.

In one famous experiment, students from rival schools watched a football game between the schools' teams. Students' assessments of the rule violations committed by each team and of the overall play were influenced (many would say biased) by which school they attended. Rather than simply recording the violations and the play, observers interpreted the action in accordance with their predispositions.[18] Recent research that seems to reflect the same phenomenon found that NBA referees' foul calls were influenced by the race of the player and the race of the referee. In the case of both African American and Caucasian players, officiating crews called more fouls against opposite-race players.[19]

Priming and Concept Accessibility

What we pay attention to and how we interpret it can be strongly affected by what else is currently on our conscious or unconscious minds. *Priming* occurs when exposure to a stimulus unconsciously influences perceptions or interpretations of a subsequent person or event. Because ideas that have been recently or repeatedly activated tend to be more accessible in our minds, such primed concepts can influence how we perceive new information.

Thus, people tend to judge their life satisfaction differently depending on whether they have just been thinking about some specific aspect of their lives such as their marriage or their job. Jurors primed with the concept of the presumption of innocence might be more likely to assert that they could ignore damaging pretrial publicity. News reports or campaign ads can prime people to think about particular issues such as crime, financial instability, or acts of heroism. Training in the law might prime lawyers to focus on issues of rights and responsibilities. And priming different character traits can influence interpretations of others' behavior; for example, a person's judgment about another's negotiation behavior might be influenced by whether notions of deception or trust are foremost in the observer's mind.[20]

In similar ways, priming can even influence behavior. Thus, for example, people who have been primed with competitive concepts subsequently behave more competitively. Those who have been primed to think about university professors perform better in trivia games. Those who are primed with concepts related to being elderly tend to walk more slowly. And priming the concept of money leads people to behave less prosocially, to prefer to work alone, and to be less likely to ask for help on a difficult assignment.[21]

Schemas, Scripts, and Stereotypes

Our construal of events and situations is also guided by basic knowledge structures known as *schemas*. Schemas define our expectations about how the world operates, fill in gaps in information, and facilitate an ability to "make inferences and judgments with heightened ease, speed, and subjective confidence."[22] Thus, people have a schema for "baby" or for "lawyer" that provides them with certain expectations and assumptions. For example, when a client walks into a lawyer's office, he will have a set of preconceptions regarding how someone in the role of a lawyer should look and behave. Such schemas serve us well most of the time, allowing us to process vast amounts of information quickly. However, because schemas may not always accurately represent the state of the world in a particular instance, our schemas can sometimes lead us astray.

The fact that we rely on our schemas may have particular importance for lawyers, whose training and experience might lead them to pigeonhole clients and cases into readily accessible categories. For example, lawyers have schemas for concepts such as "real estate deal" or "divorce" that shape their perceptions of such cases.

> The chief danger that confronts a professional, in law or in any other field, is that he will tend to fill the gap with related informational material from other similar situations in his experience. Or, he may leap ahead and begin to anticipate information that may or may not actually be involved in the situation that now confronts him.[23]

While lawyers' expertise facilitates the rapid integration of large amounts of information about the facts of their clients' cases and the relevant law, such expertise may also lead to incorrect assumptions and even erroneous memory for some distinct details.[24]

Scripts are schemas for events. Scripts structure our understanding of the typical course of an episode. For example, if we hear that Bob went into a restaurant and ate dinner, we might infer that Bob both placed an order for his meal and paid the check at the end, even though these details were not explicitly recounted. If Chris and Mark are in a car accident, they might automatically exchange insurance information because that is part of their "car accident script." A party in a negotiation may expect that a concession offered by one party will be followed by a concession from the other party because they hold a "negotiation script" that characterizes the negotiation dance in this way.[25]

Stereotypes are schemas that categorize people. Stereotypes consist of beliefs—favorable or unfavorable—about the characteristics of members of particular groups. People may hold stereotypes based on a person's race or ethnicity, gender, age, sexual orientation, weight, attractiveness, dress, athleticism, whether or not they smoke or drink, or other characteristics.[26]

Check Your Biases

To explore your own implicit stereotypes, go to http://implicit.harvard.edu/implicit/demo/.

Most of us don't like to think of ourselves as making decisions grounded in stereotypes. Yet, research has shown that we all operate on the basis of stereotypes. To some extent, reliance on stereotypes is not necessarily bad. As with other schemas, stereotypes can facilitate the rapid categorization of people and allow us to preserve our mental resources for other tasks. Thus, while it is not true that all smokers get lung cancer, it is true that smokers are at higher risk of lung cancer than nonsmokers. Of course, some stereotypes may have no basis in fact, such as the idea that members of a certain race or ethnicity are less intelligent than members of another race or ethnicity. Moreover, even those stereotypes that have a basis in truth are not true in every case. For example, men are bigger and stronger than women in general, but there are plenty of women who are bigger and stronger than many men.

Social psychologists have shown that schemas and scripts can influence how we perceive and interpret information and that those interpretations, in turn, affect a range of understandings and behaviors.[27] Specifically, preconceptions and expectations can influence how information is labeled and understood, how ambiguous information is interpreted, and the degree to which information is scrutinized. For example, when told that someone is "intelligent," we might understand the person to be "sensible, wise, insightful, and stimulating" if our impression of the person is otherwise positive. On the other hand, the same description—"intelligent"—might be understood as describing a person who is "cunning and scheming" and "detached" if we otherwise perceive that person negatively.[28]

Similarly, stereotypes have been shown to influence how information is initially processed. For example, one study demonstrated that people asked to distinguish between tools and weapons were able to identify tools more quickly when they were primed with white faces and to identify weapons more quickly when they were primed with black faces.[29] There is evidence that people pay more attention to information that is consistent with a stereotype and less attention to stereotype-inconsistent information, that people seek out information that is consistent with the stereotype, and that people are better able to remember information that is consistent with the stereotype. Such preferences for confirmation of stereotypes can make such views resistant to change.[30]

We can, however, use a variety of strategies to minimize reliance on schemas in decision making.[31] First, goals can influence the tendency to rely on particular schemas. For example, taking time and focusing attention on making an individuating assessment of another person can result in less stereotyping and increased attention to that person's distinct characteristics. Similarly, pausing to think about the unique features of a particular case may provide insight into the ways in which the case departs from the expected. On the other hand, time pressure and a focus on general impressions can increase the tendency to stereotype or to rely on other schemas.

Similarly, it can be helpful to acknowledge the reality that preexisting knowledge structures can influence perception and to actively question the basis for a particular understanding. In particular, we might reflect on our understanding and probe the assumptions that have been made, or we might solicit the insight of another person who may have a different set of schemas.

In addition, reliance on schemas tends to be reduced when counter-examples are available. For example, people are less likely to rely on negative stereotypes of

African Americans or women when they have been exposed to instances of admired African Americans or famous women leaders. Such exposure can come from objects such as photos (who is on *your* "wall of fame"?), from personal connections with individuals within the stereotyped group, or even from simply creating mental images of counterstereotypes.

> ✦ ✦ ✦ ✦ ✦
> ### Countering Stereotypes
>
> Consider the way in which one judge took steps to make sure that she had access to counterstereotypical information:
>
> > We know of a judge whose court is located in a predominantly African-American neighborhood. Because of the crime and arrest patterns in the community, most people the judge sentences are black. The judge confronted a paradox. On the one hand, she took a judicial oath to be objective and egalitarian, and indeed she consciously believed that her decisions were unbiased. On the other hand, every day she was exposed to an environment that reinforced the association between black men and crime. Although she consciously rejected racial stereotypes, she suspected that she harbored unconscious prejudices merely from working in a segregated world. Immersed in this environment each day, she wondered if it was possible to give the defendants a fair hearing.
> >
> > Rather than allow her environment to reinforce a bias, the judge created an alternative environment. She spent a vacation week sitting in a fellow judge's court in a neighborhood where the criminals being tried were predominantly white. Case after case challenged the stereotype of blacks as criminal and whites as law abiding and so challenged [even if not eradicating] any bias against blacks that she might have harbored.[32]

Confirmation Bias and Biased Assimilation

Consider Marge, a supporter of capital punishment, and David, a death penalty opponent. Marge, it turns out, is likely to be more inclined than David to notice reports of studies showing that the death penalty deters crime. And David is likely to be more inclined to notice reports of studies showing no death penalty–deterrence link. Similarly, Marge and David are likely to differentially evaluate the quality of the different studies of capital punishment and deterrence: each is likely to perceive the studies with findings that are consistent with his or her beliefs to be of higher methodological quality and more persuasive than the studies that produced contrary results (even if the studies used similar methods).³³

Marge and David are not alone. We tend to exhibit *confirmation bias* in the ways in which we seek out and evaluate information. People tend to unconsciously seek out additional information that confirms their already existing views and to disregard conflicting information, rather than attempting to systematically gather accurate information. Moreover, when evaluating information once it is obtained, there is a tendency for assessments of the information to be influenced by the extent to which the information is consistent with the attitudes or expectations of the person doing the evaluation—a tendency known as *biased assimilation.* Information that is inconsistent with expectations or beliefs is discounted and scrutinized more carefully than is expectation-congruent data. In other words, "when we want to believe an argument, we tend to ask, 'Can I believe this?' When we do not want to believe an argument, we ask, '*Must* I believe this?'"³⁵

> It is a capital mistake to theorize before one has data. Insensibly one begins to twist facts to suit theories, instead of theories to suit facts.
> —Sherlock Holmes³⁴

✦ ✦ ✦ ✦ ✦
They Saw a Protest

In a recent study, participants were presented with videotape footage of a protest and asked to evaluate whether the protesters were creating an obstruction, the extent to which the protesters presented a risk of violence, and the degree to which the protesters were engaged in persuasion as opposed to intimidation or physical interference.

Half of the participants, however, were told that the protest was being conducted outside an abortion clinic, while the other half of the participants were told that the protest took place at a campus recruitment center and was staged to protest the military's "don't ask, don't tell" policy on gays in the military.

Consistent with confirmation bias, people with different preexisting beliefs and attitudes judged the conduct of the protesters differently. Judgments were more favorable to the protesters when the described purpose of the demonstration was consistent with the participants' own beliefs and values. Conversely, participants judged protesters more harshly when the purported purpose of the demonstration was contrary to their own ideals.³⁶

> [T]he most important factor in the training of good mental habits consists in acquiring the attitude of suspended conclusion.... To maintain the state of doubt and to carry on systematic and protracted inquiry—these are the essentials of thinking.
> —John Dewey[37]

Take, as an example, a recent study in which participants were asked to review a police file, evaluate the evidence, and make decisions about further investigation. Participants who were asked to name a suspect after reviewing the file demonstrated confirmation bias in seeking out and interpreting additional investigatory information. Specifically, they were more likely (than were participants who did not name a suspect) to remember evidence consistent with the named suspect's guilt, to discount evidence inconsistent with the named suspect's guilt, and to interpret ambiguous evidence in ways consistent with the named suspect's guilt. Importantly, naming a suspect not only affected how investigators interpreted the existing evidence but also influenced the information that they ultimately had available to them because they disproportionately chose to pursue additional lines of investigation that focused on the named suspect.[38]

Interviewers have been shown to be subject to confirmation bias as well. Researchers have found that interviewers who are led to believe that an interviewee is likely guilty ask a higher proportion of questions that are consistent with the interviewee's guilt (*guilt-presumptive questions*), use more interrogation techniques early in the interview, and are more likely to judge the interviewee guilty than are interviewers who are led to believe that the interviewee is likely innocent. Interestingly, this approach to the interviews has consequences for the behavior of the interviewees as well: both guilty and *innocent* interviewees tend to display more defensive behaviors during the interview when they are questioned by someone who is predisposed to believe that they are guilty.[39] Thus, the expectations of the interviewer elicited behavior from the interviewee that was consistent with those expectations—a self-fulfilling prophecy.

One strategy that has proven helpful in countering the effects of confirmation bias and biased assimilation is to explicitly *consider the opposite*. That is, when seeking out and evaluating information, consciously and explicitly reflecting on the possibility that our preconceptions are erroneous and seeking out disconfirming evidence can serve to reduce the bias. Thus, an investigator might make a point of looking for evidence that is inconsistent with a named suspect's guilt, or an interviewer might deliberately ask questions that could reveal evidence counter to her expectations. It can also be helpful to consult others who might hold different views or have different expectations. Psychological research has found that such overt consideration of alternatives is more effective in reducing reliance on preconceptions than is simply making a good-faith effort to be unbiased.[40]

> ✦ ✦ ✦ ✦
> ### The Devil's Advocate
>
> In the history of the Roman Catholic Church, the devil's advocate was a canon lawyer who played an important role in the process of determining whether an individual would be canonized as a saint. The devil's advocate was assigned the role of making the argument for why the candidate was *not* worthy of sainthood. It was intended that the devil's advocate be a skilled skeptic, that he question the arguments made in favor of sainthood, and that he seek out evidence that would disconfirm the appropriateness of canonization. In other words, the devil's advocate formalized the process of considering the opposite.[41]
>
> Psychologists have found that authentic dissent can lead to improved decisions because engaging with dissenters leads to a consideration of additional information and perspectives. Using a devil's advocate—a person whose job it is to criticize or question an argument or position and its underlying assumptions—can also improve decision making, though not as effectively as authentic dissent.[42]

Causal Attribution and Judgments of Responsibility

Why did the business manager fire the employee? Why did the supplier breach the contract? What led to the accident in which a schoolchild was injured? Did she hit him on purpose, or was it just an accident? Why did the investor's mutual fund balance drop so sharply?

One way in which people make sense of the world is by making causal judgments, that is, judgments about what caused an outcome. Such causal judgments—including making inferences of responsibility, weighing the relative contributions of potential causes, and making predictions about others' future behavior—are often central to legal situations. Attribution theory in psychology is the study of the ways in which people make attributions of causality or responsibility, particularly attributions that are focused on understanding another person's or our own behavior.[43]

As an initial matter, it is clear that human beings often have a hard time distinguishing between patterns that are meaningful and those that are random.[44] We frequently conclude that systematic patterns exist when they do not or see patterns that differ from those that actually exist. For example, most basketball fans are believers in the existence of what is known as the *hot-hand phenomenon,* wherein a player has a better chance of making his next shot when he has made his last several shots (that is, when he is "on a roll" or "in the zone") than when he has just missed a series of shots (that is, when he is "shooting cold"). Researchers who have studied the hot-hand phenomenon, however, have examined shooting percentages across large numbers of games and have found no evidence of streak shooting.[45] Furthermore, just as we perceive patterns where there are none, we expect random events to be devoid of patterns. Consider the following example:

> When Apple first introduced the shuffle feature on its iPods, the shuffle was truly random; each song was equally as likely to get picked as any other. However, the randomness didn't *appear* random, since some songs were occasionally repeated, and customers concluded that the feature contained some secret patterns and preferences. As a result, Apple was forced to revise the algorithm. "We made it less random to make it feel more random," said Steve Jobs, the CEO of Apple.[46]

Such *illusory correlations* can make discerning causal relationships challenging. When it comes to thinking about the causes of other people's behavior, we tend to discount the extent to which behavior is influenced by various aspects of the situation in which people find themselves. The phenomenon known as the *fundamental attribution error* (or *correspondence bias*) is the tendency of observers to attribute another person's behavior to dispositional factors (those internal to the person) rather than to situational (external) factors despite what we know to be the powerful influence of situational factors on behavior. Thus, if A runs into B with a grocery cart, B is apt to view the act as deliberate or careless on the part of A rather than to attribute the collision to a spill on the floor or a sticky wheel on the grocery cart. Similarly, people attribute the views contained in a speech (for example, defending or attacking the notion that marijuana should be legal) to the speaker even when they know that the person was assigned to speak on that side of the issue.[47]

As an example of the fundamental attribution error, consider the following study: Researchers asked pairs of participants to negotiate the salary component of a job offer. Participants in the role of the job candidates were given information about their alternative to reaching an agreement with the employer; different groups of job candidates (assigned at random) were given alternatives that differed in value. It turns out that the behavior of the job candidates in the negotiation was primarily determined by the value of their alternative job. In the course of the negotiation, the negotiators in the role of the employer were able to discern these differences in the value of the candidates' alternatives. However, the employers appraised candidates with low-value alternatives as having more agreeable characters, appraised candidates with more risky alternatives as more emotionally unstable, and expressed preferences for the candidates' subsequent job assignments that were consistent with these appraisals.[48] That is, the employers attributed candidates' use of hard bargaining to their internal personality traits rather than to the external differences in situations between candidates who did and did not have good alternative job opportunities. Thus, even when people grasp the nature of the situation, they may discount the influence of those situational factors on others' behavior.

Interestingly, there is cultural variation in people's tendency to make dispositional attributions. The fundamental attribution error is commonly found in independent cultures such as the United States. While this tendency is also found in more interdependent cultures, the effect is attenuated; in other words, people from more interdependent cultures are more likely to pay attention to the whole context and to make attributions that are more strongly influenced by situational factors.[49]

✦ ✦ ✦ ✦ ✦
Culture and Attribution

Consider a study that examined the news coverage of two crimes: one in which a Chinese graduate student (Lu) shot a professor at the University of Iowa and a second in which an Irish American postal worker (McIlvane) shot a supervisor and several others. Chinese newspaper coverage of both incidents contained a smaller proportion of statements suggesting dispositional attributions and a greater proportion of statements evidencing situational attributions than did corresponding newspaper coverage in the United States:

> Causes of the Lu murder emphasized by American reporters were personality traits (e.g., "very bad temper" and "sinister edge to Mr. Lu's character well before the shootings"), attitudes (e.g., "personal belief that guns were an important means to redress grievances"), and psychological problems (e.g., "darkly disturbed man who drove himself to success and destruction," "psychological problem with being challenged," and "whatever went wrong was internal"). Causes emphasized by Chinese reporters were Lu's relationships (e.g., "did not get along with his advisor," "rivalry with slain student," and "isolation from Chinese community"), pressures in Chinese society (e.g., "Lu was a victim of the 'Top Students' Education Policy" and "tragedy reflects the lack of religion in Chinese culture"), and aspects of American society (e.g., "murder can be traced to the availability of guns"). Likewise, American reporters made reference to McIlvane's personal dispositions (e.g., "man was mentally unstable," "had repeatedly threatened violence," "martial arts enthusiast," and "he had a short fuse"), whereas Chinese reporters stressed situational factors (e.g., "gunman had been recently fired," "post office supervisor was his enemy," and "followed the example of a recent mass slaying in Texas").[50]

In an interesting turn, research has also shown that people view causation differently when evaluating their own acts as compared to the acts of others. In particular, while observers are likely to attribute others' behavior to dispositional factors, they are more likely to attribute their own behavior to situational factors—a phenomenon known as the *actor-observer effect*.[51] That is, when someone else runs into a fire hydrant, we are likely to attribute the accident to careless driving. However, if we are the driver, we are more likely to blame the hydrant, its improper placement, or a faulty mirror.

> The telephone pole was approaching. I was attempting to swerve out of its way when it struck my car.
> —Actual Insurance Claim Form[52]

The actor-observer effect works together with a number of other mechanisms to allow us to persuade ourselves that *we* did nothing wrong, or at least that we did the best that we could. Such self-justification is driven by the tension—a tension referred to as *cognitive dissonance*—that exists when a person holds two inconsistent cognitions: the belief that he is a good person who acts reasonably and the knowledge that he has engaged in an unreasonable act. The discomfort of simultaneously holding such incompatible beliefs can cause people to minimize their role in the behavior, discount the extent of the harm caused, derogate or blame the victim, or engage in other self-justificatory thinking in order to resolve the tension. The confirmation bias discussed above contributes by drawing our attention to evidence consistent with our self-justificatory view of events and allowing us to forget aspects of what happened that are inconsistent with our view of ourselves.[53]

It is easy to see how conflict can result when actors justify their own behavior but attribute their counterpart's behavior to dispositional factors. Each party may see his own behavior as a reaction to the situation or to the other's behavior but see the other's behavior as unprovoked. Consider a set of people enacting the role of world leaders engaged in a discussion of nuclear strikes. Following the exchange, people were shown statements from the interchange and asked to recall the statements that immediately preceded and followed the statements. When evaluating their own statements, people were better able to recall what had been said immediately *prior* to the statement—that is, what led them to make the statement—than what the other's response had been. In contrast, when evaluating the counterpart's statements, people were better able to recall what was said immediately *after* the statement—that is, what they themselves had said in response to the statement—rather than what they had said leading up to the statement.[54] As psychologist Dan Gilbert noted about such findings, "our reasons for punching will always be more salient to us than the punches themselves—but the opposite will be true of other people's reasons and other people's punches."[55]

Research has also demonstrated a variety of additional influences on our judgments about the causes of an outcome. For example, we tend to attribute causal significance to factors that are near an outcome in space or in time, to factors that are prominent or salient, and to factors that are similar to the relevant outcome (for example, big effects are presumed to have big causes). We are more likely to assign responsibility to another person when we judge the cause to be internal to the person, controllable by the person, and stable. That is, we tend to hold others responsible for things we think they can control but not for events we think they could not have prevented or which occurred unpredictably. Moreover, we have a tendency to latch onto readily accessible single-factor explanations for particular effects rather than appreciating that there are often a host of causal factors underlying any given outcome.[56]

Naïve Realism, False Consensus, and the Illusion of Asymmetric Insight

We have seen that people construct their reality based on where they focus their attention and as a function of how they construe information via their expectations and attributions. However, people often fail to appreciate the extent to which their own perceptions are affected by their preexisting knowledge and expectations or to recognize that other people may interpret the same basic circumstances very differently. This *naïve realism* results in the "feeling that [our] own take on the world enjoys particular authenticity, and that other actors will, or at least should, share that take, if they are attentive, rational, and objective perceivers of reality and open-minded seekers of truth."[57]

To see just one example of this *naïve realism* at work in the law, consider the U.S. Supreme Court case of *Scott v. Harris*.[58] Late one night in 2001, police officers clocked nineteen-year-old Victor Harris going seventy-three miles per hour in a fifty-five-mile-per-hour zone and attempted to stop him for speeding. But Harris sped away, and a high-speed chase ensued. The chase ended when police officer Timothy Scott rammed his cruiser into Harris's car, causing Harris to crash and rendering Harris a quadriplegic. Harris brought suit claiming that the police had used excessive force in the way in which they ended the chase and that this had violated his constitutional rights.

The chase and its aftermath were captured on videotape by cameras mounted in the various cruisers. This videotape evidence ended up being central to the Court's decision as to whether there was a genuine issue of material fact about whether Harris's conduct posed sufficient danger to the public to justify the officer's use of force. Consider how Justice Scalia, writing for the eight-justice majority, described what he saw on the tape:

> There we see respondent's vehicle racing down narrow, two-lane roads in the dead of night at speeds that are shockingly fast. We see it swerve around more than a dozen other cars, cross the double-yellow line, and force cars traveling in both directions to their respective shoulders to avoid being hit. We see it run multiple red lights and travel for considerable periods of time in the occasional center left-turn-only lane, chased by numerous police cars forced to engage in the same hazardous maneuvers just to keep up. Far from being the cautious and controlled driver the lower court depicts, what we see on the video more closely resembles a Hollywood-style car chase of the most frightening sort, placing police officers and innocent bystanders alike at great risk of serious injury.[59]

Justice Stevens, however, disagreed with this characterization of the chase (as had the U.S. Court of Appeals for the Eleventh Circuit), describing the incident as "a nighttime chase on a lightly traveled road in Georgia where no pedestrians or other 'bystanders' were present":

> At no point during the chase did respondent pull into the opposite lane other than to pass a car in front of him; he did the latter no more than five times and, on most

of those occasions, used his turn signal. On none of these occasions was there a car traveling in the opposite direction. In fact, at one point, when respondent found himself behind a car in his own lane and there were cars traveling in the other direction, he slowed and waited for the cars traveling in the other direction to pass before overtaking the car in front of him while using his turn signal to do so. This is hardly the stuff of Hollywood. To the contrary, the video does not reveal any incidents that could even be remotely characterized as "close calls." . . . There is no evidence that he ever lost control of his vehicle. . . . It is apparent from the record (including the videotape) that local police had blocked off intersections to keep respondent from entering residential neighborhoods and possibly endangering other motorists. I would add that the videos also show that no pedestrians, parked cars, sidewalks, or residences were visible at any time during the chase. . . . "At the time of the ramming, apart from speeding and running two red lights, Harris was driving in a non-aggressive fashion (i.e., without trying to ram or run into the officers). Moreover, . . . Scott's path on the open highway was largely clear. The videos introduced into evidence show little to no vehicular (or pedestrian) traffic, allegedly because of the late hour and the police blockade of the nearby intersections. Finally, Scott issued absolutely no warning (e.g., over the loudspeaker or otherwise) prior to using deadly force."[60]

Watch the Video

You can view a version of the videotape of the chase and its aftermath in *Scott v. Harris* at http://www.supremecourt.gov/media/media.aspx.

The majority of justices, however, were "happy to let the videotape speak for itself" and had "little difficulty in concluding" that Officer Scott's actions were objectively reasonable. Indeed, Justice Breyer, in concurrence, invited viewers to watch the tape for themselves:

> Because watching the video footage of the car chase made a difference to my own view of the case, I suggested that the interested reader take advantage of the link in the Court's opinion and watch it. Having done so, I do not believe a reasonable jury could, in this instance, find that Office Timothy Scott . . . acted in violation of the Constitution.

Was the Court right that the videotape spoke for itself? Following the decision in *Scott,* researchers showed a video of the chase to 1,350 people across the country and asked for their reactions. They found that a majority of respondents perceived the events in the videotape in ways that were consistent with the perceptions of the Supreme Court majority, including that Harris's driving posed a deadly risk to the public and to the police, that Harris was more at fault than were the police, and that deadly force was justified. There were, however, differences in how the tape was construed among different subgroups of respondents, with some viewers concluding that Harris's driving did not pose a deadly risk, that the police were more at fault than Harris, and that the use of deadly force was not justified. Certain groups—such as African Americans, those with lower incomes, and those with more egalitarian views—were more likely than others to depart from the Court's views. When the tape spoke, it did not say the same thing to everyone.[61] Nonetheless, naïve realism means that any individual viewer is likely to believe that others, as long as they are objective, will see the tape in the same way that they do.

Naïve realism has a number of implications that have particular relevance to the practice of law. First, people tend to overestimate the degree to which others share their perspective. The *false consensus effect* "involves an overestimation of the commonness of one's own response and reactions."[62] Thus, people believe that their behavior, choices, and beliefs are typical and, therefore, less indicative of their own character than are behaviors, choices, and beliefs to the contrary.

At the same time, however, when we are aware that others may have perceptions that differ from our own, those differences in perceptions can be magnified. In particular, we tend to overestimate the influence of factors such as ideology and self-interest on other people's attitudes and behavior, believing that such influences will cause people to have beliefs that differ wildly from our own. Thus, in one study, self-identified partisans and neutrals made judgments in a case involving interracial violence and made predictions about how their construals of the case would differ from those with other political viewpoints. While there were, in fact, differences in how the various groups perceived the case, these differences were relatively small compared to the large differences predicted by the participants.[63] Similarly, people tend to overestimate the influence of self-interest on attitudes and to believe that others are more motivated by extrinsic incentives (such as money) and less motivated by intrinsic incentives (such as learning something new, facing a new challenge, or making a difference) than they are themselves.[64] Overestimating such differences can result in unwarranted pessimism about working together and finding common ground.

Second, naïve realism has implications for the ways in which people convey information. For example, people have great difficulty conveying information with which they are familiar to someone who lacks their mental representation of the material. In one telling study, one group of people was asked to tap the rhythms of familiar songs for a second group to identify. The "tappers" (who had mental representations of the songs that included the melody and words) vastly overestimated the likelihood that the "listeners" (who heard only taps) would correctly recognize the songs.[65] (As authors, we hope we have overcome this challenge in writing this book!)

Third, secure in the belief that they see the world accurately, people tend to be confident in their abilities to persuade those on the other side and neutral third parties of the merits of their position. However, when efforts to "enlighten" the other side are unsuccessful, people are likely to conclude that such others are unreasonable, biased, and driven by improper motives. Indeed, the more the other disagrees, the more he is thought to be displaying bias.[66]

A recent series of studies demonstrated that people attribute bias to those with whom they disagree, based merely on the fact of their disagreement. Such attributions can have pernicious consequences. The studies found that once people make such attributions of bias, they are less likely to think that cooperation will be productive, less inclined to cooperate with the person with whom they disagree, and more likely to engage in highly competitive tactics when addressing the disagreement. The problem spirals and conflict escalates because when faced with such tactics, the other person is more likely to respond competitively as well, to view the disagreement as more conflictual, to be less hopeful that the conflict can be resolved, and to view the other as more biased.[67]

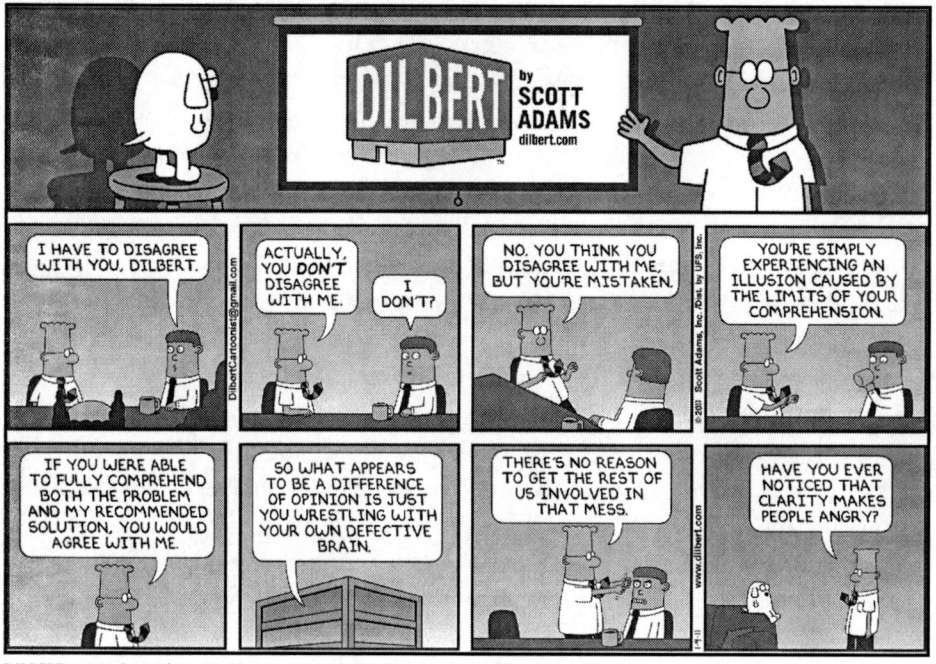

DILBERT © 2011 Scott Adams. Used by permission of UNIVERSAL UCLICK. All rights reserved.

Finally, believing that our own perceptions have particular legitimacy and that differing perceptions are the result of a lack of information, unreasonableness, or bias can also lead us to believe that we make more accurate judgments about other people than other people make about us. Indeed, "[w]e insist that our 'outsider perspective' affords us insights about our peers that they are denied by their defensiveness, egocentricity, or other sources of bias. By contrast, we rarely entertain the notion that others are seeing us more clearly and objectively than we see ourselves."[68]

This *illusion of asymmetric insight*—the notion that we know others better than they know us—can incline us to "talk when we would do well to listen and to be less patient than we ought to be when others express the conviction that they are the ones who are being misunderstood or judged unfairly" and can make us "reluctant to take advice from others who cannot know our private thoughts, feelings, interpretations of events, or motives, but all too willing to give advice to others based on our views of their past behavior, without adequate attention to *their* thoughts, feelings, interpretations, and motives."[69]

Perspective Taking

Given the challenges inherent in understanding the causes of other people's behavior and our tendency toward naïve realism, *perspective taking*—the ability to consider the viewpoints of other people and intuit their experiences, perceptions, interests, and feelings—is particularly important to the practice of law. Those who take the perspective of others are more likely to take into account situational influences on others' behavior, perceive others' interests and intentions more accurately, make less self-serving judgments of fairness, and engage in less stereotyping. As a result, considering the perspective of another helps in predicting their reactions and behavior.[70] Such insight is likely to improve a lawyer's ability to negotiate successfully, to persuade a judge, or to give advice that is useful and palatable to a client.

However, perspective taking is not automatic or easy. First, even when we are motivated to figure out the perspective of another, it can be difficult to adjust away from the anchor of our own perspective.[71] For example, when trying to judge how hungry and thirsty a group of lost hikers would be, we tend to be influenced by how hungry or thirsty *we* are.[72] Similarly, those who behave competitively are more likely than those who behave cooperatively to expect others to also behave competitively.[73]

You never really understand a person until you consider things from his point of view . . . until you climb into his skin and walk around in it.
—*Atticus Finch*[74]

Second, attempting to take the perspective of another sometimes serves to mistakenly amplify differences, real or imagined. When differences in perspective are particularly focal—as with plaintiffs and defendants, Democrats and Republicans, labor and management, or environmentalists and industry—"perspective takers [may] use their own beliefs as a point of *contrast* when stepping into the shoes of the opposing side. In these cases, it is possible for perspective takers to *overestimate* the extent to which the beliefs of opposing groups differ from their own."[75]

In similar ways, at the same time that perspective taking tends to reduce self-serving biases, it can also result in more self-interested behavior in competitive situations. This can occur when the perspective taking focuses attention on the expectation that the other will act in a self-interested manner. Such a focus can result in the expectation that others will act less fairly and be more self-serving. When perspective taking highlights these expectations, perspective takers tend to respond by acting in more self-serving ways themselves. Conversely, in cooperative situations, perspective taking is more likely to draw attention to shared concerns and does not seem to result in more self-serving behavior.[76]

In life it is hard enough to see another person's view of things; in a law suit it is impossible.
—*Janet Malcolm*[77]

> **A Perspective on Perspective Taking**
>
> Even those who think they are particularly skilled at perspective taking should assume that there is room for improvement. People do not tend to have an accurate sense of their perspective-taking ability. Indeed, self-reported ability to read others does not tend to mirror accuracy in predictions, and confidence in perspective-taking skills tends to surpass actual ability.[79]

Developing the ability to avoid these pitfalls and effectively take the perspective of others requires conscious attention. It takes effort to step outside of our own perspective and into the shoes of another. Indeed, attorneys may need to work even harder at taking the perspective of others because people in more powerful roles tend to be less likely to take another's perspective. Recent research has found that people with power, such as attorneys, are less likely to take into account another person's visual perspective, less likely to adjust for the fact that others do not have access to their private information, and less accurate at identifying emotions in others.[78] But this work is likely to pay off in a better understanding of the influences on, interests, and intentions of others.

As we have now seen, there are many factors that can influence how we construct an understanding of the events we experience. How we focus our attention, the ways in which we construe our experiences, the ways in which we tend to attribute causation, our experience of naïve realism, and our use of (or failure to use) perspective taking all have an influence on how we perceive and respond to what happens to us. Importantly, however, while we tend to be willing to believe that others' views and behaviors are influenced by where they sit, we do not fully take into account this myriad of influences on our own understandings and actions. This asymmetry is known as the *bias blind spot*.[80]

Understanding the ways in which people's understandings are shaped by the ways in which they perceive and understand the world can inform lawyers' approaches to eliciting information from clients and witnesses through interviews and depositions and reconciling the sometimes-conflicting information received, counseling clients about how to proceed, negotiating with others who have divergent perceptions, persuading others, and many other tasks. We will turn to a discussion of these implications in the second part of the book.

> ### Summing It Up
>
> - Recognize that attention is limited. Although we think we are aware of our surroundings, we miss many details as a result of the limits on our perceptual capacities.

- Think of perceivers as actively constructing what they see, relying on schemas, scripts, stereotypes, and preexisting attitudes and expectations as they interpret what they experience, fill in gaps, and resolve ambiguities.
- Keep in mind the tendency to attribute our own behavior to situational pressures but to attribute others' behavior to their innate characteristics—the fundamental attribution error.
- Consider how naïve realism can lead us to overestimate the commonality of our reactions, to have difficulty conveying information to another person who lacks our knowledge or perspective, to be overly confident in our ability to persuade, and to suppose others are biased or foolish when they do not come around to our side.
- Work to understand the perspective of others, striving to see how perspectives can differ while not overly magnifying the differences.

For Further Reading: Perception and Construal

Christopher Chabris & Daniel Simons, The Invisible Gorilla: And Other Ways Our Intuitions Deceive Us (2010).

Richard E. Nisbett & Lee Ross, Human Inference: Strategies and Shortcomings of Social Judgment (1980).

Harold E. Pashler, The Psychology of Attention (1998).

Emily Pronin et al., *Understanding Misunderstanding: Social Psychological Perspectives, in* Heuristics and Biases: The Psychology of Intuitive Judgment 646 (Thomas Gilovich et al. eds., 2002).

Lee Ross & Richard E. Nisbett, The Person and the Situation: Perspectives of Social Psychology (1991).

Carol Tavris & Elliot Aronson, Mistakes Were Made (but Not by *Me*): Why We Justify Foolish Beliefs, Bad Decisions, and Hurtful Acts (2007).

Bernard Weiner, Judgments of Responsibility: A Foundation for a Theory of Social Conduct (1995).

Memory | 2

> Memory is a complicated thing, a relative to truth but not its twin.
>
> — *Barbara Kingsolver*[1]

The movie *Rashomon*, directed by Akira Kurosawa, depicts the story of a brutal rape and murder. The eyewitness accounts of the crime, however, including the accounts given by the perpetrator and the victim (speaking through a medium), are inconsistent. Different parties remember the events quite differently. In the end, viewers never learn the "truth" of what actually transpired.[2]

Such conflicting memories are not just the stuff of movies. In 1997, Abner Louima was sodomized with a broomstick by one or more police officers in a Brooklyn police station bathroom. Several days later, probationary police officer Eric Turetzky disclosed to police investigators what he had seen on the night of the incident. A court proceeding related to the case, held four years later, was styled by the *New York Times* as "*Rashomon in Blue.*" The testimony of the three investigators, Officer Turetzky, and a police captain offered a range of descriptions of the meeting in which Officer Turetzky had disclosed what he witnessed. The witnesses offered conflicting information about who was present when Officer Turetzky arrived, how the conversation began, who conducted the interview (or even if any questions were asked), who decided to call Internal Affairs, who made the call to Internal Affairs, and whom Officer Turetzky called before he left the station following the meeting.[3] While some of the differences among the stories could have resulted because one or more of the officers were lying, many of the discrepancies were not even relevant to guilt or innocence and were more likely attributable to differences in memory.

Psychologists, police officers, and other investigators have learned that different people's descriptions of the same event can vary significantly. It is not merely that people misremember whether someone was wearing a red or a green shirt. We also do a poor job of remembering very significant events, their timing, the order in which events took place, and who was present.

Nonetheless, most people believe human memories are better than they really are. Indeed, in one recent study, most people endorsed the notion that "human memory works like a video camera, accurately recording the events we see and hear so that we can review and inspect them later."[4] But this is not the case. While it is true that people do a remarkable job of remembering a wealth of information, psychologists have also demonstrated a number of frailties that plague both short- and long-term memory. In reality, just as our perceptual abilities differ from those of seismographs (see chapter 1), so, too, are our memories unlike mechanical devices that might be counted on to store and recall accurate visual, auditory, and other details of an incident. Clients and witnesses, attorneys, and others may be unable to provide relevant and accurate details because they did not attend to or encode such details accurately at the time the event occurred (see chapter 1), because they have forgotten, or because their memories have become distorted since the event occurred.

The Workings of Memory

In chapter 1, we saw that not all details of an event attract our attention and that significant interpretation takes place as events occur. But even details that were noticed and could have been accurately reported at the time of the event may be forgotten. Working memory "holds on to small amounts of information for short periods of time—usually a few seconds—while people engage in such ongoing cognitive activities as reading, listening, problem solving, reasoning, or thinking."[5] However, to be retained, this information must be transferred from short-term working memory to long-term memory: "[T]he system must constantly discard what is no longer needed at the moment, and devote its resources to the temporary storage of incoming information. Unless special effort is made—such as repeating a sentence over and over again—information is lost from the system almost immediately after it enters."[7]

> Memory depends both on what actually happened and on how we made sense of what happened.
> —Christopher Chabris & Daniel Simons[6]

This can mean, in part, that our motivation to remember something at the time it is encoded can influence how well we subsequently remember. Being motivated to remember can incline us to pay attention to, review, and organize information in ways that result in better long-term memory. Thus, in one study, people who were given financial incentives to remember particular bits of information before they

> The true art of memory is the art of attention.
> —Samuel Johnson[8]

were exposed to that information were better able to remember that information later. Importantly, however, heightened motivation to remember that arises *at the time of recall* does *not* have this effect. By this point in the process, greater motivation "merely leads people to work hard to retrieve information, and even the most earnest search of long-term memory is ineffective when information was never stored there in the first place."[9]

So, getting information into long-term memory can be an important first step toward accurate memory. But even memories that are stored in long-term memory can deteriorate as time passes:

> At relatively early points on the forgetting curve—minutes, hours, and days, sometimes more—memory preserves a relatively detailed record, allowing us to reproduce the past with reasonable if not perfect accuracy. But with the passing of time, the particulars fade and opportunities multiply for interference . . . to blur our recollections.[10]

Probably every student has experienced the brain drain phenomenon, as information, fairly well remembered for an exam, soon begins draining from the brain. Test yourself, and you will likely find that you no longer remember things that were once deeply embedded in your memory, such as a mathematical formula, an old home phone number, how to drive to a particular location, or the name of a grade school teacher or old friend.

Not only do the details of what has happened fade over time, but what we remember is not always congruent with what actually occurred. For example, people sometimes remember events in ways that are distorted from what actually happened, combine aspects of multiple events into a single memory, fill in gaps in memory with speculation driven by their schemas or expectations, or remember events that did not happen.

> Memory is a net: one that finds it full of fish when he takes it from the brook, but a dozen miles of water have run through it without sticking.
> —Oliver Wendell Holmes[11]

Where were you when you heard that a plane had hit the World Trade Center in New York City? Or when the space shuttle Challenger exploded? How did you hear about what had happened? In one study that demonstrates the transience of memory, people provided detailed accounts of a particular salient event—how they learned about the verdict in the criminal trial of O.J. Simpson—within three days of the event. They reported where they were and what they were doing when they heard the news, as well as how they heard about it, who else was there, and how they felt about the verdict. Fifteen months later, only half were highly accurate in their recall of these details. By nearly three years after the verdict was announced, fewer than 30% of participants could accurately recall the details. This was so even though participants had reviewed their memories during the earlier sessions.[12]

In another study, attendees at a taped discussion that took place at a meeting of the Cambridge Psychological Society were contacted two weeks later and asked about their memories of the discussion. Their descriptions commonly left out over 90% of their substantive points that had been discussed, and nearly half of the recalled information was incorrect. "Respondents remembered comments that were never made, they transformed casual remarks into lengthy orations, and they converted implicit meanings into explicit comments."[13]

Conversations, in particular, may be difficult to recall in detail. Witnesses may remember the gist of a conversation but have trouble recalling what was said verbatim. Witnesses may also have difficulty remembering the specifics of who said

✦ ✦ ✦ ✦ ✦
The Vagaries of Memory

Consider the following example of how even a cherished memory can turn out to be inaccurate:

One of us (Carol) had a favorite children's book, James Thurber's *The Wonderful O*, which she remembers her father giving her when she was a child. "A band of pirates takes over an island and forbids the locals to speak any word or use any object containing the letter O," Carol recalls. "I have a vivid memory of my father reading *The Wonderful O* and our laughing together at the thought of shy Ophelia Oliver saying her name without its O's. I remember trying valiantly, along with the invaded islanders, to guess the fourth O word that must never be lost (after love, hope, and valor), and my father's teasing guesses. Oregon? Orangutan? Ophthamologist? And then, not long ago, I found my first edition of *The Wonderful O*. It had been published in 1957, one year after my father's death. I stared at that date in disbelief and shock. Obviously, someone else gave me that book, someone else read it to me, someone else laughed with me about Phelia Liver, someone else wanted me to understand that the fourth O was freedom. Someone lost to my recollection."

This small story illustrates three important things about memory: how disorienting it is to realize that a vivid memory, one full of emotion and detail, is indisputably wrong; that even being absolutely, positively sure a memory is accurate does not mean that it is; and how errors in memory support our current feelings and beliefs. "I have a set of beliefs about my father," Carol observes, "the warm man he was, the funny and devoted dad who loved to read to me and take me rummaging through libraries, the lover of wordplay. So it was logical for me to assume—no, to *remember*—that he was the one who read me *The Wonderful O*.[14]

what and to whom, who else was present, when the conversation took place, how a particular conversation fit into a series of conversations, or the context of the conversation.[15]

>
> Memory is deceptive because it is colored by today's events.
> —Albert Einstein[16]
>

Memories may be inconsistent with what actually occurred as a result of biases in what we call to mind. For example, memory tends to be biased such that it is consistent with our current experience. That is, we are likely to recall our past attitudes, beliefs, moods, or feelings in ways that are consistent with our current states of mind. Thus, if a person feels greatly dissatisfied at the present time, he will be better able to remember prior instances of dissatisfaction or will assess his state of mind in a previous circumstance to have been more dissatisfied than if he is presently experiencing a feeling of satisfaction.[17] And, as we will see in chapter 4, our recollections also tend to be colored with both the benefit of hindsight and our penchant for recalling ourselves in a favorable light.

In addition, we are more likely to remember things that are consistent with our stereotypes and other schemas and to remember things that confirm our preexisting notions (see chapter 1). For example, people who waited for a study in a graduate student office and were later asked to describe what had been in the office tended to correctly remember typical office furnishings such as a desk, table, and shelves; but they also incorrectly reported seeing items that they might have expected to see in a graduate student office but that were *not* actually present, such as books and a file cabinet.[18] And people who saw ambiguous details in a depiction of a bank robbery were more likely to interpret and remember those details in ways that were consistent with the schema for a bank robbery—a schema that prescribes, for example, that the robber almost certainly had a gun.[19]

In similar ways, we have a tendency to misremember or conflate individuals or events that share a category such as race or gender as our schemas work to guide memory (see chapter 1). Justice Ruth Bader Ginsburg put her finger on this aspect of memory bias when she noted that during arguments before the U.S. Supreme Court, attorneys frequently confused her with Justice Sandra Day O'Connor—the other woman then sitting on the U.S. Supreme Court.[20]

In a phenomenon with particular relevance to legal disputes, memories can also be distorted when people make judgments that attribute blame. In one study testing this phenomenon, study participants read a detailed description of a customer's visit to a restaurant, a visit that culminated in the customer leaving without paying for his meal. Some of the participants were provided with a justification for the customer's behavior that tended to excuse the customer's failure to pay, whereas other participants were led to accentuate blame because they were provided with negative information about the customer. When they were asked to recall the details of the event one week later, it turned out that the participants who had been given negative information about the customer were more likely to overestimate the price of the meal and were more likely to incorrectly report that the customer had also failed to pay for a predinner drink.[21]

One factor that leads to many memory errors is that people have difficulty with what is called *source monitoring*. When people try to remember something, they do not call up a perfectly accurate real-time recording of the event. Instead, they access a range of sources of information including their own "internal mental representation of the event," other basic information they have about how the world works, their schemas for how events such as this one typically happen, what they have been told by others about what happened, their experiences in other similar situations, stereotypes, what they imagined doing, and so on. A large body of psychological research has demonstrated that people have difficulty discriminating between these different sources of information. Thus, when someone tries to remember whether he turned off the stove before he left the house and seems to remember doing it, he may have difficulty determining whether he actually did it or just thought about doing it, or knows he usually does it, or remembers doing it on a different occasion. Similarly, a person may remember saying something in a meeting when she only thought about saying it, said it in a different meeting, or heard someone else say it.[22]

✦ ✦ ✦ ✦ ✦
Source Memory and the Oklahoma City Bombing

Consider how the information from two memories might become intertwined in ways that have important legal implications:

> A Ryder employee who observed [subsequently convicted bomber] Timothy McVeigh rent a van two days before the 1995 bombing of the Federal Building in Oklahoma City recalled there being two men. One was tall and fair, and fit McVeigh's description; the other was short, stocky, dark-haired and had a tattoo. It turned out that a day after McVeigh rented the van (alone), two men, who matched the descriptions of McVeigh and his supposed companion, came in to rent a van.[23]

The employee conflated the two instances in memory, leading authorities to search for both men.

One consequence of these difficulties in source monitoring is that people can be *suggestible*: exposure to information from sources other than what was actually observed can influence memories of what happened, altering details of memory or introducing new elements. For example, in one study, participants viewed a videotape of an automobile accident. Next, they were asked a series of questions about the accident, including a question about the speed of the car as it passed a barn. When asked questions about the accident one week later, 17% of participants reported having seen a barn despite the fact that there had not been a barn in the video.[24] Simply assuming a false fact in the question was sufficient to influence memory.

✦ ✦ ✦ ✦ ✦
Revisionist History?

An experiment conducted by *Slate* magazine provides another demonstration that memory is less than perfect:

> The online magazine *Slate* has a largely political audience, so last May [2010] when it showed readers a picture of Barack Obama shaking hands with Mahmoud Ahmadinejad at a United Nations conference, many were familiar with the momentous occasion. In the image, a straight-faced and upright Obama receives the hand of the Iranian President, who leans into the gesture wearing a slight grin. About half of *Slate*'s readers recalled that the handshake had taken place, and roughly a quarter remembered watching the event through various media coverage.
>
> Those are impressive figures, not because they demonstrate a high degree of political awareness on the part of *Slate*'s readership. Rather, they confirm years of psychological research showing that false memories can be implanted successfully in about 30 percent of people. In reality, the handshake between Obama and Ahmadinejad never occurred; *Slate* doctored the photo and presented it to readers as part of an online experiment designed to illustrate the fallibility of memory....
>
> Readers ... didn't know they were getting involved in a memory experiment. Those who participated thought they were giving their impressions of important political moments from the previous decade. With this understanding in mind, readers viewed images of four moments and marked whether or not they remembered seeing the event take place. They could also recall their feelings about the incident at the time it had occurred.
>
> ... All participants saw images of the same three real events as well as a fourth, randomly selected false moment, whose accompanying image and caption had been fabricated by *Slate*. Overall, readers recalled the true events more often than the manipulated ones, but the altered images did create false memories in the minds of many test participants. For instance, 26 percent of readers said they recalled seeing the Obama-Ahmadinejad handshake.

Slate found similar results for the other falsified events: 15 percent of participants recalled seeing Joe Lieberman vote to convict the impeached Bill Clinton; another 15 percent recalled watching George W. Bush and pitcher Roger Clemens relax at Bush's ranch during Hurricane Katrina; 36 percent believed they had seen a campaign ad about Reverend Jeremiah Wright aired by Hillary Clinton; and 42 percent remembered watching Dick Cheney rebuke John Edwards for mentioning Cheney's lesbian daughter during a vice-presidential debate.

Many readers described their memories of the event in vivid, certain terms. "The Chicago Trib had a big picture of this meeting," one participant wrote about the Obama-Ahmadinejad image. "Reminded me of JFK with the Russians. Naive," wrote another. When *Slate* combined the number of participants who recalled seeing the false event with those who hadn't seen it but remembered that it had happened, each of these false-memory rates jumped even higher.[25]

> Just because someone says it happened, just because the person is confident, just because the recollection is detailed, just because the person is emotional when describing it, does not mean it is true.
> —Elizabeth F. Loftus[26]

Even elaborate memories can turn out to be the result of suggestion. Researchers have demonstrated that it is possible for people to "remember" entire personal events that did not happen. For example, researchers have managed to create false memories such as being lost in a mall, meeting Bugs Bunny at Disney World (note that Bugs is *not* a Disney character!), being hospitalized, or having a particular food aversion.[27] These memories are created by exposing people to misleading information, such as a description of the event that they thought was provided by a family member or a false advertisement for Disney World that contained a picture of Bugs. People even begin to embellish the false stories, "remembering" additional details to which they had not been exposed.

✦ ✦ ✦ ✦ ✦
Internalized False Confessions

In approximately 15%–25% of cases in which convicted defendants are later exonerated, defendants had falsely confessed to the crime of which they were accused. False confessions can stem from many sources, such as the desire for publicity, an attempt to protect someone else, the belief that confessing will bring a close to a harsh interrogation, and an attempt to avoid the possibility of conviction for something worse.

In some cases, people make *internalized false confessions* in which they actually come to believe—to "remember"—that they did what they have falsely confessed to. Suspects may have been presented with false incriminating evidence, asked to imagine how the crime might have played out, or interrogated over a lengthy period of time. In some cases, a suspect will begin to distrust his own memory, conflate sources of information, and be vulnerable to suggestion. The suspect may even begin to confabulate detailed memories to support his confession, including motive. Juvenile suspects and people who are intellectually impaired are particularly vulnerable. Consider the following examples:

> [Eighteen]-year-old Peter Reilly ... immediately called the police when he found that his mother had been murdered, but he was suspected of matricide. After gaining his trust, the police told Reilly that he failed a lie-detector test, which was not true, and that the test indicated he was guilty despite his lack of a conscious recollection of committing the crime. After hours of relentless interrogation, Reilly underwent a chilling transformation from adamant denial through confusion, self-doubt, conversion ("Well, it really looks like I did it"), and eventual utterance of a full confession ("I remember slashing once at my mother's throat with a straight razor I used for model airplanes. . . . I also remember jumping on my mother's legs"). Two years later, independent evidence revealed that Reilly could not have committed the murder, and that the confession he came to believe was false.
>
> The case of 14-year-old Michael Crowe and his friend Joshua Treadway provides a more recent example. At first, Michael vehemently denied that he had stabbed his sister Stephanie. Eventually, however, he conceded that he was a killer: "I'm not sure how I did it. All I know is I did it." This admission followed three interrogation sessions during which Michael was told that his hair was found in Stephanie's grasp, that her blood was in his bedroom, that all means of entry to the house were locked, and that he had failed a lie test—all claims that were false. Failing to recall the stabbing, Michael was persuaded that he had a split personality, that "good Michael" had blocked out the incident, and that he should try to imagine how "bad Michael" had killed Stephanie. [T]he charges against the boys were later dropped when a local vagrant seen in the area that night was found with Stephanie's blood on his clothing.[28]

Experimental research in the laboratory has also shown that people can be induced to admit to offenses that they did not commit and that they can come to believe in the details of their false confessions.[29]

Misperceptions of Memory

Despite all the ways in which our memories can be faulty, however, we tend to think memory operates fairly well. That is, we don't tend to realize that we (and others) do not remember things very well. In one study, almost half the participants endorsed the notion that "once you have experienced an event and formed a memory of it, that memory doesn't change."[30] In fact, however, we seldom have occasion to question our memories, so we have no reason to notice when they are false. And when memories diverge, *naïve realism* (see chapter 1) leads us to credit the accuracy and objectivity of our own memory and to discount others' conflicting memories. Such misperceptions of memory can be problematic.

First, consider the implications of thinking we remember our own preferences when we do not. Even when thinking about something so central to our identities as our preferences about end-of-life health-care decisions, we can incorrectly remember our own preferences. In one study, researchers asked adults to imagine themselves in a series of different states of health and to indicate whether, if they were in that state of health, they would want particular medical treatments. So, for example, participants articulated what their preference for each treatment would be if they were in their own current state of health, if they had Alzheimer's disease, if they were in a stroke-induced coma with no chance of recovery, and if they had cancer but were in little pain. One year later, the same individuals were again asked to indicate their preferences. Not surprisingly, some of their preferences—just under 25%—had changed. But what was surprising was that people did not realize that these preferences had changed: in 75% of the instances in which their preferences had changed, people incorrectly remembered their prior preferences as being consistent with their new preferences. This means that a client who executed an advance directive at some time in the past may believe that it continues to reflect her current wishes when it does not because she does not realize that her preferences have changed.[31]

Second, consider how our naïve views of memory might lead us to have unrealistic expectations about what others should remember. If we expect others to be able to remember more completely and accurately than they are able to, we may end up tending to "impugn the intentions and motivations of those who are innocently misremembering."[32]

To take just one example, consider the possibility that a particular conversation that Jane had with a colleague over lunch was not seen by either of them as terribly important or out of the ordinary at the time it occurred, but that sometime later, after Jane's company has become the focus of a U.S. Securities and Exchange Commission investigation, it becomes clear that the specifics of what was said or not said during that conversation are central to resolving the regulatory issue. If Jane claims that she cannot remember what was said, what are we to make of that? Of course, it is possible that Jane is lying. Recall, however, what we have learned about memory:

knowing that something is important at the time it happens can lead to improved memory, but the fact that a person knows it is important at the time she is trying to recall does not really help.

Nevertheless, people do not do a good job at distinguishing these situations when evaluating someone's memory. In a study in which people were either given incentives to remember at the time of encoding or at the time of remembering, observers were asked to predict how well the memorizers would do in remembering the relevant information. As it turns out, the observers expected better memories from both those who were given the incentive at the time they were memorizing the information and those who were given the incentive only at the time they were called upon to recall the information. People often think that if it is important—no matter when it becomes important—it should be memorable; "[i]n short, judges mistakenly expected [people] to remember information that *became* important as though it *had always been* important."[33]

Elicitation of Memories

Given the frailty of human memory, attorneys need to know how to help people access their memories successfully. Anyone who has experienced the "tip of the tongue" phenomenon[34] knows that having information available in memory is not the same as being able to access it on demand. Psychologists have explored a number of aspects of how people retrieve and report memories, each of which has implications for attorneys' practice.

Unfortunately, our instincts about how to prompt memory are often not helpful. Many people, including attorneys, assume that if memory appears to be flagging, providing specific prompts or using a cross-examination approach will help spark the memory. Yet, if a person is seeking accurate information, this is exactly the wrong approach. Psychological research suggests that open-ended questions can elicit more accurate information than do more focused questions. Asking open-ended questions allows the interviewee time to collect his thoughts and also allows the interviewee to focus his attention on remembering the event rather than being distracted from this task by a series of interviewer questions.[35] Open-ended questions also minimize the chances that more directed questioning will limit the range of information obtained and the chances of inadvertent insertion of information into the discussion that may be subsequently "remembered" (recall the barn described above that worked its way from the question into the memory).

Open-ended questions also allow people to control the level of detail that they report in their initial responses. For example, a witness could choose to report that a particular event occurred "back in the spring" or that it happened "in April" or that it occurred "on April 10 during lunch." Research has shown that people intuitively adjust the level of detail that they report in order to choose a level of detail that favors accuracy, even at the expense of some precision, and that they are therefore able to provide a higher proportion of accurate information. This finding is consistent with other research that finds that although people may not be able to completely recreate an event from memory, the information in people's unassisted reports does tend to be fairly accurate.[36]

At the same time that people are sensitive to the accuracy of their reports, people hesitate to give answers that are not sufficiently informative. When they cannot give an answer that is both acceptably accurate and acceptably informative, they may give answers in which they are less confident. Providing people with the option to indicate that they don't know or don't remember can help to alleviate this tension and can be used to enhance accuracy. While people may also hesitate to repeatedly admit that they don't know or remember, giving them the option provides them greater freedom to report only those details in which they are sufficiently confident.[37]

Every lawyer knows that pushing clients or witnesses for additional details may sometimes be necessary. Yet, it is important to be aware of the consequences of such pressure. When necessary, people are able to adopt different accuracy and precision thresholds for their reports. That is, people can change the level of precision at which they report in order to provide more detail. Increasing the precision of the information provided, however, can come at a cost to accuracy.[38] One recent study found that when witnesses were forced to guess, more information was provided, but this new information included both more correct information *and* more incorrect information. In addition, there is evidence that "guessing" can result in the same types of source misattribution errors described above, with the witness's conjectures later being remembered as having actually happened.[39] The client or witness, therefore, should be allowed to indicate where she is less sure of such details, conjectures should be labeled as such, and both the lawyer and the client should keep in mind the potential for decreased accuracy.

Sometimes the process of asking specific questions can actually impair certain memories. For example, imagine that you are asked to view pictures of two categories of items that had been stolen from a house. Thus, you view a set of electronic items (for example, a personal computer, a refrigerator, a printer, and a video recorder) and a set of nonelectronic items (for example, a vase, a ring, a mirror, and a glass ornament). You are then questioned about some of the items from one of the categories, say, the computer and the refrigerator. How well will you be able to remember the full complement of items? People who did this task were subsequently better able to remember the items about which they had been questioned (that is, the computer and the refrigerator)—not too surprising given that they had a fair amount of practice recalling those items. More surprising, however, was that the other items from the practiced category (that is, the printer and the video recorder) were remembered *less* well than even the items in the nonpracticed category (that is, the nonelectronic items).[40] This result is an example of the phenomenon of *retrieval-induced forgetting*, whereby asking focused, detailed questions that are limited to specific aspects of the event or situation may inhibit memory for other related aspects of the situation. By using open-ended questions and encouraging the interviewee to relay even unrequested information, the interviewer may be able to minimize this problem, too.

In addition to specific questions, leading questions—questions that suggest or presuppose their answers—pose particular problems for memory. In one study, participants were shown a videotape of a car accident and were asked to describe what they had seen. When asked about the speed of one of the cars, one group of participants was asked, "About how fast were the cars going when they hit each other?" Other groups of participants were asked the same question, but the word *hit* was replaced by one of the following terms: *smashed into, collided with, bumped into,* or *contacted.* Estimates of speed varied depending on the descriptor used:

Term Used in Question	Estimated Speed of Car
smashed into	40.8 mph
collided with	39.3 mph
bumped into	38.1 mph
hit	34.0 mph
contacted	31.8 mph

In a follow-up experiment, participants who were asked about the speed of the cars when they "smashed into" each other were more likely to incorrectly remember that they saw broken glass than were participants who were asked about the speed of the cars when they "hit" each other.[41]

Importantly, it is not simply reference to a potential detail that results in these effects. While observers who are asked *leading* questions about an incorrect detail (for example, "did you see the children getting on the school bus?") are more likely than others to incorporate the detail (that is, the school bus) into their memory of the event, observers who are asked *direct* (but not leading) questions about the same detail (for example, "did you see a school bus?") are not.[42]

What else can be done to help spark memories? As a general matter, simple encouragement to the interviewee to provide more information does not tend to be helpful and can even impede accuracy. However, studies show that it can be useful to focus on facts and details rather than general feelings or overall familiarity. Thus, it is helpful to focus on the "who, what, when, and where" of the events that the interviewee is seeking to recall. In particular, reminders of the conditions under which the memories were formed (*context reinstatement*) can assist recall. Recent research has also shown that asking interviewees to close their eyes while they attempt to remember can increase the volume of accurate information that they recall while decreasing their reports of erroneous information.[43]

In addition, adopting an interviewee-centered focus to sequence questions in ways that are consistent with the interviewee's conception of the event, rather than asking questions according to a standard interview protocol or in the order that the questions occur to the interviewer, can aid people's ability to remember. The interviewer can ask the interviewee to approach the memory search in different ways, for example, recalling events in both chronological order and reverse chronological order. And, finally, avoiding confusing questions, such as those that include negatives, double negatives, jargon, or multiple parts, can increase the accuracy of interviewees' reports.[44]

Accurate Versus Inaccurate Memories

As should now be apparent, some of our memories are erroneous. While people have an impressive ability to remember lots of information, it turns out that people also have an impressive ability to remember things incorrectly and then to be certain that the incorrect memory is accurate. They are not lying; rather, they are just misremembering.

> Ignorance more frequently begets confidence than does knowledge.
> —Charles Darwin[45]

We tend to use a person's degree of confidence in his own memories as a guide to whether such memories should be trusted. The witness who expresses certainty holds more sway than does the witness who is more tentative in his conclusions. However, attorneys should be cautious about assuming that the confident witness is more reliable than the less confident witness. Psychological research has demonstrated that a person who is more confident of her memory is not necessarily more accurate than another person who is less confident. Indeed, the link between confidence and accuracy is relatively weak.[46]

On the other hand, details for which a person is confident do tend to be more accurate than details for which the *same person* is less confident. As we have already seen, people are reasonably good judges of the level of detail that they can accurately report, and they adjust their reports accordingly. Thus, details for which a particular interviewee is more confident do tend to be more accurate than details for which the same interviewee is less confident.

Similar results have been found for witness consistency. That is, across witnesses, witness consistency may be only weakly related to witness accuracy. However, for a particular witness, information that is provided consistently may be more accurate than information for which that witness is inconsistent.[47]

> ✦ ✦ ✦ ✦ ✦
> **Summing It Up**
>
> - Check the tendency to expect more from memory—our own and that of others—than it can provide. Memory is not as good as we would like to believe.
> - Keep in mind that memories may be colored by current experience, mood, hindsight, schemas and scripts, and the need to recall the self favorably.
> - Be aware of the difficulties of source monitoring, resulting in the tendency to be suggestible and the tendency to conflate aspects of different memories. Remember that the information contained in questions can become part of a memory.
> - Use open-ended questions to probe memory. When pushing for specific details, be careful to avoid leading questions and to encourage respondents to label guesses as such.
> - Avoid unduly equating confidence with accuracy.
> - Backstop memory with notes and other documentary information.

For Further Reading: Memory

Ronald P. Fisher, *Interviewing Victims and Witnesses of Crime*, 1 PSYCHOL. PUB. POL'Y & L. 732 (1995).

Ronald P. Fisher et al., *Interviewing Cooperative Witnesses*, 20 CURRENT DIRECTIONS PSYCHOL. SCI. 16 (2011).

Marcia K. Johnson, *Memory and Reality*, 61 AM. PSYCHOLOGIST 760 (2006).

Marcia K. Johnson et al., *Source Monitoring*, 114 PSYCHOL. BULL. 3 (1993).

Asher Koriat et al., *Toward a Psychology of Memory Accuracy*, 51 ANN. REV. PSYCHOL. 481 (2000).

Asher Koriat & Morris Goldsmith, *Monitoring and Control Processes in the Strategic Regulation of Memory Accuracy*, 103 PSYCHOL. REV. 490 (1996).

MEMORY FOR EVENTS (Michael P. Toglia et al. eds., 2007) (vol. 1 of HANDBOOK OF EYEWITNESS PSYCHOLOGY).

DANIEL L. SCHACTER, THE SEVEN SINS OF MEMORY: HOW THE MIND FORGETS AND REMEMBERS (2001).

Emotion | 3

> The law . . . is imbued with emotion. Not just the obvious emotions like mercy and the desire for vengeance but disgust, romantic love, bitterness, uneasiness, fear, resentment, cowardice, vindictiveness, forgiveness, contempt, remorse, sympathy, hatred, spite, malice, shame, respect, moral fervor, and the passion for justice. Emotion pervades not just the criminal courts, with their heat-of-passion and insanity defenses and their angry or compassionate jurors but the civil courtrooms, the appellate courtrooms, the legislatures. It propels judges and lawyers, as well as jurors, litigants, and the lay public.
> —*Susan A. Bandes*[1]

Emotions are inherent to the types of situations that lawyers must navigate. Lawyers' own emotions can influence their responses to clients, witnesses, cases, opponents, and colleagues. Emotions can influence the responses and decisions of opposing clients and counsel, witnesses, jurors, judges, and mediators. And client emotions surely color how clients experience the situation that led them to seek legal representation and the representation itself. The kinds of disputes that lead people to consult lawyers—divorce, breach of commercial contracts, bankruptcy, personal injury, disputes over intellectual property, employment matters, criminal charges, and many more—are themselves fraught with emotion. Legal consultations that involve planning and prevention rather than disputes—for example, estate planning, starting a business, prenuptial agreements, contract negotiation, and more—involve a mix of emotions including excitement, anxiety, hope, fear, love, and more. Litigation itself can be an extremely stressful experience, on par with the kind of stress related to job loss or relationship breakdown;[2] and, ultimately, both lawyers and clients are interested in living fulfilled lives that are subjectively happy.

> When dealing with people, remember you are not dealing with creatures of logic, but creatures of emotion.
> —Dale Carnegie[3]

It is tempting to want to try to keep emotions—both our own emotions and those of our clients—at bay. When people are blinded by anger, they may do or say things that they later come to regret and may find it difficult to negotiate advantageous agreements. Fear may prevent a client from engaging in timely planning. Elation may cause a client to neglect important aspects of an agreement. Debilitating grief may make it hard to plan for the future. Strong emotions may cause decision makers to act impulsively, focusing on short-term rather than longer-term goals, ineffectively gathering and using information, and so on.[4] Nerves may make it difficult to conduct an effective deposition, closing argument, or negotiation. In the pursuit of more rational decisions and effective performance, we might view such emotions as unimportant and as undesirable influences on decision making, particularly "when they occur at the wrong time or at the wrong intensity level."[5] After all, we have all been told that "cooler heads" tend to prevail.

> The emotional qualities are antagonistic to clear reasoning.
> —Sir Arthur Conan Doyle[6]

But it would be virtually impossible to do away with the effects of emotion. Emotions inevitably influence how events are perceived and remembered (see chapters 1 and 2). Even *incidental affect*—those moods and emotions triggered by unrelated events—have repeatedly been shown to have an influence on decision making. And, as we will see in chapter 5, it is not just current affective states that are relevant to legal decision making; people take anticipated emotions—their own and those of others—into account when making legal decisions. The question is not whether we are influenced by moods and emotions but rather which moods and emotions influence us, in what ways, under what circumstances, and how we can best utilize and manage these affective responses. Indeed, at the same time that we are cautioned about cooler heads, we are also told to "let your feelings be your guide."

Even while emotions can potentially be problematic, they can simultaneously be quite functional in helping us navigate the world. Our emotional responses direct our attention to salient aspects of our environment, provide us with information about those environments, supply information about possible responses to the conditions, and motivate us to respond to those conditions in some way. Emotions provide information about our values and goals and prompt us to act in ways that are consistent with those objectives. Displays of emotion can communicate information about our position to others and can be used as a source of information about others' frames of mind.

✦ ✦ ✦ ✦ ✦
No Decision Without Emotion?

A case study involving surgery on a patient's brain highlights the connection between emotions and decision making:

> In 1982, a patient named Elliot walked into the office of neurologist Antonio Damasio. A few months earlier, a small tumor had been cut out of Elliot's cortex, near the frontal lobe of his brain. Before the surgery, Elliot had been a model father and husband. He'd held down an important management job in a large corporation and was active in his local church. But the operation changed everything. Although Elliot's IQ had stayed the same—he still tested in the 97th percentile—he now exhibited one psychological flaw: he was incapable of making a decision.... Routine tasks that should have taken ten minutes now required several hours.... When he chose where to eat lunch, Elliot carefully considered each restaurant's menu, seating plan, and lighting scheme, and then drove to each place to see how busy it was. But ... Elliot still couldn't decide where to eat.... [W]hy was Elliot suddenly incapable of making good decisions? ... [Because] Elliot felt nothing.... He had the emotional life of a mannequin.... To Damasio, Elliot's pathology suggested that emotions are a crucial part of the decision-making process.... [W]hen we are cut off from our feelings, the most banal decisions become impossible. A brain that can't feel can't make up its mind.[7]

Lawyers who are attuned to emotions—their own emotions and those of others—are better equipped to steer a course through such waters and to capitalize on the functions of emotions in carrying out their work. Possessing an ability to be aware of their own emotions and the emotions of others, to understand the complexities of these emotional states, to use this understanding of emotions to facilitate decision making and interaction with others, and to regulate their own emotions and assist others to do the same can be a tremendous asset for lawyers in their practice. Attending to emotions and their nuances and effectively using them can help lawyers to work productively with clients and colleagues, become

> " For men decide far more problems by hate, or love, or lust, or rage, or sorrow, or joy, or hope, or fear, or illusion, or some other inward emotion, than by reality, or authority, or any legal standard, or judicial precedent, or statute.
> —*Cicero*[8] "

effective problem solvers, act as successful negotiators, and manage stress. Before we can effectively use and manage emotions, however, we must understand them.

Perceiving and Understanding Emotions

Capilano Suspension Bridge, Vancouver, B.C.

Affective states that a person might experience include specific *emotions* (such as anger, pride, happiness, fear, guilt, and shame), which tend to be triggered by identifiable stimuli and to last for a finite period of time, and *moods*, which tend to be less intense and less differentiated but which tend to last longer than specific emotions. Imagine a time when you were really angry or a time when you felt great joy. These affective experiences involve physiological effects (did your heart race?), cognitive effects (what were you thinking about?), and behavioral effects (what did you do or want to do?). Affect influences how we attend to, perceive, construe, and process information; the ways in which we remember; and how we make judgments and decisions. Affect can influence our expectations about future events and our interactions with others.

As important as it is to attend to and identify emotions—both our own emotions and those of others—this is not always an easy task. Emotions may lurk beneath the surface and be difficult to detect. And in trying to distinguish one emotion from another, we don't always get it right. In one clever study, a researcher approached people crossing the Capilano Suspension Bridge in Vancouver, British Columbia, to ask them to participate in a study. The Capilano Suspension Bridge is a 5-foot-wide, 450-foot-long footbridge that is suspended 230 feet above the Capilano River and has a thrilling penchant to shift and sway as people cross it. The bridge has been described as "one of the world's scariest" bridges. Crossing it is definitely an anxiety-producing activity. After the male participants had answered some questions, the female researcher offered them her phone number indicating that she would be happy to tell them more about the study if they were interested. Men who were approached *on* the bridge were more likely to later call the researcher—presumably interpreting the excitement generated by the bridge crossing as attraction to the researcher—than were men who were approached *after* they were on solid ground with enough time passing for the thrill of crossing the bridge to abate.[9] Despite this difficulty in identifying emotions, starting to pay attention to the kinds of things that tend to trigger our particular emotional reactions and noticing how we manifest such reactions can help us become more skilled at identifying and understanding our own emotions.

When it comes to discerning the emotions of others, we are inclined to overestimate the degree to which we can accurately read others' emotional states.[10] Attorneys, in particular, may have to make a concerted effort to pay attention to nuances of emotion because lawyers may not be naturally inclined to be good emotional detectives. It turns out that individuals who are relatively powerful tend to be less sensitive to and less accurate in judging other people's emotions.[11] But we can work to better discern others' emotional states by paying close attention to emotional cues such as facial expressions and changes in vocal quality (see chapter 7). We might be alert, for example, to whether someone displays either the one-sided smile that tends to indicate contempt or a genuine smile of pleasure, whether someone shows the raised eyebrows of fear or the lowered eyebrows of anger, or whether someone exhibits the thinning of the lips that indicates anger.[12] In similar ways, listening carefully to what is said and what is not said and making comments and asking questions designed to test our perceptions (for example, "you seem frustrated . . ." and "how do you feel about . . .") can help us to better understand the emotions of another.

✦ ✦ ✦ ✦ ✦
Noticing Emotion

Consider how paying attention to emotion might help to build a relationship with a client:

> Ellen is a partner in an accounting firm . . . [who] was faced one day with the need to present some difficult news to her client, the controller.
>
> As she began to deliver the bad news, she noticed that "the client's face was getting red, and his knuckles were getting white." We can all imagine the thousand and one emotions and thoughts that could be instantly conjured up by the active mind sitting in Ellen's chair in that moment: "How can I get out of here? There goes the account," and the like.
>
> Yet Ellen took a different approach. She paused, took a deep breath, and said, "You look a little angry." And then she waited, silently, for the client to respond.
>
> After a moment, the client shouted, "No, I'm not angry! Not at all!" He then added, "Well, I mean, not at you; I'm angry at our people. I mean, you shouldn't have to be the one to bring this news to me, it's embarrassing. I mean, I'm glad you've pointed it out. Yes, I'm angry, though not at you."[13]

Perceiving emotion and not ignoring or dismissing it allowed Ellen to draw the client out, which helped him to identify his own emotion and its causes.

Beyond simply identifying the existence of emotions, lawyers can be well served by developing a more complex understanding of emotions. In particular, it can be useful to distinguish between different emotions (for example, shame and guilt) and between moods and specific emotions. A nuanced understanding of emotion includes an awareness of the causes and consequences of different emotions and the ways in which emotions can change over time. Similarly, it is useful to understand the ways in which different emotions (even those that are contradictory) can coexist. For example, a client facing a divorce might simultaneously still feel love toward his spouse, be angry about the divorce, be anxious about the divorce process and the future, and be sad about the loss of the marriage. Similarly, a client might react with a mixture of positive and negative emotions to a "disappointing win" (a positive outcome that could have been even better) or to a "relieving loss" (a bad outcome that could have been worse).[14] Attorneys with a well-developed understanding of emotions are equipped to conduct "emotional what-if analyses," entertaining counterfactual ideas and predicting how they or another person would feel under different circumstances.[15] Correctly perceiving emotions—and their differences and trajectories—can give an attorney useful insight into his own or another's beliefs, interests and priorities, values, views of the relationship, and intentions. It is to the details of such emotions to which we now turn.

General Effects of Mood

Much psychological research has examined the general effects of being in a positive or a negative mood. Even transient moods can affect how we perceive and evaluate events, people, objects, options, causal connections, and so on. In particular, moods tend to bias perceptions and judgments in a direction that is consistent with the particular mood— the *mood congruency effect*. Those in a positive mood tend to pay attention to and recall more positive information (*affect-congruent recall*), have better recall for information that was encoded when they were in a positive mood (*affect-state dependent recall*), judge things more positively and leniently, believe that positive events tend to happen more frequently, and be more optimistic about the future. Conversely, those in a negative mood tend to pay attention to and recall more negative information, have better recall for information that was encoded when they were in a negative mood, judge things more negatively and critically, believe that negative events tend to happen more frequently, and have a more pessimistic orientation toward the future.[16]

Cognitively, positive moods tend to expand a person's thinking in ways that facilitate the integration of information, idea generation, connections between ideas, and a focus on the big picture. Similarly, positive moods can make a person more receptive to negative feedback. People in positive moods are better at solving problems requiring insight or creativity.[17] Consider people's ability to solve what is known as the Duncker task: a person is given a candle, a book of matches, and a box of thumbtacks and asked to figure out a way to attach the candle to the wall in such a way that it can burn without dripping wax on the table or floor below. Think for a moment about what you might try. People in a positive mood are more likely to be

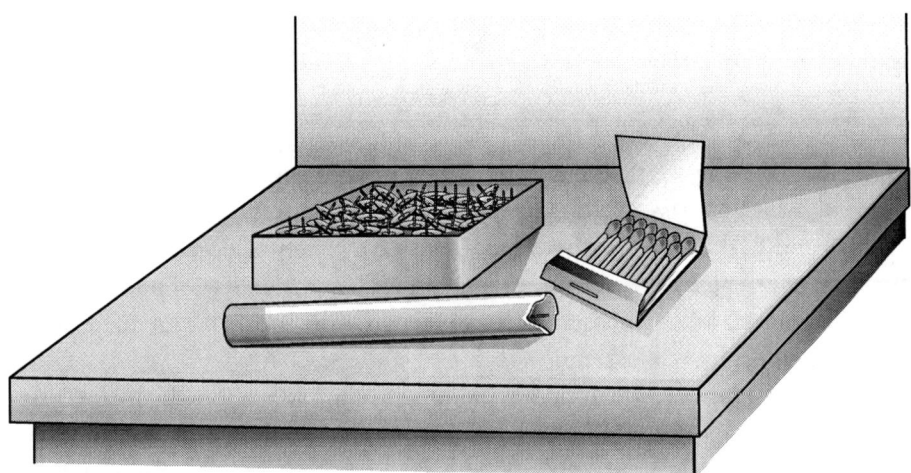

FIGURE 3.1: Dunker Task

able to reconceptualize the function of the box containing the tacks to come up with an inventive—and effective—solution: attaching the box to the wall using the tacks and then using the box as a stand for the candle.[18]

Positive mood is also associated with the use of easily accessible knowledge structures such as stereotypes and scripts (see chapter 1) as well as other shortcuts in judgment (see chapter 4). Because a positive mood signals that all is well, people may have more confidence in relying on such shortcuts, feeling less of a need to engage in more systematic processing of information.[19]

As we will see, negative moods and emotions can be more complex. People in some kinds of negative moods can be more analytical, are more likely to focus on details and task-relevant information, tend to practice more, and are more critical (searching for errors) and less likely to show confirmation bias or to make the fundamental attribution error (see chapter 1). In addition, studies have found that people in a sad mood are better able to generate concrete and persuasive arguments.[20]

These types of mood effects have been widely studied in the context of negotiation. Negotiators in positive moods tend to engage in more creative problem solving and integrative deal making, to exchange more information and propose more alternatives, to use more complex bargaining strategies involving more cooperation and fewer contentious tactics, and to make more concessions. Negotiators in positive moods tend to be more confident and to believe that they fared well in the negotiation. Negotiators in positive moods are more likely to intend to successfully reach a deal, are more likely to honor any deal that is reached, and show increased willingness to embark on joint projects in future dealings.[21]

In contrast, negotiators in negative moods tend to engage in less integrative and more competitive bargaining strategies, make less accurate judgments about the others' interests, have a narrower focus of attention and be less likely to generate alternatives, make more extreme proposals, and display lower desire to work together on future projects or deals.[22]

Emotions and Appraisal

While the most obvious distinguishing feature of different affective states is the degree to which they are pleasant or unpleasant, emotions differ in more ways than simply being positive or negative. Thus, there are a variety of negative emotions (sadness, anger, guilt, fear, shame, disappointment) and a variety of positive emotions (happiness, pride, satisfaction, hope) that are distinguishable on dimensions beyond their degree of pleasantness or unpleasantness.

How we appraise a situation has important implications for which emotions we experience. As we will see, different appraisals tend to result in different emotions. Consider, for example, a car accident in which one car hits another from behind. If the driver of the rear car realizes that he was following too closely, he may feel guilty or embarrassed. Alternatively, if he believes that the accident resulted because the other driver stopped suddenly, he is more likely to feel angry. Ultimately, emotions and attributions function in a sort of loop: "[e]motions usually occur because events have been interpreted in a certain way, and, once emotions occur, people often think in a somewhat altered manner."[23]

Consider, first, the effect of appraisals on emotions. Rather than simply stopping after assessing how good or bad we feel, we make a whole set of appraisals, often unconsciously, that serve to distinguish different types of emotions. For example, we might consider whether the relevant event is worth our attention. We might ask what we consider to be the cause of an outcome—our own conduct (in which case we might feel guilt or pride), the conduct of another person (in which case we might experience anger or gratitude), fate, or some aspect of the situation (in which case we are more likely to feel sadness)—and whether that cause is controllable. We might assess the degree to which we feel uncertain about how the situation will play out (inclining us toward sadness or fear or hope) or whether we feel that the situation is clearly understandable (making us more likely to experience anger or happiness). We might make a prediction about the degree of effort that we anticipate having to expend in dealing with the situation. We might find that we are highly motivated to take action in response to the situation or that we are not so inspired.[24]

Similarly, consider the effect of different reference points on emotions. For example, people's satisfaction with what they have tends to be influenced by comparison to what others have. In addition, satisfaction or dissatisfaction can be influenced by how well a person has done compared to his own aspirations. In appraising a situation, a person might entertain counterfactual thoughts about "what might have been"; however, someone with modest aspirations may feel happier with the same objective outcome than someone with higher expectations. Consider the findings of researchers who studied the emotions of Olympic athletes. Paradoxically, the bronze medal winners, who placed lower than the other medalists, displayed greater happiness than did the silver medalists. This seems odd, however, only until considering the salient comparison for each. The salient comparison for the silver medalists is the gold medal: "I almost won gold." For the bronze medal winners, however, the salient comparison is no medal at all: "Boy am I lucky—I just managed to finish in the medals!"[25]

This view of emotions implies that while emotions arise in response to particular events or objects, it is possible for the same event or object to elicit different emotions depending on how it is appraised by the observer. Thus, because people may have different goals, perceive the situation differently, and make different inferences, the same situation can produce different emotional responses in different individuals.[26]

Second, consider the implications of the emotions that we experience on the appraisals that we make. For a variety of reasons, those experiencing a particular emotion are inclined to make appraisals that are consistent with that emotion. When a person is already experiencing a particular emotion (for example, anger), new appraisals that are consistent with that emotion (for example, that another person is to blame) come to mind particularly easily. Thus, "when faced with a new situation that allows for several possible interpretations [as most interesting social situations do], angry people . . . focus on the actions and intentions of other people and sad people on the impersonal, situational forces."[27]

Many emotions have particular import for lawyers and lawyering. In the following sections, we will briefly examine the nature of anger and blame; guilt, shame, and embarrassment; fear and anxiety; sadness; and positive emotions.

Anger and Blame

Strong emotions are often involved when one person's conduct is thought to have contravened a behavioral norm and caused injury to another. Anger, in particular, tends to arise from many of the types of conflict that are often at issue in the legal context: violations of autonomy, perceived injustice, and violations of procedural justice (see chapter 8).[28] A person who feels falsely accused may be angry with her accuser. A negotiator may become angry when he thinks the other side has misrepresented a material fact or has made an unreasonable demand. A patient may become angry when he feels that his care provider is inaccessible or dismissive. Jurors may feel a sense of outrage that leads them to award punitive damages.

Because of the set of attributions associated with anger—primarily the attribution of harmful behavior to causes within a particular person's control—angry people tend to make dispositional attributions to the relative neglect of relevant situational factors, to perceive others' conduct as intentional, and to blame others. For example, an angry person might be more likely to attribute a car accident to the behavior of another driver than to the fact that the roads were icy. Accordingly, anger tends to result in decreased trust and a decreased concern for others' interests.[29]

Other effects of anger stem from the associated feeling of certainty. For example, angry people experience an increased desire to take some kind of action, particularly action that might serve to change the situation. As a result, anger is associated with an increase in risk-seeking behavior and with a desire to engage in retaliation and increased punishment.[30] On the plus side, anger can motivate a person to take action intended to correct injustices or to prevent future wrongs. On the other hand, when this certainty and desire to act is misdirected, punitive action may be directed against an innocent target. For example, in one study, decision makers who were induced to feel anger prescribed more punishment against an unrelated tortfeasor than did those experiencing neutral emotion.[31]

The feeling of certainty associated with anger can also lead an angry person to be less receptive to advice.[32] In addition, while some negative emotions, such as sadness, are associated with more careful cognitive processing, the certainty associated with anger tends to result in an increased reliance on more intuitive processing and schemas such as stereotypes.[33] In one study, investigating police officers were found to be less sensitive to nuances in evidence when they were angry than when they were sad.[34] Consistent with confirmation bias (see chapter 1), the search for and assessment of new evidence can be biased by a feeling of anger. And, consistent with both confirmation bias and the availability heuristic (see chapter 4), angry people are likely to find angry reasoning to be more convincing and to believe that angering occurrences are more common.[35]

Guilt, Shame, and Embarrassment

Legal representation is frequently concerned with situations that involve allegations or inferences of wrongdoing or that require the exposure of the client's personal information. Business clients may experience tax audits, allegations of deficiencies in record keeping or procedures or products, or allegations of sexual harassment or employment discrimination; individuals may be experiencing divorce, find themselves unemployed, need to file bankruptcy, or find their finances, infidelities, health records, sexual history, and other private information subjected to scrutiny. Along with other emotions, many clients will experience embarrassment in such situations, and some will experience feelings of guilt or even shame.

Embarrassment tends to arise when a person has publicly contravened some social norm of interaction or etiquette, particularly when that person believes that others will negatively evaluate his behavior. When a person is embarrassed, he is motivated to stay within the norms of social interaction and to take action to correct his missteps. It is difficult for others to continue to find fault with someone who shows embarrassment through the classic expression of embarrassment: the awkward smile and shrugged shoulders.[36]

Guilt and shame can be distinguished from the more transient and less intense emotion of embarrassment. When a person believes that she engaged in a particular wrongful or harmful behavior, she feels guilt. In contrast, when a person believes that she is a bad person, she feels ashamed. Guilt is commonly coupled with a feeling of regret and can cause us to be motivated to make up in some way for having caused harm, for example, to assist the person who has been harmed, to offer compensation of some kind, to promise not to repeat the frowned-upon conduct, or to offer an apology. But guilt can also result in the desire to avoid the person who has been harmed in an effort to avoid thinking about our less-than-stellar behavior, to avoid accepting responsibility, and to avoid the unpleasant feelings associated with guilt. Shame, on the other hand, tends to be inwardly focused and is associated with feelings of worthlessness, denial, defensiveness, and anger.[37]

Fear and Anxiety

Many aspects of legal situations can induce fear or anxiety. Many clients are anxious about the potential outcomes they face. A client may be quite apprehensive about an upcoming deposition. Still another may be anxious about even seeking legal advice. A lawyer might be anxious about negotiating with a particular opposing counsel or worry about her level of skill or preparation when contemplating trial.[38] In-house counsel might be anxious as she selects an outside attorney to handle a make-or-break litigation matter. And lawyers might feel anxious in dealing with clients' emotions.

Fear and anxiety are associated with high uncertainty about the likely outcome of a situation with potentially negative consequences and a feeling of little control over that situation. Such worry can motivate us to plan ahead for how to confront the worry-inducing situation. But the uncertainty associated with fear can also generate a desire to guard against potential harm, motivating a posture of risk avoidance. Those who are experiencing fear tend to have a narrow focus of attention on the source of their fear, to have a heightened perception of the likelihood and magnitude of potential negative outcomes, and to make more pessimistic judgments and choices. Thus, the fear of losing a job can result in choices privileging job security over salary, the fear of being duped or being a sucker can cause less exertion of effort, and the fear of failure may cause a delay of plans. In addition, the uncertainty associated with anxiety can result in an increased receptivity to advice, even bad advice. Finally, fear and anxiety tend to trigger "flight" or avoidance of the anxiety-inducing situation. Thus, for example, anxious negotiators show a tendency to avoid conflict, generate more generous first offers, make steeper concessions, and end the negotiation more quickly.[39]

Sadness

Sadness tends to result when a person attributes an unpleasant outcome to characteristics of a situation; it is often associated with loss. Thus, a client who is experiencing the loss of a loved one, a job, or a marriage; dealing with putting a parent in a nursing home; or experiencing the winding down of a business may feel sadness. An attorney might experience sadness following the loss of a case or the culmination of a project. The feeling of loss associated with sadness often prompts a search for something that can replace or substitute for the thing that is missing and can result in riskier choices. Mild sadness tends to result in more systematic processing of information, less reliance on stereotypes, a focus on details, and a greater ability to generate persuasive arguments.[40]

Positive Emotions

Positive emotions are also important to both lawyers and their clients. A lawyer may be excited to negotiate with or litigate against a particular opponent or may be energized by the challenge of appealing a novel issue. A feeling of satisfaction or pride may result from crafting a particularly creative contractual agreement or bringing a complex deal to fruition. Clients may experience a variety of positive emotions as they contemplate new partnerships (hope and anticipation), are able to patent an invention (pride), find that they were named in a will (gratitude), and successfully adopt a child (joy). Of course, both lawyers and clients presumably strive for overall feelings of happiness in their lives.[41]

We've already seen that a positive mood can expand a person's thinking, spawning creativity and flexibility. Positive emotions are also associated more broadly with productivity and success at work, good health, facility at building rewarding relationships, and greater resilience and coping. Happy people make optimistic judgments and choices, are less likely to take risks, and are more likely to be perceived as trustworthy.[42]

Happiness researchers have found that well-being is highest among those who experience and nurture close social relationships with family and friends, are truly engaged in their work and other life activities, are committed to and spend time pursuing meaningful goals, are able to savor their experiences and express gratitude for what they have, and have sufficient material means to meet their basic needs.[43]

Of particular interest to many lawyers and their clients is the complicated relationship between money and well-being. Money can, of course, ensure that a person has food and shelter, that medical bills are paid, and that basic needs are otherwise met. And it turns out that money can buy a bit of happiness: income has a positive relationship to life satisfaction such that those with higher incomes report slightly more life satisfaction. The relationship between income and well-being, however, is relatively weak; even those who are extremely wealthy are only slightly happier than other people, and the money-happiness link is subject to diminishing returns such that increases in wealth matter more at low levels of wealth.[44]

> [I]t is generally good for your happiness to have money, but toxic to your happiness to want money too much.
> —Ed Diener & Robert Biswas-Diener[45]

In addition, how we feel about money and what we do with it can also influence well-being. First, the pursuit of money tends to be negatively associated with well-being because a focus on material goals crowds out relationships and other meaningful activities.[46] Second, it turns out that discretionary income spent on experiences tends to make people happier than money spent on material possessions. Why might this be? Experiences tend to be more central to self-identify, are more conducive to social interaction (and we know that social interaction is related to happiness), and are less affected by comparisons with others than are material purchases. Experiences can be more satisfying because we are more likely to satisfice (see chapter 5) when choosing experiences rather than trying to maximize as we do when choosing material goods. And experiences tend to be increasingly satisfying over time—in a way that material possessions are not—as we relive (and revise) them in our memories.[47] Thus, a dinner out with friends, travel to another part of the world, or a visit to a national park with family is likely to have a bigger impact on well-being than a bigger TV or a new car.

Psychologist Sonja Lyubomirsky summed up the relationship this way:

> Why is it so hard for us (even myself!) to believe that money really doesn't make us happy? Because the truth is that money *does* make us happy. But our misunderstanding, as one happiness researcher eloquently explains, is that "we think money will bring lots of happiness for a long time, and actually it brings a little happiness for a short time." Meanwhile, in our effortful pursuit of such dead ends to pleasure, we end up ignoring other, more effective routes to well-being.[48]

Managing Emotions

In order to effectively use emotions, it is also important to be able to effectively regulate and manage them. There are times at which it is appropriate and even helpful to experience and express emotions. At others times, we need to be able to keep our emotions in check. Losing our cool at a city council meeting or in the middle of a deposition may not be adaptive. But we cannot count on just the right emotion to occur at just the right time to suit our purposes. Instead, we need to learn to manage our emotions.

To manage or regulate our emotions, however, does not mean to eliminate them. Instead, emotion regulation is the process of "how we try to influence which emotions we have, when we have them, and how we experience and express these emotions."[49] Rather than allowing emotions to distract from and interfere with their activities, those who are effective at managing and regulating emotions are able to "psych up, calm down, or maintain a mood, as desirable,"[50] enabling them to use their emotions—whether positive or negative—to further their tasks and goals. Similarly, those who are skilled at managing emotions are able to influence others' emotions, moderating their anger, making them more cheerful, calming them down, or inspiring them as appropriate.[52]

> Anyone can become angry—that is easy. But to become angry with the right person, to the right degree, at the right time, for the right purpose, and in the right way—that is not easy.
>
> —Aristotle[51]

> ✦ ✦ ✦ ✦ ✦
> **Failure to Regulate Emotion**
>
> The failure to regulate emotion can be detrimental to attorneys' careers.
>
> We've all encountered the "900 pound gorilla" partner who throws his weight around, intimidates other partners, excoriates hapless associates who displease him, and eviscerates the poor secretary who forgets a comma. We've seen him make embarrassing outbursts at partners' meetings, or tell off-color jokes, or beat a minor point to death.
>
> Such behavior often fails to accomplish the intended goal and can be counterproductive.
>
> In research that looked at business leaders who were pursuing promising careers and then "derailed", the single most significant factor for those who derailed was lack of impulse control. In other words, whether they were aware of their emotions or not, they allowed them to erupt in ways that got them into trouble. Lack of impulse control shows itself in inappropriate behavior such as telling off-color jokes, blowing up at people, slamming your fist down in a meeting, committing sexual harassment, etc. The emotionally intelligent lawyer is both aware of his emotions and able to head off those that will hurt others or get him in trouble.[53]

In the 1999 movie *Analyze This*, a therapist (played by Billy Crystal) tells his mob boss client (played by Robert De Niro) that when he gets mad, he hits a pillow: "Just hit the pillow. See how you feel." De Niro proceeds to pull out his gun and fire numerous rounds into the pillow. "Feel better?" Crystal asks. "Yeah, I do," responds De Niro.[54] This scene is consistent with the widespread belief that *venting*, or blowing off steam, is a useful strategy for dealing with anger. In addition to hitting a pillow or punching bag, common advice includes yelling or pounding nails.

However, it turns out that venting doesn't help to moderate anger and may instead make things worse. In particular, by focusing attention on and rehearsing the angry feelings, venting tends to keep those feelings alive, perpetuating and sometimes even intensifying them. Indeed, in one study, people who focused on venting their anger while hitting a punching bag ended up experiencing more anger and more aggression than did those who distracted themselves by hitting a punching bag for exercise.[55]

Other studies have found similar results for crying. While people tend to believe that a good cry will make them feel better, the effects of crying can vary, sometimes having a calming effect but sometimes intensifying the emotions.[56] "[C]riers who received social support during their crying episode were more likely to report mood benefits than were criers who did not report receiving social support."[57]

> ✦ ✦ ✦ ✦ ✦
> **Managing Strong Emotions**
>
> Fear, anxiety and anger operate as a double-edged sword. On one hand, they motivate us to work harder and succeed. On the other, they can cripple our efforts to perform. As is often the case, we experience insults, unfair practices and obstacles that interfere with achievement of our goals. In the high-stress environment of law firms, these challenges can disrupt our ability to not only lead, but also to perform. Because it is necessary for lawyers, especially those in leadership positions, to tolerate ambiguity and handle risk taking, a strong grasp on emotional intelligence can not only help us, but also empower us, to deal with fear, anxiety and anger, and turn them into positive emotions.
>
> [W]e can become aware of the conditions that trigger these emotions, manage ourselves to best respond to these conditions and ultimately develop a long-term plan for a constructive resolution. It is the attorney that most effectively manages stress, and responds to fear, anxiety and anger—not necessarily the one with the strongest grasp of the rules of evidence or legal technicalities—that can ultimately navigate through the many challenges and obstacles that a law career presents. The emotionally intelligent lawyer knows how to deal with unruly partners, colleagues and clients, accepts constructive criticism and overcomes such worries as "will I make partner?"[58]

However, while it seems clear that venting emotions, particularly anger, is not an optimal emotion-management strategy, *suppressing* emotions can also have its difficulties. Actively trying to monitor and suppress emotion once it occurs—the kind of thing that we might do when trying to keep a poker face—requires a great deal of energy and cognitive capacity.[59] Because efforts to suppress emotion take place *after* an emotion occurs, such efforts tend not to decrease the experience of the emotion. Indeed, thought suppression tends to have ironic effects: the monitoring required to push thoughts out of our minds ends up highlighting those very thoughts. To see how this might be so, try *not* to think about a white bear.[60] Difficult isn't it? Efforts at suppression can sometimes decrease the degree to which emotion is *expressed*, which, as we shall see, can be beneficial. But the cognitive effort involved in concealing the emotion tends to result in increased emotion and decreased memory. Those who are working to suppress their emotions also tend to increase emotion in others and to have more trouble establishing rapport.[61]

Thus, it appears that neither venting nor suppressing strong emotions is an optimal strategy. So, what can lawyers do to regulate emotion? The best strategies involve attempting to manage emotions before they occur and handling emotions effectively once the emotions are experienced.[62]

First, lawyers can exercise influence over features of a situation in order to alter the likely emotional experience by seeking out or creating conditions that are likely to produce the desired emotion and avoiding or altering those that are likely to produce unwanted emotions. For example, when needing an emotional lift, a lawyer might seek out a colleague who always has a funny spin on things, play pleasant music, or take a walk around the block. Similarly, a lawyer might seek to influence the location of a deposition, choosing a location that is likely to minimize distress for a client or, conceivably, one that might make an opponent uneasy; or a lawyer might take a break in the middle of a deposition or a negotiating session in order to allow himself or the client to calm anxieties, get control of anger, or contain elation.

Second, lawyers can focus their attention in ways that influence emotions—distracting their attention away from those things that produce unwanted emotions or concentrating on things that tend to produce desired emotions. *Rumination*—focusing attention on and rehearsing the experiences of the particular emotion, its causes, and its consequences—tends to intensify the emotion. In contrast, distraction is more likely to moderate the effects of emotion.[63] Consider, for example, an attorney who is anxious about her belief that she lacks skill at rainmaking. Ruminating about her supposed deficiencies in this area and rehearsing all the ways in which she is liable to fail in this endeavor are likely to increase her negative thoughts and pessimism about rainmaking and may even become a self-fulfilling prophecy. If, however, she distracts herself with another pleasant or engaging activity, her mood is likely to improve; thus, when she returns to the topic of rainmaking, her perspective is likely to be more positive, and she may be better able to think of creative approaches. Similarly, there may be times when an estate planner needs to focus client attention on negative health details but at other times may need to distract the client from such matters in order to convince the client to contemplate other, more positive, aspects of the future. To do so, the attorney might ask the client about her plans for an upcoming vacation or talk to the client about sports or family or other topics that the client finds uplifting.

Third, lawyers can reassess their appraisal of the situation, of its meaning, or of how others will respond to it. Because emotions are closely tied to a person's appraisal of a situation, changing the appraisal can change the emotional experience. Thus, for example, a lawyer can attribute the agitation that he feels before delivering an opening statement to stage fright, or he can elect to understand those same sensations as an indication that he is fired up and ready to go.[64] Lawyers might take into account additional information or perspectives that alter their understanding of, and emotional response to, a set of circumstances. For example, when someone is angry, a lawyer can take some time to identify the attributions he has made, consider alternative explanations, consider the other's perspective, and decide whether anger is justified or could be moderated. Furthermore, consider a client who is anxious about an upcoming deposition. The client's anxiety may be severe enough that it promises to interfere with his ability to effectively answer questions in the deposition. The attorney could assist the client in reappraising the situation, focusing on the feelings of uncertainty and lack of control that characterize anxiety. The attorney could ask the client to articulate what makes her anxious about the deposition, help the client to put those worries in perspective, reassure her that she is competent to handle the situation, and help her to formulate specific plans for how to handle both the deposition and her anxiety (see chapter 12). Such reappraisal tends to moderate the emotion.[66]

When angry, count to four; when very angry, swear.
—*Mark Twain*[65]

Fourth, lawyers can attempt to alter their experience of, response to, or expression of the emotion itself.[67] Thus, a lawyer might use exercise or relaxation techniques in order to balance her emotions. One attorney that we know takes a walk around the block before he begins a challenging deposition. In addition, a lawyer might consciously attempt to act in ways that correct for the effects of emotions. For example, a lawyer who recognizes that he is angry and feeling impelled to make a quick decision might decide to postpone the decision or to "sleep on it" in order to allow reconsideration of the decision once the intense feelings of anger have faded. An anxious negotiator may pay close attention to the concessions that she is making, knowing that her anxiety may cause her to be too quick to compromise.

Managing our emotions—particularly strong emotions—in these ways can be challenging. And it can be even more difficult when we are tired, hungry, or experiencing cognitive strain. One study found, for example, that people whose cognitive resources were taxed by their attempt *not* to think about a white bear were subsequently less able to regulate the degree to which they expressed their emotions. Another study found that people who had worked to suppress their emotional reactions to an upsetting movie clip showed less persistence in a later physical task.[68] Given these limitations, it can be helpful to have a specific plan for how to handle a situation in which strong emotion arises. For example, a negotiator could plan ahead that when she feels her shoulders start to tighten (which she has discovered is an early sign of her nascent anger), she will focus on relaxing her shoulders and suggest a five-minute break. These *implementation intentions* (see chapter 5), specifying an identifiable circumstance and a specific response, can be an effective way to regulate emotion.[69]

Using Emotions

Lawyers who understand the complexities of emotions can harness that knowledge to facilitate tasks such as thinking, problem solving, obtaining and providing information, decision making, generating persuasive arguments, and negotiating.

Emotions as a Source of Information

> Go to your bosom;
> Knock there; and ask your heart what it doth know.
> —William Shakespeare[70]

Paying attention to emotions can be a useful source of information that might not be available through other channels. Emotions signal information about our values and interests and can redirect attention to things that matter to us. A lawyer might pay attention to her emotions when considering the type of work about which she is passionate. A negotiator might glean information about an opponent's priorities from his emotional reaction to a proposal. Indeed, negotiators who more accurately recognize emotions are better able to create joint value.[71]

In addition, emotional reactions to proposed options "may incorporate factors such as moral or aesthetic values that people have difficulty articulating and which, perhaps as a result, tend to receive little weight in deliberative decision making."[72] One of the authors of this book remembers her father's advice about a test that could add some insight into the process of choosing between two colleges: flip a coin and see how you feel about the decision. That emotional reaction might contain valuable information about difficult-to-articulate priorities. Accordingly, emotional responses can provide useful information about the relative desirability of different courses of action and can help people to prioritize among competing interests. Similarly, emotions can aid ethical decision making by reminding people of important values.

> When your heart speaks, take good notes.
> —Susan Campbell[73]

Emotions as a Source of Motivation

Emotions can be an important source of motivation, providing the impetus necessary for us to implement our plans.[74] For example, a lawyer who is feeling somewhat anxious about an upcoming court appearance will be more motivated to engage in the necessary preparations. While severe anxiety can be debilitating, a mild amount of anxiety can focus attention on the task at hand and improve performance. Alternatively, a client or lawyer who feels anger or righteous indignation can be motivated to take the difficult steps that might be necessary to confront the injustice that has caused such feelings.

Emotions as a Facilitator of Thought

Emotions can be used to bolster thought processes, memory, and decision making by taking advantage of the differing characteristics associated with various emotions. Rather than simply being subject to the vagaries of emotions, we can capitalize on naturally occurring emotions or seek to generate specific emotions in order to consider problems from multiple points of view and engage in different approaches to problem solving. For example, sensing that a divorce client is in a particularly optimistic mood during a particular consultation, the attorney might ask him to revisit the options that they had discussed in a prior meeting when the client was feeling more apprehensive. While neither perspective is necessarily better than the other, the client may gain additional insight from considering his options while in different moods.

Similarly, lawyers can match tasks to the thought patterns generated by different emotions. Since those in a positive mood tend toward big-picture, creative thinking with less attention to detail, it is a good idea to engage in brainstorming—for example, thinking about alternative ways to structure a business transaction or creative ways to settle a dispute—while in a positive mood. When recognizing that they feel surprised, lawyers can push themselves to engage in additional information-seeking tasks such as asking more questions or doing further research. On the other hand, a neutral or mildly sad mood tends to be conducive to systematic, detail-oriented thinking, deductive reasoning, and identification of problems—patterns of thinking that can facilitate tasks such as checking financial statements, disclosures, briefs, or other documents for errors or reviewing the details of an agreement. Since a state of anxiety entails a greater sense of caution, this would be a good time to do tasks that involve anticipating the ways in which things could break down or to reexamine the assumptions underlying a decision or a process. Because anger focuses attention on a particular threat, it can be used to concentrate the mind on ways to confront that threat.

To the extent that there are limits on how attorneys structure their time (a brief might need to have been done "yesterday"), attorneys do not always have the luxury of waiting until the right mood for a task presents itself. But attorneys can still attempt to induce an affective state that is conducive to the task at hand. For example, a lawyer might sit in a straight-backed chair in a sterile room to do detail-oriented work but brighten his own spirits with a comfortable space and cheerful music for tasks that are more creative.[75]

Display of Emotions

Displaying or expressing emotion can serve a number of purposes. For example, as we have noted, emotions communicate information about interests and values. Displays of emotion can also provide information about a person's level of knowledge or telegraph information about how a person intends or is willing to behave. Displaying emotions can also evoke emotional reactions in other people and influence their behavior. Anger can elicit fear in another person, distress can elicit feelings of concern, embarrassment can evoke feelings of amusement or sympathy or forgiveness, and elation at the outcome of a negotiation can make an opponent feel less satisfied with the result. A person may avoid behavior that is predicted to provoke another's anger or exasperation, or, conversely, a person may strive to strategically evoke an angry reaction from another. In other instances, a person may act generously in order to stimulate a positive emotional reaction. In addition, people can "catch" the emotions of those with whom they interact through the process of *emotional contagion*.[76]

Consider a lawyer in the context of a negotiation. If she observes a positive display of emotion in opposing counsel when the negotiation turns to a particular option, she may surmise that this option is of interest and acceptable to the other side. She might then determine how to use this interest to forge agreement or to create value. If she senses guilty feelings on the part of the other side, she may expect more cooperation and make larger demands. Conversely, a display of pain, such as a grimace or a wince, might signal to her that concessions made by opposing counsel are becoming increasingly painful and may be approaching some limit. Similarly, if her opposing counsel displays anger in response to a particular proposal, she may conclude that the proposal is a potential deal breaker. She would thus need to assess how much further she is able to push for greater concessions. She might decide that further demands would not be fruitful, or she might consider further concessions that she could make. Indeed, negotiators do tend to make lower demands of and to concede more to angry opponents.[77] Given these tendencies, the negotiator will have to assess the credibility of the emotions displayed, that is, whether they are genuine or strategic (see chapter 7). Similarly, our negotiator might use such displays of emotion to signal her own interests and intentions.

Displaying emotion can also influence the development of relationships. For example, displaying signs of attentiveness and liking—making eye contact, smiling, leaning forward, asking questions that show an interest—can help to generate rapport and signal trustworthiness and can increase a willingness to disclose information, to comply with advice, or to engage in negotiation. Conversely, displays of anger tend to undermine trust (see chapter 7).[78]

All of this is complicated by the fact that we are not terribly good at gauging our own outward expressions of emotion. In particular, "people often overestimate the extent to which their thoughts, feelings, and sensations 'leak out' and are available to others."[79] Just as we tend to overestimate the degree to which we can accurately read others' emotional states, we also overestimate the degree to which others can read our emotional states, a phenomenon known as the *illusion of transparency*. While people recognize that they have more information about their own emotional states than do observers (and vice versa) and attempt to account for this lack of information when estimating how they will be perceived, they tend not to sufficiently take their privileged insight into account.[80] Thus, it is "difficult to know if we have successfully maintained a poker face"[81] or whether we have communicated the desired emotion. This is particularly true when the channel of communication provides little opportunity for signaling emotion through vocal inflection or body language (see chapter 7).

> ✦ ✦ ✦ ✦ ✦
> ### The Illusion of Transparency
>
> The tendency for people to overestimate their transparency manifests itself in a host of ways. For example, liars overestimate the likelihood that others can tell they are lying, those tasting beverages overestimate the likelihood that others can read their expressions to identify whether a drink tasted unpleasant, and observers of rule-breaking behavior overestimate the degree to which others think they appear concerned. Similarly, negotiators tend to overestimate the degree to which those on the other side can correctly identify their interests—overestimating both when they are trying to conceal those interests *and* when they are explicitly trying to convey them. Studies have also shown that innocent suspects tend to believe that their innocence will be obvious to investigators, judges, and jurors—even when that is not the case.[82] In one study, participants were recorded while they watched funny videos. Not only did they overestimate the degree to which others would rate them as expressing their amusement, but when allowed to watch themselves on video, they expressed surprise at their lack of expressiveness, leading the researchers to conclude that "people may not know just how little they show."

Thus, in addition to carefully attending to the emotional cues of others, lawyers should be sensitive to their own displays of emotions and to the possibility that they might not be sending the messages that they think they are sending or that they intend to send. Indeed, lawyers should make extra efforts to ensure that they are accurately conveying any desired emotional signals.

> ✦ ✦ ✦ ✦ ✦
> ### Summing It Up
>
> - Accept that it is impossible to do away with emotion. Emotion inevitably influences how we attend to, perceive, construe, remember, and process information.
> - Understand the nuances of mood and emotion—distinguishing anger and blame, shame and guilt, fear and anxiety, sadness, and a range of positive emotions—and the complex ways in which such affective states are experienced.

- Rather than venting or suppressing emotion, use more sophisticated techniques to regulate emotion, such as altering the situation, using distraction, reassessing the appraisal of the situation, and working to change the experience and expression of the relevant emotion.
- Use emotion as a source of information about values and interests, as a source of motivation, and as a way to facilitate thought.
- Display emotion in order to communicate values and interests, demonstrate knowledge, evoke emotion in others, and develop relationships.
- Beware of the illusion of transparency—it is difficult to assess the degree to which others can read our emotional states.

For Further Reading: Emotion

David R. Caruso & Peter Salovey, The Emotionally Intelligent Manager (2004).

Do Emotions Help or Hurt Decision Making? A Hedgefoxian Perspective (Kathleen D. Vohs et al. eds., 2007).

Emotion and the Law: Psychological Perspectives (Brian H. Bornstein & Richard L. Wiener eds., 2010).

Handbook of Affective Sciences (Richard J. Davison et al. eds., 2003).

Handbook of Emotion Regulation (James J. Gross ed., 2007).

Handbook of Emotions (Michael Lewis et al. eds., 3d ed. 2008).

Dacher Keltner & Jennifer S. Lerner, *Emotion*, in Handbook of Social Psychology 317 (5th ed. 2010).

Keith Oatley et al., Understanding Emotions (2d ed. 2006).

W. Gerrod Parrott, *The Nature of Emotion*, in Emotion and Motivation 5 (Marilynn B. Brewer & Miles Hewstone eds., 2004).

Special Issue: Emotion in Legal Judgment and Decision Making, 30 Law & Hum. Behav. 115 (2006).

Symposium, *Mindfulness, Emotions, and Ethics in Law and Dispute Resolution*, 10 Nev. L. Rev. 289 (2010).

Well-Being: The Foundations of Hedonic Psychology (Daniel Kahneman et al. eds., 1998).

Judgment Shortcuts | 4

People make a great many judgments with surpassing skill and accuracy, but evidence of dubious belief, questionable judgment, and faulty reasoning is not hard to find.
— *Thomas Gilovich & Dale Griffin*[1]

As we work our way through life, we are constantly required to make all sorts of judgments and predictions. How fast is that car coming? Am I surprised by the result of the election? Will a judge or jury find our case persuasive? Does the dispute resolution clause in the proposed contract serve my client's best interests? What kind of a plea bargain is the prosecutor likely to offer to my client? Is this client telling me the truth? How long will it take to draft this brief? Such judgments help us to "interpret the past, understand the present, and predict the future."

> Heuristics are bug ridden by definition; if they didn't have bugs, then they'd be algorithms.
> —*Anonymous*[2]

Psychological research has explored two methods by which we make such judgments: deliberation and intuition. Sometimes we engage our deliberate system of thinking, expending more effort and taking our time to systematically think through a problem. But we also routinely make intuitive judgments, coming to conclusions quickly and effortlessly without paying much attention. *Cognitive heuristics* are ways in which people simplify or take shortcuts in making judgments. Much of the time, these shortcuts are efficient routes to reasonably accurate judgments. Indeed, imagine having to carefully deliberate over every trivial judgment that we are required to make each day. However, as we shall see, reliance on these shortcuts can sometimes produce systematic errors in judgment.

Positive Illusions

In one study, civil and criminal attorneys across the country were asked to identify a case from their caseload that was expected to go to trial in the next six to twelve months. They were instructed to briefly describe the case, to state their minimum goals for the case, and to indicate the degree to which they were confident that this minimum goal (or better) could be achieved. Overall, attorneys overestimated the probability that the goal would be met or exceeded. This was true even for attorneys with many years of experience. What may be even more interesting, however, is that in hindsight attorneys seemed to believe that their predictions were well calibrated with the actual results: more attorneys reported that they had met their original goals than had in fact done so and a similar percentage reported that they were pleased or very pleased with the result. Attorneys were overconfident but didn't realize it.[4]

> Prediction is very difficult, especially about the future.
> —Niels Bohr[3]

Like the lawyers in this study, most of us tend to view the world through rose-colored glasses, often seeing ourselves and our prospects as better than they are. In particular, we have a tendency to be overconfident in the forecasts that we make, failing to sufficiently allow for uncertainty in our judgments. Therefore, for example, people routinely underestimate the time that they will need to complete a time-consuming task (the *planning fallacy*),[5] anticipate that they will enjoy their jobs and their vacations more than they actually do, underestimate the likelihood that they will suffer from ill health, predict that they will not divorce, and overestimate the likelihood that they will be awarded custody of their children in the event that they do divorce.[6] Experts, too, demonstrate overconfidence; for example, financial analysts tend to overestimate earnings, entrepreneurs overestimate their chances of success, and negotiators are overconfident about the persuasiveness of their positions.[7] In final-offer arbitration, both sides tend to be overconfident that the arbitrator will select their offer.[8] Indeed, the greater the uncertainty we face, the more overconfident our predictions tend to be.

> [O]ptimistic overconfidence is not a desirable trait for generals recommending a war or for attorneys urging a lawsuit, even if their expressions of confidence and optimism are pleasantly reassuring to their followers or clients at the time.
> —Daniel Kahneman & Amos Tversky[9]

Exposure to only one side's arguments can exacerbate this tendency. In one study, participants were given a set of details about a legal situation and asked to predict the outcome. They were provided information about either one side's arguments or the other side's arguments or information about both. Those who were given only one side's arguments failed to account for their incomplete information—even though it was straightforward to infer the arguments for the opposite side—and were less accurate in predicting the outcome than were those who were exposed to both sides' arguments. They were, however, more confident in their predictions.[10]

> ✦ ✦ ✦ ✦ ✦
> ### The Illusion of Control
> Overconfidence in our prospects for success can be exacerbated by the *illusion of control*—the tendency to overestimate our ability to control events and outcomes that are not within our control. People's assessments of the degree of control that they have over chance events tends to be inflated, and people tend to believe that they have more control over an outcome when they are in the driver's seat—for example, choosing their own lottery number or rolling the dice themselves—even when that outcome is determined by chance.[11] When attorneys are in charge of a case, they may similarly overestimate the degree to which they can control the outcome.

High confidence can sometimes be quite useful to legal decision makers. For example, high aspirations can lead to better outcomes in negotiation (see chapter 11).[12] Similarly, high confidence in an attorney may assure clients that they are being well served and may contribute to a lawyer's ability to be persuasive (see chapter 10). However, overconfident misprediction can spark undesirable litigation, can lead litigants to pass up opportunities for settlement, can lead parties to a deal to forgo reasonable contract terms, or can lead to ill-advised business decisions.[13]

> ✦ ✦ ✦ ✦ ✦
> ### Law Student Confidence
> Prospective law students tend to be more confident about their own job prospects than they are about their peers' prospects. A 2010 survey of 330 prospective law students found the following:
> Fifty-two percent are "very confident" that they will find legal employment upon graduating from law school.
> Only 16% are "very confident" that most of their peers will do so.[14]

> ✦ ✦ ✦ ✦ ✦
> **A Lack of Confidence?**
>
> Of course, sometimes we are less confident in our abilities or outcomes than we should be. In some circumstances—for example, when the task at hand is particularly easy or when success is especially likely—we can *underestimate* rather than overestimate performance. Thus, for some high-probability outcomes, people will tend to underestimate their chances of success. Similarly, while we tend to underestimate the time it will take us to complete more demanding projects (the planning fallacy), it is more likely that we will *overestimate* the time that it will take to complete a simple assignment.[15]

In addition to being overconfident in their predictions, people also tend to have unrealistically positive views of themselves and their abilities, perceiving themselves to be better than average on a variety of dimensions and perceiving themselves in more positive terms than do observers. Research has shown, for instance, that most people estimate that they are above-average drivers; that most negotiators think that they are above-average negotiators; and that people tend to think that they are more objective, fairer, and more ethical than others.[16] By definition, of course, this is not possible—despite the Garrison Keillor saying: "Welcome to Lake Wobegon, where all the women are strong, all the men are good-looking, and all the children are above average." Such biased perceptions serve a protective function—indeed, one group that tends to have more accurate self-perception are those who are clinically depressed—but such perceptions can, of course, distort predictions.

Attorneys are not immune to having overly positive views of themselves, with most attorneys assessing themselves as well above average in terms of their "ability to predict the outcome of a case, honesty, negotiation skills, and cooperativeness."[17] And in one study, a large majority of a sample of magistrate judges estimated that at least half of their peers had higher reversal rates on appeal than they did.[18]

Similarly, people's judgments are often *egocentrically biased* such that they overestimate their own role and make judgments consistent with their own point of view or interests. Because information about a person's own behavior, interests, and views is more readily available than information about others, information about the self tends to be focal. Thus, for example, people overestimate the extent to which others pay attention to them, the extent to which their knowledge is shared by others, and the extent to which others' impressions of them are consistent with their own self-assessments.[19] Similarly, negotiators tend to anticipate that an externally imposed deadline will pressure or otherwise disadvantage them more than it will the other side.[20]

Given these tendencies, it should not be surprising that people overestimate their contributions to joint projects; for example, spouses' estimates of their contributions to the work of the household typically add up to more than 100%, as do authors' estimates of their contributions to a joint work.[21] We tend, however, to perceive others through the lens of *naïve cynicism*, expecting others to take disproportionate credit for positive outcomes but underestimating their inclination to take responsibility for contributing to less agreeable results.[22] But it turns out that while people are sometimes inclined to accept insufficient responsibility for failure (see chapter 1),[23] they also sometimes overestimate their contributions to less desirable outcomes.[24]

♦ ♦ ♦ ♦ ♦
Self-Serving Bias

"If someone sues you and you win the case, should they pay your legal costs?"	85% agree
"If you sue someone and lose the case, should you pay his costs?"	44% agree[25]

Egocentric bias can also result in judgments of fairness that are biased in favor of a person's own interests or the interests of another with whom a person is affiliated (such as a colleague or client). For example, as we saw in chapter 1, sports fans from opposing teams make self-serving judgments about the fairness and conduct of the teams in the game. Similarly, the affiliation of auditors and other agents with a particular client or principal has been shown to influence the decision maker.[26] Furthermore, several studies have shown that litigants and their representatives make biased estimates of the fair settlement value of civil cases, with those on the plaintiff side making higher estimates and those on the defense side making estimates that are significantly lower.[27] Even observers who simply adopt the point of view of one side in a negotiation make judgments that are skewed by this perspective.[28]

Anchoring

If we asked you whether the average annual temperature in San Francisco was higher or lower than 558 degrees, what would you say? After berating us for asking a silly question, you would surely tell us that the average temperature is less than 558 degrees. What if we then asked you to estimate the average annual temperature in San Francisco? Would it surprise you to find that your answer would tend to be higher than that of someone who hadn't first answered our question about 558 degrees? It turns out that people's average temperature estimates are influenced in just this way even though we all know that 558 degrees is a completely implausible value.[29]

When we attempt to make an estimate—for example, the amount for which we will enter into a deal or the amount that a judge will award in a civil case—our estimates are easily colored by available numbers that do not necessarily provide information that is relevant to the judgment at hand. This phenomenon is called *anchoring* because the irrelevant values provide a starting point (or *anchor*) for a judgment; adjustments are then made away from the anchor but are often insufficient.

In the legal context, Chris Guthrie, Jeff Rachlinski, and Andrew Wistrich demonstrated that irrelevant anchors can influence judges' damage awards. One group of judges was asked to consider a motion to dismiss on grounds that a hypothetical case failed to meet the jurisdictional minimum of $75,000 in a diversity case. Because the case clearly involved more than $75,000 in damages, virtually all of the judges denied the motion. However, those who considered the motion anchored on the lower figure provided by the motion and awarded significantly less in damages than did a second group of judges who had not considered the motion.[30]

In another study, auditors were asked to estimate the prevalence of management fraud in companies audited by Big Four accounting firms. Before giving their estimates, auditors were first asked to judge whether the rate of fraud was more than ten per one thousand firms or whether it was more than two hundred per one thousand firms. Just as in other studies of anchoring, their subsequent estimates were significantly influenced by these anchors: "participants in the first condition estimated a fraud incidence of 16.52 per 1,000 on average, compared with an estimated fraud incidence of 43.11 per 1,000 in the second condition!"[31]

The potential for this sort of anchoring runs throughout legal decision making. Anchors provided by initial demands or offers, damage caps, insurance policy caps, negotiator aspirations, and the media have influenced damage awards (by judges and jurors) and settlement outcomes.[32] Similar effects have been shown for judges making criminal sentencing decisions.[33] And anchors have influenced values in negotiated deals, such as selling prices, in similar ways.[34]

Availability and Representativeness

Availability

Do more people die from motor vehicle accidents or from stomach cancer? From shark attacks or falling airplane parts? Studies have shown that most of us would say accidents and shark attacks, whereas the right answers turn out to be stomach cancer and falling airplane parts. Why do we get these answers wrong? People tend to judge the likelihood of an event by the ease with which they can recall examples of similar instances. Therefore, instances that are more available in memory or that are more fluently recalled are judged to be more common. Sometimes this tendency is adaptive: male employees of a particular company might come to mind more easily than female employees because there really are more males than females. But items can also be more accessible in memory because they are more salient, have been repeated more often, are concrete (as opposed to abstract), are more recent, or hold emotional interest. In contrast, less memorable information, such as statistical summaries, tends to hold less interest even though such information can often be more accurate. Thus, it is not surprising that we think that deaths in motor vehicle accidents are more common: we see far more stories about traffic accidents than stomach cancer in the press, and images of smashed-up vehicles tend to grab our attention.[36]

> [M]ost people reason dramatically, not quantitatively.
> —Oliver Wendell Holmes[35]

Perceptions of the legal system tend to be influenced in similar ways. Large punitive damage awards, brutal crimes, catastrophic bankruptcies, and nasty will contests tend to be more striking, seem more tangible, and garner more attention in the media than the typical case with relatively small stakes or a relatively routine resolution. Perceptions shaped by this distorted picture of the legal system can then influence decision making within and judgments about the system. For example, even attorneys overestimate the rate at which cases go to trial, plaintiff win rates, and the size of jury awards; and physicians overestimate the risk of medical malpractice suits.[37]

Representativeness

In the book (and subsequent movie) *Moneyball: The Art of Winning an Unfair Game,* Michael Lewis tells the story of how Billy Beane, the general manager of the Oakland Athletics, assembled a competitive baseball team by focusing on players who did *not* have the characteristics people tended to think of when they thought of star players (high batting averages, runs batted in, or stolen bases). Instead, Beane focused on players who were undervalued by these typical measures but who performed well in other, less stereotypical ways (such as on-base percentage). Under this system, Beane was able to create a team that was competitive with larger market teams at a significantly smaller cost. (Compare the Oakland Athletics' $40 million in salaries in 2002 with the Yankees' $126 million for the same year.)[38]

Beane was able to accomplish all that he did with the Oakland A's in part by resisting what is known as the *representativeness heuristic*—the tendency for people to base their likelihood estimates and causal attributions on the degree to which an event or object is representative of (or resembles) a particular category. As a result of the representativeness heuristic, people tend to be influenced by anecdotes or overall impressions and to ignore or be insensitive to quantitative information. This tendency can, for example, "cause baseball scouts to rely on whether a prospect matches their mental picture of a baseball player (in, say, stance or swing), rather than rely on more specific statistical predictors, such as on-base and slugging percentages, or, for pitchers, strikeouts-to-walks or ground-outs-to-fly-outs ratios."[39] Similarly, a lawyer might base her initial judgment of another's honesty on whether that person matches her idea of what liars tend to look like (we will return to this problem in chapter 7). In parallel ways, the representativeness heuristic leads us to expect that effects must resemble their causes. Thus, we may be quick to attribute ill motive to a person whose behavior has caused ill effects, to believe that the causes of (or cures for) a disease must resemble its symptoms, or to expect that a big effect must have had a similarly significant cause.[40]

> ♦ ♦ ♦ ♦ ♦
>
> **Availability and Representativeness**
>
> According to Consumer Product Safety Commission projections from data gathered in hospital emergency rooms, which of these products has the most associated injuries annually?[41]
> a. Playground equipment
> b. Home workshop power saws
> c. Cooking ranges and ovens
> d. Beds, mattresses, and pillows
>
> Answer: d

The representativeness heuristic can also lead us to ignore useful quantitative information such as the size of the sample under consideration. Consider two large companies doing hiring in a profession that tends to employ equal numbers of men and women. Company A hires approximately one thousand new employees each week. Company B hires an average of ten new employees each week. Imagine that we are concerned about patterns of gender discrimination in hiring and that we look at the last five years of hiring and examine the number of weeks during that period in which each company's hires were more than 60% male. Would you expect Company A to have more such weeks? Company B? Or would you expect both companies to have similar numbers of such weeks? Absent discrimination, most people would expect the companies to have similar numbers of such weeks. But, in fact, it would be much less likely to observe a week in which Company A hired more than six hundred men than it would be to observe a week in which Company B hired more than six men. (Think about the flipping of a coin. Which is more likely: getting more than six heads out of ten flips or getting more than six hundred heads out of one thousand flips?)[42]

The representative heuristic can also lead to misperceptions of chance events. Imagine that you are at a roulette wheel containing thirty-eight pockets (eighteen red, eighteen black, and two green). You have observed a number of spins in a row all come up red. Should you bet on black on the next spin of the wheel? Many people would predict that the wheel is now "due" to come up black. This is because a pattern in which a series of red spins is followed by black seems more representative of the random process that is generating the outcomes than is yet another red. However, on any individual spin of the wheel, the odds of coming up black or red remain unchanged (slightly less than 50%) and are not influenced by previous spins. This tendency to mispredict is known as the *gambler's fallacy*.[43] The gambler's fallacy may lead clients involved in a succession of cases or deals to expect to have a success following a series of losses or unsuccessful deals because they believe that they are due for a win.

Affect Heuristic

Judgment is also affected by a phenomenon that psychologists call the *affect heuristic*—using emotions as a basis for judgment. A person's first reaction to a stimulus is often an intuitive affective response, that is, a feeling of like or dislike. Consistent with these reactions, people may make judgments based on gut level impressions, using their feelings toward the object of judgment as a guide (see chapter 3).

Thus, for example, people may rely on their general feelings toward something, such as nuclear power or cellular phones or pesticides or genetically modified foods, to make judgments about its risks and benefits. Similarly, it turns out that attitudes about regulation can be driven by emotion. For example, people tend to demand regulation of behaviors related to particularly dreaded risks (such as cancer) more than they demand regulation of behaviors related to other, less dreaded risks (say, accidents) even if the latter are more common.[44] We also might expect people to evaluate others (clients, lawyers, opponents, suppliers, insurers) or courses of action (doing nothing, filing a lawsuit, signing a document) based on their general affective reactions toward those people or actions.

Relying on a global feeling can be functional: "[a]lthough analysis is certainly important in some decision-making circumstances, reliance on affect and emotion is a quicker, easier, and more efficient way to navigate in a complex, uncertain, and sometimes dangerous world."[45] At the same time, however, these gut reactions may sometimes depart in important ways from the judgments that might have been reached through more deliberative analysis. Ultimately, the affect heuristic

> works beautifully when our experience enables us to anticipate accurately how we will like the consequences of our decisions. It fails miserably when the consequences turn out to be much different in character than we expected. In the latter circumstances, the rational actor becomes, to borrow the words of Amartya Sen, the rational fool.[46]

Hindsight Bias

A related bias—*hindsight bias*—is the tendency to unconsciously overestimate the likelihood that we would have assigned to an outcome once that outcome has actually occurred. In a form of Monday morning quarterbacking, people predicting the outcome of an event after the fact are more certain that they would have predicted the actual outcome than are those who attempt to predict in foresight. That is, we have a tendency to feel that we "knew it all along," making it difficult to assess in hindsight the predictions that we would have made in foresight. Only when an outcome is really surprising will we experience a feeling that we "would never have predicted that."[47]

Hindsight bias is likely to affect a variety of legal judgments. For example, a decision maker, such as a judge or juror, who is asked to evaluate the reasonableness of particular conduct will know that harm has in fact occurred. Hindsight bias can, therefore, affect judgments about the range of risks that were foreseeable, whether a particular risk was foreseeable, the likelihood that a particular risk would materialize, and the likely severity of harm risked. The risk of loss is likely to seem greater once harm has occured, and any precautions taken are likely to seem less reasonable.[48]

Similarly, hindsight bias can make decisions by defense counsel seem less competent once the defendant has been convicted, can make the outcome of deal negotiations seem predictable once the deal has been struck or has fallen through, can make the basis for a motion seem more or less meritorious once the motion has been sustained or rejected, can make a corporate officer's predictions seem fraudulent once they have proven to be erroneous, or can make the success or failure of a business venture seem preordained.[49]

Because hindsight bias makes such outcomes seem predictable, this phenomenon makes it difficult to learn from experience. When we "knew it all along," we can have difficulty appreciating the extent to which we mispredict before the fact and, accordingly, it is difficult to use this information to make better predictions in the future. "In a world where everyone 'knew it all along,' there is no incentive to learn and very little left to learn."[50]

A related phenomenon, *outcome bias*, occurs when people judge the quality of a decision based on its outcome; for example, decisions resulting in negative consequences are judged to have been bad decisions. In one study, people given information about the up-front risks and benefits related to a medical treatment decision and asked to judge the quality of that decision, judged the same decision more favorably when the treatment turned out to be successful than when it did not.[51]

Judgment Heuristics	
Heuristic	Description
Positive Illusions	
Overconfidence	Failing to sufficiently allow for uncertainty in our judgments.
Unrealistically Positive Views of Self	Perceiving ourselves to be "better than average" and in more positive terms than observers.
Egocentric Bias	Overestimating our own role and making judgments about events in ways that are consistent with our own perspective or interests.
Anchoring	Beginning with irrelevant values as a starting point for a judgment and then making adjustments—often insufficient ones—away from the anchor.
Availability	Judging the likelihood of an event by the ease with which we can recall examples of similar instances.
Representativeness	Basing a likelihood estimate on the degree to which an event or object is representative of a particular category.
Affect Heuristic	Making judgments based on gut level impressions; using feelings as a guide.
Hindsight Bias	Tendency to unconsciously overestimate the likelihood that we would have assigned to an event once the outcome is known.

Debiasing

Sometimes our intuitions are useful, resulting in efficient and accurate judgments about the world. Sometimes the most available example is the right one, sometimes a cause does resemble its effect, and sometimes our gut feelings lead us to the right assessment. Accordingly, it would not be prudent to completely disregard intuitive judgments and engage in thorough research or deliberation about every question that we encounter. However, as we have seen, our intuitive judgment shortcuts can produce systematic errors in judgment. Thus, when errors are likely or when the judgment has important consequences, it is important to recognize the range of common errors in judgment and to engage in deliberative efforts to correct any errors in our intuitive reactions.

> The instantaneous "thin-slicing" of information, which drives intuitive thinking, necessarily disregards the realities of most complex disputes; if those disputes could have been resolved by "thinking without thinking," the parties themselves would have done it before retaining counsel.
>
> I doubt that Malcolm Gladwell, in writing *Blink*, intended to inspire an entire generation of attorneys to bypass the dorsal lateral prefrontal cortex and shoot directly from the amygdala, making rapid judgments, strategic decisions and settlement recommendations sparked by split-second reactions to briefs, memoranda, statutes, witnesses, adversaries and judges. Attorneys and clients do not expect accountants, engineers, physicians and psychologists to rely on intuitive judgments to calculate their tax liability, design bridges, diagnose illnesses and evaluate mental competence; and they should not exempt themselves from clients' justified expectation of objective judgment untainted by hunch, suspicion, intimation, instinct, premonition and impulse. Since attorneys and clients would be alarmed if judges based their decisions entirely on intuition, they should be no less alarmed when they find themselves indulging in the same intellectual shortcut. When decision makers feel the impulse to "go with your gut," they should question whether they are relying on intuition because it is accurate or because it is easy.[52]

There are several steps that people can take to attempt to debias judgments. Perhaps most straightforwardly, when there are data available that speak to the judgment, they can be obtained and used. A lawyer negotiating a deal can gather information on similar, previous deals. A lawyer negotiating a settlement can obtain information on trial verdicts in similar cases. Independent confirmation of facts can be sought. Seeking such information can help to ensure that any judgments are made on a solid factual foundation.

✦ ✦ ✦ ✦ ✦

Using Facts in Judgment

Lawyers are well advised to seek out factual information to inform their judgments. This is true even in areas in which they might be considered expert. One study found that trial lawyers' estimates of various trends in civil litigation—the percentage of cases resolved through trial, plaintiff win rates, and average damage awards—departed significantly from the actual figures as calculated by the Bureau of Justice Statistics.[53] It seems that lawyers, like others, can be influenced by the way that cases are reported in the media.[54]

One of the most effective, and broadly applicable, methods for debiasing judgment is to consider why the judgment might be wrong by generating counterarguments, considering weaknesses, considering the opposite, or including a devil's advocate in the process of deliberation. Such deliberation procedures can minimize (although perhaps not completely eliminate) the effects of overconfidence, hindsight bias, self-serving bias, anchoring, and other biases.[55]

Attorneys, of course, are not strangers to the notion of considering the arguments on the other side of their position. However, according to Russell Korobkin, law professor and author, attorneys must be particularly careful about how they assess such counterarguments:

> [Lawyers] are fully aware that their adversary will make contradictory arguments, have thought about what those arguments might be, and very often have identified the opposing side's best arguments in advance.... [When asked] to identify the weaknesses of their case or identify their opponent's likely arguments, lawyers are able to do so quickly but are equally ready to provide a detailed account of why they would prevail in court despite those weaknesses. This lawyerly skill–no doubt honed in law school courses in which professors ask students to make arguments and anticipate counter arguments–suggests a tendency to identify undesirable facts and arguments *for the purposes of generating responses rather than for the purpose of conducting an objective evaluation* in a way that could substantially lessen the force of the overconfidence bias.[56]

Thus, it can be helpful, for attorneys in particular, to focus on the strength of any counterarguments. Korobkin suggests that attorneys adopt the perspective of a *disagreeable adjudicator*—that is, a person who is predisposed to take the opposing position—in evaluating why their judgment or position might be incorrect.[57] Moreover, generating explanations for how an alternative outcome might result has been shown to make those outcomes seem more plausible.[58]

> " Don't delude yourself. Try to discern the real argument that an intelligent opponent would make, and don't replace it with a straw man that you can easily dispatch.
> —Justice Antonin Scalia & Brian A. Garner[59] "

Similarly, it can also be useful to adopt an *outside perspective*, one that concentrates on making predictions based on what is known about a range of similar instances or cases. The following story about the planning of a high school curriculum project, related by psychologist Daniel Kahneman, illustrates this principle:

> When the team had been in operation for about a year, with some significant achievements already to its credit, the discussion at one of the team meetings turned to the question of how long the project would take. To make the debate more useful, I asked everyone to indicate on a slip of paper their best estimate of the number of months that would be needed to bring the project to a well-defined stage of completion: a complete draft ready for submission to the Ministry of Education. The estimates, including my own, ranged from 18 to 30 months. At this point I had the idea of turning to one of our members, a distinguished expert in curriculum development, asking him a question phrased about as follows: "We are surely not the only team to have tried to develop a curriculum where none existed before. Please try to recall as many such cases as you can. Think of them as they were in a stage comparable to ours at present. How long did it take them, from that point, to complete their projects?" After a long silence, something much like the following answer was

given, with obvious signs of discomfort: "First, I should say that not all teams that I can think of in a comparable stage ever did complete their task. About 40% of them eventually gave up. Of the remaining, I cannot think of any that was completed in less than seven years, nor of any that took more than ten." In response to a further question, he answered: "No, I cannot think of any relevant factor that distinguishes us favorably from the teams I have been thinking about. Indeed, my impression is that we are slightly below average in terms of our resources and potential."[60]

When contemplating a particular case, our "forecasts of future outcomes are often anchored on plans and scenarios of success rather than on past results."[61] Therefore, it can be quite helpful to adopt or obtain a broader view that takes into account what is known about the past, looking specifically at other similar projects or cases in order to make predictions about the instant one.

Consulting with others is also a useful way of making more accurate judgments. First, it is possible that others can be more objective about our situation because it may be more natural for them to take the outside view. And, second, averaging multiple individual predictions or judgments is a powerfully effective way in which to improve accuracy. In part because of the representativeness heuristic, people tend to believe that averaging leads to average performance. But it turns out that the *wisdom of crowds* can actually lead to improved performance.[62]

It is a mathematical principle that the average of two estimates will be no further from the true value than the average difference of the individual estimates from that true value, and it can sometimes be more accurate. But this *averaging principle* is not intuitive to most people. Accordingly, even when we seek the opinions of others, we do not tend to make optimal use of the estimates provided. Instead, we tend to choose one prediction or the other rather than averaging them. When we choose, we frequently choose the prediction that turns out to be less accurate. And when we do consider another's judgment, we tend to give it too little weight. Many factors incline us to rely too heavily on our own estimates, including overconfidence, anchoring, naïve realism (we assume that another's estimate that is different from ours must be biased), not wanting to appear indecisive—and a failure to appreciate the statistical benefits of simply averaging.[63]

❖ ❖ ❖ ❖
The Averaging Principle

To see how the averaging principle works, imagine that two attorneys make independent estimates of the number of client documents that will have to be revised in the wake of a new financial regulation.

> One possibility is that both estimates depart from the true value in the same direction, that is, they are both too low (or both too high). Thus, imagine that the estimates are forty and fifty and that it turns out that the true number is sixty. The two individual estimates are off by fifteen contracts on average (one is off by twenty, and the other is off by ten). Similarly, the average of the two estimates (i.e., forty-five) also departs from the true value by fifteen.
>
> The other possibility is that the two estimates will bracket the true value, one on either side of it. For example, the two estimates might be fifty and eighty. The individual estimates are still off by fifteen on average (one is off by ten, and the other is off by twenty). But now the average of the two estimates (i.e., sixty-five) is only off by five. Thus, the error that results from averaging the estimates will always be equal to or less than the average error of the individual estimates.[64]

Consider a study in which attorneys were asked to predict jury verdicts in a series of cases. Attorneys' initial estimates varied widely, with attorneys both underestimating (63.7%) and overestimating (32.1%) the actual verdicts. When given the opportunity to use a second attorney's estimates to inform their second estimate, more than half of the attorneys (53.1%) completely ignored the new information and stood firm on their original estimates; another large proportion (29.5%) adjusted toward the second opinion but moved less than halfway toward it. Overall, attorneys moved approximately 19% toward their partner's estimates. Consistent with the averaging principle, this movement resulted in increased accuracy, but attorneys still tended to be less accurate, on average, than they would have been had they simply averaged the two estimates (their own and that of their partner). Finally, attorneys who were given the opportunity to discuss their estimates with a second attorney improved their accuracy still further, as much as they would have by simply averaging their initial estimates. Interestingly, this improvement persisted into attorneys' final independent judgments.[65]

To maximize the effectiveness of combining multiple estimates, it is important to seek input from others who are substantively informed, such as other lawyers. At the same time, while it is common for attorneys to seek second opinions from colleagues,[66] seeking additional input from others who are likely to see things in exactly the same way is not likely to be useful. Instead, lawyers should solicit input from informed people who are nonetheless likely to draw on different perspectives and to make different assumptions.

Moreover, simply obtaining additional opinions from well-informed people with alternative perspectives is not enough to ensure that the full benefit of the information is captured. Because attorneys, like others, are inclined to overprivilege their

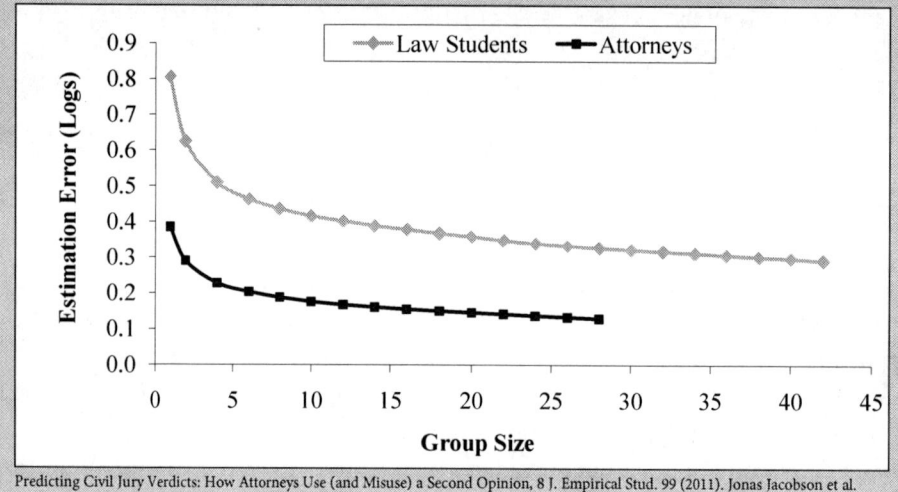

How Many Opinions?

Consistent with the averaging principle, one or two additional estimates can lead to increasingly accurate predictions. Note, however, that while additional gains can be generated by averaging the estimates made by even larger numbers of attorneys, the rate of increase diminishes as additional estimates are incorporated.[67]

Predicting Civil Jury Verdicts: How Attorneys Use (and Misuse) a Second Opinion, 8 J. Empirical Stud. 99 (2011). Jonas Jacobson et al.

own assessments, attorneys would be well served by giving their colleagues' judgments more weight than they would naturally be inclined to give, to average them or use their median value, and to engage in discussion that leads to a joint estimate even if, ultimately, they rely on their own judgment.[68]

Even when it is not possible to get a second or third opinion, it is still possible for people to get some of the benefit of the wisdom of crowds by accessing the *crowd within* their own minds by generating multiple judgments or predictions. While capitalizing on the crowd within does not improve accuracy to the same degree as consulting a crowd of others, averaging multiple estimates or predictions generated by a single person has also been shown to improve accuracy. Simply coming up with a second estimate helps a little bit. But what is more helpful is to generate a second estimate that is based on some different knowledge, assumptions, or perspectives. Sleeping on it and then coming up with a new estimate, considering the opposite or taking into account what a disagreeable adjudicator might think, and taking a different perspective are all ways to generate less redundant estimates.[69]

Finally, it is useful to obtain feedback about the accuracy of judgments when possible. Prompt feedback about the accuracy of judgments has been shown to improve future judgments. To take one example, weather forecasters are fairly accurate—when they say that there is an 80% chance of rain, it rains about 80% of the time. This is largely because forecasters get regular, immediate feedback.

In addition to information about the accuracy of judgments, it is also useful to seek out feedback about the reasons for success and failure. It is not sufficient to chalk up a success to great lawyering or having a great case (or to attribute failure to bad luck); it is important to examine the reasons for the success (or failure) so that those factors can be replicated (or avoided).[70] Similarly, it can be helpful to document predictions ahead of time and to refer back to them later to avoid the biasing influence of hindsight.

✦ ✦ ✦ ✦ ✦
Summing It Up

- Recognize the tendency to be overconfident, to commit the planning fallacy, to hold unrealistic views of the self, to overestimate our own role and, to make judgments consistent with our own point of view or interests.
- Consider the ways in which anchoring, availability, and representativeness influence judgments by causing us to be swayed by irrelevant values, to judge an event's likelihood by the ease with which we can recall similar events, and to base our estimate of an event's likelihood on the degree to which the event is representative of other similar events.
- Be aware of the ways in which emotion can influence judgments (the affect heuristic).
- Recognize the tendency of people to think that they "knew it all along"—hindsight bias. Outcomes can seem deceptively obvious once they have occurred.
- Obtain and use relevant data before making a decision, and obtain and review feedback afterward.
- Consider the opposite, consult the hypothetical disagreeable adjudicator, obtain an outside perspective, and capitalize on the wisdom of crowds (including the crowd within) as strategies for making better judgments.

For Further Reading: Judgment Shortcuts

Max H. Bazerman, Judgment in Managerial Decision Making (4th ed. 1998).
Heuristics and Biases: The Psychology of Intuitive Judgment (Thomas Gilovich et al. eds., 2002).
Heuristics and the Law (Gerd Gigenzer & Christoph Engel eds., 2006).
Judgment Under Uncertainty: Heuristics and Biases (Daniel Kahneman et al. eds., 1982).

Daniel Kahneman, Thinking Fast and Slow (2011).

Richard Nisbett & Lee Ross, Human Inference: Strategies and Shortcomings of Social Judgment (1980).

Simple Heuristics That Make Us Smart (Gerd Gigerenzer et al. eds., 1999).

Decision Making   5

> As much money and life as you could want! The two things most human beings would choose above all—the trouble is, humans do have a knack of choosing precisely those things that are worst for them.
>
> —*Albus Dumbledore*[1]

Legal actors must make decisions in a wide variety of legal contexts. Disputants must decide whether to initiate settlement discussions and whether to agree to a proposal for settlement. Attorneys must decide whether to take on a client, what to request in discovery or due diligence and how to respond to such requests, what motions to file and what arguments to make in them, how to respond to motions filed by the other side, and so on. Lead attorneys must decide which tasks to delegate to junior attorneys and how to structure the work team. Attorneys and clients must decide how to structure a proposed transaction and what terms to include. While philosophies differ regarding how directive lawyers should be in helping clients make decisions, both directive and nondirective lawyers, in order to be effective, need to understand how clients structure and make decisions. Although some decisions are reserved for the client and others are the domain of the attorney,[2] it is important to understand the decision-making process from both perspectives in order to be an effective lawyer.

Decision-Making Strategies

In making decisions, we might strive to obtain all of the pertinent information, fully analyze all of the relevant options, and make explicit trade-offs among all of the relevant dimensions of the decision problem. Indeed, in some abstract models, decisionmakers are assumed to (1) perfectly define the problem, (2) identify all criteria, (3) accurately weigh all of the criteria according to their preferences, (4) know all relevant alternatives, (5) accurately assess each alternative based on each criterion, and (6) accurately calculate and choose the alternative with the highest perceived value.[3]

Yet, in the real world, there are a variety of reasons that this sort of decision making based on full information does not take place. First, we do not and generally cannot make decisions based on full information. Gathering information is costly, time consuming, and sometimes impossible. For example, when clients decide whether to try to negotiate a resolution to their situation prior to commencing litigation, they and their lawyers must assess how the opposing party might respond to settlement proposals both prior and subsequent to the commencement of a lawsuit. They must also consider what the likely costs (financial and otherwise) of a lawsuit would be and what the likely results of a lawsuit might be. Absent a crystal ball, none of this information is completely foreseeable, particularly given that background facts will continue to change. The more different options under consideration and the greater the number of relevant considerations, the less likely it is that all of the potentially relevant information will be considered.

Second, even if we could gather all the relevant information, we lack the time and capacity to consider a nearly infinite number of options. As we have already seen, human beings rely on a variety of cognitive strategies, or heuristics, that depart in predictable ways from an idealized judgment model. But were we to try to make decisions based on full information, we would often not be able to make any decisions at all.

Thus, while an approach to decision making based on assumptions of perfect rationality and full information may seem ideal, it is for good reason that both lawyers and clients use a variety of decision-making strategies that depart from this model. They may make some decisions by examining options one by one until they find an option that satisfies a predetermined set of minimum requirements—a process known as *satisficing*.[4] When decision makers satisfice, they do not compare all of the options and attempt to find the best one; rather, they settle for the first good enough or minimally acceptable option they encounter. An entrepreneur who uses this strategy to find a location at which to open a restaurant might look at properties until he finds one that will work for his purposes and is within his budget. Following a somewhat similar strategy—*elimination by aspects*—decision makers eliminate options that do not meet some threshold for a particular attribute.[5] Thus, our entrepreneur might eliminate options from the set under consideration that are not near public transportation. This process is continued with successive attributes (whether it is at least 2,400 square feet, whether it would support a liquor license) until a single option remains.

Other strategies include choosing the option that rates the highest on the attribute that is deemed to be the most important, choosing the option that is better on a majority of attributes, choosing the option chosen last time or based on the attribute used the last time, choosing the first option that comes to mind, and choosing an option based on what other people have chosen under similar circumstances. Each of these strategies may fail to provide the best course of action, yet such strategies are used because of the costs and limitations of alternative choice processes and may sometimes be the most preferable under such circumstances. Indeed, there is evidence that people who satisfice are more content with their choices than are those who attempt to maximize.[6]

Information Gathering

Setting aside the costs of gathering information, it is generally useful to gather lots of information and generate lots of options. However, when people do attempt to gather more information to guide their decision making, they may not always act optimally. We have already seen that people tend to seek out and pay attention to confirming information to the neglect of information that is contrary to their existing beliefs or preferences (see chapter 1). And we have seen that information that people already possess may not be remembered accurately (see chapter 2).

In addition, people sometimes spend time and resources seeking information that is irrelevant in the sense that knowing the information would not alter their decision. For example, in one study, people were asked to decide whether to book a vacation at an attractive price that was about to expire, to decline to book the vacation, or to pay a small fee to preserve the option to purchase at the sale price for two additional days. The majority of people who were told that they had just passed a major exam *and* the majority of people who were told that they had failed the exam chose to purchase the vacation. However, people who were told that they would learn the results of the exam the following day tended to choose to defer the decision about the vacation until they learned whether they passed or failed. Thus, when the information (pass or fail) was available at the outset, it did not influence most decisions about the vacation. Nonetheless, people in the group that lacked the information preferred to wait for this information before making a decision, apparently failing to recognize that the information would not otherwise affect their decision.[7]

Not only can the process of searching or waiting for irrelevant information be costly, but it can also change the nature of the decision, turning information that initially had no value into information that influences the decision. Because people do not want to conceive of themselves as seeking out irrelevant information, the fact that they have sought the information implies that it is relevant and worthy of attention. In one study, the majority of students considering a protest over campus bookstore prices chose to settle with the university even when it was clear that the university would not take disciplinary action against them if they engaged in the protest. However, when it was unclear whether or not the university would take disciplinary action, most students chose to wait until this information was available; and, once it was clear that no discipline would ensue, the majority chose to protest rather than to settle.[8] In another study, people (nurses) who were tested to see if they were suitable organ donors were more willing to donate kidneys to relatives than were those who were not tested but who were instead simply informed from the start that they matched.[9] In both cases, waiting for the information imbued it with importance to the decision in a way that altered the decision that would have been made if the same information had been available at the outset.

In sum, it is often tempting to seek out more and more information, to do more interviews, to issue more interrogatories, to request more documents, to take more depositions, to do more independent research, to wait and see—particularly when a decision is difficult.[10] "Seeking more information before making a decision is alluring and quickly achieves two goals: it simultaneously delays the decision while enhancing the decision maker's image as a thoughtful, inquisitive and objective deliberator."[11] And sometimes it will be quite beneficial to obtain additional information that is relevant to a particular decision. But, at other times, the attorney and client will already have sufficient information to make a decision. And when additional information exceeds our capacity to use it well or even distorts the decision at hand, it is not clear that the benefits outweigh the costs. Thinking carefully about the uses to which information will be put and how knowing particular information will (or will not) change a decision can help attorneys limit the costs of unnecessary information gathering.

Evaluation of Options

Once information is gathered, options must be assessed. One might think that people (like computers) would be able to objectively analyze the pros and cons of an option and decide whether that option maximizes their interests. However, it turns out that people's evaluations of options are influenced not only by the substance of those options but also by the way those options are presented.

Framing

People's willingness to take risks is affected by whether they believe they are facing a potential gain or a potential loss. In a body of work known as *prospect theory*, psychologists Daniel Kahneman and Amos Tversky have shown that people are *risk averse* toward moderate- to high-probability gains and *risk seeking* toward moderate- to high-probability losses.[12] Consider the following choices (simplified to exclude consideration of attorney fees and other costs):

> Imagine that you are a plaintiff in a lawsuit. You have been offered $48,000 to settle the case. You estimate that you have a 50% chance of winning at trial and receiving $100,000 and a 50% chance of losing and receiving nothing. Which would you choose?

> Imagine that you are a defendant in a lawsuit. You can settle the case for $48,000. You estimate that you have a 50% chance of winning at trial and paying nothing and a 50% chance of losing and paying $100,000. Which would you choose?

Prospect theory suggests that most people will tend to prefer to take the settlement in the first example (showing risk aversion in the face of a gain) but to go to trial in the second example (choosing risk in the face of a loss).

When it comes to low-probability gains and losses, the pattern is different. It turns out that people tend to be risk averse toward low-probability losses but risk seeking toward low-probability gains. We know, for example, that people are willing to pay a little bit up front to insure against large, but low-probability, risks. And we know from the abundance of lotteries that many people are very willing to spend a little to obtain a very low chance of winning a large payout.

In addition to all of this, we have particular reactions to losses and to feelings of certainty. We tend to be *loss averse*, such that "losses loom larger than gains" and a loss of a given size tends to be more aversive than a gain of comparable size is attractive. Furthermore, we tend to overweight the value of sure things. This *certainty effect* makes us willing to pay more to increase the odds of a positive outcome from 99% to 100% than we might pay to increase the odds from 75% to 80% and makes us willing to pay more to reduce the risk of harm from 1% to zero than we might pay to reduce it from 5% to 1%.

❖ ❖ ❖ ❖ ❖

The Last 10 Percent

Consider the certainty effect in the context of a toxic torts case. Supreme Court Justice Stephen Breyer describes how this phenomenon played out in a case in which he ruled as a circuit judge, *United States v. Ottati & Goss Inc.*,[13] which involved the cleanup of a toxic waste disposal site:

> The site was mostly cleaned up. All but one of the private parties had settled. The remaining private party litigated the cost of cleaning up the last little bit, a cost of about $9.3 million to remove a small amount of highly diluted PCBs and "volatile organic compounds" (benzene and gasoline components) by incinerating the dirt. How much extra safety did this $9.3 million buy? The forty-thousand-page record of this ten-year effort indicated (and all the parties seemed to agree) that, without the extra expenditure, the waste dump was clean enough for children playing on the site to eat small amounts of dirt daily for 70 days each year without significant harm. Burning the soil would have made it clean enough for the children to eat small amounts daily for 245 days per year without significant harm. But there were no dirt-eating children playing in the area, for it was a swamp. Nor were dirt-eating children likely to appear there,

> for future building seemed unlikely. The parties also agreed that at least half of the volatile organic chemicals would likely evaporate by the year 2000. To spend $9.3 million to protect nonexistent dirt-eating children is what I mean by the problem of "the last 10 percent."[14]

While one might think that "a gain is a gain and a loss is a loss," it turns out that people evaluate options by comparison to reference points, and the characterization of options as gains or losses is highly manipulable. For example, imagine that the Centers for Disease Control and Prevention (CDC) is considering two alternative approaches to a pandemic flu outbreak that is expected to kill six hundred people in the United States. If Program A is adopted, two hundred people will be saved. If Program B is adopted, there is a one-third probability that six hundred people will be saved and a two-thirds probability that no one will be saved. Between A and B, which program would you recommend the CDC adopt? Now imagine that, instead, you have the following two options: If Program X is adopted, four hundred people will die. If Program Y is adopted, there is a one-third probability that no one will die and a two-thirds probability that six hundred people will die. Which program would you recommend: X or Y? Now note that the options in both instances are the same, except that Options A and B are framed as gains (that is, the number of lives saved) and Options X and Y are framed as losses (that is, the number of deaths). However, when presented with Programs A and B, most people are risk averse and choose to save two hundred people (Program A). In contrast, when presented with Options X and Y, most people are risk seeking, choosing Program Y.[15] Thus, how the options are framed can have a significant influence on decision making.

> ✦ ✦ ✦ ✦ ✦
>
> ### Losses, Gains, and the Brain
>
> Neuroscientists have investigated how making decisions about gains and losses are related to activity in the brain. They have found that decisions about gains are related to activity in the parts of the brain that are associated with the "anticipation and receipt of monetary rewards." Somewhat surprisingly, they have found that decisions about losses are not associated with increased activity in the parts of the brain that are related to negative emotions. Instead, decisions about losses are associated with a *lack* of activity in the brain's reward centers.[16]

A number of implications flow from these insights. First, people may demand more to give up something they already possess than they would be willing to pay to acquire that same item—a phenomenon referred to as the *endowment effect*. For example, in one study, half of a group of students were given coffee mugs. Students with mugs were asked to indicate the price at which they would sell the mug, and students without mugs were asked to name the price at which they would buy a mug; trades would then be executed as determined by the responses. However, few trades were executed because mug owners consistently set selling prices that were higher than the prices set by buyers.[17] More generally, this means that

> a party may demand more to abate a nuisance than it would pay for the right to inflict the nuisance, a real property owner in an eminent domain action may insist on compensation far greater than the fair market value of the property, the amount of an injunction bond will be disputed because the enjoined party places a higher value on the deprivation of a previously exercised right than the enjoining party places on the power to restrain the exercise of that right, and a retail tenant in a shopping center will demand more money to vacate the premises early than it would pay to remain there.[18]

Second, people tend to prefer the status quo over other options because the potential downsides of a change loom larger than the potential gains—a tendency known as the *status quo bias*. Thus, people tend to prefer to stick with their current entitlements and tend to gravitate toward default rules. In one telling example, the states of New Jersey and Pennsylvania both offered two different levels of automobile insurance coverage: one level had a higher premium and entailed the right to sue, and a second level had a lower premium and no right to sue. However, the states differed in one important respect: in Pennsylvania the default policy comprised the higher-priced, more comprehensive policy with a discount available for those who would waive the right to sue; in New Jersey, the default policy was the lower-priced policy with an option to pay more to obtain the right to sue. Although the policies in the two states were similar, more drivers in Pennsylvania (75%) opted to purchase the more comprehensive policy than did drivers in New Jersey (20%), with most drivers in each state opting for the default policy.[19] Similarly, employees tend to choose whatever health insurance or retirement plan is designated as the default, and people who receive an inheritance tend to hold it in whatever form it was received.[20]

Third, people experience *penalty aversion*. Compare your reactions to the price structures of the following two gas stations:

Station A: $3.90 per gallon, with a $0.05 discount for using cash

Station B: $3.85 per gallon, with a $0.05 penalty for using a credit card

In both cases, those who pay cash will pay $3.85 per gallon and those who pay with a credit card will pay $3.90 per gallon. Nonetheless, customers have very different reactions to the two pricing structures. Station A has set the reference price at $3.90 with a gain for users of cash; Station B has set the reference price at $3.85 and imposed a penalty—a loss—for credit card users. Customers tend to prefer the station that provides for a discount for cash even though the two stations' prices are equivalent.[21]

A fourth implication is that people tend to find a particular option less attractive when considered among other options than when it is considered in isolation—a phenomenon known as *option devaluation*. When people compare options, they typically compare the pros and cons of the options. Because losses loom larger than gains, the negative features will assert prominence in this comparison, and each option will look less attractive than it would have on its own.[22]

Finally, a tendency to avoid losses can incline people to overweight *sunk costs*— that is, costs that have already been incurred. Because such costs are not recoverable, decisions about whether to invest additional resources (for example, time or money) should not take them into account. Nevertheless, decision making is often influenced by such previous investments. For example, one study found that theater season ticket holders who had paid more for their tickets were more likely to attend the performances than those who had paid less.[24] In the same vein, we can all probably think of an occasion on which we ate more than was advisable because we had paid good money for the food. And managers have difficulty pulling the plug on projects in which they have invested resources even when they would be better off cutting their losses. Lawyers similarly may have difficulty walking away from a case or a deal once they have invested resources in pursuing it. Have you have heard or expressed sentiments like the following?

> If you find yourself in a hole, stop digging.
> —Will Rogers[23]

"We've come too far to walk away now."
"We've put too much into this to let it tank."
"If you had made us that offer six months ago, we might have had a deal."[25]

If so, you have seen sunk costs in action.

Contrast and Compromise

As we have already seen with the example of option devaluation, the selection of a particular option can be influenced by the nature of the full set of options under consideration.

Another possibility—a *contrast effect*—can occur when one option resembles, but is inferior to, another option. The contrast between these options can increase the attractiveness of the better option relative to others in the set. To see this more clearly, imagine a dispute over a piece of property. A disputant might consider two options:

1. Sell the property and divide the proceeds
2. Accept a particular sum of money from the other party and allow her to keep the property

Now imagine that there is a third option under consideration: the other party will keep the property in exchange for the same sum of money, but payments will be made over time—an option that is similar but inferior to the second option. Although people do not tend to choose this inferior third option, including it as one of the array of options under consideration causes more people to choose the lump-sum payment option rather than choosing to sell the property and divide the proceeds.[26]

To take another example, consider a study of the impact of expert testimony. Trial court judges were asked to evaluate the credibility of expert witnesses in a child custody dispute. One group of judges was asked to indicate which of two experts of similar quality was more credible, the expert for the father or the expert for the mother. A second group of judges was asked to evaluate these same two experts plus a second expert for the father; this third expert's credentials were of significantly inferior quality as compared to the father's other expert. Even though no judge in this later condition chose the inferior expert, more judges asked to select from the three experts chose the father's better expert (72%) than when this contrast was absent (54%).[27]

A *compromise effect* can occur when an extreme option is included among the options under consideration. Because people are averse to choosing what appears to be an extreme option (*extremeness aversion*), the introduction of an extreme option makes other alternatives appear to be more moderate choices and, hence, more attractive.[28] Would it surprise you to know that when a store introduces an extremely high-end, high-priced item—for example, a very expensive camera—sales of the next-priciest camera tend to increase? This is because the extreme option makes the next-priciest option seem more moderate.

This sort of compromise effect has been demonstrated in studies of legal decision making as well. In one study, people considering a land purchase were more likely to select a particular property when it was a moderate choice among the options considered than when it was at the extremes of the range of options considered (see sidebar).[29] Similarly, the introduction of an extreme verdict option can change jurors' verdicts, making other verdicts seem more moderate.[30]

❖ ❖ ❖ ❖ ❖
Compromise Effects

You represent a property management company that specializes in building and managing apartment complexes that are located on relatively inexpensive plots of land and that target undergraduate and graduate students. The company seeks to build a two-hundred-unit apartment complex on a fifteen-acre plot of land and has hired you to negotiate and purchase a plot. You have been in discussions with several property owners and have negotiated the best deals you can with each. You must now choose one of the following to recommend to the company.

> Consider the following two options:
>
> BlueAcre—Located in an open field seven miles from the university campus, BlueAcre is available for $150,000.
>
> RedAcre—Located in a residential neighborhood one mile from the university campus, RedAcre is available for $250,000.
>
> Which property would you choose?
>
> What if you had considered the following additional option?
>
> YellowAcre—Located in a residential neighborhood one-half mile from the university campus, YellowAcre is available for $580,000.[31]

Inaction Inertia

Not only can currently contemplated options influence choice, but so, too, can options that were previously considered and not chosen. *Inaction inertia* is the "tendency of a person to omit action when he or she already has passed up a similar, more attractive opportunity to act."[32] In other words, once a decision maker has chosen not to avail herself of a particular option, she will also tend to pass up a subsequent option that is less attractive than the forgone one even if this option would still be a gain.

For example, imagine a defendant who passes up an offer to settle a case for $10,000, thinking that she can push the plaintiff to settle for a lower figure. But imagine that the plaintiff does not settle for less and withdraws the offer to settle for $10,000. Down the road, the defendant is likely to find settling for $12,000 particularly unattractive even if the defendant thinks it is likely that a trial would result in liability of $15,000. Similarly, a buyer who has turned down an offer for the purchase of widgets at $1 per widget hoping to get a better price may later devalue an offer of $1.10 per widget even if the best alternative offer at that time is $1.20 per widget. Thus, we "do not consider the merits of current opportunities independently of past choices" but rather compare current opportunities to recalled superior, but missed, opportunities.[33] It can be helpful to think about how to recharacterize the prior option: "if the initial missed opportunity is somehow made to look less attractive than it previously did, regret over taking a related offer dissipates and inaction inertia is diminished."[34] Perhaps, for example, the widget buyer might focus on the possibility of delivery delays by the supplier of the $1 widgets.

Delaying a decision can also change how options are evaluated. In particular, choosing to delay a decision can engender feelings of doubt about the most prominent or default options. Having put off a decision, the decision maker might think, "If that option was such a good one, why didn't I jump on it?" This doubt can lead the decision maker to shy away from prominent or default options in favor of a less prominent or nondefault option even if in the absence of delay he would have chosen otherwise.[35] Thus, similar to the effects of deferring a decision in order to seek

> ### Deal or No Deal
>
> Imagine a contestant on the game show *Deal or No Deal* faced with twenty-six numbered briefcases, each one holding a different amount of money ranging from one penny to $1 million. The contestant chooses one of the briefcases and may keep it (and its contents) unless she chooses to relinquish it in exchange for an amount of money offered by the "Banker." As the game is played, the contestant is faced with a series of such offers of varying magnitudes.[36]
>
>
> NBC via Getty Images
>
> Viewers of *Deal or No Deal* have inevitably seen hapless contestants pass up deals that would have been financially advantageous—in part because the offer was lower than offers that they passed up earlier in the game. This is inaction inertia in action.

more information, simply choosing to delay the decision can change the decision that we make.

Choice and Time

Many legal decisions unfold over a period of time. Clients do long-term estate planning. Contracts are negotiated to govern relationships over time. Settlements are negotiated to compensate for losses that include past and future harm and may be structured to pay out over time or contingent on some future event. But because immediate consequences are experienced differently than those anticipated in the future, the temporal characteristics of decision options can have a significant influence on decision making.

Consider, first, the time value of money. Assuming positive interest rates and consistent tax rates, it is economically better to receive $100 today than to receive the same $100 one year from now: if we had $100 now, we could invest it at some rate of interest so that it would be worth more than $100 one year from now. (And, for the same reasons, we would be better off paying $100 one year from now than paying it today.) However, our decisions are not completely consistent with this basic principle.

On one hand, when asked to indicate the amount of money that they would have to receive in one year so that they would be indifferent between receiving that amount then or $15 now, the median response was $50—implying that they would require a greater-than-threefold return![37] On the other hand, people routinely give interest-free loans to state and federal governments by setting their income tax deductions low enough that they receive refunds each year. And teachers and professors frequently give interest-free loans to their school districts and universities by choosing to spread their nine-month salaries over a twelve-month period. While many would argue that these behaviors are reasoned techniques that force saving, these are costly methods of doing so.

In addition, people often have different requirements for expediting as opposed to delaying gains and losses. First, gains are discounted more than losses (the *sign effect*). In other words, people tend to require high payments to delay a gain (imagine a plaintiff demanding substantially more to receive a later payment) but are not willing to pay as much to delay a loss (imagine a defendant being unwilling to pay as much in order to delay the same payment). In some cases, people would even prefer to bear a loss sooner rather than later to avoid the dread of anticipating a negative outcome. Second, people will demand more to delay a gain than they will pay to expedite the same gain by the same amount of time (the *delay-speedup asymmetry*).[38] As we will see in chapter 11, attorneys can capitalize on these asymmetries to forge agreements.

It also turns out that the timing of the outcome of the decision influences choices. Imagine that we offered you a choice between receiving $50 now or $100 in six months. Now imagine that, instead, we offered you a choice between receiving $50 in twelve months or $100 in eighteen months. In either case, the choice is the same—a doubling of money over a six-month period. (And note that a year from now, the second choice will have become identical to the first choice.) However, people do not experience these choices as being the same. Most people would take the $50 when it is offered immediately, but most would take the $100 when the time horizon is longer. In other words, we want the $50 if we can have it immediately; but if we have to wait, we might as well wait a bit longer and get the $100.[39]

Finally, people have preferences for improving sequences in outcomes. For example, imagine being given a choice between several different jobs. Each job entails the same work and will last for five years, and each pays an equal amount in total (undiscounted) wages. However, Job A pays the most in the first year, with a decline in salary for each subsequent year; Job B pays an equal amount in each year; and Job C pays the least in the first year, with increases in salary in each subsequent year. Economic considerations would prescribe taking Job A: the additional salary can be invested for additional earnings; employees who decide to quit prior to the end of the five-year period would come out ahead; and so on. However, perhaps viewing the year-to-year decreases in Job A's salary profile as losses to which they are averse and out of a concern that they will not be able to save appropriately to maintain steady or increasing consumption, most people prefer Job C.[40]

Reactive Devaluation

Finally, the evaluation of an option may also depend on where that option originated. In theory, options would be evaluated objectively without regard to their source. However, psychological research has found that proposals often appear less appealing when they are offered by an opponent—a phenomenon known as *reactive devaluation*. In one study, researchers asked participants to evaluate a proposal for nuclear disarmament between the United States and the Soviet Union. When the proposal was described as originating with the Soviets, the proposal was viewed as unfavorable to the United States; but when the same proposal was described as originating on the U.S. side, it was viewed as favoring the United States. Thus, "the very act of offering a particular proposal may diminish its apparent value or attractiveness in the eyes of the recipient."[41]

A number of explanations for this effect have been offered, including that people assume that the proposal is a result of private information known only to the other side and thus must favor that side, that people ascribe lower value to proposals favored by the other side (an explanation based on the value of spite), that they view such proposals as signaling a willingness to make further concessions and increase their own aspirations, or simply that they see the option as less appealing once it is possible.[42] Thus, decision makers should be careful not to dismiss a particular option because of its source, nor should they get overly attached to an option simply because it was their own proposal. As we discuss in chapter 11, attorneys involved in negotiation and mediation can also work to make offers in ways that will not trigger reactive devaluation.

Emotions and Decision Making

Although we have seen that it is tempting to think of decision making as an analytical process in which the costs and benefits of different courses of action are dispassionately weighed and compared to goals, we have also seen that emotions influence decision making. As we learned in chapter 3, emotions can influence how we perceive and remember, how we make judgments, and how we engage in analysis. Recall also that emotions can provide useful information about the decision maker's values and priorities that might be difficult to articulate. Decision making is also complicated by the difficulties we encounter in predicting how we will experience the outcomes of our decisions.

Affective Forecasting

Good decision making depends, in part, on the ability to anticipate or predict how we will feel about our choices once we have made them. To what extent will a client, for instance, be more satisfied with settlement X or settlement Y? To what extent will a client feel vindicated following a favorable jury verdict? Recent research in psychology has explored how well people perform in predicting their future emotional states. This research has found that people are reasonably accurate in predicting (1) the valence or direction of their future emotions, that is, whether something will make them feel good or bad; and (2) the specific emotion they will feel, for example, whether they will feel sadness or anger. On the other hand, however, this research has demonstrated that people are not very good at predicting the intensity or duration of these anticipated emotions:

> In a score of studies, people have been shown to mispredict how they will feel after relocating a household, breaking up with a romantic partner, losing an election, receiving a gift, learning they have a serious illness, failing to secure a promotion, scoring well on an examination, failing to lose weight, reading tragic stories, winning a football game, receiving personality feedback, being insulted, tasting food, and so on.[43]

Other studies have demonstrated a similar inability to predict the emotions that will follow the denial of tenure, the results of a pregnancy test, or the death of a spouse.[44] And we saw in chapter 3 that people have difficulty predicting how venting their emotions will make them feel.

In similar ways, it can be difficult to predict our own behavior in future circumstances. Consider a study that examined how women predict they will respond to sexually harassing interview questions. When contemplating such a situation in foresight, women tend to anticipate that they will take some kind of action to protest such questions, such as confronting (or at least reporting) the interviewer, refusing to answer the question, or leaving the interview. But when actually asked sexually harassing questions in an interview setting, most interviewees simply answer the questions.[45] Furthermore, consider a negotiator anticipating a tough negotiation. One study found that in foresight, negotiators facing a negotiation with a competitive counterpart tend to predict that they will be tough themselves and hold their ground. But when they actually engage in a competitive negotiation, they tend to give way and become more compromising. "[F]orecasters predicted that winning, not being bullied, and going head-to-head would be more important motivators, while actual negotiators stated that avoiding an impasse and making sure the interaction goes smoothly were more important."[46]

There are many reasons why people err in making such predictions. Sometimes people lack experience with the event and do not know what to expect, making accurate predictions difficult; or they may fail to accurately remember their previous emotional reactions and so are unable to use them to make accurate predictions. In the absence of this experiential knowledge, people may fall back on theories about what influences their emotional well-being. Unfortunately, these theories are sometimes faulty. For example, people tend to overestimate the degree to which income and status will affect their well-being and to underestimate the importance of social factors, such as time with friends and family.

In addition, there are various ways in which a decision maker's attention is drawn to particular aspects of the alternatives. For example, people tend to fall prey to *focalism* or a *focusing illusion* in that they focus on a particular aspect of the event in making their prediction and do not take into account the countervailing emotional influences of other aspects of the event or of other life experiences. Thus, someone contemplating a move to a new house might focus on the nice big kitchen and less on how his family, work, and social life will continue pretty much as before. Moreover, people may be disposed to an *isolation effect*, in which they "disregard components that the alternatives share, and focus on the components that distinguish them," thus overweighting unique attributes of the options.[48] For example, when a person is contemplating whether she would be more satisfied locating her new restaurant in the space available on First Street or in the one three blocks over, her focus might be drawn to the differences in the volume of street traffic and the sizes of the kitchens, to the neglect of all of the features of the two locations that are similar. In addition, people tend not to account for the degree to which their own dispositions will influence their responses. A fundamentally shy person may not become more party loving even if she moves to Las Vegas. And, finally, people tend to suffer from *immune neglect* as they underappreciate the ways in which their psychological immune system will buffer them from the emotional fallout of future events. Indeed, most of us do tend to recover fairly well even from terrible catastrophes such as the death of a loved one or a serious injury.[49]

> Nothing in life is quite as important as you think it is while you are thinking about it.
> —Daniel Kahneman[47]

It turns out that one really good way to figure out how a particular experience will make you feel is to find out how that same experience made someone else feel. In a line of research testing this *surrogation strategy*, researchers asked people to predict their affective responses to future experiences. Some people were given information about the nature of the upcoming event itself; others were only given information about how a prior participant (a surrogate) had rated his own affective reaction to the event. The researchers found that people made more accurate predictions of their own reaction when all they had was information about how another person experienced the event. Ironically, however, the participants believed that information about the event would be more helpful to their own assessment than the surrogation information. Because the power of surrogation is counterintuitive, people are prone to overlook its ability to help them make more accurate affective forecasts.[50]

Decision Regret

One particular emotion that people anticipate and take into account when making decisions is regret. Regret is "the painful feeling a person experiences upon determining she could have obtained a better outcome if she had decided or behaved differently."[51] When making decisions, people anticipate the prospect that they will experience regret following the decision. They expect to experience more regret for negative outcomes when they must choose one option and reject other possibilities, when they act rather than fail to act, when they miss their goal by a narrow margin or come close to succeeding but do not, when they receive feedback about what the outcomes of unchosen options would have been, or when they have made an atypical choice. Taking into account this anticipated regret, people make decisions that they think will avoid or minimize the amount of regret that they expect to feel. This inclination to avoid anticipated regret means that people will take into account not only the expected outcome of the decision itself but also "the feelings associated with the outcomes of foregone options."[52]

However, people's predictions about their postdecision regret are not always correct. In particular, as described above, people are not terribly accurate in predicting the intensity and duration of their future emotional reactions. Indeed, recent studies have shown that people may anticipate feeling more regret than they ultimately experience. One reason for this may be that decision makers tend to evaluate options differently once they have made a decision, changing their evaluations in ways that may help to minimize regret. Psychological research has found that the act of "making a decision can lead to selective memory for information supporting that decision."[53] Studies have found that for a variety of decisions that people make (for example, choosing job candidates, roommates, or blind dates), people are more likely to attribute positive aspects of the choices to the option they have chosen. In other words, not only are favorable aspects of the chosen option likely to be correctly associated with that option, but favorable aspects of the nonchosen option are likely to be incorrectly associated with the chosen option. Such postdecision effects on memory can serve to minimize postdecision regret. To put it more simply, once we decide something, we have a tendency to make ourselves happy with that decision so that fears of subsequent regret are often overstated.

Thus, while taking into account the regret that one is likely to experience following a decision is often helpful, encouraging a careful and creative analysis,[54] it can also sometimes contribute to less optimal decision making. Overweighting or incorrectly assessing anticipated regret may be detrimental to decision making, resulting, for example, in a greater willingness to settle below an initially determined reservation price or causing people to place too high of a premium on the ability to change their minds in instances in which such flexibility is not valuable.[55] These choices may not be optimal.

Not Deciding

At times, people prefer not to make a decision. When making a decision is unpleasant—because, for example, the decision is anxiety producing, it is difficult to make the necessary trade-offs, the decision requires accepting a particular path and foreclosing others, or the decision requires taking responsibility for its outcome—people might attempt to avoid making a decision.

Often, this decision avoidance manifests itself in attempts to delay making the decision. For example, as we have already seen, people have a tendency to seek out additional information, thereby delaying their decision, even when the information does not inform the decision. In addition, people might simply *procrastinate*, that is they might choose to "delay an intended course of action *despite* expecting to be worse off for the delay."[57] The more difficult the decision, the more willing people are to defer choice, even when such deferral is costly.[58]

> Not to decide . . . is to decide.
> —Harvey Cox[56]

Similarly, a decision maker might attempt to avoid making a decision by making a *nondecision*—choosing an option that preserves the status quo or requires no action. We have already seen that people tend to prefer the status quo (*status quo bias*). In addition, because people anticipate experiencing more regret when they act and it turns out poorly than they do if their failure to act results in harm, there is a tendency to prefer options that entail inaction to options that require action. This *omission bias* can result in a tendency to avoid taking action to make a decision.[59] In addition, people have a tendency to make "decisions" that keep other options open even when such decisions mean a postponement of a final decision and even when keeping options open entails a cost.

Consider one clever study examining this tendency to want to keep options open. Participants played a computer game in which they saw three doors. Clicking on a door opened it (but generated no payment). Once a door was open, the player could either click within the room and receive a payment or click to open another door. Players were given a limited number of clicks to use as they wished. In one version of the game, each of the three doors was available to the player at any time. In a second version of the game, when the player clicked "on a door or within a room, the doors to the *other* two rooms were reduced in size by 1/15 of their original width. A *single* door-click on a shrinking door revitalized it to its original size and the process continued. Once the door reached zero, it was eliminated." The researchers found that switching between doors was more likely to occur in the version with the shrinking doors: people were willing to "spend" a click to keep the door available even when the door produced smaller payoffs than the others and was, thus, not needed to maximize the players' gains. This was true even when players knew that some doors had lower payoff distributions than others.[60]

At times, postponing a decision is prudent: additional information may be necessary, or it may take time to generate attractive options. However, sometimes postponing or avoiding decisions can result in lost opportunities: the search for additional information might be costly (and can alter decisions), an offer might expire, or someone else might outbid us. Moreover, we have seen that maintaining the opportunity to reverse a decision can get in the way of being satisfied with the chosen option.[61] Thus, when faced with a sense of indecision, the decision maker should explore the reasons underlying the indecision and address them directly. For example, if additional information is actually necessary, the decision can be deferred while the relevant information is acquired. If a decision is difficult because the decision maker has not clearly articulated his needs and goals, steps should be taken to clarify these preferences. If delay is resulting from a desire to keep options open simply for the sake of keeping options open or from concerns surrounding anticipatory regret, these concerns can be met head-on to allow the decision maker to move forward with the decision-making process.

Structuring Decision Making

There are many ways in which decisions can be structured. One of the most commonly recommended approaches is to consider the pros and cons of each alternative.

Psychologists have examined the effects of structuring decisions in certain ways, including articulating reasons for making a particular decision (pros and cons, for example), valuing decisions based on the particular ways in which they are made, structuring a decision as an exercise in choosing or rejecting options, considering options jointly or separately, and making use of deadlines.

✦ ✦ ✦ ✦ ✦
Advice from Benjamin Franklin

In a letter to Joseph Priestley, Benjamin Franklin contemplates the challenges of decision making and how to address those challenges:

> When ... difficult Cases occur, they are difficult, chiefly because while we have them under Consideration, all the Reasons pro and con are not present to the Mind at the same time; but sometimes one Set present themselves, and at other times another, the first being out of Sight. Hence the various Purposes or Inclinations that alternately prevail, and the Uncertainty that perplexes us.
>
> To get over this, My way is to divide half a sheet of paper by a line into two columns, writing over the one Pro, and over the other Con. Then, during three or four days consideration, I put down under the different heads short hints of the different motives, that at different times occur to me, for or against each measure.... I find at length where the balance lies; and if, after a day or two of further consideration, nothing new that is of importance occurs on either side, I come to a determination accordingly. And, tho' the Weight of Reasons cannot be taken with the Precision of Algebraic Quantities, yet, when each is thus considered, separately and comparatively, and the whole view before me, I think I can judge better, and am less likely to make a rash step.[62]

Reason Giving

People seek to make decisions they can justify—to themselves and to others. Thus, given options that are similarly attractive, people tend to choose the one that they are best able to explain or defend. And, as we have seen, people will sometimes change their memory for or evaluation of the attributes of different choice options in order to justify a choice they have made. This desire to make choices that are correct, or at least justifiable, leads people who are faced with a decision to engage in a search for reasons on which to base their choice.

Often this focus on the underlying reasons for making a particular decision can be quite helpful, stimulating deliberative consideration of options and leading decision makers to be more satisfied with their choices.[64] However, focusing on reasons is not without its pitfalls. In particular, the "reasons that come to mind are often fleeting, are limited to what is introspectively accessible, and are not necessarily those that guide, or ought to guide the decision."[65] This can result in several different problems.

> So convenient a thing it is to be a reasonable creature, since it enables one to find or make a reason for everything one has a mind to do.
> —Benjamin Franklin[63]

First, it turns out to be very easy to recruit reasons to support preferred decision outcomes whether or not such reasons actually underlie the decision and whether or not the use of such reasons results in the best choice. Indeed, it can be easy to produce justifications for even questionable decisions. Such justifications allow us to rationalize our decisions (both publicly and privately) and to maintain an *illusion of objectivity* such that we believe ourselves to be making decisions using objective criteria.[66]

As an example of how such effects occur, consider a study that explored the effect of race on peremptory challenges and the reasons provided to justify strikes. Lawyers in the role of prosecuting an African American defendant were presented with a pair of prospective jurors—a journalist who had written about police misconduct and one who believed that statistics (including forensic lab analyses) were often manipulated—and asked which of the two they would strike. The researchers varied the race of the two jurors: in some conditions the journalist was black and the other juror was white, and in some conditions this was reversed. In both cases, the black prospective juror was more likely to be challenged than was the white juror. Not surprisingly, however, few participants mentioned race as a factor in their decision. Instead, they cited to other (nondiscriminatory) characteristics of the potential juror, such as his journalistic background or his skepticism of statistics. The study thus found that even when race influenced peremptory challenges, race-neutral reasons were readily provided as justification.[67]

In addition, people have intuitions about what types of reasons are appropriate bases for a decision. Specifically, people tend to more heavily weigh reasons that are economic, quantifiable, or related to the central function of the decision than they are to weigh factors that are less concrete. These tendencies, known as *lay rationalism*, may "stem from a general desire to base one's decision on things that are 'real'—i.e., substantive, material, and concrete, and not on factors that are ethereal or purely psychological."[68] In some cases, a focus on these quantifiable factors will lead to an objectively superior choice (and the decision maker may gain some degree of satisfaction from making what she believes is a "rational" decision). However, less concrete factors can sometimes have a greater influence on our actual experience.

Finally, focusing on the reasons for preferences can alter those preferences. Sometimes it is difficult to identify the reasons for a particular preference. In attempting to justify such a preference, people will focus on reasons that come to mind easily, reasons that are plausible justifications, and reasons that are easy to articulate. Sometimes, these easily recruited reasons are consistent with the decision maker's true underlying preferences. At other times, however, these easily articulated or seemingly plausible reasons lead in a different direction from the reasons that actually underlie a preference. In such instances, people may alter their choices to be consistent with the reasons they have been able to articulate.

In one study, for example, people were given the opportunity to choose a poster from a set of five that included two popular art posters and three more humorous (and less popular) posters. Some people were asked to describe the reasons why they did or did not like each of the posters, and others were not. Interestingly, those who were required to articulate their assessments of the posters were more likely to pick one of the humorous posters, and they were ultimately less satisfied with their choice than were those who had not been required to think about their reasons for liking the poster they chose. Particularly when the reasons for a preference are hard to identify or articulate (such as preferences about art), when the decision maker lacks detailed knowledge about the choice options, and when the easily accessible plausible justifications are at odds with underlying preferences, focusing on reasons can actually reduce satisfaction with decisions.[69]

In contrast, thinking about reasons can be more useful when the decision is more analytical or quantitative in nature and when "good" reasons that are consistent with the decision maker's actual preferences are made salient.[70] Thus, it may be quite important to allow sufficient time to thoroughly engage in such a decision-making strategy.

Preferred Decision-Making Approaches

People judge their satisfaction with a decision not only based on their valuation of the substantive outcome but also based on their satisfaction with the processes by which the decision was made. For example, as noted above, a decision maker might derive value from making what she feels is a rational decision based on objective criteria. Similarly, she might believe that making a decision quickly is a bad decision process.[71] Alternatively, a decision maker might value making a decision in what he sees as an ethical manner. Such process preferences can influence the ways in which the decision maker evaluates the merits of the decision outcome.

Relatedly, psychological research has found that people may prefer to engage in decision-making strategies that are consistent with whether they are oriented toward *promotion*, with an eye toward accomplishment, aspirations, and attaining positive outcomes, or *prevention*, with a focus on safety, obligation, and avoiding negative outcomes. Those with a promotion focus are

> It's not whether you win or lose, it's how you play the game.
> —*Grantland Rice*[72]

likely to emphasize the positive feelings associated with attaining a positive outcome and to prefer an *eager* decision-making strategy that seeks to ensure positive outcomes and to avoid missing opportunities. In contrast, those with a prevention focus are likely to emphasize the negative feelings associated with a negative outcome and to prefer a *vigilant* decision-making strategy that seeks to ensure the avoidance of negative outcomes and to avoid making mistakes. This matching of decision-making strategy to motivational orientation can lead decision makers to be more engaged in the decision-making process, to show a greater degree of persistence, and to feel greater satisfaction with the ultimate decision.[73]

In addition, people may approach a decision-making task differently depending on their *need for closure*, that is, the extent to which they have a need to arrive at a conclusion. Those who have a high need for closure tend to dislike ambiguity and have a strong desire to get to a final answer quickly. Thus, they are likely to engage in activities designed to facilitate closure, to process less information and jump to conclusions, to be distressed by conflicting opinions or evidence, and to be less likely to generate many hypotheses or to comprehensively entertain alternative perspectives. In contrast, those who have a low need for closure are more likely to suspend judgment, are likely to gather more complete information, and are willing to try out many hypotheses and perspectives. Those with a high need to avoid closure can be reluctant to commit to a particular decision.[74]

Selection Versus Rejection

A choice may also depend on whether the decision task is approached as one in which an option is selected or one in which one or more options are rejected. When acting affirmatively to choose an option, attractive features of the options tend to be salient, and the decision maker is oriented toward finding reasons to accept one of the options. In contrast, when deciding which option(s) to reject, the downsides of each option are the focus, and the decision maker is oriented toward finding reasons to reject options. Accordingly, an option that has both strong positives (that is, reasons to choose that option) and strong negatives (that is, reasons to reject it) may be both more likely to be chosen *and* more likely to be rejected.

In one study examining child custody decisions, the researchers found that a parent with significant strengths (for example, high income or a close relationship with the child) and significant drawbacks (for example, a heavy travel schedule or health problems) was more likely to be chosen over a parent who was average on all dimensions when people were asked to determine to whom custody should be awarded. However, when people were asked to evaluate the same two parents and determine to whom custody should be denied, they were also more likely to reject that same parent.[75] The structure of the decision, therefore, changed the substance of the decision made.

Joint Versus Separate Evaluation

As we have already seen, the evaluation of options can be influenced by the context in which those options are assessed (for example, contrast and compromise effects or the effects of time perspective). One contextual circumstance that can influence choice is whether the options are considered jointly or separately. In some cases, whether options are evaluated jointly or separately can have powerful effects on decision making.

Imagine that you are going to hire a computer graphics assistant for your office. The assistant will primarily be responsible for creating trial exhibits and other visual aids. Consider Candidate A, who has a GPA of 3.0 (on a 5.0 scale) and has created seventy exhibits for a law firm as an intern over the last two years. As a measure of the candidate's value to you, how much would you be willing to pay this candidate? Now consider Candidate B, who has a GPA of 4.9 (on the same 5.0 scale) and in the last two years has created ten exhibits. How much would you be willing to pay this candidate?

When faced with a similar problem, people rating the candidates in isolation indicated that they would be willing to pay Candidate B (high GPA) more than they would be willing to pay Candidate A. However, when considering the candidates jointly, people tended to assign higher pay to Candidate A (lots of experience) than to Candidate B.[76]

Why might such *preference reversals* occur? Well, it turns out that GPA tends to be easier to evaluate than does experience. When considering these candidates one at a time, it is relatively easy to assess whether a particular GPA is good or bad. In contrast, it is harder to know how to assess the value of having created a particular number of exhibits. When options are evaluated separately, attributes of the options that are harder to assess tend to have a smaller impact on decisions. On the other hand, when evaluating options simultaneously, the comparison makes this assessment easier (seventy seems significantly better than ten), and this attribute becomes more influential. (The factors that were easy to assess remain so, but their relative influence diminishes.)

As another example, consider two alternative outcomes in a dispute between two partners over joint sales revenue:

>Settlement 1: $600 to self and $800 to partner
>Settlement 2: $500 to self and $500 to partner

When evaluating these outcomes separately, most people give higher ratings to the equal allocation in Settlement 2 than they do to the manifestly unequal allocation in Settlement 1. However, when asked to jointly consider both options and choose the one they would prefer, most people choose Settlement 1, the settlement with the higher payoff to themselves.[77] (Note, however, that the unfairness of a decision does matter to people. We will return to this topic in chapter 8.) In this example, money was the dimension that was difficult to assess. Even though money is a relatively objective measure, it can still be difficult to assess how desirable (or aversive) receiving (or paying) a particular amount is in the abstract. Here, the equitable division seemed fair and earned higher marks until people saw that they could do better for themselves by accepting a somewhat less equitable division.

Similarly, it may be difficult to assess whether $5,000 is a good or bad settlement of a claim without reference to what the injuries were or for what amount other similar cases have tended to settle. Likewise, it may be hard to evaluate an offer to sell widgets for $5 apiece without reference to the type of widget, the quality of the widgets, or the typical selling price for similar widgets. It is such difficulties in evaluation that can lead to differences in preferences in joint and separate evaluation.

At least in some instances, joint evaluation can result in decisions that are suboptimal:

> [C]onsider an audio store that carries two models of loudspeakers of equal price. One model looks attractive and the other looks ugly. The ugly-looking model has a slightly lower distortion level and thus sounds slightly better. For most nonaudiophile consumers, the appearance of a speaker is easy to evaluate independently, and its sound quality is not. The sound quality of a speaker can only be appreciated when it is compared directly with another speaker. When consumers are in the store and are making a purchase decision, they are typically in [joint evaluation mode]; they can easily compare one model against the other. Through the comparison, the difference in sound quality becomes salient. In this situation, many people may end up buying the better-sounding but ugly-looking model. However, once people have purchased a set of speakers and brought them home, they are usually in the [separate evaluation] mode; they enjoy (or suffer with) whatever they have bought and do not actively compare it with the forgone alternative. In [separate evaluation mode], the difference in sound quality between the ugly and the attractive models may not make any difference in one's consumption experience, but the difference in appearance may. Thus, people who bought the ugly model may not enjoy its sound quality any more than those who bought the good-looking model, but the former group of consumers may be constantly bothered by the ugly appearance of the speakers they bought. The moral of this example is that when making decisions, people may put too much weight on difficult to evaluate attributes and be too concerned with differences between options on those attributes that will make little or no difference in [separate evaluation], hence little or no difference in actual consumption experience.[78]

Thus, in some circumstances, people may overestimate the difference that a quantitative variation in some characteristic (such as sound quality or income level) will have on their satisfaction with an option. This is known as the *distinction bias*. This is more likely to happen when evaluating (subtle) differences in magnitude than it is when the difference between the options is more qualitative in nature (for example, really bad sound quality versus good sound quality).[79]

So what does all of this mean for how to structure decision-making processes? Certainly, a combination of joint and separate evaluation can be useful. Importantly, joint evaluation can often be extremely valuable. In particular, joint evaluation makes it easier to compare difficult-to-evaluate attributes of the options and helps to make explicit the inevitable trade-offs among options. This comparative perspective can be invaluable to a decision maker.

At the same time, however, in some cases it might be useful to think separately about decision options at some point in the decision process. Particularly when an important criterion for the decision is quantitative in nature or the outcome of the choice will be experienced without the comparison, separate assessment can be useful. In other words, there is some utility to matching the mode in which the decision is made (joint or separate) to the way in which the outcome of that decision will be experienced.[80] While it may be impossible to completely ignore what is known about other options on the table, taking steps to isolate the evaluation of an option can provide a useful perspective.

Deadlines

When a decision maker is experiencing difficulty in making a decision or carrying out decision-related tasks (for example, gathering relevant information), deadlines can help structure a decision task to minimize the effects of procrastination or other delays. "Many things never get done not because someone has chosen not to do them, but because the person has chosen not to do them *now*."[81] Deadlines can provide an incentive to do a task sooner rather than later. Thus, when delegating the task of obtaining a valuation of marital assets to a client in a divorce case, setting a deadline by which the client will report back with the information can be more effective than leaving the task more open ended. In addition, as long as they do not define a period of time within which it is not possible to complete the task, shorter deadlines can result in more timely decisions. Short deadlines (seemingly paradoxically) are also less likely to be missed: the more distant the deadline, the longer the delay in both beginning and finishing the task.[82] Finally, breaking down the task into concrete steps and using more frequent, periodic deadlines can also be useful.[83]

Group Decision Making

Sometimes decisions are made by groups: trial teams, practice groups, law firm management committees, corporate boards, families, and many others. Groups are, of course, made up of individuals, and group decisions can be subject to the same sorts of influences as can the decisions of their individual members. The process of group deliberation, however, introduces some distinctive dynamics that can influence decision making. For example, groups can benefit from the separate reasoning processes of their members, from the ability to combine different information or perspectives, and from identifying and correcting members' errors. On the other hand, working in groups introduces the need to foster interpersonal relationships, the need to adopt some process for reaching collective decisions, and the possibility of group conformity.[84]

First, consider how groups share information. One of the benefits of working in groups, of course, is that groups can capitalize on the collective wisdom of many minds (see chapter 4). Each group member potentially has access to different information and perspectives. This should mean that the group has access to more ideas than would any individual group member. In some instances, the pooling of unshared information can even lead to the discovery of superior options. In addition, there can be a "stimulating effect of exposure to others' ideas"[85] such that the flow of discussion among group members leads to the generation of new ideas.

However, group discussion can also interfere with the generation of ideas. In particular, *production blocking* occurs when the "usual melee of group discussion tends to interfere with our ability to get a productive train of thought started, or can effectively 'derail' an ongoing train of thought."[86]

In addition, group members may be reluctant to express their views due to concern about negative evaluation by other members of the group. Whether this reluctance is driven by self-censorship or by a group norm that discourages dissent, such editing results in less information available to the collective. Consider a system like that used by the U.S. Supreme Court. When the Court meets to discuss a case, each Justice offers his or her views of the case in descending order of seniority. That is, the most senior Justice expresses his or her view of the case first. In some settings, such a system could result in false consensus to the extent that those lower in the hierarchy are inclined to echo what their superiors have already voiced. Systems in which the more junior people are encouraged to speak first or that preserve anonymity (perhaps via electronic brainstorming or survey software) can be helpful, though this anonymity may often not be realistic in a law firm setting.[87]

A related finding is that groups have a tendency to focus their discussion on information that is shared by all group members, neglecting unique information that is held by individual group members. Unshared information is both less likely to be mentioned and less likely to be repeated and considered in subsequent group discussion.[88] Thus, we see an "interesting paradox . . . groups are created to share information, yet they end up spending their time discussing already shared knowledge."[89] It can be useful, therefore, to make a point of eliciting relevant information from group members and even to assign one or more group members to "be responsible for certain categories of information and making sure that knowledge of who knows what is shared among the group members."[90]

Beyond the sharing (or lack of sharing) of information, groups also need to pay attention to the ways in which consensus (or seeming consensus) is reached within the group. Consider the effects of *pluralistic ignorance* and the *illusion of consensus*:

> [I]ndividuals often publicly endorse decisions and attitude positions that they view as normative for their membership group despite having private reservations

regarding such views or holding less extreme positions than those endorsed by the group. Moreover, in such settings, the individuals involved assume that similar (extreme) endorsement from other group members reflects their true feelings. Stated differently, pluralistic ignorance describes a situation in which each "member of a group or society privately rejects a belief, opinions, or practice, yet believes that virtually every other member privately accepts it." As a result, each individual assumes that the group consensus is more united and extreme than it actually is.[91]

Despite group members' knowledge of their own private reservations and their awareness that they have not expressed them, they misjudge the implications of other people's failure to express contrary views as an indication that the group has converged on an acceptable consensus.

Such beliefs can have implications for the behavior of group members. One study found that people tended to believe that their teammates subscribed to a more competitive approach than they did. And this belief led people to act more competitively when their outcomes were linked to the outcomes of their teammates.[92] Similarly, an attorney might privately think that a deal should not proceed but continue to work toward it, believing that the others on his team think that the deal is the appropriate course of action.

It is not just illusory consensus that can be problematic for groups. Group deliberation can also change the nature of the consensus reached. In particular, initial or emerging group leanings can lead to more extreme group decisions. Specifically, groups have a tendency to make decisions that are more extreme—in the direction of the initial leanings of the individual group members—than would individual decision makers. This means that if the initial leanings of the individual group members are risk seeking, the eventual group decision is likely to be even riskier than the decisions of individual group members. Conversely, if the initial leanings of the individual group members tend toward greater risk aversion, the eventual group decision is likely to be even more risk averse. These *choice shifts* tend to occur as group members discuss their reasons for their leanings. The arguments proffered by individual members of the group will tend to be in line with their own initial leanings. Because group members with similar leanings may have different reasons for holding similar positions, individual group members may be exposed to additional reasons to support their leanings. In addition, positions that are in line with the prevailing group sentiment are more likely to be expressed as group members edit their contributions in light of the emerging group position.[93]

Thus, it can be useful to take steps to ensure that group members are encouraged to express divergent views, that the group has access to a broad range of information, and that seeming consensus is questioned. For example, groups should strive to avoid suppressing contrary views and to actively encourage group members to present divergent views. The group might invite outside perspectives by consulting experts and other nongroup members such as an outside consulting attorney. Group leaders might refrain from stating their own views at the beginning of the discussion to minimize the likelihood that others will simply agree. One device that has been shown to be particularly useful in ensuring more complete discussion is to formally assign someone to play the devil's advocate (see chapter 1). To ensure that this role is fully enacted, it is important to communicate to the devil's advocate the importance of making her counterarguments as effectively and persuasively as possible. In addition, *second-chance meetings* can be held at which group members can revisit conclusions and reexamine lingering concerns.[94]

Implementation of Decisions

Gentlemen, I take it that we are all in complete agreement on the decision here.... Then I propose we postpone further discussion of this matter until our next meeting to give ourselves time to develop disagreement and perhaps gain some understanding of what the decision is all about.
—Alfred P. Sloan, General Motors[95]

Once a decision has been reached, it needs to be implemented. In some instances, this is relatively straightforward: a lawsuit is filed, a check is written, a phone call is made. At other times, it can be challenging to carry out the decision. Deciding to exercise more may be the first step, but it doesn't always get us to the gym. We may decide to control our anger or to get our anxiety in check, to hold firm in a tough negotiation, or to buckle down and get a brief written. A decision may result in a set of tasks that the lawyer or client must complete to carry out that decision—and those tasks must get done. But carrying through is not always easy.

Psychological research has shown that having a firm goal (exercising more) and sheer force of will are not always sufficient to achieve that goal. All sorts of factors can conspire to throw us off the track. We might have trouble getting started: "Where is the gym?" or "I'll start tomorrow." And we can get derailed once we start: "I was just too busy this week."[96] In addition, as we saw in chapter 3, limits on our processing capacity can result in limits on our ability to regulate our behavior. Indeed, researchers have likened our capacity for self-control to that of a muscle that can get fatigued (but that can also be strengthened through exercise).[97] In one study, for example, people had to memorize a number so that they could report it to a researcher down the hall. On their way down the hall, they were given the opportunity to choose a snack: either a piece of chocolate cake or a fruit salad. Those who were trying to remember a seven-digit number exercised less self-control than those trying to remember a two-digit number and were much more likely to choose the chocolate cake![98] Even the processing required to make a decision can itself impair subsequent self-control.[99]

But psychologists have shown that formulating specific *implementation intentions* can help to counteract these effects. An implementation intention is an if-then

The road to hell is paved with good intentions.
—Proverb[100]

statement that specifies how we will behave in a future situation. In particular, the statement anticipates and articulates a specific triggering circumstance or feeling followed by a detailed statement of what we will do on that occasion. Thus, we might say, "When I walk into the lobby of my building, I will turn to the right and take the stairs up to my fourth-floor office." Similarly, we might say, "When I feel myself under pressure to make a concession, I will tell Joe that I need to make a phone call and take a five-minute break." When the trigger occurs, the response is to automatically follow. Specifying the trigger as well as the specifics of the behavioral response in this way has been shown to be effective in furthering the desired goal-directed behavior.[101]

◆ ◆ ◆ ◆ ◆

Summing It Up

- Reflect on whether additional information is actually needed in order to avoid spending resources on irrelevant information and risking that such information will take on a life of its own.
- Consider how framing and loss aversion can result in the certainty effect, the endowment effect, status quo bias, penalty aversion, option devaluation, and the overweighting of sunk costs.
- Keep in mind that options are evaluated differently when they are considered in relation to different option sets, when they are considered in different time horizons, and when they are offered by the other side.
- Understand the difficulties inherent in making predictions about future emotions, reactions, or behaviors.
- Appreciate the allure of not deciding—the temptation to procrastinate, the pull to avoid taking action, and the appeal of keeping doors open.
- Structure decision-making processes to account for the illusion of objectivity and the appeal of lay rationalism, participants' preferred decision-making approaches, the differences between choosing and rejecting options, and the differing information available in joint versus separate evaluation.
- Use group processes that facilitate information sharing and dissent.
- Develop implementation intentions to increase the odds of following through with decisions.

For Further Reading: Decision Making

JOHATHAN BARON, THINKING AND DECIDING (3d ed. 2000).
ROBIN M. HOGARTH, EDUCATING INTUITION (2001).
DANIEL KAHNEMAN, THINKING FAST AND SLOW (2011).

Daniel Kahneman & Amos Tversky, *Choices, Values, and Frames*, 39 AM. PSYCHOLOGIST 341 (1984).

Daniel J. Keys & Barry Schwartz, *"Leaky" Rationality: How Research on Behavioral Decision Making Challenges Normative Standards of Rationality*, 2 PERSP. ON PSYCHOL. SCI. 162 (2007).

RANDALL KISER, BEYOND RIGHT AND WRONG: THE POWER OF EFFECTIVE DECISION MAKING FOR ATTORNEYS AND CLIENTS (2010).

JOHN W. PAYNE ET AL., THE ADAPTIVE DECISION MAKER (1993).

BARRY SCHWARTZ, THE PARADOX OF CHOICE: WHY MORE IS LESS (2004).

SIMPLE HEURISTICS THAT MAKE US SMART (Gerd Gigerenzer et al. eds., 1999).

TIME AND DECISION: ECONOMIC AND PSYCHOLOGICAL PERSPECTIVES ON INTERTEMPORAL CHOICE (George Loewenstein et al. eds., 2003).

Timothy D. Wilson & Daniel T. Gilbert, *Affective Forecasting*, 35 ADVANCES EXPERIMENTAL SOC. PSYCHOL. 345 (2003).

Persuasion and Social Influence | 6

I would rather try to persuade a man to go along—because once I have persuaded him, he will stick. If I scare him, he will stay just as long as he is scared, and then he is gone.
—Dwight D. Eisenhower[1]

The tasks of persuasion and influence are central to the work of attorneys. Attorneys persuade others to engage in deals, create contracts, and accept settlement offers or demands. Attorneys work to persuade courts and other tribunals—through motions, briefs, testimony, and oral argument—that their positions are correct. Similarly, attorneys work to persuade administrative agencies, city councils, and other government entities. Attorneys also use persuasion in working with clients or colleagues. And, of course, attorneys are subject to others' efforts to influence them.

Lawyers tend to have facile, analytical minds; expertise in logical argument; and an instinct about what is persuasive or what will influence others to comply with their wishes. Understanding the psychology of persuasion and influence can build on these intuitions. By knowing more about how, and under what conditions, persuasion efforts tend to be effective and understanding the science underlying how people influence each other, lawyers can hone their ability to accomplish their desired ends.

> [Lawyers] are constantly endeavoring to come to agreements of one sort or another with people, to persuade people, sometimes when they are reluctant to be persuaded.
> —Harvard Law School Dean Erwin Griswold[2]

Two Paths to Persuasion

The most prominent models of persuasion in psychology are dual-process models that posit the existence of two routes to persuasion: a more deliberative central route in which persuasive messages are carefully processed and a more intuitive or peripheral route in which processing is more superficial.[3] The central route involves deliberative, effortful, and elaborative thinking in which the content of the proffered arguments is processed systematically. Pros and cons are weighed, attention is given to multiple perspectives, and the evidence for the arguments offered is scrutinized carefully. When a message is processed through the central route, persuasion is dependent on the content of the message, the decision maker is more likely to distinguish strong and weak arguments, and the strength of the arguments is likely to be influential. Because it is based on systematic processing of the evidence, persuasion that occurs through the central route tends to be more stable and enduring than that achieved through the peripheral route.[4]

In contrast, the peripheral route involves more superficial, less effortful, and more automatic processing. Because peripheral processing is less systematic and deliberative, persuasion can depend more on heuristic or peripheral cues that may not be linked to the actual quality of the message. Thus, a decision maker might be swayed by factors such as the length of the message or the number of arguments it contains rather than by the quality of those arguments. Strong arguments may become less persuasive while weak arguments have more influence. The decision maker might be more swayed by the attractiveness or apparent expertise of the persuader, such as an honorific title, rather than by whether the source of the message actually possesses expertise that is relevant to the topic at hand.

People are more likely to process information systematically through the central route when they are both motivated and able to do so. Lacking either the motivation or ability to so process, they tend to fall back on peripheral cues. Some people, by virtue of their personality attributes, are generally disposed to process information systematically.[5] But motivation to process systematically is also more likely across a wide variety of people when the topic is personally engaging to them or highly relevant to their objectives or when they will be held accountable for their decisions.[6] Motivation by itself, however, is not enough. Deliberative processing is more likely when people are able to systematically process the message, that is, when the message is understandable, the decision maker has sufficient background knowledge to scrutinize the message effectively, there is sufficient time to carefully consider the message, and other distractions are minimal. In contrast, when the decision maker is not interested, when he is distracted or tired, or when the message is hard to understand or ambiguous, peripheral or heuristic processing is more likely to appear.[7] But even the "deliberate use of more effortful strategies does not preclude the possibility that less effortful processes continue to operate."[8]

> ✦ ✦ ✦ ✦ ✦
> **Clarence Darrow and Peripheral Processing?**
>
> Consider the following example of how one famous attorney attempted to use distraction to induce peripheral processing in jurors:
>
>> The famous advocate Clarence Darrow (1857–1938) is reputed to have employed the tactic of distraction to prevent the jury from hearing his opponent's closing arguments. Darrow would insert a wire inside his cigar so that when he smoked it the ash would grow long without falling. He would smoke it during his opponent's closing, and as the ash grew increasingly long, the jury (it is said) would become increasingly fascinated and not be able to attend to the opponent's arguments.[9]
>
> As psychologist Michael Saks pointed out, however, this distraction was probably not enough to interfere with jurors' hearing of the message but may have interfered with their ability to process the message more deeply:
>
>> An ash growing on a cigar is probably easy enough for a juror to monitor while still hearing closing arguments. But it would demand enough attention to interfere with [jurors' ability to note the argument's weaknesses]. Thus, Darrow's tactic, while having intuitive appeal and being terribly clever, probably *increased* his opponent's effectiveness.[10]

Thus, the targets of persuasion may process information differently depending on whether they are processing that information systematically or heuristically. Here is why this matters for persuasion: aspects of the message, its source, the context, and so on can have different effects depending on the ways in which the message recipient is processing and can even influence the extent of processing itself.[11] For example, when the level of processing is low, the physical attractiveness of the source may operate as a heuristic cue with attractive sources being more persuasive. When the level of processing is higher, the target is likely to make more discriminating judgments; thus, the attractiveness of the source won't be as persuasive unless it is relevant to the subject of the message, for example, when the source is trying to sell a beauty product.

Similarly, consider the potential effects of emotion on persuasion. As we saw in chapters 3 and 4, affect can operate as a heuristic: someone in a positive mood is more likely to form a positive evaluation of the proposal at hand, particularly when processing is peripheral. In contrast, when processing is systematic, emotion might be carefully assessed for its value as information relevant to the question presented. In either case, affect can influence the interpretation of ambiguous information. In addition, emotion can influence the degree of processing in which people engage, with some emotions (for example, happiness and anger) triggering heuristic processing and others (for example, sadness) producing more careful processing. Emotion can even influence persuasion by affecting people's confidence in and, consequently, reliance on the thoughts that they generate in response to a persuasive appeal.[12]

Thus, as we will see, characteristics of the source of the message and of the message itself can have an important influence on the persuasiveness of the message. The nature of these effects, however, can differ depending on the ways in which the message is processed.

Source Credibility

Sources that appear to be credible are more persuasive. To be highly credible, a source must have relevant *expertise*—the knowledge and ability to provide information that is accurate and useful to the decision at hand.[13] For example, the more knowledgeable an air conditioner repairman appears to be, the more likely a customer will be to follow his recommendation to buy a new system. An attorney can claim expertise in a case when she clearly knows the case and has an exhaustive knowledge of the record. Such expertise increases the credibility of the statements made by the source.

> [T]he man who wishes to persuade people will not be negligent as to the matter of character . . . he will apply himself above all to establish a most honourable name among his fellow-citizens; for who does not know that words carry greater conviction when spoken by men of good repute . . . ?
> —Isocrates[14]

In addition to being expert, sources that are perceived to be *trustworthy* are viewed as more credible and, hence, more persuasive. Sources that are seen as objective and perceived as intending to provide accurate and useful information are more credible. Thus, those who argue against their own self-interest or admit to weak points in their arguments are perceived to be more credible.[15] The air conditioner repairman is likely to build credibility by suggesting that the customer could wait to buy a new system or by suggesting a less expensive system. Criminals are more effective than noncriminals when arguing in favor of tougher sentencing.[16] And a plaintiff's attorney who admits that any claim for punitive damages is a long shot may be more credible when she stands firm on her demand for compensation for pain and suffering. In contrast, an attorney who lies, overstates his case, or mischaracterizes precedent is less likely to be seen as trustworthy—and, accordingly, will not be as persuasive.

The persuasiveness of expert and trustworthy sources derives, in part, from a desire to come to accurate conclusions. But we also tend to operate from a heuristic that prescribes that "experts" can be trusted. Thus, the apparent expertise or trustworthiness of a source can have a greater impact under conditions of low deliberation; and we can be influenced by nonexperts who look like experts, experts with nonrelevant expertise, and so on. In contrast, when the message recipient is motivated and able to process systematically, the seeming expertise and trustworthiness of the source are less influential as the message itself is more carefully scrutinized.[17] Indeed, indications that a source is not trustworthy can increase the motivation to scrutinize a message. When such increased elaboration occurs, even a message from an untrustworthy source can be persuasive when it turns out to be of high quality (and even less persuasive when it turns out to be weak).[18] For example, we might not trust the opposing party, but that does not preclude the party from crafting a way to structure a transaction that is creative enough to warrant our attention.

> [P]erhaps the most valuable thing the lawyer brings into the courtroom when he is an advocate is his reputation. His reputation for candor and soundness is worth three points in his brief and a marvelous opening for his oral argument. If his reputation is bad, I don't care what he says or how he says it—he is climbing a glass mountain in shoes covered with oil.
>
> —Hon. Charles D. Breitel[19]

As a general matter, the expressed confidence of a source tends to influence judgments of the source's credibility—sources who express a higher degree of confidence tend to be perceived as more credible—even though, as we saw in chapter 2, the relationship between confidence and accuracy is tenuous.[20] At the same time, the extent to which a source is known to have been accurate in providing information can affect the credibility of the source. Inaccuracies, whether they relate to important details of the topic at hand or to more peripheral details, can damage credibility.[21] But, interestingly, such errors tend to have a more deleterious effect on sources who have expressed a high degree of certainty. A highly confident source who is later shown to have made an error is no longer trusted to give useful signals of confidence, while a source who is shown to have made an error in making a statement about which she expressed low confidence is now thought to be well calibrated and, hence, more credible.[22]

To see this point more clearly, consider a study in which participants assessed the credibility of two witnesses to a car accident: one who stated that he was highly confident about what had happened in the accident and other details about the same day and a second witness who expressed confidence about the details of the accident but less confidence in recalling peripheral details about the day. Later, it became clear that each witness had made erroneous statements about some peripheral detail relating to their day. Prior to this revelation, the highly confident witness was judged to be more credible. But after the errors became known, the less confident, but better-calibrated, witness was found to be more credible.[23] People assess the credibility of their advisers in similar ways.[24] Accordingly, in order to avoid losing credibility, attorneys should strive for accuracy in their dealings with clients, negotiating counterparts, and judges.

A person's manner of speaking or delivery can also affect his perceived credibility. Those who speak in a *powerless* manner—speech that includes verbal hesitations (such as *um*, *well*, or *you know*), false starts, intensifiers, and verbal hedges (such as *I think* or *kind of*)—tend to be perceived as less credible than those who speak in a more *powerful* manner in which such features are absent.[25] Similarly, the more fluent or easy to understand a communication is, the more credible and, hence, persuasive it tends to be.[26] It can also be useful to match style of delivery to the decision-making orientation of the audience. Recall our discussion of the distinction between promotion and prevention focus from chapter 5. Those with a promotion focus are oriented toward achieving positive outcomes and capitalizing on opportunity, while those with a prevention focus are most concerned with avoiding negative outcomes and mistakes. An *eager* delivery style—more animated, forward-leaning posture, open gestures, quick pace—tends to be more persuasive for those higher in promotion focus. In contrast, a more *vigilant* delivery style—slower, backward-leaning posture—can be more effective with those who are prevention focused.[27]

Finally, the number of sources can also influence the persuasiveness of the appeal. Because message recipients tend to believe that divergent sources have come at a problem from different perspectives and have access to different information, increasing the number of sources tends to increase the degree of attention to and processing of the message. Thus, three different strong arguments in favor of a proposition given by three different sources tend to be more persuasive than the same three arguments given by a single source. Conversely, three weak arguments given by three different sources tend to be less persuasive than the same three arguments given by a single source.[28] Accordingly, when the arguments are sound, it can be useful to marshal a number of sources or to evoke multiple external authorities for support, for example, citing precedent from multiple jurisdictions or calling upon multiple appraisers.

Message Characteristics

In addition to the credibility of the source, the message itself can be more or less persuasive. Not surprisingly, higher-quality arguments are more persuasive.[29] As we have already seen, this is particularly true when the audience is motivated and able to effectively attend to the quality of the arguments. Thus, for engaged audiences, arguments that are logical, well constructed, and relevant will tend to be more persuasive.

It is also the case that what is persuasive may vary with the characteristics of the audience. For example, when thinking about a topic such as capital punishment, some people may be more persuaded by arguments based on religion or morality. Others may find legal arguments more compelling, while still others may be most persuaded by empirical research on whether the death penalty deters crime.[30] In the realm of a lawsuit, one defendant may be more persuaded to settle in order to cut her losses, another may be swayed by a desire to "do the right thing," and another may find the idea of putting the problem behind her more compelling than anything else.

Similarly, members of different cultures may be differentially persuaded by arguments about benefits to the individual and arguments about benefits to the collective. Persuasion in independent cultures tends to be about getting other people to understand the "true" facts and providing them with reasons for making concessions. People from such cultures are more likely to appeal to logic and rationality to persuade, putting forward facts, reasons, and cost-benefit analyses. But for members of interdependent cultures, persuasion is focused on the demands of the social context, and concessions are obtained by focusing attention on the obligations of social role. People from such cultures would be more likely to appeal to emotion, social roles and obligations, or relationships as a basis of persuasion.[31]

Recall that the quality of the arguments in a message matters the most when the audience is motivated and able to systematically process the message. Accordingly, to present a high-quality message in a convincing manner, it is important to do so in a way that focuses the attention and cognitive effort of the audience on the substance of the message.

For example, to increase the audience's ability to systematically process, a message should be easy to understand. This does not mean that the point must be elementary or that analytically complex arguments are off-limits. Nonetheless, unnecessarily complicated and confusing arguments are less persuasive than those that are made more clearly. Indeed, messages that are processed more easily or fluently are more likely to be perceived as true, are easier to remember, and inspire more confidence. Thus, difficult-to-read fonts, obscure or overly technical language, illogical arguments, convoluted sentence structures, poor grammar, examples that are difficult to imagine, and arguments that are hard to believe can interfere with the persuasiveness of the underlying message.[32] We will return to this point in the next chapter.

Likewise, messages that are concrete rather than abstract tend to be easier to understand, more memorable, and, ultimately, more persuasive.[33] To take a simple example, look at the following list of words:

    camel
    beach ball
    mountain
    fork
    bumblebee
    snowplow
    flower
    skyscraper
    computer

After reviewing the list, see how many of the words you can remember without looking back at the list. Now try the following list:

    justice
    complacency

friendly
smooth
hate
order
feminism
moral
success

Notice that the concrete words (the words that describe tangible things) are easier to remember. Concrete examples or analogies can help people to remember by capitalizing on this *concreteness effect* and by making unfamiliar material seem more familiar.[34]

To see how making abstract statistical information concrete can increase its persuasiveness, consider the following demonstration used by Geoff Ainscow and his group Beyond War in the 1980s to illustrate the magnitude of the world's nuclear arsenal:

> He always carried a metal bucket to the gatherings. At the appropriate point in the presentation, he'd take a BB out of his pocket and drop it into the empty bucket. The BB made a loud clatter as it ricocheted and settled. Ainscow would then say, "This is the Hiroshima bomb." He then spent a few minutes describing the devastation of the Hiroshima bomb—the miles of flattened buildings, the tens of thousands killed immediately, the larger number of people with burns or other long-term health problems.
>
> Next he'd drop ten BBs into the bucket. The clatter was louder and more chaotic. "This is the firepower of the missiles on *one* U.S. or Soviet nuclear submarine," he'd say.
>
> Finally, he asked the attendees to close their eyes. He'd say, "This is the world's current arsenal of nuclear weapons." Then he poured 5,000 BBs into the bucket (one for every nuclear warhead in the world). The noise was starling, even terrifying. "The roar of the BBs went on and on," said Ainscow. "Afterward there was always dead silence."[35]

> The death of a single Russian soldier is a tragedy. A million deaths is a statistic.
> —*Joseph Stalin*[36]

By making the statistic tangible, Ainscow made it easier for the audience to comprehend and thereby increased his persuasive impact.

In similar ways, individual stories or anecdotes tend to be more persuasive than abstract information or statistics. Such stories tend to be more memorable than dry statistics, and we are more likely to empathize with an individual than an abstraction.

Let a 6-year-old girl with brown hair need thousands of dollars for an operation that will prolong her life until Christmas, and the post office will be swamped with nickels and dimes to save her. But let it be reported that without a sales tax the hospital facilities of Massachusetts will deteriorate and cause a barely perceptible increase in preventable deaths—not many will drop a tear or reach for their checkbooks.[37]

Research has repeatedly found that people respond more to identified people (or even specific unidentified people) than to statistics. For example, people are more willing to help identified victims and more inclined to punish identified wrongdoers.[39] Similarly, people have a tendency to ignore statistics, focusing instead on individual cases even when those cases are atypical or misleading.[40] Thus, it can be important for an attorney representing a class of plaintiffs to highlight individual class members' stories, for policy arguments to be tied to anecdotes that illustrate the effects of the policy on individual actors, or for potential consequences to be linked to individuals.

> If I look at the mass, I will never act. If I look at the one, I will.
> —Mother Teresa[38]

Consider another example of the effect that individuating details can have on persuasiveness. In one study, researchers asked participants to review the evidence relating to "Mrs. Johnson's" fitness as a parent. Some pieces of evidence were presented in relatively abstract terms: "Mrs. Johnson sees to it that her child washes and brushes his teeth before bedtime." Other pieces of evidence were elaborated with an additional, irrelevant, but concrete, detail: "He uses a Star Wars toothbrush that looks like Darth Vader." For half of the participants, the evidence favoring Mrs. Johnson was abstract, while the evidence against her was concrete. For the other half of the participants, the favorable evidence was concrete, and the opposing evidence was abstract. How did participants judge Mrs. Johnson's fitness as a parent? They judged her to be fitter as a parent when the favorable arguments included concrete details than they did when the unfavorable arguments were the ones that were concrete.[41]

Some aspects of a message can increase the degree to which people systematically process information when they are not already doing so but can distract them when they are already processing at a high level. For example, rhetorical questions can increase the engagement of audiences with low involvement, making them more sensitive to the quality of the arguments presented. At the same time, however, for audiences who are already engaged, rhetorical questions can be distracting and can even make them less sensitive to the quality of the arguments.[42]

✦ ✦ ✦ ✦ ✦

Order of Arguments

Psychological research has demonstrated a *primacy effect*—information that is presented early in an interaction tends to capture attention and to influence the processing of information that follows it. In addition, research has demonstrated a *recency effect* such that information presented later is easier to remember. Thus, information and arguments that are presented early and late in a presentation or writing can be more persuasive than are those that are buried in the middle.[43]

> Forewarned is forearmed.
> —Proverb

To be most persuasive, the presenter must address the weaknesses in his own argument. Putting forth a *two-sided argument*—that is, one that acknowledges the opposing position and refutes it—can be more effective than a one-sided argument, particularly with an audience that is engaged and processing systematically. We have already seen that acknowledging opposing arguments and addressing them can increase credibility by making the source of the message appear evenhanded. But providing a two-sided argument can also reduce the amount of counterargument that is self-generated by the audience and provide the audience the tools with which they can argue against later opposing arguments.[44]

The effectiveness of two-sided arguments works through what is known as *inoculation*. Drawing on a medical analogy, the notion of inoculation is that exposure to a relatively weak opposing message to which the audience can straightforwardly generate counterarguments builds resistance to (that is, the ability to counterargue) a later stronger opposing message. In addition, a two-sided message can serve as a forewarning of later counterarguments, preparing the audience to counterargue when the later message is presented.[45]

Similarly, acknowledging weaknesses can allow the presenter to "steal the thunder" of an opponent by disclosing potentially damaging information before such information can be revealed by the opponent. Presenting damaging information before an opponent can do so allows the presenter to characterize and label the information in ways that are more favorable, increases credibility by making the presenter seem fair and objective (because the presenter is admitting to information against her interest), changes the degree to which the information is interpreted as damaging, and minimizes counterarguments by inoculating the audience.[46]

To see this more clearly, consider a study of mock jurors in which researchers compared the credibility of an expert witness under three conditions: where there was no evidence of bias, where bias was raised by the other side on cross-examination and only then addressed by the witness, and where the same bias was first raised and addressed by the witness on direct examination. The witness who raised the potential bias himself (stealing the other side's thunder) was seen as more credible, more prepared, more convincing, and more trustworthy than was the witness about whom the other side raised the bias. In fact, the witness who raised the bias himself was not seen as any less credible than the witness about whom no bias had been raised.[47] In similar ways, corporate clients who get out in front of negative publicity can make themselves seem more credible and the relevant crisis less severe.[48] And an attorney can build credibility in negotiation or mediation by raising and addressing the weaknesses in his own case. While stealing thunder may not always completely wipe out the effect of the negative information, it has frequently been shown to decrease the damage.

> ✦ ✦ ✦ ✦ ✦
> ### Head in the Sand?
>
> Failing to address an opponent's strong arguments can damage an advocate's credibility and sacrifices the opportunity to counter those arguments. In one recent case involving motions to dismiss for forum non conveniens, the U.S. Court of Appeals for the Seventh Circuit sharply chastised counsel for failing to cite relevant precedents:
>
>> When there is apparently dispositive precedent, an appellant may urge its overruling or distinguish or reserve a challenge to it for a petition for certiorari but may not simply ignore it. . . . The ostrich is a noble animal, but not a proper model for an appellate advocate.[49]
>
>
>
> The court also took the unusual step of including a picture (shown at right) in its opinion.

Finally, what about the number of arguments put forward? As a general matter, it might seem reasonable to think that adding more arguments would increase persuasion. Even if an additional argument is not very strong, it certainly shouldn't hurt . . . right? Well, when the level of processing is low, the sheer number of arguments relied on can serve as a heuristic cue (more arguments must be better), increasing persuasion regardless of argument quality. But what might surprise you is that when processing is high, the number of arguments by itself does not increase persuasion. Instead, the quality of the arguments is central: additional strong arguments increase persuasion, but additional weak or irrelevant arguments can actually decrease persuasion. In particular, weak arguments can distract from better ones and can lead to increased counterarguing. Even if a stronger form of the argument is later provided, inoculation is likely to result in increased resistance to that later message.[51] Thus, cluttering a motion or brief with flimsy or tangential arguments or peppering a negotiation with weak points can dilute an argument, making the stronger points less persuasive.

> ❝ [A] weak argument does more than merely dilute your brief. It speaks poorly of your judgment and thus reduces confidence in your other points. As the saying goes, it is like the 13th stroke of a clock: not only wrong in itself, but casting doubt on all that preceded it.
> —*Justice Antonin Scalia & Brian A. Garner*[50] ❞

Influence Tactics

There are myriad ways in which human beings attempt to influence each other. Some of these involve changing the incentives that another person faces. For example, we can attempt to convince another person to assent to a particular negotiated agreement by sweetening the deal or otherwise making a concession. Alternatively, we could use negative incentives such as threats—as Don Corleone says in *The Godfather*, "I'm gonna make him an offer he can't refuse."[52] *Psychological influence*, however, has been described as "the effort to positively influence another party's attitude towards a given idea or proposition *without* changing the incentives or objective information set of the other party."[53] Such efforts tend to play on the range of intuitions and rules of thumb that guide our behavior. As we have seen before, these intuitions often help us to successfully navigate the world, but they can sometimes lead us astray. It is to these means of influence to which we now turn.

Before we launch into our discussion of some of the methods of psychological influence, we should note one simple but sometimes-overlooked way of obtaining compliance: *asking* for what we need or want. It turns out that we tend to underestimate the degree to which others will comply with a direct request for assistance.[54] And failure to ask can be costly. In one study, the failure to negotiate starting salary was associated with a 7.4% difference in starting salary—a difference that when factoring in raises and interest becomes even more significant over time.[55] Asking for agreement to a continuance, commitment to a particular contract term, the institution of a particular workplace accommodation, or a particular way of structuring a settlement may be all that it takes to secure agreement. We realize, however, that in many instances more will be needed.

The Psychology We've Already Discussed

Already in this book, we have seen a number of psychological phenomena that can be used to influence others. For example, in chapter 1, we learned that people's understanding of the world is constructed through their subjective construal of what they see and experience. One implication of this is that sometimes persuasion can result from changing the ways in which people interpret a particular set of facts.[56] Similarly, taking the perspective of the target of influence can help a person formulate a more persuasive argument. For example, lawyers who can perceive how a prospective client might find their services valuable are likely to be more effective rainmakers. In addition, it seems clear that introducing different perspectives can have a persuasive effect because different viewpoints can highlight and make salient different slices of information. One person's clunker might be another's collector's item.

In chapter 3, we saw the ways in which emotion can influence thinking. Consider, too, the variety of influences on judgment and decision making that we discussed in chapters 4 and 5. The effects of the ways in which options are framed, reference points and anchors are evoked, options are considered in context, concepts are primed to be available in memory, and decisions are structured suggest a range of techniques for influencing others.[57]

Reciprocity

You scratch my back, and I'll scratch yours. You take the kids to the library on Saturday; your spouse takes them to the movies on Sunday. Your waiter includes a mint with your check, hoping for a better tip.[58] A survey firm includes a dollar in the envelope containing the survey that it wants you to fill out and return. The grocery store offers you a free sample of a new product. When someone does something for us (entertains the kids, gives us a mint or a dollar or a sample, buys us a drink), there is a human tendency to want to return the favor. This *reciprocity norm*—that "we should try to repay, in kind, what another person has provided us"[60]—has been described as "one of the strongest and most pervasive social forces in all human cultures."[61]

Life cannot subsist in society but by reciprocal concessions.
—*Samuel Johnson*[59]

This felt need to reciprocate can be quite functional, furthering cooperation and civility. In fact, reciprocation underlies the back-and-forth nature of the negotiation process in which the two sides alternate making concessions until a deal can be reached. The parties can be comfortable making concessions knowing that the norm of reciprocity will push the other side to respond in kind. And, indeed, we tend to be quite dissatisfied when we make unreciprocated concessions or "bid against ourselves."[62]

At the same time, however, the reciprocity norm can be used to elicit concessions in response to seeming concessions that aren't really concessions. For example, psychologists have found that the recipients of apologies feel a great deal of social pressure to accept an offered apology even when the proffered apology is unconvincing or patently insincere.[63]

Or, consider the following scenario described by psychologist Robert Cialdini:

> I was walking down the street when I was approached by an 11- or 12-year-old boy. He introduced himself and said he was selling tickets to the annual Boy Scouts Circus to be held on the upcoming Saturday night. He asked if I wished to buy any tickets at $5 apiece. Since one of the last places I wanted to spend Saturday evening was with the Boy Scouts, I declined. "Well," he said, "if you don't want to buy any tickets, how about buying some of our chocolate bars? They're only $1 each." I bought a couple and, right away, realized that something noteworthy had happened. I knew that to be the case because (a) I do not like chocolate bars; (b) I do like dollars; (c) I was standing there with two of his chocolate bars; and (d) he was walking away with two of my dollars. . . .
>
> His request that I purchase some $1 chocolate bars had been put in the form of a concession on his part; it was presented as a retreat from his request that I buy some $5 tickets. If I were to live up to the dictates of the reciprocation rule, there had to be a concession on my part. As we have seen, there was such a concession: I changed from noncompliant to compliant when he moved from a larger to a

smaller request, even though I was not really interested in *either* of the things he offered.[64]

This exemplifies what is known as the *rejection-then-retreat*, or *door-in-the-face, technique*. The requester makes a large request that is likely to be rejected. The requester then makes the concession of retreating from that request and making a less onerous request instead. The reciprocity norm dictates that this concession be met with a reciprocal concession, that is, agreement to this scaled-back request.

This technique has been used to obtain agreement to significant commitments. For example, Cialdini and his colleagues used the reciprocity norm to get college students to agree to chaperon a group of juvenile delinquents on a trip to the zoo: When they simply asked students to take on this responsibility, only 17% agreed. However, if this request was preceded by a request to mentor juvenile delinquents for two hours a week over a two-year period—a proposal that was refused by all of the students—half of the students (50%) agreed to chaperon the zoo trip.[65]

◆ ◆ ◆ ◆ ◆

Reciprocity and Television Writing

The writers and creators of network television programs use the reciprocity norm in negotiating with network censors over indecorous language in television programs:

> The rules of engagement in this routine warfare are understood by everyone involved. Standards editors often tell one another, "Give them seven notes so you can negotiate." The writers, in turn, put "asshole" in the script a few times as "censor bait," knowing they'll have to cut it but hoping to keep two "bitches" and a "balls" in exchange.[66]

Reciprocity is also evident in the *that's-not-all technique* used by marketers, in which a person makes an initial offer and then, before waiting for a response to that proposal, immediately makes an improved offer. The sweetening of the offer, then, appears to be a concession that calls for reciprocation.[67]

The reciprocation instinct can also work against influence, with negative behavior evoking a negative response.[68] Thus, for example, a disputant who has been treated badly by an opponent may be inclined to dig in his heels. Moreover, research has found an asymmetry between reciprocating to positive acts such as giving and negative acts such as taking. Specifically, while people tend to reciprocate positive acts with equivalent positive acts, they are more likely to reciprocate negative acts with responses that are harsher. This asymmetry can cause conflict to escalate as each side reciprocates with increasingly harsh responses.[69]

Scarcity

"Limited time offer!"

"Act now—only three tickets left at this price!"

"Well, we've got another interested buyer. This place might not be on the market much longer."

"My client is only willing to leave this offer open until tomorrow at 5:00 p.m."

Such statements derive their influential power from our reactions to *scarcity*.[70] We want what we can't have. We infer that an item or opportunity is in short supply because others want it—and if others want it, it must be valuable. We worry that we will lose the chance to take advantage of the opportunity, deal, or item; and we are averse to losses (see chapter 5). We worry that we will regret missing out (see chapter 5). We want to win. All of this means that we can be influenced by deadlines, limited availability, and competing offers.

Consistency and Commitment

There is a human tendency, particularly in independent cultures, to want to appear to be consistent in our views and behaviors. As a result, once we've acted in particular ways or made particular commitments, particularly when those commitments are made actively or publicly, we feel compelled to act in ways that comport with those prior behaviors or commitments.[71] To recognize the truth of this, just think about the ways in which "flip-floppers" and "wafflers" are denigrated in political campaigns.

Consider one exploration of the tendency toward consistency and commitment in which researchers compared juries that used open voting procedures to those that used secret ballots. In close cases, open voting—in which each juror made a public commitment to his initial position—was found to result in more hung juries.[72] Having made a public commitment to their initial position, the jurors were reluctant to change their position. Legal counselors, writers, and negotiators can capitalize on this tendency by appealing to their audiences' previously enunciated positions.

One technique that derives from this tendency is the *foot-in-the-door technique*. The requester makes a relatively minor, innocuous request, the sort with which it is easy to comply. Once compliance with the small request has been obtained, the requester moves on to a more substantial request. Wanting to behave in a manner that is consistent with her prior behavior, the target agrees to this larger request even though she may not have done so if approached with this request in the first place. Thus, in one study, more people were willing to allow an unattractive billboard promoting safe driving to be erected on their lawn if they had first agreed to display a small (three-inch-square) sign or to sign a petition.[73] Similarly, people are more apt to decide to donate bone marrow if they are not asked to make this ultimate decision until after they have already complied with smaller preliminary steps, for example, discussing donation with a medical provider or undergoing a blood test to see if they are a match.[74] In the same way, a lawyer may lead a buyer to a larger order by first starting with a small one or may persuade a client to trust her with all of the client's legal business by first convincing the client to hire her to work on a single deal.

Another technique that capitalizes on the desire to be consistent is *low-balling*. The target is asked to agree to an initial request that, it turns out, has not been fully and clearly specified. Once the target has agreed, the details of the offer are revealed: hidden costs, an error in calculating the price, a price that doesn't include all of the relevant features. But because the target has already committed, he is still likely to go through with the deal.[75]

Think about how the tendency to act in ways that are consistent might be used to facilitate negotiation. When a lengthy negotiation gets tough, a lawyer might evoke principles of commitment to argue for sticking it out: "We've put so much into this and have come so far. Let's not let all of our efforts go to waste." Furthermore, the pull of the desire to be consistent suggests that it can be useful for a lawyer to elicit commitment from a counterpart to a guiding principle with which the lawyer hopes that counterpart will consistently act. Convincing an opponent to publicly state his bottom line could be counterproductive in that it will be difficult to later obtain concessions that are or seem inconsistent with that stated position. In contrast, consider what might happen if the lawyer obtains commitment to a more useful principle, for example, "what is in the best interests of the children" or "the prevention of future medical errors like this one." Capitalizing on the commitment to this principle, the lawyer could frame proposals for concessions in ways that would be consistent with the principle.

Finally, consider the phenomenon of *escalation of commitment*—the tendency for someone who has begun a project or a negotiation to become increasingly committed to continuing with it even when it is longer sensible.[76] Overweighting sunk costs (see chapter 5), paying attention to evidence that confirms the initial investment (see chapter 1), being motivated to justify our prior engagement (see chapter 5), and wanting to behave consistently with previous decisions, we are hesitant to reevaluate and can become more invested in closing the deal than in striking the right deal or walking away. Interestingly, when presented with situations in which they might be tempted to escalate their commitment, people predict that they will not escalate. But when later faced with the situation, what do they do? They escalate. In fact, the less that people predicted that they would escalate commitment and "the more they believed that they would be able to remain rational and avoid being ensnared, the more they negotiated and actually escalated their commitments."[77] Rather than assuming that we won't be ensnared, it is more effective to set (in advance) thresholds beyond which will we not go and focus accountability on the decision-making process rather than on the outcome of the decision.[78]

Liking

People are more persuaded by and more likely to comply with the requests of someone they like. Thus, we are more influenced by people we like; those with whom we are familiar; those who are attractive or famous; those with whom we have positive associations; those with whom we have developed good rapport (see chapter

7); and those we find to be similar to ourselves or with whom we share interests, goals, or even names or birthdays. Even brief interactions and conversations with another person can increase liking and persuasion, as can remembering the other person's name.[79] Similarly, *ingratiation*—conforming opinions to those of another, complimenting or otherwise flattering the other person, and so on—can increase liking and, hence, persuasion as long as the ingratiation is not so transparent that the target begins to mistrust the flatterer's motives.[81] To the extent that many of these factors are extraneous to the merits of the topic of persuasion or request, they are likely to have a greater impact when the decision maker is processing peripherally or heuristically.

> The main work of a trial attorney is to make a jury like his client.
> — Clarence Darrow[80]

> Remember that a person's name is to that person the sweetest and most important sound in any language.
> — Dale Carnegie[82]

Lawyers, Liking, and Negotiation

The influence of liking and familiarity on persuasion can be seen in research findings on legal negotiation. First, there is evidence that lawyers who deal with each other routinely are less likely to reach impasse, settling more often and more quickly.[83] In addition, there is evidence that negotiators who have a chance to get to know each other and develop a sense of rapport are better able to consider a broad range of options, are more likely to reach agreement, and are more willing to work together again.[84]

Social Proof

Imagine that you are sitting in a room filling out paperwork when you become aware of smoke entering the room through a vent. What would you do? Would it matter if you were alone in the room? Psychologists Bibb Latané and John Darley investigated precisely this question. Study participants found themselves answering questionnaires in a room as the smoke started to waft in. After several minutes had passed, sufficient smoke had come into the room to obscure the vision of those present. When they were alone in the room, most participants (75%) got up and reported the smoke. But a fascinating thing happened when there were other people present in the room. When there were three naïve participants in the room together, only 38% of the time did at least one of them report the smoke. And when the other two people in the room were confederates of the experimenters who were instructed to remain impassive, only 10% of participants reported the smoke. Why such a big difference? It turns out that the presence of other people can influence how we interpret what is going on around us, particularly when what is transpiring is ambiguous. When we do not know what is happening or what we should do, we look to other people for clues about how to behave. Looking to others for social cues often provides useful information—but not always. As the researchers noted,

> [i]f each member of a group is, at the same time, trying to appear calm and also looking around at the other members to gauge their reactions, all members may be led (or misled) by each other to define the situation as less critical than they would if alone. Until someone acts, each person only sees other nonresponding bystanders, and, as with the passive confederates, is likely to be influenced not to act himself.[85]

✦✦✦✦✦

Bystander Apathy?

Many of the studies on bystander behavior, including the study of the smoke-filled room, were conducted in the wake of the murder of Kitty Genovese in a residential neighborhood in New York City in 1964. Following the attack, the New York Times reported that at least thirty-eight of Genovese's neighbors had observed the attack but had not intervened—or even called the police—even though the murder had unfolded over the course of thirty minutes.[86]

The behavior of the participants in the smoke-filled room is an example of the operation of *social proof*—looking to what others are doing or thinking in order to determine what we should do or think.[87] Social proof is the theory behind laugh tracks and is the driving force behind fashion trends. We laugh along with the laugh track or studio audience, we look skyward when we see others doing so, we all face the same direction in an elevator (even when it's backward), we pay attention to what others are watching on television or wearing, and we look to others to determine which fork to use or which bread plate is ours. But as the smoke-filled room example demonstrates, we also look to others to inform more consequential behaviors: how to react in what is potentially an emergency situation, how to behave as taxpayers, whether to engage in file sharing, how to treat the environment, or how much dissembling is permissible in negotiation.[88]

Standing Backwards

For a humorous example of the elevator phenomenon, watch "Social Proof Elevator," a segment from *Candid Camera*, http://www.ebaumsworld.com/video/watch/1057680/.

The power of social proof, which can lead us to follow the actions of even a single individual, means that lawyers can establish norms for behavior by modeling the desired conduct. For example, an attorney might draw a negotiation counterpart into a joint problem-solving process by exhibiting her own curiosity about finding joint gains and using a collaborative approach to the negotiation. In similar ways, the amount of money that others were compensated for a similar injury, the prices paid for similar properties, or what a colleague did in a similar situation can be influential.[89]

The behavior of the participants in the smoke-filled room is also an example of *pluralistic ignorance* (see chapter 5), that is, the mistaken belief that others do not share one's understanding or perception of the world: "No one else seems to think anything is wrong. It must be nothing."[90] In such cases, it is misperceived social information that influences behavior. Despite people's awareness that their own failure to react belies their own underlying concern, they misjudge the meaning of other people's failure to act as an indication that there is nothing to be concerned about. In the legal context, imagine a lawyer who thinks that her colleagues all approve of a particular billing practice—though they do not. Or imagine a client who proceeds with a deal, without expressing a nagging reservation, because others seem to think the deal is sound—though they do not. Perceptions of group beliefs can also be misperceived because of a tendency to infer that a belief that is frequently expressed is a belief that is widespread—even if it is merely repeatedly expressed by only one or a handful of people.[91]

Thus, *descriptive norms*—what others do—can provide information about what is appropriate behavior. But what others do can also exert a normative influence on behavior: we sometimes go along with the group because we want to avoid the social disapproval associated with departing from social *prescriptive norms*.

✦ ✦ ✦ ✦ ✦
Please Call Again

Knowing about the power of descriptive norms, we cringe every time we hear radio fund-raisers make their pitch for donations by noting how many listeners don't pledge. Such an approach can be counterproductive because it ignores the power of social proof, sending the message that the normative behavior—that is, the behavior engaged in by most other similarly situated people—is *not* to pledge. Thus, Cialdini recommends telling listeners that "if operators are busy, please call again" (implying that so many calls are coming in that they are having trouble keeping up) rather than telling them that "operators are waiting, please call now" (suggesting that no one else is calling).[92]

Consider an experiment conducted by psychologist Solomon Asch. Participants in Asch's experiment were asked, each in turn around the table, to indicate which of a set of three possible lines matched the length of a target line. The problems were relatively easy, and things went smoothly until the fourth problem, when the first respondent confidently gave an answer that was clearly incorrect. Each respondent around the table, not including the last one, then proceeded to give the same, incorrect answer. The last respondent, it turns out, was the only naïve participant in the study; the others were confederates of the experimenter. When the real participant's turn came, he had to decide whether to conform to the incorrect answer that represented the consensus of the group or to go against the group to give the answer that was obviously correct. The same dilemma presented itself on numerous additional problems as the experiment proceeded.

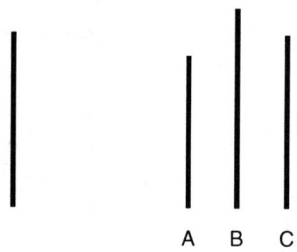

Asch Compliance Experiment

How did participants respond? While 25% of participants remained independent and gave the correct answers, 75% conformed to the group's wrong answer on at least one problem, and 50% conformed their answer to the group's answer on at least six of the problems. Subsequent experiments demonstrated that the size of the group establishing the norm did not have to be large; a three- or four-member group in which each person gave the wrong answer was enough. However, the incorrect responders did have to be unanimous—a single dissenter who gave the correct answer was enough support to permit the naïve participant to remain independent.[93]

Opportunities for conformity pressures to operate are rampant in legal settings: a police officer might conform to a group norm of illegal behavior within a department, a lawyer might conform his risk assessment to those expressed by others on the team, a client might act in ways that conform to the culture of her workplace, or a prosecutor might make a charging decision that conforms with the expressed views of others in the office.[94]

Obedience to Authority

We have seen that credible authorities can be more persuasive than individuals without particular expertise (when the audience is processing systematically) and that expertise or authority can serve as a heuristic cue (when the audience is processing more peripherally). But authorities can also have a different kind of effect on compliance. Specifically, people have a tendency to comply with those who are in authority or who are perceived to be in authority.[95] As with most of the influence tactics we have examined, obedience to authority can be a good thing. Imagine what might happen if firefighters tried to fight a raging fire without a chain of command or if hospital personnel attempted to conduct emergency surgery with everyone in the surgical suite questioning each order. But our tendency to comply with authority is not limited to such situations.

Consider the most famous studies of the psychology of obedience, studies conducted by psychologist Stanley Milgram.[96] Participants were told that they were participating in a study of learning and were assigned to the role of either a "learner" or a "teacher." The two would sit in adjoining rooms but would be able to hear each other. The learner was to learn sets of word pairs. For each wrong answer, the teacher was to administer an electrical shock to the learner, beginning at 15 volts (labeled *slight shock*) and increasing the intensity of the shock in 15-volt increments until eventually reaching 375 volts (labeled *danger severe shock*) and ultimately 450 volts (marked *XXX*).

> We do what we're told.
> —*Peter Gabriel*[97]

In fact, all of the actual study participants were assigned to the teacher role; the learners were confederates of the researcher and were not actually shocked. Once the experiment began, the confederate learner answered numerous questions incorrectly and made increasingly distressed responses to the resulting shocks (grunts, demands to be released from the experiment, agonizing cries of pain, and, eventually, failure to respond).

If at any point the teacher balked, the experimenter responded with one of a series of prompts: "Please continue." "The experiment requires that you continue." "It is absolutely essential that you continue." "You have no other choice; you *must* go on."

Under these conditions, fully 63% of participants continued to administer shocks to the maximum level. Milgram, who had run the initial experiment to establish a baseline condition in which no one complied, was amazed.

Milgram ultimately conducted eighteen variations on this study, shedding light on a variety of factors that influenced compliance. For example, compliance increased to over 90% if the participant worked together with another (confederate) participant to carry out the experiment but it was the peer who actually administered the shocks. In contrast, compliance was reduced to 30% when the learner was in the same room with the teacher and the teacher had to physically place the learner's hand on a plate to administer the shock. Similarly, compliance was reduced to 20% when the experimenter was not present but relayed his instructions via telephone, or when it was another ostensible participant (rather than the experimenter) who indicated that the participant should continue. Social proof also affected compliance: if the participant was in the presence of two disobedient peers, compliance dropped to 10%. And when no authority was exerted and teachers were allowed to select the level of shock they would administer, the mean level of shock administered throughout was only a "slight" shock, and only one participant gave the maximum shock. Similarly, if a second experimenter gave conflicting instructions, not a single participant continued to administer shocks.

To say that a substantial proportion of participants obeyed the experimenter is not to say that they calmly and blithely followed his orders. Many of the participants attempted to resist in some way, for example, expressing their own discomfort, making sure the experimenter was aware of the learner's distress, and stating that they wouldn't participate anymore. But, in the end, many of these same participants continued to administer shocks when told that they "must continue." As psychologists Lee Ross and Richard Nisbett noted, "the Milgram experiments have less to say about 'destructive obedience' than about ineffective and indecisive *dis*obedience."[98]

How would you have reacted if you had been a participant in Milgram's experiment? Interestingly, we tend to have a blind spot here as well. Milgram described the experimental task, but not the results, to another set of participants and asked them how they thought they would conduct themselves in such circumstances. To a person, they all responded that they would defy the experimenter. And when asked how they thought others would behave in the same circumstances, they predicted that virtually all participants would resist. Yet, we know that many participants who were placed in the actual experimental circumstances did not resist. Milgram concluded that when predicting how we would respond, we "show little insight into the web of forces that operate in a real social situation."[99]

The Milgram studies suggest uses in the legal realm. For example, the studies demonstrate that attorneys can be persuasive by invoking authorities such as judges or experts. But obedience to authority also has some more complex implications. Because attorneys themselves may often be seen as authorities, attorneys need to be especially aware of their ability to influence others in these ways. In working with nonlawyer clients in particular, attorneys may need to pay careful attention to the ways in which they can act to preserve client autonomy. At the same time, it is important for attorneys themselves to attend to the effect that an authority figure—for example, a boss, a client, or a judge—may have on them.

Channel Factors and Tension Systems

When we attempt to persuade someone to comply with our wishes, our attention is often focused on how to compel the person to do what we want him to do, that is, what carrots and sticks to impose to motivate the desired action, what reasons or new information will be persuasive, and so on. But psychologist Kurt Lewin noticed that, often, motivation or information is not the sticking point. For example, someone may both understand the value of recycling or of getting vaccinated against H1N1 and want to engage in such behaviors but not actually put his soda can in the recycling barrel or get himself down to the health department to get his shot. In such cases, providing more information or incentives may not be what is needed. Lewin's insight focused on shaping behavior by using *channel factors*—relatively minor changes in the relevant situation that can have a significant influence on behavior by leading, or "channeling," people in a particular direction.[100] Thus, rather than spending copious amounts of time and money to provide information about the compelling reasons that someone should recycle her office paper, we might simply place a designated recycling basket under her desk or next to her trash can. Similarly, providing a map and getting people to specify a good time to go to the health department can increase the number of people getting vaccinated.[101]

Lewin also pioneered the notion that situations can be thought of as *tension systems* in which both driving and constraining forces work to shape behavior. This means that to change behavior, a person can either increase the driving forces that are pushing toward the behavior or decrease the constraining forces that are getting in the way of the desired behavior. Note that increasing driving forces will increase the amount of tension in the system but that decreasing the constraining forces will decrease tension.[102] Thus, figuring out what is preventing the desired behavior and removing that barrier can frequently be a more effective strategy than trying to compel a particular behavior change. Those who are trying to change behavior, however, often overlook simple barriers.

To see this point more clearly, consider a company that introduced a new online time-billing system. The company provided the online system, it provided training on how to use the system, and it mandated that people use the system. But many employees continued to submit their billings on paper. Just as the company was getting ready to announce that it would withhold the paychecks of those who didn't use the system, an adviser called for a time-out:

> "Wait," he said. "Do we know *why* people aren't doing the online time sheet?" The executives assumed that the [employees] were Luddites or simply obstinate—classic labels inspired by the Fundamental Attribution Error. [The adviser] persuaded the executives to do a bit more investigation.
>
> The employees who turned in paper time sheets were asked why they weren't using the online tool. Paper was easier, they said. Skeptical, the interviewers asked if they could observe the employees while they filled out the online time sheet. The results were telling.
>
> Lots of employees started grousing as soon as they encountered the "wizard" that was built into the online tool. Ironically, the wizard was intended to help people fill out the form. Think of the annoying paper clip guy in Microsoft Office who wants to help you write a letter. Now imagine that you have no choice but to accept his "help." When the executives killed the wizard, allowing people to skip directly to the form itself, compliance rates rose immediately, and within a few weeks everyone was using the online tool.[103]

Thus, when seeking to change behavior, it can be vitally important to ask, "Why not?" This can allow any such barriers to be addressed directly. It might be easy to lower the costs of compliance by changing a system, offering a guarantee, or finding a work-around.

Resistance

As with many of the psychological phenomena that we have covered so far, we tend to have a blind spot when it comes to assessing our own susceptibility to influence attempts. Indeed, we tend to see ourselves as invulnerable to persuasion and to believe that others are more persuadable than we are.[104] Ironically, these very beliefs can interfere with efforts to resist persuasion. "Far from being an effective shield, the illusion of invulnerability undermine[s] the very response that would have supplied genuine protection."[105] In contrast, a healthy concern over the possibility that we might be fooled facilitates the type of analysis necessary.[106] Thus, the first step toward resisting unwanted persuasion is to recognize the possibility that we might fall sway to social influence.

But when it comes to resisting influence, one complicating factor is that not all influence attempts should be resisted. Many deals are mutually beneficial, authorities sometimes do know best, reciprocation is often appropriate, and social norms are sometimes well grounded. Indeed, in this context, "unrelenting cynicism or stubbornness can be as costly as gullibility."[107] Sometimes it is wise to follow the dictate of an old saying: "Don't cut off your nose to spite your face." Good decision makers need to discriminate between instances in which it is beneficial to allow themselves to be persuaded and instances in which it is not.

Accordingly, we must ask whether a source that is held out as an expert is truly someone who possesses expertise that is relevant to the question at hand. We should glean knowledge from social proof but should be wary of instances in which such proof is contrived. It is often appropriate to reciprocate a concession but important to watch out for apparent concessions that aren't really concessions. Nonconcessions should not demand reciprocation. We should look behind deadlines to determine which ones are real. Decision makers need to evaluate options on their merits, not solely as framed by another or in an option set defined by another. Thinking about the full range of options and rephrasing offers into multiple frames can help with this task. We must be willing to adjust our position or decisions rather than being a slave to consistency. Good decision makers flip-flop if the merits require it. And it is important to question authority, consider the opposite, and be a devil's advocate.

This kind of discrimination requires systematic processing so that decisions, options, and arguments are evaluated on their merits. We know that to process systematically, we must be motivated and able to do so. Motivation comes from recognizing that we can be swayed by a range of influences. The ability to process systematically in order to be able to resist influence when appropriate is facilitated by having knowledge about how persuasion and social influence operate. Knowledge of the tactics of persuasion and social influence allows us to keep an eye out for instances in which such tactics are being used and to scrutinize the relevant information and options.[108] In addition, we can work to create the conditions under which systematic processing is possible, engaging in sufficient preparation so that we have objective information on which to rely, paying close attention, taking the time necessary to make a good decision (watch out for deadlines), and minimizing distractions (watch out for multitasking).

◆ ◆ ◆

In considering how to act in order to persuade others—such as negotiation counterparts, courts and other tribunals, government officials, and clients—it is useful to keep in mind the long view:

> As the best influence professionals have long realized, to the extent that dishonest or high pressure tactics work at all, they work only in the short run. Their long-term effects are malignant—undermining trust and damaging the reputation of the practitioner who employs them. Thus, the deceptive or coercive use of social influence principles within professional relationships in not only ethically wrong, it's pragmatically wrongheaded.
>
> Yet the same principles, if engaged appropriately, can influence decisions in a positive way. When the similarities are authentic, the windows of opportunity truly closing, the authority legitimate, the commitments freely made, the obligations genuine, and the social proof real, the resultant choices are likely to benefit everyone.[109]

Persuasion based on peripheral processing, coercion, or deceitful tactics is more likely to lead to buyer's remorse, deals falling through at the last minute, a breakdown of trust, and ongoing conflict. In contrast, persuasion that results from deliberation and that is based on legitimate influence is likely to result in more durable agreements.

◆ ◆ ◆

Summing It Up

- Distinguish between two different routes to persuasion: an effortful deliberative route and a more intuitive peripheral route. Deliberation requires both the ability and the motivation to think critically.
- To be persuasive, work to establish credibility by demonstrating expertise and trustworthiness.
- Increase persuasiveness by taking the perspective of the audience, focusing their attention on high-quality messages, offering concrete examples, and presenting two-sided messages.
- Influence others peripherally by paying attention to the effects of reciprocity, scarcity, consistency and commitment, and liking.

- Take account of social context to increase influence by attending to the ways in which people are influenced by social proof and authority.
- Ask "Why not?" and think about how to use channel factors to elicit desired behavior.
- Critically distinguish between circumstances in which it is beneficial to allow yourself to be persuaded and instances in which it is not, and use knowledge of persuasion techniques to resist undesirable persuasion.

For Further Reading: Persuasion and Influence

Timothy C. Brock & Melanie C. Green, Persuasion: Psychological Insights and Perspectives (2d ed. 2005).

Shelly L. Chaiken et al., *Persuasion in Negotiation and Conflict Situations*, in The Handbook of Conflict Resolution: Theory and Practice 144 (Morton Deutsch & Peter T. Coleman eds., 2000).

Robert B. Cialdini, Influence: Science and Practice (5th ed. 2009).

Chris Guthrie, *Courting Compliance*, in The Negotiator's Fieldbook 371 (Andrea Kupfer Schneider & Christopher Honeyman eds., 2006).

Richard E. Petty & John T. Cacioppo, Attitudes and Persuasion: Classic and Contemporary Approaches (1996).

The Science of Social Influence: Advances and Future Progress (Anthony R. Pratkanis ed., 2007).

Donna Shestowsky, *Psychology and Persuasion*, in The Negotiator's Fieldbook 361 (Andrea Kupfer Schneider & Christopher Honeyman eds., 2006).

Interpersonal Communication   7

> I know that you believe you understand what you think I said, but I'm not sure you realize that what you heard is not what I meant.
> —Robert McCloskey[1]

In late 2001, attorney Kenneth Feinberg was selected to administer the September 11th Victim Compensation Fund that was created in the wake of the September 11 terrorist attacks. As Feinberg began the task of administering the fund and working with the families who were eligible for payment from the fund, he learned an important lesson about communication:

> Not surprisingly, the communication style I'd developed over the years proved less than ideal for this new challenge. I tend to be straightforward and businesslike, especially when I'm trying to explain a complex plan to a group of lawyers. My preferred approach is to dive in head first: "Hello, ladies and gentlemen. I'm here to explain how the 9/11 fund will work. Please hold your questions; we'll allow plenty of time for those later. Let's start at the beginning. The statute authorizes the following procedures . . ."
>
> I should have realized that this kind of neutral, authoritative, purely factual presentation would strike the 9/11 families as brusque and callous. Instead, it took me a while to realize the effect I was having and adjust my approach. Looking back, I should have started every meeting in a quieter, more empathetic way—expressing sympathy, offering words of respect and condolence, and inviting the families to start the conversation. . . .[2]

Communication and interpersonal interaction are central to the work that attorneys do. Attorneys spend much of their time communicating in some form with clients, colleagues, witnesses, other attorneys, courts, insurance company representatives, and others. Attorneys who can communicate well with their clients will build better relationships with those clients, be better able to obtain relevant information from them, and be better able to provide information and advice to those clients. Such skills are crucial for effectively serving clients, sustaining client relationships, and developing business. Indeed, studies have found that clients independently value good relational skills in their attorneys.[3] But the value of good communication is not limited to client relationships. Good communication with other attorneys can result in more effective negotiation and mediation. Effective communication with witnesses means more valuable depositions. And good communication with the court can mean the difference between a clear and persuasive argument and one that is confusing and fails to have the desired effect.

The Complexities of Human Communication

Many attorneys may wish that they could (or even believe that they can) communicate with others automatically and seamlessly, as if people were computers that could be networked. In this vein, Feinberg (quoted above) expressed his desire to be "straightforward and businesslike." But, for better or worse, human communication is not always so straightforward. Whereas computers communicate exclusively using strings of unambiguous numbers, human communicators rely on a jumble of information gleaned from inference, social convention, memory, body language, and shared knowledge, as well as from the relevant verbal or written expressions. The advantage of human communication, then, is that it can be saturated with meaning and rich with nuance. At the same time, human communication is rife with the ambiguities of language and dependent on interpretation. Understanding can be complicated by the use of humor, sarcasm, euphemisms, and idioms. Communication often depends on a shared base of knowledge, and the meaning of a communicative expression can change depending on the context. Communicators often have multiple, concurrent goals for their exchanges, goals that may include a clear exchange of information but that may also include impression management, persuasion, bluffing, puffery, monitoring the reactions of their audience, building relationships, and managing the flow of the conversation.

> Communication is for being understood and for being misunderstood, to convey old word meanings and to create new meaning, to tell it as it is and to fabricate lies that conceal what is, to solve problems and to create new problems and conflicts.
> —Klaus Fiedler

Given that the wish for computer-like communication is not going to be granted in the foreseeable future, it is important for attorneys to understand the ways in which humans communicate. We begin by describing some of the nuances of human communication before turning our attention to a number of ways in which attorneys can communicate more effectively.

Perspective Taking in Communication

Think about what it means to communicate with another person. In order to communicate effectively, it is useful to know how each person understands the situation and what information about the topic of conversation each person has and doesn't have. On the one hand, giving information that the other already has or explaining things that the other already understands can be tedious and even condescending. Children express this frustration to their parents frequently, not hesitating to note, "You told me that already." Assuming a shared base of understanding, however, when such a foundation doesn't exist can result in serious miscommunication. Imagine a mother who does not understand that her son needs to be hospitalized when the pediatrician says that he needs to be "admitted for a workup" or a child who doesn't understand that "look both ways" means to look to the left and the right to see whether cars are coming.

Shared Understanding in Communication

When the [hotel in which then-Vice President of the United States Calvin Coolidge was staying] was evacuated after a fire, a marshal stopped Coolidge from heading back to his suite.

"[But] I'm the vice president," Coolidge insisted.

The marshal let him proceed at first but then reconsidered, "What are you the vice president of?"

"I am the vice president of the United States," came the indignant reply.

"Come [back] down," said the marshal, "I thought you were vice president of the hotel."[5]

Unfortunately, it can be very difficult to know what another person knows. And it can be particularly difficult to appreciate differences between what we ourselves know and what another knows. Because we often overestimate the degree to which others share our perspective and because we have difficulty ignoring what we know, we tend to overimpute our own knowledge and perspective to others. Therefore, even when we are aware that others have information that we do not, we fail to take into account their privileged knowledge. Conversely, even when we know that we possess relevant knowledge that others lack, we often fail to account for the others' lack of knowledge and expect those people to act as though they share our privileged information. This is known as the *curse of knowledge*.[6]

Because we have such a deep knowledge of what we mean to say, we may gloss over key assumptions or fail to provide complete explanations. Given our own knowledge, what we say makes sense to us, and we assume that it will be understandable to others even when it is not. We saw an example of this in chapter 1 when we considered the difficulty experienced by people asked to estimate the likelihood that another person would be able to correctly identify a song whose rhythm they tapped. Recall that "tappers" were unable to set aside their own mental representations of the songs—representations that included words and melodies in addition to rhythm—and significantly overestimated their listeners' success. Similar results have been found in negotiation situations, with negotiators proving unable to ignore their privileged information in making predictions about their counterparts.[7] Thus, in communicating with others, attorneys need to pay close attention to the details of their own knowledge and the extent to which it is shared—or not.

This self-monitoring, however, is complicated by the fact that communicators tend to misjudge how well they have conveyed their message. Writers of headlines surely believe that their captions clearly describe the underlying news story—even when the captions turn out to be fodder for comedy routines: "Drunk Gets Nine Months in Violin Case" or "Kids Make Nutritious Snacks" or "Red Tape Holds Up New Bridge." When speakers utter ambiguous sentences (for example, "Angela shot the man with the gun"), they have a particular meaning in mind (either that Angela used a gun to shoot the man or that Angela shot the man who had the gun). Consequently, they overestimate the extent to which a listener would understand the sentence in the way it was intended.[8]

Conversational Norms

Successful communication often involves the exchange of information via conversation. Such exchanges typically rely on a set of mutually understood *conversational norms*. For example, participants in a conversation tend to expect that the information provided by a speaker will contribute to the ongoing conversation. Contributions are expected to be relevant. And contributions are expected to be informative, but not more informative than is needed. (We all know people who don't seem to "get" this norm and are therefore thought to be tedious.) Many legal discussions, however, including interviews, counseling sessions, depositions, and negotiations, deviate from typical conversations and the norms of such conversations in ways that have implications for attorneys' ability to maximize their effectiveness.[9]

The above-listed conversational norms imply that a speaker does not need to contribute information that the other already has. Such information is an unnecessary contribution to the conversation. But attorneys often call upon clients or witnesses to violate this conversational norm by, for example, asking them to repeat themselves so that the attorneys can verify their understanding. Thus, attorneys will often ask questions to which they have already received an answer. However, "[u]nless the person asked has reason to believe that the questioner did not understand the answer given in response to the first question, he or she is likely to interpret the second question as a request for new information" and will provide an answer that differs in some way from the answer to the previous iteration of the question.[10] Such inconsistencies can be problematic in many legal contexts. On the other hand, attorneys may attempt to capitalize on this conversational tendency by asking the same question again in the hope of eliciting inconsistent statements. Attorneys interviewing clients and preparing witnesses for depositions need to explain clearly what is expected from them.

Typical conversational norms also counsel that a speaker should not contribute to a conversation in a way that is uninformative. Such a norm may tempt people to provide responses that are more precise than their underlying knowledge would support and to hesitate to admit to a lack of knowledge. Accordingly, as we noted in chapter 2 and will discuss in more detail in chapters 9 and 11, attorneys should be alert to such pressures, encouraging clients to indicate when they are unsure or are merely offering a conjecture.

Similarly, in the context of an interview or a deposition, a client or witness will usually be expected to report information at a higher level of detail than would be expected in a typical conversation. In normal conversation, people tend to summarize their descriptions, emphasizing and sharpening some aspects and eliminating others. Whereas a client might simply tell her friends, "I was discriminated against," her attorney will need her to provide details as to when, where, how, and why she believes she was mistreated.

On other occasions, such as in the context of a deposition, however, a client might be advised to limit her answers in ways that would seem unnatural in typical conversation.

The classic example involves a simple request:

Q: Do you happen to have the time?
A: Sure, it's almost 2:30.

That is the wrong answer, of course, because it went beyond the actual question. In a deposition, if nowhere else in human interactions, the correct answer is simply "yes." If the lawyer wants more information, he will have to ask another question. In the world of litigation, this makes perfect sense.[11]

Conversely, an attorney who is deposing an adverse witness might hope to get the witness to fall back into his normal patterns of conversation so that he will volunteer additional information or make inconsistent statements.

Nonverbal Communication

Human beings communicate volumes through body language, facial expressions, and voice. Indeed, it is virtually impossible not to communicate *something* nonverbally—even impassivity communicates. More actively, we wave, smile and frown, and use our hands to indicate distance or patterns of movement. We lean in or away from a conversation partner, make or break eye contact, tap our pens on the desk, nod or shake our heads, roll our

> He speaketh not; and yet there lies
> A conversation in his eyes.
> —Henry Wadsworth Longfellow[12]

> As the tongue speaketh to the ear so the gesture speaketh to the eye.
> —Francis Bacon[13]

eyes, cross our arms, give a thumbs-up, get tears in our eyes, and make a myriad of other movements or expressions. Such gestures, postures, and facial expressions all convey messages to others. Similarly, the ways in which words are spoken—for example, tone of voice, inflection, rate of speech, accent, or patterns of pausing—hold additional information. Other behaviors communicate as well: turning on loud music, arriving late for a meeting, and offering a cup of coffee all send a message.

Nonverbal displays can serve as an important source of information. By supplementing or illustrating a verbal expression, expressing emotion, or communicating expectations, nonverbal signals add to the messages conveyed by the words that are spoken. A facial expression, for example, may suggest uncertainty or anger even when the language used conveys confidence or agreement, and the use of air quotes may help to convey skepticism about the meaning or applicability of the words used. In addition, nonverbal signals can help to coordinate the communication interaction. For example, nonverbal displays facilitate turn taking and demonstrate that a person is paying attention. Similarly, as we will see, nonverbal displays, including mimicry, can facilitate the development of rapport. In these ways and more, nonverbal signals add richness and nuance to human communication.[14]

✦ ✦ ✦ ✦ ✦

Thin Slices and Malpractice

Psychologist Nalini Ambady and her colleages conducted a clever study to explore the association between surgeons' tone of voice and whether they had been sued for malpractice.

First, the researchers recorded conversations between patients and their surgeons during a regular consultation. Half of the surgeons had been previously sued for malpractice and half had not. The researchers created four 10-second clips of each surgeon's voice. Each clip was "content filtered" so that the surgeons' vocal quality—tone of voice, speed, pitch, and cadence—was recognizable, but the substance of the conversation was not. Observers then listened to the clips and rated them on whether the surgeons' voices displayed various qualities—for example, warmth, concern, hostility, professional, competent, and dominance.

The researchers found that these ratings were associated with whether or not the surgeons had been previously sued. In particular, the more dominant and the less concerned the surgeon's tone was rated, the more likely the surgeon was to have been sued.[15]

On the whole, we are able to discern a great deal from even thin slices of nonverbal behavior. For example, ratings of teachers given on the basis of just of few seconds of silent video of the teachers' classroom behavior are remarkably similar to evaluations by students in the teachers' classes.[16] But people vary widely in their abilities to effectively read others or to project a desired impression. Indeed, facility with nonverbal communication involves a range of different skills, including noticing the nonverbal cues displayed by others; interpreting these perceived cues accurately; and expressing attitudes, emotions, and ideas through nonverbal cues accurately and effectively. Each of these facets of nonverbal communication can present complications.

In particular, it is important to remember that nonverbal displays are not necessarily a perfect window into a communicator's state of mind. First, consider that nonverbal cues seldom have a single evident interpretation. For example, a particular facial expression or shrug of the shoulders might be interpreted as disinterest when it really reflects confusion. "[N]o 'dictionary' of nonverbal cue meanings exists in which we can simply look up a cue and find out its meaning. Thus we must constantly be on guard against simple interpretations and simple cause-and-effect explanations of observed behavior."[17] Similarly, there are cultural differences in the meanings that are attached to particular nonverbal displays. Gestures that are innocuous in some cultures may be obscene in others. For example, the U.S hand gesture for OK (with the thumb and forefinger forming a circle) has a sexual connotation in some European cultures. Likewise, the meanings of nonverbal behaviors such as eye gaze and facial expression can vary across cultures.[18]

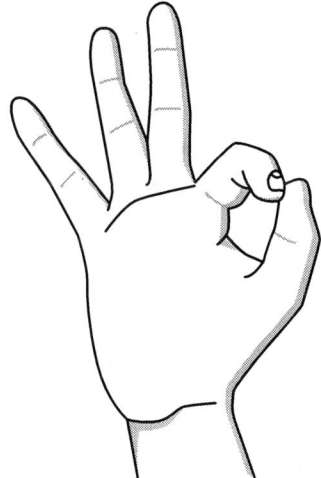

In addition, people routinely rely on theories about the association between particular nonverbal cues and particular mental states—theories that often turn out to be erroneous. For example, as we will see later in the chapter, in attempting to detect deception, people often rely on a variety of cues that they incorrectly think are associated with deception. And just as with interpretations of other sorts of information, our interpretations of nonverbal signals are colored by our moods, our prior expectations, and so on (see chapters 1 and 3).

To complicate things further, nonverbal signals can be sent either unintentionally or intentionally by an individual. Sometimes nonverbal cues are automatic and unconscious. Indeed, sometimes nonverbal expressions belie a verbal message. For example, a negotiator might claim that he is not angry, but his red face suggests otherwise. At other times, nonverbal signals may be consciously controlled. For example, a speaker might intentionally adopt a particular expression or posture in order to accurately express his state of mind. On the other hand, a speaker might adopt a particular expression or posture in order to give a contrary impression, perhaps by exaggerating, minimizing, or masking a particular feeling. For example, a negotiator may attempt to effect a poker face to avoid giving away private information.

People may be more or less successful in such attempts to consciously control their nonverbal expressions. Some nonverbal behaviors (for example, crossing or uncrossing arms) are easier to control than others (for example, a spontaneous smile or a particular negative emotion). And people's ability to control their nonverbal expression may also depend on the intensity of the underlying experience: disguising intense anger is more difficult than covering up minor annoyance.

In addition, the conscious control of nonverbal behavior is complicated by the fact that nonverbal signals are more accessible to the receiver than to the one displaying the behaviors. "In interpersonal interactions . . . people never know as much about their own nonverbal behaviors as do the people with whom they are interacting."[19] We do not see our own facial expressions or hear the tone of our own voices in exactly the same ways as others do. Nonetheless, the illusion of transparency (see chapter 3) means that we tend to believe that we can accurately read others' mental states and that our mental states are transparent to others. All of this makes it difficult to get an accurate read on how well we are communicating nonverbally. Indeed, "[p]eople high in sensitivity to nonverbal cues are not necessarily those who appraise their own skills highly."[20] Thus, it is a good idea for all attorneys to pay close attention to how they express and interpret nonverbal communication.

Communication Mediums

We communicate through many different mediums: face-to-face, over the telephone, and in writing. In our high-tech society, electronic forms of communication have also become ubiquitous. E-mail, instant messaging, and text messaging are now used for an array of communication purposes ranging from a quick confirmation of the time of a meeting to extended and complex negotiations. Video calls and videoconferencing are common as well. The unique characteristics of these different forms of communication can have important implications for how a communication encounter unfolds. Thinking about these characteristics can help in deciding which medium to use for a particular communication and how best to use a particular medium.[21]

❖ ❖ ❖ ❖ ❖
Lawyers and Communication Technology[22]

"I'll only unplug when I'm sleeping or on vacation."	26%
"I mainly use my digital devices during business hours."	27%
"I'm always wired; even the restroom isn't off-limits."	47%

First, modes of communication differ in the extent to which they create a record of the exchange. Letters, e-mails, and even instant and text messages generate a running log of the communication. Such a "paper" trail, or archive, makes it possible to return to the text (though not other aspects) of the conversation. In contrast, unless they are recorded, face-to-face and phone conversations are less permanent.

Second, in contrast to communication in real time, some forms of communication, such as e-mails or letters, are asynchronous, lacking the immediate give-and-take of face-to-face conversation. Indeed, such exchanges can play out over hours, days, or longer. This inherent asynchrony can have its benefits. Asynchrony affords communicators the opportunity to think through their responses and to choose their words carefully, and it minimizes the likelihood that they will be dominated by quick-talking counterparts.[23] For these reasons, e-mails and letters tend to facilitate the offering of more complex arguments or offers.[24]

There are also, however, downsides to this asynchrony. Longer messages present the risk that attention will be focused on only part of the communication. In face-to-face conversations, there are constant opportunities to instantly self-correct errors, to ask for clarification, or to recognize and preempt potential disagreement. When communicating via e-mail or letter, in contrast, there are time lags between messages and fewer opportunities to quickly catch and clarify misunderstandings. Unfortunately, we do not always fully take into account this asynchrony—evidencing a *temporal synchrony bias*.[25] Thus, people may expect immediate responses to e-mail messages even when such responses are impractical. They may make assumptions about meaning rather than clarifying. In addition, they may exchange less information. For example, one study found that people negotiating via e-mail were less likely to ask each other about their interests and capabilities and less likely to ask for clarification than those negotiating face-to-face.[26] Similarly, people negotiating via e-mail have been found to exchange less information about preferences and capabilities than those negotiating via instant messaging, a communication medium that facilitates more frequent "speaking" turns.[27]

Third, different forms of communication vary in the degree to which nonverbal and contextual information is available. For example, face-to-face conversation is a *rich* form of communication, one in which participants can draw on a range of verbal and nonverbal cues in helping them to navigate the communication encounter. In contrast, e-mail, text messaging, and instant messaging are *lean* forms of communication, relying on text and occasional emoticons to communicate. The myriad aspects of nonverbal communication on which people rely to understand each other—head nods, vocal inflection, body positioning, eye contact, and so on—are not available. Other forms of communication, such as phone communication, video calling, and videoconferencing, fall somewhere in between. Phone communication allows the possibility of vocal cues. And video-mediated communication further allows for the transmission of some additional nonverbal cues.

The absence of nonverbal cues can minimize the possibility of inadvertently and nonverbally communicating a message that was not intended. However, the same lack of nonverbal cues can make it difficult to establish rapport.[28] In addition, a lack of nonverbal cues and the inhibition of efforts to seek clarification mean that the same statement can be more ambiguous in electronic than in face-to-face communication. Such ambiguity affords more room for preconceived expectations and stereotypes to influence how statements are interpreted.[29]

Moreover, when the medium through which people are communicating provides little opportunity for signaling emotion through vocal inflection or body language, it can be particularly difficult to communicate about emotions. Consider e-mail. Studies of people attempting to communicate sarcasm, sadness, anger, and humor via e-mail have found that e-mail senders are overconfident about the receivers' ability to accurately determine the emotional content of the message. When they consider their own words, e-mailers hear them with the inflection that they would use if they were speaking them. Recipients do not have access to that additional information, but e-mailers fail to account for the lack of such cues to emotion that are inherent in the e-mail context. Even when they were allowed to use emoticons, people continued to be overconfident about the degree to which they were able to communicate emotion.[30]

Finally, communicators using different modes of communication experience different degrees of connectedness. In particular, those communicating via electronically mediated means tend to experience a greater sense of social distance, more anonymity, and less accountability than they do when interacting face-to-face or by phone. Some people may prefer to communicate via mechanisms that provide a greater sense of social distance, particularly those who are less extroverted.[31] Interestingly, the relative anonymity of electronic communication can result, for better or worse, in greater disclosure.[32]

The greater social distance associated with electronically mediated forms of communication can also result in a tendency to feel less constrained by social norms. Indeed, legal ethics experts have noted that "lawyers' tendency to be risk-averse seems to fade away on the Internet. 'They're disclosing confidences, talking about pending matters, they take potshots . . . like everyone else.'"[33] Consistent with this observation, researchers have found that e-mail communicators engage in more negative communication behavior (such as flaming) than do those who communicate by less impersonal means.[34] E-mail negotiators tend to develop relationships more slowly and expect to trust their opponents less. Consistent with these expectations, they do tend to perceive their opponents as less credible and trust them less. This lack of trust can lead to less cooperation and more deception.[35] Hard bargaining tactics such as threats, ultimatum offers, and appeals to the other's obligations can be more damaging in electronic communication as the lack of nonverbal and contextual cues, lack of opportunity to clarify, and greater social distance contribute to an escalation of conflict.[36]

>
> ## Lawyers and the Internet
> Consider just a few examples of ill-advised electronic communications by attorneys:
> - An attorney defending a wrongful death case "e-mailed a photograph of the overweight deceased, lying naked on an emergency room table, to a friend, along with his own lewd and disparaging commentary."
> - An e-mail from a lawyer to a candidate for a legal secretary position: "[I]n addition to the legal work, you would be required to have sexual interaction with me and my partner, sometimes together sometimes separate. This part of the job would require sexy dressing and flirtatious interaction with me and my partner, as well as sexual interaction. You will have to be comfortable doing this with us."
> - A prosecutor "took pictures of a crime scene and posted them on her Facebook page, along with comments from law enforcement talking about the crime and crime scene."
> - A criminal defense attorney complained on a courthouse blog that a judge "was an 'evil, unfair witch' with an 'ugly, condescending attitude.' He also suggested she was 'seemingly mentally ill.' His beef? The judge allegedly wasn't giving defense lawyers enough time to prepare for trials."[37]

Attorneys should be aware of these dynamics when they engage in different forms of communication. In particular, when communicating electronically, attorneys should be vigilant for miscommunication, attempt to generate a back-and-forth flow of information to the extent possible, make a point of asking for information and clarification, and strive for good manners. In order to build rapport, it can be quite useful to engage in some non-task-focused communication prior to conducting business or negotiation via e-mail. In one study, half of a group of e-mail negotiators were asked to engage in a brief telephone call to get to know each other prior to beginning their electronic negotiation. Negotiators who "schmoozed" in this way developed better rapport. Consequently, they were able to consider a broader range of possible outcomes, were more likely to reach an agreement, and were more interested in working together in the future.[38]

Culture and Communication

As we have already seen, cultural differences can be reflected in different styles of communication. For example, cultures differ in terms of the meaning that is attributed to silence in an interaction, the degree of formality that is expected, the appropriateness of interruptions, understandings of the meaning of eye contact, the contours of personal space, conceptions of time, the importance of perspective taking, and the appropriateness of self-disclosure.[39]

One distinction that is commonly drawn is that between *low-context communication* and *high-context communication*. Low-context communication is associated with independent cultures and consists of communication in which the meaning is explicit in the words themselves and that can be understood without reference to the context in which the communication occurs. High-context communication, in contrast, is associated with interdependent cultures and tends to be indirect and highly dependent on context for its meaning. For example, low-context communicators will be more likely to say "no" when they mean "no," while a high-context communicator's refusal may be more implicit. Furthermore, in interpreting a contract, a low-context communicator might be more likely to rely on the text of the contract, while a high-context communicator might be more inclined to rely on what is known about the relationships between the parties to the contract and the circumstances under which the contract was signed. And, as we saw in chapter 6, low-context communicators are also more likely to appeal to logic, facts, and reasons to persuade; while high-context negotiators are more likely to appeal to emotion, social roles and obligations, and relationships as a basis of persuasion.[40]

Consider how a negotiation interaction might differ for a low-context and a high-context negotiator trying to assess the other side's interests. A low-context negotiator would be more likely to follow the "script of asking the other party questions about his preferences and priorities, . . . reciprocating with information about [her] own preferences and priorities, and thereby slowly building a complete understanding of the tradeoffs in the negotiation and [then] formulating multi-issue proposals to capture those tradeoffs." On the other hand, a high-context negotiator would prefer to gather and disclose information more indirectly, making many, often multifaceted, proposals and drawing "inferences about the other parties' priorities from the patterning of proposals and counterproposals."[41]

While there are broad cultural differences in communication style, different situations within a culture might also nudge an individual toward a particular communication style. For example, a person might tend toward more high-context communication when interacting with others with whom she shares a history, such as a family member or a close friend, as compared to a stranger.

Communication between those employing different styles of communication can be complicated. For example, "[h]igh-context people are apt to become impatient and irritated when low-context people insist on giving them information they don't need. Conversely, low-context people are at a loss when high-context people do not provide *enough* information."[42] Attorneys who are sensitive to such possibilities are likely to get more out of a communication encounter and to be able to navigate such encounters more effectively.

Lying

Another difference between computerized and human communication is that computers don't lie. When a computer provides information to another computer, the information may be flawed, but the computer itself is simply conveying information. Humans, in contrast, may sometimes make deliberate misstatements. This means that effective communicators must be alert to and work to address the possibility of dissembling.

> Ask no questions, and you'll be told no lies.
> —Charles Dickens[43]

While there is a lot of folklore regarding how to distinguish liars from truth tellers, it turns out that identifying liars is extremely difficult, even for experts. Many of the cues that we think are associated with deception are not. Many of the cues that are actually associated with deception are subtle and not easily detectable. In addition, many cues to deception can also be associated with other states, such as stress, that are likely common to legal clients, witnesses, or negotiators. Indeed, across a variety of studies, psychological research has found that people are not very adept at distinguishing those who are lying from those who are telling the truth—performing at levels that are little or no better than chance.[44] Moreover, there is little correlation between our degree of certainty that we have identified a liar and our accuracy.[45] Apparent experts do not tend to perform any better than laypeople, though, ironically, they do tend to be more confident in their judgments.[46] Thus, although many attorneys may believe that they are quite good at figuring out whether clients or opposing counsel are lying based on whether they blink, look away, or tap their fingers, they are probably wrong as often as they are right.

A primary reason why people are unable to reliably distinguish lies and truths is that we pay attention to the wrong things. Psychological research has identified a number of cues that people believe are related to deception. In particular, people strongly believe that liars avert their gaze, smile, engage in lots of movement (such as shifting positions, making hand and foot movements, and making gestures of illustration), and have more disturbed speech (including hesitation, pauses, and slower speech). Many of these anticipated cues are thought to be associated with nervousness and, hence, lying.

However, many of these purported indicators do not in fact prove reliable in distinguishing liars and truth tellers.[47] For instance, the cue most commonly believed to indicate deception—averted gaze—has not been shown to distinguish liars from truth tellers. Similarly, while people anticipate that liars will display more movement, studies have shown either no differences or that liars tend to make fewer movements. A decrease in movement may result from attempts to compensate for the expectation that they will show an increase in motion or from a cognitive effort to carry out the lie. In the same way, higher rates of blinking and speech disturbances do not appear to distinguish liars from truth tellers. People also tend to incorrectly associate trustworthiness with attractiveness.[48] The stereotype of the shifty-eyed, fidgety liar who looks like a weasel apparently does not serve us well. Accordingly, it is important that attorneys not rely on stereotypes about lying that do not accurately discriminate between liars and truth tellers.

All of this is made even more complicated by the fact that much of the time we are not dealing with others who are blatantly lying but instead with persons who hold varying versions of reality. As we saw in chapters 1 and 2, different factual accounts can result from, among other things, differences in what was attended to, differences in how events were construed or interpreted, and differences in what was remembered. In addition, self-presentational concerns can lead us to emphasize certain aspects of the story or gloss over others.

> Telling the whole truth and nothing but the truth is rarely possible or desirable. All self-presentations are edited. The question is one of whether the editing crosses the line from the honest highlighting of aspects of identity that are most relevant in the ongoing situation to a dishonest attempt to mislead.[49]

In addition, because people tend to judge active conduct or commission more harshly than inaction or omission (see chapter 5), *lies of omission* are not seen to be as serious as affirmatively false statements.[50] Thus, it is likely that attorneys will more frequently encounter such misleading omissions than outright lies. For example, a client may fail to inform the attorney of particular details, or opposing counsel may gloss over certain specifics during a negotiation. Such omissions may simply be a function of a different understanding, a failure to remember, or a need to be viewed positively.

Some such omissions may be deliberate. Notwithstanding attorneys' incantation of the attorney-client privilege and exhortations to their clients to be forthright, some clients may believe that their attorneys will represent them more effectively if they are not aware of certain skeletons in the clients' closets. Clients may also fear that if they disclose damaging information to the attorney, the attorney will feel compelled to disclose it to the opposing side or to a finder of fact. If outright lies are difficult to discern, surely it is even more difficult to discern nuances of omission, shading, positive spin, or subtle editing.

While it is true that detecting lies is difficult, psychological research has more to teach regarding the detection of liars than simply admonishing us to be careful about our intuitions. There are some dimensions on which liars do tend to differ from those who are telling the truth. Liars tend to offer fewer details, give accounts that are less plausible and coherent, and speak with more vocal tension and higher pitch—though the size of these effects can be quite small.[51] Unfortunately, these cues can also be present for other reasons; for example, a high pitch could be a sign of lying or a sign that the person is upset or nervous for some other reason (such as the stress of being questioned or being asked to talk about personal information). Similarly, lack of detail or coherency can reflect poor memory rather than lying. Thus, cues such as these should be seen as signals that are worth pursuing further in order to get more information or verification rather than as fail-safe indicators of lying.

Indeed, looking for inconsistencies between the interviewee's story and information obtained from other sources of information can be an effective way to identify areas for further probing. In attempting to distinguish truth from lies, people often rely on information from third parties, their own prior knowledge, any physical evidence, and so on.[52] To the extent that an interviewer has access to other sources of information—for example, additional witnesses, documents, or physical evidence—such information can be used to craft more probing questions. Waiting to raise contrary information until late in an interview (or until a subsequent interview) provides an opportunity for such inconsistencies to surface and can lead to improved accuracy in detecting deception.[53]

When dealing with multiple witnesses, inconsistencies in their reports may or may not indicate lying. It is clear from the research we have reviewed so far on perception, construal, and memory that two people's understanding and memory of a single event can vary widely. Similarly, complete consistency may not be a reliable indicator of deception either. Witnesses who tell harmonious stories may be providing accurate reports about an event, or they may have colluded to "get their stories straight." Psychological researchers have found it helpful to ask such witnesses questions that they might not have anticipated and, therefore, would have been less likely to have included in their discussion. Questions about unanticipated details tend to elicit more divergent answers from pairs of liars than they do from pairs of truth tellers.[54] Similarly, asking an individual witness the same unanticipated question multiple times (perhaps in different ways) over the course of an interview or series of interviews can uncover contradictions because such details are less likely to be part of a rehearsed lie and have to be made up on the spot.[55]

In addition, paying particular attention to changes in the behavior of the particular speaker may be revealing. While one individual's speech and behavior may simply differ from those of another person (for example, higher pitch) even when they are telling the truth, making distinctions among people difficult to draw, changes in an individual's behavior may be more predictive and worth following up with additional questions or verification. Thus, just as within-person confidence is more useful in assessing memory than are cross-person comparisons (see chapter 2), within-person behavior is more useful in identifying lying.[56]

Another strategy that has proven useful in separating liars from truth tellers is asking the person to recount the relevant information in reverse chronological order. Telling a story in reverse order is cognitively challenging, especially for those who are already laboring under the cognitive demands attendant to lying (formulating and remembering the lie, suppressing the truth, monitoring

> For all the talk of reading hands and watching tells, it turns out that the single most important determinant is familiarity with your opponent's playing style. . . . The baseline . . . needs to be observed over time so that meaning can be attached to repeated anomalies.
> —Steven Lubet[57]

and attempting to control demeanor, and monitoring the listener's reactions). Indeed, there is evidence that liars telling their stories in reverse chronological order show more signs of cognitive load, providing fewer auditory details, speaking slower and with more hesitation, and demonstrating increased movement in the legs and feet. And, importantly, observers are somewhat better able to detect lies when people tell their story in reverse chronological order.[58]

Finally, recent research has found that when people are asked direct questions, they are less likely to lie by omission. Instead, in responding to direct questions, people are more likely to answer with either the truth or with an express misstatement. In contrast, in the absence of a direct question, people tend to either tell the truth or to lie by omission. For example, the seller of a used car may fail to mention some sporadic issues with the car's brakes. When confronted with a direct question, however, a strategy of omission is more difficult to carry out. Some people who might have preferred to omit the relevant information will choose to tell the truth rather than tell a lie. Thus, while asking direct questions may increase the risk of a direct lie, such questions may also be more likely to produce clear statements that can then be subjected to verification or become the focus of warranties.[59]

Ultimately, successful lie detection may depend on keeping an open mind as to whether someone is lying. Many people begin their assessment with a predisposition that influences their judgment. For example, laypeople tend to hold a bias in favor of judging statements to be truthful (*truth bias*), while law enforcement officers tend to hold a bias in favor of detecting deception. This is a form of the confirmation bias that we discussed in chapter 1. In contrast, avoiding commitment to a conclusion about whether a person is lying until all of the available information has been processed allows a person to pay closer and more sophisticated attention to nonverbal cues, to focus closely on nuances of language, and to use corroborating or disconfirming information.[60]

❖ ❖ ❖ ❖ ❖

Polygraph Testing and Neuroimaging

"For as long as human beings have deceived one another, people have tried to develop techniques for detecting deception and finding truth."[61] In recent years, polygraph testing and lie detection through neuroimaging have received the most attention. But the search for an accurate lie-detection device has been more challenging than many would hope.

Polygraph tests—a staple of movie and television crime investigation—involve measuring a variety of physiological processes such as heart rate, blood pressure, respiration, and galvanic skin conductivity. The idea is that these physiological responses are linked with the nervousness that is likely to be associated with deception. Unfortunately, many of these responses can also be linked to other states that are likely common to those who might be the subject of a polygraph test, for example, anxiety about simply taking the test or the stress experienced by truthful examinees who have been accused of wrongdoing. In addition, practiced liars may be able to undertake countermeasures to dampen the physiological responses measured. The National Academy of Science has lamented the state of the science on which polygraph techniques are based,[62] and the U.S. Supreme Court has noted that "[t]here is simply no consensus that polygraph evidence is reliable."[63]

Scientific advances in neuroscience and neuroimaging techniques such as functional magnetic resonance imaging (fMRI) have more recently captured the popular and legal imagination.[64] Developing scientific techniques promises the ability to measure relevant activity in the brain. However, it is a significant leap from the current state of neuroscience to the ability to use such techniques as lie detectors in legal settings.[65]

Development of Effective Communication

As we have seen, human communication is very rich. This richness provides great potential but also can conspire to make communication difficult. An awareness of these complexities suggests a number of ways in which attorneys can strive to communicate clearly and effectively. Clear communication is facilitated by trying to take the perspective of the conversation partner or audience, paying attention to conversational norms, paying attention to nonverbal signals, being sensitive to the features of the mode of communication, paying attention to cultural differences in communication, and carefully taking into account the potential for dissembling.

Many attorney communication tasks revolve around eliciting information from others. Attorneys routinely need to obtain information from clients in order to effectively represent them, from witnesses to facilitate the preparation of a case, from negotiation counterparts in order to put together an acceptable deal or settlement, and from regulators in order to obtain permission for clients to proceed with their projects. In addition, much of what attorneys do involves conveying information to others. Attorneys provide information about the law and advice to clients; convey information to the court in the form of briefs, motions, and oral argument; convey information to negotiation counterparts in order to facilitate mutually beneficial exchanges; and help clients formulate disclosures to a variety of audiences. A number of skills are central to each of these broad tasks, including building trust, establishing rapport, and listening. We discuss each of these in turn before we focus more specifically on facilitating disclosure and conveying information.

Building Trust

To trust is to "accept vulnerability based upon positive expectations of the intentions or behavior of another."[66] Trust is central to legal relationships and can be an important factor in establishing good communication. In particular, people tend to be more willing to share information (particularly sensitive or personal information) with those whom they trust.[67] Similarly, those who are trusted may be perceived as more credible (see chapter 6). And a client who trusts his attorney may be more likely to go to the attorney for advice and to refer others to the attorney for help. At the same time, betrayals of trust tend to evoke particularly strong negative reactions.[68]

> Research shows that people trust those who treat them like adults and give them accurate information and don't make promises they can't keep.
> —Baruch Fischhoff[69]

Clients experience trust in their attorneys when they rely on the attorneys to act in ways that are consistent with the clients' well-being, that is, acting with fidelity to their interests and acting competently in doing so. In contrast, clients who do not believe that their attorneys will act competently and on their behalf experience distrust. Accordingly, clients who trust their attorneys may be more willing to consider and follow the attorneys' advice.[70]

Trust can be quite valuable in negotiation settings as well. Negotiators who trust each other may be more willing to exchange information, to rely on the information provided, to cooperate and search for mutually beneficial solutions, and to negotiate in the future. In contrast, distrustful negotiators may withhold information and be unwilling to rely on statements made by their opponents.[71]

Trust can be facilitated in a variety of ways. As an initial matter, existing reputations, expertise, and institutional structures—such as the requirements and norms of professional responsibility—can lay a foundation for a relationship of trust. But trust can also be built over time as a person acts consistently and predictably, competently, and with integrity and honesty.[72]

Beyond this, trust is influenced by patterns of communication and interpersonal interaction. In particular, attorneys with good relational skills are perceived as more trustworthy. Specifically, people can build trust through the ways in which they listen and communicate openness and concern for the other's needs. Such openness and interest can be shown through behaviors such as shaking hands, open-palmed gestures, sharing personal information, and listening carefully. In addition, communicating in such a way as to provide information that is accurate and to provide explanations for actions also contributes to a sense of trust. For example, adviser explanation of and elaboration on the information provided has been shown to be associated with trust.[73] Consider a businessperson who has consulted an attorney about starting a new small business. The attorney could simply tell her that she needs to incorporate her business. A greater degree of trust could be fostered, however, by briefly explaining the nature of incorporation and the benefits that it can provide. In similar ways, shared control and participation in decision making tends to foster a sense of trust. In particular, psychological research has found that criminal defendants whose actual participation in their cases was congruent with their level of desired participation were more trusting of their attorneys.[74]

Establishing Rapport

Good communication is also facilitated by a sense of rapport between the communicators. When the participants in a conversation attend to each other, show a sense of mutual consideration for each other, and feel a sense of responsiveness to each other such that they are "in sync," they are experiencing rapport.[75] Psychological research has found that rapport can result in increased trust and more cooperative interactions. More generally, people tend to remember and disclose greater amounts of information and feel less need to present themselves in a positive light when they feel comfortable and at ease. Finally, people may be more willing to consider and comply with professional advice when they have a trusting and comfortable relationship with their adviser.[76]

When rapport is disrupted, communication can sometimes be taxing. For example, when communicators have difficulty coordinating on a joint task or some aspect of the communication violates social norms or expectations, the encounter can be high maintenance. In such cases, performance on subsequent tasks tends to be weaker and self-regulation impaired.[77]

Studies have found that feelings of rapport are facilitated when people spend some time getting to know each other. Engaging in small talk, schmoozing, or discussing personal or shared interests can provide the opportunity to develop a connection.[78] Recent research has even found evidence that physical feelings of warmth can influence perceptions of interpersonal warmth. Researchers have found that people holding something warm, like a cup of coffee, perceive others as having warmer personalities.[79] In addition, a variety of behaviors related to posture and orientation—such as directly facing the other person, leaning forward, and not crossing one's arms—are associated with assessments of rapport in interpersonal interactions. Nonverbal behaviors that signal attentiveness and coordination, such as smiling and nodding, are also related to the development of rapport.[80]

Recent research has focused, in particular, on *mimicry* and the role it plays in communication and the establishment of trust and rapport. If you have ever found yourself adopting the accent of someone with whom you were speaking or feeling compelled to yawn when someone else does, you know what this sort of mimicry is like. Indeed, human beings tend to unconsciously mimic those with whom they interact—the *chameleon effect*—copying facial expressions; imitating speech patterns; and mirroring behaviors such as posture, gestures, and other movements.[81]

This mimicry serves a social purpose, resulting in a range of interpersonal effects. For example, mimicry results in greater rapport, liking, trust, and feelings of similarity. Mimicry also results in interactions that unfold more smoothly and in more cooperative behavior. Those who mimic others are better at identifying others' emotional states. And those who mimic can be more persuasive. In one study, waitresses who mimicked their customers by repeating their orders back to them received larger tips than did waitresses who did not mimic.[82] In another study conducted at a Fortune 500 corporation, researchers found that some midlevel managers performed better in a business interview setting when their behavior was mimicked than when it was not.[83]

Mimicry is usually unconscious and is more common in those who feel rapport with, take the perspective of, or desire to affiliate with another person.[84] But mimicry can also be done consciously. In one study of the effects of mimicry on negotiation, the researchers asked some of the participants to consciously mimic their negotiation counterpart. These participants were instructed as follows:

> Successful negotiators recommend that you should mimic the mannerisms of your negotiation partner to get a better deal. For example, when the other person rubs his/her face, you should too. If he/she leans back or leans forward in the chair, you should too. However, they say *it is very important that you mimic subtly enough that the other person does not notice what you are doing*, otherwise this technique completely backfires. Also, do not direct too much of your attention to the mimicking so you don't lose focus on the outcome of the negotiation. Thus, you should find a happy medium of consistent but subtle mimicking that does not disrupt your focus.[85]

The researchers then compared the negotiation results of mimickers and nonmimickers in two different negotiations.

The first negotiation involved a mix of distributive, integrative, and compatible issues. When one of the parties mimicked the other, the negotiators created more joint gain (with more mimicking associated with more joint gain). Mimickers captured more of this joint gain; that is, mimickers had better individual outcomes than nonmimickers. A second study involved a negotiation in which agreement on price alone was impossible. In fact, agreement was only possible if sellers disclosed particularly sensitive information to the buyer. Negotiations in which the buyer mimicked the seller were more likely to result in agreement (67%) than were those in which the buyer was not instructed to mimic the seller (12.5%). Buyers who mimicked their sellers were trusted more, and this trust facilitated the sharing of the crucial information. Importantly, mimickers were able to achieve these effects in response to a relatively simple instruction about mimicking, and none of those participants who were mimicked guessed that they were being mirrored. The researchers also examined the effects of mimicry on a negotiation involving a purely distributive issue, finding no effects of mimicry on outcomes.[86] Read together, these studies suggest that subtly mimicking a negotiation counterpart can benefit negotiators when negotiations turn out to involve integrative issues, while not hurting them in purely distributive settings. With this research in mind, negotiators also should be cognizant that a negotiation counterpart may be consciously or unconsciously attempting to mimic their behavior in order to gain a negotiation advantage.

Listening

To foster good communication, it is vitally important for attorneys to listen carefully and also to demonstrate that they are paying attention. At a basic level, if the attorney does not attend to the information that someone is providing, she is likely to miss important data. For example, a lawyer who is not listening carefully is likely to miss information about a client's goals or preferences, a negotiation counterpart's interests or constraints, or a witness's insights or contradictions. Similarly, an advocate who does not listen to a judge's questions is more likely to give an answer that is nonresponsive or to miss what was intended as a friendly question.

> If you are not listening, you are not learning.
> —Lyndon Baines Johnson[87]

In addition, people like to feel that someone is listening when they speak. In one study in which criminal clients were asked to rate a range of lawyer characteristics, respondents rated "listening skills" as the most essential lawyer characteristic.[88] Another survey found that business and legal professionals believe that listening is the most important communication skill.[89] Indeed, an attorney's ability to listen can make the lawyer-client relationship more productive. Consider how one professional described his attorney's ability to listen:

> [She] asked all the right questions and proved to be an excellent listener.... [S]he was hearing what I was saying as well as listening. In doing that, she was able to direct my thinking along lines I hadn't considered. She showed me a different way to think about the case.[90]

> It is the province of knowledge to speak and it is the privilege of wisdom to listen.
> —Oliver Wendell Holmes[91]

People are more likely to trust another when they perceive that the other is listening to them. Accordingly, studies have shown that people have a tendency to convey more detail in their answers when the listener is attentive and not distracted and to be more receptive to advice offered by good listeners.[92]

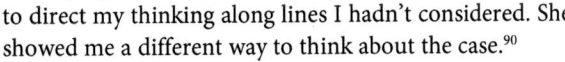

✦ ✦ ✦ ✦ ✦
Advisor as Listener

"Jack Welch, [former] CEO of General Electric, has high praise for Steven Volk, a corporate lawyer to whom Welch turned when GE's subsidiary NBC acquired Financial News Network in 1991. 'He is really a great advisor,' says Welch. 'He listens better than anybody else.'"[93]

While the importance of listening may seem self-evident, we tend to pay more attention to what *we* say in conversations than to what the other person has said. Indeed, people tend to remember more of their own statements and to remember those statements more accurately than the statements made by another. Recall the study we described in chapter 1 in which participants were better able to recall another person's statements when they had responded to them and to remember how they had responded to the other person's arguments than they were able to remember how the other person had responded to them or what had led the other person to make a particular argument.[94] Good listening does not come naturally.

To listen well, it is important to minimize distractions. Riffling through papers, engaging in side conversations with colleagues, checking e-mail or text messages, and similar behaviors distract from the task of listening. As in other contexts, our attention is limited and such multitasking (see chapter 1) draws resources away from the task at hand, which in this case is listening. In addition, attorneys need to be conscious of the extent to which such behaviors may inadvertently signal a lack of attention.

✦ ✦ ✦ ✦ ✦

Listening for Emotion

As we saw in chapter 3, emotions can provide information and signal values. Thus, in listening to clients, witnesses, negotiation counterparts, and others, attorneys should listen for and respond to both the substantive content of the message and the emotions underlying it:

> [I]f the message carries any emotional flavor at all (and most do), then *not* to use emotive colorings or tones in our acknowledgement sends the message that we are not listening.
>
> A client who says "We do 300,000 transactions a day here" has a feeling about that number. It is not enough to know whether 300,000 is above or below the competition, or higher or lower than last month. The client may be proud of that number, or proud of simply knowing it. Or he may be bored by the number, or embarrassed by it, or any number of things.
>
> The advisor who listens passively (using only "mm-hmm") is sending a message that only the rational content matters, that the feelings of the one conveying the information are irrelevant. The effective advisor knows that the emotional data is every bit as valid and important as the rational data.[95]

Studies of professionals, including lawyers, police interviewers, and physicians, have found that they are prone to interrupt early and often. One study showed that lawyers interrupt their clients more often than people interrupt one another in the course of normal conversation.[96] Another study, of legal services lawyers, showed that they interrupted clients ten times during the course of an interview, approximately once every three minutes.[97] Research shows that interjecting a large number of specific questions can make it difficult for the questioner to listen to the answers provided by the respondent because the questioner is concentrating on framing the next question rather than focusing on the answer to the instant question. In addition, as we discussed in chapter 2, psychological research has documented the benefits to memory that come from listening to, and not interrupting, people's answers to questions. Being peppered with questions makes it hard for the speaker to focus her attention on retrieving information from memory and expressing herself clearly.

> When you take the time to actually listen, with humility, to what people have to say, it's amazing what you can learn.
> —Greg Mortenson[98]

Thus, in order to both listen effectively and appear to be listening effectively, lawyers should typically let their counterpart talk without interruptions. Similarly, it is useful for lawyers to focus on listening to the answers provided rather than to assume that they know what the other will say or be preoccupied with what to say or ask next. A good listener uses follow-up questions to probe for additional details: "Can you tell me a bit more about that?" A good listener also uses follow-up questions to clarify that she has understood what the speaker has said: "So, you've said that . . . Have I got that right?" Such questions indicate to the speaker that the listener has heard him, verify the listener's understanding, and invite any necessary clarification or elaboration. Such active listening motivates speakers to continue.[99] And, as we will see in the next chapter, being listened to in this way can also make the speaker feel that he has been treated in a procedurally just manner.

✦ ✦ ✦ ✦ ✦

Investing in Listening

Listening well takes time. But good listening doesn't just improve communication with the current conversation partner; it also continues to pay off.

> Listening well takes work. It requires a willingness to invest time and energy without any guarantee of results. But you get a lot back. "Inevitably," says [Santa Fe lawyer Merit] Bennett, "[even] if you don't take the case, the person will tell other people about you, and you'll get another case. They will tell ten or twenty people that I'm the greatest lawyer around and that I helped them, when all I did was have a conversation and listen."[100]

Avoiding Talking Like a Lawyer

Q: What do you get when you cross the Godfather with a lawyer?
A: An offer you can't understand.

> Legalese—you mean jargon? Legal jargon? Terrible! Terrible! I would try to avoid it as much as possible. No point. Adds nothing.
> —Justice Stephen G. Breyer[103]

Lawyers, in their use of language, "often adopt a style that does not communicate all that well, at least to the general public."[101] Legal communication—including statutes, contracts, briefs, Miranda warnings, and jury instructions—can be difficult for laypeople, and even those who are legally trained, to understand.[102] And when lawyers "talk like lawyers" when communicating with clients and witnesses, confusion can result.

Legal language at its worst is characterized by long and complex sentences. Lawyers' speech and writing is often distinguished by too many clauses; the use of jargon, Latin words and phrases, and arcane expressions (such as *aforesaid*, *to wit*, and *hereby*); ritual phrases (such as *comes now plaintiff* or *further affiant sayeth not*); and the absence of pronouns. Legal communicators also have a tendency to use many words when one (or a few) will do or to use big words when simple ones will do. For example, lawyers might use the words *in the event of* rather than *if*, *subsequent to* rather than *after*, *commence* or *initiate* rather than *begin*, *desist* rather than *stop*, or *the instant case* rather than *this case*. Law also contains an abundance of redundant phrases: *cease and desist*; *will and testament*; *true and correct*; *give, devise and bequeath*; *any and all*; *aver and attest*; *null and void*; and many others.[104]

All of this can be counterproductive. Perhaps not surprisingly, simpler expression is cognitively easier to process and easier to understand. But what might be more surprising is that the *fluency* of communication—or the ease with which communication is processed—translates into better memory for the underlying message and more confidence in the truth of that message. And, as we saw in chapter 6, fluency in processing also leads to more persuasion.[106]

> It is more fun to talk with someone who doesn't use long, difficult words but rather short, easy words like "What about lunch?"
> —Winnie-the-Pooh[105]

While some people think that using complex constructions and big words will make them sound more intelligent, it turns out that this is not so. In an article appropriately titled *Consequences of Erudite Vernacular Utilized Irrespective of Necessity: Problems with Using Long Words Needlessly*, psychologist Daniel Oppenheimer reported the results of a series of studies in which he found that readers rated the authors of simpler, more fluent texts as being more intelligent.[107]

All of this is true for legal communication as well. In one study, researchers found that using shorter sentences, using simpler words, and removing archaic terminology made legal contracts more comprehensible.[108] And in another study, judges and their clerks were asked to read excerpts from legal briefs and motions for rehearing. Briefs written in traditional legal prose were found to be less understandable and less persuasive than were the same briefs when they were rewritten in plain

English. Moreover, the authors of the more understandable briefs were judged to be more effective advocates than their counterparts who used legalese.[109]

Facilitating Disclosure

In many legal encounters, obtaining information can be quite valuable. Client interviews seek to elicit information relevant to the legal representation. Depositions are conducted in order to learn more about what the witness knows. Legal negotiators seek to figure out the interests and constraints of their counterparts. Integrative bargaining, in particular, often requires the parties to disclose private information to each other. Lawyers' ability to claim value for their clients can be significantly affected by what they are able to determine about the other side's bottom line. In all of these cases, eliciting the disclosure of information from others is essential.

Yet, the people with whom we are communicating will not necessarily be eager to disclose. While disclosure can be quite valuable, it can also be quite risky and make the discloser vulnerable to exploitation. Certain disclosures may be embarrassing or seem inappropriate and so may not be easily forthcoming.[110] Effective disclosure can also be hampered by differences in speakers' and observers' notions of what amounts to a telling disclosure. Speakers tend to think that they are revealing a great deal about themselves and the intensity of their feelings when they make statements about their values. However, observers tend not to find such statements as revealing as do the speakers. In contrast, speakers tend to believe that they are not revealing much about themselves when they make off-the-cuff remarks, while observers tend to believe that such remarks are informative. This is known as the *illusion of asymmetric insight*.[111] Moreover, recall that the illusion of transparency (see chapter 3) leads people to believe that their internal states—emotions, beliefs, motives—are more transparent to others than they are. Thus, people can feel that they have disclosed information about such states to others when they have not.

All of this means that the ability to facilitate improved disclosure can be an important legal skill. As noted above, building trust and rapport can be essential for drawing out disclosure. People are much more likely to disclose intimate or sensitive information to those whom they like or trust. In addition, people tend to respond to signs of interest, such as smiling or nodding, by disclosing more. Similarly, simply prompting another to continue can encourage greater disclosure.[112]

The fluency of communication can also influence disclosure. Difficulty understanding the written or verbal questions posed tends to produce an elevated sense of risk, which inhibits disclosure. In contrast, cognitive fluency tends to increase disclosure. Even something as simple as the legibility of a font can affect disclosure, with people disclosing more on questionnaires that are formatted in an easy-to-read font than they do when the questions are more difficult to read.[113] Attorneys can make it easier for others to disclose to them by attending to the fluency of the interaction, for example, avoiding jargon in favor of simpler terms and making sure that questions are easy to follow.

Finally, psychological research has shown that the physical environment can have implications for disclosure. Certainly, obvious physical issues such as noise, excessive heat, or excessive or deficient lighting can be problematic. However, research reveals that even environments that avoid such problems can still differ quite substantially in how conducive they are to effective disclosure.

Most importantly for disclosure in legal contexts, research has shown that people are more willing to disclose relevant personal information in surroundings that appear private.[114] Thus, it can be conducive to disclosure to make sure that the space is one in which the parties to the communication can be alone without others intruding or overhearing. It can be helpful for attorneys to make sure that their clients know that they have taken steps to ensure privacy, such as shutting a conference room door or asking a secretary not to interrupt an interview. And, as we saw above, people may perceive the relative anonymity of electronic communication media as providing a measure of privacy.[115]

In addition, people have preferences about their *personal space*—"the area individuals maintain around themselves into which others cannot intrude without arousing discomfort."[116] Intrusion into someone's personal space can cause distress, inhibit disclosure, and result in a negative impression of the intruder. While personal space preferences vary by individual and among cultures, a comfortable social distance is usually between four and twelve feet.[117] Because individuals may differ in terms of the distance at which they are comfortable interacting and because people may feel more comfortable when they have some control over interaction distance and orientation, disclosure may be facilitated by having several seating options or chairs that can be moved so that people can select their seating.

Finally, studies have found that people disclose more in "warm" rooms with pictures on the walls, soft lighting, and rugs as contrasted with "cold" settings with bare walls and harsher lighting. Relatively uncluttered offices have been shown to elicit more favorable reactions as compared to messy offices, and there is some evidence that indicia of expertise (for example, diplomas) increase observers' perceptions of competence.[118] Thus, attorneys might strive to provide neat, warm, and professional spaces within which to communicate in instances in which disclosure is central.

Conveying Information

In addition to eliciting information from others, there are many contexts in which lawyers need to convey information to others. For example, lawyers are frequently called upon to explain the various aspects of legal doctrine or procedure to their clients, they may need to explain a client's position to an opponent, and they are often required to explain their position to a judge. In addition, lawyers provide information in the form of advice to their clients on a regular basis.

Teaching and Learning

Legal communication that requires an attorney to convey information to others can be construed as a process of teaching and learning. Many attorneys have never worried much about the implications for legal practice of how people learn. They tend to think that if they say something to a client, witness, judge, jury, or opponent, that person will absorb it. Psychologists, on the other hand, have studied the limitations that learners experience and have demonstrated a number of ways in which to improve the transfer of information.[119]

First, as we have seen, psychologists have found that people's processing capacity is limited. Thus, it can be useful to excise unnecessary information from a presentation so that the learner can focus on what is most important. In addition, learning can be facilitated when the relevant material is divided into manageable segments. Working with, rather than against, people's intuitions when presenting information can also be helpful. For example, expressing two quantities in the same units eliminates the need to engage in conversions, and visual displays or quantitative expressions in which higher numbers indicate "more" of something are more easily processed than those that fight this intuition. In short, "[p]eople tend to comprehend more and make better informed decisions when the presentation format makes the most important information easier to evaluate and when less cognitive effort is required."[120]

Second, it is easier to learn things that are concrete as compared to those that are abstract. As we saw in chapter 6, concrete examples or analogies tend to be easier to understand and to remember. (Which of the word lists presented in that chapter could you better recall?)

Third, psychologists have found that people learn by building on what they already know. We have already seen that it can be difficult, but important for clear communication, to think about how the world looks from another person's perspective and to be alert to the ways in which another's knowledge differs from our own. In addition, existing knowledge can provide an organizing structure for the processing of new information. Thus, taking into account people's existing knowledge and beliefs—for example, by drawing analogies with familiar contexts—can improve learning.

Fourth, we know that people take in and process information via multiple channels. While it is not clear that different people learn better through different modalities,[121] it is useful to utilize multiple methods of presenting information. For example, people tend to learn better when words are supplemented with visual representations such as pictures or diagrams. Similarly, learning can be aided by the use of decision aids such as flowcharts or decision trees. Ultimately, people may rely on a mix of learning strategies, and their preferences may vary with the type of learning task.

Finally, we know that people do not always ask questions when they do not understand or want more information. Studies that compare the perspective of patients with that of doctors are particularly illuminating: while doctors report believing that patients will ask follow-up questions if they want more information, patients prefer that doctors provide them with information without expecting them to ask.[122]

Giving Advice

Effectively communicating advice is central to the attorney-client relationship. Louis Brandeis put it this way: "Your law may be perfect, your ability to apply it great, and yet you cannot be a successful adviser unless your advice is followed."[123]

> A lawyer's time and advice are his stock in trade.
> —Abraham Lincoln[124]

There are many factors that influence the degree to which people are receptive to advice from others. Two of these factors—that people are more receptive to advice they solicit and to advice for which they have paid—are inherent in most, but not all, legal representations.[125]

More importantly, though, people tend to rely more on advice—even advice that is not what they want to hear—when they receive that advice from someone they trust. Conversely, they may reject even good advice if they lack trust in the adviser.[126] As we have seen, people tend to trust their advisers more and weigh their advice more heavily when those advisers provide needed expertise and when they appear to be well intentioned. With regard to the relative expertise of the adviser, advice tends to be relied upon more when the adviser has relevant education or experience; when the advisee lacks her own foundation of relevant knowledge, increasing the relative value of the advice; and when the decision at hand is a difficult one. Advice given by more confident advisers is also more likely to be followed, perhaps because advisees use confidence as a proxy for expertise.[127] But expertise is not the only important factor. Advisees also tend to be more receptive to advice if they believe that their adviser is ethical, motivated to help them succeed, and has their interests at heart. In addition, advisees rate advice as being of higher quality if the advice and its delivery demonstrate respect for the advisee.[128]

The type of advice offered may also influence receptivity. One study of advisee preferences for different types of advice examined five different types of advice: recommendations in favor of an option, recommendations against a particular option, information about the available options, suggestions about how to structure the decision-making process itself, and social support. Across a range of decision-making contexts, study participants rated all five types of advice positively. This suggests that each of these forms of advice may have its place. The most highly rated forms of advice were

> I cannot . . . advise you what to determine, but if you please I will tell you how. . . .
> —Benjamin Franklin[129]

the provision of information about alternatives and recommendations in favor of a particular option.[130] Thus, consistently providing information about the relevant options, even when other forms of advice are provided as well, may be an effective way to improve receptivity to advice. In similar ways, providing information about and explanations for the advice given can improve receptivity to that advice. As we noted above, advisers tend to be more trusted when they elaborate on the advice that they provide.[131]

> ✦ ✦ ✦ ✦ ✦
> **Summing It Up**
>
> - Recognize that communication is enriched and complicated by the ways in which it is infused with inference, interpretation, social convention, context, body language, culture, and shared knowledge.
> - Replace misleading intuitions about liars with more psychologically informed lie-detection strategies: use direct questions to address the tendency to lie by omission, impose cognitive load to make lying more difficult, watch for changes in behavior, and keep an open mind.
> - Build trust and rapport in order to establish credibility, facilitate the sharing of information, and increase receptivity to advice.
> - Improve listening by minimizing distractions, resisting the urge to interrupt, and asking follow-up questions.
> - Effectively convey information by taking the audience's perspective into account, avoiding jargon, breaking information into manageable segments, capitalizing on the audience's intuitions and existing knowledge, using multiple channels of communication, and providing advice in different forms.

For Further Reading: Communication

Silvia Bonaccio & Reeshad S. Dalal, *Advice Taking and Decision-Making: An Integrative Literature Review, and Implications for the Organizational Sciences*, 101 ORGANIZATIONAL BEHAV. & HUM. DECISION PROCESSES 127 (2006).

Charles F. Bond Jr. & Bella M. DePaulo, *Accuracy of Deception Judgments*, 10 PERSONALITY & SOC. PSYCHOL. REV. 214 (2006).

Tanya L. Chartrand & Rick van Baaren, *Human Mimicry*, 41 ADVANCES EXPERIMENTAL SOC. PSYCHOL. 219 (2009).

Bella M. DePaulo et al., *Cues to Deception*, 129 PSYCHOL. BULL. 74 (2003).

PAUL EKMAN, TELLING LIES: CLUES TO DECEIT IN THE MARKETPLACE, POLITICS, AND MARRIAGE (2001).

Nicholas Epley & Eugene M. Caruso, *Perspective Taking: Misstepping into Others' Shoes*, in HANDBOOK OF IMAGINATION AND MENTAL SIMULATION 295 (Keith D. Markman et al. eds., 2009).

MARK L. KNAPP & JUDITH A. HALL, NONVERBAL COMMUNICATION IN HUMAN INTERACTION (6th ed. 2005).

RICHARD E. MAYER, APPLYING THE SCIENCE OF LEARNING (2010).

THE SAGE HANDBOOK OF NONVERBAL COMMUNICATION (Valerie Manusov & Miles L. Patterson eds., 2006).

Norbert Schwartz, Cognition and Communication: Judgmental Biases, Research Methods, and the Logic of Conversation (1996).

Aldert Vrij et al., *Pitfalls and Opportunities in Nonverbal and Verbal Lie Detection*, 11 Psychol. Sci. Pub. Int. 89 (2010).

Justice 8

> This is a court of law, young man, not a court of justice.
> —*Oliver Wendell Holmes Jr.*[1]

Did the September 11th Victim Compensation Fund create a just solution for the victims of the 9/11 terrorist attacks? Is a particular will provision, custody agreement, contract term, or deportation decision fair? Is the structure of the tax system just? Was a person treated justly as she was subjected to a search of her vehicle or applied for welfare benefits or was considered for a promotion at work? What does *justice* mean anyway? Jerry Facher, one of the big firm defense lawyers made famous in the book and movie *A Civil Action*, once notoriously said after a court session, "The truth? The truth is at the bottom of a bottomless pit."[2] Could the same be said about justice?

While we may not often think explicitly about what we mean when we consider justice, achieving a sense of justice is frequently a core concern of legal clients. People want results that comport with their notions of justice and fairness—notions that may or may not be in sync with the requirements or practicalities of the law. Ultimately, the perceived legitimacy of legal results is influenced by the extent to which the results are considered just.[3]

While it is tempting to assume that people are results oriented and will feel treated justly if they receive a lot of money, avoid having to pay a lot of money, or manage to stay out of jail, psychological research shows that such a conception of justice is too narrow. Instead, people pursue a range of goals and often care a great deal about various types of justice. In particular, people are concerned with the distributive fairness of their outcomes; with the procedural fairness of the processes they experience; and with reestablishing a sense of justice though retribution, reconciliation, or other means.[4]

Distributive Justice

While most people understand the need for compromise in a well-functioning society, it is clear that people resist agreeing to or complying with outcomes that do not comport with their notions of substantive fairness. Models of *distributive justice* attempt to explain how people determine whether an outcome is substantively fair. It turns out that the distributive fairness of an outcome can be judged by a number of different metrics, including principles of *equality, equity,* or *need*.[5]

Equality is distribution by equal shares: a testator might divide her estate equally among her three children, or a dinner group might divide a restaurant tab equally rather than attempt to figure out how much each individual diner consumed and therefore owes. Equality can be a "straightforward decision-making heuristic when dividing outcomes because it is easy to implement and widely accepted as valid"[6] and is commonly applied in situations in which social relations and cooperation are important, such as within families or among friends.

But while equal shares can be a straightforward and useful baseline distribution, such a distribution is not without complications.[7] First, equal divisions may be inefficient. The classic story of two sisters who are arguing over an orange provides an example. An equal division, that is, cutting the orange in half, does not provide the most efficient solution if one sister wants to eat the flesh of the orange but the other wants the peel in order to make a cake.

Second, in some instances the dimension on which a split should be accomplished may not be clear. Imagine a testator who has two children, one with a single child and another with four children, and who wants to split his estate based on principles of equality. To make an equal division, should he distribute the estate equally across the two families or divide by the number of grandchildren?

Third, the seeming fairness of equality can make a particular division appear fair when it may not be. Consider the following example:

> You visit a car dealer and go on a test drive. You return to the salesperson's cubicle in the showroom. The car has a list price of $18,000. After a short discussion, you offer $15,500. The salesperson counters with $17,600, you counter with $16,000, he counters with $17,200, you counter with $16,400, and he reduces his price to $16,800. You act as if you will not make another concession and threaten to visit another dealership. The salesperson then says earnestly, "You look like a nice person, and I can see that you really like the car. My main concern is that you get the car that you want. *I assume that you are a reasonable person, and I want to be reasonable. How about if we split the difference—$16,600?"*
>
> Many of us would quickly accept the salesman's offer. After all, a 50-50 split sounds fair. Yet, careful consideration reveals that this 50-50 split, like most 50-50 splits is quite arbitrary. The final two numbers on the table could have been $16,000 and $16,400, and the 50-50 split would have sounded just as fair, but the resulting price would have been $16,200, or $400 less. The fairness of a 50-50 split depends on the comparative fairness of the two numbers used as anchors for the split. A rational decision maker must be aware of the influence of a seemingly fair 50-50 split and

realize that other 50-50 alternatives are easy to generate. Just because an offer can be considered fair does not mean that it is optimal. Other equally fair outcomes may exist that would be better for you.[8]

Other metrics for evaluating distributive justice depart from strict notions of equality in some way; for example, different shares might be justified on the basis of rights or relative contributions or needs or abilities or efficiency rather than on a per capita basis.[9] In particular, distribution based on equity involves evaluating substantive fairness based on the relative contributions of the relevant actors, for example, a salary raise pool that is divided among workers based on "merit" or a distribution of loss that is divided among tortfeasors based on their contribution to the harm caused. Such a metric is more likely to be found in market relationships, in situations in which productivity is the focus, and in situations that involve competition. In contrast, distribution based on need involves channeling resources to those with the greatest need and is often seen in situations in which increasing welfare is a focal goal.[11]

[I]t is hard to imagine a more pervasively justifiable principle of making allocation decisions than the principle of equality.
—David Messick[10]

Which of these metrics is chosen by an individual or a group in a particular situation depends in part on their goals, the relationships among the parties, and the type of resource at issue. Consider, for example, how distributions might differ if the goal in a particular situation is to foster productivity as compared to fostering harmony. Furthermore, consider how a distribution might differ in an arm's-length transaction as compared to a familial relationship. To consider a specific example, reflect on how we might choose to distribute organs for transplant as compared to how we might distribute the last piece of peach pie. In some instances, two or more metrics might be used in combination so that, for example, distribution is based on need until some threshold is achieved, and then a principle of equity is used from that point forward; or equity might be preferred up until such a method becomes too inefficient.

People from different cultural backgrounds may prefer different metrics or may apply different bases for equitable distributions. For example, people from independent cultures are more likely to favor distributive rules based on norms of equity, while those from more interdependent cultures tend to privilege fairness norms based on equality or need. Similarly, while two people from different cultures may both value equitable distribution, one of them may prefer to distribute resources based on seniority, and the other may prefer a productivity-based system of distribution.[12]

Interestingly, applying the "wrong" metric in a particular situation or relationship can evoke particularly negative reactions. A *taboo trade-off* results when a distribution or exchange occurs that is inconsistent with the norms of the relationship, such as trading money for organs or babies or a whistle-blower's silence. Such

> Justice is a bone-deep urge toward fairness in things large and small. It's the human journey toward a better world.
>
> —*Plaintiff-side Attorney Elizabeth J. Cabraser*[14]

distributions or exchanges are often seen as being particularly inappropriate and unjust.[13]

The availability of different metrics for evaluating the substantive fairness of an outcome makes it possible for individuals to hold and defend very different interpretations of whether a particular outcome is just. In addition, we have already seen that differences in perception (see chapter 1) and memory (see chapter 2) can result in different understandings of what is fair. Moreover, recall that we also tend to conflate what is fair with what benefits us and that we tend to make unrealistically positive assessments of our own contributions to joint projects (see chapter 4). If we think that we have contributed more or have been hurt more or are more skilled, then we may think that we are more deserving of resources. As we have seen, those on different sides of a dispute are likely to have different perceptions of what a fair resolution would be and of what an objective observer or a judge would find to be a fair solution. In similar ways, we are also more likely to think of ourselves as engaging in fair actions than others and to think that others are more likely to engage in unfair actions than we are.[15] Finally, people who have experienced what they see as unfair losses tend to feel more entitled, as a matter of distributive justice, to claim a bigger piece of the available pie.[16]

It is also clear that in assessing justice, we are concerned about how we fare relative to others. We would sometimes rather take a substantively inferior outcome as long as others' outcomes are similar to ours than a better outcome that involves others receiving even more than we do. Similarly, as we will see, we are sometimes willing to incur costs in order to punish another person and will sometimes give up a benefit in order to assist another person.[17] Consider the following examples:

- Imagine that you are graduating from law school. After a few interviews, a law firm in which you are very interested makes you an offer of a position as an associate attorney at a salary of $140,000 per year. The offer is not negotiable. You think $140,000 per year is a tremendous amount of money. You like the firm. You like the practice area. And you like the location. However, right before you are about to accept the offer, you find out that the same firm is offering another new associate $160,000. You do not see any characteristics that make the other individual more qualified than you. Will you still accept the offer? Imagine that you have a second offer at a firm that is similar to the first but at which all new associates receive $130,000. Which offer will you take?[18]
- Imagine that you and a colleague are given the opportunity to play an *ultimatum game* with the following rules: Your colleague will be given $100. Your colleague will then determine how much of the $100 to give to you and how much to keep for herself. If you deem her proposal to be acceptable, you will

each keep the designated amount. However, if you reject her proposal, all of the money will be forfeited. If your colleague decides to give you $10 and to keep $90 for herself, will you accept the offer?

If you are like most people, both of these offers bother you. This is not because either of these outcomes—accepting an attractive job that pays $140,000 per year and gaining $10—is a bad thing in the abstract. Rather, it is the comparison between your outcome and the other person's outcome that creates the discomfort. A salary of $140,000 for an associate attorney might seem acceptable in the absence of comparative information but begins to seem unfair if an equally qualified candidate is offered $160,000, and your colleague's blatant violation of a norm of equality makes your gain of $10 seem unfair in light of her gain of $90. Indeed, responders in such ultimatum games routinely reject offers that consist of less than 20% of the total stake even though that means they walk away with nothing. Proposers, however, are sensitive to the norms at play here, frequently offering fifty-fifty splits and on average keeping less than 70% of the stake.[19]

Consider another example: Imagine a dispute between you and your neighbor over the property taxes owed on a disputed strip of property. The percentage of the property owned by each of you is unclear. How would you react to a proposal that you pay $400 of the tax and your neighbor pays $200? Again, this resolution might bother you. Given no information about relative ownership, the norm of equality might suggest that each of you pay half of the outstanding tax bill. But what if the alternative were a higher total tax bill of which each of you would pay $500? Evaluated in isolation, this seems like a more equitable outcome. And, indeed, in isolation people tend to find this second proposal more satisfactory. However, it is possible to focus people's attention on their own objective outcome. For example, when considering the two proposals simultaneously, a person's concern for the size of his own payout ($400 or $500) can override concerns for fairness and lead people to accept the first, unequal, proposal (see chapter 5).[20] Thus, the relative importance of concern for fairness and concern for the quality of a person's own outcome can be influenced by situational factors (such as whether a person considers options jointly or in isolation), as well as by factors like the size of the disparity in outcomes.

Such reactions are deeply engrained. Even nonhuman primates dislike inequalities, reacting negatively, for example, when offered a less attractive reward (say, a slice of cucumber) when another monkey has received a more attractive reward (say, a grape) for exerting the same effort.[21] And brain research has found evidence that unfair offers such as those in the ultimatum game are associated with activation in areas of the brain that have been linked to negative emotions such as anger and disgust.[22] Other research has found evidence that fair offers are associated with activation in the emotional reward centers of the brain, suggesting that fairness has an intrinsic positive significance. Interestingly, unfair offers that are accepted despite their unfairness are not associated with activity in these reward structures but are instead associated with emotion regulation parts of the brain, suggesting that in order to facilitate the acceptance of an economically beneficial though unfair offer, people must overcome their negative reaction to unfairness.[23]

Finally, as we saw in chapter 5, it is common for people to make evaluative judgments against an existing baseline. The same is true for fairness reactions. Consider a retailer who takes the opportunity to raise the price of necessary supplies following a natural disaster even though his own costs have not risen. Most people would say that such opportunistic price increases are unfair. This is because the pre-disaster prices of lumber or water or bread serve as reference points for assessing the fairness of the prices of these items post-disaster.[24] Similar baselines resulted in negative customer reactions to moves by airlines to impose fees for services (for example, checked luggage) that they previously provided for free and to the Coca-Cola Company's ill-fated proposal to introduce vending machines that charged more for Coke on hot days when demand was higher.[25]

Procedural Justice

We have seen that people care deeply about the substantive fairness of their outcomes. But distributive justice is not the only facet of justice about which people are concerned. Perceptions of *procedural justice* relate to the fairness of the processes, procedures, and rules by which a substantive decision is reached. And, as it turns out, people's evaluations of the justness of a system are often determined as least as much by the extent to which they assess the system to be procedurally fair as by the system's substantive outcomes. The research on procedural justice demonstrates that when people believe that a decision-making procedure is fair, they are more likely to believe that the outcome produced by that procedure is fair (even if it is negative), have more respect for and trust in the institution or decision maker, are more willing to comply with the decision or agreement reached, are more satisfied with the outcome, and have more positive opinions of the social policies that are formulated under the procedure. Conversely, the benefits of positive outcomes can be undermined by procedures that are seen as unfair.

The notion that the fairness of the procedure can matter just as much as the substantive outcomes produced by that procedure is one that many lawyers find hard to believe: "The procedural justice hypothesis goes against the strong intuition of many people that they and others are motivated by [monetary] self-interest. Lawyers in particular are often found to hold this view of human motivation quite vigorously."[26] While achieving superior monetary outcomes can indeed be an important motivator, we have seen that we tend to overestimate the effects of this sort of self-interest on behavior (see chapter 1). Furthermore, decades of research have consistently demonstrated the robust effects of procedural justice.

To say that people place a high value on the procedural justice of the legal processes with which they engage is not to say that people would prefer to lose or to receive distributively unfair outcomes: "On the contrary, no one likes to lose. However, people recognize that they cannot always win when they have conflicts with others. They accept 'losing' more willingly if the . . . procedures used to handle their case are fair."[27] For example, among workers who have been laid off, those with more positive perceptions of the fairness of their treatment by their former employer are less likely to sue than are those who perceive that the procedures used by the employer were unfair.[28]

Consider also a study that looked at individual and business litigants who participated in a court-mandated nonbinding arbitration program to resolve cases with amounts in controversy ranging from a few thousand to several million dollars. Decisions about whether to accept the arbitrator's decision or to reject the award and proceed to trial were more strongly associated with litigant perceptions of the procedural justice of the arbitration than with the size of the arbitration award.[29] And among fathers who lose custody of their children, those who perceive their custody hearings as having been more procedurally fair are more likely to stay involved with their children.[30] Such effects have been shown with regard to procedures in courts, mediation and arbitration procedures, civil commitment procedures, treatment by the tax system, treatment by the police, and many others.[31]

So, if the perceived fairness of the procedure at issue can have such powerful effects, what is it that leads people to assess a procedure as fair? Procedural justice researchers have identified a variety of concerns that people take into account in making judgments about the justness of a procedure.

First, people are concerned about *voice*—having an opportunity to participate in the process, to state their case, to provide their views on what might be a just result. Second, consistent with popular notions that "justice is blind" and that playing fields should be level, people care about the *neutrality* of the process or forum. A procedurally just process is one in which decision makers are unbiased, decisions are based on rules and objective criteria that are consistently applied, and explanations are given for the decisions reached. Third, the *trustworthiness* of the authority or process is important. People prefer processes in which the relevant authority is concerned about their interests and well-being, listens to their arguments, and genuinely tries to reach the right result. Finally, a procedurally just process is one in which participants are treated with *dignity* and *respect*. In making these evaluations of procedural fairness, people tend to be concerned both with whether the formal rules are fair and whether individuals act fairly in carrying out those rules.[32]

These features of procedures are considered important because they address people's "twin worries of exploitation and exclusion."[33] First, when evaluating the features of a decision-making procedure, people are concerned with the quality of the decisions produced (because they do not want to be exploited). Thus, procedures are considered to be fairer to the extent that they incorporate the sorts of features—the opportunity for voice, neutrality, trustworthiness, and respect—that are thought to produce fair outcomes. People may be better situated to evaluate the fairness of

> ✦ ✦ ✦ ✦ ✦
> **The Importance of Voice**
>
> Psychologist Tom Tyler studied the traffic courts in Chicago and how people experience them. He found that most traffic cases in which the ticketed party appeared were dismissed. He "assumed that the court felt that it was too much trouble to actually contest such cases (for example by making the police officer appear and testify) so they just dropped them." In his exit interviews with traffic court participants, he encountered
>
>> one woman who came out after having her case dismissed and she was really angry. She understood that she had no fine and no record but she had taken pictures to show that the no parking sign that led to her ticket was not visible from the street and the judge would not look at them. So, even though she won, she was angry that she had no voice. She could not present her evidence in court.
>
> Because she had not experienced procedural justice, even a favorable substantive outcome was not satisfactory.[34]
>
> James Nelson, the former chief judge of the Los Angeles Municipal Court, had a similar experience:
>
>> "I had a case in which a lady had sued a dry cleaner for damaging her clothing," he recalls. "Well, when she got through presenting her case, I wasn't even clear about whether or not she was suing the right dry cleaner. She just didn't seem to have a case. So as soon as she was done, I said that the judgment was for the defendant.
>>
>> "At that point, the dry cleaner almost attacked me. I thought he was going to jump over the bench and grab me, so I said, 'Sir, sir, I just ruled in your favor. The case is over.' But he was furious. He said, 'I wanted to tell you about what this woman did!' And at that moment, I realized that most people would rather be heard than win."[35]

their treatment than they are to evaluate the justness of a particular substantive legal outcome. For example, a person who is sentenced to two months in jail for having defaced a building with graffiti may more easily be able to judge whether he feels he was treated fairly at the trial than whether such a sentence is appropriate for such a crime. Thus, procedural fairness can operate as a tool for judging substantive fairness.[36]

Second, the manner in which an individual is treated communicates something about the degree to which others in the system value him. Being listened to, provided with explanations, and treated according to defined rules signal that a person is worthy of consideration. Therefore, "treatment with dignity and respect are important because they tell people that they have status within the group."[37] In contrast, treatment that does not evidence dignity and respect conveys a message that the individual lacks status within the community—a message of exclusion.

Concerns about procedural justice are strikingly universal. Notably, both attorneys and clients tend to be influenced by the same aspects of a procedure in making assessments of procedural justice. And, like their clients, attorneys' decisions are associated with the procedural justice of a procedure. Attorneys, for example, are more inclined to accept the nonbinding decision of an arbitrator when they assess the arbitration procedure as more procedurally just.[38] Likewise, there is marked similarity in the features that underlie perceptions of fair procedures across cultures.[39] Cross-cultural research on procedural justice finds only minor variations in the importance that people from different cultures place on the inferences they make about the meaning of fair treatment. For example, people from independent cultures tend to place greater value on the status recognition that comes from being treated fairly than do those from interdependent cultures, and people from cultures that are high in power distance tend to be more comfortable with hierarchical authorities as compared to those from cultures that are low in power distance and prefer a more consultative type of authority.[40] Beyond these minor variations in emphasis, reactions to procedural justice are remarkably consistent.

While much procedural justice research has been conducted with regard to processes involving third-party decision makers or facilitators such as courts, police, employers, arbitrators, and mediators, procedural justice also matters in the context of bilateral negotiation. Of course, negotiators understand and expect that their negotiation counterparts will be partisan rather than neutral. But they nonetheless expect and hope that the other party will listen to their position (voice), act in good faith (trustworthiness), and treat them with respect and dignity. Negotiators who treat each other in a procedurally just manner display less divergence in their notions of what a fair agreement would be, are less likely to reach impasse, tend to reach agreement more quickly, and are more satisfied with and willing to accept negotiated outcomes.[41] Moreover, research has found that negotiators who are procedurally fair are able to claim as much value in a distributive negotiation and also to produce more joint gains where such gains are possible.[42]

Procedures also matter to people when they receive assistance from service providers, including professionals such as lawyers. For example, imagine being given a choice between two different financial advisers: one who tends to provide average financial returns but a high-quality experience (that is, the adviser treats you respectfully, allows you to participate, and pays attention to your needs and concerns) and a second that provides little in the way of process but above-average financial return. Which would you choose? When a sample of TIAA-CREF participants were asked this question, more than half of them (62%) expressed a preference for the advising that provided a high-quality process.[43] Similarly, as we saw in chapter 7, doctors who fail to provide explanations and who communicate poorly with patients are more likely than other doctors to be sued.[44] Furthermore, neglect of client matters and failure to communicate are the most common complaints made about lawyers to disciplinary authorities.[45] Thus, even though it is tempting to think that it is solely professional expertise (analytical skill and knowledge of the law) that is the defining feature of the assistance sought by clients, it is clear that features of the process are also central to effective representation of clients. Indeed, a procedurally just attorney might pay particular attention to providing the client with opportunities for voice, providing clear explanations, showing respect by returning phone calls, and demonstrating trustworthiness by acting in accordance with the ethics of the profession.[46]

Interestingly, people do not always predict the important role that procedural justice will play in their evaluations of legal processes. Indeed, people tend to use different criteria to evaluate procedures before and after experiencing them. When selecting a procedure, people tend to focus on their sense of whether the procedure will favor them substantively. But when evaluating a procedure that they have already experienced, they tend to focus on procedural justice concerns:

> For example, a defendant in a civil lawsuit might choose a particularly contentious litigation option based on his or her belief that the option will lead to less exposure to unfavorable decisions in the case, but then evaluate the experience unfavorably based on elements of the process he or she encountered (and chose!). The irony is all the more striking because, as we noted above, the ultimate acceptance of the outcome will be more closely linked to the experience of procedural fairness than to satisfaction with the outcome.[47]

Reestablishment of Justice

We want to believe that the world is fair, that people get what they deserve. Conversely, we find it distasteful to discover that the world may not be just after all. Accordingly, when we encounter instances of injustice, we experience a sense of outrage that motivates us to restore justice in some way.[48]

Sometimes people change their perceptions of the situation, the victim, or the perpetrator in order to restore a sense of justice. For example, particularly when other avenues for restoring justice are unavailable, there is a tendency to denigrate the victims of harm and to conclude that they got what they deserved. Believing that a crime victim "asked for it," that an employee deserved to be fired, or that someone living in poverty is lazy allows people to maintain a belief in a just world. An injured person might even question whether she brought the harm on herself. Similarly, there can be a tendency to justify existing systems as legitimate and to conclude that any inequities they produce are deserved or otherwise justified.[49]

But sometimes an opportunity to rectify the harm more directly is available. We might seek or offer compensation, an apology, or other remediation. We might distance ourselves from offenders by refusing to engage with them—ostracizing a person whom we think has done wrong, organizing a boycott, or attempting to generate negative publicity. We might seek governmental action. A lawsuit might be filed or criminal charges brought. Those accused of wrongdoing in a lawsuit can not only make their denials but also sometimes bring claims of their own against their accusers. At times, victims or observers might be moved to engage in self-help or vigilante justice.

Retribution

Some offenses are so egregious that they give rise to a sense of moral outrage that demands punishment. The violations that trigger such feelings of *retributive justice* can vary across individuals and cultures. For example, those from independent cultures have stronger reactions to rights violations, while those from interdependent cultures respond more strongly to failures to live up to obligations. And, as we saw in chapter 1, people from different cultures may place differing emphasis on such factors as the intentionality of the actor or the social context in which he is embedded.[50] Once triggered, however, retribution "is concerned primarily with the elimination of a sense of injustice" that results from an offense and implicates issues of whether, what kind, and how much punishment is warranted.[51] In addition, it can be important to people that the offender not simply be punished—that is, not simply experience suffering—but that the offender understand that his suffering has been imposed as a consequence of his misdeed.[52] This is consistent with the often-expressed need to "send a message."

> If you prick us do we not bleed? if you tickle us do we not laugh? if you poison us, do we not die? and if you wrong us, shall we not revenge?
> —*William Shakespeare*[53]

Punishment might be aimed at a variety of goals, including utilitarian goals such as deterrence, incapacitation, and rehabilitation and retributive goals such as making sure an offender receives her just deserts. Although psychologists have found that many people tend, in the abstract, to strongly support deterrence arguments, when setting specific punishments they tend to be more influenced by aspects of the offense that are considered relevant to retribution than by those relevant to deterrence.[54] Punishment, then, is often aimed primarily at providing the offender with her just deserts. At the same time, however, features of the offense and attributions of the causes underlying it can make one or the other of these goals prominent.[55]

As with other types of justice, perceptions about appropriate retribution can vary by where one sits. In particular, psychologists have found that because there is a *magnitude gap* in the assessment of wrongdoing such that the "scope, importance, and lasting consequences of a transgression are generally larger for the victim than for the perpetrator," it is difficult for victims and perpetrators to agree on the degree of punishment that would be proportionate to the original wrong. Punishments that, to the injured party, seem fair tend to seem excessive to the recipient of that punishment. Thus, the original wrongdoer may come to see herself as a victim who deserves to strike back.[56]

People anticipate that exacting punishment will be emotionally satisfying. "Revenge is sweet" goes the common saying, or, as Alfred Hitchcock more colorfully put it, "[r]evenge is sweet and not fattening."[57] Indeed, those who believe that punishing a person who has wronged them will be cathartic tend to punish more severely.[58] Sometimes taking revenge does reduce feelings of anger.[59] However, as with other predictions of future emotions (see chapter 5), our experience is not always as we anticipate. Consider a study that examined the effects of allowing participants to punish someone who had induced them to act cooperatively and then took advantage of their trust. Paradoxically, while participants anticipated that punishing the offender would make them feel better, those who punished actually ended up feeling worse than those who did not have the opportunity to punish. In acting to punish an offender, people end up thinking more about the offender and the offense, and this rumination may result in increased negative emotions (see chapter 3). Sometimes, as Francis Bacon put it, "[a] man that studieth revenge keeps his own wounds green."[61] Interestingly, this affective cost was not experienced by those who witnessed someone else punish the offender, suggesting one reason why it may be particularly satisfying for the state to exact punishment on a victim's behalf.[62]

> Therein lies the defect of revenge: it's all in the anticipation; the thing itself is a pain, not a pleasure; at least the pain is the biggest end of it.
> —*Mark Twain*[60]

Restoration of Justice

The restoration of justice is simultaneously concerned with providing just deserts, reasserting a shared commitment to the violated norm, reestablishing the standing of the victim, and alleviating the harm to the victim and the community that resulted from the violation at issue. Accomplishing each of these goals may be deemed more or less important in the context of a particular offense or by those with different cultural backgrounds. Furthermore, different types of sanctions or other responses may be differentially able to accomplish each of these goals. Thus, a prison sentence may be seen as effectively punishing an offender and communicating the value of the violated rule to the community but be seen as less effective at accomplishing rehabilitation. Community service might be viewed as effectively restoring the harm done to the community while providing a moderate punishment but be seen as less effective at restoring the victim.[63] Ultimately, there are an endless variety of mechanisms through which justice might be restored in some way in particular contexts: rehiring an employee who was wrongly terminated, repairing property that was damaged, compensating an injured person for her expenses, drafting a new agreement that defines a future relationship, and retracting false statements.

One mechanism through which a person might attempt to restore justice is by offering an account of the conduct that led to an injury. For example, a person might attempt to deny, explain, excuse, justify, or apologize for the behavior that purportedly led to harm. Apologies, in particular, may have a role to play in restoring justice. In some cases, "[p]aying monetary damages may help take care of the financial consequences of an injury, but it may take an apology to 'wipe the moral ledger' clean and construct understandings of the injury and the relationship which both parties can accept."[64] Indeed, the popular press is full of stories describing injured claimants who claim that they would not have filed lawsuits had apologies been proffered, settlement negotiations stalled for lack of apology even after the financial issues were resolved, and disappointed claimants who settled despite not receiving apologies. Consider the 2009 settlement reached in a contentious case involving the wrongful death of actor James Woods's brother. The case only settled when the CEO of the defendant hospital admitted that errors were made and apologized to the Woods family. Woods, who claimed that what he wanted was "justice," said, "It was all I ever needed to see in my life, one human being saying to another human being 'I'm sorry for your loss.'"[65]

Psychological research has shown that apologies can change the attributions people make about the behavior that led to the harm, can ease negative emotional responses, can change the way disputants are viewed by each other and society, can reinforce the societal norm that was violated, and can result in a decreased need to punish.[66] In addition, researchers have found that apologies can decrease the likelihood that potential claimants will seek legal advice following an injury, can lower the amount of money sought by claimants in settlement negotiations, and can increase the likelihood that a claimant will accept a particular offer of settlement.[67]

Of course, the offering of apologies can be complicated in the context of a legal dispute, and attorneys may worry that any apology will be viewed as an admission and will lead to more certain legal liability. Perhaps not surprisingly, then, research has found that while lawyers assess apologies and the information communicated by apologies in ways that are similar to the assessments made by claimants (making similar assessments, for example, of the remorse conveyed and similar predictions about the apologizer's likely future behavior), attorneys are more attuned to the liability implications than are their clients. Specifically, attorneys expect cases in which an apology has been offered to settle at higher, rather than lower, dollar amounts.[68] These different understandings of apologies

> may lead attorneys on both sides to resist settlement or to push for trial where their clients might otherwise prefer to settle. Conversely, attorneys may not entirely understand their clients' or opposing clients' resistance to settlement in the absence of apologies. This may lead attorneys on both sides to dismiss claimant requests for apology and may result in a reduced ability to "bring [the] client along" to accept a settlement. In addition, defense attorneys may advise their clients against apologizing because their perspective suggests that apologies will lead to *less* favorable settlement terms in addition to any increased liability risk. Any of these disconnects

may interfere with attorneys' ability to settle cases to the best satisfaction of their clients.[69]

> ✦ ✦ ✦ ✦ ✦
> **Summing It Up**
>
> - Be aware of a range of justice considerations when working with clients, opposing counsel, witnesses, opponents, and decision makers.
> - Bear in mind the different metrics that can underlie a concern for distributive justice—including equality, equity, and need—and the ways in which people compare their result to the outcomes of others or to other baselines.
> - Recognize the importance of procedural justice and the desire for voice, neutrality, trustworthiness, dignity, and respect—understanding how perceptions of procedural justice relate to compliance, satisfaction, and judgments of legitimacy.
> - Take into account the experience of moral outrage that demands punishment and a consideration of just deserts while recognizing that punishment is evaluated differently by those who experience it and those who mete it out (the magnitude gap).
> - Understand the need to restore justice in order to reaffirm the shared values of the community, to reestablish the standing of the victim, and to assuage the effects of the injury done to the victim and to the community.

For Further Reading: Justice

Kevin M. Carlsmith & John M. Darley, *Psychological Aspects of Retributive Justice*, 40 ADVANCES EXPERIMENTAL SOC. PSYCHOL. 193 (2008).

John M. Darley & Thane S. Pittman, *The Psychology of Compensatory and Retributive Justice*, 7 PERSONALITY & SOC. PSYCHOL. REV. 324 (2003).

Morton Deutsch, *Equity, Equality, and Need: What Determines Which Value Will Be Used as the Basis of Distributive Justice?*, 31 J. SOC. ISSUES 137 (1975).

HANDBOOK OF JUSTICE RESEARCH IN LAW (Joseph Sanders & V. Lee Hamilton eds., 2001).

THE JUSTICE MOTIVE IN EVERYDAY LIFE (Michael Ross & Dale T. Miller eds., 2002).

E. ALLAN LIND & TOM R. TYLER, THE SOCIAL PSYCHOLOGY OF PROCEDURAL JUSTICE (1988).

Dale T. Miller, *Disrespect and the Experience of Injustice*, 52 Ann. Rev. Psychol. 527 (2001).

Psychological Perspectives on Justice: Theory and Applications (Barbara A. Mellers & Jonathan Baron eds., 1993).

Tom R. Tyler et al., Social Justice in a Diverse Society (1997).

Interviewing Clients and Witnesses   9

The art and science of asking questions is the source of all knowledge.[1]

Despite what we see on television and in the movies, many attorneys spend far more time working with clients and witnesses than they do participating in trials and hearings.[2] This chapter explores the implications of the psychological literature for each facet of the interview process. By applying what we have learned about perception, memory, communication, and other aspects of psychology, attorneys can develop improved interviewing skills, which will help them be more effective attorneys who win more cases, close more deals, and have more satisfied clients. Chapter 10 then offers suggestions as to how psychological insights can help attorneys counsel their clients more effectively.

Interviews with clients have much in common with interviews with prospective witnesses, but substantial differences also exist. The attorney builds a much closer relationship with the client and also knows that conversations with clients are protected by attorney-client confidentiality. On the other hand, issues related to perception, judgment, memory, perspective taking, trust, and rapport are just as important in witness interviews as they are in client interviews. As we proceed, we will treat these subjects together where possible but draw distinctions as needed. We consider the interview process chronologically.

Preparing for the Client Interview

Gathering Pre-Interview Information

Some lawyers, especially those in certain practice areas such as plaintiff-side personal injury, follow the practice of most doctors and have prospective clients fill out a written survey prior to meeting with the attorney. In other law offices, the prospective client meets first with a paralegal or secretary, who may gather preliminary information from the prospective client. Still other attorneys may chat with the potential client fairly briefly, by phone, prior to having the potential client come to the office.

It does seem like it would be efficient to have clients fill out forms or be interviewed prior to meeting the attorney. Information obtained in advance may serve as a starting point for further exploration and may allow the lawyer to think about or research issues in advance. Alternatively, the preliminary information may reveal to the attorney that she is not interested in the case, saving both the attorney and the client the time and cost of an initial interview.

Although surveys do have these advantages, they also have some significant downsides. First, surveys may give the impression that the attorney does not care a great deal about the potential client. In contrast, sitting together face-to-face is a great way for the attorney to show the potential client that she is concerned about the client's problems. If the client is considering multiple firms or attorneys, the client may feel more comfortable with the one that was able to establish a connection. And, as we saw in chapter 7, establishing rapport and building trust will make it easier for the potential client to speak more clearly and to remember and disclose events more completely. Second, to the extent that attorneys rely heavily on surveys, they are more likely to succumb to misconceptions that may be created by stereotypes or the other judgment shortcuts that we described in chapters 1 and 4. Similarly, surveys may tend to lead attorneys to pigeonhole disputes into certain categories, whereas in-person interviews provide the opportunity for the client to give a more nuanced explanation of her situation. A claim that the attorney initially thought involved only divorce may actually turn into a major fraud claim once the attorney learns from the wife that the husband was conspiring with his business partners to hide assets. A request that an attorney help a small business draft its articles of incorporation may lead to the attorney doing other contractual or intellectual property work on the company's behalf over a longer term. While it is true that few, if any, attorneys would rely exclusively on a written survey, the attorney who relies too much on the written survey is at greater risk of missing body language or other cues that might have been revealed in person and may never ask questions that would have been asked if more information were gathered face-to-face. Although we do not urge the abolition of all pre-interview surveys, we do suggest that attorneys consider whether and under what circumstances the benefits gained from such tools outweigh the costs.

Pre-interviews with paralegals or other staff members avoid many of the drawbacks of surveys. In particular, if the paralegal meets with the prospective client in person, she will have the opportunity to read voice and body language clues that might aid her in obtaining a more complete story from the client. Moreover, a paralegal may have more time than the attorney to spend with a client, allowing the paralegal to start building a relationship with the client and obtain more information. If the paralegal is particularly empathetic and good at listening, the paralegal may be even better able to build initial rapport with the potential client than the attorney might be. One family law attorney of our acquaintance who claims that she "do[esn't] do needy" has gone out of her way to hire paralegals who are more empathetic.

Nonetheless, to the extent that the paralegal relies on an interview script and focuses primarily on filling in blanks in a form, the screening interview will have less psychological value. Some clients may expect to or even insist on meeting with the attorney rather than someone else. Moreover, if the critically important relationship is that between the attorney and the client, the attorney will ultimately need to establish her own relationship with the client in order to be an effective counselor. Meeting personally with the client will make a statement to the client that the attorney cares about the client and will likely help ease the client's fears.

An initial phone conversation between the attorney and the potential client can also be useful. Like the written survey, this conversation can save the attorney time and save the potential client both time and money. Unlike the written survey, however, preliminary phone conversations allow some back-and-forth between the attorney and the client and can therefore be helpful in beginning to establish a relationship and build rapport. Of course, attorneys may have other, nonpsychological reasons for deciding that preliminary phone conversations are not a good idea, such as the fact that the attorney is not likely to bill for time spent on such conversations.

Setting the Stage

The typical attorney interviews clients in either a conference room or the attorney's office. Sometimes attorneys interview clients or prospective witnesses in other settings, such as the witness's home, hospital room, or a public restaurant. Does any of this matter?

Most lawyers probably do not aspire to be feng shui specialists, but there are aspects of the physical setting, as discussed in chapters 6 and 7, that have implications for interviews. One of the most critical factors for the client or witness is perceived privacy because many people will not want to share their personal business in a public setting. Thus, the attorney should select an interview locale that is likely to provide privacy in order to facilitate disclosure.[3]

Clients will get an initial impression of the attorney from the waiting area: a neat, attractively furnished, and well-lit waiting room can communicate competence and put clients at ease.[4] If an attorney keeps a neat and comfortable office with diplomas or other awards on the wall, the intimate office setting can be appropriate.[5]

Alternately, attorneys who have messy or otherwise unimpressive offices may want to conduct interviews in a nice conference room.

Regardless of the setting, the attorney should consider offering the client a choice of seating options and should ensure that physical distance is sufficient for the client to feel comfortable. Whereas some attorneys feel that it is always appropriate to sit across a table or desk from a client or witness and others feel it is always best to sit side-by-side with the interviewee, psychological research demonstrates that there is no ideal seating that is appropriate for all interviewees. Instead, seating may need to vary by interviewee, depending perhaps on factors such as the ages, genders, and cultural backgrounds of the interviewee and the attorney. A younger female interviewee may be comfortable sitting next to a middle-aged female attorney, but an older male interviewee might be nervous sitting too close to an unfamiliar female and be more comfortable sitting across a table. Attorneys should use interview settings that have movable chairs and are conducive to alternative arrangements so that they can vary the seating as needed.[6]

Similarly, although many attorneys would probably like to think that is it their brain and not their appearance that is relevant to interviewees, psychological research shows that people's appearance plays an important role in how they are perceived.[7] Perhaps longtime clients will not care if the attorney dresses down, but with new clients or witnesses the attorney must be careful to create a good first impression that builds confidence, establishes credibility, and generates comfort. To some degree, the attorney's style of dress and grooming may depend on his clientele and setting. Attire that works in Hawaii may not play well in New York City, and corporate clients may expect a different style of dress than do entertainers.

Conducting the Interview

Establishing a Good Relationship with the Interviewee

In the movie *Legally Blonde*,[8] Elle Woods (played by Reese Witherspoon), a bubbly student at Harvard Law School working as an intern, helps defend a famous fitness instructor, Brooke Taylor Windham, who is accused of killing her elderly husband. Brooke is not comfortable with the lead counsel, who is unfriendly and insinuates that he believes Brooke is guilty. In response, Brooke is not forthcoming with information, including her alibi. Law student Elle, using her sparkling personality and common interests, talks to Brooke and brings her a gift basket in jail. Brooke comes to trust Elle and is ultimately willing to reveal her alibi to Elle.

What does Elle understand about psychology that the more experienced lawyer does not? It is true that demonstrating competence and expertise in the law is an important foundation for a trusting relationship. And helping clients to understand the terms of the attorney-client privilege will also likely help the client trust the attorney. But expertise and the existence of the privilege will not always be sufficient to create a trusting relationship with the client. Clients also need to know that the attorney cares about the client as a person and is willing to set aside his own personal interests when necessary. Communicating in an open manner, using body language to communicate a genuine concern for the client, demonstrating an understanding of the perspective of the client, and being willing to explain when issues or procedures are unclear can all be important to building a trusting and comfortable relationship. Clients who trust and have a good relationship with their attorney will be more forthcoming in response to the attorney's questions.

Although it may be more difficult to create a trusting relationship with a witness than with a client, establishing some level of rapport and trust with witnesses can also be helpful. The witness who trusts and feels some rapport with an attorney will be more inclined to provide more complete information and may be more willing to make the effort to appear to testify in difficult circumstances. Thus, in working with both clients and witnesses, the attorney should take steps to build relationships, create rapport with the interviewee, build a foundation of trust, and demonstrate an understanding of the interviewee's perspective.

> ✦ ✦ ✦ ✦ ✦
> **Offering a Warm Drink**
>
> Recall that research has found that people holding a warm drink perceive others as having warmer personalities (see chapter 7). Offering a client a cup of coffee or tea can help to create a feeling of rapport.

At the outset of the interview, a foundation of rapport and mutual understanding can be initiated by engaging in a period of small talk that provides an opportunity for the lawyer to get to know something about the interviewee and even for the discovery of shared interests. Rather than being a waste of time, chatting about mutual acquaintances, shared geographical backgrounds, sports, or other comfortable topics can provide the opportunity to develop a connection and increase the client's or witness's level of comfort.[9] Engaging in effective schmoozing of this nature is something of an art form; it requires good listening skills and good memory, and a standard line may not be sufficient for all interviewees. An elderly female client may not warm to a conversation about sports, or, then again, she may happen to be an avid Yankees fan.

Recognizing Differences

Attorneys should also be attuned to the possibility that individuals' culture may lead them to have different preferences than might be natural to the attorney. Some interviewees may, for example, find handshakes or the use of first names to be too informal or may find the straight gaze of many attorneys to be insulting. Even assumptions about physical space and time can vary by culture. Americans typically feel comfortable standing about four to twelve feet apart from each other for personal conversations, but some other cultures prefer either more or less physical space. Regarding time, when the typical American sets an interview for 2:00 p.m., he means that it should commence at close to 2:00 p.m. (except, perhaps, when it comes to doctors' offices?); but in some other cultures, setting an appointment for 2:00 p.m. actually means that it is expected to commence much later.[10]

Attorneys who conduct interviews also need to be aware that people's values and sense of the world may differ, sometimes substantially, with their background. Different cultures may place varying degrees of importance on goals such as maintaining relationships or creating relational capital, protecting autonomy, expanding social networks, achieving justice, saving face, vindicating rights, achieving economic gains in the short or long term, protecting collective interests, or laying a foundation for the future. Clients from more independent cultures may be primarily concerned with their own individual success, with economic outcomes, and with the present. Clients from more interdependent cultures may be more highly attuned to how their behavior has affected or will affect the social standing of the broader group with which they identify, how they are viewed by that group, the joint success of the parties, how relationships are affected, and the interplay between past and future.[11] In addition, a client may be concerned about the "cultural consequences" of her actions, that is, the consequences of "taking steps that are out of her culture's norm."[12] Such differing perspectives may have a significant impact on how clients interpret events, how they seek to resolve problems, and even whom they think should participate in an interview.

So what's a good attorney to do? Is it enough to say, "I don't discriminate and I always act in good faith, so I don't need to worry about any of this"? Unfortunately, this is not good enough. We are not always aware of our stereotypes and expectations, and attorneys who are unaware of cultural differences will inevitably step on toes and miss cues. Yet, at the same time, it is obviously not practical, even if it were desirable, for attorneys to do extensive cultural research on each potential client or witness.

For attorneys, then,

> [t]he task here is to appreciate and respect the differences among your clients, but without resorting to stereotypes or stubborn myths about race, sex, ethnicity, and culture. To ignore likely differences in culture is an invitation to malpractice in counseling; to presume you know what those differences will be once you know your client's race or sex or cultural background is an invitation to dehumanize or reify your client, and to assume generalizations that may not apply to him.[13]

Balancing this task has been referred to as "informed not-knowing"[14] and requires attorneys to have some knowledge of the potential differences among cultures, a willingness to keep an open mind about how another person sees the world, and flexibility in responding to different and sometimes unexpected perspectives.[15]

The most important thing for attorneys to do is to recognize that things they take for granted are not taken for granted by everyone else. Attorneys can also improve their cultural understanding by making it a point to meet with people from other backgrounds or to read books or see movies about people different from themselves. While cultural sensitivity alone cannot solve all cultural dilemmas (such as the client who simply does not think women can or should be attorneys or the attorney who believes that all people from a certain background tend to be greedy), at least the culturally attuned attorney will have a head start on spotting the issues and looking for possible resolutions.

Questioning and Listening

As we discussed in chapter 7, interviews are different from typical conversations in many ways: interviewees are required to provide information that the interviewer already has, asked to repeat themselves, and must try to remember details that are fuzzy. Consequently, as another preliminary matter, attorneys should explain to their interviewees how the interview will be different from the patterns of a normal conversation. Similarly, attorneys can attempt to help interviewees understand from the outset the importance and appropriateness of indicating when the interviewees are not sure about the information that is being requested.

❖ ❖ ❖ ❖ ❖
Guidance on How the Interview Will Proceed

It is important for the attorney to give preliminary explanations so that the client understands the interview procedure.

Attorney: Thank you so much for coming in to discuss your situation, Mr. Min. Let me tell you a little bit about how this interview will work. First, I will ask you to tell me about the problem that has brought you here today. Please give me all the details, even if they don't seem to matter now. Next, I will follow up with some questions. I may ask about matters that seem unimportant. I may need to ask you to repeat some things so that I can be sure I have all the necessary details. And it is possible that I will need to ask some questions that are painful or, at times, even offensive. Please know that if I do so, it is with the intention of helping you rather than causing you any insult or harm. As your attorney, I will need to understand all aspects of your situation. If you don't know the answer to any of my questions, please let me know that; people usually don't remember every detail, and that is OK.

Talking less and listening more, as well as more effectively, will help the attorney to take another person's perspective and build trust and rapport. Most attorneys, like most nonattorneys, probably think that they are fairly good listeners. In fact,

>
> Clients come to lawyers to be heard. In fact, when you deal with your clients, listening is the more important half of the communication equation.
> —Lawrence J. Vilardo[16]

though, many of us do not listen as effectively as we might. In particular, multitasking—such as by formulating the next question rather than listening to the answer already being provided, thinking about how to demonstrate our expertise, glancing at a smartphone or other mobile device, or letting our minds wander to other tasks while the client is answering—can get in the way of effective listening. Similarly, it is easy to be unduly guided by stereotypes and preexisting expectations, placing the client's problems into predetermined categories rather than listening carefully to and exploring the details of the client's situation. To battle these tendencies, attorneys need to try to focus more attentively on their clients and witnesses, paying attention to what the interviewees say and also to their tone and body language.[17]

Once the interview begins, it is easy to become a Socratic law professor, seeking to extract facts as quickly and efficiently as possible. This method of obtaining information, however, is often not conducive to building an effective relationship. In particular, interrupting interviewees' answers is a false efficiency that is likely to prevent lawyers from gathering complete information. As we saw in chapter 7, attorneys tend to interrupt frequently, but psychologists have shown that interruptions disrupt memory and cause interviewees to feel disrespected and to believe that there is a lack of procedural justice. Psychological studies have shown that interviewers can create better rapport and, therefore, obtain more information by engaging in an effective back-and-forth with their clients. Some may choose to use the specific approach of "active listening" advocated by many teachers of interviewing and counseling.[18] At a minimum, attorneys need to establish a friendly and comfortable rapport with their interviewees in order to be effective interviewers.

It is also critically important that attorneys be perceived as listening carefully. Even if the attorney believes that he is exceptionally able at multitasking and can hear the interviewee well while also focusing on another task (a belief that tends to be belied by the research discussed in chapter 1), the attorney needs to realize that if the interviewee believes the attorney is not focusing, he likely will not provide as much information during the interview. Thus, the attorney should use his face, words, and body to show that he is listening carefully and should avoid pen tapping or other nervous tics that might be seen as reflecting boredom or inattention. The attorney should also ask appropriate follow-up questions, resist the impulse to interrupt excessively, and express an understanding of clients' and witnesses' difficult situations.

Addressing Emotions

Finally, attorneys must develop some comfort with interacting with clients and witnesses at an emotional level as described in chapter 3. Interviewees may, for example, be angry, upset, or depressed. Interviews may also trigger emotional responses in attorneys themselves. An attorney who has gone through a nasty divorce may become angry when he interviews a client whose situation is similar.

> ✦ ✦ ✦ ✦ ✦
> ### "I Went to Law School So I Wouldn't Have to Deal with Emotion"
>
> Spouses Helaine and Dwight Golann, a psychologist and a law professor/mediator, conceived the following dialogue addressing the phenomenon of lawyers not wanting to deal with emotion:
>
> Lawyer: The fact is, I sometimes don't feel that I'm being professional when I work with emotions. It's not what lawyers do.
>
> Psychologist: That's interesting—What *does* make you feel as if you're acting like a professional?
>
> L: Dealing with facts and arguments, analyzing issues, generating strategies and, most important, solving problems.
>
> P: Well, those are clearly professional activities, and they are often invaluable to clients. My only concern would be not to rush into them too soon. In an emotional situation—and people who feel that they've been hurt or treated unfairly are often quite emotional—people can't really listen until they feel they've been heard. You might think that you can predict their story because you have heard so many similar ones, but even if you are right, they won't feel heard until they've told it. In fact they may need to review the story with you in order to hear it themselves, and become open to different ways of resolving the problem. Rushing to analyze can get in the way of disputants figuring out what is important to them.[19]

Some lawyers may resist talking about emotions because they think it is "inefficient." Urged in a conference to spend more time on clients' emotional needs, one lawyer reportedly stated, "I don't really have time to focus on my clients' feelings and psychological issues."[20] But, as the lecturer responded, if you are ignoring your clients' emotional needs and concerns, you are not doing a good job as an attorney and not being very efficient after all.[22] Emotions can be useful in providing insights that the interviewee may not directly express. If a client appears to become upset in discussing a particular subject, that may be a hint to the attorney to circle back to that topic later in order to try to uncover additional facts. If a client appears angry or upset about something and has not yet told a story that would seem to provoke anger or upset, the attorney can attempt to seek out the rest of the story. Emotions can also provide important clues

> " The great gift of human beings is that we have the power of empathy.
> —*Meryl Streep*[21] "

about values and goals, particularly those that might be hard to articulate. Ignoring emotions ignores the information contained in them; makes it harder to establish a relationship; and may mean that it takes longer to get the information that is needed, if that information is even forthcoming at all. In addition, a client who does not feel that her emotional concerns have been heard may keep trying to raise them with the attorney, potentially requiring the attorney to spend even more time on such issues. Accordingly, developing some skill in recognizing and identifying emotions, for example, by working from facial or vocal cues, can be quite valuable. While attorneys should not try to convert themselves into therapists, a job for which they presumably have no adequate training, they also should not act as if interviewees' problems can somehow be stripped of their emotional content.

> ✦ ✦ ✦ ✦ ✦
>
> ### Emotional Clues
>
> Ms. Jones goes to see an attorney because she believes she was treated improperly by a police officer. She reports that the police officer gave her a ticket for supposedly running a red light even though she is sure she did not run the light. The attorney notices that Jones seems to be extremely upset about this event, more so than she might have expected.
>
> Attorney: Ms. Jones, you appear to be very nervous or upset by this event. I noticed that as we have been talking, you have been tapping the table a lot and rubbing your arms a lot. Is there anything else that happened that you have not mentioned yet that you want to discuss?
>
> Ms. Jones: Well, kind of, but it is so embarrassing.
>
> Attorney: Please, go ahead. That is one reason we go to attorneys—so we can tell them things we don't want to tell to anyone else and know the attorney will keep the information confidential.
>
> Ms. Jones: Well, it is just that as the officer was giving me the ticket, I swear he was looking down my blouse; and then as I was walking back to my car, he actually reached over and touched my butt.

It is important to remember that emotions are often complex and overlapping. A divorcing client might be both angry and relieved, or even guilty and exhilarated. An attorney who senses that a divorcing client feels relief or even exhilaration may intuit that the client may want to sell the marital house or property in order to move on with his life more completely. An attorney who intuits that a client negotiating a business deal is very nervous may be able to help that client uncover specific concerns that the attorney can help resolve.

> ✦ ✦ ✦ ✦ ✦
> ### Overlapping Emotions
>
> Identifying and addressing a client's conflicting emotions will help to ensure that the client is ultimately pleased with the way in which a matter is handled.
>
> Attorney: I may well be wrong, but I sense that while you are excited about this business opportunity, you are also rather nervous. If I am right, can you try to tell me why you are feeling nervous?
>
> Client: Well, I had not really thought about it that way, but I think you are right that I am nervous. I think this deal is going to pan out great; but it is just that if it goes bad, I will have lost my whole life's savings.
>
> Attorney: That is certainly an important and valid concern. Let's work together to think about any ways we might restructure this deal a bit to reduce the pressure on you. Maybe we can think about finding a way to give you some assurance that the deal will work, or maybe we can find some ways to spread that risk more broadly.

While emotions can often be helpful, it is sometimes the case that an interviewee may be so emotional that it is difficult for him to focus or communicate effectively. In these situations, the attorney may want to try to help the client manage his emotions. As we discussed in chapter 3, neither venting nor trying to suppress emotions is likely to be an effective technique. Instead, the attorney can expressly recognize the emotion and reassure the interviewee that experiencing emotion is normal, while being careful not to reinforce negative perceptions or to encourage the interviewee to generate new justifications for his anger. Instead, approaches such as distraction, reappraisal, deep breathing, or taking a break can be effective. Thus, if an interviewee is very angry or upset, the attorney may want to take a break from the interview, offer the interviewee a chance to take a walk or get some coffee, change the subject for a bit, or even suggest that the client take some deep breaths.

> ✦ ✦ ✦ ✦ ✦
> ### Dealing with a Client's Anger
>
> How an attorney handles a client's anger will impact the interview.
>
> Attorney: So, Mr. Lefkowitz, tell me what brings you here today.
>
> Mr. Lefkowitz: My gd *@&*ing business partner is trying to screw me, that's what. After all these years and everything I have done for him, now he is trying

> to squeeze me out. I just can't believe it, and I am not going to put up with it. I want you to squelch him like a bug.
>
> Attorney: Mr. Lefkowitz, I can see you are still very angry about what happened. That's understandable. This may not work for you, but when I am very angry about something, I sometimes find it helpful to take some deep breaths and think about the ocean for a few minutes. It may sound hokey, but it does actually work for me.

While it is important to be sensitive to interviewee emotions and to read those emotions for clues, attorneys should not become overconfident about their ability to know what someone else is thinking. Recall that studies have shown that we tend to be overconfident in our ability to accurately read others' emotions. Thus, it can be very helpful for the lawyer to check in with the interviewee to verify that his understanding is accurate.

> ◆ ◆ ◆ ◆ ◆
>
> **Dealing with a Client's Feelings of Guilt**
>
> Mrs. Nelson is a mother whose two-year-old child was seriously injured when he fell off some playground equipment. In telling the story, Nelson has emphasized her own failure to adequately supervise her child, leading the attorney to suspect that her guilt over the incident may be leading her to put excessive blame on herself.
>
> Attorney: Mrs. Nelson, thank you so much for that account of how your son was injured. I appreciate that it must be terribly painful for you to retell that story. Nonetheless, I need to ask you to go over aspects of the event once again so I can be sure I understand exactly what happened. Can you start by describing for me in detail the equipment from which your son fell? [Attorney follows up as needed to get more detail.]
>
> Attorney: Can you also tell me whether you recall seeing any signs posted on the equipment regarding the age at which children should be permitted to use the equipment?

Questioning

Attorneys who conduct interviews need to ask questions that are clear and understandable to the interviewee. As we described in chapter 7, a lack of fluency inhibits disclosure, and confusing questions make it difficult for interviewees to give accurate answers.²³ Thus, attorneys must use terms that will make sense to the interviewee and should generally avoid legalese.

When conducting the interview, it is useful to begin with open-ended questions rather than questions that can be answered yes or no or that provide only a limited number of options. Open-ended questions allow the interviewee lots of flexibility in providing an answer, giving clients and witnesses the freedom to tell their story in a manner that makes sense to them and encouraging them to tell a more complete story. Closed questions can cause lawyers to superimpose their own schemas on the interview, making it difficult for interviewees to fully tell their story. For example, asking "What happened next?" rather than "Did the police arrive right away, or did it take a little while for them to get there?" allows the interviewee to provide details that the attorney might not have thought to ask about.

Another advantage of open-ended questions is that they allow interviewees, and particularly clients, to explain their interests and nonlegal concerns. The attorney should not ask the client a question that assumes that a lawsuit should be brought: "What do you hope to get out of this lawsuit?" Rather, the attorney should ask the client to describe her concerns more generally: "What brings you here today?" or "What resolution are you seeking to the problems you have described?" In some instances, a lawsuit may be the best approach; in others, the client would be better served by another approach, such as finding a new job, seeking an apology, taking political action, or bringing her concerns to the media. Similarly, a corporate attorney might use open-ended questions to explore the client's interests and how they relate to various business structures. Even in a criminal case, when representing someone charged with a crime who obviously needs legal assistance, the attorney should probe broadly to determine whether the client's legal needs may extend beyond the initial problem of which the attorney is aware. When clients are permitted to express their desires in a more open-ended manner, new solutions may present themselves.²⁴

Allowing clients to speak fully in response to open-ended questions may also address clients' desire for procedural justice as described in chapter 8. Clients may crave having their concerns heard, even if only by the attorney. The lawyer who cuts off clients unnecessarily, demanding that they "get to the point," may ultimately prolong the battle because clients may be unwilling to settle or resolve their claim until they feel like their complaints have been fully heard. Witnesses, too, may sometimes feel a need for this sort of voice.

Allowing interviewees to tell the story in their own way, and asking broad questions before narrowing in, will also aid memory. As we discussed in chapter 2, witness and client memories are far from perfect, and clients' own confidence in their memories is not necessarily a reliable indicator of the accuracy of those memories. Specifically, asking open-ended questions allows interviewees to provide a level of detail with which they are confident and that will therefore be more accurate. When an attorney requires an interviewee to try to provide more precise details for an event that the interviewee does not remember clearly, the attorney must proceed carefully so as not to tarnish the accuracy of those memories.

> ✦ ✦ ✦ ✦ ✦
> **Procedural Justice in Action**
>
> When one of the authors was practicing law, interviewing prospective clients who believed they might have been treated illegally at work, she frequently had to tell those clients that they probably did not have a claim that it made sense to pursue in court. She often explained that while what happened to the prospective client may have been unfair, it would be hard to prove that it was illegal. She similarly had to tell many clients that while they might have a legitimate legal claim, the financial and other costs of bringing that claim might well outweigh the prospective benefits. Although most clients no doubt would have preferred to hear that they had a viable lawsuit, many of these presumably disappointed clients seemed to leave the office happier than when they had entered. Many stated that having the opportunity to explain their story to an attorney who listened carefully and provided feedback made them feel like they had received some kind of hearing for their claim. This was procedural justice in action.

Attorneys who are familiar with the psychological literature will resist the urge to simply encourage interviewees to better probe their memories. Not only are such appeals unlikely to be productive, but also they are apt to be counterproductive. Attorneys must be very careful not to influence the memories of interviewees. As we saw in chapter 2, it is surprisingly easy to sway people's memories. Asking questions in certain ways can cause people to think that they remember events that never happened. Asking particular questions rather than others can cause interviewees to remember some portions of an event but not others.

So, what is the ethical attorney to do? At a minimum, attorneys must be conscious of the way in which they ask questions so that they try not to inject information that the interviewee has not already volunteered. If the interviewee has not said that the other driver sped through the intersection, the attorney should not assume a fast rate of speed. Let the interviewee tell her story first; then use her own words, where possible, to seek additional information. Be wary of asking interviewees to speculate or guess because once they do, they may begin to think they remember that information. Attorneys can also ask clients and witnesses to retell their story in chronological or reverse chronological order, suggest that interviewees close their eyes as they seek to remember, ask them to focus on details of the setting that may not be directly relevant to the legal problem, and try to get clients and witnesses to focus more on facts

> ✦ ✦ ✦ ✦ ✦
> ## Nonleading Questions
>
> Attorney: Tell me everything you can recall about how the accident happened.
>
> Client: Well, I was just driving down Pecos, minding my own business, when suddenly this big green truck came out of nowhere and slammed into me.
>
> Attorney: Where were you on Pecos?
>
> Client: I was right at the intersection of Wigwam, in the right-hand lane.
>
> Attorney: Which direction were you driving?
>
> Client: I was driving east toward the elementary school.
>
> Attorney: Do you know how fast you were going?
>
> Client: Honestly, no. I would think I was probably going thirty or forty.
>
> Attorney: How fast would you say that big green truck was going?
>
> Client: I really have no idea, but it had to have been going pretty fast.
>
> Attorney: You say you were "minding your own business" when the truck hit you. Do you recall specifically what you were doing?
>
> Client: Actually, I think I was trying to find a decent radio station. That plus looking where I was going, of course.
>
> Attorney: At what point did you realize that the green truck was going to hit you?
>
> Client: I never did, until it happened, so I had no time at all to try to avoid it.

and less on surrounding emotions. Furthermore, attorneys can resist the temptation to interrupt interviewees, disrupting memory and causing the interviewees to omit key aspects of their narration. These devices will not solve all memory lapses but will at least prompt memories that otherwise might have been forgotten.

Attorneys should also be careful as to how and when they use documents to help interviewees enhance their memories. Documents can be helpful in refreshing memory, but documents can also be incomplete or erroneous. If documents are used too early in the interview, they may actually cause clients to forget or neglect matters they otherwise would have reported. Furthermore, they may cause witnesses to "remember"

✦ ✦ ✦ ✦ ✦
Assisting Client Recall

Attorneys can have a huge impact on the kind and amount of recall that a client experiences.

Attorney: Thank you for that description of your meeting with Ms. Bing. You have told me that you do not remember the date when the meeting took place or who besides you and Ms. Bing may have been present at the meeting. However, I am going to ask you do a little exercise with me that some of my clients how found useful in stimulating their memory. I am going to ask you to try to remember a few of the details of the meeting that, while they are not directly related to the lawsuit, may help you remember other aspects of the meeting. For example, do you remember what time of day the meeting took place?

Client: Yes, I know it was first thing in the morning.

Attorney: Do you recall what you or Ms. Bing was wearing?

Client: I have no idea what I was wearing—a suit I assume. But I do have an image of Ms. Bing wearing a black pantsuit and some really spiky red heels. I remember thinking that it was ironic that she looked so good on a day when she was saying such mean things to me. Oh, and I remember she had just taken off her fancy fur coat. I guess the meeting was in the winter; I at least remember that much.

Attorney: Try to envision where you were each positioned in the room. Were you sitting? It may help to shut your eyes as you try to recreate the situation.

Client: Yes, we were both sitting at that little side table Ms. Bing has, across from her desk. I remember she kept fiddling with this little Christmas angel she had on the table, and I thought that was pretty ironic, too. You know, come to think of it, our meeting had to have been right around Christmas for her to have that angel on the desk. And you know what else I remembered is that as we were sitting there, about halfway through the meeting, Mr. Bruce came into the room, too.

something reflected in the document that did not actually happen. Thus, we suggest that attorneys first question clients without reference to documents and then go back and question them again using available documents. While this approach may be more time-consuming, it is more likely to produce a more complete set of memories.

It will also often be appropriate to interview clients and witnesses on multiple occasions. There are several reasons why multiple interviews might be helpful. First, people sometimes experience *reminiscence*—the ability to remember information in later interviews that they were unable to recall initially.[25] Second, there is evidence that retrieval-induced forgetting (see chapter 2) is transient.[26] Thus, temporarily forgotten information might be recalled in a subsequent interview. Third, recall that people in more positive frames of mind are more likely to recall positive aspects of an experience and vice versa (see chapter 3). A client in a patent dispute, for example, may remember different things during her initial upset over the litigation than she is able to remember during later interviews when she is less agitated. Similarly, a client in the middle of a divorce may focus on different facets of his memories when he is feeling angry than he does when he is feeling more optimistic about the future. On the other hand, repeating errors tends to reinforce them.[27] Repeat interviews increase the opportunity for suggestion, so attorneys need to be careful to use high-quality interview techniques throughout the process.

Of course, an interview cannot and should not be conducted solely through open-ended questions, and some interruptions may be necessary. After hearing the gist of the interviewee's story, the attorney may need to ask pointed questions to get at issues not covered in responses to open-ended questions. Attorneys also need to ask follow-up questions to try to get a broader picture because clients' and witnesses' recounting of the "facts" are undoubtedly affected by their expectations, interests, and perspectives. And attorneys will need to probe interviewees' answers to ensure that the interviewees are describing things that they know and not just what they assume based on the kinds of schemas, scripts, or stereotypes that we described in chapter 1 or their assumptions about others' use of such stereotypes. For example, realizing that people have a tendency to blame others' dispositions rather than the situation for bad outcomes (see chapter 1), that a person who feels angry may construe the facts to put more blame on someone else, or that a person who feels guilty may understand the facts in a way that places more blame on herself (see chapter 3), the attorney should be sure to explore the varying potential causes of the problem that occurred. Recognizing that the client or witness may be doing some Monday morning quarterbacking as a result of hindsight bias (see chapter 4), the attorney can ask questions to test whether things that seem obvious in the present would have been obvious in the past. Similarly, as we discussed in chapter 7, direct questions are a good way to discern whether interviewees may be lying.

✦ ✦ ✦ ✦ ✦
Asking About Other Perspectives

Client Linda Loozer, a forty-eight-year-old single mother, has just told a story about how her financial adviser, Barney Bucks, led her to make a series of investments that caused her to lose all of her savings.

Attorney: Thank you for sharing that with me. You and your family must be upset about this turn in your financial fortune. I am really sorry that this has happened. As you know, it is my job to help you think about how your claim might be received by a judge or jury. To do that, we will need to try to think about this situation from Mr. Bucks's perspective as well as from yours. You have told me that Mr. Bucks encouraged you to buy the Shakky Enterprise stock. What specifically did he say about that stock?

Client: Well, Barney said that it was a great stock that he highly recommended.

Attorney: Did Barney mention anything about the investment carrying any risk?

Client: Oh, you know that investment advisers always give you that malarkey about "nothing is a sure thing" and "we can't guarantee any return"; but overall he was very high on the stock, and told me he thought it would bring a great return.

Attorney: Try to put yourself in Barney's shoes for a moment. If we sue Barney for giving fraudulent investment advice, how do you suppose Barney will respond?

Client: Hmm, that's a hard one. I guess he will start out with some choice curse words. But after that, I guess they will just try to emphasize all those mealy-mouthed words that we were just talking about and try to blame the whole thing on me being greedy.

Attorney: Why might he try to blame you for being greedy?

Client: Well, you know that investment advisers always offer the safe choices, and I did not go for those because I made clear to Barney that I needed to get more money for my kids' education. The bonds and things he was offering as the supposed safe choices just were not going to get me the return I needed.

Attorney: I am here to help you and to help you make the decisions that are best for you, but as we do that, I want you to at least consider the possibility that a judge or jury might think you had some share of responsibility for the choice to go with the riskier investment. Can you do that?

Client: I suppose. . . .

✦ ✦ ✦ ✦ ✦
Considering Confirmation Bias

Carl Cementa, a contractor, is worried that Henrietta Homemaker may sue him due to alleged defects in the patio he installed for her.

Attorney: Carl, you have said that you are worried Henrietta may sue you based on what you see as a frivolous claim that her patio was improperly designed. Can you tell me a little bit more about your relationship with Henrietta prior to the time that this dispute arose?

Carl: Ya know, I knew she was trouble from the get-go. Some clients are just a pain, and I need to get smarter about just dumping them early on.

Attorney: Can you tell me a bit more about that? How did you know Henrietta was trouble?

Carl: Well, for one thing, she kept asking me to make minor little changes on this job that was only a small job in the first place. You know how some of these dames are—they just can't ever make up their minds. First they want paving stones, then they want bricks—but, oh, how about gravel? And why not a canopy—can we make that work? No sooner would I give her one proposal than she had five more "what ifs" to consider.

Attorney: For comparison purposes, Carl, can you tell me about one of the clients you have had recently who has been really good to work with?

Carl: Sure. Take Dan Torres. He is a real down-to-earth guy—says what he wants, up front, without a lot of dancing around. Of course, we had to talk a few things through, but it wasn't one of these back-and-forth and back-and-forth deals. I did a pretty similar project for him as I did for Henrietta, but it just wasn't a headache.

Attorney: Ok, thanks, that is helpful. Now let me ask you to do a little thought experiment. Suppose it had been Dan, rather than Henrietta, who had called you to say that he had a drainage problem with his patio. Do you think you would have responded in the same way as you did with Henrietta?

Carl: Well, probably not, because I know Dan is not a flake.

Attorney: Do you think it might be possible that your interpretation of and reaction to Henrietta's report about the drainage was affected by your earlier impression that she was a flake?

Similarly, attorneys need to guard against their own biases and be conscious of how their interviews may be affected by their own preconceptions. An attorney's training and experience may lead her to pigeonhole particular clients or claims into categories based on her prior experiences. While this can, of course, be useful, it can also be dangerous because the assumptions made can sometimes take the interview down a path that misses the mark.

> ✦ ✦ ✦ ✦ ✦
> ### Problems with "Setting the Problem"
>
> Consider the following true story of a medical resident who was called upon to interview a middle-aged man who had arrived at the emergency room complaining of chest pain:
>
> Resident: [immediately upon approaching the patient] Have you ever had heart trouble?
>
> Patient: No.
>
> Resident: Have your parents had heart trouble?
>
> Patient: No.
>
> Resident: How about your siblings or other relatives?
>
> Patient: No, Doc. How come you're asking all these questions about heart trouble?
>
> Resident: Because I think that the reason you are having chest pain is that you are having a heart attack.
>
> Patient: Well, Doc, I think the reason I am having chest pain is that a tractor ran over my chest this afternoon.[28]

To counter her own presumptions, the attorney should consider outside perspectives and ask additional, disconfirming questions to ensure that she is getting a complete picture of the situation. For example, an attorney who practices estate planning may typically represent heterosexuals and therefore tend to assume that all of her clients are heterosexuals. That attorney will want to make a special effort to remind herself that gay and lesbian clients have estate planning needs, too, and that these days a client may be married to a person of the same gender. An attorney who is representing a seemingly well-spoken, middle-class high school student who has been charged with stealing a car should remember that the student may well have some skeletons in her closet. Even if the student reminds the attorney of her own daughter, who never got into any trouble, the attorney will need to ask the student about any prior criminal or disciplinary record, about who her friends are and any problems they may have had, about problems within the student's family, and so on. An attorney who realizes she tends to be more sympathetic to business than to consumer interests should make extra efforts in her questioning of business representatives to ensure that she has obtained all of the information that might be favorable to the consumer's position. Attorneys' preconceptions may also lead them to reject particular cases as not financially viable, whereas upon further inquiry it might turn out that the claim is in fact strong.

Confirming Accuracy

Attorneys always need to remember that the information they obtain in interviews from clients and witnesses may not be accurate. Such inaccuracies can be due to the ways in which clients and witnesses have inaccurately construed events, heuristic thinking, faulty memories, or even lying. What can attorneys do to try to catch or deal with such inaccuracies?

Catching and Dealing with Lies

Attorneys worry, probably with reason, that some clients and witnesses may lie to them. However, whereas some attorneys have great confidence in their own ability to sniff out liars, the literature reviewed in chapter 7 shows that very few of us are in fact able to accurately and consistently detect lying. Thus, rather than relying on our own—likely erroneous—ability to detect lying based on body movement, facial tics, or other mannerisms, it is usually better to focus on keeping an open mind, withholding judgment about the client or witness's veracity while seeking additional information through further questioning and from other witnesses or documents.

To the extent that attorneys feel compelled to try to determine when interviewees are lying, psychologists have shown that they likely need to change their approach. Although many people believe that liars avert their gaze, engage in lots of movement (e.g., shifting position, hand or foot movements), smile, and have more disturbed speech (e.g., hesitation, pauses, slower speech), many of these anticipated cues do not turn out to be associated with lying. The characteristics that do seem more closely linked to lying include offering fewer details, giving accounts that are less plausible and coherent, and speaking with somewhat more vocal tension and higher pitch. However, because these speech characteristics can be present for other reasons (for example, simple nervousness or stress), we suggest that they should be seen as a signal to probe further or to seek additional verification rather than as a reliable indication of lying. And, of course, the lack of these cues is no guarantee that the speaker is telling the truth.

The literature on lie detection also suggests that attorneys can stay alert to changes in the behavior of an interviewee (see chapter 7). While some people simply tend to give more details or speak in a higher pitch, when the pitch of a particular person's voice changes or the level of details that the interviewee provides lessens, the attorney should pay attention and follow up.[29] As we saw in chapter 7, a change in pitch, for example, might signal an increase in tension stemming from deceit. Attorneys can also ask interviewees to tell their stories in reverse chronological order, which increases the difficulty of maintaining a lie and increases the likelihood that any lies will be detected.[30]

It is also important to remember that multiple witnesses often report the same incident quite differently based on their different perceptions, construal, and memories even if no witness is lying. Some attorneys might assume that if three coworkers give three different versions of a conversation that they heard, one or more of them are likely lying. Yet, the psychology-savvy attorney will think about this in a more nuanced way: if three coworkers recount identical versions of the conversation, they may have conferred prior to the interview to agree on key details and cook up a story to tell to the attorney, or they may all be telling the truth; if the coworkers did not compare notes in advance, it is entirely likely that differences in memory, perception, and construal would lead three different honest people to report the same event somewhat differently. Questions designed to more thoroughly explore the stories of multiple witnesses are useful, particularly those that might be unexpected and, therefore, less likely to have been discussed by witnesses attempting to get their stories straight.

Confirming Interviewees' Accuracy

While attorneys do need to be alert to the possibility that a client or witness is lying, we think it is more common that interviewees attempt to be truthful but fail to report all of the relevant details in an accurate manner. For example, positive illusions may lead people to exaggerate their own capabilities, confirmation bias may lead people to make assumptions that are not justified, difficulties with source attribution may lead people to mischaracterize who said what, and schemas or scripts may lead people to fill in details that fit the schema but that did not actually happen. How can attorneys deal with the fact that interviewees, while trying to be truthful, may nonetheless be reporting inaccurate information due to issues with perception, preconceptions, biases, and memory failure? The short answer is that the interviewer should look for confirmation and probe for contrary evidence. As President Reagan famously said in referring to relations with the Soviet Union, "trust but verify."

Even when interviewees seem to be honest and seem to know what they are talking about, attorneys should always attempt to confirm—and to disconfirm—their stories by talking to additional witnesses and by searching out documents, videos, computer records, and other materials that may give an independent report on the events that supposedly transpired. As people more often mislead through omission than by making actual false statements, it is also a good idea to question all interviewees thoroughly and to ask follow-up questions whenever possible to root out omissions. Direct questioning minimizes the likelihood that the interviewee will lie by omission and is more likely to result in clear statements that can then be checked.[31]

If the attorney finds documents or other witness statements that conflict with the interviewee's story, it is important to remember that such discrepancies do not necessarily mean that the original interviewee was lying. The interviewee may merely have suffered a memory lapse, or the other documents or interviewees may be in error. As noted above, to the extent that attorneys use documents to verify an interviewee's veracity, it is best to conduct an extensive interview first in order to elicit the interviewee's complete story before introducing the documents that might or might not be consistent with that story. As we have seen, raising inconsistent evidence late in an interview or even in a later session can be effective at surfacing deception.[32]

Remembering the Interview

Just like those of their clients and witnesses, attorneys' own memories are fallible. Thus, attorneys must take steps to ensure that they accurately record and recall discussions with their clients and witnesses. Attorneys can take notes during or after the interview, ask someone else to be present and take notes, or record the interview session. Recognizing that some methods of bolstering memory may interfere with attorneys' efforts to create a comfortable atmosphere and build rapport or may even destroy the privileged nature of the interview, the trick is to balance the use of aids for memory with the need to establish the necessary rapport and protect client confidences.

For example, if supporting the attorney's memory were the only goal, making video recordings of all interviews might make sense. However, from the standpoint of establishing rapport, many clients may not appreciate the presence of a camera, and the creation of any recording always creates risks of disclosure, notwithstanding the attorney-client privilege and work product doctrine. The discoverability of recordings of interviews varies significantly from jurisdiction to jurisdiction and according to the type of interview.[33] Thus, attorneys would be foolish not to at least take substantial handwritten notes, which most interviewees see as less intrusive and which are least likely to be discoverable. If remembering a particular interview is going to be critically important, it may be worth investigating the desirability of recording the interview given that the attorney likely can't trust her memory to be anything close to perfect.

❖ ❖ ❖ ❖ ❖
Summing It Up

- Set the stage for an effective interview by paying attention to how best to obtain preliminary information from the interviewee and providing a venue that conveys competence and a sense of privacy.

- Create a good working relationship by establishing trust, displaying an understanding of the interviewee's perspective, and taking the time to establish good rapport.
- Effectively gather information by listening well, focusing only on the task at hand; minimizing interruptions; addressing the interviewee's emotions; and working to avoid making unfounded assumptions.
- Ask questions that are understandable, that begin by seeking open-ended responses, that assist recall, that follow up on specific details, and that test assumptions.
- Detect lies by watching for changes in behavior, asking direct questions, making it more difficult for the interviewee to maintain the lie, and seeking both confirming and disconfirming evidence.
- Find ways to effectively support your own memory for the details of the interview.

For Further Reading: Interviewing

Ronald P. Fisher et al., *Interviewing Cooperative Witnesses*, 20 CURRENT DIRECTIONS PSYCHOL. SCI. 16 (2011).

Ronald P. Fisher, *Interviewing Victims and Witnesses of Crime*, 1 PSYCHOL. PUB. POL'Y & L. 732 (1995).

STEFAN H. KRIEGER & RICHARD K. NEUMANN JR., ESSENTIAL LAWYERING SKILLS: INTERVIEWING, COUNSELING, NEGOTIATION, AND PERSUASIVE FACT ANALYSIS (2d ed. 2003).

Martine B. Powell et al., *Investigating Interviewing*, in PSYCHOLOGY AND LAW: AN EMPIRICAL PERSPECTIVE 11 (Neil Brewer & Kipling D. Williams eds., 2005).

Counseling Clients | 10

[G]ood counsellors lack no clients.
—*William Shakespeare*[1]

Imagine a client sitting in a lawyer's waiting room. He may be nervous, angry, or upset. He may be excited about a possible new venture. As he waits for the lawyer to assist him, the lawyer will feel the weight of her responsibility. In this chapter, we examine six important ways in which attorneys can use psychology to improve their counseling of clients: broadening the focus of the consultation, challenging preconceptions, assessing the likelihood of success, choosing among alternatives, dealing with strong emotions, and using persuasion effectively.

Broadening the Focus of the Consultation

Some lawyers have a "tendency . . . to view their clients as walking bundles of legal rights and interests rather than as whole persons whose legal issues often come deeply intertwined with other concerns—relationships, loyalties, hopes, uncertainties, fears, doubts, and values—that shape the objectives they bring to legal representation."[2] Although it is often tempting to compartmentalize a client's problems into a single category, attorneys, by focusing on a particular problem, may fall prey to the satisfaction of search phenomenon (see chapter 1) and be less likely to spot additional issues.[3]

To combat the tendency to pigeonhole clients into broad categories, lawyers should remind themselves that a client may have multiple problems and that the issues that are more salient at first may

> What makes this person different from any other client I've served? What does that mean for what I should say and how I should behave?
> —David H. Maister et al.[4]

not even turn out to be the most central issues. Attorneys may try to spark their own curiosity in their client's situation by varying the way in which they interview the client, challenging themselves to learn more about the client, and reminding themselves that learning about the client's broader situation can help them better represent the client.[5] Attorneys may even want to use checklists to ensure that they inquire broadly about the client's possible legal concerns.[6] Attorneys should also remember that clients' preferences may change over time and that because clients may not even be aware that their preferences have changed, it is unlikely that they will think to apprise their attorneys of the change. Thus, attorneys will want to check in with clients periodically to assess their current desires and needs.[7]

It is also useful to remember that a single problem can have multiple solutions and that others may see the world and those solutions quite differently than we do. Naïve realism (see chapter 1) can cause us to incorrectly assume that our views and values are widely shared, making it difficult to see when a client's preferences diverge from our own. In addition, attorneys, like others, may often rely on lay theories of what motivates other people—theories that are not always correct. While an adviser, believing that her individual preferences differ from those held by others, might discount these presumed motivations when making a decision for herself,[8] she might wrongly allow such presumed preferences to guide her advice to her client.

In particular, it is easy to conclude that clients are primarily focused on money.[9] Attorneys may focus on money because they think it is what most clients want or because they think it is what our legal system delivers best or because monetary relief often helps fund the legal representation. But there is also evidence that attorneys tend to be more analytical and less emotional in their general approach to counseling than are their clients.[10] And, advisers tend to assume that advisees are more motivated by external motivations than is the adviser and, therefore, may tend to privilege monetary considerations over other concerns.[11] Attorneys' distance from the underlying issues faced by their clients may remove them from the interpersonal aspects of the situation and thereby enable them to counsel the client in ways that can avoid some psychological pitfalls. At the same time, however, such detachment may also lead the attorney to focus on the financial aspects of the matter to the neglect of other considerations.

> When a feller says it hain't the money but the principle o' th' thing, it's th' money.
> —Frank McKinney "Kin" Hubbard[12]

Clients, too, are undoubtedly concerned about the financial aspects of their situations. However, research has shown that the range of client concerns is often much broader. In particular, many clients will have a need for information, for justice (procedural, distributive, and retributive), for apology, and for reform that might help others, as well as for other nonmonetary personal satisfaction. Conversely, some clients may be focused narrowly on litigation and beating an adversary in court, failing to recognize that this approach may not serve their own interests.

Whoever said money can't buy happiness simply didn't know where to go shopping.
—*Bo Derek*[13]

✦ ✦ ✦ ✦ ✦
What Did the 9/11 Victims Want?

A study of 9/11 victims who were given the chance to choose between participating in the September 11th Victim Compensation Fund or pursuing litigation found that they made their choice based on factors far beyond merely "satisfying private material ends." Specifically, they sought information, accountability, reform, and punishment. And, as one commentator put it, they saw litigation as a potential way to connect with their community and express their citizenship.[14]

The Quest for Information

Why did the train crash? Why didn't the other company deliver the product as promised? Will the government target for demolition the property that we are thinking of buying? People crave information to help them understand the position they are in, to give them a solid basis for their business transactions, and to simply make sense of their world. Indeed, studies have shown that one of the central reasons people pursue legal claims is to obtain an explanation for what has happened.[15]

Recognizing that clients are often on a quest for information and have a need to obtain explanations, the attorney can counsel the client about the ways in which particular approaches can or cannot provide the answers that the client seeks. Similarly, an attorney might explore with his client the mechanisms by which his client might be able to comfortably provide information to the other side. In other words, attorneys can explain the pros and cons of litigation, in the context of the client's case, as an information-gathering tool. Clients, particularly those who have not previously engaged in litigation, often assume that litigation will allow them to find out the truth and to learn about their opponent's true actions and motivations. They frequently envision a courtroom scene in which their fierce advocate will deftly pry answers from the opponent in cross-examination, as in the famous scene from the movie *A Few Good Men*:

Col. Jessep (Jack Nicholson): You want answers?

Lt. Daniel Kaffee (Tom Cruise): I think I'm entitled to them.

Jessep: You want answers?

Kaffee: I want the truth!

Jessep: You can't handle the truth![16]

However, although the discovery and trial processes do allow for information gathering to some degree, most experienced attorneys would agree that the truth, to the extent there even is a single truth, often remains buried or hidden throughout litigation. Indeed, the adversarial nature of litigation can sometimes block the discovery of information that might have been revealed in a less adversarial setting.

Given the limitations of litigation as an information-gathering tool, the attorney should help the client consider other possible means of obtaining answers: meeting informally with people who might have those answers; participating in mediation; or using nonlegal approaches, perhaps involving the media or governmental entities. For example, a community may fear that a local manufacturer is polluting the air or water. While litigation may be one means to try to determine whether the company's activities are harmful, going to the press or a governmental regulator may prove cheaper, quicker, and more effective.

✦ ✦ ✦ ✦ ✦
A Conversation About the Quest for Information

Client: OK, so I was fired yesterday after fifteen years of service and never a critical performance review. The boss just came to my office, said she was sorry (and, oh yeah, she looked real sorry) and I would need to pack my things and leave immediately. I was pretty much in shock. I asked her, "What? Why?" And she wouldn't say a thing. Just "I'm sorry, your position has been eliminated, and you need to leave immediately." She even said that if I would not leave, she would need to call security. As if I, a sixty-year-old lady, was going to make some kind of trouble that she would need to call security.

Attorney: Wow, it sounds like that must have been a hard experience for you.

Client: What really gets me more than any of the rest of it is why? Why me? Why would they do it? I mean, do they think I stole something? That's how they are acting. Or is this just part of the belt-tightening they have been talking about for

> the last six months? That is why I need to sue. I need to find out what is really going on here and what my options are.
>
> Attorney: I think I understand how you are feeling. When something like this happens and it just seems to come out of nowhere, we have a really strong need to try to figure out why. Let's talk about some of the ways I might be able to help you get that information. . . .

When counseling a transactional client, an attorney can also make good use of her knowledge of the client's quest for information. Clients' desire for information to help them make decisions is understandable and often appropriate. Obtaining accurate information can help clients avoid mistakes grounded in biases and speculation. At the same time, we have also seen that clients who are trying to make decisions may have a tendency to seek information that is not really needed because it will not affect their ultimate decision (see chapter 5). They may seek information merely to confirm the decisions they have already made, in which case the time and money spent obtaining the information is not likely to be well spent (see chapter 1). And, the certainty effect may lead people to seek a degree of confidence that is either not possible or not worth the cost of the search (see chapter 5). Thus, if the attorney senses that a client is hesitating to commit to a transaction because the client does not have complete certainty regarding how the transaction would work out, the attorney might remind the client that complete certainty is rarely possible.

In short, the attorney must help the client find a balance between seeking too little and too much information. We discuss further implications of these phenomena in chapter 12, where we focus on discovery and due diligence.

The Quest for Justice

Explicitly focusing on clients' strong interests in justice (see chapter 8)—whether procedural, retributive, or distributive—is central to effective legal counseling. Just as attorneys may be able to speak to clients' desire for procedural justice through the ways in which they conduct interviews with their clients (see chapter 9), so may attorneys provide clients a sense of procedural justice through the counseling process. To do so, attorneys should listen to the client's point of view, explain the process and the reasoning underlying the advice given, and treat the client with dignity.

> If you want peace, work for justice.
> —Pope Paul VI[17]

Attorneys can also consider litigation clients' desire for procedural justice as they help them consider alternative legal strategies. Specifically, attorneys should recall that their clients may have a strong interest in having their voice heard or in presenting their claims to a neutral, not just in receiving a particular substantive outcome. Some clients will find it very meaningful to have an opportunity to meet with the opposing party in a settlement conference, mediation, arbitration, or trial in order to explain their perspective to their opponent or a third-party neutral. For such clients, it is possible that a monetary settlement cannot entirely take the place of the opportunity to provide their perspective in a setting in which they are treated in a dignified fashion.

Procedural justice concerns can be relevant to business transactions as well. A contractor, for example, might feel better or worse about having her bid on a project rejected depending on whether she perceived the bidding process to be fair. Knowing this, an attorney who is counseling a client about establishing a bidding process would want to help that client create a process that will be perceived as fair by all participants, ensuring that all bids are reviewed in a neutral manner, that the process is transparent, and that all participants in the bidding process have a chance to adequately present their proposals.

Of course, the attorney should also consider his client's desire for distributive justice. In litigation, for example, many plaintiffs and defendants may be concerned about equity and substantive fairness. If an attorney recognizes that her defendant client may oppose a settlement on fairness grounds even though the settlement may be cheaper than going to court and defending against a particular claim, the attorney can use this knowledge to counsel the client more effectively. For example, a company sued for discrimination may resist giving a higher salary to the plaintiff even though the litigation costs of fighting the higher salary may exceed the salary differential. Similarly, some criminal defendants may refuse to plead guilty to a crime they did not commit even if the only sanction would be probation. In the transactional setting, a business may refuse to pay more than $25 per container to its supplier, even though it knows it can't get a better deal elsewhere, if it is aware that the supplier recently gave a lower price to another buyer.

Clients may also have goals related to their sense of retributive justice, that is, a felt need to punish the other party. For example, one family of a 9/11 victim refused to settle its wrongful death claims against the United States and other defendants even though most other plaintiffs had already settled for damages.[18] The family members recognized that settlement would have been quicker and easier but insisted that they were less interested in money than in exposing how defendants' "conscious choice[s]" had led to their loved one's death and holding the defendants accountable for their wrongdoing.[19] Even in a business setting, some clients' strong desire for retributive justice may lead them to choose or avoid particular transactions: "I will never sell my hotel to that bigoted jerk. He should suffer for the harm he has inflicted on others."

Instead of trying to convince the client that her interest in justice is irrational and may cost money or risk jail time, the attorney should assure the client that he understands her justice concerns while helping the client to think about how these concerns relate to her other interests. In some instances, the client may decide to set aside her interest in relative fairness or in exacting retribution for the sake of her own overall payout (see chapter 8). An attorney representing a defendant in a criminal case might help the client consider how her desire for retribution against a codefendant relates to other potential concerns, such as her own well-being or security. On other occasions, the attorney can help the client consider the extent to which retributive or distributive justice might be fairly obtained. For example, a client might want to think about how to make sure someone loses his job or is pursued in a criminal case. Although these remedies might not be available in civil litigation or through a business transaction, a civil attorney can nonetheless help a client think about the pros and cons of making a report to a district attorney's office, sending a letter to a supervisor, publicizing concerns in the press, or taking other steps that could potentially satisfy the need for retribution.

Attending to clients' desire for justice also highlights the need for attorneys to be aware of the potential importance of apologies (see chapter 8). Some clients involved in a dispute may feel moved to make an apology, and others may find it difficult to move forward in the absence of an apology. A business client might feel that she cannot proceed with a transaction unless her counterpart apologizes for a past wrong. A client's desire for an apology may stem from a need to be treated fairly, a need to understand what happened, a need to achieve retribution or restoration, or a need to be reassured that an offense will not recur. A client may feel the need to make an apology due to a desire to acknowledge responsibility or a need to express sympathy. Thus, the attorney needs to be prepared to help the client think through the nuances of apologies, guiding the client in considering both the legal risks and benefits of giving or accepting an apology and any psychological implications of such an action.

In addition, the attorney can help the client assess the sincerity of a proffered apology as well as the logistics of a desired apology, such as whether the apology should be written or oral, whether a private or a public apology is most appropriate, who should author the apology, and how the apology should be worded. Although many clients may not have thought through these issues, they may be critically important to determining the other party's willingness to issue an apology and whether the apology will satisfy the recipient party. For example, a company might be willing to state that it is sorry that an individual was harmed as long as it does not have to do so publicly or as long as it does not need to admit liability. Conversely, the recipient party may place particular value on an acknowledgement of wrongdoing. In some instances, it may be appropriate for both parties to apologize to each other.

The Quest for Reform

Some clients are interested in influencing future individual or institutional behavior. Thus, an estate planning client may be looking for ways to help his heirs make more of themselves, an entrepreneur may wish to leave a legacy to the world, or a civil rights activist may want a juvenile detention facility to change how it disciplines child detainees. Studies of claimants have shown that many are motivated by

✦ ✦ ✦ ✦ ✦
An Apology from Massachusetts Institute of Technology President Charles Vest

September 8, 2000

Dear Mr. and Mrs. Krueger,

I am grateful that Rosalind Williams and I were able to talk with you and come to understand even more deeply your family's unimaginable anguish over Scott's death. Despite your trust in MIT, things went terribly awry. At a very personal level, I feel that we at MIT failed you and Scott. For this you have our profound apology.

The death of Scott as a freshman living in an MIT fraternity shows that our approach to alcohol education and policy, and our freshman housing options were inadequate. I am deeply sorry for this.

Scott's death galvanized us to action. It impelled us to greatly intensify our consideration and accelerate our actions with regard to alcohol, our housing system, and other issues of student life and learning. Starting in 2002, when additional housing has been constructed, all of our freshmen will be required to live for their first year in residence halls. Our approach to alcohol education as well as to policies regarding its use—and their enforcement—have been greatly strengthened. We are building a stronger sense of community and community responsibility. All this takes longer than I would like, and will never be perfect, but MIT is, and will be, a better institution for having undertaken substantial change.

I am a parent, and have devoted my entire career to teaching and academic administration because I believe in young people and in the importance of their education. The death of your son has profoundly affected me. My MIT colleagues and I will continue to apply the lessons of this tragedy and make MIT the better for it.

It is with great respect and personal gratitude that I thank you for the opportunity to meet in person. With your help, I now have a greater understanding of your terrible loss and of MIT's responsibilities to its students and their families.

I understand that you wish to make this letter public. You certainly have my permission to do so.

Sincerely yours,
Charles M. Vest[20]

Before the Kruegers filed a lawsuit, Vest requested a meeting with them to discuss a settlement. At that meeting, Vest apologized. Following the meeting, the case was settled, and Vest issued this formal apology.[21]

prevention of the same thing happening to someone else.[22] Stella Liebeck, who was initially awarded substantial compensatory and punitive damages in her "hot coffee" case against McDonald's, originally wrote a letter to the company stating she had "no intention of suing for unreasonable recompense" but instead merely wanted the company to check and reevaluate their coffee heating procedures and pay some of her medical expenses.[23] Similarly, claimants in cases of medical injury are commonly concerned about effecting changes to underlying systems in order to prevent future injuries, perhaps by requiring hospitals or drug companies to change their procedures or doctors to attend educational seminars.

Understanding these reform goals can prompt the attorney to explain to the client the extent to which different approaches might or might not be useful in achieving such goals. Perhaps a lawsuit will help to spark such reform. If a lawsuit appears unlikely to bring about the reforms of interest to the client, the attorney should discuss with the client other ways to potentially achieve such goals.

The Quest for Other Nonmonetary Outcomes

Beyond their concerns for information, justice, or reform, clients may also care a great deal about things that have minimal or uncertain monetary value. Symbolic gestures, for example, can have important meaning to clients.

✦ ✦ ✦ ✦ ✦

The Gold Watch

Imagine the following scenario: Bobby Rizzo worked for the Percyville Police Department for twenty-nine years prior to being terminated for an alleged abuse of his office. (Rizzo brought the teenage son of a neighbor to the emergency room for treatment of a head injury and incorrectly stated that the boy was his own son so that the boy could receive immediate treatment.) Bobby challenged the termination on various grounds.

Rizzo's attorney assumes that Rizzo is primarily interested in a monetary settlement, the continuation of health care benefits, and the restoration of his pension. These items are indeed of interest to Rizzo, but it turns out that Rizzo also cares a great deal about receiving the gold-plated watch that the department awards to all employees who retire after having completed at least thirty years of satisfactory service. Unless Rizzo's attorney recognizes the importance of the watch to Rizzo, the attorney may lose an opportunity to settle the case on terms satisfactory to Rizzo. While the watch may have relatively little monetary value, it clearly has great emotional import to Rizzo. "It's a pride thing," said Rizzo. "I earned that watch."

> ✦ ✦ ✦ ✦ ✦
> ### Apple and the Beatles
>
> Apple Inc. launched iTunes in 2003, but it was not until late 2010 that music lovers could buy tunes by the Beatles on the site. Why? Because litigation over a trademark—the "apple"—complicated a deal. No doubt the dispute had a significant monetary component, but surely both sides' affection for the apple icon played a role.
>
> A deal between Apple Corps, which was founded in 1968 and holds a variety of rights to the Beatles' catalog, and Apple Inc. (founded in 1977 as Apple Computer) held great promise for both sides. But until the two companies could reach agreement on trademark litigation that dated back to 1978 (shortly after the founding of Apple Computer), finding Beatles tunes on iTunes was not to be. A 1981 settlement between the two sides included a noncompete clause in which Apple Computer agreed not to compete in the music business. But litigation over whether Apple Computer had violated the clause—by establishing iTunes, for example—continued for years. Finally, an agreement in which Apple Inc. took control of the trademark and licensed it back to Apple Corps paved the way toward negotiations over adding the Beatles' songs to iTunes.[24]

Defendants may also have nonmonetary concerns that are not easily translated into dollars. For example, a newspaper publisher may be disinclined to settle cases alleging defamation for fear of diminishing the reputation of the newspaper. A products liability client may make concessions in order to minimize publicity or to avoid bad precedent.

Business clients, similarly, may care a great deal about what might to others appear to be a minor or cosmetic matter, such as the name of a joint venture restaurant or the type of advertising for a particular product or service. Clients' personal history

> ✦ ✦ ✦ ✦ ✦
> ### Cliff Lee and the Philadelphia Phillies
>
> In 2010 renowned baseball pitcher Cliff Lee shocked many when he accepted an offer from the Philadelphia Phillies that paid substantially less than he could have obtained from the New York Yankees. It seems that Lee was attracted by nonmonetary concerns such as his desire to win a championship, his family's attraction to Philadelphia, and his own liking for the Philadelphia franchise. "Boy, he must have really loved those cheesesteaks." said one sports commentator.[25]

Respecting Memories

Consider the ways in which an estate planning client may bring with her a host of nonmonetary concerns:

> A financial adviser came to [psychologist Frank] Murtha for advice about an elderly widow whose money was tied up in stocks from the company where her husband had worked for decades. The adviser wanted her to diversify her assets to lower her investment risk, but the woman refused. The adviser asked Murtha how to get her to reconsider.
>
> "What it boiled down to was that letting go of these positions was letting go of her husband," Murtha says. "The financial adviser was saying, 'You're at risk,' and what she heard was 'Your husband put you at risk.' Once the financial adviser realized this, he could work with his client to acknowledge the loss she felt." He and the client took one of the shares of the stock and framed it, and she was able to bring herself to sell some of the rest.[26]

may enter into what might from the outside look to be "just business." To the extent that attorneys fail to find out about clients' nonmonetary concerns, they may be unable to help their client to successfully resolve a dispute or close a business transaction.

The Quest for Litigation

For some disputing clients, litigation may seem to be the goal itself rather than a means of achieving other goals. Author Bruce Winick noted that

> [c]lients may come to the law office demanding that their attorneys "sue the bastards." They are there to interview the attorney for the role of trial lawyer. Litigation is the goal, and they are ready for war. In interviewing the lawyer, they are not looking for a peacemaker, but for a pit bull.[27]

In such cases, it is possible that the client's litigious posture may have resulted from how she construed the situation or from her fundamental understanding of the role of a lawyer (see chapter 1). The client might be making dispositional attributions consistent with the fundamental attribution error and either not paying enough attention to situational factors or focusing on one actor as the sole cause of a complicated situation. Similarly, the client might be assuming that others clearly see the world as she does and attributing bias and even malevolence to another actor, who instead may have acted out of more benign motives. In such instances, the attorney can sometimes help the client understand that there may be multiple and complex perspectives on a given situation, understand how litigation is likely to work out, and consider the extent to which litigation is and is not likely to serve the client's underlying needs and desires. In other instances, of course, the attorney may simply want to refuse to represent such a client. "With life as busy as it is, and with our personal lives often neglected at the expense of our work, some cases simply are not worth taking."[28]

> ✦ ✦ ✦ ✦ ✦
> **The Client's Frame**
>
> At times it is the attorney's frame that needs to be broadened so that the attorney takes into account the whole range of a client's interests and goals. At other times, the attorney needs to help the client expand his own frame. Consider the following example:
>
> > [A farmer] and his wife decide that they want to retire. They ask their lawyer to transfer ownership of the farm to their three children as equal partners. Specifically, they tell the lawyer that they want her to draft them a grantor retained income trust (GRIT) that during their lifetimes transfers ownership of the farm to their children. They have a friend who did this, they explain, and they hear that the technique minimizes estate tax liability, which is of great concern to family farmers.
> >
> > The lawyer informs the couple that the tax laws have changed so that a GRIT will not achieve these ends. Moreover, in the course of the consultation, she learns that two of the children play different roles in running the farm, reflecting their different interests and talents, and that the third child has moved to New York City and has not been involved in the farm at all. The lawyer points out that the trust and tax issues are relatively minor compared to the questions about how the children will participate harmoniously in running the farm and share in its profits (or losses). She knows from experience with other family businesses that whatever stability in family relations may exist while the parent is actively running the enterprise often dissolves upon the parent's retirement or death. The clients' problem frame—"how do we set up a GRIT?"—failed to capture important dimensions of their actual problem: How should we structure our estate plan to best provide for our children? Helping her clients develop a better problem frame was an important aspect of the lawyer's job.[29]

Challenging Preconceptions

In the 1994 movie *Disclosure*,[30] based upon the book by Michael Crichton, Michael Douglas's character is sexually harassed by his female boss, played by Demi Moore. A lawyer representing such a figure might have had to work to overcome schemas indicating that women do not sexually harass men. As attorneys consider their clients' situations and possible solutions to their problems, attorneys should remind themselves to guard against their own schemas, stereotypes, and other preconceptions. The company that, in the attorney's experience, has always employed honest, hardworking employees may have employed a criminal this time. The individual who lives in a poor part of town and wears inexpensive clothes may be very wealthy. The client who happens to be whiny may actually have a legitimate grievance.

In addition, the attorney may need to help the client get beyond her own stereotypes and preconceptions. For example, a prosecutor working with police officers may realize that a particular officer tends to assume that most or all members of a particular race or ethnicity are criminals. This assumption may not only cause the police officer to wrongly search or accuse innocent people but also cause the officer to miss opportunities to get good information from law-abiding members of the group.

A lawyer may realize, similarly, that a client is potentially being affected by confirmation bias (see chapter 1) in that she tends to see and hear data better when it accords with her preexisting views. For example, an attorney who is advising a local government that is seeking to improve its system for fining parking violators may realize that the mayor assumes that people are inherently dishonest and seek to avoid their tickets by cheating whenever possible. The mayor therefore interprets all nonpayments as deliberate attempts to avoid paying a debt that is due. Yet, perhaps people who have been fined simply lack information as to where to send the payment, are deterred by having to obtain a cashier's check to make the payment, or merely want a chance to tell their story and explain why they believe the ticket was erroneous. Through careful questioning, the lawyer can help the mayor see these possibilities and think about any changes that might be made to the system.

✦ ✦ ✦ ✦ ✦

Sage Advice from Ben Franklin

In his autobiography, Benjamin Franklin explains that whereas in his youth he tried to win arguments by asserting his position with great vehemence, he later decided he could learn from the Socratic method and be more effective by asking questions and being less assertive of his own views:

> I . . . dropt my abrupt contradiction and positive argumentation, and put on the humble enquirer and doubter[,] . . . [later] retaining . . . the habit of expressing myself in terms of modest diffidence, never using when I advanced any thing that may possibly be disputed, the words certainly, undoubtedly, or any others that give the air of positiveness to an opinion; but rather say, I conceive, or I apprehend a thing to be so and so, it appears to me, or I should think it so or so, for such and such reasons[.] . . . This habit, I believe, has been of great advantage to me, when I have had occasion to inculcate my opinions, and persuade men into measures that I have been from time to time engag'd in promoting. . . .[31]

Of course, attorneys themselves may also be affected by confirmation biases. The good news is that there is some evidence that people merely advising others show smaller confirmation biases than people who make decisions for others as well, presumably because they take seriously the responsibility of presenting all sides of the issues. On the other hand, people who are engaged in making decisions on behalf of others show an increased preference for information supporting their position.[32] To combat their own tendency toward confirmation bias, attorneys should remind themselves of the phenomenon; work to provide the client with full information; and, where economically feasible, bounce ideas off of other people less likely to be affected by the same biases, for example, other attorneys in the office, staff in the office, or even people outside the office (bearing in mind client confidentiality).

Attorneys and clients may have preconceptions that range far beyond prejudices and biases about categories of people or other entities. For example, preconceptions about the nature of attention, perception, and memory can impact the way clients or attorneys see their situation and thus may impact the way in which attorneys should counsel their clients. A client who does not recognize the limitations of her own ability to perceive and remember the world may be overly confident that her own perceptions or memories are correct. This overconfidence, in turn, can be an impediment to entering into a deal or resolving a dispute. For example, a client who is "sure" that a business partner failed to make the last three deliveries in a timely fashion might understandably be reluctant to enter into another contract with that partner. Perhaps, though, the client's memories or perceptions are not entirely accurate. Careful questioning, providing counterevidence, and reminding clients that "there are at least two sides to every story" can be helpful. Ideally, the lawyer can lead the client to recognize that all of us have cognitive limits and that many of us have misconceptions about the extent of these limits.

Assessing the Likelihood of Success

One of an attorney's most important tasks is to try to help the client accurately predict his likelihood of success in pursuing or defending a particular claim; in negotiating a successful deal; or in obtaining legislation, publicity, or other results that meet the client's needs. Yet, even with great expertise, no attorney has a crystal ball that enables him to predict the future or assess the cost of a particular approach with certainty. Instead, the attorney must do her best to make accurate predictions by relying on her knowledge of similar situations. Unfortunately, however, both attorneys and clients can be affected by predictable biases as they attempt to make these assessments.

Dealing with Positive Illusions

Lawyers, like their clients, are often overly optimistic about both their own skills in particular and their clients' prospects for success more generally (see chapter 4).[33]

Moreover, lawyers and clients tend to make self-serving judgments about their cases and positions. As we saw in chapter 4, studies have shown that when two groups of attorneys are provided identical hypothetical case files, those acting as the plaintiff's attorneys tend to believe that the plaintiff's case is much stronger than do those attorneys acting as representatives of the defendant. Similarly, lawyers engaged to counsel a business seeking a zoning variance in order to complete a particular construction project are likely to overestimate the chances of positive results. And, like the student who underestimates how much time her homework will take, attorneys will often underestimate the amount of time and effort necessary to accomplish a given task, prevail on any particular point, get a signed contract, or achieve a settlement. It can be hard to step back from these judgments and the role of advocate to offer more objective judgments.

Overly optimistic analyses can be problematic to the extent that they lead attorneys to reject alternatives that might have yielded superior results. Just as a general's overly optimistic predictions about the ease or success of a military invasion may lead to poor decisions, so may attorneys' overconfidence cause them to incorrectly counsel a client to reject a good settlement or deal. One recent study found that during the period studied, 61% of plaintiffs and 24% of defendants obtained results at trial that were the same as or worse than they could have obtained in settlement, and the average cost of such decision errors was $43,100 for plaintiffs and $1,140,000 for defendants.[34] Similarly, the attorney who erroneously counsels the client to reject a contractual offer from one party because the attorney is overly confident about the outcome of a negotiation with an alternate party has not served the client well.

Positive illusions do have their benefits. As we will discuss in the next chapter, the negotiator who aims high will likely increase her odds of obtaining a favorable deal. Similarly, the advocate who has confidence in her client's position and demonstrates that confidence will surely be more help to that client in litigation or arbitration than the advocate who is only able to see the weaknesses in her client's position.[35] Nonetheless, in order to help their clients make good choices, lawyers need to be able to see the options clearly, not just through overly rosy glasses.

To counter positive illusions, attorneys need to be aware that their judgments can be affected in this way and consciously question their own assumptions. It can be helpful, as we discussed in chapter 4, for attorneys to consider the opposite and to try to see the issues from the perspective of a disagreeable adjudicator who is not inclined to favor their side. From this standpoint, a litigator who finds herself believing that her client's claims or defenses are extremely strong should go through the case on an issue-by-issue basis and question each piece of the analysis. Can we really win on Point A? Point B? What evidence do we have? Are the precedents all in our favor? What would the disagreeable adjudicator say? What are the best arguments that favor the other side? As the lawyer goes through each element, she should force herself to play devil's advocate and make arguments as to why the claim, defense, or transaction will fail. One attorney, a litigator and corporate counsel with more than forty years of practice in major law firms, offered this advice:

> The tool that I find most useful at this stage [of understanding a client's position] is the mathematician's practice of inverting the proposal or the tentative conclusion. Write or think through the opposite proposal or conclusion to determine whether it is equally or perhaps more convincing. If so, retreat to the library for more thought and critical analysis.[36]

Another strategy is to consult with others; another lawyer at the litigator's firm who has not been working on the particular project may be able to offer a perspective that is more realistic. Finally, attorneys can take the outside view when making predictions by reminding themselves of the class of similar cases (see chapter 4). For example, in addition to thinking about the unique features of a particular case when considering whether a motion to dismiss will be granted or whether a variance will be obtained, the attorney can think carefully about how such motions or requests have fared in other, similar instances. By considering the opposite and making the contrary arguments, focusing on all of the elements of a challenge that must work in order to achieve success, and taking an outside perspective, the lawyer may be able to shed some of her irrational exuberance.

Lawyers may also need to rein in their clients' positive illusions, and this can be a difficult balancing act. In criminal cases, for example, defendants may often be overly optimistic that the jury will believe their story or acquit them. Attorney Abbe Smith had a client, Kelly, who rejected a plea bargain for a five- to fifteen-year sentence in favor of defending herself against a felony murder charge that presented the possibility of life imprisonment. She rejected the plea because "[s]he could not imagine that the jury would find her guilty when she *wasn't*. It was as simple as that."[37] As we saw in chapter 3, it is quite common for people to believe that their innocence will be transparent. The jury did, however, find Kelly guilty. Similarly, attorney Ian Weinstein had a client who was convinced the jury would acquit him on charges of dealing drugs because he was a nice guy:

> I had replied, "I'm not sure the jury will see it that way, but there is still a lot we don't know about the evidence."
>
> "I know," he responded, smiling, "But I know myself. People like me. No jury will convict me. They don't convict people they like, do they?"
>
> "You're exactly right about that." I told him, "If someone likes you, they believe you and they will try to think of reasons why you are right. But we will have to think long and hard about how to let the jury get to know you. A trial is very different from a social event and even liking some people isn't enough to get over strong evidence."
>
> "They'll like me." . . . [my client] said to himself, as much as to me, "They won't convict me."[38]

In such instances, one of an attorney's most important functions is to serve as a voice of reason, telling clients when they are being unrealistic about their likelihood of success in their pursuits and saying no when appropriate.

> ✦ ✦ ✦ ✦ ✦
> ### Conveying Bad News
>
> Asking questions can be an effective strategy for delicately conveying an unpleasant assessment. One law partner said,
>
> > Where a client has a really weak case . . . and I know it's going to be an issue, instead of saying to the client, well I think you fucked up here, I'll say . . . I know this is going to be an issue. How would you respond if you are asked this?
>
> Similarly, the attorney can make it clear that the legal risks that the client faces do not necessarily reflect the moral value of the claim or the attorney's personal view of whether or not the client was wronged.[39]

This role can be challenging. One observer termed the difficulties that some lawyers experience in giving clients the straight story *the curse of compassion*.[40] However, attorneys need to make a special effort to explain potential risks and downsides clearly and to try to make sure that clients are not just hearing the positive and tuning out the negative. "It's human nature for us to want to hear good news when something bad has happened."[41] In breaking bad news or saying no to a client, attorneys must be clear. If the attorney is not clear, the client may not hear the no. Saying that "this course of action may have some risks" may not get through to a client who strongly believes that what he wants to do is wise, profitable, and ethical. Thus, the attorney will need to be explicit: "If you structure the deal in the way that has been proposed, I see a significant likelihood that you and your firm could be accused of fraud."

At the same time, a client may feel that an attorney who spends too much time warning of downsides will not be a successful advocate. To be an effective counselor, then, the attorney must be respectful of the client, listen to his point of view, provide the reasons underlying her assessment, tailor her message to her client's needs, and listen carefully to the client to discern whether he has or has not heard the downsides described by the attorney. An attorney who is credible and who retains the trust of her client will be more successful in conveying disappointing news (see chapter 7). We have repeatedly seen lawyers and accountants who are unable to walk this line brought down in scandals, such as those surrounding the demise of Enron.[42] Of course, attorneys will sometimes need to disassociate themselves from a client who is intent on a course of action that is illegal or unethical. We will return to these difficult matters in chapter 14.

> ✦ ✦ ✦ ✦ ✦
> ### Weighing Benefits and Risks
>
> It is important for the attorney to make sure that the client is aware of the reality of his situation, which means being frank about any weaknesses in the case.

> Attorney: Ms. Employee, I have heard your account of the way you were treated at work. As you explain things, it certainly sounds like you were treated very unfairly. It seems that you have endured a very difficult set of events, and I understand why you are hurt and angry. I see why you would like to bring a lawsuit in order to prove that you were wronged and prevent others from being similarly mistreated. Unfortunately, I have to tell you that from a purely legal perspective, there are some potential weaknesses in your claim. First, in our jurisdiction, employment is called "at will." That means that, in general, an employer can fire an employee for a good reason, a bad reason, or no reason whatsoever as long as that reason was not discrimination on the basis of something like race, gender, or age. Now I know that you believe that you were in fact discriminated against, but our challenge will be how to prove that in a court of law. We will need to present your case using the witnesses and documents we can find. The reality is that some of those witnesses may not tell the truth because they will be afraid of losing their own jobs. And even if helpful documents exist, they are in the company's files and may not be accessible to us. On top of it all, the law requires us to prove discrimination rather than requiring your employer to prove lack of discrimination. So, we have to assess the positives and negatives of bringing a claim in light of these factors. I am not saying that you should not bring a lawsuit. Indeed, I am ready to represent you should you decide to make that choice. But I want you to think through the likely benefits and risks carefully and make the decision that you think will be best for you.

Finally, attorneys may sometimes want to enlist third parties in conveying bad news to their clients. For example, an attorney who needs to say no to a client may want to let her know that another attorney or another department within the firm has raised concerns regarding the proposed transaction. Similarly, an attorney who needs to convey bad news to a client may find it helpful when an early neutral evaluator,[43] mediator, or opposing attorney highlights the weaknesses in the client's position. In this way, the attorney can maintain the client's trust in her as an advocate while providing an opportunity for the client to consider the risks of her position.

✦ ✦ ✦ ✦ ✦

Using Third Parties to Convey Bad News

> Attorney: I support you and your case, but I think that we do need to take seriously the issues raised by our early neutral evaluator. Mr. X is a very experienced attorney in this area and has a good feel for how these cases tend to be resolved.

> He has highlighted a number of weaknesses in our position, and we need to think about what those mean for how we want to proceed.

Dealing with Availability and Anchoring

As lawyers and clients assess the likelihood of success of a particular claim or venture, they will often be strongly influenced by information that is highly available in their minds.

> "Once you tell a client the value of a case, he or she will never forget it."
> —Mark Wolfe[44]

Imagine, for example, that a particular lawyer, A. Terney, has brought many employment discrimination suits against various local employers. Assume further that one of those claims, brought on behalf of Missy Mintz against Jones Construction for sexual harassment that occurred over a period of five years, recently went to court and resulted in a $2 million award for Mintz. This is, by far, the most successful of the discrimination claims that Terney has brought. Most of the other employment discrimination claims that Terney has brought have settled for amounts less than $100,000. The one other claim brought by Terney that went to court in the past five years, a claim for age discrimination, resulted in a defense verdict. Shortly after the large Mintz verdict was handed down, another employee, Cindy Lewis, consults with Terney regarding her possible claim of gender discrimination against employer Mitchum Construction. Although the availability of the Mintz verdict may highlight the possibility of a high award, both the attorney and the client need to be careful not to be excessively influenced by that result. The Mintz claim was brought by a different plaintiff against a different construction company and involved different facts. While the recency and the vividness of the Mintz verdict may cause it to be foremost in the minds of Lewis and her attorney, both should consider that verdict as only one of many results in employment discrimination cases, including those in which plaintiffs had less success.

Similarly, attorneys need to be sensitive to other anchors that might serve to fix clients' expectations and predictions (see chapter 4). Such anchors, including jury verdicts in other cases or sales figures from other transactions, might come from media reports, well-meaning friends, prior experiences, or other sources. In particular, attorneys need to be careful about providing early assessments or other information that might anchor clients' perceptions, expectations, or choices. We have seen that it is difficult to adjust away from such salient figures even where those figures clearly have no basis in reality (such as whether the temperature in San Francisco is in excess of 558 degrees!). So, imagine the significant impact that numbers provided by attorneys can have on their clients during the course of a counseling session. If an attorney says to the client, "I would hope to be able to get you a price in the

> ✦ ✦ ✦ ✦ ✦
>
> **Keeping Client Expectations Realistic**
>
> Attorney: You have asked me to give you a sense of how this claim might fare if we were to file a complaint in court, and I will do the best I can to answer your question. Unfortunately, my experience is that it is almost impossible to make these sorts of predictions at such an early stage of representation. The strength of your claim and the response we receive will likely depend in part on both facts and law that we have not yet investigated. You have told me the story, from your perspective, as best you can, and I find it a very compelling story. But as we go on to pursue this claim, we will learn more and more. We will not only learn more about what different people believe happened, but we will also learn more about who is willing to testify, what documents still exist, what insurance is available, the extent of defendants' assets, and how the other side intends to respond to our initial claims. For now, I can tell you that most claims are ultimately resolved before trial, whether in a settlement, in mediation, or on the basis of pretrial rulings. It is often good that cases settle because trials are always a huge gamble and are time consuming and expensive.
>
> Client: I understand all of that, but I would still like you to give me at least some kind of estimate of what I could win in a settlement or in court. How else can I decide whether to pursue this matter?
>
> Attorney: Sure, I appreciate that. Let me at least tell you what I would initially ask for on your behalf if you were to retain me to handle this matter. We know that your BMW, worth $20,000, was totaled in the accident; and we know that you suffered a strained wrist, which, fortunately, now seems to be mending well. If I were to represent you, I would seek compensation for the loss of your vehicle, for the cost of your medical treatments, and for the pain and suffering you have endured. I can promise you that I and everyone else in my office will work as hard as we can to get you all available relief. But, beyond that, we will need more time to see how this dispute develops. And you should know that plaintiffs very rarely get everything they seek in either litigation or settlement. I hope you give me and my firm the opportunity to work with you on this matter. If you are ready, we can move on to discuss what our financial arrangements might look like.

neighborhood of $30,000," it is likely that the $30,000 figure will provide a readily accessible anchor point for the client even though the attorney's statement was fairly noncommittal and not meant as a guarantee.

Such anchoring may later prove problematic for the relationship between the attorney and the client and for the process of decision making. If information learned later in the representation leads to the conclusion that a price as high as $30,000 is highly unlikely, the client may be disappointed or angry, refuse to enter into a settlement for a lower amount even though it would serve her best interests, or even seek new representation.

Dealing with Hindsight Bias

As we discussed in chapter 4, once people know the outcome of an event, they have a tendency to believe that they would have predicted that outcome. Thus, in hindsight, people have a tendency to believe that a bad outcome was more foreseeable (and, thus, possibly more preventable) than they would have believed in foresight. As a form of Monday morning quarterbacking, this hindsight bias can lead clients to believe that it is obvious that an actor should have known that his actions would cause harm. The best way for attorneys and clients to attempt to rid themselves of hindsight bias is to consider a divergent outcome and rethink the inferences made. That is, people who want to make sure that they are making an objective assessment of whether British Petroleum (BP) was negligent in failing to take steps to ensure that the blowout preventer used in the Gulf of Mexico was functioning properly could ask themselves whether they would have assessed BP's actions differently had a major spill not occurred. After all, while the fact that a major spill occurred is evidence that the blowout preventer did not function properly, the mere fact of malfunction does not mean that BP was necessarily negligent with respect to the blowout preventer. Rather, the proper question is whether BP took reasonable steps to ensure that the blowout preventer was working properly prior to the blowout.

Hindsight bias can also influence the decisions of judges, arbitrators, and juries.[45] While rules of evidence or substantive law sometimes minimize the impact of hindsight bias, for example, by allowing defendants to show that the approach they took was customary in the field, the reality is that hindsight bias may play a role in the decision of a judge or a jury. Thus, hindsight debiasing may not be necessary for the purpose of making an accurate prediction of how the legal system would likely assess a particular claim or defense. In fact, it is possible that lawyers who try to completely rid themselves and their clients of hindsight bias might actually be less effective at predicting case outcomes than those who did not. But hindsight debiasing may nonetheless be particularly helpful when attempting to reach common ground in negotiations (see chapter 11). Settlements can be hindered by antagonism toward an opponent as well as by disparate predictions regarding trial outcomes.

Dealing with the Representativeness Heuristic: The Gambler's Fallacy

Sometimes attorneys need to counsel clients who have fallen under the influence of the gambler's fallacy. Just as some people mistakenly believe that if the coin flip has landed on tails ten times in a row, it is now due to land on heads (see chapter 4), so may a corporate client express the view that having recently lost five workers' compensation claims, it is due for a victory in the sixth. The attorney can help the client make a more accurate assessment by carefully explaining that the losses in the earlier claims would not make the client more likely to win this claim. Indeed, if the claims had anything in common, those prior claims could possibly be used, by plaintiffs, to support arguments in the pending matter.

Choosing Among Alternatives

One of an attorney's most important counseling tasks is to help clients choose among various alternatives. In helping clients make such choices, some attorneys are quite *directive*, explaining that it is their duty to provide clients with the "right" answers regarding how to handle their issues. Such attorneys may tell clients "this is what you need to do" or "this is what I suggest you do." Other attorneys are more *client-centered*, believing that attorneys need to be solicitous of their clients' special needs and interests because certain answers may be right for some clients but not for others. Such attorneys provide information but ask their clients to make the ultimate decision.[46] Attorneys' perspectives on this important issue appears to vary by practice area, with criminal defense attorneys being more directive than corporate attorneys, for example.[48] Attorneys with either leaning can benefit from greater understanding of the psychology of choice. As we saw in chapter 7, advisees tend to value a variety of different types of advice, including advice that provides information about the available options, advice in the form of a recommendation, and advice about how to structure the task of decision making.

> It is not enough for a professional to be right: An advisor's job is to be helpful.
> —David H. Maister et al.[47]

The Decision-Making Process

Attorneys, whether by character or training, often aspire to a highly reasoned decision-making process in which decisions are made after obtaining full information. While decision making based on full information and abstract logic has its benefits, we have also seen the limits of such an approach (see chapter 5). Obtaining full information may be too costly and time consuming to pursue in all instances, making satisficing a more realistic goal. Reasoned analysis can privilege easily quantifiable interests over those that are equally valid but hard to measure. Some reliance on emotion is essential to the process of decision making (see chapter 3).

Clients, too, will have their own preferred approaches to decision making: some clients will rely on instinct; some clients may view a decision from either a promotion perspective (trying to make decisions that ensure positive outcomes and take advantage of opportunities) or a prevention perspective (trying to make decisions that minimize harm and avoid mistakes); some clients will have a deep need for closure, and others will be much more comfortable with suspending judgment, considering other perspectives, and entertaining alternatives; and some clients will be inclined to avoid making a decision at all (see chapter 5).

Matching the decision-making process to the client's preferred approach can make the client more engaged in and satisfied with the process. Thus, attorneys should attempt to strike a balance in which they respect the value of these different decision-making processes while at the same time engaging the client in a deliberative process. For example, a lawyer might remind the client that a particular decision is hers to make and ask the client if she would find it useful for the lawyer to help her work through an analysis of the costs and benefits of the various options.[49] The attorney can help promoters to also think about possible future harm and help preventers to also consider possible future benefits. And the attorney can explain to the client the consequences of avoidance or delay and can impose deadlines to help clients make decisions.

Tendency to Gather Irrelevant Information

Remember the protestors who initially preferred to settle with the university even when they were told up front that the university would not discipline them for protesting, but who ultimately decided to protest rather than settle if they instead learned later that protesters would not be disciplined (see chapter 5)? As we have seen, people have a tendency to keep seeking information even when that information is irrelevant. And once people have gone to the effort of gathering it, even previously irrelevant information suddenly gains a significance that it did not have before. Gathering information is often essential to support good decisions. Yet, as we will discuss further in the context of discovery and due diligence (see chapter 12), lawyers need to gird themselves against this quest for irrelevant information to avoid overinvesting in investigation and discovery while putting off decisions that can be made sooner rather than later.

The desire for more information can also tempt clients and lawyers to keep options open as they attempt to learn more about their available opportunities. As we saw in chapter 5, however, the tendency to keep options open, like the tendency to seek additional information, can sometimes lead to nonoptimal decisions and can delay the process of psychologically adapting to a decision. Sometimes it is best to proceed with a decision even without gathering all of the information that could be relevant.

✦ ✦ ✦ ✦ ✦
Assessing the Relevance of Desired Information

Client: I am trying to figure out what to do with this proposed leasing agreement. We have been leasing our executive golf carts from Carly's Carts for five years and have only been moderately satisfied with the product. At $3,200 per month for twenty carts, the price is right. But the carts break down so frequently that we are often short, which can be embarrassing. We could go with this offer from Superior Carts at $3,300 per month for twenty-five carts with their special money-back guarantee. But, they want to lock us in for a year, whereas we are month to month with Carly's. Or, we could just buy our own carts and solve the problem that way. My real problem is I feel like we don't have enough information. Aren't there a lot more cart companies out there? And can't we find out more about the repair records? It would also be good to know things like how much our employees and guests use the carts, whether the people who use the carts are disabled or just lazy, and whether the carts actually save employee time as we originally envisioned. So, my inclination is to continue renting from Carly's while we keep these other options open. What do you think?

Attorney: From what you say, the Carly's option does not sound particularly desirable. Although the carts are cheap, they break down a lot and have caused you problems. To me, it sounds like this would be a good time either to lease from a different vendor or to purchase your own carts. I understand your desires to keep your options open with the month-to-month lease, and to gather more information; but in my experience it is often possible to make a bad choice due to trying to keep all options open or seek out endless information.

Client: Why isn't it better to keep my options open?

Attorney: There is nothing per se wrong with keeping options open, but the problem here is that it comes at a cost. You have to keep the contract with Carly's, which you yourself have said is not a good contract.

Client: And why wouldn't we want to get all the information possible so that we make the best decision?

Attorney: Information is usually good, and you may want to gather some additional information, such as finding a few more competing bids. But some of the information that you stated you wanted may not actually be relevant. For example, you said you wanted to know who was using the carts and why. But if you learned that your employees were using the carts because they were lazy rather than because they were disabled, would that really cause you to get rid of the carts? Or might you decide to keep the carts because otherwise your employees would complain or fail to get their work done efficiently?

Client: Hmm. I am starting to understand what you are talking about. Maybe we should just bite the bullet, get some bids, and find the best deal we can now.

Presenting Options

As we saw in chapter 5, the way in which options are presented will affect the attractiveness of these options to both attorneys and clients. While it is not surprising that people prefer gains to losses, what is more remarkable is how easily our preferences can be swayed by presenting identical choices as either gains or losses. We have seen that framing can influence decisions as widely varied as settling a civil case and choosing a disease control strategy. Similarly, obtaining a particular price in the sale of a property can be viewed as either a gain or a loss, depending on the point of comparison. Consider a property in Las Vegas that was purchased for $200,000 in 2000, was assessed at $400,000 in 2007, and is now being offered for sale in a real estate market that has declined a great deal since 2007. If the seller can get $240,000 for the property, she might view that as a gain relative to the initial purchase price in 2000 and relative to the prices that others are getting in a poor market. On the other hand, if the seller views the $240,000 relative to the property's high-water price in 2007, she will view the proposed sale as a loss and perhaps insist on holding onto the property until its value rises closer to that level.

The attorney also needs to be careful about the way that she characterizes a client's options. By placing relatively greater emphasis on the pros or cons of an option, the attorney can significantly impact the client's decision. For example, imagine an attorney discussing the development of a new internal dispute resolution procedure with his corporate client. If the attorney highlights the procedure's potential for dramatically cutting punitive damage awards and decreasing the average payment per claim, the procedure will sound very attractive. Yet, if the attorney focuses on the new system's potential for increasing the number of payouts to claimants, the procedure will not sound as desirable. Thus, the attorney must work to be evenhanded in presenting both the pros and cons of a particular choice.

◆ ◆ ◆ ◆ ◆

Counseling Mrs. Jones

Ethicist and law professor William Simon once had a client, Mrs. Jones, who was charged with leaving the scene of a minor traffic accident without stopping to identify herself. Jones, who was African American, insisted that she was innocent of this infraction and that in fact it was the other driver, who was white, who falsely accused Jones. The evidence supported Jones's version of the facts, and she believed she was a victim of racism.

The prosecution offered a deal in which Jones would plead nolo contendere and receive a disposition of six months' probation. Simon gave Jones the choice of taking the plea or going to court, made it clear that the decision was hers to make, and ended the conversation by stating, "If you took their offer, there

> probably wouldn't be any bad practical consequences, but it wouldn't be total justice." Jones immediately stated that she wanted to go to trial.
>
> A few minutes letter, according to Simon, Simon's friend, a more experienced attorney, reopened the conversation with Jones:
>
>> He didn't tell her what he thought she should do, and he went over the same considerations I did. The main differences in his presentation were that he discussed the disadvantages of trial last, while I had gone over them first; he described the remote possibility of jail at slightly greater length than I had; and he didn't conclude by saying, "It wouldn't be total justice." At the end of his presentation Mrs. Jones . . . decided to accept the plea bargain.[50]
>
> Clearly, the way the choices were characterized made a huge difference. As Simon characterized the options, Jones would lose justice by accepting the plea bargain, whereas Simon's friend characterized the same option such that Jones would gain peace of mind by accepting the offer.

The structure of the decision-making process itself can also influence clients' choices. We saw that when people are choosing among options, they tend to focus on the comparative positive attributes of the options; whereas when people are asked to reject one of several options, they focus more on the relative negative attributes of the choices. Thus, the way in which the attorney characterizes the decision-making process can impact how the client will see her choice.

Accordingly, attorneys need to be alert to the characterization of options as gains or losses or as opportunities to choose or reject options and consider both frames. Attorneys should be alert for instances in which clients, opposing attorneys, or others state that a particular option will allow someone to win, advance, gain, save, or come out ahead. The attorney should ask herself whether that same option might be reframed as a loss, a failure to win or advance as much as possible, or an expenditure. Similarly, if a particular option has been presented as a loss to be avoided, the attorney should consider whether there is a way to reframe that potential loss as a gain. Because neither a gain nor a loss characterization is necessarily right or wrong, the attorney should try to view the choice from both perspectives before trying to help the client decide which choice is preferable. Similarly, the attorney should try to use both choosing and rejecting verbiage when possible so that clients examine both the positive and negative attributes of their options.

It is similarly useful to be aware of the high value that people often place on what they already possess. We learned in chapter 5 that people tend to prefer the status quo to a change and that they may value a current endowment simply because it is theirs. Recall that students who randomly received mugs in an experiment

> ✦ ✦ ✦ ✦ ✦
> **Discussing Options**
>
> Client: I need your help in deciding whether to take the severance package they are offering. Human Resources says that I can increase my pension benefits by 15% if I retire now instead of waiting another two years as I had originally planned.
>
> Attorney: [hears alarm go off in her head] OK. As it has been presented, that does sound enticing, and it may ultimately be the right choice for you. But before we evaluate the package, let's make sure we understand all the aspects of the option they are offering. We will need to consider not only the increase in your pension but also the decrease in your earnings over the next two years, how much your pension would increase if you were to keep working, how all of this will affect your health insurance and any other benefits, and, of course, how you feel about retiring instead of working. That is, we have to compare their offer to what you would receive if you continued working, as well as to what you would receive if you retired now without the severance package.
>
> In this counseling session, the attorney recognizes that while the Human Resources department has chosen to emphasize the gain side of the offer (increased pension benefits), there also may be loss aspects of the offer that need to be considered.

perceived the mugs as more valuable than students who did not receive a mug (see chapter 5). Yet, through discussion, the attorney may help the client to see that trading a current entitlement for something new may actually bring the client greater monetary or other benefits.

> ✦ ✦ ✦ ✦ ✦
> **Selling the Farm**
>
> Client: I can't even think about selling the farm. It has been in our family for three generations, and it is part of our heritage. My grandmother would probably rise out of her grave and kill me if I sold the farm. Plus, I still think farming is going to make a great comeback in this area as soon as the economy turns around.
>
> Attorney: I hear you, and certainly I don't see it as my role to convince you that you need to make the sale. If you decide that holding onto the farm is your best

> option, then that is what we will do. As you think about it, you may want to consider what would happen if you did sell the farm. Ms. Lazarus has offered $1.5 million for the farm. If you were to make that sale, you would net $300,000 after paying off the mortgage and your other bills. What do you think you would do with that money? Another way to think about this is to imagine that you did not own the farm at all but did have $1.5 million. Would you buy the farm, or would you do something else with that money?
>
> Client: Well, I know what my grandmother would say. She would want me to put it toward paying off our house and toward the kids' college education.
>
> Attorney: OK. So how do you compare those options—keeping the farm and continuing to operate it, or making payments toward the house and the college funds?
>
> Client: Hmm. It is not such an easy decision. My grandmother did believe so strongly in maintaining economic security and in education. Maybe she would be OK with me selling the farm. I have to think about this a bit more. . . .

Sunk Costs

As we saw in chapter 5, most of us have a hard time accepting that it is sometimes best to cut our losses, recognize that certain costs are simply sunk, and move on without trying to recoup those costs. Attorneys will be more effective if they can bring themselves to accept certain costs as sunk in their own practice (deciding, for example, that it no longer makes sense to invest resources in a case that appears weak) and also if they can help their clients to understand that some losses are best forgotten.

> About half the practice of a decent lawyer consists in telling would-be clients that they are damned fools and should stop.
> —Elihu Root[51]

Imagine, for example, a very angry client who consults an attorney because she believes she was defrauded in a deal with a former friend. The client, Sue Ellen Bates, explains that her friend Louanne sold her a car that turned out to be a real lemon. The car cost $4,000, and the mechanic says it is not safe to drive and probably not repairable for less than $3,000. Louanne had assured Sue Ellen the car was in great shape.

Unfortunately for Sue Ellen, the amount at stake in this dispute is so small that it may not make sense to hire an attorney to take the case. Were Sue Ellen to pay an attorney by the hour to handle the case, the attorney fees might well exceed the amount in dispute. Those attorney fees would not likely be recoverable as part of the litigation. Moreover, most attorneys would not want to handle a matter like this on a contingent fee basis. Thus, without necessarily using the term, the attorney may need to explain the concept of sunk costs to Sue Ellen.

> ✦ ✦ ✦ ✦ ✦
> **Dealing with Sunk Costs**
>
> Attorney: From what you say, it sounds like you were treated badly—and possibly even defrauded—by Louanne. It must be disturbing to think you have been mistreated by your own friend.
>
> Client: It really is. I am so angry and sick about this that I have been yelling at everyone in my life for the last two weeks. I need to find a way to make Louanne pay for what she did.
>
> Attorney: Unfortunately, I am not sure that it makes economic sense to retain me to file a lawsuit regarding this matter. If I took this case, I would have to charge my regular hourly rate of $150 per hour, and it would not take long before I would have run up a bill of another few thousand dollars. In our legal system, even if you win, you would be responsible for paying my fees. And although I know that you feel that you have lost quite a bit of money in this transaction, there is not enough money at stake for me to be able to handle this case on a percentage or contingent fee basis.
>
> Client: So what does that mean? She cheats me and she just gets away with it? I can't let that happen.
>
> Attorney: Well, you do have some options besides hiring me to represent you. For example, you could file a lawsuit on your own, without representation. You could do this in small claims court, or, if Louanne agreed, you could try to resolve this matter in mediation through our Neighborhood Justice Center. I can give you some information about both of those options if you are interested. But hiring me to represent you in this matter would basically just throw good money after bad. Even if you won the claim, you would end up owing me money.
>
> Client: But how can I just let her get away with this?
>
> Attorney: You don't have to let her get away with it. You can pursue the options we have discussed, including hiring me to bring a lawsuit. But you do need to understand that bringing a lawsuit could be costly in the ways we have discussed. Sometimes it is best to just cut your losses and walk away.

Comparison of Options

We have also seen that the ways in which an option is considered in the context of other options can diminish or heighten its attractiveness (see chapter 5). Just as customers in a camera store or auto dealership tend to opt for the midprice choice, so, too, may clients avoid extreme options and select the seeming middle choice (the compromise effect). Similarly, we have seen that the contrast effect leads people to value a particular option more highly if a new option is added to the available choices that is similar, but inferior, to that option. Furthermore, option devaluation leads many of us to value an option more highly when considered on its own than when considered among other options. Recall, too, that some options are more easily evaluated in comparison to a set of alternatives but that it can also sometimes be useful to think about how a decision will be experienced in the absence of salient information about comparisons.

❖ ❖ ❖ ❖ ❖

Investment Gone Wrong

Imagine a scenario in which an investor has gone to see an attorney for advice on how to handle the fact that, based on a broker's advice, he invested $10,000 in a particular stock that has now plummeted to a value of roughly zero:

Attorney: As I see it, we really have three options here. You can, of course, do nothing and just accept that you have lost your $10,000 investment. You can bring an individual claim seeking to recover those losses. Or we can try to affiliate with other people who have suffered similar losses and see whether we can turn this into a bigger case that might even yield punitive damages.

To a client who has a tendency to avoid the extremes, the middle option—an individual lawsuit—may appear to be the most attractive choice. But imagine if the attorney had presented some different choices:

Attorney: As I see it, we really have three options here. First, you can bring an individual claim against the broker, trying to recover some or all of that $10,000. Second, we can expand the set of defendants, and you can bring a claim against both the broker and the investment house, arguing that the investment house is responsible for the bad advice provided by the broker. Third, we can try to affiliate with other people who suffered similar losses and see whether we can turn this into a bigger case that might even yield punitive damages.

Again, the client may be drawn to the middle option, but notice that it is a different middle option!

Recognizing that any comparison (or lack thereof) can influence decision making, it can be tempting for an attorney to take a vow of silence or to limit the extent to which she generates additional options for consideration. However, good counselors need to think creatively about alternative solutions and must inevitably discuss options with clients. Thus, as with framing, attorneys can best consider options with their clients by being conscious of the array of options presented and helping their clients consider options and make comparisons in a variety of ways.

Decisions for the Future

All decisions implicate the future. We make choices now that will affect how events transpire going forward. Sometimes we can be fairly certain of the impact that our choices will have. If we buy a U.S. savings bond that is scheduled to yield $1,000 in ten years, we can be reasonably confident that it will have that payout. The effects of other choices are more uncertain. When we decide to reject a settlement proposal, we do not know how the trial will turn out. We might reject a buyer's offer without knowing what another buyer will pay for the property. We have already seen the difficulties that optimism bias can cause when making predictions about the future, but counseling clients about the future also raises other significant challenges.

We have seen that even when people can do a good job of predicting the nature of a future event, they are often not very good at predicting how that event will make them feel (see chapter 5). Things that they think will ruin their lives (even losing a job or a piece of property) turn out to have a more transitory impact. People are often surprisingly good at coming to terms with a bad turn of events and regaining their fundamental equilibrium. Similarly, things that they think will bring them great pleasure (even lottery winnings) do not necessarily do so, at least not to the extent or for as long as they had expected. And while it is a common belief that money and material possessions in particular will make people a lot happier, we have seen that the link between money (and especially material possessions) and happiness is fairly weak.

In addition, people have a tendency to make decisions aimed at minimizing anticipated regret. Studies have shown that people may choose to settle a claim rather than take a dispute to trial to avoid a later comparison between the trial verdict and the forgone offer. Although focusing on anticipated regrets can have the advantage of causing people to think thoroughly about their decisions, too much emphasis on regret avoidance does not necessarily yield maximum satisfaction.

Attorneys can help their clients deal with the problem of trying to predict future emotional states by asking them to conduct an emotional "what if" analysis (see chapter 3) to try to imagine how several different courses of action might play out. Because the attorney knows more about some options (such as going through the pretrial process) than the client, the attorney may want to provide factual information before having the client try to imagine how she would feel if a particular option were chosen. The attorney may also want to provide the client with information about the experiences of others. While we have often stressed that every client is different and that every client needs to make her own decision based on her own values, it turns out that knowledge of others' responses—even those of a stranger—can help us better predict our own future feelings. And the attorney can help the client to minimize the focusing illusion by highlighting other relevant aspects of the client's circumstances (see chapter 5).

✦ ✦ ✦ ✦ ✦
Considering the Future

Attorneys are called *counsel* for good reason: their job involves counseling clients not only about the law but also about nonlegal aspects of the case.

Attorney: I think I have a pretty good understanding of your situation, and I have tried to give you an understanding of the pros and cons of litigation. The tough decision is going to be yours—whether you want to file a lawsuit.

Client: I am thinking that I do want to, for a couple of reasons. First, I am really mad at those jerks for ripping me off, and I want to get the satisfaction of seeing them squirm. Second, I think I would be really mad at myself in the future if I let this go—I would always wonder if I could have beaten them in court.

Attorney: OK. That may, indeed, be the best decision. But let me play the devil's advocate for just a bit. A lot of my clients tell me what you just told me—that they want to bring a lawsuit so that they can see the other side suffer. But what I have often seen is that the litigation doesn't necessarily play out the way the client thought it would. For one thing, no one tends to have a particularly good time in litigation, including my clients. Being a party to a lawsuit requires you to keep reliving these events and requires you to spend a lot of time and emotional energy on the lawsuit. Of course, my office and I will do a lot of the work, but you will be personally involved as well, for example, spending one or more days being deposed, preparing for that deposition, and searching out various documents that we need for the litigation. As for making the other side squirm, remember that since most cases eventually settle, only a very small percentage of cases actually end up in trial. Plus, even assuming that we do get the folks from Bad Guys Inc. on the stand, most of my clients have not found the experience as satisfying as they would have thought. Often the other side just sticks to its guns and denies everything that you and your witnesses have said. And, of course, they may throw just as much dirt at you as we are able to throw at them.

Client: Sure, I get all that. But I just don't want to give up on litigation and then regret that for the rest of my life.

Attorney: I understand that, and again I am not saying that it would be a bad decision to litigate, but I do want you to really think this through. It is very common for people to make decisions that they think preserve their options so as to minimize future regret. But the reality is that most decisions both open and close some doors. For example, if you do make the decision to litigate, you will never know how things would have panned out if you had instead chosen to forgo litigation. So, what I am suggesting is that rather than focusing on try-

> ing to minimize future regrets, you instead try to imagine in some detail what your life might look like if you litigate and then also try to imagine in some detail what your life might look like if you did not litigate. Then, having tried to imagine those results, consider both the pros and cons of the courses of action we have discussed. You might even want to make up a list of the likely pros and cons and then do your best to pick the option that you think will make you feel best. You may want to talk this decision over with some members of your family or close friends because sometimes other people know you as well or better than you know yourself, and perhaps some of them will have had to make a similar decision. It may give you a little comfort to know that whatever decision you make, you may come to believe that it was the best decision. Psychologists have found that many of us have a tendency to grow more comfortable with the decisions we ultimately make.

Even when future benefits or losses are clearly identified, clients frequently have difficulty valuing those consequences (see chapter 5). Thus, clients may struggle with the financial implications of receiving or paying money at a future point in time or over a period of time, make decisions that are economically inconsistent, and overvalue the benefit of getting an immediate payment. In both litigation and transactional settings, attorneys often have to help their clients compare alternative offers or demands that include both future and present payments or benefits. The attorney's role is complex. A math professor or statistical consultant might see this role as simply helping the client maximize his monetary gain or minimize his monetary loss. Once the relevant variables—such as interest and tax rates—are estimated, a formula can be used to choose the best option by comparing the present discounted value of the alternatives. Even math-challenged attorneys can provide a similar accounting analysis by using software programs to help clients better understand the consequences of these sorts of choices. Attorneys may, however, have to go further if the client's goals are not simply to maximize or minimize the present discounted value of his payment.

◆ ◆ ◆ ◆ ◆
Considering Options

> Consider the following scenario in which the attorney helps the client visualize the consequences of the various available options:
>
> Attorney: As you know, the buyer, XYZ, is willing to structure this deal in either of two ways. First, XYZ is willing to pay cash for your property and to make that cash payment at the time of closing in the next month or so. The second option

would spread the payment over the next five years with interest. Based on our current predictions about interest rates over the next few years, I can tell you that the payment over time is a better deal for you financially. After taking into account estimates of the relevant interest rates and taxes, the present value of the cash offer is $250,000, and the present value of the payments over time is $325,000. However, I realize that there may be more to your decision, so tell me what you are thinking about as you compare the option of immediate payment to the option of payment over time.

Client: Well, I would definitely love to get my hands on that money as soon as possible. I am not sure how long I have to live, and there are lots of trips I would like to take before I go. So, sooner is better than later. But I also worry about how getting an immediate payment would impact my relationship with my ex-husband and my grown children. Maybe if my ex knew I just got a windfall, he would try to get his hands on that money. And maybe my kids would start worrying about how to inherit that money. Plus, I do worry about the uncertainty of it all. What if XYZ goes broke before I get all my money, or what if the prediction regarding the interest rate is way off? Maybe I am better off just getting the money sooner rather than later and dealing with the relationship issues.

Attorney: These are all very important concerns, so let's try to think them through. I will consult with the divorce experts at our firm to see what the implications of either payment would be with respect to the support you are paying to your ex-husband. They will need to see a copy of your divorce agreement. We can also think about whether there are alternative options we might present to XYZ, such as extending payment over two years rather than five, or whether we might want to involve a third party that could, for example, give you a loan based on XYZ's promise to make future payments.

Dealing with Strong Emotions

Given all that we know about the importance of emotion (see chapter 3), how should the attorney handle emotions that arise in the counseling process? We suggest four steps: pay attention to the emotions experienced by both attorney and client, take emotion into account when embarking on particular counseling tasks, attempt to regulate the client's emotions when appropriate while recognizing constraints on the ability to control the emotions of others, and attempt to regulate the attorney's own emotions.

First, rather than trying to eradicate client emotions, counselors should be alert to those emotions as they can provide important clues to clients' deeply held values and interests. Sometimes a client's emotional state will be fairly obvious, and sometimes it will not. Angry clients may yell or even pound the table, and upset clients may cry. Other clients will be more restrained. Learning to recognize facial and body language clues that may reveal client emotions can be quite helpful. In addition, attorneys can benefit by becoming more knowledgeable about the subtleties of emotion. The seemingly angry client may also feel worried or scared, and the sad client may also feel proud or hopeful as to a different and possibly better future. Few of us experience emotions on a single dimension.

✦ ✦ ✦ ✦ ✦

Suing One's Mother

Paying attention to client emotions can be the key to effective counseling:

> Peter Biagetti is a senior litigator at the prestigious Boston law firm of Mintz, Levin, Cohn, Ferris, Glovsky and Popeo.
>
> A property developer who wished to sue his own mother, a partner in the family real estate business, had hired Biagetti to represent him. Biagetti got ready for the case, and a court date was set. Just before the first hearing, Biagetti met the developer on the steps of the courthouse. The developer seemed to hesitate, his body language suggesting indecision, reluctance, and some kind of discomfort. Biagetti saw a man who was wrestling with a dozen issues that had to do with family pride, personal success, recognition, and filial love.
>
> He knew that the lawsuit could resolve only one issue, and a relatively minor one at that. Drawing on the common background he shared with his client, he decided to comment on what he saw. "I told him that I found it hard to imagine how it must feel to go into litigation with his mother. I said I didn't think it was something many sons could go through with."
>
> The developer might have upbraided his lawyer, told him to mind his own business, just do his job and get on with it. But he didn't. Instead, he stopped and looked at Biagetti. The developer decided not to press the lawsuit. Biagetti commented later: "I think he respected that we'd girded for battle, but were not so bellicose as to want to crush his mother. We settled the matter on the court-house steps."
>
> Soon after the settlement, the developer sent more work to Biagetti's firm, and eventually he decided to use Mintz, Levin for all of his business and family legal needs.
>
> Another lawyer might not have sensed his client's underlying concerns, been blind to his courthouse hesitation, been unwilling to forgo the revenues of a potentially lucrative trial, or (most important of all) not felt enough affinity for him to speak up. But in this case, the client drew back a curtain and the lawyer was willing to look through the window. This is how a trusted advisor relationship often begins.[52]

Emotion can also affect the decision-making processes of both the lawyer and the client. Clients' emotional states may, for example, affect their analytical capabilities, their degree of impulsiveness, their tendency to rely on stereotypes or scripts to gather new information, their focus on short- or long-term interests, their degree of creativity, or their tendency to procrastinate. People in positive moods tend to be more creative and flexible but less analytical. People in neutral or sad moods tend to be more careful and focused on details. It is also clear that emotion can impact clients' preference or distaste for particular options. For example, particular emotions may make clients more or less interested in apologizing or accepting responsibility, may affect their degree of trust or concern for others, and may affect their attitude toward risk.

Emotion can also impact the attorney-client relationship, specifically the likelihood that the client will really hear what the attorney has to say. For example, people in more positive moods are likely to be more receptive to advice and even to negative feedback. Those who are feeling anxious may be highly receptive to advice, even bad advice. And those who are angry are likely to be less trusting and less collaborative. As in many life activities, timing is critical in counseling. When a client is distraught or shaking with anger, it is not a good time to have him think through complicated issues and make tough choices. It may be difficult for the client who is sobbing about her mother's recent demise to think through all the tax implications of changing her estate planning documents. On the other hand, a few weeks later when the client is still sad but no longer distraught, it may be a good time to ask her to think through those issues. Indeed, we have learned that sad people can be better analysts. Similarly, if an attorney is working with a client to plan a new business, it can be a good idea to take advantage of the client's obviously ebullient mood to do some creative work on the company's financing structure while saving the drudgery of proofreading corporate bylaws for a day when the client is more pensive. Of course, some projects have rigid timelines, and an attorney will not always have the luxury of juggling tasks according to the mood of the client or attorney. But attorneys can be both more efficient and more effective when they capitalize on or create emotions that are conducive to particular tasks.

To the extent that clients' emotions are effectively preventing them from fully participating in a counseling session and the discussion cannot be deferred, the attorney can attempt to help the client moderate his emotion using the same techniques we suggested for client interviews (see chapter 9). Acting to distract the client from a source of distress, allowing him time to take some deep breaths or even to go for a short walk, helping the client to reappraise the situation, or assisting him in formulating concrete steps for going forward can all help him to manage strong emotions.[53]

Finally, attorneys should take steps to ensure that their own fears, anger, happiness, and other emotions do not taint the advice they give to clients. One way to do this is to build in ways to deliberate about important advice. Sleeping on crucial matters can give the attorney a chance to see how different moods affect her thinking. Similarly, the attorney might consult with others in her office before making an important decision. Snap judgments may reflect emotion rather than adequate analysis.

Using Persuasion Effectively

The best advice in the world is useless if the lawyer cannot persuade her clients to accept that advice. Just as knowledgeable professors may be lousy teachers, so, too, may knowledgeable attorneys be ineffective counselors.

While attorneys should be cognizant of the ethical subtleties of whether and how they exert influence over clients,[55] influence is inevitable and also often appropriate. To be persuasive, the advice given must be credible. And, as we have seen, credibility stems from both the expertise and trustworthiness of the source (see chapter 6). Thus, it is important that attorneys be prepared for counseling sessions in order to demonstrate the necessary expertise. Similarly, building trust and establishing rapport are just as critical to providing effective counsel to clients as they are to obtaining full information from clients in interviews. In chapter 7, we outlined a variety of ways in which attorneys can seek to build trust and establish rapport with clients through the way they communicate, such as by paying attention to nonverbal cues and by creating a warm environment.

> To listen well is as powerful a means of communication and influence as to talk well.
> —*John Marshall*[54]

❖ ❖ ❖ ❖ ❖

Rapport as Persuasion

In chapter 9, we described how building relationships with clients makes a lawyer a better interviewer. In similar ways, building rapport with clients can help a lawyer to be more persuasive. Consider the true story of a lawsuit brought against a large corporation that allegedly allowed contaminated water to infiltrate a local community, causing severe health problems. The plaintiffs' law firm had to contend with significant reluctance on the part of the clients and prospective clients to cooperate in a massive lawsuit against an intimidating corporation. In the film version of the story, Julia Roberts portrays Erin Brockovich, a spirited file clerk who uses her interpersonal skills to build clients' trust. In contrast to her austere attorney colleagues, Erin is sincere and personable. She visits the homes of the injured clients and empathizes with them regarding their illnesses and sufferings. While one of the other attorneys on the case interviews clients by telling them to give only the facts and to "reserve sentimental indulgences," Erin encourages the clients to speak freely, listens to how the clients are feeling, and takes an interest in their lives. In turn, the clients trust Erin and are willing to cooperate with her because they believe that she is looking out for their best interests. Ultimately, when the clients become frustrated with the litigation process and almost withdraw, Erin is able to convince them to stay with the litigation.[56]

In addition, as we learned in chapter 6, clients are more likely to trust advisers who provide the reasoning underlying their advice:

> [A] key to business success is thinking through reasons before giving opinions and advice and, in doing so, giving your clients a full and thoughtful account of how you reached your decision. Your clients will be more likely to follow your advice if they understand and appreciate the reasons behind it. Good reasoning makes advice—even if it's not the answer they want—easier to believe in.[57]

◆ ◆ ◆ ◆ ◆

Getting Advice Implemented

It is often said that the most valuable thing a lawyer sells is his judgment. I believe that to be true—but only when the judgment is accepted. The ability to gain agreement, in my opinion, makes the difference between a good lawyer and a great one. Acceptance depends on how thoughtful and objective your analysis is and how effectively you have communicated it to your client. Recently, an investment banker and I were engaging in the postmortem of a failed merger. We initially congratulated ourselves for having spotted the key issue and for reaching what later proved to be the right advice. But we quickly realized that being right was of little solace and reward when the merger had cratered precisely because our client rejected our advice. Good advice has little value if it is not communicated in such a way that it is followed.

My point is simple: Making the right judgment is important, but getting it implemented is more important. Here psychology may be as important as the law—the art of persuasion in and out of court is little understood and less appreciated in most law schools. However, it is a skill that lawyers must learn to master.[58]

Further, as we saw in chapter 6, there are a variety of additional ways in which attorneys might persuade clients. For example, an attorney might point out that the client's current position is inconsistent with values that the client has expressed in the past, using the client's need for consistency to move the client's thinking forward.

Attorneys may also be well served by paying particular attention to channel factors (see chapter 6) that will make it easier for clients to carry out required tasks such as finding needed records or analyzing the pros and cons of various options. For example, the attorney might give the client a list of exactly which documents are needed, provide the client with a map showing how to get to the office where the documents are stored, or provide the client with a sheet entitled "Pros and Cons" to help the client start to make a list that might otherwise be difficult.

In addition, it can be important to recall that clients' cultural backgrounds may affect which persuasive tools will be most effective. For example, clients from

> ✦ ✦ ✦ ✦ ✦
> **Influence Through Identifying Inconsistency**
>
> Consider the following scenario in which the attorney convincingly, but politely, argues that the client might not be looking at the issue with the appropriate perspective:
>
> Attorney: I understand your concern that your son Joe, at age thirty-five, may still not be mature enough to manage the extensive wealth that he would stand to inherit. At the same time, I have heard you say in other contexts that taking on major responsibilities is the best way to build character. You certainly know your son far better than I do, but perhaps by age thirty-five he will be ready to take on the responsibilities of managing significant assets and even learn and grow from that experience.

a low-context culture are likely to be more responsive to logic, facts, and reasons, whereas clients from high-context cultures might be more responsive to persuasion based on social roles, relationships, or obligations.

Finally, when lawyers counsel their clients, they are, in part, acting as teachers. We have seen that effective teachers use multiple methods to convey their messages (see chapter 7). Thus, it may often be useful to use visual aids to communicate information to clients. The attorney could use a whiteboard or piece of paper to make a list of options or costs and benefits, or the client could write out her own list.

Visual aids can also be useful for conveying concepts that many people have difficulty understanding, such as probabilities, interest payments, and differences in magnitude. For example, the attorney might use a series of bar graphs to help the client understand how compound interest will help a lump sum payment grow substantially over the next twenty years, or the attorney could use a decision tree drawing to show that a plaintiff must prevail on many different points at trial in order to be entitled to a judgment. Videos, too, can sometimes be useful for providing clients with an understanding of events, such as depositions, that the clients may not have experienced before.

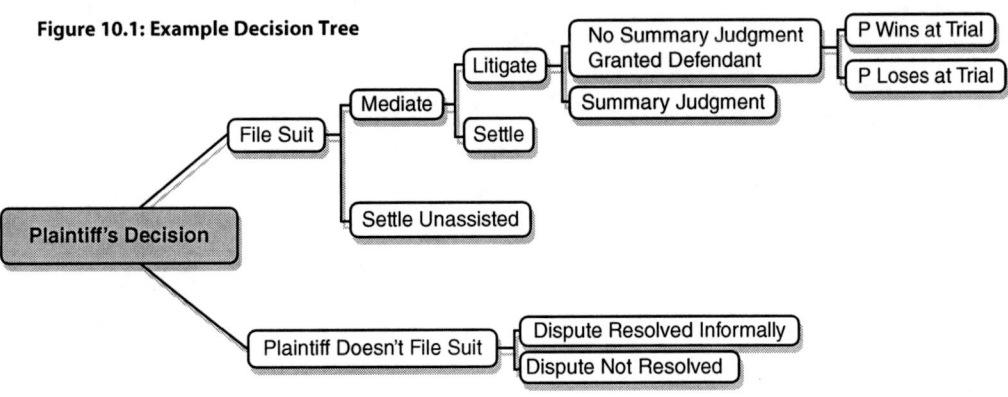

Figure 10.1: Example Decision Tree

Good teachers also know that important lessons often need to build on existing knowledge. Thus, attorneys should try to present information in ways that tap into a client's experiences. For example, if a client has been involved in litigation before, his attorney can draw on those experiences in discussing his options. In contrast, when counseling a client who has no experience with litigation, an attorney will not be able to take any knowledge for granted and will need to explain more about the nature of the process and the available options. In doing so, the attorney should strive to use clear and understandable language with a minimum of legalese (see chapter 7). The attorney can try to use facets of the client's background to make these explanations clearer; for example, if the client is a civil engineer, she may readily understand an analogy between building a bridge and preparing a case for trial.

◆ ◆ ◆ ◆ ◆
Learning by Doing

Attorney: I appreciate your interest in obtaining an apology from the defendant. We will need to give some serious thought to what kind of apology might be both meaningful for you and also feasible for the defendant to give. This may sound a little unusual, but perhaps you can try putting yourself in the role of the school superintendent and giving the sort of apology you think you would like to hear. That may help us figure out both what apology would be valuable to you and what apology the superintendent might be in a position to give.

Similarly, important lessons may need to be repeated, so attorneys should not assume that their clients heard and retained everything that was said at a prior session. And given that confused clients will not necessarily ask clarifying questions, attorneys need to be sure to invite questions and offer clear explanations even when no questions are asked.

◆ ◆ ◆ ◆ ◆
Summing It Up

- Broaden the focus of consultation to consider the client's desire for information, justice, reform, monetary and nonmonetary recompense, and litigation.
- Challenge client preconceptions by paying attention to instances in which schemas—including stereotypes—and preferences or attitudes influence their judgments.

- Effectively assess the likelihood of success by watching out for optimism and self-serving biases, the effects of availability and anchoring on predictions, and the gambler's fallacy. Consider the views of an imagined disagreeable adjudicator and seek outside perspectives.
- Improve the process of decision making by paying attention to how the client approaches decisions, considering what information is relevant, and reflecting on how to best describe and compare options.
- Deal appropriately with emotions by paying attention to emotion, taking emotion into account in the counseling process, and attempting to regulate the emotions of both client and attorney.
- Be a credible adviser by demonstrating expertise and trustworthiness, establishing rapport, providing reasons, using channel factors, and being a good teacher.

For Further Reading: Client Counseling

THE AFFECTIVE ASSISTANCE OF COUNSEL: PRACTICING LAW AS A HEALING PROFESSION (Marjorie A. Silver ed., 2007).

John M. A. DiPippa, *How Prospect Theory Can Improve Legal Counseling*, 24 U. ARK. LITTLE ROCK L. REV. 81 (2001).

Chris Guthrie, *Better Settle Than Sorry: The Regret Aversion Theory of Litigation Behavior*, U. ILL. L. REV. 43 (1999).

Chris Guthrie, *Framing Frivolous Litigation: A Psychological Theory*, 67 U. CHI. L. REV. 163 (2000).

Chris Guthrie, *Panacea or Pandora's Box? The Costs of Options in Negotiations*, 88 IOWA L. REV. 601 (2003).

RANDALL KISER, BEYOND RIGHT AND WRONG: THE POWER OF EFFECTIVE DECISION MAKING FOR ATTORNEYS AND CLIENTS (2010).

Russell Korobkin & Chris Guthrie, *Barriers to Litigation Settlement: An Experimental Approach*, 93 MICH. L. REV. 107 (1994).

Russell Korobkin & Chris Guthrie, *Psychology, Economics, and Settlement: A New Look at the Role of the Lawyer*, 76 TEX. L. REV. 77 (1997).

Jeffrey J. Rachlinski, *A Positive Psychological Theory of the Value of Judging in Hindsight*, 65 U. CHI. L. REV. 571 (1998).

TAMARA RELIS, PERCEPTIONS IN LITIGATION AND MEDIATION: PARALLEL WORLDS OF LAWYERS, PLAINTIFFS, DEFENDANTS AND GENDERED PARTIES (Cambridge Press 2008).

Negotiating and Mediating   11

> The propensity to truck, barter, and exchange one thing for another . . . is common to all men, and to be found in no other race of animals. . . . Nobody ever saw a dog make a fair and deliberate exchange of one bone for another with another dog.
> —*Adam Smith*[1]

Most lawyers spend a great deal of time thinking about and conducting negotiations. Transactional attorneys negotiate purchases, sales, leases, licenses, and permits. Litigators typically focus on negotiations even while they are simultaneously preparing a case for trial. Indeed, one of the greatest mental challenges attorneys face is how to maintain the partisan belief that will help them prevail while simultaneously recognizing the weaknesses in their position and the interests of the other side that will help them to craft an acceptable agreement.

> [An] almost galactic scope of disputes . . . are subject to resolution by negotiation [by attorneys].
> —*James J. White*[2]

Attorneys employ a range of approaches to negotiation including *distributive* techniques for dividing a fixed pie and *integrative* methods for trying to expand that pie.[3] Psychology offers useful insight into both of these approaches. While many have examined how psychological phenomena can impede agreement, we will also discuss the ways in which psychology can enhance the prospects for agreement. After discussing negotiation, we examine how lawyers can also draw on psychology in representing their clients in mediations.

A Psychologically Expanded Model of Negotiation

According to the traditional economic model of bargaining, people make decisions—such as whether to enter into a settlement, plea agreement, or deal—by trying to maximize their *utility*, or overall satisfaction. Under this model, a negotiator decides whether to enter into an agreement by comparing the expected utility of the particular agreement to the expected value of the best alternative to the agreement (referred to as the best alternative to a negotiated agreement or BATNA).[4] Thus, in the criminal or civil litigation context, a person would compare the anticipated value of the settlement or plea bargain to the likely results of continuing toward trial. A sophisticated calculation would take into account the predicted probabilities of various future resolutions (a later settlement or plea, dismissal on motion, winning at trial, losing at trial) and the value or cost of each of these to the decision maker. Such calculations would include adjustments for all anticipated benefits and costs of settling or proceeding toward trial, such as attorney fees and related expenditures and nonmonetary costs and benefits (publicity, the impact on future relationships, and emotional fallout). In nonlitigation settings, the economic approach to bargaining posits that decision makers compare the anticipated value of the proposed deal to alternative courses of action. For example, a person who has been offered the opportunity to buy a house would consider such factors as the characteristics and prices of alternative houses and whether it might make more sense to invest the money in the stock market and continue to rent a home.

Given the complexities of human perception, memory, judgment, decision making, and emotion, taking into account psychological research can help lawyers identify ways in which people routinely and predictably deviate from this standard economic model. In many instances, such departures can impede our ability to reach optimal negotiated agreements. Anger or optimistic overconfidence may, for example, lead us to reject agreements that we might be better off accepting. In other instances, however, we may jump at agreements that a utility maximizer would not accept. Loss aversion, for example, may cause us to reject risks that could be worth taking; and overconfidence may cause us to take risks that are ill advised, such as closing on a transaction that may be undesirable.

> There are many situations in which less-than-rational agents may reach agreement while perfectly rational agents do not.
> —Daniel Kahneman & Amos Tversky[5]

The psychological aspects of the dynamics between the lawyer and the client—with lawyers handling negotiations as agents for clients—can also complicate negotiations. The lawyer-client interaction is particularly important because attorneys largely conduct negotiations outside the presence of their clients. After initially consulting with the client, the attorney typically acts as a conduit, expressing the client's concerns to the other side and reporting back to the client on the negotiation counterpart's interests, demands or offers, and concerns. These communications will inevitably be filtered through the attorney's own perspective, and the manner in which the attorney conveys any proposal will influence how the client responds.

Negotiation presents particular challenges for attorneys as they must simultaneously adopt the roles of advocate and adviser. It is very easy for agents to align their perspectives with those of their clients. We saw in chapter 4 that even partisan *observers* tend to adopt a perspective that is similar to that of the principal actor. And we saw that attorneys tend to evaluate cases in ways that are consistent with the interests of their clients. This alignment has a benefit, as we will see, because in negotiating deals and settlements, attorneys should aim high and display confidence in their clients' position.

> Discourage litigation. Persuade your neighbors to compromise whenever you can. . . . As a peacemaker the lawyer has superior opportunity of being a good man. There will still be business enough.
> —Abraham Lincoln[6]

However, in addition to an advocate, the client needs an adviser who can provide a more dispassionate analysis of her options and prospects for success. It can be challenging for the attorney to engage in partisan negotiations with the other side and simultaneously provide the client with objective advice.[7] It can also be challenging for an attorney to balance the desire to maintain good rapport with the client with the need to provide accurate advice.

The fact that attorneys often conduct negotiations outside the presence of their clients is particularly significant to the extent that the attorney has interests or perspectives that diverge from those of the client. Although the rules of legal ethics make clear that clients—not attorneys—should ultimately make the decision as to whether or not to enter into a negotiated agreement,[8] the divergent perspectives and incentives of attorneys and clients can impact the negotiation.[9]

Attorney decisions are not only influenced by the attorney's assessment of the client's case and best interests but are also potentially influenced by the decision's impact on the attorney herself including implications for the attorney's reputation, her need to manage her own time, and personal financial considerations. For example, repeat-player attorneys who negotiate against one another frequently may be able to use the reciprocity aspect of persuasion (see chapter 6) to convince one another to settle in situations that might not serve a particular client's best interests.[10]

✦ ✦ ✦ ✦ ✦

Attorney Self-Interest

Sometimes the attorney's self-interest is blatant and can lead attorneys to recommend against settlements that serve the client's best interests or in favor of settlements that do not. Renowned plaintiffs' lawyer Gerry Spence considered how a lawyer's financial constraints might influence how a lawyer advises his client about settlement. While presenting a very confident face to the adversary, the lawyer who needs a quick settlement to pay the bills might present a more negative picture to the client:

> This is a tough case, Helen. Our expert is a little mushy on his conclusion, and you can never predict what a jury will do. They could turn you loose with nothing. Nothing, Helen! We got money on the table. Not enough, but "a bird in the hand. . . ." And what that s.o.b. defense attorney can do to you on cross-examination! He's a vile reptile. Yes, Helen, I hate to say this, but I don't think we can win.[11]

Constructing Initial Proposals

Under the standard economic model of negotiation, constructing an initial proposal should be a fairly simple task. The attorney should (1) explore the client's preferences to figure out what will satisfy the client, (2) help the client assess the probability of achieving various levels of satisfaction under alternative paths, and (3) help devise a proposal that is calculated to maximize the client's satisfaction given the relevant constraints. However, psychology shows that none of these tasks is straightforward and that additional tasks may be important as well.

Assessing What the Client Wants

Typically, one of the first steps that an attorney takes in undertaking a negotiation is to figure out what the client wants to accomplish. Deciphering what the client wants, however, is not as easy as one might imagine.

Clients themselves will not necessarily know what will provide them with the most satisfaction. As we saw in chapter 5, we have difficulty predicting our responses to future events or outcomes—making mistakes about the degree and duration of our reactions. Thus, clients may think they know what they want but may make choices and decisions that do not serve their long- or even short-term interests.[12] Clients' lack of knowledge of and experience with the legal system can amplify the challenge of predicting what would be a satisfying outcome.

The focusing illusion (see chapter 5), in particular, can result in the incorrect prediction of future emotions as people focus on isolated aspects of a future situation to the neglect of other likely influences. A person who is ending a marriage, for example, may be focused on a desire to put an adulterous soon-to-be-ex spouse through the litigation ringer rather than on other aspects of postdivorce life. Students tend to focus on certain features of their job offers—in particular, the salary and whether the offer is from a prominent employer—rather than on other features of the offer such as location, medical benefits, or the nature of the work itself.[13] We saw in chapter 5 that people tend to focus more on economic or quantifiable factors—exhibiting lay rationalism—perhaps because they believe such factors to be more "real." Yet, the less concrete factors may in fact have a large impact on how clients feel.

To help the client keep the big picture in mind and get a better handle on what will be most satisfying in the long run, the attorney can draw focus to a range of relevant aspects of the situation, particularly those that are less salient or less concrete. In addition, although clients may find it hard to believe, we have seen that knowing how a peer reacted to a similar set of circumstances can help people to make more accurate assessments of their own emotional reactions (see chapter 5). Thus, the attorney can offer the perspective of other clients who have experienced similar choices.

❖ ❖ ❖ ❖ ❖

Sharing the Experience of Others

Attorney: Mrs. Brown, I understand th t to want to punish Mr. Brown by going to trial. Many of my c ilar thoughts when going through nasty divorces. Howev you to know that most of them haven't necessaril The trial itself doesn't do much to change their fe heir spouse, nor does it result in their spouse suff p suffering themselves. And you may find that w gs behind you, you will be able to focus on all of t hat make you happy. Thus, while the decision as to ent demand is entirely yours, I would counsel you to think at you hope to gain by going to trial and whether there might be a btain those same benefits through a settlement.

It can also be useful to suggest that clients employ a scoring system in which they assign values to various interests, including those that might be less concrete. For example, a home buyer might easily get carried away by the fabulous mountain views afforded by a particular property. However, an attorney might help the client to list all of the various attributes that the client is looking for in a house (for example, size, location, type of construction, and age) and to place an estimated value on each of these attributes. The attorney and the client would then be better able to construct an offer that more fully reflects the client's entire mix of preferences. While it may not be possible to perfectly identify and value every relevant feature, making the effort to list and value a range of considerations will help both the attorney and the client think more broadly.

Compounding the difficulty that clients have in making predictions about their own future satisfaction is the fact that attorneys may make unfounded assumptions about what they think will make their clients happy. It is all too easy for an attorney to focus on the negotiated resolution that she would want if she were in the client's shoes, forgetting that the client's perspective may be very different. The attorney who is not fond of water, for example, may have a difficult time appreciating the great importance that the client places on having a swimming pool.

Similarly, the attorney may not recognize the extent to which her own personal or institutional interests affect her sense of what the client wants. Consider the class action lawsuits filed after the decision in *Brown v. Board of Education*.[14] According to legal scholar Derrick Bell Jr., lawyers leading civil rights groups were fervently opposed to anything less than full desegregation, in part because contributors to civil rights groups took that position even though such a remedy was not desired by all "victims of segregated schools."[15]

Likewise, an attorney who focuses more on the assumed immediate needs or desires of a particular client may not recognize that the client is willing to set aside solutions that might best serve her own personal interests in order to better achieve a resolution that would help a broader segment of society.

> ✦ ✦ ✦ ✦ ✦
>
> **Long Wait in the Emergency Room**
>
> Mrs. Grigorich is a client whose injuries were exacerbated when she was kept waiting too long by hospital emergency room staff. She believes that the hospital staff was rude to her and ignored her in part because she is very overweight.
>
> Attorney: The settlement offered by the hospital would pay all of your medical bills, compensate you for the time you lost from work as a result of having been hospitalized for extra days, provide you with an additional payment of $10,000, and pay your attorney fees. I strongly recommend that you take the settlement. It gives you everything and more than I expect you could get in court.
>
> Mrs. Grigorich: But have they taken steps to make sure that this never happens again to someone else? And would they apologize to me for what they did?

People are complex and so, too, are the ways in which they achieve life satisfaction. Clients may seek compensation, vengeance, fair and dignified treatment, apologies, reform, and an array of other goals in their legal interactions (see chapter 10). Moreover, as we saw in chapter 8, people have many different ways of thinking about justice. In addition, people from different cultures tend to emphasize varying objectives in a negotiation, for example, placing different degrees of importance on goals such as maintaining relationships or creating relational capital, protecting autonomy, expanding social networks, saving face, vindicating rights, achieving economic gains in the short or long term, protecting collective interests, or laying a foundation for the future.

But clients' complexities may not always be easily visible to the attorney. For example, as we discussed in chapter 10, attorneys may assume that clients are primarily concerned about money, whereas their actual concerns may be much broader. Attorneys may also monetize disputes that clients, at least initially, do not perceive in primarily monetary terms. A study by Tamara Relis found that

> [plaintiffs'] explanations of why they sued and what they were seeking from the legal system are thickly composed of extralegal aims of principle. . . . Yet, plaintiffs' objectives of obtaining admissions of fault, acknowledgments of harm, retribution for defendant conduct, prevention of recurrences, answers, and apologies remain invisible to most lawyers throughout the duration of litigation and mediation.[16]

Clients, too, may overemphasize the extent to which money will make them happier. Plaintiffs in civil litigation often aspire to substantial monetary awards, and defendants seek to avoid paying such awards. In transactions, the monetary aspects of a deal are often more prominent than other issues even though those other issues may prove to be equally or more important. This focus on money is understandable. Attorneys and clients may both share Oscar Wilde's view: "When I was young I thought that money was the most important thing in life; now that I am old I know that it is."[17] On the other hand, even popular culture disputes the idea that money can buy happiness. As Paul McCartney sings, "money can't buy me love."[19]

>
> Money is better than poverty, if only for financial reasons.
> —Woody Allen[18]
>

As we know from chapter 3, psychological research shows that both perspectives on money have some truth to them. Money can be helpful in permitting clients to achieve basic levels of comfort and security. The financial aspects of the agreement can be extremely important when there are bills to pay. And people do typically care about how they are treated as compared to others (see chapter 8). A client, therefore, may value getting a deal that is financially comparable to that received by others who are similarly situated. At the same time, however, sometimes holding out for those last dollars may not make the client more satisfied in the long run. As we have seen, obtaining more money has diminishing returns and does not necessarily make people as happy as they think it will. Thus, it is important to help clients think about both the monetary and the nonmonetary aspects of a potential agreement.

Clients' nonmonetary interests can open a wealth of negotiating opportunities because sometimes the nonmonetary item that would make one party happy is relatively inexpensive for the other to provide or can even serve both sides' interests. Perhaps a thank-you, a handshake, a certificate, an apology or explanation, a reprimand, or a fairly simple reform of procedures would help to resolve a matter that would otherwise go to trial. Perhaps providing delivery on a particular date or renaming a product is easy for the supplier and crucial to the buyer. Institutional reforms—such as securing additional training for the defendant or its employees, improving signage or labeling, changing bureaucratic processes, or changing living or working conditions—might be mutually beneficial.

In short, attorneys need to make a concerted effort to ensure that they have a good understanding of what their clients really want and that they counsel clients to more effectively predict what will bring them future happiness or satisfaction. Rather than depend on assumptions, the attorney should marshal all of her interviewing skills (see chapter 9) to find out what a particular client might be looking for in a negotiated agreement. By asking lots of questions, providing information about other clients' experiences, and helping the client to test her assumptions, the attorney and the client can get a better sense of what it is that the client most wants. Similarly, the attorney can glean information about the client's preferences by watching for and following up on emotional and other nonverbal cues (see chapters 3 and 7). Attorneys should also remember that what people want can change over time and that people do not always remember that they used to want something different (see chapter 2). Thus, for attorneys who engage in extended negotiations, it will be important to reconfirm clients' goals as time passes.

Assessing What the Other Side Wants

While it is important to carefully consider what the client wants, the attorney and the client also should spend some time thinking about and trying to learn about their negotiation counterpart. Eliciting information from the other side about its needs, interests, and obstacles will help to make the negotiation productive and make it easier to structure a proposal that maximizes both joint and individual gains. Thus, as an initial matter, good negotiators will work to good interviewers by drawing on the lessons of chapter 9.

> To be successful, you have to be able to relate to people; they have to be satisfied with your personality to be able to do business with you and to build a relationship with mutual trust.
> —Trump Org. Exec. VP & Sr. Counsel George H. Ross[20]

To learn about a negotiation counterpart, it is desirable to try to build rapport and to establish a degree of trust. As we saw in chapter 8, negotiators understand and expect that their negotiation counterparts will not be neutral but will act as advocates for their own interests. This, however, does not preclude establishing a relationship of trust appropriate to the circumstances. For example, the two sides may be able to trust that neither will lie to or deliberately try to harm the other. Such a relationship of trust can be important to effective negotiation (although, of course, naïve trust can be detrimental). In particular, to the extent that negotiators trust each other, they will be more comfortable sharing the kind of information that can lead to agreements that expand rather than merely divide the pie.

> ✦ ✦ ✦ ✦ ✦
> **Nelson Mandela as Negotiator**
>
> In his account of Nelson Mandela's negotiation with the leaders of the South African apartheid regime, conflict resolution expert Robert Mnookin describes the steps that both sides took to try to ensure that they could trust one another, notwithstanding a sordid history and significant political differences. For example, during the first of their several meetings, government official Barnard confided in Mandela that he was worried that he would not be able to communicate effectively in English. Mandela responded respectfully, "I can follow Afrikaans quite well. If I don't understand something, I will ask you." Furthermore, Mandela established rapport with each of the government officials: one was "surprised and flattered" that Mandela remembered him from their first meeting some thirty years prior. Although their policy differences were significant, these "simple gestures" allowed the two parties to negotiate respectfully and effectively. In return, the government relocated Mandela from prison to more comfortable accommodations during the negotiations. Eventually, the successful negotiations between Mandela and the leaders of the apartheid regime led to the dismantling of apartheid in South Africa.[21]

Perspective taking can be particularly beneficial for assessing the other side's interests. Negotiators who take the perspective of their opponent—trying to understand what their counterpart is both thinking and feeling and being "relentlessly curious about what is really motivating the other side"[22]—can more effectively devise a proposal that will appeal to the other side and overcome the tendency to assume that what is good for one side must be detrimental to the other.[23]

One of the best ways to learn about a counterpart's interests and concerns is to ask about them. Thus, if the lawyer is representing a ballet company that is negotiating over the potential hire of a new principal dancer, she would want to ask why the dancer is considering joining a new company, what the dancer is looking for in a new contract, what forms of compensation are of interest, and what additional concerns the dancer might have. To be most effective, such questions should be specific and should be formulated so as to disconfirm any assumptions that the lawyer might have (see chapter 1).

> " Don't assume you know the other side's story. If you think you do, you're probably wrong. Even if you turn out to be substantially right, you will still be more effective if you begin with an attitude of curiosity about how the other side sees the world.
> —Robert H. Mnookin, Scott R. Peppet & Andrew S. Tulumello[24] "

Inquiries to a counterpart should also focus on possible impediments to settlement (see chapter 6). Finding out about the other side's constraints can often lead to a more successful deal. If the principal dancer is reluctant to accept an offer of employment because she is hesitant to take her young child out of the school she loves, the company might help her to find a particularly suitable school in the new locale. Consider the experience of one Fortune 500 company:

> A few years ago, Chris's company entered into negotiations with a small European firm to buy an ingredient for a new health care product. (Some details have been changed to protect the companies involved.) The two sides settled on a price of $18 a pound for a million pounds of the substance annually. However, a disagreement developed over terms. The European supplier refused to sell the ingredient exclusively to the U.S. firm, and the U.S. firm was unwilling to invest in a product that was based on an ingredient its competitors could easily acquire. With considerable hesitation, the U.S. negotiators sweetened the deal, offering guaranteed minimum orders and a higher price. To their shock, the supplier still balked at providing exclusivity—even though it had no chance of selling anything close to a million pounds a year to anyone else. The negotiation seemed to be at a dead end, with the U.S. negotiators out of ideas for pushing through a deal. Even worse, the relationship had deteriorated so much that neither side trusted the other to continue bargaining in good faith.
>
> At that point the stymied U.S. team brought in Chris to help improve relations. He did more than that. After listening to the facts, he asked the Europeans a simple question: Why? Why wouldn't they provide exclusivity to his corporation, which would buy as much of the ingredient as they could produce? The response surprised the Americans. Exclusivity would require the supplier's owner to violate an agreement with his cousin, who bought 250 pounds of the ingredient each year to make a locally sold product. Armed with this new knowledge, Chris proposed a solution that allowed the two firms to quickly wrap up a deal. The European firm would provide exclusivity with the exception of a few hundred pounds annually for the supplier's cousin.
>
> In retrospect, that solution seems obvious. But as we've seen in real-world negotiations, as well as in classroom simulations with seasoned deal makers, this type of problem solving is exceedingly rare. That's because most negotiators wrongly assume that they understand the other side's motivations and, therefore, don't explore them further. The U.S. team members initially failed because they thought they knew why the supplier was being difficult: Clearly, they assumed, the Europeans were holding out for a higher price or didn't want to lose out on future deals with other customers.[25]

Offering multiple proposals for consideration at the same time can also be useful for gaining perspective on a negotiation counterpart's preferences:

> We could structure this in a variety of ways. For example, we could consider the following: (1) delivery of five thousand widgets in one week at a price of $3 per widget; (2) delivery of one thousand widgets tomorrow, with the remaining four thousand to be delivered in a week, at a price of $3.10 per widget; or (3) delivery of five thousand widgets tomorrow at a price of $3.50 per widget. From your perspective, how do these compare?

By devising multiple proposals that are all equally acceptable to the client but that differ in subtle or not-so-subtle ways, the attorney can gain information about the relative importance of different issues to the other side. Even if none of the proposals is acceptable to the other side, obtaining reactions to different alternatives can provide a great deal of insight that will be useful as additional proposals are created.

To the extent that the lawyer has contact with the opposing principal, the lawyer can also closely observe that principal's reactions and outward expressions of emotion for additional information about his interests, preferences, and constraints. If a personal injury plaintiff is angry, then perhaps an apology would be welcome. If the seller of a property shows signs of being anxious and desperate to make a sale, then perhaps a lower but speedy offer is in order. Even when the parties have not had a chance to meet, the attorney and the client can try to anticipate whether a negotiation counterpart might be experiencing anger, jealousy, fear, or an array of other emotions (see chapter 3).

In thinking about the other side's needs, negotiators Roger Fisher and Daniel Shapiro suggest that it can be helpful to pay attention to five core concerns: appreciation, affiliation, autonomy, status, and role. Note how these five concerns relate to the notion of procedural justice discussed in chapter 8. Fisher and Shapiro suggest that by using these concerns as a lens, negotiators can do a better job of understanding their counterparts and themselves, devise better proposals, and engage in a more productive negotiation process.[26]

◆ ◆ ◆ ◆ ◆
Paying Attention to Underlying Concerns

Law professor Leonard Riskin describes how familiarity with the five concerns emphasized by Fisher and Shapiro might help hypothetical longtime business partners Jack and Phil negotiate more effectively about Jack's ongoing role in their company, PJB:

> Using the core concerns as a lens to understand Jack . . . Phil might realize that Jack:
>
> 1. Thinks that Phil does not appreciate his contribution to PJB;
> 2. Is concerned about his affiliation with Phil and with PJB;
> 3. Feels a need for autonomy in decision-making about PJB and his relationship to it;
> 4. Is concerned about his status in relation to Phil, Phil, Jr., and PJB; and
> 5. Believes that he does not have a fulfilling or appropriate role in PJB.

Thus, Phil should be able to see that Jack's core concerns were significant in the evolution of the conflict and would remain important to Jack during the negotiation. . . .

Phil's new insights about Jack would enable him to use Jack's core concerns as a lever to attempt to stimulate positive emotions in Jack. For

> instance, Phil might express appreciation for Jack's commitment to PJB, his strong relations with customers, his willingness to travel, and other interests or perspectives that Jack expresses during the negotiation. Phil might build affiliation with Jack by recalling their long history of work and friendship; by sitting in such a way as to convey closeness; by initiating in-person, rather than email contact, and talking about the real issues in their relationship. In addition, he could respect Jack's autonomy in the negotiation by consulting with Jack before making any decisions about negotiation procedure. He might propose a brainstorming process or ask Jack to suggest options for addressing various issues. He could acknowledge Jack's status as a founder of the firm, as a great boiler salesman, as an expert on boilers, as a good golfer, and a bon vivant. Finally, Phil could try to ensure that Jack had a fulfilling role in the negotiation (i.e, a role that has "a clear purpose," is "personally meaningful," and "is not a pretense"), with lots of opportunities to speak freely and to influence the focus, procedures, and outcome.[27]

The lawyer can also gain perspective on a counterpart's interests by providing that counterpart with information about his own or his client's needs and interests. Disclosing information can trigger the reciprocity norm (see chapter 6), resulting in reciprocal disclosure.[28] Thus, it can be helpful to commence a negotiation by sharing information with a counterpart in the hope that the favor will be returned. In addition, the lawyer may be able to pick up information by observing the counterpart's reaction to the disclosure. As many negotiation experts have pointed out, there is a strategic tension between sharing information, which can help both sides achieve joint gains, and guarding information, which may be important for achieving individual gains. Accordingly, it can be important to disclose information incrementally and to be clear that disclosure must be a two-way street.[29]

Devising a Proposal

Having gathered lots of information and considered multiple perspectives, a negotiator must eventually structure a proposal and consider how best to convey it to the other side. Just as it is important to think about the other side's interests, preferences, and constraints, it is also useful to think about how a negotiating counterpart will be affected by the proposal itself and the way it is presented.

Be Ambitious

Research has demonstrated an important link between negotiator aspirations and negotiation outcomes. For example, in the transactional context, negotiators with more challenging goals tend to negotiate more advantageous final sales prices than do negotiators with lower goals. Negotiators with more challenging aspirations similarly tend to have higher expectations for their performance in the negotiation, exchange more information, and make more exacting demands. They also tend to be willing to devote more time to the negotiation, slower to make concessions, and more willing to bluff.[30]

> Always aim your goals and aspiration for the moon, because even if you don't make it, you'll always end up reaching the stars.
> —Anonymous[31]

Challenging aspirations can also anchor other negotiation judgments (see chapter 4).[32] By making a particularly low offer, for example, a buyer may be able to influence seller's aspirations or even her sense of how much an item is worth, although there is, of course, less room to sway the valuation of an item whose worth can be objectively determined. The question of how extreme is extreme enough but not too extreme will turn on the information that the negotiator is able to obtain about his counterpart's perspective and alternatives and what the negotiator is able to justify with reasons (see chapter 5).[33]

Starting with a more extreme negotiation position also gives the negotiator the chance to make concessions designed to elicit reciprocal concessions from the other side. The negotiator might proceed as follows:

> Joe, as you know, my client demanded $2 million in his complaint, and I don't have to tell you that he very sincerely believes his claim is worth at least that much. Given that we have now decreased our demand to $1.2 million, I think it is only fair that you raise your initial offer of $100,000 by a comparable amount to $900,000. Then maybe we can just split the difference and resolve this claim of copyright infringement for $1.05 million. Whaddya say?

Recall that the psychology underlying distributive justice (see chapter 8) may also lend credibility to this split-the-difference approach.

At the same time, attorneys and clients must be careful not to sink themselves with their own ambitious initial demands by becoming anchored to those demands. If the client starts to believe that her initial demand of $380,000 for the sale of her house is a "fair" demand, then she may have a hard time accepting a lower amount even though it is almost inevitable that the buyer will offer less. Given that even irrelevant numbers can act as anchors, it seems likely that numbers the client believes have been fairly calculated can have an even greater impact.[34]

Hoist with Their Own Petard

In the class action environmental litigation depicted by Jonathan Harr in the book *A Civil Action*, plaintiffs and plaintiffs' attorneys became anchored to the extravagant punitive damages demand made by plaintiffs at the suggestion of Harvard Law School Professor Charles Nesson. Nesson urged that the plaintiffs

> make a demand of more than half a billion dollars—a year's profits from the two defendant companies—in order to "ring alarm bells in corporate boardrooms."[35] Having made the demand, plaintiffs' counsel found it impossible (until they had lost many claims at trial) to settle the case for a lower figure.

Negotiators must also recognize that those who hold more challenging aspirations are more likely to be dissatisfied with the results of the negotiation, given the same objective outcome, than those with less challenging goals. In other words, although parties who are more ambitious tend to achieve objectively better results in negotiations, such ambition may also lead to subjective disappointment as those who seek the most are not likely to get all they hope for and are more likely to compare their outcome to something even more favorable.[36]

Thus, while we do not counsel attorneys to avoid making high demands or low offers, we do counsel them to remind themselves and their clients that extreme demands and offers are just starting points in most negotiations. Attorneys can note that although it may feel disappointing to make an aggressive offer that will inevitably be rejected, such offers can often ultimately lead to better results. In addition, when the negotiation has concluded, satisfaction can be improved by making a favorable comparison to the bottom line goals rather than by focusing on the highest aspiration.[37]

> ◆ ◆ ◆ ◆ ◆
> **The Negotiation Dance**
>
> Consider the ways in which an attorney can prepare his client for the negotiation process:
>
> Attorney: As you know, we're at the point where we need to begin to fashion an offer in this case. The way legal negotiations typically work is that both sides start pretty far apart in the negotiation, and then over time we tend to move closer and closer toward a resolution. Some people refer to this as the negotiation dance. I tell you this because I think our discussion today should have two parts. First, I want to work with you to come up with terms we think would be reasonable terms for resolving the defamation claim that the plaintiff has made against you. But then, after we have come up with those terms, we'll also talk a bit about the strategy for this negotiation. The offer we decide to make after today's meeting won't be our final offer—it will be a lot lower than where we'll end up and is just a starting point for the negotiations. If we are able to settle this dispute, we will likely have to give the plaintiff quite a bit more than we will offer today. Does that make sense to you?
>
> Client: Sure, I get it. Today is just a starting point.

Be Creative

To craft the most effective agreements, negotiators need to be creative and open-minded in structuring their proposals. It is common, particularly in independent Western cultures, for people to be affected by a *fixed pie bias*. That is, we tend to assume that interests are incompatible—that one side's gain is necessarily another side's loss.[38] Legal settings, in particular, can elicit these sorts of assumptions. People tend to associate law with competitiveness (rather than cooperation). When primed with legal concepts they perceive situations as more competitive, perceive others as more untrustworthy, and make more competitive decisions.[39] Relatedly, many of us tend to assume that others are more selfish than we are (see chapter 1). When such differences are overestimated, it is hard to work together and find common ground.

> I have had a philosophy for some time in regard to [this treaty], and it goes like this: the Russians will not accept a . . . treaty that is not in their best interest, and it seems to me that if it is in their best interest, it can't be in our best interest.
> —U.S. Congressman Floyd Spence[40]

The assumption of a fixed pie is so engrained that it can cause negotiators to compromise (that is, to divide a seemingly fixed pie) even when no compromise is needed:

> Leigh Thompson has shown that even when two sides want the exact same outcome, negotiators often settle for a different outcome because they assume that they must compromise to reach agreement. She developed a negotiation simulation that included two issues that were compatible; the parties had the exact same preference. From an objective standpoint, there was nothing to negotiate on these issues, as no real conflict existed. Yet 39 percent of negotiators did not agree on the mutually preferred outcome on at least one of the two compatible issues![41]

When negotiators assume a fixed pie and fail to share information that might reveal compatible interests and supportive creative solutions, suboptimal deals can result.

While some pies really are fixed in size, many are not. However, creativity is often required to see that interests may be aligned. Negotiations that appear to turn on a single issue can be recharacterized as involving multiple issues that permit one side to gain without causing equivalent harm to the opposing party. For example, although both Company A and Company B may have insisted that they needed exclusive control over a disputed trademark, perhaps this issue could be resolved using a license that gives some control to each company. In a case involving a claim of wrongful termination, a new job might be created that will provide income to the offeree and services to the offerer. Stretching payments over time may be beneficial to both sides of a transaction. Furthermore, apologies, institutional reform, and community service can be useful components of mutually beneficial dispute resolution.

> ✦ ✦ ✦ ✦ ✦
> ### Recognize the Power of Apology
>
> Recall the letter of apology provided by MIT President Charles Vest to the parents of Scott Krueger, a young man whose death was attributed to excess alcohol consumption at a fraternity party (see chapter 10), and the apology issued by Kent Hospital to actor James Woods and his family following the death of Woods's brother (see chapter 8). By changing the assessments that people make about the harm that occurred, the motivations of the relevant actors, or the extent to which respect has been shown, apologies can be central in helping the parties to reach agreement.
>
> While apologies will not always be appropriate, attorneys should ask themselves whether an apology might be meaningful to an opposing party and whether the client might be interested in receiving or willing to give an appropriate apology. If so, attorneys can arrange meetings between clients to allow for personal interaction or can help their clients to provide written apologies.

A range of psychological insights can be useful in developing creative proposals. A creative corporate attorney, for example, might capitalize on what she knows about framing (see chapter 5) by seeking to limit benefits for newly hired or newly unionized workers rather than restricting benefits previously granted to the union. Furthermore, recognizing that thinking about the near term focuses attention on the details while a longer time perspective focuses attention more globally, a negotiator who is trying to get a counterpart to make repairs to a property might consider changing the temporal focus of the discussion, shifting attention from the immediate term (in which logistical impediments may seem formidable) to discussion about undertaking repairs over the next several years, making those actions seem more feasible (see chapter 5).[42]

> ✦ ✦ ✦ ✦ ✦
> ### Charitable Contribution in Lieu of Punitive Damages
>
> Plaintiffs sometimes desire punitive damages as a way of shaking up a defendant. But defendants often object to putting a punitive damages payment into the pocket of plaintiffs and their attorneys. Creative plaintiffs' attorneys have forged settlements by suggesting that the plaintiff forgo the punitive damages component of the claim and instead have defendants make substantial contributions to legal services or charitable organizations.[43]

Similarly, the attorney representing Dr. X, the inventor of a new product that he claims can deodorize odoriferous shoes, might recognize that Dr. X has a much higher tolerance for risk than do the stores in which he is trying to place his product and so might propose a consignment agreement. Under such an agreement, the stores, which prefer less risk, would not need to pay Dr. X for his product until it was purchased by customers; and Dr. X, who is more tolerant of risk, would bear most of the risk that the product might not sell. Recognizing different orientations toward risk—across individuals, situations, and even ways of engaging in mental accounting[44]—can also help attorneys structure more creative settlements. For example, repeat players can often afford to be more risk neutral, evaluating overall risk over a stream of outcomes. By contrast, people who are rarely involved in litigation, such as most plaintiffs in personal injury suits, may not feel as if they can afford to lose a case at trial.

Attorneys should not assume that their clients share the attorneys' preferences about risk. Differences between the attorney and the client might be accentuated because the money or other gains or losses at issue would primarily belong to the client and not the attorney. Accordingly, it can be helpful for attorneys to discuss risk tolerance with their clients and to alert clients to instances in which they express preferences that are contrary to the rules of probability. Such discussion can equip the client to make educated decisions that are consistent with her own risk preferences.

While we have seen that being creative and brainstorming options can aid development of a proposal, it is also true that the generation of too many options can impede good decision making: "people often have great difficulty selecting the value-maximizing option when multiple options are on the table; that is, the very presence of multiple options has a tendency to induce people to make suboptimal decisions."[45] Thus, as the attorney works with the client to develop a proposal, the attorney should be careful not to overwhelm the client with limitless choices and should help the client develop tools to choose among various creative options.

Recognize the Importance of Fairness and Justice Norms

In constructing and presenting offers, an attorney should consider how the other side will perceive the fairness of the offer. People tend to care a great deal about fairness and justice even though they may not always agree about what is fair or just (see chapter 8). Furthermore, people may accept a proposal that is objectively less beneficial if they are convinced that other similarly situated people have accepted a comparable deal or if special circumstances seem to warrant a deviation from what otherwise might be the norm. Consider the following:

> Prosecutor Ramirez: Mr. Limberger, your client has been charged with arson in the second degree, which carries a penalty of up to ten years in prison and a fine of up to $10,000. We are willing to offer your client a plea agreement. In these circumstances, it is the regular practice and custom of this office to offer your client this deal: if she pleads guilty to the lesser charge of arson in the third degree, she will serve just four years in state prison and pay a fine of $5,000.

Apart from whether this plea agreement is truly fair in the grand scheme of things, the prosecutor has increased the likelihood that the defendant and her lawyer will find it acceptable by presenting the plea as consistent with the office's typical practice and, therefore, unbiased or at least not comparatively unfair (see chapter 8).[46] Such a characterization also takes advantage of the influence of social proof (see chapter 6) by at least intimating that others have taken similar offers. Of course, were the recipient of such an offer to investigate and learn that the offer is not in fact consistent with office policy, such a characterization by the prosecutor would likely backfire.

In similar ways, recognizing a negotiation counterpart's special claims to fair or just treatment can also make an offer more attractive.

> Ms. Jones, your client Smith Recording Studio has sued my client, Video Enterprises, claiming that my client damaged some of the Smith Recording equipment by improperly installing additional amplifiers. This allegation particularly pains my client as it has greatly appreciated its relationship with Smith Recording over the years. As you know, we do not believe that any of our workers did or could have damaged the Smith equipment. Nonetheless, we think it would be fair and appropriate to recognize the value of our longstanding business relationship by crediting Smith Recording in the amount of $500 on its next bill.

Presenting Proposals

In addition to the substantive content of a proposal, the way that a proposal is presented can be quite important. In particular, to the extent that the negotiator anticipates that the counterpart will resist the proposal, the negotiator should try to structure the proposal and its presentation in a way to reduce that resistance.[47]

To Whom Should the Offer Be Conveyed?

Savvy negotiators, like children, know that it may be better to address an offer to one member of a team than to another. Even though parents may well consult with one another on many issues, one parent or the other may be the softer touch when the child asks to get that special treat. Similarly, one member of the board of directors may be more receptive to an idea than another, or one member of a legal team more amenable to talking settlement. Attorneys should remember that they have the power to ask to negotiate with or against particular negotiators.

As we have seen, in traditional negotiation, attorneys are the conduits through whom proposals flow. If the substance of proposals were all that mattered and if that substance could always be conveyed verbatim and with the same inflection and other nonverbal cues, it would not matter that the proposal was conveyed to a client through an intermediary. However, we have seen that interpretations are malleable, that no two people will likely see the world in exactly the same way, and that communication is complicated. As many of us learned while playing the childhood game of "telephone," every transmission of a message is an opportunity for distortion. Thus, even though an attorney may intend to be a completely accurate conduit for a proposal, and while the ethical attorney will surely attempt to convey the key terms of a proposal accurately, it is quite possible the proposal may transform in transmission due to changes in language or emphasis.

> ✦ ✦ ✦ ✦ ✦
> ### The Attorney Conveys an Offer
>
> In the example below, notice the differences between the way an employer's offer is originally conveyed and the way it is then presented to the client employee:
>
>> Employer's attorney to employee's attorney: As you know, my client, ABC Industries, denies that it engaged in any discrimination in failing to promote your client, Jenny Renteria, to be a senior account representative. ABC Industries also denies that Ms. Renteria was subjected to any illegal sexual harassment. Nonetheless, we believe Ms. Renteria to be a very capable account representative and we have valued her services greatly over the past fifteen years. Because we think so highly of Ms. Renteria's work and because we would hate to lose her services as an account representative, we are hopeful that we might find a mutually beneficial solution to the dispute that has arisen here. Might Ms. Renteria be interested in a settlement that would transfer her to our Second Street office? We understand that office is closer to Ms. Renteria's home. Her title would remain what it has been, account representative, but the nature of the Second Street office would allow her to expand her job responsibilities somewhat, and we would therefore increase her pay by $1.50 per hour. Her new boss would be Jane McDougal, who has the reputation of being one of our best managers. I really think Ms. Renteria would enjoy her new position.
>>
>> Employee's attorney to employee: Well, I got a call from ABC's attorney, and, as I feared, they are not offering much on the settlement front. They are still completely denying that they engaged in any discrimination or sexual harassment. As a result, they are not willing to give you the promotion. The only thing they are willing to do is to transfer you to another office where you would remain an account representative. On the upside, you would get a pay increase of $1.50 per hour.
>
> Although the plaintiff's attorney's summary is not substantively inaccurate, and likely would not be found to be unethical, the client is far less likely to be attracted to the offer as conveyed by her attorney than she might have been to the offer as conveyed by the defendant's attorney.

Given that receiving attorneys may inadvertently influence how offers are understood, it can be beneficial for attorneys to communicate offers directly to opposing parties when possible. As we will see later in the chapter, one of the potential benefits of mediation is that it allows attorneys and clients to speak directly with opposing parties. But an attorney may request the opportunity to meet personally with the other side outside of mediation as well. An attorney may also consider providing a written rather than verbal offer to her negotiation counterpart. Although the ethical rules do not explicitly require an attorney to convey the written offer itself (as opposed to a verbal restatement) to the client,[48] it is likely that the opposing attorney will provide the letter to her client.[49]

✦ ✦ ✦ ✦ ✦
Meeting with the Decision Makers

In the course of the environmental litigation described in Jonathan Harr's book *A Civil Action*, plaintiffs' attorney Jan Schlictmann repeatedly requested that Beatrice Foods' attorneys, Jerry Facher and Neil Jacobs, allow Schlictmann to meet directly with the "decision-makers" for defendant Beatrice Foods:

> Schlictmann . . . thought that Facher was acting in an arrogant, insulting manner, . . . [b]ut Schlictmann didn't let himself feel offended. The first goal in any negotiation was to keep talking, and talking to Facher was the first step to a real negotiation. "We don't have to talk numbers now," said Schlictmann. "Let's get the decision-makers together first."
>
> "You want the decision-maker?" said Facher. "I'm it. You want Mr. Beatrice Foods? He's sitting right here. Tell me what you want. Make it reasonable, and I'll accept, and we can get on with our lives."
>
> "We can't just throw numbers at each other," said Schlictmann. "That doesn't work. We need to set aside some time so we can discuss this—your people and my people—in a neutral place."
>
> Facher grunted at this. "Why don't you bring your clients up here? They're the decision-makers, aren't they? Let me hear them say no to a million dollars."
>
> Schlictmann demurred. They had reached an impasse.[50]

Although both Schlictmann and Facher rejected each other's early attempts to meet with their clients, it can sometimes be wise to request or to agree to such meetings. While there are sometimes countervailing concerns, such as a client's busy schedule or the fear that she will be inappropriately pressured by opposing counsel, allowing the client to hear directly from the opposing party or attorney may ultimately serve the client's interests by better educating him as to the other side's interests and arguments. Note that the plaintiffs did eventually settle their claims with the other major defendant, W. R. Grace, following a series of meetings in which the executive vice president and general counsel for W. R. Grace participated directly.

At the same time, attorneys will also want to consider whether it is best *not* to speak directly to an opposing client but instead to have an opposing attorney or mediator convey the message. If an attorney is aware that an opposing client (perhaps a divorcing husband) is very angry and therefore likely to reject any proposal made by his wife or her attorney, it may be best to allow the husband's trusted attorney to be the intermediary who delivers all messages.

When Should the Offer Be Conveyed?

Once an attorney has a handle on her client's interests and has worked to understand the interests of the other side, should she make the first offer? Negotiation research finds that making the first offer can result in an economic benefit by defining the starting point for negotiation.[51] Recall that initial numbers can anchor judgments even when the initial numbers have no particular relevance and even in negotiations conducted by experienced negotiators (see chapter 4). Particularly when the value of the subject of the negotiation is unclear, making the first offer can focus the valuation of that item at a desired level. For example, imagine that a young painter is selling a work of art to a gallery. Because the painter's work has only recently been discovered, its value is not yet clearly established. If the gallery starts the negotiation by offering the painter $300, the ultimate sale price will likely be much lower than if the artist starts the negotiation by demanding to be paid $20,000 for the work. Along these lines, a real-world art dealer recently bemoaned the fact that he once sold an Andy Warhol painting for $375,000 and just two years later saw other Warhol paintings being sold at auction for $26 million and $71 million.[52]

On the other hand, there can also be psychological benefits to being the party that responds to an opponent's first offer. In particular, when a party lacks the information necessary to accurately assess the subject of the negotiation and set an ambitious anchor, waiting to hear the other side's starting point can be valuable. Perhaps the other side's initial offer will be more favorable than the demand that the responding party would have made. The responding party also has the opportunity to capitalize on both the anchoring phenomenon and the norms of reciprocity and fairness in defining the contours of the zone of agreement. Thus, if our artist starts the negotiation by demanding $20,000 for his piece, the gallery might respond by offering just $300. These two numbers will set the bounds of the bargaining range as the parties bargain toward an ultimate price. Similarly, to the extent that splitting the difference is an attractive heuristic for compromise (see chapter 8), defining the difference to be split can be beneficial. In addition, if the responding party can make it clear that in providing a counteroffer she is already giving ground on a particular issue, the opponent is likely to feel a pull to reciprocate by giving some ground as well (see chapter 6).

To balance out these different psychological effects, we suggest that making the first offer is most sensible when the negotiator has enough information about the other side's goals and interests to make an offer that is neither too disadvantageous nor ludicrously ambitious. Absent sufficient information to make a good first offer, it is better to wait to gather that information or to allow the other side to make the first offer.

> ✦ ✦ ✦ ✦ ✦
> **First Offers and Satisfaction**
>
> Ironically, while making the first offer can result in greater objective gains, it can simultaneously result in lower subjective satisfaction. One study showed that the party making the first offer tends to suffer increased anxiety, presumably as a result of worrying that the first offer was not sufficiently ambitious.[53]

The negotiator may also want to try to anticipate whether his counterpart is likely to be particularly receptive to a proposal at a given point in time. For example, anticipated regret (see chapter 5) may be more salient at certain points, such as on the eve of trial or of a key ruling.[54] In other words, a party facing the risk that the judge's ruling on summary judgment could go against her may be particularly interested in settlement in order to avoid the future regret of having declined a settlement and then lost the case on summary judgment. Similarly, a prospective tenant's offer to lease a major property may look particularly attractive to the owner at a time when many other tenants' leases are about to lapse.

Countering Concerns About the Source of the Proposal

We have seen that reactive devaluation (see chapter 5) causes people to value the content of a proposal less if it is put forward by the other side. To try to counter this phenomenon, lawyers should look for opportunities to put offers on the table indirectly. As we will see later in the chapter, mediation is an excellent process for dealing with reactive devaluation because offers and acceptances can be conveyed through the mediator.

> " Please accept my resignation. I don't want to belong to any club that will accept people like me as a member.
> —Groucho Marx[55] "

Absent mediation, attorneys should think creatively about using other third parties, such as business associates or allies, as intermediaries to convey offers, as well as acceptances. In international political negotiations, neutral third countries are often used as agents in this fashion. Consider the approach taken by one negotiator:

> The chairman of the council . . . was a prominent figure in the Soviet hierarchy. At some council meetings he would adopt a very noncollaborative stance. This especially occurred when there was some flare-up of antagonistic relations between the United States and the Soviets. . . . In the midst of such episodes, I felt that I was (or would be) a victim of reactive devaluation. I therefore either refrained from making new proposals, waiting for a more propitious time, or engaged in a bit of creative manipulation: I would meet separately with a council member and in private discussions lead him to generate a variant of the proposal I wanted introduced. Coming from the council member of country XYZ, the proposal did not evoke the knee-jerk reactive devaluation that I wished to avoid.[56]

Attorneys can also work to deflect reactive devaluation by clients on both sides by discussing potential deals with one another before making proposals to the clients. For example, the attorneys representing an athlete and a team in negotiations for a new contract might work with each other to develop a proposal—with each inquiring whether a particular figure would meet the other side's needs and indicating that it might be adequate from his perspective—before running it by their clients. In the end, both the player and the owner might think that they and their lawyer, rather than the other side, had initiated the proposed salary figure and that the other side only reluctantly accepted it, thereby reducing the resistance that might otherwise have resulted from reactive devaluation.

The Dynamics of Negotiation

Much negotiation consists of a back-and-forth "dance" that involves both explicit and subtler communication of information and the exchange of proposals. The ways in which negotiators interact with each other during this dynamic process significantly influence how proposals are shaped and agreements are forged.

Building Relationships

Credibility is central to negotiation and can be earned or damaged over time. As we have seen, negotiators who trust each other tend to be more willing to disclose information to each other, to rely on information provided, to cooperate and search for mutually beneficial solutions, and to negotiate with each other in the future.[57] Thus, attorneys must always remember the importance of building and maintaining a good reputation. Whereas musician Marvin Gaye reportedly said that "negotiation means . . . getting the best of your opponents,"[58] psychologists and experienced negotiators might recommend taking a longer-term view.

Attorneys can demonstrate their competence, and thereby enhance their credibility, by always being thoroughly prepared for a negotiation, by listening to their counterpart, and by providing reasons and explanations for their positions (see chapters 6 and 7). An attorney who is commencing negotiations with someone she does not know might also try to obtain a reference that would impress her counterpart.

It is also important to build rapport with the negotiator on the other side. We have seen that negotiators who have had a chance to develop rapport with the other side tend to consider a broader range of options, are able to elicit more information, are more likely to reach agreement, and are more willing to work together in the future (see chapter 7). To take advantage of the power of liking (see chapter 6), a negotiator might draw on shared interests to create a bond ("how about that game last night?"), offer a compliment ("I just love those shoes you are wearing today— where did you get them?"), subtly mimic a counterpart's posture (see chapter 7), or

> ✦ ✦ ✦ ✦ ✦
> ### An Introduction
>
> Julie: Mary, I'm going to try to purchase a major tract of land from the city on behalf of my client, Vista Development Group. I've never dealt with anyone from the city before, have you?
>
> Mary: Sure, I deal with Lucinda Fingle over there all the time. We have a very good relationship.
>
> Julie: Would you be willing to introduce me or put in a good word for me?
>
> Mary: No problem. I'm always happy to do a favor for an old friend. I'll set up a lunch.

offer a warm drink to create a feeling of personal warmth (see chapter 1). At times an attorney can blend liking and reciprocity, perhaps by buying a counterpart lunch or treating her to a round of golf (see chapter 6).

Finally, the attorney can try to use the negotiation process to achieve procedural justice (see chapter 8). People care deeply about how they are treated and want to voice their concerns, seek trustworthy processes, and be treated with dignity and respect. By attending to these concerns, an attorney can create more joint and individual gains for her client.

> ✦ ✦ ✦ ✦ ✦
> ### Rapport and Deceit
>
> While there are many benefits of establishing rapport with a negotiation counterpart, there are also some pitfalls of which to be wary. In particular, one study demonstrated that "negotiators seeking to build or maintain rapport may be more likely to deceive their partners than to disappoint them with the truth."[59] However, the same study also showed that negotiators who are aware of this danger can better resist the temptation to be unethical.

Interpreting Counterparts' Behavior

At times, particularly in the dispute context, it can be quite difficult to reach agreement because each side is ready to assume that its view of the world is right and that the other guy has it all wrong. Confirmation bias, then, often leads us to become even more convinced of our own perspective. We have learned that we naturally see ourselves in more favorable terms than we see others and that we may attribute others' mistakes to character flaws while we link our own to situational context (the fundamental attribution error). Hindsight bias can also sharpen divides as it may lead us to conclude that mistakes were, or certainly should have been, predictable when perhaps the problem was not so obvious in foresight (see chapters 1 and 4).

> If you come to a negotiation table saying that you have the final truth, that you know nothing but the truth and that is final, if you are not willing to accept anything, you will get nothing.
> —Harri Holkeri[60]

Sometimes a client's assumptions regarding a counterpart's prior behavior may influence the client's evaluation of a settlement offer.

> Consider the situation of Rubbermaid's contract to supply their kitchen and bath products to WalMart. About a year into the contract Rubbermaid asked WalMart to reopen negotiations. Rubbermaid was having margin problems with the contract they had negotiated with WalMart. Why? The situational attribution is that the cost of their raw materials increased dramatically with the rise in oil prices over which they had no control. The dispositional attribution is that Rubbermaid did not negotiate a very good contract; they should have thought about this contingency and planned for it. The dispositional attribution casts aspersion on Rubbermaid's management—a generalization of perceptions. Such perceptions at their most cynical might be that Rubbermaid intentionally avoided negotiating a contingency in the contract based on raw material costs because they hoped to take advantage of lower raw material costs and planned to reopen negotiations if raw materials became more expensive, which would have implications for WalMart's willingness to renegotiate the contract and their negotiating behavior. In contrast, the situational attribution implies no bad faith bargaining but events outside of parties' control make reopening negotiations perfectly reasonable.[61]

Remembering, and even delicately reminding one another, that behavior can be strongly influenced by the pressures of the situation can help forge agreement. Here, Walmart's attorney might help Walmart think through how it characterizes Rubbermaid's action and what implications that characterization has for Walmart's negotiation position. Specifically, the attorney might encourage Walmart to consider the possibility that Rubbermaid acted in good faith. The attorney might also help Walmart to see that its willingness to reopen the negotiation should not depend exclusively on Walmart's characterization of Rubbermaid's past action. While the possibility that Rubbermaid acted in bad faith is a relevant factor to consider in deciding whether a future deal is advisable, Walmart might also decide that there is reason to believe that a similar breach is unlikely to recur or that the risk of continuing bad faith is not sufficient to scuttle a profitable deal. By using their own experience and credibility to emphasize that an opposing counterpart or attorney may have alternative and valid perspectives or motivations, attorneys can help their clients find mutually beneficial middle ground.

In similar ways, it can be important to think carefully about how to understand the behavior of an opponent within the negotiation. As we saw in chapter 1, when a negotiator takes a tough position, we may attribute that behavior to the negotiator's supposedly disagreeable personality rather than to the fact that the counterpart may simply have a good alternative to a negotiated agreement. In order to find out more about why counterparts have behaved in ways that the negotiator finds objectionable and to allow the negotiator to more successfully extract concessions, the negotiator can take the perspective of counterparts and remember that their behavior is influenced by their circumstances; that their misstatements may reflect memory limits rather than deceit (see chapter 2); and that their unwillingness to budge from a position may not reflect stubbornness but rather the effects of anchoring, optimistic overconfidence, a reluctance to abandon sunk costs, or a feeling that they have been disrespected (see chapters 4, 5, and 8).[62]

It also may be "beneficial for negotiators to encourage their *partners* to do some perspective taking."[63] Psychological research has found that negotiators tend to achieve better outcomes when they negotiate with someone who is able to take their perspective.

Finally, it can be important to assess whether a negotiation counterpart is providing truthful information. As we saw in chapter 7, we often rely on unreliable cues to deception. However, attorneys can minimize a counterpart's incentive to lie by being prepared and informed and by asking lots of specific questions. Attorneys can also gather information from other sources to check the accuracy of statements made by negotiation counterparts, watch for changes in counterparts' manner that might signal deception, and listen carefully to the nuances of counterparts' statements.[64]

Conveying Information

As attorneys share information and attempt to persuade the other side, it is important for them to pay particular attention to principles of good communication. They should convey information in clear and concrete terms, avoid legalese, provide information in multiple ways, and use visual aids when helpful (see chapter 7).

To express ourselves most effectively, it is important to become attuned to the perspective of our negotiation counterparts. Some psychologists have called this process *tuning*—taking account of our counterpart's information, opinions, and knowledge in expressing our own message.[65] Thus, just as any good communicator or teacher will try to take account of his audience, negotiators need to consider the background, culture, and experiences of their negotiation counterparts, tailoring the message accordingly.

Sometimes, expressing emotions can be a useful way to convey information about positions or interests. For example, the expression of positive emotions can signal the negotiator's openness to exploring a particular option, and the expression of disappointment in the counterpart can lead to cooperation.[66] Expressing anger over a particular proposal can elicit concessions from the other side—particularly when the other side does not have good alternatives—by signaling to the opponent that the negotiator will not back down from her position.[67] A negotiator in an international political context may angrily threaten war if his country's wishes are not respected, and a union negotiator may angrily threaten to strike if management does not comply with some of the union's demands. Even the appearance of apparent irrational anger can be useful in some situations. Game theorist Thomas Schelling pointed out many years ago that one driver can gain an advantage in the "negotiated" game of chicken by ripping his steering wheel off and throwing it out the window.[68]

> ✦ ✦ ✦ ✦ ✦
> **Anger as a Double-Edged Sword?**
>
> We have seen that expressing anger over a proposal can lead the counterpart to make concessions, but communicating anger can also have its perils. In particular, research has found that negotiators are more likely to deceive angry opponents, that the expression of anger can backfire and lead to less favorable outcomes when the consequences to the other side of nonagreement are low, that angry emotions can be contagious and lead to a desire to retaliate, and that negotiators are disinclined to negotiate again in the future with counterparts who have expressed anger.[69]

Silence, too, can be a means of signaling thoughts and intentions. Indeed, some cultures are renowned for their effective use of silence in negotiations.[70] Silence in response to an offer may be interpreted as a lack of interest, or silence may elicit more information from the other side. Of course, as with all communication, silence can be misconstrued. Thus, it is often useful to inquire further into the meaning of silence.

As we attempt to communicate with negotiation counterparts, it is important to remember the illusion of transparency, that is, we are not as adept at conveying our thoughts and emotions as we think we are (see chapter 3). In addition, we sometimes try to make our points indirectly, fearing that our words will cause defensiveness or anger or will leave too much of a trail. A major league ball club may not want to state in words that the aging star player is no longer worth $750,000 a year but may be willing to raise an eyebrow to express its feelings about such a salary proposal. However, the raised eyebrow that seemed so obvious may not be perceived or understood by the opposing party. Thus, it is important to pay close attention to how well a counterpart seems to understand what we have attempted to convey.

Relatedly, we have seen that the mode of communication will have a big impact on a negotiator's ability to convey information effectively (chapter 7). In-person negotiations will include body language, appearances, and physical setting. Written negotiations, by contrast, will focus negotiators more intensely on the meaning of words, while telephonic negotiations will include the tenor of those words. Negotiators may, in the interest of speed, efficiency, or clarity, prefer to conduct some negotiations in writing. However, they will need to be cognizant that the lack of personal presence may make rapport building more difficult, that misunderstandings may occur due to loss of nuance and temporal asynchrony, and that the creation of a paper trail can sometimes make it more difficult for negotiators to change their positions.

Presenting Options

Negotiations typically involve discussion of a set of alternatives or options. We saw in chapter 5 that the frame in which potential decisions are presented often makes a difference in how options are perceived. Thus, the way in which attorneys present options and alternatives to those options can help them succeed in negotiations. Consider how the framing of various options would likely affect negotiation counterparts' assessment of those options:

- Highlighting the potential losses of an alternative will make that alternative more unattractive:
    If your client rejects this offer and goes to trial, you face a substantial risk that you will lose, and your client will end up with no car at all; whereas if you accept this offer, your client will be able to buy a nice used car or to use the settlement to lease a BMW just like the one that he lost in the accident.
- Characterizing an option as the standard way of doing things can play to a counterpart's bias in favor of the status quo and thus make that option more appealing.[71] A negotiator representing a buyer, for example, might suggest that it is "standard practice" in the industry for the seller to pay all shipping costs or for the seller to take on the risk that the product will be damaged during the course of shipment.
- Providing a proposed contract as the basis for negotiation can allow the negotiator to capitalize on the pull of default provisions. Counterparts will be less likely to negotiate changes to terms that seem to be part of a standard form. Drafting the contract can also provide a significant advantage because although nondrafters may focus on certain key contractual provisions, such as price, they tend to focus less on less prominent, but potentially important, provisions such as those pertaining to timing, scope, or publicity.[72]
- Recognizing penalty aversion and presenting a price differential as a bonus or discount, rather than a penalty, will help to make that choice attractive. Similarly, imposing or highlighting an effective penalty if the offer is rejected, such as an increase in closing costs or interest due, can push the other side toward agreement.

- Disaggregating the pieces of the offer that the counterpart will find attractive will highlight these gains, and aggregating the pieces of the offer that the counterpart is likely to find less attractive will minimize the sense of loss. For example, in making an offer regarding the sale of a business, the negotiator should separately highlight the attributes that the buyer will likely find positive, such as an early closing date, a reasonable price, and the seller's willingness to provide names of existing customers. If there are aspects of the offer for which the buyer might have less enthusiasm, such as the need for a formal letter of credit, an indemnification clause, and limitations on the permissible scope of the business, these should be aggregated into a single request.

Simultaneously proposing multiple options can also be a useful technique for providing a context within which options are to be selected. As we now know, the perceived value of a proposal may vary substantially depending upon how it compares to other options (see chapter 5). Options can look different when they are considered in isolation than when they are considered in comparison to other options. Negative features tend to loom particularly large when we are looking to reject options, and positive features tend to be salient when we are choosing. Furthermore, we know that people tend to be attracted to a middle option and will be drawn to the better of two similar options as compared to a third, dissimilar option.

Of course, in employing any of these strategies, an attorney must be careful not to be perceived as manipulative or even dishonest. For example, a supposed penalty that has been created only to encourage closing a deal might cause ill will and thereby backfire. As always, things that are good in moderation may not be good in excess.

Persuading and Eliciting Concessions

To be effective as negotiators, we must convince others to make desired concessions, to help us to devise creative options, and to accept the agreements that we believe serve our client's interests. In addition to thinking about how to most effectively present options, it can be useful to draw on a range of persuasive tools to achieve these ends (see chapter 6).

> Negotiation consists of assessment, persuasion, and exchange.
> —Robert J. Condlin[73]

Negotiators are often highly motivated and able to focus on the relevant issues. Accordingly, the attorney can use her advocacy skills—highlighting the strengths of her position and the weaknesses of her opponent's position—to persuade a negotiation counterpart that a particular resolution makes sense. In addition, providing reasons or justifications for positions can be quite persuasive.[74] Although the logic of argumentation will come naturally to attorneys, it is also important to think carefully about how to make those arguments the most persuasive.

> ✦ ✦ ✦ ✦ ✦
> **Concessions as Losses and Gains**
>
> Because losses loom larger than gains (see chapter 5), it is likely that negotiation counterparts will differently assess the value of the same concession. The negotiator making the concession will see the concession as a loss—something she is giving up—and is likely to value it more highly than the negotiator on the other side who is the beneficiary of the concession and sees it as a gain. Assisting the parties to objectively value concessions, therefore, can help to forge agreement.

Good persuasion involves simple, clear, direct communication and arguments that are tailored to the circumstances and interests of the other side (see chapter 6). For example, rather than state, "It is well known that juries in our jurisdiction never award punitive damages to plaintiffs in disability suits," it may be more effective to say, "Because your client did not come across as very sympathetic in her deposition, it is highly unlikely that a jury in our jurisdiction would award her punitive damages." Similarly, it can be helpful to remember that people from different cultures or holding different perspectives may not be persuaded by the same arguments. Thus, arguments about the importance of protecting family relationships or ensuring future amicable dealings will work better in some contexts than in others.

Effective negotiators also employ a range of indirect persuasive strategies to prompt concessions by the other side (see chapter 6). For example, drawing on the psychology of reciprocity, an attorney might highlight his own concessions for the opponent so that the opponent feels compelled to make concessions as well. Because a concession is likely to seem more significant to the side that makes it than it does to the side that receives it (see chapter 5), it can be helpful to identify the concession and draw attention to its import.

> ❝
> [T]he vast majority of writing on negotiation has ignored the element of interpersonal influence. Since negotiators spend a great deal of time trying to persuade each other to agree to their desired outcome, this seems a glaring omission.
> —Deepak Malhotra & Max Bazerman[75]
> ❞

The negotiator can also try to evoke reciprocation by employing the door-in-the-face strategy, that is, following a rather extreme offer or demand with a more modest proposal (see chapter 6). Alternatively, the negotiator can try to stimulate reciprocal concessions by laying out an initial offer and then immediately improving that offer (the that's-not-all technique) (see chapter 6):

Joe, my client really wants to seal the deal with your client today if at all possible. Thus, we are not only willing to provide you with the premises for the discounted rate of $2,200 per month for the next two years, but we are also willing to throw in the cost of renovations, up to a limit of $5,000.

Savvy negotiators can also capitalize on the psychology of consistency and commitment to persuade others to their position (see chapter 6). For example, the attorney can use the foot-in-the-door technique to get a counterpart's initial commitment to a modest proposal or concession and then try to parlay that commitment into the completion of a larger deal. Similarly, in negotiating a transaction, the attorney might try to broker agreement on the broad outlines of a deal, hoping to generate commitment to the deal such that later decisions on the finer points will be made in ways that are consistent with that initial agreement.

Knowing that people have difficulty moving away from their publicly expressed commitments, a savvy negotiator might look for prior expressed commitments that could be helpful or ask for a counterpart to agree on some general principles that could be used to forge an agreement. For example, a plaintiff's attorney suing a corporate defendant might cite to general language in the corporation's mission statement that the company seeks to enhance public health. A defense lawyer attempting to negotiate a plea agreement might reference a prosecutor's prior statement that incarceration imposes high costs on taxpayers and society as a whole. Applying the same principle, good negotiators will avoid pushing their counterparts to make statements or bottom-line positions from which it will be hard to move away.

Negotiators might also try to use the traditional low-balling approach by first obtaining agreement to one set of terms and then backing away from those terms to some degree (see chapter 6):

> Mary, I have just a few provisions that my client has asked me to add to the deal that we worked out yesterday. First, Human Resources insists that the terms of our agreement need to remain confidential. Second, in-house counsel has asked me to ensure that your client pay any taxes that the IRS might assess on the settlement were they to do an audit. I think it is highly unlikely that the IRS would poke into this. I assume you have no problem with those minor additions to our agreement?

This approach can be effective in the short run. Needless to say, however, developing a reputation as an attorney who routinely makes such "minor" additions can wreak havoc with the lawyer's credibility and diminish the effectiveness of this strategy.

Negotiators might also try to obtain agreement by imposing a deadline, evoking concerns about scarcity (see chapter 6). For example, the negotiator might let a counterpart know that a particular offer can only remain on the table for a limited period of time:

> Attorney: My client, Linda, would like to lease these premises to your client, Bob. Frankly, Linda likes Bob and likes the idea of his running a skateboard concession in the very spot where Linda's dad used to run a similar business. However, Linda also needs to get this property leased out as quickly as possible in light of her own financial situation, so if Bob cannot accept this offer by tomorrow afternoon, Linda is going to need to make a deal with Fred, who is interested in leasing the premises to open a tattoo parlor.

Fearing the loss of the other side's interest, the lessee may go ahead and commit to a deal even though it is less attractive than he had hoped. Of course, invoking scarcity

> [K]eeping negotiation deadlines secret is a mistake.... Negotiators obtain better outcomes when they tell their opponents about their final deadlines. Moreover, negotiators who keep their deadlines secret increase the risk of an impasse.
> —Francesca Gino & Don Moore[76]

must be employed cautiously because a savvy counterpart may successfully call the bluff:

Mike, you have said that this offer is "take it or leave it" and that you will take it off the table by the end of the day. However, my client and I don't like those games. Why can't you give us a few days more to consider your offer?

Ironically, given the power of deadlines, we often fail to inform our counterpart of our own time constraints for fear that knowledge of our predicament will give the other side an advantage. Disclosing our deadlines, however, informs the other side that their time is short as well. Indeed, recent studies have found that negotiators who disclose their deadlines to the other side achieve better-negotiated outcomes. Thus, it can be persuasive to be forthcoming with a counterpart about the existence of a deadline.[77]

◆ ◆ ◆ ◆ ◆

Misperceiving the Impact of Deadlines

Externally imposed deadlines, such as the expiration of a tax regulation that allows a particular deal, impact both sides. Each negotiator, however, tends to believe that the pressure of such deadlines will harm him more than it will harm the other side. Under this impression, a negotiator may hurry to reach agreement and accept less advantageous terms. Focusing on how the deadline might also impact the counterpart can moderate this misperception.[78]

Appeals to authority or social norms can also be persuasive (see chapter 6). A negotiator, for example, can cite to the authority of someone who is respected or to a social norm favoring agreement:

Joe, I really hope we can close this shopping center deal today. Bert Jones [chairman of the local chamber of commerce], whom I know we both respect very much, told me just yesterday that he thinks it would be very beneficial to the city's business community if we could clarify the status of this property that has been vacant for so long.

Recognizing the tendency to overweight sunk costs (see chapter 5) can also help the negotiator to be persuasive:

Your client has already invested more than $2 million in this project. It would be a real shame to let all that money go down the drain. I strongly urge you to invest the additional million, which will help us to make this project successful and help you to recoup your investment.

And, finally, given the nature of reactive devaluation (see chapter 5), the attorney may want to seem to resist or take time to think about a proposal rather than endorsing it too eagerly. If the other side believes that a negotiator has accepted the proposal with reluctance, it may be less likely to devalue the proposal. Feeling as though it is getting a fair deal will increase the other side's satisfaction and likely their compliance and willingness to negotiate in the future.

> My father said: "You must never try to make all the money that's in a deal. Let the other fellow make some money too, because if you have a reputation for always making all the money, you won't have many deals."
> —J. Paul Getty[79]

Dealing with Emotion

Emotions can also be central to negotiations. As we have seen (see chapter 3), emotions can affect cognitive processing, convey information, cause an emotional reaction in a counterpart, or operate as an incentive for a counterpart (who might, for example, strive to avoid making someone angry).[80]

Some take the position that negotiators should try to take the emotion out of negotiation. For example, Howard Baker, former Senate majority leader and chief of staff to President Ronald Reagan, reportedly stated that "the most difficult thing in any negotiation, almost, is making sure that you strip it of the emotion and deal with the facts."[81] Similarly, Leonard Riskin observes that "[n]egotiators—especially those trained in law—commonly . . . try[] to exclude emotions from negotiation and to focus solely on 'objective' factors."[82] Those who would exclude emotion from negotiation seem to strive for a world in which negotiators take on the character of Mr. Spock of *Star Trek* fame. Of course, this is impossible.

However, although emotion can be potentially problematic, it can also be quite helpful to negotiators. Recall that positive moods are more conducive to big-picture creative thinking than are neutral or sad moods (see chapter 3). Thus, it is not surprising that studies have shown positive moods are more conducive to information sharing and collaboration in negotiation and that happier negotiators achieve greater joint gains. Less intuitively, studies have also shown that happier negotiators also achieve greater individual gains in integrative negotiations than do negotiators who express more negative or neutral affect.[83] Thus, at least in some contexts, it can be worthwhile for negotiators to try to put themselves and also their counterparts in a good mood. Conversely, since those in sad moods tend to focus on the details, it can be wise to capitalize on sad or neutral moods to review the fine print before finalizing an agreement. Furthermore, we have seen that expressing anger can sometimes result in more favorable outcomes.

> It is becoming increasingly clear that in order to become a truly skillful negotiator, it is important not only to employ cognitive strategies and skills but also to be emotionally intelligent.
> —Delee Fromm[84]

Sometimes, however, emotions such as anxiety can undermine a negotiator's performance.[85] And negotiators must be wary of negative emotions that can spiral out of control and lead to impasse in a negotiation that might otherwise have succeeded. Even when impasse is avoided, experiencing anger in a negotiation can result in spiteful behavior and less concern for the counterpart's interests. This can lead to a less accurate view of what the other side needs to reach agreement and, ultimately, less joint gain.[86] To avoid such situations, negotiators must become adept at managing emotions—their own and those of their counterparts.

Thus, a litigator who knows that fear may cause her to shy away from trial can remind herself not to cave in as the trial date nears and can seek to bolster her own resolve by bringing in a more confident co-counsel for moral support. A transactional attorney who is aware that she tends to be overly excited by the prospect of closing deals can try to calm herself down prior to negotiation. A negotiator who is anxious about negotiating can engage in some reality testing to come up with a realistic assessment of the risks and possible responses.

✦ ✦ ✦ ✦ ✦

A Fit of Pique

Elected officials are no more immune to their own emotions than anyone else. In fact, a politician's pique purportedly led to a temporary shutting down of the U.S. government:

In 1995, President Bill Clinton and a number of American dignitaries traveled to and from Israel on Air Force One to attend the funeral of Israel's Prime Minister, Itzak Rabin. Newt Gingrich, then Speaker of the U.S. House of Representatives, was on board and hoped to use the long flights to negotiate the budget with President Clinton. According to President Clinton's spokesperson, however, he "just didn't feel like negotiating the budget with the Speaker" after a long day hosting former presidents, secretaries of state, and congressional leaders. Nonetheless, Gingrich felt offended by Clinton's unwillingness to negotiate. To make matters worse, when the plane landed at Andrews Air Force Base, Gingrich had to exit through the rear door, rather than joining the President and others who left through the forward door. In reaction to Clinton's behavior, Gingrich admitted, he deliberately added provisions to a spending bill that he knew would prompt a presidential veto and precipitate a "shutdown" of the government. "This is petty, but I think it is human," Gingrich explained. "You just wonder: Where is their sense of manners? Where's their sense of courtesy?" Newt Gingrich has plenty of company in succumbing to strong negative emotions in situations of conflict. . . .[87]

The psychological studies of mood in negotiation demonstrate that mood is surprisingly easy to influence, even by small acts such as offering a cup of coffee or a cookie, playing pleasant music, or pumping in good smells.[88] Similarly, making polite conversation and giving out compliments are easy ways to improve another person's mood. Techniques such as counting backwards from ten, taking a break, tensing and relaxing leg muscles, or thinking about a more peaceful scene can help a negotiator get his own negative emotions such as anger under control. And we have seen (see chapter 3) that reappraising a situation is often the best way to take the edge off intense emotion.

> [M]anaging emotions does not mean removing the emotional aspect of negotiation. Rather, it means developing a set of strategies to effectively monitor, shape, and influence our own and others' emotional expressions so as to better achieve our goals in negotiations.
> —Leigh Thompson et al.[89]

Negotiators can also try not to provoke undesirable emotions such as anger in a counterpart. For example, in expressing disappointment with a counterpart, the negotiator might be careful not to be accusatory or to cast blame unnecessarily. Instead, the negotiator can try to share his own feelings, ask the counterpart to share her perspective, apologize for any misunderstanding, and try to help the counterpart save face.[90] Being aware that emotions can be contagious (see chapter 3), we must sometimes rein in our tendency to mimic when that would be unproductive.

At times, an attorney may be able to strengthen her position for the value-claiming portion of the negotiation by portraying her client as somewhat angry or extreme while still seeking to maintain positive emotions in the negotiation.

> Attorney Jones, we've worked together successfully before, and I am quite confident that we can work together very successfully in this case as well. Like you, I am completely convinced that it would serve both our clients' interests to resolve this matter amicably and quickly before either party runs up more legal bills. Nonetheless, you do need to know that my client feels very strongly about what has happened to her and her family as a result of actions she attributes to your client. She is pretty angry, and we're going to have to be attentive to that as we strive to work this matter out.

Responding to a Counterpart's Proposal

Once an attorney has received a proposal, psychology also provides guidance regarding how to convey the proposal to the client, how to evaluate it, and how to respond. The attorney must be conscious of how the approaches employed by his negotiation counterpart may make a proposal look unduly appealing.

Conveying Offer to Client

Although the *Model Rules of Professional Conduct* require that attorneys convey all settlement offers to their clients,[91] they do not describe *how* attorneys should convey offers to their clients. Yet, we have seen (in this chapter and in chapter 10) that the manner in which proposals are conveyed to clients will inevitably have a huge impact on whether the client finds them attractive. Even an attorney who aspires to allow clients to make their own choices, free of attorney influence, cannot avoid influencing client choices. Thus, as the attorney considers how to convey an offer to her client, she should think about her own vision of the appropriate attorney-client relationship and remember that her method of conveying proposals will have a significant impact on the client.

Recall, for example, the reactive devaluation phenomenon that may cause a client to resist or reject a proposal simply based on its source (see chapter 5). An attorney might counter this phenomenon by letting the client know that an agreement was forged jointly. In addition, attorneys can help their clients direct their focus to the merits of any proposal rather than to the source from which it came.

Evaluating the Offer

In addition to conveying an offer to the client, the attorney will typically help the client evaluate that offer by comparing it to her other available choices. The client's BATNA (best alternative to a negotiated agreement) may be an anticipated trial, an alternative transaction, or no transaction at all. Yet, while it might seem simple to compare an offer to its possible alternatives, we have seen that a variety of psychological phenomena can make this task difficult.

As an initial matter, negotiators should be careful to resist the anchoring effects of the other side's proposal, articulating a preliminary counterposition prior to hearing its first offer and focusing on the other side's likely BATNA or bottom line in order to call to mind reasons why such an offer might be extreme. This variant of the consider the opposite (see chapter 1) strategy has been shown to be an effective means of limiting the anchoring effect of first offers.[92]

It is inevitable that we will not have complete information about a proposal, the alternatives, or how the decision will impact us in the future. How should the attorney and the client deal with these informational lacunae? We learned in chapter 5 that we may delay decisions while we seek information that is not logically necessary. On the other hand, time pressures can cause us to process information less systematically than we would with more time; and some of us—probably many lawyers—have a high need for closure, which may lead us to make decisions too quickly. If an attorney recognizes that she (or her client) is seeking too much information, she should remind herself and her client that they will never have perfect or complete information. But if, on the other hand, the attorney realizes that she or her client is acting too quickly or without adequate information, she might try to slow down the decision-making process.

In trying to compare a proposal to its alternatives, the attorney should also be aware that both clients and attorneys are likely to be affected by positive illusions (such as overconfidence and egocentrism), availability (being unduly affected by prior, particularly memorable, litigation outcomes, settlements, or deals), the affect heuristic (relying on gut-level impressions or feelings), and the representativeness heuristic (being overly impacted by anecdotes and ignoring relevant quantitative information) (see chapter 4). One additional challenge is the need to balance truth and accuracy on the one hand with rapport on the other (see chapter 10). Inevitably, clients may feel a bit let down, if not sold out, when their attorney points to the downsides of a favored option or emphasizes the need to compromise, but the attorney has an obligation to help clients thoroughly analyze all aspects of relevant proposals.

Each of these influences on judgment can be countered, in part if not in whole, by being more systematic in evaluating the alternatives. Consider Barb, a plaintiff who injured her back after she slipped on the highly waxed floor of a Las Vegas casino. She was out of work for a month and alleges substantial continuing pain but has now returned to work. Barb is inclined to reject the casino's offer of $35,000 because she has read about cases in which plaintiffs in personal injury cases were awarded millions of dollars in damages. She points, in particular, to "that McDonald's coffee-spill case."[93] To counter this very available example, Barb's attorney can explain how the facts of her case differ and provide Barb with statistics describing jury verdicts and settlements in cases that are more similar to hers. The attorney might also tell Barb that certain verdicts tend to get a lot of publicity precisely because they are so unusual but that such cases (including the McDonald's case) are often reversed or reduced on appeal or settle for much lower amounts. Barb's attorney can use similar techniques to help Barb navigate away from other anchors, such as a prior settlement demand, that may have come up earlier in the course of the negotiation.

It can also be helpful to systematically consider each element of the case. Imagine that to prevail on her claim against the casino, Barb would need to show that (1) the casino staff was negligent, (2) the parent corporation she is suing was responsible for the act of the subsidiary management company, and (3) the back injury was due to the fall and not a preexisting injury. The plaintiff would also have to establish the nature of her damages and prove that the damages related to the injury that took place at the casino. The plaintiff's attorney should try to work carefully with the client to come up with objective estimates of—rather than intuitions about—the probability of prevailing on each point.

In addition to assessing the likelihood of success on individual elements of the case, it can be useful to get a better understanding of how all of the pieces of the case fit together. For example, if the probability of prevailing on each of three independent issues is 60%, the probability of prevailing on all three is just 21.6% (that is, 0.6 $\times$ 0.6 $\times$ 0.6). A client or attorney may have an intuition that the odds are fifty-fifty that they will prevail at trial. However, once the case is broken down into its elements and estimated probabilities assigned to those elements, the client or attorney may realize that the overall odds are worse than she originally thought.

As we saw in chapter 10, using decision trees to break down the alternatives can also be helpful, particularly in complex cases.[94] A tree might show, for example, that

> ✦ ✦ ✦ ✦ ✦
> **Evaluating a Settlement Offer**
>
> Attorney: Now that we've received an offer of $35,000 from ABC Casino, we need to figure out how that offer compares to what we think might happen at trial.
>
> Client: Well, I can tell you that right now. The offer stinks, and we would do a whole lot better if we went to trial.
>
> Attorney: I appreciate that you have that initial thought, and I, too, want to believe that you would do a lot better if we took the claim to court; but the hard lesson that I've learned over the years is that we'll ultimately be better off if we try to do a close analysis of the odds of success rather than just go with our gut. I think I do my clients a real disservice if I take them to court when a careful analysis might actually lead us to conclude that it is better to take a settlement offer. Does that make sense to you?
>
> Client: Yeah, I guess. So what do we do now?
>
> Attorney: What I suggest is that I explain all the different pieces of our claim and give you my sense of the chances that we can prove each part of the claim based on the evidence we have so far and based on my knowledge of how other cases have proceeded. Does that work for you?
>
> Client: OK.
>
> Attorney: So, one thing we have to show is that the casino was negligent or careless in the way it handled the waxed floor. It may seem obvious to us, but there are some cases in which people have made a similar claim but a jury found no liability. Sometimes a jury finds that the person who slipped should have been looking at the floor more carefully, walking more carefully, or wearing different shoes. What I did was try to collect a number of similar cases from our jurisdiction and from around the country. Considering how those cases played out and given that it seems that you are the only one who slipped on the floor that night, my sense is that we have roughly a 60% chance of establishing this piece of our case.
>
> Client: OK. Is that it?
>
> Attorney: No, now we also need to think about our chances of succeeding on the other pieces of our claim. . . .

Barb could lose her case on summary judgment and recover nothing (an estimated 10% probability). If summary judgment is denied (an estimated 90% probability), then Barb might either prevail (an estimated 20% probability) or lose (an estimated

80% probability) at trial. If Barb does win at trial, her total recovery is estimated to be $200,000. The decision tree displays these possibilities and shows the plaintiff's expected recovery to be $36,000.

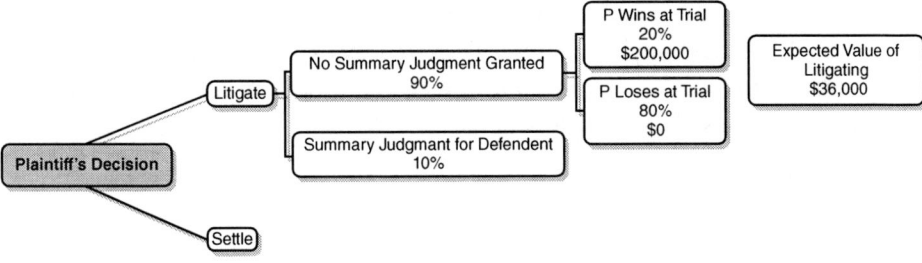

Figure 11.1: Decision Tree

Given confirmation bias, the fundamental attribution error, and naïve realism (see chapter 1), attorneys may have to push themselves hard to think carefully about all of the strengths and weaknesses of the case. Attorneys who work in close-knit groups or offices may be impacted by a group form of the fundamental attribution error, leading some to call this the *ultimate attribution error*.[95] The attorney's motives—such as a desire by prosecutors to imprison criminals, a desire by public interest attorneys to help their clients, or a desire of defense attorneys to help their clients better themselves—can heighten these tendencies.[96] Thus, it is important to keep in mind the disagreeable adjudicator in order to give due weight to the arguments on the other side (see chapter 4). In addition, it can be helpful to solicit independent perspectives on the strengths and weaknesses of the client's position, remembering that aggregating such estimates can improve prediction (see chapter 4). In a larger case, the attorney might also use surveys or mock juries to try to get a sense of how others view the case.[98]

> Because prosecutors and defense attorneys are not unaffiliated individuals who come to each case without any preconceived notions ... but instead are members of well-defined groups who are likely to have well-formed stereotypes ... about the other group's behavior, they are more likely to process information in a biased manner.
> —Rebecca Hollander-Blumoff[97]

While the preceding discussion has focused on psychological factors that may push a client to reject an agreement she would do better to accept, we have also seen that psychological factors can sometimes tempt clients to accept offers they should reject. Attorneys discussing offers with their clients should pay attention to how phenomena such as framing, reactive devaluation, escalation of commitment, scarcity, apologies, anchors, defaults, reciprocity, liking, and the grouping of options can influence evaluations of particular offers (see chapters 4, 5, and 6). Similarly, the attorney should pay attention to how the client perceives the offer in terms of how it compares to offers made to similarly situated parties and whether it seems fair according to some external criteria (see chapter 8).

If the attorney believes, for example, that a negotiation counterpart is trying to attract his client to an offer by emphasizing certain aspects of the offer but deemphasizing other, less attractive aspects of the offer, the attorney can remind the client to also focus on the less obvious aspects of the offer.

> Attorney: I know it is tempting to jump on this offer because Confections Inc. is offering a very nice price for your property. However, before you agree, I suggest you consider some other aspects of the offer as well. For example, are you confident that Confections Inc. is sufficiently profitable that it will be able to pay the portion of the price that will fall due in a year? And are you sure that the use that Confections Inc. has in mind for the property will not cause any harm to your adjacent operations?

Similarly, if the attorney sees that an opponent has used framing or introduced extraneous options to make an offer particularly attractive, the attorney can show the client how the offer can be reframed, or considered in a different context, in which case it may become somewhat less attractive.

> Attorney: They have offered us three different options: (1) we can sell the painting, and you and Berta can divide the proceeds; (2) you can accept $5,000 from Berta and give her the painting immediately; or (3) you can keep the painting for a year and then provide it to Berta once she has paid you $5,000 over the next year. Two of the options involve Berta paying you for the painting, either now or over time. Berta seems comfortable with either payment plan, and we haven't identified any advantages to you of keeping the painting for a year and delaying payment; so it seems as though between those two options, the immediate payment would be preferable. Thus, I'd like to propose that we set the extended payment option aside and focus carefully on the other two options. Does that make sense to you?

Attorneys can also help clients to see how other contextual factors influence decisions, to view offers from various perspectives, and to approach decisions in different ways. For example, it is predictable that a defendant will object to "paying off" a plaintiff whom he feels does not have a strong or valid claim. Thus, defense counsel may explain that the defendant should not think of the potential settlement as a payment to the plaintiff but rather as the defendant's purchase of financial security (eliminating the risk of a hefty verdict), peace (no more squabbling and picking sides), and full use of her own and others' time (some of which otherwise would have been devoted to litigation defense). Thought of in these terms, the proposed settlement may seem more palatable. There are, of course, many other ways that counsel might characterize a proposal to make it more or less attractive to the client.

We have also seen that clients may find it tricky to evaluate offers involving future conduct or payments (see chapter 5). Attorneys can counsel their clients about the difficulty in valuing future payments and help the client with these calculations. Some clients will not realize that in most economic environments, a promise to pay $10,000 in a year is worth less than a promise to pay $10,000 in a month. The attorney might even be able to help the client understand the ways in which present and future payments can be converted into one another. For example, the attorney might note that a proposed stream of future payments could potentially be converted into an immediate payment by a bank. Furthermore, attorneys might teach their clients how to use smartphone applications to make present-value calculations. In addition, if a counterpart has asked the attorney's client to commit to something that will occur in the future, the attorney can remind the client that an action that may sound easy because it is not immediately required may appear more difficult when the future arrives.

To ensure that accepting the offer would actually serve the client's best interests, the attorney should help the client carefully analyze the proposal in context by, for example, pointing out that the fact that the opposing attorney seems to be a nice guy should not be relevant, that reciprocation is not always appropriate, that others' acceptance of similar proposals does not mean the proposal would necessarily be a good deal for the client, that the urgency or scarcity imposed by a deadline may be artificial, or that sometimes a client's best interests are served by not reaching an agreement. Similarly, the attorney will want to help the client think through whether an apology is genuine and whether that matters to the client,[99] as well as whether other aspects of the settlement are satisfactory to the client.

✦ ✦ ✦ ✦ ✦

Analyzing an Apology

Although Hospitals Inc. has issued an apology to the attorney's client, the attorney recognizes that it may not be sufficient.

Attorney: As you heard, the president of Hospitals Inc. has apologized profusely for the way you were treated in the hospital waiting room and has assured you that changes will be made in hospital policy to ensure that no one in the future is cursed at by hospital security personnel. Perhaps you will want to ask for more specifics on the training or other measures that the hospital will implement?

Attorneys and clients should formulate specific implementation intentions to help them resist undue pressure to accept offers (see chapter 5). For example, the attorney and the client might decide in advance that they will not agree to pay more than a certain amount without doing substantial analysis or consulting others. Similarly, they might agree never to accept an offer without taking at least forty-eight hours to fully consider the terms being proposed, allowing themselves time to work through their initial emotional reactions.

Finally, it is important to recognize that, in considering offers, clients will not always reach the decisions that attorneys think are best. Criminal defense attorney Abbe Smith has stated that she would use virtually any tool of persuasion short of breaking her clients' arms to encourage them to take a plea agreement that she thinks serves their best interests.[100] In her book, *Case of a Lifetime*, Smith tells the story of Kelly, a client who chose to go to trial on felony murder charges rather than plead guilty to a lesser charge. Kelly could not imagine that a jury would find her guilty when she was innocent. But she was found guilty of felony murder and sentenced to life in prison. After Kelly had served ten years in prison, the trial court granted her habeas petition. The state appealed, but Kelly was offered a chance to plead guilty and be sentenced only to time served (meaning that she would be freed from prison). However, according to Smith,

> Kelly refused the plea offer. She told [her attorney at the time] that she couldn't do it, couldn't plead guilty to a crime she did not commit. The crime was too horrible. She didn't think she would be able to live with herself if she admitted having taken part in a senseless, brutal murder of a teenager that she had had nothing to do with. She didn't think she would be able to look herself in the mirror. She didn't think she would be able to face anyone she knew.[101]

The appeals court reversed the trial court's grant of the habeas petition, and Kelly remained in jail for nineteen more years. From Smith's perspective, Kelly should have taken the plea. However, Kelly maintained that she would never have taken a plea.[102] Each attorney must ultimately struggle with how hard to push a client to take the attorney's advice. Attorneys' conclusions will vary based not only on their model of lawyering but also on how confident they are that they know what is best for their clients.

❖ ❖ ❖ ❖ ❖

Fee Negotiation

At the same time the attorney is helping the client decide whether and how to enter into an agreement with the opposing party, the attorney and the client may also be thinking about renegotiating the terms of their own fee agreement. An attorney representing a claimant on a contingent fee basis may, for example, agree to reduce her fee if the client agrees to accept a particular settlement offer. The attorney may have calculated that she is better off taking a smaller percentage of the proposed settlement rather than putting additional resources into the case. Conversely, the attorney who prefers to go to trial may agree to cut her fee if the client rejects the settlement.[103]

Clearly, such downward fee adjustments can influence the client's interest in the proposed agreement. While we will not discuss the ethical or practical

> implications of such discussions, we do see one psychological concern. In opening any such discussions, the attorney needs to beware of anchoring the client on the idea of a reduced fee. If the parallel negotiation does not result in an agreement that includes a reduced fee, the client may see paying the original fee as a "loss" and react adversely.

Mediation

With the growth of both court-mandated programs and contractual mediation provisions, it has become increasingly common for attorneys to use mediation to help their clients resolve disputes and negotiate agreements. Yet, taking on the task of representing clients in mediation may require attorneys to adopt a different mindset than the adversarial rule-oriented mindset with which many are familiar. As Leonard Riskin famously put the matter, "[t]he philosophical map employed by most practicing lawyers . . . differs radically from that which a mediator must use."[104]

> Mediation is a process in which an impartial third party acts as a catalyst to help others constructively address and perhaps resolve a dispute, plan a transaction, or define the contours of a relationship.
> —*Carrie J. Menkel-Meadow et al.*[105]

Attorneys who are familiar with psychology can be particularly effective as representatives in mediation. As mediation is essentially facilitated negotiation, it is no surprise that many of the skills that will most help attorneys effectively represent clients in mediation are those already discussed in this chapter. There are, however, some ways in which mediation is different than nonfacilitated negotiation. The presence of a mediator, who can help parties and attorneys examine their own views and communicate with one another more effectively, is critically important.[106] The mediator may work this magic not only in joint sessions but also as he meets separately with each side in private caucuses. In addition, while represented parties often do not directly participate in legal negotiations, they are more likely to participate in mediation. These features of mediation offer a variety of psychological opportunities and also present a few challenges.

Psychological Opportunities Offered by Mediation

We have seen that prospects for agreement may be impeded where one or both sides are affected by correspondence bias and naïve realism, that is, assuming that actions are motivated by ill will or bad character rather than driven by situational constraints or differing perceptions (see chapter 1). Conflicting memories can also pose an impediment to agreement. It can be difficult to find common ground when both sides are "sure" that their own memories of relevant events are correct.

But we have learned (see chapter 2) that memories are not as good as we tend to think they are.

Mediators can use a variety of techniques to get disputants to question their assumptions. Most directly, mediators can expressly question whether the attributions that one side is making are correct. As law professor Russell Korobkin notes,

> the mediator might concede that it is *possible* that the adversary is a malicious, obnoxious jerk but suggest that the mediator finds another hypothesis more *plausible*—and then provide an account of the events that is consistent with the observed outcome but attributes a more situationally-dependent motivation for the adversary's actions.[107]

Mediators can also ask disputants why they are sure that their view of the facts or the opponent's motives is correct. By requiring disputants to think through their assumptions, the mediator may lead them to question their validity. Similarly, by having disputants and their attorneys describe their views to one another, the mediator can help them see that alternative views are possible. To the extent that the confidentiality of mediation communications is afforded by statutes or contract as well as by the evidentiary rules that cover all settlement discussions, participants may feel freer to express their interests and concerns more openly than in other settings.[108]

Similarly, as we have seen, prospects for agreement may be limited where one or both sides are overly optimistic or anchored to unrealistic aspirations (see chapter 4). As we have discussed, it can be challenging for attorneys to be completely objective about their own client's case, and they may also hesitate to emphasize the weaknesses

---

◆ ◆ ◆ ◆ ◆

Seeing Different Perspectives

In a mediation that mediator Frank Scardilli handled between Sisters of the Precious Blood and Bristol-Myers Co., the Sisters accused Bristol-Myers of marketing infant baby formula in an unethical and dangerous manner which they believed contributed to serious illness and death of infants. Bristol-Myers, by contrast, viewed the Sisters as unduly self-righteous and regarded itself as highly responsible and ethical. Scardilli notes:

> I struck often at the theme that it was dangerous to assume that one with whom you disagree violently is necessarily acting in bad faith. Moreover, I stressed to both that I had become fully and firmly convinced that each of the parties was acting in compete good faith, albeit from a different perspective. I strove to get each to view the matter through the eyes of the other. . . .

After extensive mediation—and after Bristol-Myers voluntarily changed certain of its practices—the matter settled.[109]

in their own client's case for fear that the client will see such negativity as a lack of faith in the client or the case. When parties attend the mediation, however, they can be educated by the other side or the mediator about the weaknesses in their positions.

A good mediator can begin to break down biases and resistance to agreement by asking probing questions regarding, for example, the strengths and weaknesses in an argument. Additionally, a mediator can ask the lawyers to present arguments that they think the other side might make as a means to help them see issues in the dispute from an adversary's perspective. The mediator can suggest that the lawyers consider the views of the imaginary disagreeable adjudicator and have the lawyers provide the explanations that they think the judge might provide if their clients lost in court. Generating such explanations will enhance the likelihood that the attorney will be able to imagine the judge actually ruling against her client.[110]

Mediators, and opposing counsel and clients, can also help disputants get beyond judgments based on hindsight; reliance on availability, affect, and representativeness; or undue focus on sunk costs (see chapters 4 and 5). Mediators can, for example, suggest that each side look at data that may reveal judgment errors. Simply talking through sunk costs using lay terms may help a person realize that it does not make sense to throw additional good money down the drain just because some losses have already been suffered.

> Mediator: Mr. Jones, I know that you are very upset that the trucks your company bought from Jalopies Inc. are not performing as well as you had hoped. I understand that you believe that Jalopies Inc. committed fraud that caused at least $100,000 worth of damage to your company. At the same time, however, before you make the decision to reject their offer of $50,000 to set this matter to rest, you may want to consider what the costs will be of continuing this litigation. Specifically, you may want to consider both the financial costs of further litigation and also the emotional or morale costs to you and your company. At some point you may decide that it makes sense simply to cut your losses and accept the settlement rather than to continue to spend additional money to try to recoup that loss.

Similarly, a mediator can point out that mistakes that seem obvious after the fact may not have been obvious at the time.

> Mediator: Ms. Lucero, I appreciate that you are confident that Ms. Chan must have been aware that she was not doing a good job when she repaired your chimney. It did, after all, fall apart just six months after she had completed her work. Nonetheless, perhaps you can appreciate Ms. Chan's explanation that she simply could not foresee the possibility of the ice storm that ultimately seems to have contributed to your chimney's demise. Sometimes we find it easier to predict things when we look backward than it might have been at the time.

A more evaluative mediator may counter such judgment biases even more directly by offering her own views on the dispute.

> Mediator: Mrs. Juarez, you have stated that you are absolutely sure that you will recover significantly more than the $20,000 defendant has offered if you reject the settlement and take your claim to trial. However, I have to tell you that I have

> handled lots of these kinds of cases, and in my experience it is quite rare for a plaintiff with your type of claim to recover much more than the $20,000 you have been offered. Indeed, in my opinion, it is quite possible that you could lose your case altogether if the jury finds that your injuries were due to your prior skiing accident and not this recent car crash.

Although attorneys may discount the views expressed by mediators as strategically geared to enhance settlement prospects, the views of a well-respected mediator are likely to make a dent in the thinking of most attorneys and their clients.

A mediator can also help break an impasse by serving as an intermediary to help the parties avoid reactive devaluation (see chapter 5). Whereas a party might devalue an offer that comes from the opposing party, the mediator can present an offer or idea as a neutral proposal.

> Mediator: I don't know for sure whether Mr. Randolph will go for this, but might you be interested in a deal in which your company, in return for a complete release, paid Mr. Randolph the back pay he claims he is due but not the punitive or compensatory damages or attorney fees he has also sought?

In some instances, a client or attorney may be resisting a proposed settlement due to his frame of reference (see chapter 5). For example, the defendant party may be comparing the plaintiff's demand of $15,000 to a finding of no liability. In order to make settlement more likely, the mediator will want to highlight a different reference point so that the defendant compares the plaintiff's demand to the defendant's expected loss if the case goes to trial. Few, if any, cases are so clear that the expected loss at trial would be zero.

> Mediator: Joe, I know that you are expecting that the jury will find for you if this case goes to trial, but I have to tell you that in my experience, there is always an element of surprise at trial. You just never know who will be on that jury, how the witnesses will present, and so on. Ms. Roth is claiming at least $150,000 in compensatory and punitive damages, not to mention your anticipated legal fees. If she has even a 10% chance of prevailing, you will be taking a significant risk. And I believe your attorney said it could easily cost another $20,000 to take this case to trial. In comparison, paying $15,000 may result in significant savings.

The mediation process can also help fulfill disputants' desire for procedural justice. As we discussed in chapter 8, disputants desire the opportunity to voice their concerns to someone who is neutral and trustworthy and who will treat them with dignity and respect. Although this neutral would traditionally have been a judge, mediators now often fulfill this role. To the extent that the mediator and both sets of parties and attorneys treat the participants with dignity and respect and allow them to voice their concerns, the mediation process can allow disputants to feel that they have been heard. Once heard and treated with dignity and respect, the disputants may be better prepared to settle. As one experienced litigator states: "Having an opportunity to open up about their feelings and speak at length about their experiences with a neutral party can help clients achieve a sense of catharsis and closure, without the specter of a public trial."[111]

The presence of the parties can also make apologies more possible and more powerful. Consider a lawsuit in which parents sued a doctor for medical negligence.[112] The mother went into labor on her physician's day off. The physician attended to the mother when the fetal monitor strips showed signs of distress. But when her labor appeared to return to normal, he left to play golf. Thirty minutes later, the mother was again in distress, but the golfer doctor did not make it back to the hospital before the baby died. The parents were extremely upset with the doctor and blamed their child's death on the doctor's lack of caring. Although the physician's lawyers resisted a meeting between the doctor and the family, the doctor pushed for such a meeting. The mediator, Eric Galton, then asked the parents (in caucus) whether they would like to meet with the doctor, and the mother stated, "Yes, I would very much like to meet with *my* doctor." Galton described what happened next:

> The physician is escorted to the parents' room. As the physician enters the room, he stops just outside the door. The mother is seated ten feet away.
>
> For several minutes, no words are exchanged. No one even moves. Suddenly, the mother gets up, tears begin to flow, and she holds out her arms. The physician goes over to the mother. As they embrace, the physician says, "I'm sorry. I'm so sorry." The mother, patting the physician's back, responds, "It's okay, we forgive you." The husband comes over and joins the embrace. The lawyers, standing on the opposite ends of the room, appear mystified. The physician, father and mother sit together and talk for ten minutes.[113]

The formidable power of apology should no longer be surprising.[114] Indeed, as one experienced personal injury litigator has noted, "Often, one of the first things my clients tell me is that they want to hear an apology."[115]

Similarly, parties who participate directly in mediation may find it easier to communicate about other kinds of nonmonetary relief and to deal with other emotional issues (see chapters 3 and 7). Talking directly may allow parties and their attorneys to pick up subtle emotional cues that will help them learn more about each other's interests. Moreover, parties may find value in expressing their anger to each other. On the other hand, some direct confrontations can blow up a negotiation, and it is for this reason that some mediators prefer to keep parties separated during much of the mediation. As we discuss below, mediators need to make tough judgment calls regarding when in-person communication will be most helpful.

◆ ◆ ◆ ◆ ◆

The Science of Influence

Reflecting high mediator interest in learning about the psychology of persuasion, the American Bar Association Section of Dispute Resolution invited psychologist Bob Cialdini to give a plenary lecture on persuasion—*Using the Science of Influence to Improve the Art of Persuasion*—at its annual meeting in 2002.

Some—likely most—mediators will use their persuasive skills (see chapter 6) to convince disputants and attorneys that agreement is their best option. Using their own apparent expertise, expressing themselves simply and clearly, controlling the physical setting, managing information exchange, imposing or lifting deadlines, and using reciprocity and liking can help disputants and attorneys find ways to agreement. Many mediators use simple approaches like providing food or drink to ease the path toward settlement. Mediators may also use more sophisticated persuasive tools, such as securing agreement on broad guiding principles and then characterizing more specific options as consistent with those principles.[116]

Psychological Challenges Posed by Mediation

> Mediators in different practice settings and with differing ideological perspectives may well disagree about specific goals and methods of persuasion, but most mediators engage pervasively in persuasion activities.
> —James H. Stark & Douglas N. Frenkel[119]

Although mediation can enhance the prospects for agreement, some potential psychological dangers may lurk. As we have seen, to the extent that clients participate directly in the mediation, they will be exposed to the mediator, opposing counsel, and, often, opposing parties. Mediators are often judged (or judge themselves) by their success in helping disputants reach agreement. We have noted that mediation provides an opportunity for the mediator to be persuasive, but this "opportunity" also has its dangers—particularly when used to push disputants and their attorneys to a result that the mediator finds desirable but that does not serve the parties' actual or perceived best interests.[117] Although the worst mediator practices would presumably be prohibited by ethical rules, the constraints on mediators' persuasive capabilities are not clear.[118] In chapter 14, we will revisit the realistic limits of ethical regulation.

Opposing counsel may similarly attempt to use their access to a client to accomplish a settlement that might not serve the client's best interests. Counsel

Mediator Pushes Settlement

One attorney, seeking to help his clients rescind an agreement reached in mediation of a civil rights lawsuit brought by the parents of a seventeen-year-old killed by Texas police officers, described the nature of the mediation as follows:

> [E]verything he [the mediator] said to them was, "Your family is going to be destroyed in this case. You got zero"—and if he said it once, he must have said it 40 times—"you got zero chance of success on this and your family is just going to be destroyed"—and he really harped on that.[120]

can, for example, use tools of persuasion, play to parties' interests in avoiding losses or recouping sunk costs, or frame choices and issues in a way favorable to their own position. For example, according to attorney Lawrence M. Watson, defense attorneys can use mediation as an opportunity to confront plaintiffs with prodefense statistics and data and thereby encourage plaintiffs to settle their cases on terms that are more favorable to the defense.[121]

In the typical attorney-to-attorney negotiation a client's own attorney can help temper opponents' persuasive efforts through the ways in which she conveys and discusses offers with the client. But clients who participate directly in mediation may be more susceptible to opponents' influence than they would be in traditional attorney-to-attorney negotiations and may also risk emotional exposure and confrontation.

> There is growing evidence . . . that at least some court-connected mediators are engaging in very aggressive evaluations of parties' cases and settlement options (i.e., "muscle mediation") with the goal of winning a settlement, rather than supporting parties in their exercise of self-determination.
> —Nancy A. Welsh[122]

The assurances of confidentiality often afforded in mediation may also lull disputants into making disclosures that may not serve their best interests. While the extent of confidentiality will vary by jurisdiction or contract, few if any mediations provide absolute confidentiality. However, even when mediators are careful to note that confidentiality is not absolute, participants may still feel comfortable with high levels of disclosure. Research has shown that disclosure is not deterred by nuanced assurances of confidentiality ("this is confidential except . . .").[123]

Finally, the immediacy of mediation can tempt attorneys and clients to make speedy decisions, enhancing the pressures for closure (see chapter 5) that many clients will feel in any event.[124] Indeed, mediators and some court orders may require that a decision maker be present and able to resolve the matter right away. Mediators may well push for speedy decisions and may urge disputants to sign an agreement or at least an overview of an agreement on the spot. Escalation of commitment can work together with time pressure to cause people to make agreements that they may later regret (see chapter 6). And sometimes social norms and authority are evoked to encourage quick settlement (see chapter 6): "The judge really wants you to settle this matter today."

Mediation as a Benefit for Clients

While we have spelled out a number of psychological risks of mediation, we do not urge that attorneys avoid mediation. Rather, we suggest that there are a variety of ways in which counsel can handle mediation in order to maximize its psychological benefit for their clients and minimize any potential harm.[125]

Given the importance of the mediator's role in the mediation, an attorney should attempt to choose a mediator who will be effective and ethical in leveraging this unique role. To the extent that an attorney can identify the most likely impediments to agreement in a particular case, the attorney can look for a mediator whom she thinks would be effective in dealing with that particular set of problems. Thus, if the attorney believes that both sides are overly optimistic, she could search for a mediator who will be effective in imparting a dose of reality. To the extent that the attorney believes that an apology would help resolve the dispute, she should endeavor to find a mediator who could be particularly effective in facilitating an apology.

Once the mediator has been selected, the attorney can use premediation communications with the mediator (if permitted) to try to begin to shape the mediator's understanding of the issues and approach to the dispute. Using premediation caucuses to develop trust and rapport with the mediator has been associated with achieving higher-quality settlements.[126] Premediation contacts may also offer a good opportunity "to begin cultivating a working relationship with [the] mediator and educating him about [the] client's interests and what impediments may be impeding the case's resolution."[127] If, for example, an attorney can convince an evaluative mediator that the other side's position is unreasonable, perhaps the mediator will lean a bit harder on the opponent to moderate her settlement position. Even mediators who characterize themselves as facilitative are undoubtedly subject to influence. On the other hand, taking too adversarial of an approach can lead to impasse.

The attorney will also want to think carefully about the roles of the lawyer and the client in the mediation. It is tempting to limit the client's role in the mediation so as to minimize the chances that the client will undermine the presentation of the case or be taken advantage of or harmed in some way by either the mediator or the other side. However, we have seen the many potential benefits of direct client participation in mediation. Thus, an attorney should carefully consider the characteristics of her client, the mediator, the other side, and the impediments to agreement. Often, but not always, this analysis will lead an attorney to have the client play an active role in making opening statements, presenting ideas, and listening directly to statements by opposing counsel or clients.[128]

In addition to focusing on mediators', attorneys', and clients' roles in mediation, knowledge of psychology can help the attorney better prepare her client to take advantage of the opportunities provided by mediation. For example, to the extent that an attorney thinks it would be desirable to have her client treat the opposing client with dignity, listen to his concerns, or apologize for things that have occurred, the attorney needs to explain these potential benefits of mediation to the client and help the client think about how best to behave in the mediation. The attorney can similarly work with the client to communicate effectively and craft her message to be more persuasive (for example, using two-sided arguments). The attorney can also prepare the client for how the mediator and the opposing side will do their best to help the client see another side to the story. The attorney may want to acknowledge that while considering other viewpoints might initially be distressing, gaining such additional perspectives can actually be quite helpful. A client who is not properly

✦ ✦ ✦ ✦ ✦
Preparing for Mediation

In order to properly prepare the client for mediation, the attorney should give detailed instructions.

Attorney: Mrs. Goldstein, let me tell you a little bit more about what to expect during the mediation. As I've explained, the mediator will be doing her best to help us see if we can resolve this matter amicably prior to trial. As your attorney, it's my job to represent you and protect you as best I can. If Johnson Inc. proposes a settlement that I think is good, I will recommend that you take it. But if the company proposes something that I think does not serve your best interests, I will suggest that you reject the offer. The final decision will be yours.

During these discussions, the attorney for Johnson Inc. and Vice President Smith will be doing their best to help us to see the dispute through their eyes and to see the strengths of their side of the dispute. We'll be doing them the same favor. In some ways, this may be uncomfortable. We all want to believe that we are 100% right and that the judge or jury is 100% likely to find in our favor. However, having represented many clients and attended many mediations, I have now learned, sometimes the hard way, that there are almost always at least two sides to every story. Rather than reject out of hand what opposing attorneys or clients are saying, I have found that it is important to listen carefully to their perspectives and to learn from what they are saying. In the end, if there are weaknesses to any aspects of our position, it is best that we learn about them sooner rather than later. The mediator, too, will be trying to get all sides to learn from each other and to see all sides of the arguments. So, I ask you to keep an open mind and be prepared to view the world through different eyes. At the same time, let's agree that you and I will talk privately before agreeing or reacting to any terms that Johnson Inc. may propose. If you feel yourself getting ready to jump on an offer, I want you to ask me if we can take a break. Does all that make sense?

prepared for mediation can derail what might otherwise have been a psychologically positive experience.

At the same time, the attorney will also want to use her mediation preparations to protect the client from falling prey to an opponent's or mediator's persuasive skills, pressure, or even manipulations. For example, the attorney may want to caution a client to consult with the attorney privately before making any concessions. Preparing a client for mediation should also include alerting the client to the specific maneuvers that an opponent or even a mediator may use in mediation. An attorney may have experience with a particular opposing attorney and know that he is likely to try to scare the client into settling by playing to her risk aversion, or the attorney may have reason to believe that opposing counsel will try to use charm or reciprocity to try to influence the client to accept a settlement that might not be advisable. To protect her client against such risks, the attorney may warn the client of the opposing counsel's or mediator's typical approach and tell her that if either the attorney or the client senses the opposing attorney trying to mislead the client in any way, they should call for a caucus.

Finally, both the attorney and the client should try to plan in advance and create implementation intentions (see chapter 5) for how they will handle the time pressures of mediation. As we have seen, more time can sometimes help a person process an important decision more completely: he may realize upon reflection that his instinctive reaction was not a good one. Thus, attorneys and clients may want to be prepared to insist on taking the time to review an important decision. While such insistence may not please the mediator, it may be important to ensuring a satisfactory decision.

✦ ✦ ✦ ✦ ✦
Summing It Up

- Creatively structure negotiation proposals by considering what the client and the other side will find desirable. To determine interests, take the parties' perspectives, ask questions, build trust and rapport, consider impediments, watch for emotional cues, glean information from reactions to multiple proposals, and consider a broad range of interests.
- Make proposals effective by considering to whom they are best presented, the timing of their presentation, and how they should be conveyed.
- Pay attention to the dynamics of the interaction between negotiation counterparts: build good working relationships; be aware of how phenomena such as confirmation bias, the fundamental attribution error, naïve realism, and hindsight bias color interpretations of others' behavior; work to clearly and persuasively convey the intended information; and pay attention to and regulate emotion.
- Help clients to effectively evaluate proposals by thinking systematically about the need for information, the strengths and weaknesses of their position, and the likelihood of success.
- Capitalize on the unique features of mediation—the presence of the parties and a mediator—to provide opportunities to address biases and assumptions and provide a sense of procedural justice. Protect clients from being pushed into disadvantageous agreements by the mediator, opposing parties or attorneys, or the pressures of the situation.

For Further Reading: Negotiation and Mediation

Richard Birke & Craig R. Fox, *Psychological Principles in Negotiating Civil Settlements*, 4 Harv. Negot. L. Rev. 1 (1999).

Roger Fisher & Daniel Shapiro, Beyond Reason: Using Emotions as You Negotiate (2005).

Michele J. Gelfand & Jeanne M. Brett, The Handbook of Negotiation and Culture (2004).

Rebecca Hollander-Blumoff, *Just Negotiation*, 88 Wash. U. L. Rev. 381 (2010).

Russell Korobkin, *Psychological Impediments to Mediation Success: Theory and Practice*, 21 Ohio St. J. on Disp. Resol. 281 (2006).

Russell Korobkin & Chris Guthrie, *Psychological Barriers to Litigation Settlement: An Experimental Approach*, 93 Mich. L. Rev. 107 (1994).

Deepak Malhotra & Max H. Bazerman, Negotiation Genius: How to Overcome Obstacles and Achieve Brilliant Results at the Bargaining Table and Beyond (2007).

Robert H. Mnookin, Scott R. Peppet & Andrew S. Tulumello, Beyond Winning: Negotiating to Create Value in Deals and Disputes (2000).

Michael W. Morris & Dacher Keltner, *How Emotions Work: The Social Functions of Emotional Expression in Negotiations*, 22 Res. Organizational Behav. 1 (2000).

Andrea Kupfer Schneider & Christopher Honeyman, The Negotiator's Fieldbook: The Desk Reference for the Experienced Negotiator (2006).

Jean R. Sternlight, *Lawyers' Representation of Clients in Mediation: Using Economics and Psychology to Structure Advocacy in a Nonadversarial Setting*, 14 Ohio St. J. on Disp. Resol. 269 (1999).

Leigh Thompson, The Mind and Heart of the Negotiator (4th ed. 2009).

Discovery and Due Diligence | 12

Most cases settle, and victory is not in the scathing cross, but in the tedious review of documents. Success is in the details, the expertly drafted interrogatories or request for records, and in the ingenious strategy to obtain the statement allegedly protected by privilege. For it is Discovery which we do. The motions, the papers, the depositions. . . . This is the numbing, ditch digging work that determines the winner.[1]

Civil litigators in the United States spend a significant proportion of their time on discovery. While lawyers in some countries (and even within the United States) may view this attachment to discovery as odd or unfortunate, it is currently a fact of U.S. civil litigators' lives.[2] Criminal litigators are less focused on discovery, but they, too, must exchange relevant documents. And transactional attorneys similarly spend a significant amount of time doing factual research (due diligence) on the companies with which they are involved.

One important insight provided by psychology is that our substantial investment in and use of discovery and due diligence may not always be entirely justified. Thus, it is important to make informed decisions about what information to seek in discovery or due diligence, how to most effectively acquire the desired information, how to share information appropriately, and how to best use the information obtained.

> [I]n the practice of law most of the working time of a litigator is spent in the discovery phase.
>
> —David I. C. Thomson[3]

> For having lived long, I have experienced many instances of being obliged, by better information or fuller consideration, to change opinions, even on important subjects, which I once thought right but found to be otherwise.
>
> —Benjamin Franklin[4]

Deciding What Information to Seek

Obtaining additional information can facilitate the preparation of a case for trial or settlement and can provide a more complete understanding of a proposed transaction. At the same time, however, it can be costly to gather and analyze additional data. Some of the data collected may not be worth the investment. In addition, gathering information can be tedious and frustrating; valuable information can be difficult to identify; and the resulting disclosures can result in embarrassment, emotional distress, or economic harm.

◆ ◆ ◆ ◆ ◆

Planning for Discovery or Due Diligence

The planning fallacy (see chapter 4) may lead attorneys to underestimate how long a particular discovery or due diligence project will take. Such underestimates can be costly for both clients and attorneys.

In formulating plans for discovery and due diligence, lawyers should remember that people tend to be overconfident about their prospects for success (see chapter 4). Ironically, "the less information decision makers have about a decision, the more confident they feel about their decisions."[5] Obtaining more information can help battle this overconfidence. Indeed, many medical malpractice plaintiffs drop their claims without receiving any compensation because they learn in discovery that their claims were not as strong as they had initially thought.[6]

However, it is also important to remember that overconfidence with respect to the quest for information itself can lead litigants and deal makers "into territory where they do not belong."[7] As lawyers think about discovery or due diligence early in the process, it is tempting to have the attitude of a child on Christmas Eve: Santa is coming, and more presents are better than fewer. Yet, as we saw in chapter 5, we sometimes seek information that is not useful to our decisions. Moreover, additional information does not always help us as much as it should. Confirmation bias may lead us to seek and then use information to confirm our existing beliefs rather than to challenge these views (see chapter 1). The certainty effect may cause us to overspend on information in a misguided attempt to reduce uncertainty to zero (see chapter 5). And the escalation of commitment phenomenon may cause us to throw additional good money after bad, ignoring costs that should be viewed as "sunk" (see chapter 5). An attorney who has spent $15,000 on unsuccessful depositions might feel compelled to notice even more depositions so that she will have something to show for that big investment, whereas sometimes the wiser course of action may be to pull the plug on a case that is just not working out. "An effective lawyer . . . must be ready to back away from a promising claim or a theory that doesn't quite pan out, even though it was worth pursuing for a while."[8]

In addition, the investigating attorney should be attentive to her own incentives to seek information. For example, the due diligence attorney is charged with ensuring that there are no hidden skeletons or problems and can even be sued for failing to find problems that should have been discovered before the closing. And because due diligence and defense attorneys will typically be compensated by the hour, some investigating attorneys may have incentives to conduct a very in-depth investigation. Yet, no search can be infinite, and the client certainly will not want to pay for an unbounded investigation.

The challenge, then, is to do the right amount and the right kind of discovery and due diligence, but not to go overboard. To this end, attorneys may want to take an outside perspective (see chapter 4) as a means of thinking about whether to seek certain depositions or request particular documents. To make a more realistic assessment of which informational searches are likely to be worthwhile, the attorney can consider the productivity of information gathered in prior comparable situations. In addition, the attorney should consider the potential impact of each individual piece of information that might be sought. If the information shows "X," will it significantly help or harm the client's position? Upon reflection, the information being considered may not be useful after all because the litigation will focus on a different issue altogether or the transaction will proceed unaffected.

To see how this kind of analysis might be helpful, consider an instance in which the information sought might have been useful only for proving an ill-advised alternative defense or counterclaim. During the course of the environmental litigation brought by members of a community against two companies that they accused of polluting the water and causing cancer, as described by Jonathan Harr in his book *A Civil Action*, defense counsel spent numerous days in depositions asking detailed questions about how much bacon and peanut butter the plaintiff families had eaten, presumably on the theory that defendants could blame the plaintiffs' cancer on regular food consumption.[9] However, many trial lawyers would counsel that trying to blame common foods was likely to backfire, making efforts to pursue those questions a waste of time and money.

Attorneys may also consider that many requests for information are a form of negotiation (see chapter 11). For example, Rule 26(f) of the Federal Rules of Civil Procedure and similar state court rules require litigants to meet early in the case to arrange for initial disclosures and to develop a comprehensive discovery plan that will be submitted to the judge for approval. Parties often engage in horse trading as they construct a discovery plan: "If you let me depose three of your people, I will give you leasing documents, just for the Minneapolis office, for the past seven years."

It can be useful to be ambitious in proposing an initial discovery plan. Thus, a party that seeks to obtain five years' worth of e-mail with respect to one hundred of the company's current employees may want to start by asking for seven years' worth of e-mail with respect to three hundred current and former employees. If rejected, this ambitious "ask" can set up the door-in-the-face persuasion technique (see chapter 6) in the hope that subsequently backing off of this request will trigger the responding party's sense of reciprocity and lead him to accede to the more limited request. Similarly, an ambitious initial "ask" may set a high anchor for an assessment of the level of discovery that is appropriate (see chapter 4). An attorney who emphasizes all of the requested discovery that she is *not* getting may be able to induce her opponent or the judge to grant at least part of the outstanding request.

It may also be possible to draw on the foot-in-the-door technique (see chapter 6). Once the opponent has conceded that one of the key company employees can be deposed, the party seeking discovery can use this as a rationale for allowing even more discovery: "You let us depose Miss Jones, from accounting, so I don't see how you could reasonably object to our deposing her boss, Mrs. Smith, as well." Judges, too, can be urged to be consistent with their own prior favorable rulings.

So, too, can attorneys draw on the principle of liking and their ability to establish credibility and trust in negotiating requests for information (see chapter 6). Those who have built relationships with other attorneys may be more successful in obtaining information. Pointing to respected colleagues who have handled discovery or due diligence requests in a particular way (capitalizing on social proof) or evoking the predilections of the judge (as an authority) can also be persuasive.

Dealing with Written Requests for Information

> Discovery . . . is a mechanism that is expressly designed to enable participation and voice[,] . . . provid[ing] both parties with the opportunity for meaningful participation by allowing them access to information that will form the basis for their presentation to the court.
>
> —Rebecca Hollander-Blumoff[10]

Preparing Interrogatories and Document Requests

To be effective as information-gathering tools, interrogatories and document requests should be written in clear and understandable language (see chapter 7). Similarly, we have seen that evasion is less likely when the question posed is direct and is phrased broadly enough to cover the information requested (see chapter 7).

But interrogatories and document requests can do more than simply request information. Because the primary purpose of interrogatories and document requests is to gather the requested information, it is easy to think of these requests as comparable to grocery lists meant to accomplish a workmanlike task rather than as documents to be crafted with an eye toward persuasion. The ready availability (in a firm, on the Internet, and elsewhere) of standardized forms for such requests enhances this focus even when (as time permits) the form requests are tailored to the case at hand.

Although we do not seek to persuade readers to think of interrogatories or document requests as potential works of literature, any document that will be read by opposing parties, judges, a lawyer's own clients, or even jurors can have a psychological impact. The phrasing of an interrogatory or document request might prime a relevant concept (see chapter 1) or anchor the other side's perception (see chapter 4).

In the context of discovery in particular, the scope and nature of requests for information can indirectly highlight the viability, strength, or breadth of a claim or defense. Consider, for example, an interrogatory submitted in *Jones v. Clinton*, in which Paula Jones, a former state of Arkansas employee, sued President Bill Clinton for allegedly having sexually harassed her while he was governor of Arkansas. Jones submitted the following interrogatory to Clinton:

> *Jones v. Clinton*, Interrogatory 10
> Please state the name, address, and telephone number of each and every individual (other than Hillary Rodham Clinton) with whom you had sexual relations when you held any of the following positions:
> a. Attorney General of the State of Arkansas;
> b. Governor of the State of Arkansas;
> c. President of the United States.[11]

Although Jones no doubt expected Clinton to object to the interrogatory, which he did on grounds of relevance and privacy, and although the court ultimately limited the permissible time frame of the plaintiff's inquiry and found that she could only inquire as to state or federal employees with whom Clinton may have had a sexual relationship,[12] the broad nature of Jones's interrogatory may have helped convince Clinton and his lawyers that it would be wise to try to settle the claim.

Responding to Interrogatories and Document Requests

Responding to interrogatory and document requests is an important part of the discovery process, and document responses are also important to due diligence work. Depending on the nature of the case or transaction, responding to informational queries can be as simple as providing a few written answers or going through a handful of documents provided by the client, or as complicated as going through thousands upon thousands of documents. No matter the scope of the task, the responding legal team must diligently review all interrogatories, document requests, and potentially responsive documents and decide whether and how to respond. The team must consider whether requested materials are sufficiently relevant. In the discovery context, the attorneys must also consider whether the documents are protected due to a privilege, the work product doctrine, or the excessive cost or scope of the proponent's request.

Few attorneys view the task of responding to interrogatories and document requests as particularly scintillating. For this reason, the task is often delegated to junior attorneys or paralegals. Document production may involve sitting surrounded by boxes of documents and files in warehouses for hours or days on end. The task of identifying and then reviewing all electronically stored documents is often more difficult. Even when computers are used to conduct an initial search of electronic documents, humans must program the computer and review the identified documents.[13]

Scintillating or not, however, attorneys' lapses with respect to document production have led to the disgrace of some respected attorneys and vaunted firms. To take just one recent example, consider the fact that the attorneys who represented Qualcomm Inc. failed to produce forty-six thousand "critical" documents in a major lawsuit.[14] The magistrate judge in charge of the case initially concluded that

> one or more of the retained lawyers chose not to look in the correct locations for the correct documents, to accept the unsubstantiated assurances of an important client that its search was sufficient, to ignore the warning signs that the document search and production were inadequate, not to press Qualcomm employees for the truth, and/or to encourage employees to provide the information (or lack of information) that Qualcomm needed to assert its non-participation argument to succeed in this lawsuit.[15]

Ultimately, the judge concluded that "[t]he fundamental problem in this case was an incredible breakdown in communication."[16] Had the Qualcomm attorneys been more aware of the psychology that can lead to such problems, they may have been able to avoid a highly embarrassing, costly, and time-consuming investigation into their alleged improprieties and the resulting sanctions. Even when there is no conscious effort to behave in an unethical fashion or to deliberately hide documents, there are a number of ways in which such lapses can happen (see chapter 14).

✦ ✦ ✦ ✦ ✦

The Case of the Missing Suitcase

Another infamous discovery debacle dates back to major antitrust litigation that took place in the 1970s between the Eastman Kodak Company and Berkey Photo Inc. Kodak's attorney, a senior partner at a major New York litigation firm, failed to turn over a whole suitcase of documents on which Kodak's expert witness had relied. When questioned at a deposition as to the whereabouts of the suitcase, the senior partner lied, saying he had discarded the documents. An associate, seated next to the senior partner at the deposition, whispered a correction to the senior partner; but the senior partner maintained his lie, and the associate did not speak up. Eventually the lie came out, the jury awarded Berkey $113 million, and Kodak fired the firm.[17] Large-firm attorneys questioned years later about the nondisclosure in the case found it hard to believe that their legal brethren could be so incompetent or unethical.[18] Psychology provides some important explanations.

First, the evaluation of document requests can be influenced by our tendency to make judgments consistent with our own interests. This inclination can lead us to interpret the substance of documents and the nature of the rules in such a way as to not require disclosure. Just as football fans are more prone to see the fouls made by the other team and attorneys focus on those documents and arguments that are most helpful to their case or position (see chapters 1 and 4), so may the disclosing attorney be disposed to gloss over harmful documents. Similarly, we are likely to interpret and apply any possible privileges or other exemptions in a way that minimizes disclosure. This is likely to be particularly true when we are facing a loss (see chapter 5), such as when the document could seriously hurt our case. Underproduction is the likely result. (We will return, in chapter 14, to a detailed discussion of these and other pressures and why it is that other attorneys tend to think that *they* would have been impervious to such pressures and would have produced the requested material rather than evade production.)

There is also a tendency for respondents to interrogatory and document requests to avoid answering the queries or to draft evasive or even misleading responses. Consider the following interrogatory filed in *Washington State Physicians Insurance Exchange & Ass'n v. Fisons Corp.*[19] and the corresponding response:

> Interrogatory No. 2: Can Theophylline cause brain damage in humans?
>
> Answer: See general objections [set forth in two pages] attached hereto as Exhibit A and incorporated herein by reference. This interrogatory calls for an expert opinion beyond the scope of Civil Rule 26(b)(4), and is, in any event, premature. Furthermore, this interrogatory appears to call for an opinion based on medical knowledge after January 19, 1986, whereas the relevant time frame is on or before January 19, 1986. In addition, this interrogatory is not reasonably calculated to lead to discovery of admissible evidence under CR 26(b)(1). This interrogatory is also vague, ambiguous and overbroad. For example, the term "cause" is vague and ambiguous in that it does not specify whether it includes indirect, as opposed to direct, causes. The term "brain damage" is similarly vague and ambiguous and is overbroad as to time and scope. For example, it is unclear whether the term "brain" includes the entire central nervous system; it is further unclear whether the term "brain damage" includes temporary as well as permanent changes.[20]

While the court found that this kind of answer, alone, was not sanctionable, it found that the defendant had engaged in sanctionable conduct by failing to produce two "smoking gun" documents discussing the link between theophylline (the primary ingredient of the defendant's drug, Somophyllin) and health dangers to children. The defense team's excuse was that the documents pertained to theophylline but did not specifically mention Somophyllin.

In similar ways, there can be incentives not to produce material in response to due diligence document requests. For example, a seller's optimism about its health and its interest in seeing a deal completed may lead the seller not to produce documents that might put the target company in a negative light.

Finally, as we discussed in chapter 1, studies have shown that people engaged in search tasks may not notice additional instances of a phenomenon once they have identified a first instance. Recall, for example, the radiologists who do poorly at identifying a second anomaly once they have found the first. Once attorneys and nonattorneys have found documents that are responsive to their counterpart's request, they should remember to keep up their zealous efforts to identify any additional relevant documents.

To protect against their own and their clients' possible tendency not to see damaging documents or to exaggerate legitimate excuses for nonproduction, attorneys should remember to take the perspective of the disagreeable adjudicator (see chapter 4), thinking about how an outsider—particularly one disinclined to give the attorney the benefit of the doubt—would view the document. In addition, it is important not only to emphasize to clients and subordinate attorneys and paralegals that all questionable documents should be provided to the attorney but also to create a culture in which members of the team are not hesitant about being the bearers of bad news. In addition, the lead attorney should continually remind herself of her own tendency to overprotect documents and question whether she is truly doing her best to meet her discovery or due diligence obligations.

Putting appropriate systems in place is a good method of guarding against human fallibility.[21] An attorney who is charged with producing documents in response to discovery or due diligence requests should make sure a system is in place to (a) adequately communicate with all people who might have custody over relevant documents, (b) spell out to all such people the full scope of material that is requested, (c) make sure that he is aware of all document storage systems and locations, and (d) ensure that everyone involved with document production knows who is ultimately responsible for defining the scope of the search.

The adversarial nature of litigation contributes to the instinct to resist providing informative responses in discovery. However, attorneys should consider that complying more fully with discovery requests can sometimes be beneficial to a client's interests. First, providing impressive interrogatory and document responses can communicate to the other side that the respondent's position is strong, thereby enhancing the settlement position. Second, the process of working with the client to prepare discovery responses can enhance the attorney's relationship with the client and help the client to prepare for any future deposition.[23] In the due diligence context, being forthright can protect the attorney from charges of ethical misconduct and can protect the client from being sued for fraud or breach of contract.

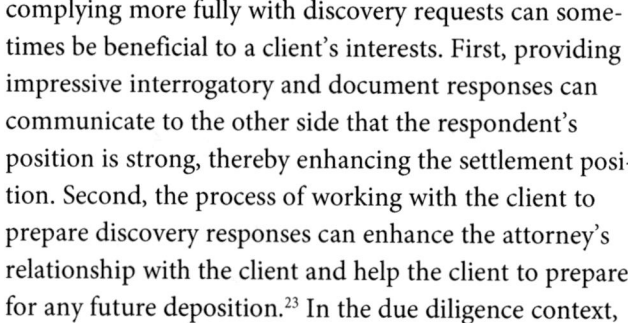

> As poker players might put it, "good things can happen when you show your hand."
> —Steven Lubet[22]

Conducting and Defending Depositions

Depositions are a critically important part of U.S. style litigation. Unlike other forms of discovery, which are attorney-dominated, depositions give attorneys a chance to interview prospective witnesses directly. From a psychological standpoint these face-to-face meetings provide great opportunities and great risks. The questioning attorney has a chance to obtain information from the witnesses' statements and demeanor, and also to make an impression on the witnesses and opposing attorney. Although the defending attorney will be present at the deposition, the rules of civil procedure sharply limit her ability to participate in the deposition itself.[24] Thus, the defending attorney has to use her witness preparation to both make the most of this opportunity and protect her witness and case from being derailed by the opposing attorney.

Conducting the Deposition

Attorneys conduct depositions for a variety of purposes and often have multiple objectives for a single deposition. Different purposes may call for different psychological approaches.

Deposition, taking: Seven hours of pretending to be a sociopath while locked in a room with an amnesiac and a compulsive obstructionist.
—*Mark Herrmann*[25]

The most common purpose for taking a deposition is to gather information. The questioning attorney hopes that through skillful questioning she can obtain information that will help bolster her client's position. The attorney also seeks to learn about the other side's best evidence so that she can come up with additional arguments and evidence to undercut her opponent's position. The information gathered through a deposition may also pertain to the witness, such as whether the witness seems credible, whether the witness can be shaken from her testimony, or whether the witness retains a calm demeanor under pressure.

Depositions are also sometimes used to preserve testimony from witnesses who the attorney knows or suspects will not be available to testify at trial. Under such circumstances, the deposition will more closely resemble a trial. The attorney is not in information-gathering mode but is instead attempting to set out known information in a way that will most impress the judge or jury.

Depositions inevitably have a third purpose that dovetails with both of the first two. Because preparation for trial is always done with an eye toward settlement, one goal of depositions is to improve the client's settlement position. A deposition that yields significant new information or that shows that the deponent will be a particularly strong (or weak) witness may convince one or both sides to change their settlement positions.

Introducing the Deposition

Most attorneys spend a few minutes at the outset of the deposition informing the deponent why she is being deposed, setting out ground rules, and making sure that the deponent is not in a condition (such as being ill or on drugs) that would interfere with the deposition. While the introduction serves many other purposes, it can also give the questioning attorney a chance to build a relationship with the deponent. As we discussed in chapter 9 on interviewing, building trust and rapport with an interviewee can be key to encouraging the interviewee to answer questions more completely and to probe her memory more effectively. The same is true in a deposition.

Building trust and rapport with neutral or nonaligned witnesses, such as the person who just happened to be standing on the corner when the traffic accident occurred, can be relatively straightforward. Through body language, the use of open-ended questions, and attentive listening, the questioning attorney can attempt to demonstrate that the attorney is interested in what the deponent has to say. A deponent who feels that she has had a chance to tell her story to someone who cares about her perspective will likely experience a greater sense of procedural justice (see chapter 8) and more rapport (see chapter 7) with the questioning attorney. Whereas comfortable witnesses are more likely to give more complete answers, uncomfortable deponents may be more likely to default to responding, "I don't recall," or to giving short or even evasive answers.

◆ ◆ ◆ ◆ ◆

A Trust-Building Deposition Introduction for a Neutral Witness

The opening moments of a deposition will cover many issues. In part, the deposing attorney can use this time to put the witness at ease.

Attorney: Good morning, Mrs. Ozer. As you may know, I am June Jones, the attorney representing Michael Adams in the lawsuit arising out of his involvement in a car accident on June 14, 2008. We understand that you saw at least part of what happened that afternoon, so we would like to ask you some questions about what you saw. Your knowledge could be very important to the just resolution of this lawsuit.

Have you ever been deposed before? . . .

Some witnesses are nervous about their deposition, but there is really no need for you to be nervous. I'm going to ask you a series of questions about what happened on June 14. If you don't understand any of my questions, just tell me, and I will be happy to rephrase them. The court reporter will make a record of my questions and your answers and will then send you the transcript to review and correct, if necessary, before it becomes final. Does that sound OK?

Also, just let me know if you need to take a break or if you want some coffee or water or whatever. I don't expect that this deposition will take very long, but you are welcome to take a break at any time. All right?

Even when a witness is associated with the opposing party, it can be possible for a questioning attorney to build a relationship with that witness. While some adverse witnesses will resist all such rapport-building efforts, others may begin to feel a degree of comfort with the opposing attorney.

To see this potential, consider a deposition taken during the environmental litigation described in Jonathan Harr's *A Civil Action*. As explained by Harr, Al Love was deposed because he had worked in the sheet metal department for defendant W. R. Grace. Plaintiffs' attorney Jan Schlictmann, however, realized that Love also lived in the neighborhood that had allegedly been affected by the polluted water. Schlictmann, therefore, asked Love how many children he had and inquired as to all their names and ages. Schlictmann then went on to ask Love his opinion about the smell and taste of the water he and his family used at home. The defense attorneys—one of whom was said to have been reading a newspaper during the deposition—inserted a series of objections. According to Harr, those objections disturbed Al Love because he "could not understand why [defense attorneys] Cheeseman and Frederico were objecting to questions about his family's health." Cheeseman was supposed to be on his side, but it seemed as if Schlichtmann was his ally, not Cheeseman. As the deposition progressed and Schlictmann probed further into the health problems of Love's children, one of the defense attorneys purportedly "snorted" and scoffed at what he thought was an "irrelevant matter." Through his handling of the deposition, Schlichtmann was able to forge a connection with Love—while Cheeseman managed to damage any rapport that he had with Love. Indeed, a few weeks after the deposition, Al Love contacted the lead plaintiff, Anne Anderson, and eventually Jan Schlictmann. Setting aside the question of whether it was ethical for Schlictmann to meet with Love,[26] these events demonstrate the potential for establishing rapport with even an adverse witness.[27]

Asking Questions in Depositions

We saw in chapter 7 that lawyers need to make a special effort to communicate clearly. This is also true when taking depositions.

To the extent that the deposing attorney seeks to make a useful evidentiary record, he must be sure not only that each question and answer is clear but also that each question and answer is freestanding. Yet, such speech patterns are different from those used in a typical conversation. As we discussed in chapter 7, normal conversations tend to be fast paced, free flowing, and interruption filled. Thus, when the goal is making a clear record, the deposing attorney must consciously shift away from traditional conversational norms and ensure that the deponent does so as well.

But sometimes the goal of the questioning attorney is simply to obtain as much information from the deponent as possible. Because deponents are typically coached to keep their answers short and not to volunteer information, it can sometimes be challenging to get the deponent talking. Here, it will often serve the questioning attorney's interest for the deponent to fall into normal conversational patterns and answer questions quickly without giving her attorney the chance to inject objections: "[N]o matter how much she is prepared, sandpapered, woodshedded, cautioned, or admonished, a typical deponent will never be more than tenuously committed to the proposition that monosyllabic answers are best. Instead, the natural tendency to amplify and explain will always be lurking in the background."[28]

> ♦ ♦ ♦ ♦ ♦
> ### Avoiding Extraneous Language
>
> In addition to using simple English, Jim McElhaney advises attorneys to avoid useless introductions and needless tag endings.
>
> | Useless Introductions | Needless Tag Endings |
> |---|---|
> | It's true, is it not, that . . . | Isn't that true? |
> | Isn't it a fact that . . . | Isn't that correct? |
> | In fact, didn't you . . . | Right? |
> | Are we correct in assuming that . . . | That is correct, is it not? |
> | | Isn't that not so? |
> | Tell the ladies and gentlemen of the jury, if you would please, . . . | |
>
> "Useless introductions and needless tag endings may look like they make your questions more powerful, but the opposite is true. They make your questions weak by hiding what you really want in a pile of verbal clutter." [29]

Open-ended questions are often a very effective means of both getting the deponent to talk and helping the deponent to remember more about the events in question. The questioning attorney is often well advised to ask lots of who, what, when, where, and why questions. Even the smartest and most educated deponents may give in to conversational norms that incline them to explain more fully. Thus, in an information-gathering deposition, it is better to start with a request like "Tell me everything you can remember about the accident you witnessed on July 5" than to ask a series of yes or no questions such as "July 5 was a clear day, right?" or "Would you say that the van was driving very quickly?"

Silence can also be a very effective way to get the deponent talking. The inclination to fill empty spaces in conversations (see chapter 7) can induce witnesses to volunteer information that they otherwise might have kept to themselves. In particular, if the questioning attorney can make herself pause after the witness appears to have finished answering a question—rather than rushing to ask the next question—the witness may continue to talk in order to fill the silence.

> " Never forget the power of silence, that massively disconcerting pause which goes on and on and may at last induce an opponent to babble and backtrack nervously.
> —*Lance Morrow*[30] "

Questioning attorneys should also remember that deponents, like all of us, want to be viewed in a positive light.[31] They may, for example, want to be seen as

> ### President Clinton Succumbs to the Urge to Talk
>
> Did any witness ever suffer a greater talking bias, to worse effect, than President William Jefferson Clinton? A Yale-educated lawyer, Rhodes scholar, former constitutional law professor, and Arkansas attorney general—not to mention consummate politician and debater—he understood the litigation process far better than most other witnesses. In the crucible of cross-examination, however, when brevity could have been the soul of his defense, he simply could not restrain himself.
>
> > "I don't know why his lawyers didn't tell him, 'You don't have to answer any questions about your private life, Mr. President. Let them sue you. Take the heat. You don't have to answer.'"
> > —Chris Matthews[32]
>
> Clinton's moment of truth came on August 17, 1998, when he appeared for questioning before a grand jury empaneled by Special Counsel Kenneth Starr.... The president's lawyers had obviously counseled him that short answers were essential, and at first it seemed that he understood.... [B]ut it was not long before Clinton was disastrously (from his perspective) expanding on his responses....
>
> The prosecutor was pursuing a line of questioning about events in the *Jones* case [in which Jones had accused Clinton of sexual harassment]. During the president's deposition Clinton's lawyer had asserted that "there is absolutely no sex [with Monica Lewinsky] of any kind in any manner, shape or form with President Clinton."
>
> "That statement is a completely false statement," asked the prosecutor. "Is that correct?"
>
> "It depends on what the meaning of the word 'is' is," the president famously replied. "If 'is' means is and never has been ... that is one thing. If it means there is none, that was a completely true statement.
>
> The tortured equivocation was quite unnecessary. Clinton could just as easily have answered "yes" or "no," neither of which would have damaged him as much as the slippery explanation.[33]

competent and knowledgeable. Thus, it can be effective for the attorney to ask the deponent for help and to show gratitude for any explanatory assistance that the deponent can provide. When the questioning attorney says that she does not understand something about the deponent's company and hopes that the deponent can help her understand it better, it may prompt the deponent to try to be helpful and to give complete answers.[34]

Deposition of Company Vice President in Oil Spill Suit

A particular deponent may want people to think well of the organization or company for which she works. Consider a deposition taken of a company vice president in a lawsuit against ABC Corp. alleging that ABC was negligent in the operation of its oil drilling operation. Imagine that ABC's legal team is trying to pass as much of the liability as possible to a subcontractor, Drilling Inc., that worked on the drilling operation. Notice how the plaintiff's attorney first tries to use flattery to build rapport with the witness and then tries to use the witness's interest in boasting about her company to support the plaintiff's claim that the company was responsible for the acts of its subcontractor.

Attorney: I really appreciate the time you are spending with me today, Ms. Big. Given your extensive knowledge of ABC, I'm confident you'll be able to help me gain a better understanding of how the company is set up.

Ms. Big: Well, I'll certainly do my best.

Attorney: Can you please describe for me the current organizational structure of the company? I would like to know what all the divisions are, who heads each, and what their responsibilities are.

Ms. Big: Sure, . . . blah, blah, blah, blah. . . .

Attorney: Now, can you tell me a bit about ABC Corp.'s reputation in the drilling world?

Ms. Big: Well, I think we've got a great reputation. We're certainly the largest drilling operation in terms of dollars and barrels pumped.

Attorney: How has your safety record been over the last three years?

Ms. Big: I think we have a great safety record. Like any company, we've received occasional citations, but we respond quickly to any problems. The explosion in January 2010 was a freak event that no one could really have predicted.

Attorney: Tell me how you have achieved what you call your "great safety record."

Ms. Big: Well, we set clear standards, and we have a good team for making sure that our standards are met.

Attorney: To the extent you use subcontractors, do you lose all control over that safety record?

Ms. Big: No, of course not. We set standards that our subcontractors are required to follow.

> Attorney: Is there anyone at ABC Corp. who is responsible for ensuring that subcontractors are living up to their safety obligations?
>
> Ms. Big: Yes, . . .

In similar ways, the questioner can push the deponent to guess at answers to questions about which she really should not speculate. Deponents may be embarrassed when they don't know the answer to a question—especially when the questioner seems to expect them to know the answer—and will guess (often incorrectly) in order to appear knowledgeable.[35]

> ♦ ♦ ♦ ♦ ♦
>
> **Softball Goes Foul**
>
> Some deponents will resist the urge to speculate. For example, in the Department of Justice's antitrust lawsuit against Microsoft, the following exchange took place between Steve Houck, the government's lawyer, and Bill Gates:
>
> Q. I'll give you a softball question. Would you agree that Microsoft is the world's most respected computer software company?
>
> A. Some people would agree with that, some people wouldn't.
>
> Q. What's your opinion?
>
> A. I think we are the most—if you took it on a statistical basis, yes, we'd be the most respected software company.[36]

Memory lapses (real and purported) are important impediments to obtaining information in a deposition. In addition to commencing the deposition with open-ended questions, there are a number of techniques (see chapters 2 and 9) that the questioning attorney can use to help deponents remember as much as possible. Asking deponents to describe events in chronological order or to visualize a scene can prompt memory for additional details. And when a deponent responds that she cannot remember a particular event at all, the questioning attorney may want to encourage her to remember any details that she can.

> " Every man's memory is his private literature.
> —Aldous Huxley[37] "

Once a deponent's memory seems to have been exhausted, the questioning attorney may want to use more specific questions or documents to help stimulate or contradict deponents' memories. The careful use of specific questions might, for example, be used to see if the deponent can confirm information gathered from other sources, such as documents or other witnesses' testimony.

> ✦ ✦ ✦ ✦ ✦
> ### Remembering Planning Meeting in New York
>
> In the following exchange, the witness initially has no recall of attending a certain planning meeting. However, the attorney's deft questioning evokes some memories.
>
> Attorney: You have said that you have no recollection of attending a planning meeting for the Barbados Bridge Project that took place in McMillan Corp.'s New York City office on July 3, 2007. Is that correct?
>
> Witness: Yes, I just don't remember.
>
> Attorney: Well, let's think about July 4, 2007. Do you remember being in lower Manhattan to watch the fireworks that evening?
>
> Witness: Oh, now that you mention it, I think I do remember that. It was a really great show.
>
> Attorney: So, let's work backward. Do you think you went to New York just to watch the Fourth of July fireworks in 2007?
>
> Witness: No, I am sure I didn't. I must have been there to attend a meeting. I guess it just could have been that Barbados Bridge Project meeting.
>
> Attorney: Well, I don't want you to guess. Were you at a meeting the day before those fireworks?
>
> Witness: Yes, I definitely was at a meeting. I know it was downtown. I remember eating lunch at the South Street Seaport in fact. So, yes, I think I was at that bridge project meeting after all. In fact, I remember that Sarah Taylor was there, too, and that she gave an excellent presentation on the project.

Of course, it is also true that too much pushing or leading can cause people to misremember or conflate events (see chapter 2). Perhaps the witness saw the Fourth of July fireworks in New York in a different year altogether and has now combined the two events in her mind. Unfortunately, we have seen that it is not always possible for questioning or defending attorneys to distinguish accurate from inaccurate memories, which is why corroborating information can be so important.

A similar technique can also be used to prompt additional thoughts by unsettling deponents. Consider the approach taken by attorney David Boies in the Microsoft antitrust litigation:

> Perhaps [Boies's] favorite strategy was to find a document or record showing that the witness, or someone related to him, had said something provocative in the past. Boies would read the old statement back to the witness word-for-word, without

saying where it came from, and then ask him if he agreed. A theoretical example: Mr. Smith would you agree that, at the time, you wanted to help Microsoft "bury Netscape six feet under?" To that, under the normal scenario, Mr. Smith would say, "Oh no. I would never say something like that," after which Boies would produce the document quoting him saying exactly those words and ask, "Does this refresh your recollection?"[38]

Once shown the contradicting document, the deponent may remember additional facts or feel the need to offer an explanation.

Given how easy it is to influence people's memories (see chapter 2), attorneys must carefully consider the timing of showing documents to deponents. Imagine, for example, a deponent who remembers that there were four people present at a particular meeting. Once she sees meeting minutes that indicate that only three people were present, the deponent may come to believe that only three people were actually present. Yet, documents are not always correct. Thus, if an attorney is seeking to plumb the depths of a witness's memory, it is better to try to exhaust the witness's memory before introducing the contents of a document. Then, having exhausted the unassisted memory, the attorney can use the document to attempt to spark additional or different memories.

Of course, the use of documents will vary depending upon the goals of the deposition. If the attorney has a document that she thinks presents her client's position in a favorable light, she may want to frame the discussion around that document to focus the deponent on aspects of the situation that are consistent with that advantageous portrayal.

As discussed in chapter 9 regarding interviewing, the questioning attorney should also use careful and active listening techniques to make sure that she obtains all possible information and follows up on any hints that the deponent may drop. In particular, the questioning attorney needs to be careful that her schemas and assumptions (see chapter 1) do not lead her to miss promising leads. The famous (or infamous) 1921 trial of anarchists Nicola Sacco and Bartolomeo Vanzetti provides an example of a questioner missing such a hint. Sacco and Vanzetti were charged with a murder that occurred in connection with a robbery. One of the main pieces of evidence was Sacco's possession of a Colt pistol that was allegedly used to commit the murder. A portion of the direct examination of the ballistics expert by the prosecutor went as follows:

> Q. Have you an opinion as to whether bullet No. 3 [Exhibit 18] was fired from the Colt automatic, which is in evidence [Sacco's pistol]?
>
> A. I have.
>
> Q. And what is your opinion?
>
> A. My opinion is that it is consistent with being fired by that pistol.[39]

In retrospect, it is easy for us to see that although the expert says the bullet *could* have been fired by Sacco's pistol, he does not definitively state that it *was* fired by

Sacco's pistol. Yet, the defense attorney was apparently not listening closely because he did not pursue the idea that the bullet may have come from another Colt automatic rather than Sacco's pistol—a possibility that the expert admitted following the trial. Although many believed (then and now) that Sacco and Vanzetti were wrongly accused and convicted due to their political beliefs, they were put to death by electrocution on August 23, 1927. Attempts to seek a new trial based on the expert's posttrial admission regarding the ambiguity of the ballistics evidence were unsuccessful.[40]

After the questioning attorney has elicited all the information she thinks she can get from a deponent, she may want to use closed-ended questions to confirm or sum up the deponent's views on a particular subject. These summary questions can ensure that the attorney correctly understood the witness and can also be very useful if the case eventually goes to trial because they more concisely combine the key aspects of different answers.

◆ ◆ ◆ ◆ ◆

Defense Attorney Cross-Examines a Coroner

In crafting summary questions, it is important for the questioning attorney to avoid making unwarranted assumptions, as suggested by the following old joke:

Attorney: Before you signed the death certificate, had you taken the pulse?

Coroner: No.

Attorney: Did you listen to the heart?

Coroner: No.

Attorney: Did you check for breathing?

Coroner: No.

Attorney: So, when you signed the death certificate, you weren't sure the man was dead, were you?

Coroner: Well, let me put it this way. The man's brain was sitting in a jar on my desk. But I guess it's possible he could be out there practicing law somewhere.[41]

One final issue to consider in crafting deposition questions is the timing of the questions. As we discussed in chapter 3, it takes mental effort to self-regulate. Most deponents are likely to make a concerted effort to answer questions carefully and analytically and to keep their emotions in check. However, our capacity for self-regulation is not limitless. Thus, a questioning attorney may want to save certain kinds of questions for later in the deposition, when the deponent is likely to be less able to control her answers effectively.

✦ ✦ ✦ ✦ ✦
Using the Deposition to Tell a Story

As we will explain in chapter 13 in greater detail, stories have great psychological power. Just as litigators are counseled to tell stories with their trial evidence and in their writing, so, too, can they seek to use their depositions to tell stories by "thinking about how a witness's testimony fits into the broader story [the attorney is] attempting to tell and how that testimony will contribute to the coherence of that overall story."[42]

David Boies's deposition of Bill Gates, in the antitrust suit brought by the United States against Microsoft, is once again informative:

> Throughout every case Boies tries, he focuses on the litigation as a morality play. He determines the facts and the basic principles of law that apply and develops a theme that resonates around them to give the jury or judge a compelling reason to decide in favor of his client.
>
> With Gates, the morality play Boies constructed was about credibility. . . . To focus on technology might have permitted the case to turn on a software developer's persuasive explanation to an unsophisticated trier of fact. . . . But by calling into question the honesty and stability of the witness, Boies made it easy for the judge and jury to doubt anything Gates might say on the stand. And Boies focused on credibility in various ways through the deposition.
>
> "They came in saying, 'I know more than you do.' True," says Boies. . . . "But if I can't believe you, it doesn't matter. It was very important from day one of the Microsoft case to attack their credibility.[43]

Consider, too, the defense of a home builder who was sued over alleged construction defects by a class of homeowners:

> We settled the class action through an agreement under which the homebuilder inspected, evaluated, and, where necessary, made repairs to the class members' homes. We then filed third-party claims on behalf of the homebuilder against various subcontractors who constructed the homes, including the bricklayers who laid the exterior brick on the homes. One of the themes we used in that case was "you have to stand behind your work." The theme worked because it was simple, it was supported by the facts, it captured what most jurors in our Midwest venues already believed, and our client was on the right side of that theme because it had already stood behind its work by making the necessary repairs to the class members' homes on its own dime. Now, we were asking the subcontractors to stand behind their work.[44]

Using this theme to guide the depositions taken in the case proved to be effective.

Dealing with Lying and Evasion

Some deponents lie. Some simply fail to be forthcoming. An opposing party or someone who is loyal to the other side, for example, may fail to volunteer helpful information. Indeed, we have seen that people are more likely to evade and obscure than to state an outright falsehood (see chapter 7). Many deponents may seek to cast their responses in a particular way even if they are not inclined to lie directly. Use of charged language, nuances in phrasing, or quibbles over the meaning of words can all shade the meaning of the testimony. In this regard, recall Bill Clinton hedging about the meaning of the word *is* or Bill Gates splitting hairs over the meaning of such words as *we*, *concern*, and *market share* in his multiday deposition in the antitrust proceedings against Microsoft.[46]

> The pure and simple truth is rarely pure and never simple.
> —*Oscar Wilde*[45]

Many (if not most) deponents will also suffer from memory lapses, forgetting or misremembering information, events, and conversations (see chapter 2). Such lapses in memory may be neutral, or they may be slanted (often unconsciously) to protect the deponent's view of the world. For example, a witness may remember her favorable employment evaluation better than she recalls any unfavorable evaluations. But memory lapses—even those that unconsciously support the deponent's own position in the case—are far different from deliberate lies.

Unfortunately, as we saw in chapter 7, it is not easy to differentiate lies from memory lapses. During his 2007 perjury trial, Scooter Libby, Vice President Dick Cheney's chief of staff, defended himself on the ground that he could not recall exactly whom he told what regarding the identity of CIA employee Valerie Plame.[47] And during the deposition of Rudolph Giuliani, former New York mayor, about his proposal to dispossess certain taxi drivers of their taxi licenses, Giuliani repeatedly claimed that he did not recall particular events or details that apparently did occur.[48] Were Libby and Giuliani lying or simply forgetting? In Libby's case, jurors did not believe him and found him guilty of various crimes. But many of us have higher expectations for memory than are justified. As we discussed in chapter 2, people erroneously assume that we will remember things that turn out to be important even though they may not have been seen as important, and thus memorable, at the time they initially occurred.

Attorneys can use a variety of techniques to identify and deal with the evasive deponent—though it may not be possible to stop a person who is determined to lie. First, the attorney may craft questions that are designed to uncover or prevent evasion. For example, if the attorney asks, "Did you ever hear Clint Jones say anything derogatory about Mary Beth Sweet?"—the witness may simply say "no." However, questions that are framed

> You never know how much a man can't remember until he is called as a witness.
> —*Will Rogers*[49]

more broadly to cover written as well as verbal comments and questions that specifically inquire as to whether, to the witness's knowledge, any other person has stated or written that Jones had any negative views with respect to Sweet may elicit additional information that would not have been volunteered in response to the narrower question. By asking the deponent specific, direct questions, the attorney can minimize the possibility that the deponent will be able to elide disadvantageous information.

Second, the attorney must be attuned to the fact that the witness may be using evasion or careful wording to avoid a direct lie. If the witness states, "I never heard Mr. Jones say anything derogatory about Mary Beth Sweet at work," the questioning attorney should immediately realize that she needs to query the deponent about statements that Jones may have made *outside* of work. Similarly, the attorney can watch carefully for changes in the deponent's demeanor when certain topics are broached. Follow-up and restated questions can be very useful in minimizing evasion.

✦ ✦ ✦ ✦ ✦

A Giant or a Dodger?

Some deponents will provide evasive answers and attempt to dodge a question by dissembling or answering another question altogether. Consider how baseball player Barry Bonds—accused of illegal steroid use—answered a grand jury question about whether his trainer had ever injected him:

> I've only had one doctor touch me. And that's my only (sic) personal doctor. Greg, like I said, we don't get into each other's personal lives. We're friends, but I don't—we don't sit around and talk baseball, because he knows I don't want—don't come to my house talking baseball. If you want to come to my house and talk about fishing, some other stuff, we'll be good friends, you come around talking baseball, you go on. I don't talk about his business. You know what I mean? That's what keeps our friendship. You know, I am sorry, but that—you know, that—I was a celebrity child, not just in baseball by my own instincts. I became a celebrity child with a famous father. I just don't get into other people's business because of my father's situation, you see....[50]

"This rambling and disjointed answer ... led to [Bonds's] conviction on obstruction of justice, for dodging the question he was asked and offering such an egregiously unrelated answer."[51]

Recent research has found that it can be difficult to detect evasive answers, particularly when the respondent answers a question that is similar to the one asked and when the listener's attention is not focused on detecting evasion.[52] Thus, attorneys would do well to focus their attention on the specifics of the deponent's answer so that they don't miss the artful dodge.

Third, the attorney can attempt to make it more challenging for a deponent to maintain a lie. For example, the attorney can try asking questions in an unanticipated order or can ask the deponent to give his version of events in reverse chronological order. Similarly, the attorney can ask the deponent about peripheral details that she is less likely to have thought about and practiced integrating into her story. As we discussed in chapter 7, responding to these kinds of questions takes greater cognitive effort and makes it harder for people to keep track of their lies.

Finally, an attorney may use documentary or other evidence to catch the witness in a lie. When a deponent is lying, the attorney can expect that the deponent will stick to the lie as long as possible, resisting any corrections. In contrast, when a deponent is simply suffering a memory lapse, even an unconsciously biased memory lapse, the deponent may be willing to allow that her memory is incorrect or possibly incorrect. Thus, the questioning attorney may want to probe the deponent's confidence and show the deponent documents or video that reflect a different reality. Confronted in this manner, the deponent who is simply suffering a memory lapse may be willing to admit that she is not sure about the memory or even to correct her stated version of the facts. At times, it can be useful to wait to raise contrary information until late in the deposition in order to provide an opportunity for such inconsistencies to surface. Alternatively, the questioning attorney may choose not to try to catch and disprove the lie in the deposition, instead preferring to allow the witness to commit herself to the lie and subsequently using other evidence to disprove that lie at trial or during settlement negotiations.

Undermining Detrimental Deponent Testimony

Sometimes deponents give testimony that is unfavorable to the questioning attorney's case. By drawing on psychology, the questioning attorney can take a number of steps to try to remove the sting from such testimony either at the deposition or at trial. First, the questioning attorney may want to challenge the deponent's perception of the events being discussed and to identify anything that might have distracted the deponent's attention. We have seen (see chapter 1) that it is very easy for people to miss important things (like gorillas entering the room) and to draw connections that did not exist (such as assuming that they are still talking to the same person after an interruption). Thus, the questioning attorney may want to ask about what else the deponent was focusing on at the time or to make inquiries regarding physical conditions, such as distance or lighting, that may have limited the deponent's perception.

Similarly, the questioning attorney may try to cast doubt on the deponent's memory for certain events (see chapter 2). For example, we know that people commonly rely on scripts (see chapter 1) in remembering and may get mixed up as to whether a particular activity followed the script on a certain occasion. (I know I always brush my teeth before bed, but can I really remember if I did it that night?) In addition, because we know that memories typically fade over time, the questioning attorney will want to make clear not only how long ago the events happened but also what, if any, steps the deponent took to memorialize her initial observations. If no contemporaneous notes were kept, the validity of her memory may be subject to question. Drawing on knowledge of difficulties in source monitoring (see chapter 2), attorneys can explore the possibility that conversations that the deponent had between the time of the events and the deposition have introduced aspects of the "memory."[53]

Finally, the questioning attorney can highlight any sources of bias that may have caused the deponent to see, hear, or remember events differently from how they actually occurred. For example, the questioning attorney will want to bring out the fact that the witness is a personal friend of the party for whom she just gave favorable testimony or that the witness was previously involved in litigation against the party about whom she gave negative testimony. Because people are willing to see bias in others, highlighting the potential biases of the witness can be helpful.

Scaring Deponents

Some questioning attorneys try to scare deponents or to make them uncomfortable. Practitioners of this approach might defend it on the ground that fearful deponents are more truthful or perhaps even that they can be cowed into submission or settlement. According to one leading deposition text,

> some witnesses react to aggressive questioning and control with something like a "whipped dog" syndrome. These witnesses become meek and malleable, willing to agree to almost anything suggested by the deposing lawyer. Sometimes this defeated attitude is accomplished by shocking the witness with difficult or embarrassing questions at the beginning of the deposition; other times by pressing the witness who is unsure of his facts into repeatedly admitting, "I don't remember." Sometimes the witness will react in the opposite manner. Through persistent and aggressive questioning, the witness can be angered until he is tempted to lash out with intemperate responses that can often be quite revealing and helpful.[54]

To accomplish this end, deposing attorneys may act in nasty ways, speak aggressively, wear intimidating glasses, or seat deponents such that they must look into the blinding sun.[55] An acquaintance of one of the authors of this book tried to make deponents uncomfortable by deposing them in a conference room where they had to look at a ghastly, bloody work of art.

In addition to being ethically questionable, the scary approach to depositions may not be effective. First, as we have already seen, the questioning attorney may be able to get more information by being pleasant. More troubling, however, is evidence from the criminal setting that using strong interrogation techniques such as isolation, confrontation with false evidence of guilt, and minimization of blame can substantially increase the risk that people will confess to crimes they did not commit.[56] Indeed, as we saw in chapter 2, some people who are subjected to such tough interrogation techniques even come to falsely believe in their own guilt, particularly when they are vulnerable due to factors such as age, mental retardation, or psychopathology.

To take just one example of the pernicious effects of such tactics, consider the confessions elicited in the case of the Central Park jogger:

> In 1989, a female jogger was beaten senseless, raped, and left for dead in New York City's Central Park. . . . Within 48 hours, solely on the basis of police-induced confessions, five African American and Hispanic American boys, 14 to 16 years old, were arrested for the attack. All were ultimately tried, convicted, and sentenced to prison. The crime scene betrayed a bloody, horrific act, but no physical traces at all of the defendants. Yet it was easy to understand why detectives, under the glare of a national media spotlight, aggressively interrogated the boys, at least some of whom were "wilding" in the park that night. It was also easy to understand why the boys were then prosecuted and convicted. Four of their confessions were videotaped and presented at trial. The tapes were compelling, with each and every one of the defendants describing in vivid—though, in many ways, erroneous—detail how the jogger was attacked, when, where, and by whom, and the role that he played. . . . Collectively, the taped confessions persuaded police, prosecutors, two trial juries, a city, and a nation.
>
> Thirteen years later, Matias Reyes, in prison for three rapes and a murder committed subsequent to the jogger attack, stepped forward at his own initiative and confessed. He said that he had raped the Central Park jogger and that he had acted alone. Investigating this new claim, the Manhattan district attorney's office questioned Reyes and discovered that he had accurate, privileged, and independently corroborated knowledge of the crime and crime scene. DNA testing further revealed that the semen samples originally recovered from the victim—which had conclusively excluded the boys as donors (prosecutors had argued at trial that the police may not have captured all the perpetrators in the alleged gang rape, but this did not mean they did not get some of them)—belonged to Reyes. In December 2002, the defendants' convictions were vacated. The case of the Central Park jogger revealed five false confessions resulting from a single investigation.[57]

False confessions such as those by the teens in the Central Park jogger case can occur when the suspect confesses in order to escape an aversive interrogation (the suspects in the Central Park jogger case said that they confessed because they thought that if they did, they would be able to go home), to obtain an explicitly or implicitly offered reward, or to avoid a threatened negative outcome.[58]

While we are not aware of studies of the impact of "scary" techniques used in civil depositions, we think that it is reasonable to infer that some such approaches might cause a deponent to make false admissions or statements merely in order to end an unpleasant deposition as quickly as possible. Such false admissions or statements are unlikely to ultimately serve the attorney's interests. It is generally problematic to craft a trial or settlement around false information. And even if a deponent makes a damaging false statement in a deposition, other information may ultimately be revealed at trial that will contradict that statement and thus seriously undercut its value. Ultimately, psychologists have found that more respectful approaches are often more productive—even in the interrogation setting—than are more dominating approaches, which often lead to denials or false statements.[59]

Dealing with Emotions in Depositions

Though depositions are often rather dull affairs, they can be very emotional, particularly for the deponent. In particular, deponents are often anxious because they are navigating a process with which they are unfamiliar and of which they are not in control. They may be anxious about being the focus of attention, about not being able to perform well, or about being asked questions that will require them to harm themselves or other people or entities about whom they care. Some deponents become very upset as they speak about difficult material; others become extremely angry and frustrated. Anger is often triggered by the fact that the relevant procedural rules allow the questioning attorney fairly free rein to interrogate (and even insult) the deponent. Deponents may feel trapped in such a situation and strike out in response. In a deposition described in Harr's *A Civil Action*, a very angry deponent deliberately poured water all over a fancy conference table. Some deponents have done and said even more extreme things during depositions, including swearing at the questioning attorney, making threats, or actually engaging in physical violence.[61] A deposition made famous (or infamous) after it was posted on the internet shows renowned Texas personal injury attorney Joe Jamail questioning an obviously furious deponent. The deponent angrily tells Jamail, "You have a case of incipient verbal diarrhea!"—and the deposition continues to go downhill from there.[62]

> In short, being a witness at a deposition is a horrible experience.
> —David M. Malone et al.[60]

Questioning attorneys may want to handle deponent emotions in different ways depending on their goals. To the extent that inappropriate anger may not play well to a judge or jury,[63] attorneys may be happy to test whether they can incite deponents' anger. In addition, an angry deponent may occasionally blurt out damaging information in a fit of pique. Weathering a deponent's anger during a deposition may be worth it if it improves the settlement value of the case.

At the same time, however, an angry deponent is often not likely to be forthcoming with information, so the attorney who is trying to obtain information at the deposition may want to try to diffuse that deponent's anger. In particular, the attorney can help to manage witness anger by remaining calm herself, staying focused on the process, and distracting the witness with questions on another subject before circling back to the sensitive topic (see chapter 3). Offering a break can also help, particularly if the attorney can suggest a break as he senses anger starting to build rather than waiting for it to explode.

Dealing with a crying or visibly upset deponent can also be difficult. Crying and other displays of distress, if perceived as genuine and proportionate to the harm experienced, may add to a witness's appeal.[64] Thus, the attorney who learns that an opposing client cries when talking about his dead son may decide that he does not want to let that case go to trial. In Harr's *A Civil Action*, defense attorney Jerry Facher, after attending such a deposition, famously stated, "'You think you're going to put those families on the witness stand and break everybody's heart. You think the jury's going to pull out their handkerchiefs and dab their eyes.' Facher shook his head resolutely. 'It will never happen. Those families will never see the light of day.'"[65]

In the context of the deposition, showing genuine concern for a deponent's sadness—such as by offering a glass of water, a tissue, or a break in the questioning—can be a way for the questioning attorney to try to establish rapport with the deponent. This demonstration of empathy may help the attorney obtain more information from the witness. In addition, because mild sadness can lead to more deliberative processing, the questioning attorney might take the opportunity to ask a sad witness questions about details. If the deponent is more than mildly upset, however, her emotion may interfere with her ability to remember events well or to recount them clearly. An attorney who is conducting an exploratory deposition will, therefore, want to try to calm the upset deponent as best he can.

Attorneys, like deponents, can sometimes become emotional during depositions, most commonly experiencing and expressing frustration and anger. A quick search of the Internet for deposition videos will produce any number of examples of attorney anger in depositions, such as Joe Jamail's response (including profanity, shouting, and physical threats) to being insulted by a deponent in the manner recounted earlier.[66]

✦ ✦ ✦ ✦ ✦

Deposition Disorder

A Miami lawyer was recently sanctioned for his conduct at a videotaped deposition. As described by the referee's report, the two opposing attorneys began speaking forcefully to one another, and then the defending attorney attempted to place an exhibit sticker on the questioning attorney's laptop. The questioning attorney "very briefly touched [opposing counsel's] hand, then attempted to run around the table towards [him]." Next, the questioning attorney "proceeded to forcefully lean over the deposition table, lambast [opposing counsel] in a tirade while proceeding to tear up the evidence sticker, wad it up and flick or toss it in the direction of [opposing counsel]." The referee found that all of this had quite an impact on the people present at the deposition: the deponent stated that she was very scared; the court reporter stated, "I can't work like this"; and the questioning attorney's own consultant tried to calm him and suggested that he "take a Xanax."[67]

Attorneys who know that they have a tendency to get angry, particularly in depositions, can take some steps to try to regulate their emotions. First, as we discussed in chapter 3, venting, though sometimes popularized as an anger management tool, is not usually a good way to regulate emotion. Instead, redirecting focus is likely to be more productive. Thus, rather than dwelling on the source of the angry feelings, the defending attorney can try to focus her attention on considering one question at a time, or the questioning attorney can temporarily shift her questioning to another topic. Recall, as we discussed in chapters 3 and 5, that it is more effective to make specific self-regulatory plans than to simply try to do better. Thus, rather than merely making a general effort not to get angry, an attorney should identify a particular trigger and plan a specific response, such as "Whenever I feel my blood pressure beginning to rise, I will ask to take a short break and use those breaks to distract myself, call someone who can help me change my state of mind, or take a short walk." Attorneys can also prepare themselves for depositions or help themselves let go of lingering emotions postdeposition by exercising, taking a walk, meditating, or listening to music rather than ruminating on subjects likely to cause distress.

Preparing the Witness for Deposition

Many attorneys recognize that preparing their own witnesses for deposition is important and, therefore, devote significant time and energy to this task. Of course, the time allocated to witness preparation will vary depending on the witness and the stakes involved in the case. The typical deposition preparation consists of a review of the substantive facts in the case and a recitation by the attorney of a lengthy list of dos and don'ts. In addition, attorneys commonly provide their clients with a written guide to depositions that spells out this advice. Some attorneys have their clients view videos that discuss or illustrate depositions. Spending time preparing witnesses for depositions and attention to psychology can help minimize the stress associated with depositions, help make sure that the witness is able to give the best deposition testimony that she can, and better prepare witnesses for typical deposition pitfalls.

> Witnesses who stumble, perspire, twitch, sneer, lose their tempers, or otherwise cannot deliver a smooth presentation are forgotten or not believed.
> —William M. McErlean et al.[68]

✦ ✦ ✦ ✦ ✦
Hiring an Expert Psychologist Consultant

In very large cases, attorneys may also hire consultants to help them prepare their clients for depositions.

Trial consultants come in all shapes and sizes. There is no such thing as a "licensed trial consultant." Anybody can hang out a shingle and call

> himself or herself a "trial consultant" or a "jury consultant." But the ones who tend to get hired for the "bet your company" cases, and the ones who have tended to have a real impact on the practice of law, are usually social scientists and psychologists who hold doctoral degrees. So, with the trial consultants comes the "science" and "psychology" of persuasion and effective communication.[69]

Preparing Witnesses for Differences Between Conversations and Depositions

As an initial matter, attorneys need to help their clients and other witnesses understand that depositions do not follow the same patterns as other conversations (see chapter 7). As we have noted, whereas in normal conversations we interrupt each other frequently, make guesses, change subjects rapidly, leave thoughts incomplete, and finish each other's sentences, depositions are different:

> The purpose of a conversation is to have an interesting, easy-flowing exchange between two people. Anything one person doesn't know or remember is an obstacle to that flow, to be avoided or worked around. A deposition, by contrast, is intended, in part, for discovery—to discover what the witness knows. To explore—and push—the boundaries of that knowledge in a question-and-answer environment requires asking questions until the witness no longer recalls or knows the answers, and then to keep going just to be sure.[70]

If a deponent follows the normal rules of conversation, she may give her defending attorney heart failure by volunteering objectionable information or creating a confusing record. Thus, in preparing the witness, the defending attorney should explain that normal conversational norms do not and generally should not apply in a deposition.

In particular, recall that the norms of conversation prescribe that contributions to a conversation should be informative (see chapter 7). This norm underlies the difficulty that many of us have in only answering the specific question posed. When someone asks us if we have the time, for example, we infer that an informative answer would actually tell the time. Good witness preparation may include describing the norm of informativeness and excusing the witness from following that norm. In this context, witnesses may need to be reminded of the importance of listening (see chapter 7) to the specific question that is asked. Witnesses who listen carefully can also learn to "ask for clarification, state that the question as asked cannot be answered, or . . . define the word(s) out loud and answer that question. . . . : 'If you're asking me if I was going inappropriately fast, my answer is no.'"[71]

> ♦ ♦ ♦ ♦ ♦
> **Listening Test**
>
> Try the following listening exercise:
>
>> A simple test that lawyers can use with witnesses is to have them repeat the questions out loud before they are allowed to answer. It is amazing how often untrained witnesses can't repeat the question accurately. And if they can't repeat it out loud, it's hard to argue that they have heard the question accurately.[72]

Recall, too, that conversational norms prescribe that there is no need to contribute information to the conversation that the other already possesses and that this can lead people to conclude that questions that are repeated are asking for new or different information (see chapter 7). Such a tendency can lead the witness to create seeming inconsistencies in her testimony. Thus, witnesses must be informed that in depositions they might be asked the same question repeatedly (sometimes in different ways) and that they should be prepared to repeat themselves.

Defending attorneys will want to give concrete instructions to help the witness implement her goals (see chapter 5). Thus, in preparing the witness, an attorney might say the following:

> Slow down. Take your time. Make sure you have heard and understood the entire question before trying to answer. Pause after every question and repeat it silently to yourself. Count to five or ten if necessary after every question to prevent yourself from rushing your answers.

> ♦ ♦ ♦ ♦ ♦
> **Silence**
>
> Although many people are uncomfortable with silence, good witness preparation involves helping the witness to become comfortable with periods of silence:
>
>> "The secret to becoming a very good witness, even just a safe one, is *silence*. . . . [I]t's only during silence that a witness can really become crystal clear about the question and the answer it demands. . . . You will have a huge edge if you teach your witness to use silence."[73]

It can be helpful to put all of this advice in a context with which the witness is familiar (see chapter 7). For example, one analyst suggested making an analogy to a well-known card game:

> I tell my clients that depositions are like the childhood card game *Go Fish*. The other side wants to take your cards. If they get all your cards, you lose. If they say, "Do you have any tens?" and you don't, the truthful answer is "No." The last thing on earth you want to say is "No, but I've got some sixes and jacks." You don't want to show your full hand until we get to trial.[74]

Of course, depending on the circumstances, the attorney might have a different purpose in defending a deposition and might not object to the witness volunteering certain information. Whatever the attorney's strategy, the attorney should give concrete advice to the deponent on how to implement that strategy.

❖ ❖ ❖ ❖ ❖
"Do You *Know* That Happened?"

In everyday conversation, we make a host of assumptions without stopping to examine them. The attorney can help clients step back from these assumptions when responding to deposition questions. In particular, the attorney might help clients to avoid relying on scripts (see chapter 1) as they relay their answers. Consider the following example:

> Let's say your witness arrived to work Monday morning at 8:00. On the way to his office he stopped by the mailroom and dropped off some letters that needed to be mailed. The mailman usually arrives between 9:45 and 10:00 a.m. At 11:00 a.m. your witness returns to the mailroom to make some copies and he notices that the letters are no longer there. Can he honestly testify about what happened to those letters? No. Is it likely that the mailman picked them up between 9:45 and 10:00 a.m.? Sure but he cannot testify to that. Unless your witness saw the mailman take the mail from the out box, he can only assume that everything went as it normally does. He cannot present that information as fact. That does not mean he cannot explain the normal routine. He just needs to make it very clear that he did not see it with his own eyes. So if he were asked if the letters went out in Monday's mail, the correct answer is, "I don't know."[75]

Helping Witnesses Make a Good Impression

As we have discussed, depositions can allow the questioning attorney to assess how compelling a particular witness will be in front of a judge or jury. As we saw in chapters 6 and 7, the credibility and persuasiveness of a witness will turn on not only her substantive expertise but also her ability to communicate effectively and the extent to which she is perceived to be trustworthy and reliable. Some witnesses who are truthful can fail to make a good impression due to their attire or physical or verbal mannerisms. Excessive sweating, for example, may make a witness appear dishonest when the only problem is that the witness is too warm.

Thus, just as political candidates and media personalities may receive coaching on presentation, so, too, may such preparation be useful for witnesses, particularly important witnesses in a big case. Attorneys may want to have other members of their team help them to evaluate what, if any, problems may haunt a particular witness. Sometimes an attorney who has worked with the witness closely over a period of time may no longer be able to judge the witness's demeanor as effectively as might another person who has never met the witness before.

One simple way to help the witness make a good impression is to prepare the witness for how to dress. Thus, although many attorneys may hesitate to discuss witnesses' attire, perhaps because they do not want to think of themselves as fashion consultants or because they do not want to intrude on witnesses' personal space, it is important to make sure that witnesses dress both appropriately and comfortably.[76] It may not be sufficient to simply tell a witness to "be sure to dress nicely." The witness's idea of dressing nicely may be dressing to go out clubbing in a low-cut dress or dressing as if for a wedding in a rented tuxedo. Neither is probably the most advisable deposition attire.

> ✦ ✦ ✦ ✦ ✦
>
> **Deposing Minnie?**
>
> Not talking with a witness about what to wear to a deposition can occasionally result in some curious consequences.
>
> > Imagine, if you will, the distress of a new assistant United States attorney in Texas whose principle witness (a secretary with a federal agency) appeared in court dressed like Minnie Mouse—complete with short red skirt, long black tail and mouse ears. It was the day before Halloween, and her supervisor had ordered everyone in the office to come to work in costume. Because the attorney had not told her what to wear, she had not brought a change of clothes with her to work.[77]

Videotaping key witnesses and then reviewing the recording with them may help witnesses overcome worrisome physical or verbal mannerisms. While most of us do not enjoy watching recordings of ourselves, doing so can help the witness become aware of twitches, finger pointing, or hemming and hawing. Some may recall the first debate of the 2000 presidential election in which the media focused on Al Gore's habit of sighing while George W. Bush answered questions. To emphasize how strongly this mannerism came across to the American public, Gore's advisers made him watch a *Saturday Night Live* parody of the debate in which he appeared to be "an overbearing know-it-all."[78] Emphasizing the differences between a deposition and other situations that the client has experienced can help to soften this advice to

> ✦ ✦ ✦ ✦ ✦
> **Helping Witnesses Communicate**
>
> Consider how a team of lawyers and trial consultants handling a fraud case used video to effectively work with an important witness.
>
> > [The witness] was a dynamic and engaging speaker . . . whom jurors wanted to trust. But his explanations regarding the handling of certain checks struck mock jurors as internally inconsistent, which caused low reliability ratings and undermined all the good will he otherwise was able to establish. The witness's explanations, in fact, were not logically inconsistent, but he could easily see, upon a video replay, that the apparent inconsistency resulted from an incomplete explanation. Once that was corrected, his reliability ratings with mock jurors and, in turn, his overall credibility, soared.[79]

beware of physical mannerisms. Rather than challenging witnesses' usual ways of communicating and presenting themselves, the attorney can suggest that different behavior is appropriate in the deposition setting.[80] Having identified any particular quirks, the attorney can give the witness very specific implementation advice for how to deal with them (see chapter 5). For example, the attorney might say, "Anytime you notice yourself beginning to tap on the table with your pen, just put the pen back in your pocket."

It is important, however, not to overcoach witnesses to the point that they no longer seem genuine. In addition to the successes, we have all seen the dangers of coaching people to overcome their mannerisms. In the second presidential debate of 2000, after receiving coaching to remedy his off-putting mannerisms, Al Gore's performance was still criticized. This time, instead of appearing aggressive and arrogant, he was critiqued by some as appearing too "reticent" and "too willing to agree with Bush."[81] Four years later, some blamed overcoaching for John Kerry's loss to George W. Bush. Fritz Hollings, former Democratic U.S. senator, commented thus:

> He [Sen. John Kerry] was a good fellow; he's still one of the finest. But he got overcoached. He had too many consultants, too many pollsters, and really too many in that they call it "Noah's Ark." He had two or three of everything. And he never could make up his mind.[82]

> ✦ ✦ ✦ ✦ ✦
> **Witness Preparation**
>
> Good litigators can use the psychology of learning (see chapter 7) to structure their preparation of witnesses for maximum effect. Knowing that cognitive

> capacity is limited and that repetition aids learning, attorneys should carry out witness preparation across multiple, short meetings in order to keep the focus of the witness's attention.[83] Similarly, attorneys should focus the witness's attention on the most important points:
>
>> At the beginning of the practice deposition it is never a good idea to start reading your long list of dos and don'ts. It is possible that several of the items on your checklist will come naturally to the witness. Reserve those things as compliments to go with the constructive criticism you will need to offer in other areas. For example, if the witness already has good posture but does not project his or her voice you might say, "I notice that you are sitting up straight and that is great because that is something that people do not always seem to do on their own. Keep doing that. I also need you to speak up a little like you will in court. The courtroom is bigger than this room so you will need to make sure everyone can hear you." If you were to go through your list first you would have undoubtedly told the witness to speak up so everyone can hear, but you would have given those instructions along with 20 other things, including sit up straight, which the witness is already doing. Giving a long list at the very beginning reduces the likelihood that the witness will remember the areas with which he or she is having trouble.[84]

Dealing with Client Memory

Another way to help deposition witnesses be effective at depositions is to work with them on their memory lapses. A witness's possession of apparent good memory, including good memory for details, can help boost his credibility and make him more effective as a witness.[86] Conversely, when a witness is shown to have lied or made a mistake about one aspect of his testimony—particularly when the erroneous statements were made with confidence—his credibility as a whole will suffer.[87] Yet, as we saw in chapter 2, the reality is that our memories are far from perfect.

> I'm always fascinated by the way memory diffuses fact.
> —Diane Sawyer[85]

In *The Buffalo Creek Disaster*, author and lead attorney Gerald Stern describes obtaining an answer in a deposition that seemed almost too good to be true. One of the top managers for the defendant, Pittston Coal Company, described how, a few days before the occurrence of the horrendous flood at issue in the case, several mining officials sat in a car and chatted about whether they should take measures to prevent the dam from overflowing. "To this day, however," said Stern,

> I do not know if this conversation actually occurred. Mr. Spotte and Mr. Dasovich and Mr. Yates could not remember any such conversation, even though Mr. Kebblish (the deponent) said it took place in the close confines of an automobile. Maybe

Mr. Kebblish wanted only to believe the conversation took place. At least it showed some effort on his part to avert the disaster, though not much. Maybe Mr. Spotte, Mr. Dasovich, and Mr. Yates wanted only to forget such a conversation took place. They had ignored Mr. Kebblish's concerns that they get an emergency overflow into the dam. Often in traumatic situations such as this we can remember only what we want to remember and are truly incapable of remembering what in fact happened—a kind of psychic numbing like that suffered by the survivors. Or maybe it's like [legendary attorney] Thurman Arnold often said, "The things I remember best never really happened."[88]

Stern ultimately attributes the differing descriptions of the event to memory differences among the witnesses rather than to prevarication.

The imperfections of memory have many implications for deposition preparations. First, the defending attorney will want to normalize, for the deponent, the fragility of memory. Because many of us tend to believe that memory is better than it really is, we may feel uncomfortable when we find that we are unable to remember something. We may also be unwilling to recognize that something we think we remember did not in fact happen the way that we clearly recall it happening. Faced with such imperfections the deponent may be tempted to guess rather than admit lack of memory, yet this may prove disastrous for the litigation. Normalizing the frailty of memory by establishing that memories are poorer than people realize can liberate the witness to admit that she simply does not recall.

❖ ❖ ❖ ❖ ❖
Normalizing Faulty Memory

Attorney: As you go into your deposition, I want you to remember that most of our memories are not as good as we think they should be. Lots of things that happen never get coded for retrieval in our brains, and even information that is initially stored tends to deteriorate over time. Most people find that they can't remember even things that were once almost second nature, like their phone number or address from a number of years ago.

Client: Gee, I am glad it's not just me.

Attorney: The reason I am emphasizing this is because the opposing attorney may try to make you feel guilty or stupid because you can't remember something. This, in turn, may lead you to try to guess at something that you don't really remember. Please, though, don't guess and don't speculate. If you remember, you should, of course, answer the question. But if there is something you don't recall, you should feel comfortable in telling the attorney—over and over if necessary—that you just don't recall.

Client: OK, I will.

Alerting witnesses to the frailty of memory may also help them deal with being confronted with a document that is contrary to their stated memory. Such a witness may be able to calmly say, "Interesting. That is not the way I remembered things." In contrast, a less prepared witness might be angry or scared and tempted to say things she might later regret.

If you tell the truth you don't have to remember anything.
—Mark Twain[89]

Of course, we are by no means suggesting that attorneys use the fragility of memory as an excuse to coach their clients to conveniently "forget" facts that they indeed remember. We have already seen the skepticism directed at Scooter Libby and Rudy Giuliani for their purported failures to remember. To take another example, consider former Attorney General Alberto Gonzales's testimony in Congress about the scandal arising out of the termination of a large number of U.S. attorneys. Many viewed as evasive, if not dishonest, his repeated statements that he could not recall the details of the process leading up to those terminations.[90] There is a fine line between permissibly preparing a witness for deposition or trial—for example, using documents to help the witness refresh her memory or helping her tame her mannerisms—and inappropriately coaching that witness to say something that she does not remember or believe or to conveniently forget something that she actually remembers. Fans of the book and film *Anatomy of a Murder* may remember the scene in which defense attorney Paul Biegler (played by James Stewart in the film), flirts with this ethical line when he tells his client Lieutenant Manion (played by Ben Gazzara) about the available defenses to a charge of murder before hearing his client's account of what happened. Manion is savvy enough to pick up on his attorney's hint that he "must have been crazy" when he killed his wife's lover.[91] We have also seen that merely asking questions about an event may affect a witness's memory—not only the memory for that event but also for other events as well (see chapter 2).

Yet, if attorneys were to stop preparing their witnesses at all in order to allow clients' "true" memories to be explored at the deposition, such unprepared witnesses could be subject to manipulation by well-prepared questioning attorneys. When asked leading or misleading questions or when presented with inaccurate documents, unprepared witnesses might confirm events that did not occur. And seemingly forgetful witnesses are not likely to be deemed credible.

So, what is the ethical attorney to do? We suggest that witness preparation should be done, but that it should be done carefully. The defending attorney should question the witness about matters that may be discussed at the deposition but should be careful not to plant ideas in the witness's mind. Thus, rather than ask, in preparation, "How fast was the other car speeding when it smashed into your car?," the defending attorney might ask, "What do you remember about the accident?" or "How fast do you think the other car was traveling?" Attorneys should also recall that people have a tendency to calibrate their own answers to maximize accuracy (see chapter 2). A witness may say that a car was going "fast" or "at least sixty miles per hour" but may be uncomfortable attempting to be more specific. Thus, rather than push a witness to "recall" more detail (such as whether the car was going approximately seventy miles per hour), the preparing attorney may be better off helping the witness explore what she can say accurately (e.g., whether the car was going faster than other cars in the stream of traffic) and also helping the witness resist attempts by the questioning attorney to provide more detail than is justified.

Similarly, defending attorneys should be careful in how they use documents to prepare witnesses. The questioning attorney will almost certainly have reviewed key documents to prepare for the deposition, and she may also use those documents to examine the deponent. Familiarizing the deponent with such documents levels the playing field. At the same time, however, the defending attorney should remember that the simple act of reviewing the documents may influence the witness's memory. Thus, just as we suggested to the deposing attorney, the defending attorney may want to first review what the deponent remembers without the aid of the documents. The witness can then review the documents, and the defending attorney can help the witness focus on any inconsistencies between her memory and the documents or among the various documents. Perhaps the witness will be able to resolve such inconsistencies, or perhaps she will find that she cannot. Either way, she will be prepared.

◆ ◆ ◆ ◆ ◆
Helping Witnesses Tell Their Story

Helping witnesses understand the themes of the case can also be an important part of witness preparation. Consider, again, the home-building case described earlier in which the theme of the defense was "You have to stand behind your work." Imagine how this theme might help a witness communicate effectively and with less anxiety:

> A witness who understands and believes in the case theme is typically more confident and better positioned to handle difficult or unanticipated questions. In one of our homebuilder cases, a superintendent who worked in the field overseeing the construction of the homes was grilled in deposition about the homebuilder's responsibilities during construction: "Isn't it true that the homebuilder had a responsibility to the homeowner to oversee the construction of the home?" But, where a witness has fully embraced an effective theme, it is hard to throw the witness off. The superintendent's answer: "Yes. That's why we stood behind our work and paid to have every home repaired. But, now the subcontractors are refusing to stand behind their work that they did for us."[92]

Addressing Witness Emotions

Just as questioning attorneys must be aware of deponent emotions, so, too, must defending attorneys address witness anxiety when they prepare a client for deposition. Such nervousness may negatively impact the witness's performance by interfering with the witness's ability to understand questions, to remember relevant information, to speak articulately, or to follow counsel's instructions. Excessive anxiety may also make the witness less believable, more argumentative, or too malleable.[93] Thus, in addition to helping witnesses understand the need to stay on their toes and be alert to possible mischief by opposing counsel, attorneys need to help witnesses manage the inevitable anxiety.

As an initial matter, it can be quite useful to normalize the witness's anxiety (see chapter 3). By reassuring witnesses that their emotional reactions to depositions are common, the attorney can help the client to remain calm:

> Don't be nervous about being nervous. Everyone is nervous, and that's OK. You *should* be nervous: This is an important process. Moreover, I *want* you to be nervous. It's the best way to sustain the kind of energy and intensity required to handle this process properly.... [J]ust think about what it is you do when you're nervous, and deal with that. For example, if you talk too fast when you're nervous, make an extra effort to slow down. Whatever it is, do the best you can, but don't worry about it.[94]

Similarly, the attorney can help the client identify the sources of her anxiety and put them into perspective. The attorney should specifically ask the witness if she is nervous about any aspect of the upcoming deposition and then address those fears directly. Imagine, for example, a witness who has indicated that he is too frightened to testify:

> Attorney: What are you afraid will happen?
>
> Witness: I'll freak out.
>
> A: What does *freak out* mean?
>
> W: You know, lose it.
>
> A: What would that look like? Suppose I saw a movie of it with no sound.
>
> W: I would be all shaky and then faint.
>
> A: Have you ever fainted before?
>
> W: No.
>
> A: Why would you faint?
>
> W: I would just be really nervous.
>
> A: You probably would be. Many people are. But people don't usually faint from that.

W: OK. I probably wouldn't faint, but I'd get all nervous and shaky.

A: OK. So, you'd be shaky. Then what would happen?

W: I would shake and look all crazy.

A: Look all crazy how?

W: Shaky and scared.

A: And then what?

W: Everyone would see me nervous.

A: And they'd think what?

W: That I was freaking out.

A: And then what?

W: They'd think I was crazy.

A: Because you were nervous on the stand? Do you think they would expect you to be nervous?

W: Well, kind of nervous. But not like this.

A: It sounds like it would look like you were shaking and nervous.

W: Yeah.

A: And then what?

W: That's it.

A: It sounds like you are afraid of looking nervous when you are doing something that makes people nervous.

W: Yeah.[95]

By helping the client or witness to articulate her fears and what the ultimate consequences are likely to be, the attorney may be able to help the witness make those fears manageable. The witness who feels more secure will likely be more effective than one who is overly nervous as long as the security does not rise to the level of overconfidence.

In addition to addressing anxiety about an upcoming deposition, attorneys should prepare witnesses for other emotions they may experience during the deposition. As we have seen, depositions are not just cold, rational, information-gathering sessions. First, as we have observed, some questioning attorneys may deliberately try to scare or bully deponents in order to cause them to give more favorable answers or so that they appear to be lacking in confidence or untruthful. Second, deponents will often face a range of additional emotional reactions during the deposition: "[c]lients facing the prospect of being a witness may come to you displaying a full range of emotions and attitudes, from overwrought to overconfident."[96] Some emotions, such as guilt, can cause deponents to say things that are not true and that could be very damaging to their case; for example, a deponent might blurt out, "It's all my fault!" Anger can cause deponents to make comments that they later regret or that reduce the settlement value of the case. Of course, not all displays of emotion are bad. A deponent who displays controlled anger or upset in an understandable situation may impress opposing counsel and potentially a jury, thereby increasing the settlement value of her case.

To help the deponent confront her emotions, it may be wise for the defending attorney to simply talk to her in advance about these issues. Because some witnesses might think that responding angrily to the questioning attorney will help their case, the defending attorney should counsel the witness to try to keep her cool. By warning a client that the opposing attorney may look at the deponent critically, raise her voice, put her in an uncomfortable seat, and so on, the defending attorney can help the deponent steel herself against such tactics. The defending attorney will be most effective if she can help the client identify specific scenarios and suggest useful responses (see chapter 5). For example, the defending attorney might say, "If you feel the opposing attorney is getting you angry, I want you to silently count to ten before answering her question." (We noted earlier that counting before answering can also help a witness resist the urge to get into a conversation with the questioning attorney, so this technique may do double duty.) In addition, the defending attorney might suggest that if the witness finds any aspect of the physical environment to be uncomfortable, she should immediately voice such concerns.

Given the possibility that attorneys may raise their voices or even appear to melt down during depositions, defending attorneys should warn clients that this may occur. It is better that a client be psychologically prepared for a possible attorney shouting match than that the witness be completely shocked or scared by what transpires during the deposition. Letting witnesses know that attorneys sometimes lose their cool, even sometimes doing so deliberately as an intimidation technique, may help the witnesses maintain their own equanimity. Again, it is usually best to be specific, for example, to suggest that the witness sit silently if any attorneys start blowing off steam. Of course, in warning the witness about all of these possible problems, the attorney must use her discretion so as not to make the witness even more nervous.

On the other side of the equation, it is also important to prepare the deponent to deal with the seemingly charming opposing attorney—a figure who may be even more dangerous than the obvious jerk. As we have discussed, by establishing rapport with the witness, a questioning attorney may be able to obtain a great deal of information and perhaps even some admissions. Thus, the defending attorney should warn the witness in advance about getting too comfortable with the questioning attorney.

It can be quite helpful to work with the witness in an environment similar to that in which she will be deposed and to engage in some practice questioning by an unfamiliar attorney.[97] Learning by doing can be more effective than attempting to learn only by reading or hearing a lecture (see chapter 7). And becoming familiar with the process can help the deponent to confront and then overcome fears that she may have. In many cases, merely talking about possible emotional reactions will not be as useful as doing some role-playing of the deposition in advance. If the deposing attorney or someone else playing the questioning attorney can trigger the deponent's

> ✦ ✦ ✦ ✦ ✦
> **Too Nice to Be True?**
>
> Attorney: Mrs. X, I want to tell you a bit about Attorney Mendoza, who will be questioning you at the deposition. I have seen Mr. Mendoza conduct depositions in the past, and I can tell you that he comes across as a very friendly, nice guy. In a way, of course, this is great news. I'd be very surprised if he tried to scare or browbeat you. On the other hand, you do still need to keep your guard up. Sometimes the seemingly charming guys are the ones who end up tricking you into saying things you don't really believe. So, listen to his questions carefully, and remember at all times that he is the opposing attorney and not your friend.

likely emotional reactions, the deposing attorney can then help the deponent deal with these emotions in advance.

Defending the Deposition

Although state and federal rules of civil procedure have been written to minimize the role that defending lawyers can play in the deposition,[98] defending attorneys can take a few important steps to help protect their witnesses and provide them with emotional and psychological support. First, in addition to preparing the witness ahead of time, the defending attorney should try to enhance the comfort of the deponent by meeting with the deponent prior to the start of the deposition. The attorney can use this meeting to answer any last-minute questions and to allay any lingering concerns. Similarly, the defending attorney should seek to arrange the seating in a manner designed to ensure the comfort of the deponent. Although court reporters often insist that the deponent sit right next to them so that they can more easily hear the witness, the attorney may want to seat herself between the deponent and the court reporter. In this way, as the deponent looks toward the court reporter, she will also see the familiar face of her own attorney.[99]

> *Deposition, defending:* Seven hours locked in a room with a compulsive talker and a sociopath.
> —Mark Herrmann[100]

Second, attorneys should be careful about allowing witnesses to engage in small talk with opposing attorneys or anyone on the opposing team, including secretaries and paralegals. Although the ethical rules prohibit attorneys from conversing directly with represented clients except during the deposition itself, some attorneys seem to believe that it is acceptable to engage in small talk regarding weather, sports, and so on. While these topics themselves may be harmless, it is risky, psychologically, to let the witness establish a comfortable rapport with opposing counsel. A witness who becomes comfortable with opposing counsel may let down her guard against misleading questions or volunteer answers that her attorney would have preferred she not provide. The defending attorney should warn the client to avoid such conversations and should stay with the client whenever possible.

Third, the defending attorney should use breaks to further protect her deponent. Although the jurisdiction's rules may or may not permit the defending attorney to speak with her deponent about the substance of her testimony during a break,[101] it will usually at least be acceptable for the attorney to give the client a chance to get a cup of coffee, eat lunch, use the restroom, or talk with people other than the attorney. Depending on the jurisdiction, much more may be possible as well. Thus, the defending attorney should observe the testifying witness carefully at all times to try to discern if she is tiring, getting angry, or becoming too conversational with the opposing attorney. If the defending attorney sees something problematic happening, she should not hesitate to call for a break to try to straighten matters out.

Fourth, the defending attorney should be attentive to situations in which an objection may be appropriate. Although "coaching" objections are clearly barred by many rules of procedure and although attorneys often reserve all objections except as to form, attorneys do typically retain the right to object to questions that are worded in a confusing or unfair fashion. It is wise to object to such questions not only from an evidentiary perspective but also because making occasional objections can reassure the witness. When a defending attorney simply sits silently for hour upon hour, the deponent may begin to doubt that the attorney is there for her.

"I Object!"

Question: Do you still beat your wife?

Objection: That question assumes something that has not been proven. My client has never admitted nor have you shown that he ever did beat his wife.

Debriefing the Client

Postdeposition debriefing can help the client process what occurred at the deposition. Such meetings, even if just a short conversation or a shared meal following the deposition, can help maintain a solid relationship with the client and can also allay any postdeposition anxiety. The debriefing can help to build the foundation for future discussions of case strategy and possible settlement. Of course, if a postdeposition meeting is held, the attorney should be positive and not berate the client for mistakes that may have been made during the deposition.

Dealing with Videotaped Depositions

Videotaped depositions are quite different from ordinary depositions. The purpose of a videotaped deposition is not just to obtain information but also to preserve the information in a form that can be used at trial. Such depositions may, for example, be used for a witness (even the attorney's own client) who is in precarious health or for an expert whose schedule does not allow appearance at trial. Videotaped depositions can also be used to impeach witnesses at trial.

The addition of the visual and auditory dimensions to the deposition is critically important. Consider a political example:

> When presidential candidates Richard Nixon and John F. Kennedy debated in [1960], those who heard the first debate on the radio pronounced Nixon the winner. But the 70 million who watched television saw a candidate still sickly and obviously discomforted by Kennedy's smooth delivery and charisma. Those television viewers focused on what they saw, not what they heard. Studies of the audience indicated that, among television viewers, Kennedy was perceived the winner of the first debate by a very large margin.[102]

One writer put it this way:

> [O]ne of the lasting lessons of the debate was that television is not about rhetoric; above all, it is about pictures. On that level, Kennedy was the clear winner. He seemed self-assured, youthful, vibrant. By contrast, Nixon appeared defensive, and the bright studio lighting exaggerated his jowls and sunken eyes. As the hour wore on, the pancake makeup he used to hide a five o'clock shadow became streaked with perspiration.[103]

In taking or defending a videotaped deposition, attorneys must pay attention to these sorts of cues. It is even more important than it is in traditional depositions to discuss body language and appropriate dress with the deponent. Witnesses should be taught to display body language that shows honesty and confidence rather than dishonesty, fear, or arrogance (see chapter 7). Since body language tends to be amplified on camera, witnesses must be taught (if possible) to avoid mannerisms such as playing with their pen or their hair.

The attorney may also want to prepare the witness somewhat differently for answering questions at a videotaped deposition. While a witness may genuinely not recall the details of facts that transpired months or even years earlier, it may look bad to the jury or judge if the witness repeatedly has to say, "I don't recall." As we highlighted in our discussion of the Scooter Libby litigation, jurors don't necessarily have a good understanding of memory, nor will the judge necessarily permit them to be educated regarding the nature of memory. Thus, the witness may want to give short explanations as to why he may not recall the details of a particular meeting, such as the fact that he has attended roughly two hundred meetings since the date of the meeting in question. Of course, a witness who has too many such explanations will sound defensive, so both the witness and the preparing attorney will have to use their discretion and common sense to meet this concern. Sometimes it will be better to simply say, "I don't know" or "I don't recall."

Similarly, although witnesses are often instructed to take a few moments before answering a question in a typical deposition, taking a lengthy pause in a videotaped deposition may lead the jury to conclude that the witness is not being honest. Thus, while a witness may still be better off hesitating than answering too quickly without thinking, the costs of hesitation are higher in a videotaped deposition. Witnesses can, however, be instructed to briefly pause before answering questions even in a videotaped deposition, particularly if they pause before answering every question. As one commentator notes:

> It is similar to living near train tracks. If the train comes on a regular, consistent schedule, you stop noticing the noise pretty quickly. However, if the train comes intermittently, you will notice it every time it passes through. Pausing works the same way. Inconsistent pausing is noticeable, even annoying. It can cause jurors to be suspicious of answers that are given after a pause, which decreases the witness's credibility. But if the pause is consistent, beginning with the reply to, "Please state your name for the record," jurors will never notice.[104]

Given all of this, it can be even more helpful to make a practice video as part of the preparation for a videotaped deposition than to make one for a nonvideo deposition. In reviewing the practice video, the attorney can work with the deponent to try to solve any problems that are evident in the video.

✦ ✦ ✦ ✦ ✦

Interviews in Due Diligence Reviews

Due diligence reviews consist primarily of document analysis. Attorneys look at relevant draft transactional documents, contracts, leases, regulations, corporate minutes, and records of litigation. Depending on what is revealed in these documents, the due diligence attorneys may also conduct interviews and site visits to ensure that the company being investigated has been presented in an accurate light. To the extent that attorneys conduct interviews as part of their due diligence work, they should follow the suggestions that we have set out in chapter 9.

Reviewing Information Obtained through Discovery and Due Diligence

After attorneys have obtained material through discovery or due diligence, they must review that information and work it into their files and strategy. Here, too, psychology offers some insights.

>
> True genius resides in the capacity for evaluation of uncertain, hazardous, and conflicting information.
> —*Winston Churchill*[105]

First, attorneys must guard against confirmation bias and biased assimilation. As we learned in chapter 1, our tendency is to interpret new information in ways that are consistent with what we previously knew or believed or with our theory of the case. We scrutinize information that is inconsistent with our prior views more closely—trying to find errors or exceptions—than we do information that is consistent. Thus, we do not easily abandon our initial views, and this may be even more so when we have been retained to represent one side in a dispute or transaction.

Confirmation biases may cause an attorney who is reviewing the information obtained in discovery or through due diligence to gloss over or reject information that is helpful to the other side and to ignore weaknesses in supportive materials. Naïve realism (see chapter 1) may make it difficult to see how others might view the case or transaction differently. Such biases may cause the attorney not to settle cases that should be settled, to fail to prepare adequately for trial, to pursue deals that are ill advised, or to pass up deals that would be worth pursuing. To guard against these problems, the attorney should look specifically for information that she predicts the other side will use to support its position. She should also look specifically for weaknesses in the materials that she thinks are helpful to her own position or materials that would disconfirm her own assumptions.

>
> The pre-trial deposition-discovery mechanism established by Rules 26 to 37 is one of the most significant innovations of the Federal Rules of Civil Procedure. . . . [They] serve (1) as a device . . . to narrow and clarify the issues between the parties, and (2) as a device for ascertaining the facts. . . . Thus civil trials . . . no longer need be carried on in the dark. The way is now clear . . . for the parties to obtain the fullest possible knowledge of the issues and facts before trial.
> —*Hickman v. Taylor*[106]

Attorneys should also be alert to the possibility that information obtained through discovery or due diligence might not be as useful for forging agreement as they might hope. The optimistic drafters of the broad discovery rules believed that sharing pretrial information would help the parties ascertain the facts and bring them closer together. Similarly, the point of due diligence is to obtain concrete information on which to base a decision so that parties to a transaction do not have to rely on their prior assumptions. However, we have seen that it is not so easy for disputing parties to reach a common understanding, and parties may use due diligence to confirm rather than disconfirm their prior conceptions (see chapter 1). In fact, "shared information, if it is open to multiple interpretations, is likely to be interpreted egocentrically by the disputants, which can cause beliefs to diverge rather than converge."[107] Attorneys and clients will have to work hard to get beyond these divergences.

Similarly, in reviewing the information provided, the investigator should also take into account the conflicting interests of some of the parties to the transaction or case. For example, if an underwriter has compiled an evaluation of the proposed deal, the attorney should discount that evaluation if the underwriter is being compensated on a contingent fee basis out of the proceeds of the sale. As we will see in chapter 14, this can be hard to do.

> . . . Diligence is the Mother of good Fortune.
> —*Don Quixote*[108]

Recall that it can be helpful to assume the posture of a disagreeable adjudicator (see chapter 4). By trying to disconfirm her own or others' biases, the attorney can more likely gain a complete picture of both the favorable and unfavorable evidence in the case. Companies are also wise to use law firms and other third parties, such as accountants, to do due diligence work on proposed transactions because such outsider companies will not necessarily be as invested in ensuring that the transaction goes through.[109]

As they seek and review the information obtained, attorneys should pay attention to the degree to which they or their clients have a need for closure (see chapter 5). Those with a high need for closure—that is, those who are apt to process less information, to jump to conclusions, and to less thoroughly entertain alternatives—may need to push themselves to suspend judgment and continue to engage in analysis with an open mind. In contrast, those with a low need for closure—that is, those who are more likely to suspend judgment, to continue to gather information, and to thoroughly consider many different angles—may need to push themselves to curtail their search for and analysis of information and make the decisions at hand.

Finally, attorneys who do locate a document or a set of facts that might reflect negatively on the case or transaction should remember to continue their search for additional possible problems. Just as a radiologist who has located a single anomaly can miss others (see chapter 1), so, too, may a case or proposed transaction have multiple issues.

♦ ♦ ♦ ♦ ♦
Summing it Up

- Remember that while information can be very useful in countering optimistic overconfidence, it is also costly and may not bring all of the hoped-for benefits. In conducting discovery and due diligence, be wary of overconfidence, the tendency to seek unnecessary information, and confirmation bias. Carefully consider the need for each request, and make an extra effort to search out disconfirming information.

- Deploy persuasive techniques when engaged in a negotiation over information, using liking, reciprocity, anchoring, and the door-in-the-face and foot-in-the-door techniques.
- When propounding interrogatories and document requests, remember that they can have a persuasive impact.
- Beware the tendency to overlook, discount, or hide pertinent information when responding to interrogatory and document requests.
- To conduct effective depositions, make appropriate use of open- and closed-ended questions and documents, build rapport, work with emotion, and tell an effective story.
- To prepare witnesses for depositions and to defend those depositions, warn witnesses about the communication patterns of depositions, normalize the fragility of memory and witness anxiety, and help witnesses make the best impression possible.
- When reviewing information obtained in discovery or due diligence reviews, guard against confirmation bias, biased assimilation, and the tendency to view information in a way that serves your own or your client's interests.

For Further Reading: Discovery and Due Diligence

Diane R. Follingstad, *Preparing the Witness for Courtroom Testimony: Modifying Negative Behavior Through Employment of Psychological Principles*, 20 TRIAL 50 (1984).

Roy Futterman, *Advanced Witness Preparation Using Psychological Techniques*, in THE SCIENCE OF COURTROOM LITIGATION: JURY RESEARCH AND ANALYTICAL GRAPHICS 93 (Joanna Gallant et al. eds., 2008).

DAVID M. MALONE ET AL., THE EFFECTIVE DEPOSITION: TECHNIQUES AND STRATEGIES THAT WORK (2007).

William M. McErlean et al., *The Evolution of Witness Preparation*, 37:1 LITIGATION 21 (2010).

Dennis P. Stolle & Mark D. Stuaan, *Defending Depositions in High-Stakes Civil and Quasi-Criminal Litigation: An Application of Therapeutic Jurisprudence*, 4 W. CRIM. REV. 134 (2003).

Writing 13

> Writing is easy. All you do is stare at a blank sheet of paper until drops of blood form on your forehead.
> —*Gene Fowler*[1]

The lawyers portrayed on television and in the movies lead a pretty glamorous life. They spend a lot of time trying cases in the courtroom, meeting with clients, and dining at nice restaurants. In contrast, lawyers in real life spend a great deal of their time writing. They write letters, contracts, pleadings, motions, appellate briefs, statutes, instructions to associates and paralegals, and many other documents.

Writing involves a great deal of cognitive effort, much more than is required for reading or digesting new information. Good writing requires collecting information, generating ideas and strategies, and translating these into text.[3] Thus, the good writer needs both substantive knowledge and expertise in the delivery of the message. Good writing also requires extensive revision—the ability to look back at one's writing and to determine what works and what does not:

> "There is no such thing as good writing. There is only good rewriting.
> —*Justice Louis Brandeis*[2]"

> To revise a text for an audience is a very complex task. It requires the reviser to comprehend the goals of the text, to predict how well the text will accomplish those goals for the intended audience, and to propose better ways to accomplish those goals when the reviser perceives the text to be faulty.[4]

In short, good writing—whether in the form of an appellate brief or a more standardized document such as a contract, will, or set of corporate bylaws—draws on the psychology of persuasion, emotion, perception, communication, judgment, and decision making.

In this chapter, we first discuss two broad psychological themes that are important for all types of writing. Then we provide additional insights that are significant for particular kinds of legal writing: briefs, complaints, letters, and contracts.

General Psychological Guidance for Writers

> The power of clear statement is the great power at the bar.
> —Daniel Webster[5]

Psychology dictates that good writers convey ideas and information clearly and accessibly and take into account the nature of their audience.

Clarity and Accessibility

We've seen that people's processing capacity is limited. Thus, writers can enhance audience comprehension by focusing on the most important information and organizing material into clear, manageable segments (see chapter 7). In addition, recall that a message that is processed easily (or fluently) is more believable, inspires more confidence in the truth of the message, is more memorable, and is ultimately more persuasive as well (see chapters 6 and 7). Thus, writing clearly and directly is a key to good writing: "All the careful strategy in the world will be of no assistance to you unless you write clearly and forcefully. And clarity and power are above all the fruit of simplicity."[6]

Cosmetic concerns are important, too: the skilled use of font size, spacing, and white space can help make a document more readable.[7] As the authors of one legal writing text put it, "[a]ll is lost in the end . . . if no one cares to read the document."[8]

✦ ✦ ✦ ✦ ✦

Extreme Lack of Clarity

The U.S. Court of Appeals for the Seventh Circuit recently found a complaint to be so poorly drafted that it affirmed dismissal of the lawsuit with prejudice and issued an order to show cause why the attorney should not be disciplined. Consider just one sentence from the complaint:

> Stanard and attendees, were stunned on the day of the family-oriented event, when an even more menacing law enforcement presence was created when Nygren's armed deputies, without prior consent or permission, warrant or probable cause, arrived, not a part of any agreement and a surprise and upset when it arrive, uninvited, on and entered and trespassed on Plaintiff property with drug-sniffing "K-9" dogs, obviously and unfortunate that Defendants were "looking for trouble" where there was none as distinct from "looking to serve."[9]

Organization

Effective organization is essential for making writing clear and accessible and provides a structure to help the reader process the text. Good writers employ road maps to help orient the reader to how the writing is organized and use topic sentences to highlight the concepts contained in each paragraph. Writers can also reinforce good organization by repeating the key points in introductions and conclusions.

Brevity

While road maps and even occasional repetitions are valuable, brevity is also a key to good writing. Multiple surveys of judges have demonstrated the high value that judges place on conciseness.[10] Judge Alex Kozinski of the U.S. Court of Appeals for the Ninth Circuit stated, "[W]hen judges see a lot of words they immediately think: LOSER, LOSER. You might as well write it in big bold letters on the cover of your brief."[11] Brevity is effective for other readers as well because it directs attention to the best and most important arguments. Readers do not always have the processing capacity or motivation to sort through large amounts of rhetorical chaff to find the high-quality wheat. Moreover, as discussed in chapter 6, weaker arguments can distract the reader from the stronger arguments and can fuel the reader's inclination to generate counterarguments to the writer's positions.

✦ ✦ ✦ ✦ ✦

Brief Tweets

In a humorous nod to the importance of brevity, the Texas Bar recently sponsored a contest asking competitors to write a Twitter-length (140 characters) brief.[12]

Word Choice

Word choice is also critical to clarity: "You would have no confidence in a carpenter whose tools were dull and rusty. Lawyers possess only one tool to convey their thoughts: language. They must acquire and hone the finest, more effective version of that tool available. They must love words and use them exactly."[13]

As we saw in chapter 7, attorneys have a penchant for using big words, complex sentence structure, jargon, and lots of words. But these tendencies are often indulged at the expense of clear communication and, ultimately, persuasiveness. Consider the following statement of a question presented in a brief:

> A lawyer should keep in mind that the purpose of communication is to communicate, and this can't be done if the reader ... doesn't understand the words used.
> —*Bryan Garner*[14]

> Whether there was a violation of the OSHA rule requiring every incident-investigation report to contain a list of factors that contributed to the incident, when the investigation report on the June 2002 explosion at the Vespante plant listed the contributing factors in an attachment to the report entitled "Contributing Factors," as opposed to including them in the body of the report?[15]

Think about your experience in trying to read the passage. Note how difficult it was to process the statement and to understand exactly what question the court is to consider. Did you have to reread portions of the statement in order to see how the various clauses related and to discern its meaning? Now compare the following rewritten question:

> OSHA rules require every incident-investigation report to contain a list of factors that contributed to the incident. The report on the June 2002 explosion at the Vespante plant listed the contributing factors not in the body of the report but in an attachment entitled "Contributing Factors." Did the report thereby violate OSHA rules?[16]

This version is much easier to understand.

> " Legalese annoys almost anyone who reads contracts—whether client, lawyer, or judge. Obscure words and phrases, hailing from times past, clutter provisions and make them difficult to understand.
> —Tina L. Stark[18] "

Although lawyers may believe that using jargon and writing complexly will impress readers with their expertise, studies have shown that readers tend to have the opposite reaction.[17] Readers are more impressed by simple and clear writing than they are by complexity and jargon (see chapter 7). Thus, attorneys should avoid terms like *render* and *disbursement* and instead use words like *make* and *spend*. It is particularly important to write clearly and simply when writing letters to people, such as clients, who may not be familiar with legal terms or law practice.

Using Examples

As we discussed in chapters 6 and 7, people tend to better understand and remember concepts when they are conveyed through concrete examples. Individual examples tend to stick with us; generalized statistics and abstract concepts do not. Concrete examples also increase the impact of a point. Recall from chapter 6 the image of BBs pouring into a bucket to demonstrate the firepower of the world's nuclear arsenal. Or think of the commercial that uses body bags to represent the death toll from smoking. Remember, also, how much easier it was to remember a word list comprised of objects than one made up of abstract concepts. Ultimately, using specific examples will help make writing clearer and more memorable.

Hickman v. Taylor, the case in which the Supreme Court first enunciated the work product doctrine, can help to illustrate the importance of concrete examples in legal documents. Justice Murphy's majority opinion justified creation of the doctrine in part by using a series of policy arguments:

> Were such materials [notes of witness interviews] open to opposing counsel on mere demand, much of what is now put down in writing would remain unwritten.

General Psychological Guidance for Writers

An attorney's thoughts, heretofore inviolate, would not be his own. Inefficiency, unfairness and sharp practices would inevitably develop in the giving of legal advice and in the preparation of cases for trial. The effect on the legal profession would be demoralizing. And the interests of the clients and the cause of justice would be poorly served.[19]

> Like the measured length of a coastline, which increases as the map becomes more specific, the perceived likelihood of an event increases as its description becomes more specific.
> —Amos Tversky & Derek J. Koehler[20]

This statement is most effective to the extent that it gives a specific example: lawyers failing to take notes at all. However, the reader is left to ponder about the meaning of *unfairness* and *sharp practices* mentioned in the opinion. The Justices might have made their point more clearly by more explicitly explaining that some lawyers would mooch off their opponents' discovery efforts (unfairness) and that some unscrupulous lawyers might even insert fake interview notes into the documents provided to an opponent (sharp practices). Enabling the reader to envision a particular instance makes the message more powerful.

Engaging Multiple Channels

Since people take in and process information via multiple channels, it is useful to present information to readers in different ways (see chapter 7). Although some may be skeptical of the link between law and art,[21] pictures and charts can help make words come to life.

> A picture can be worth a thousand words— but only if a reader can decipher it.
> —Stephen M. Kosslyn[22]

For example, a verbal description about changes in company profits over time might be accompanied by a graphic to illustrate the relevant trend. A description of facts might be accompanied by a timeline that visually emphasizes the sequence of relevant events. Similarly, imagine an attorney handling a case involving the alleged infringement of a patent on liquid crystal display (LCD) technology:

> [T]he main arguments you wish to advance relate to how LCD television screens and computer monitors are constructed. . . . You may use an example of how the general method of display involves polarizing plates which act like venetian blinds. A graphic illustrates that Venetian blinds open or close to let light pass through or to block the light. This concept of Venetian blinds can then be connected to the appearance of different displays on various devices when the "blinds" are essentially open or closed.[23]

By presenting the description in both words and pictures, the advocate is better able to convey her message, helping her audience to both understand and remember it.

While it is not yet in vogue to routinely include actual pictures in legal writing, it can be effective for the lawyer to at least paint a verbal image to win readers over to her position.

> If you want to win a case, paint the Judge a picture and keep it simple.
> —John W. Davis[24]

For example, [consider] the following scene: A woman is being held by her arms and roughly dragged out of her house into a police van. The police and the van are carefully described, as is the way in which she was held and pulled. All of these images support her claim that she was subject to government persecution. But what other accessory details can we discover from her? Imagine the scene for yourself. What do you see? Do you see her feet as she is dragged? What kind of shoes is she wearing? . . . [I]n response to our query, she disclosed that the police dragged her through a bed of daisies that she had planted, tramping them and breaking their stems. Destruction of flowers is not grounds for asylum. It does, however, make the scene come to life.[26]

The greatest possibilities of visual display lie in vividness and inescapability of the intended message.
—John W. Tukey[25]

Audience Perspective: In the Reader's Shoes

We have seen that it is critically important to be able to understand the perspective of the people with whom we are attempting to communicate (see chapter 7). Thus, regardless of whether writing is good or bad, the effectiveness of writing necessarily depends on the audience for whom the writing is intended. The good writer, like all good communicators, should try to imagine the experiences, perceptions, interests, existing knowledge, feelings, and mindset of her audience, using that awareness to refine her writing.

The good writer should remember that her audience likely does not see the world in entirely the same way as she does. Thus, writing that is clear and persuasive to the author will not necessarily be clear and persuasive to the reader. Think back to how wrongly confident people are that others will be able to identify a song whose rhythm they tap (see chapters 1 and 7), and recall how hard it can be to effectively convey information to a person who lacks our perspective and background. Good writers make a concerted effort to overcome this naïve realism and curse of knowledge, consciously trying to account for things that they know but that their audience does not. One practical way to address this difficulty is to share drafts with readers from a variety of perspectives who can point out deficiencies in a piece of writing.

Because people learn by building on what they already know, good writing needs to take into account people's existing knowledge and beliefs—for example, by drawing analogies with familiar contexts. Writers often employ common aphorisms—such as not letting foxes take charge of the chicken coop or putting old wine into new wineskins—as a means of connecting new ideas to concepts that may be more familiar to their audience. Good writers also try to gear their writing to their readers' likely concerns. Some readers will care more about following rules, others about the content of particular policies, others about certain kinds of morality, and others more about efficiency. Addressing the reader's particular perspective makes the writer more effective.

When writing a brief to a busy trial court judge, for example, the lawyer must remember that such judges are not necessarily prepared to research the law or facts in-depth or to pore over a lengthy brief. The writer must, therefore, succinctly provide the judge with the key information, including relevant legal standards and analysis of relevant cases. One of judges' most frequent complaints about legal writing is that many attorneys effectively dump a large number of cases in their laps without adequately digesting or analyzing them. While keeping the writing concise, the attorney must remember that the judge is likely not as expert as the attorney in the particular legal issues presented by the case. Thus, the attorney should not hesitate to offer careful explanations and to connect the dots for the judge.

> With due respect to judge and jury and to the procedural constraints of the law itself, cases are decided not only on their legal merits but on the artfulness of an attorney's narrative.
> —Jerome Bruner[27]

Moreover, it can be helpful to recognize that readers who are decision makers are typically engaged in trying to balance a range of different goals and concerns. Judges, for example, may seek to balance their desire to follow precedent, their preferred policy goals, and the constraints of their workload and the need to manage their docket.[28] Clients may similarly attempt to balance their need for closure, their financial obligations, and their desire for recognition or retribution. Taking a broad view of the likely concerns of the audience can help lawyers to envision a broader set of issues and arguments that might be addressed.

Similarly, the attorney should always try to remember the perspective of the reader when drafting documents for clients. In striving for clarity, it is important to remember that terms that are clear to a sophisticated reader may be less clear to others. For example, while there are, of course, a variety of subjects that lawyers need to cover in a retainer letter (such as the scope of representation, billing rates, possible termination of the relationship, and dispute resolution), the attorney should consider the ability of the client to understand the substance of the letter. In addition, the attorney should consider how the client will perceive its tone.

Briefs

Briefs directed to trial court and appellate judges (as well as to arbitrators) are intended to persuade the reader of the correctness of the writer's position. Modern psychological studies support the wisdom of looking to some ancient philosophers and classical rhetoric to improve our writing:

> Aristotle and Quintilian, those classic teachers of oratory and rhetoric, taught that a persuasive written or oral presentation contains three elements:
>
> Ethos: The ethics, integrity, and character of the advocate;

Pathos: The emotions that the advocate instills in the audience; and

Logos: The logic or reason that supports the advocate's argument.[29]

While no appeal to psychology can turn an argument based on bad logic into a pearl, properly emphasizing the credibility of the author (ethos) and using stories to evoke emotions (pathos) can greatly strengthen written work.

Credibility

> [P]ersuasive discourse depends as much on the advocate's character and credibility, or ethos, as it does on the logic of the argument or the emotional content of the case.
> —Michael Frost[30]

Credibility is key to effective communication and influence (see chapters 6 and 7). If, through her writing, the lawyer can demonstrate her credibility, then her statements in a brief will more likely be accepted. If, on the other hand, the lawyer is found not to be credible, then her writings will be viewed with skepticism.

As we have seen, two key components of credibility are expertise and trustworthiness. In her writing and otherwise, the attorney must demonstrate that her assertions are based on sound facts, law, and policy. If the attorney is found to have ignored or incorrectly described a case or statute, her credibility with the judge will plummet, and she will be less effective in arguing her case and other cases as well. Even seemingly superficial aspects of writing may influence a reader's general assessment of expertise. For at least some readers, typos and spelling errors may cast doubt on the writer's overall competence.

To be deemed trustworthy, the attorney will need to deal with contrary rules and precedents in a forthright manner. Because no lawyer is ever lucky enough to be called upon to present a perfect case, lawyers must inevitably contend with at least some facts and law that might seem to favor the opponent's position. Psychology can help an attorney figure out how best to deal with such adverse material. While ethical rules require disclosure of some of the most damaging information,[31] attorneys have discretion regarding whether and how to disclose more than the minimum required by the ethical rules. As we saw in chapter 6, it can be most persuasive to present two-sided arguments that directly confront and rebut adverse facts, precedent, and legal arguments. Evenhanded presentation can increase credibility, minimize the likelihood that the reader will generate counterarguments, and provide the reader with the tools to respond to counterarguments presented by an opponent. In contrast, ignoring the opponent's arguments damages credibility and weakens defenses to those arguments once they are made.[32]

In confronting adverse authority, attorneys may also need to consider the reactions that judges or juries may have to particular parties or witnesses. For example, people may feel sympathy for an injured person, particularly where the harm does not seem to result from her own actions. A Nevada case, *Wood v. Safeway*, posed an extreme challenge for defense counsel in this regard. Plaintiff Jane Doe, a mentally handicapped woman, had allegedly been raped and impregnated during the course of her employment at a Safeway grocery store by a man, Emilio Ronquillo-Nino, who did janitorial work at the store. Safeway filed and ultimately won a motion for summary judgment, arguing that the plaintiff's only source of relief was workers' compensation and that the store was not responsible for the janitor's deliberate misdeeds.[33] Rather than ignore the sympathy that a finder of fact would likely have for this plaintiff, a defense attorney would want to confront it directly. Imagine the effect of writing something along the following lines in the brief supporting Safeway's motion for summary judgment:

> While Ms. Doe admittedly suffered a terrible wrong, it would also be wrong to hold Safeway directly responsible for her injuries. Instead, Ms. Doe can properly seek relief through our workers' compensation system, which is designed to protect employees from workplace harms. She can also seek relief from the perpetrator of these wrongs, Mr. Ronquillo-Nino, who should be held responsible for his horrendous acts.

Of course, fact finders might be skeptical of, rather than sympathetic toward, a plaintiff, in which case plaintiff's counsel would need to confront such hostility.[34] Similarly, defense counsel may have to address fact finders' perceptions of the defendant.

A Good Story

The best legal advocates have long recognized that facts, themes, and stories are essential building blocks of a persuasive case. Teachers of trial advocacy like renowned trial attorney Gerry Spence consistently remind their students that "[i]f we are to be successful in presenting our case we must not only discover its story, we must become good storytellers as well. Every trial, . . . every argument for justice is a story."[35] While logic and evidence are central to the strength of legal arguments, logic alone is not as powerful as logic connected to a story.

A great story is like a well-crafted joke—deliciously brief, immediately memorable, eminently repeatable and virtually impossible to dismiss.
—Kenneth Albers[36]

The importance of telling a good story has been borne out in psychologists' research on juror decision making. One set of studies found that mock jurors were more likely to find in favor of the side that presented its evidence in the order of a story supporting its view rather than in an order based on how the witnesses happened to testify or how the judge might instruct on the legal issues, thus departing from a clear causal and chronological narrative. The most effective stories are those that account for the evidence (*coverage*) and that are internally consistent, plausible, and complete (*coherence*).[37]

The importance of stories may also relate to the representativeness heuristic, that is, events tend to be perceived as more probable when they are more easily visualized (see chapter 4). One study (which was conducted before the Katrina

> As the amount of detail in a scenario increases, its probability can only decrease steadily, but its representativeness and hence its apparent likelihood may increase.
> —Amos Tversky & Daniel Kahneman[40]

flooding and the Fukushima earthquake), found that people believed it more probable that (1) an earthquake would occur in California and cause a flood leading to the drowning of one thousand people than that (2) a flood would occur *somewhere in North America* and lead to the drowning of one thousand people.[38] Logically, of course, (2) includes (1) because California is within North America and floods would include floods caused by earthquakes. Thus, the probability of (2) occurring must be greater than the probability of (1). Yet, people tend to view the possibility of such a disaster occurring in California to be more likely.[39]

Stories derive their power from the way they connect to how we perceive the social world, drawing on our tendency to look for patterns, relationships and meaning in what we observe in the world (see chapter 1).[41] Indeed, many of the ways in which we understand the world are encapsulated in a set of commonly understood stories, metaphors, and narratives. Such stories allow us to "understand one domain of experience in terms of another."[42]

By connecting to concepts and narratives with which the reader is already familiar, stories can tap into preexisting schemas about commonly understood characters or story lines. For example, an attorney writing a brief on behalf of fishermen harmed in the BP Gulf oil spill may want to tap into perceptions of corporate greed. An attorney writing a brief advocating on behalf of a juvenile charged with vandalism may well try to tell a story of an innocent child who has been let down by her parents or "the system." Evoking these sorts of shared narratives can induce readers to fill in gaps in ways that are consistent with such schemas and prime concepts upon which readers will draw when interpreting ambiguous facts, precedent, or policy (see chapter 1).

> We see and understand the world through "stock stories." These stories help us interpret the everyday world with limited information and help us make choices about asserting our own needs and responding to other people.
> —Gerald P. Lopez[43]

Stories also provide a structure—including a setting and protagonist, a problem, reactions, goals, actions, and consequences—that helps readers understand the information provided and into which the readers can incorporate new information as they are exposed to it. Consider the case against a hypothetical pharmaceutical company, Mostly-Super-Drug Company (MSD), the producer of a painkiller (Mercox) that has been withdrawn from the market after being associated with an increased risk of cardiac arrest:

> In one narrative, the plaintiff's protagonist would be MSD and the story would begin ten years prior to the trial, when MSD is competing with another major drug company to be the first to market with a painkiller ("problem"). In one likely narrative, MSD's "reaction" is intense motivation to market a drug with "plans" and

"actions" to push Mercox through FDA approval and onto the market. Sub-goals include securing FDZ approval for Mercox, the actions in that sub plan involve applications for approval and various activities of MSD's scientists and executives to secure approval (such as rushing the requisite clinical trials tests of Mercox). Another sub-goal is, following FDA approval, to distribute the drug and aggressively to persuade physicians to recommend it to patients. The "outcome" is a poorly tested, improperly labeled drug, being prescribed by ill-informed physicians. The "consequences" are deaths of patients, due to the cardiac side-effects of Mercox. The fate of the victim in the instant case would be a narrative embedded in the "outcome" component of the overarching story of corporate greed.

> [N]arrative . . . corresponds more closely to the manner in which the human mind makes sense of experience than does the conventional, abstracted rhetoric of the law.
> —Steven L. Winter[44]

The plaintiff is likely to present several "embedded narratives" within the larger story of corporate greed, desperation, and misconduct. For example, there might be an embedded story about MSD's efforts to respond to the "problem" of a negative study result, perhaps by suppressing publicity, attempting to mislead physicians about the implications of the study, and obscuring warnings to patients.[45]

But consider how an alternative story also fits this narrative structure:

In one defense narrative, MSD is again the protagonist but now the "problem" is defined as patients' needs for effective drug therapies. Thus, MSD's goal is to produce useful drugs, while balancing the benefits and costs of any artificial therapy, and behaving in a fiscally responsible manner to preserve reasonable shareholder profits. It would probably be wise to note that profitability means not introducing new drugs heedless of adverse consequences for users, as this destroys profits and the company's ability to make profits. Then, with the focus on the goal of responsible production, plans and actions to produce effective drugs are described in the case of Mercox. This would be the place to emphasize the implementation of multiple trial studies of efficacy and side effects, the quick reaction to signs of adverse consequences, the high volume response by physicians to the warnings and press releases (indicating their efficacy, etc.). The defense may also want to tell a second story, this one with the victim/plaintiff as the protagonist. A story that begins with the victim's struggles with ill-health ("problem"), emphasizing the many features of his background, lifestyle, and prior problem-incidents. His "reaction" is to be concerned and to take medication to prevent further health incidents, but a heart attack ("outcome") results from his prior disposition and (ideally for the defense) a precipitating incident.[46]

Note how the different stories might shape the ways in which the reader interprets ambiguous information. In a similar way, a particular piece of evidence, such as an e-mail asserting the need for speedy approval of the drug, might be interpreted differently under the two versions of the drug story.[47]

Of course, different readers may be naturally inclined to draw upon different scripts and schemas. When some readers think about corporations, they may think of greed or self-interest; other readers may think of competence and efficiency. Similarly, whereas mention of the military evokes patriotism and honor for some,

> The explanatory stories that people find compelling are simple; are concrete rather than abstract; assign a larger role to talent, stupidity, and intentions than to luck; and focus on a few striking events that happened rather than on the countless events that failed to happen.
> —Daniel Kahneman[48]

for others it may connote violence or blind obedience to authority. Good writers understand the sorts of stories that are likely to be effective for a particular reader and use them to frame the argument. In addition, good writers seek to tell the story to go beyond these natural inclinations, priming the schemas and conveying the messages that are beneficial to the writer.

Stories can also affect our decisions and judgments by influencing our emotions, thereby subtly incorporating the pathos that Aristotle and Quintilian saw as so key to persuasion. As we saw in chapter 3, emotions influence the ways in which we perceive the world, our judgments and decisions, and the ways in which we communicate. Even judges admit to being affected by emotions at the workplace at least occasionally.[49] Thus, it can be useful to tell stories that we hope will build emotion, such as sympathy or anger, in the listener:

> The effective use of emotion involves creating a response in the audience that makes the audience *want* to do things your way. It means the audience not only believes at an intellectual level that you are right, but feels it at a gut level and wants to do something about it.[50]

In similar ways, stories can evoke justice considerations by putting events in a context that primes a reader to think that a particular result is or is not fair and just (see chapter 8). A judge or jury will likely be more interested in punishing a defendant, whether civilly or criminally, if that defendant acted deliberately or maliciously and is unrepentant than if the defendant simply made a onetime understandable mistake. Thus, when BP defends itself in litigation arising out of the oil spill in the Gulf of Mexico, it will try to tell a story of unfortunate and unforeseeable disaster, whereas plaintiffs will try to tell a story of corporate greed and shortcuts that predictably caused harm to innocent third parties.

Using Facts

> It may sound paradoxical, but most contentions of law are won or lost on the facts.
> —Justice Robert H. Jackson[51]

Facts are critically important for telling a story, fostering understanding of the relevant law, and building support for a position. As we saw in chapters 6 and 7, making concepts more concrete tends to make them easier to understand, seem more familiar, more persuasive, and easier to remember. Moreover, once a particular set of facts—facts that favor one side or damage the other side—has lodged in the reader's mind, it may be difficult to counter those facts with "mere" logic.

Therefore, while it is easy to focus more on the law than on the facts in drafting briefs and motions, it is important for attorneys to pay particular attention to how they use the facts to tell the story in a brief. One obvious place to direct this focus is, not surprisingly, the "facts" section of the brief. There should rarely be any doubt as to which side wrote a particular facts section of a brief. While dishonesty and hyperbole in describing the facts are improper and unwise, and while attorneys wants to appear to be trustworthy to maximize their persuasiveness (see chapter 6), they should select and emphasize those facts that will present their case in the most favorable light:

> So, when legal advocates look at the facts of the case, we should ask ourselves: what are my most emotionally powerful, memorable facts? Is this a story of injustice (requiring the court to step in)? A story about redemption? A story about how bad things sometimes happen that cannot be fixed by the legal system? How do these facts make the reader feel? Angry? Sad? Satisfied that justice has been done?[52]

Take, for example, *Roper v. Simmons*, the case in which the Supreme Court ruled that imposing the death penalty on juvenile offenders was unconstitutional.[53] In their briefs, the petitioner (the State) and the respondent (Simmons) described the underlying facts—of how seventeen-year-old Christopher Simmons came to kill Shirley Crook—in quite different ways. First, consider the Brief for Petitioner and its focus on "The Murder":

> In early September 1993, Simmons, then age seventeen (now 28), discussed with his friends, Charlie Benjamin, fifteen, and John Tessmer, sixteen, the possibility of committing a burglary and murdering someone. On several occasions, Simmons described his planned crime: find someone to burglarize, tie the victim up, and ultimately push the victim off a bridge. Simmons assured his friends that their status as juveniles would allow them to "get away with it."
>
> On September 8, 1993, Simmons arranged to meet Benjamin and Tessmer at around 2:00 a.m. to carry out Simmons's plan. The trio met at the home of Brian Moomey. When Simmons and Benjamin left to commit the burglary, Tessmer returned home.
>
> Simmons and Benjamin found a window cracked open at the rear of Shirley Crook's home. They opened the window, reached through, unlocked the back door, and entered the house. Simmons turned on a hallway light; the light awakened Mrs. Crook, who was home alone. She sat up in bed and asked, "Who's there?" Simmons entered her bedroom and recognized Mrs. Crook as a woman with whom he had previously had an automobile accident. Mrs. Crook apparently recognized Simmons as well.
>
> Simmons ordered Mrs. Crook out of bed and, when she did not comply, Simmons forced her to the floor with Benjamin's help. While Benjamin guarded Mrs. Crook in the bedroom, Simmons found a roll of duct tape, returned to the bedroom, and bound her hands behind her back. The two also taped shut Mrs. Crook's eyes and mouth. They placed Mrs. Crook in the back of her minivan. Simmons drove the van from Mrs. Crook's home in Jefferson County to Castlewood State Park in St. Louis County.
>
> Simmons parked the van near a railroad trestle that spanned the Meramec River. When he and Benjamin began to unload Mrs. Crook, they discovered that she had freed her hands and had removed some of the duct tape from her face. Using Mrs. Crook's purse strap, the belt from her bathrobe, a towel from the back of

the minivan, and some electrical wire found on the trestle, Simmons and Benjamin bound Mrs. Crook again, restraining her hands and feet and covering her head with a towel. Simmons and Benjamin walked Mrs. Crook to the railroad trestle. There, Simmons bound her hands and feet together, hog-tied fashion, with the electrical cable, and covered her face completely with duct tape. Simmons then pushed her off the railroad trestle into the river below. At the time she fell, Mrs. Crook was alive and conscious. Simmons and Benjamin threw Mrs. Crook's purse into the woods and drove the van back to the mobile home park across from the subdivision in which Mrs. Crook lived.

Later that day, Simmons returned to Moomey's home and bragged that he had killed a woman "because the bitch seen my face." Meanwhile, Mrs. Crook's husband Steven returned home from an overnight trip and discovered that she had not gone to work as scheduled. When he did not hear from her by that evening, he filed a missing person's report.[54]

Now contrast this portrayal with excerpts of the facts taken from Simmons's brief:

[A]fter learning that Christopher Simmons and his friend Charles Benjamin may have been involved in the crime, police arrested Simmons, a 17-year-old high-school junior with no previous criminal convictions, at his school. Simmons was taken to the police station, where he waived his *Miranda* rights and was interrogated. Simmons initially denied involvement in the crime. After nearly two hours of interrogation, during which police accused him of lying, falsely told him that Benjamin had confessed, and explained that he might face the death penalty and that it would be in his interest to cooperate, Simmons began to cry and asked to speak to one of the detectives alone.

Simmons told the detective that, in the early morning of September 9, he and Benjamin met at the house of Brian Moomey, an adult friend of both Simmons and Benjamin. After trying and failing to wake Moomey, Simmons and Benjamin went to Mrs. Crook's house, planning to burglarize it. The two gained entry through an open window at the back of the house. Their entrance woke Mrs. Crook, who sat up in bed and asked, "Who is there?" Simmons recognized Mrs. Crook as someone with whom he had been involved in a minor car accident immediately after receiving his driver's license. Believing that Mrs. Crook had also recognized him, Simmons "panicked." He and Benjamin took Mrs. Crook out of bed, bound her, put her in the back of her mini-van, and drove to Castlewood State Park in St. Louis County, where Simmons pushed her from a railroad trestle into the Meramec River.[55]

Not surprisingly, the State emphasized the deliberateness and ghoulishness of Simmons's crime. The State may have noted the husband's discovery of his wife's disappearance in order to cause the Justices to imagine how they would have felt if their own spouses had disappeared from the home. In contrast, Simmons's brief emphasized Simmons's youth, the fact that he was in high school, and the fact that his crime resulted from panic rather than a premeditated act. While we can't be sure how these alternative statements of facts influenced the Justices,[56] we can see that both sides made an effort to use the facts of the case to effectively present their positions.

The facts should not simply be mentioned once and then forgotten. In addition to including a good statement of facts at the beginning of the brief, it is essential that the attorney weave the facts throughout the rest of the brief, using them to persuade the reader of the merits of his position.

Early Sections of the Brief

Rather than being dull requirements, the early sections of a brief—the introduction, statement of facts, and statement of questions presented—provide an ideal opportunity to make a good impression and to set the stage for the argument.[57] In particular, the writer can use these early sections of the brief to prime concepts and themes that will be favorable to his client and to capitalize on confirmation bias and biased assimilation by evoking an initial perspective that readers will seek to confirm (see chapter 1). For example, if a defendant in a personal injury case can make the point early on that the plaintiff is a malingerer or is prone to exaggerating her injuries or blaming others for her own problems, readers may well look for evidence that confirms such a depiction and discount arguments and evidence that might otherwise have supported the plaintiff's claims.

Consider, for example, *McDonald v. City of Chicago*, in which the Supreme Court determined that the Second Amendment right to keep and bear arms limits states' ability to enact gun control legislation.[58] An examination of some of the briefs filed in the case shows that both sides were adept at setting out their most sympathetic positions very early in the brief. For instance, a group called Jews for the Preservation of Firearms Ownership (JPFO) filed an amicus brief on the side of the gun owners, arguing that the gun control legislation was unconstitutional. The rules governing Supreme Court amicus briefs require that amici—at the outset—describe their interest in the matter at hand. Rather than treating this section of the brief as a mere administrative hurdle, JPFO used this initial section to plead its position quite effectively:

> Jews for the Preservation of Firearms Ownership ("JPFO") is a non-profit tax-exempt Wisconsin corporation with more than 5,000 members and many more Internet-based supporters. Not a lobbying group, JPFO is an educational organization with a vital interest in preserving the individual right to keep and bear arms. Based upon original historical research and analysis, JPFO has observed that the 70 million innocent civilians murdered in the 20th Century's eight major genocides were direct victims of "gun control" laws and policies that disarmed them.[59]

Combining the organization's educational pedigree with its interest in preventing future holocausts was an artful way to gain support for the group's position. Even the name of the group, Jews for the Preservation of Firearms Ownership, nicely employs the psychology of loss aversion (see chapter 5).

Respondent City of Chicago sounded very different themes in the statement of facts that began its brief in the same case:

In 1982, Chicago enacted a handgun ban, along with other firearms regulations, because "the convenient availability of firearms and ammunition has increased firearm related deaths and injuries" and handguns "play a major role in the commission of homicide, aggravated assaults and armed robbery." . . . Under Chicago's ordinance, "[n]o person shall . . . possess . . . any firearm unless such person is the holder of a valid registration certificate for such firearm," and no person may possess "any firearm which is unregisterable." . . . Unregisterable firearms include most handguns, but rifles and shotguns that are not sawed-off, short-barreled, or assault weapons are registerable. . . . Registerable firearms must be registered before being possessed in Chicago . . . and registration must be renewed annually. . . . Failure to renew "shall cause the firearm to become unregisterable."[60]

Thus, the city emphasized that the regulation was needed to protect public safety and that the regulation was reasonable and limited because many weapons in fact could be registered. Each side in the case was clearly aware that it was important to begin to tell its story as early in the brief as possible.

Describing Alternatives

The way in which choices are presented to a decision maker can have a large impact on how those options will be perceived. Thus, as litigators present judges with choices, they should be mindful of how judges may be affected by the grouping of options (contrast and compromise effects), that judges may be more concerned with present than future impacts, and that judges may seek to avoid future regrets (see chapter 5). Sometimes our established jurisprudence fits nicely with such psychology. For example, a party seeking a temporary restraining order must try to show that the defendant's conduct is likely to cause imminent and irreparable harm. Thus, the plaintiff will naturally emphasize harms that will take place soon and those that might cause significant regret if not avoided.

In a more traditional lawsuit, a party can also try to present arguments to the court in a way that will capitalize on the judge's likely attitudes toward choice. For example, a defendant in a lawsuit alleging libel might emphasize that any harm to the plaintiff's reputation is speculative and not immediate. A defendant in a construction defect lawsuit might emphasize its counterclaim against the plaintiff for nonpayment so that the judge will be tempted to choose a compromise outcome that neither party has a claim; absent the counterclaim, the judge might be tempted to find that the defendant was liable for some but not all of the defects alleged by the plaintiff. A plaintiff bringing a tort claim for which some of the damages are speculative might emphasize that unless the plaintiff is awarded damages now, he will have no remedy if, at a future date, causation becomes even clearer.

We have also learned that some people have overall attitudes toward decision making that could be relevant as parties write their briefs. While we hope that few judges are affected by decision avoidance, some do have that reputation. If an attorney appears in front of such a judge, she will want to try to structure the matter so that the judge's nondecision will be helpful to her client and not to the opposing party. Thus, if the parties are in a discovery dispute, a party requested to provide documents may want to choose simply to file an objection and refuse to provide the documents rather than file a motion for a protective order, which would require the judge to take an affirmative step to order nondisclosure.

How issues are characterized can also have a significant impact on how decision makers are likely to view those issues. For example, recall that some people tend to focus on promoting well-being, whereas others seek to prevent harms (see chapter 5). If the attorney can identify whether the judge assigned to her case tends toward either of these perspectives, she can try to appeal to that underlying philosophy. Thus, in a child custody dispute, the attorney might emphasize either improving the child's well-being or preventing harm to the child. Along similar lines, judges may respond differently to an argument depending on whether they are asked to choose one outcome or reject an alternative outcome. We learned in chapter 5 that when choosing, a person tends to focus on the positive attributes of options; and when rejecting, a person tends to focus on the negative attributes of options. Thus, a person involved in a dispute might select either the choosing or the rejecting terminology depending on whether he is more likely to win the issue based on positives or a lack of negatives.

Finally, we seek to avoid losses and tend to reject courses of action that will cause certain losses (see chapter 5). Thus, each side should try to set up or frame its theory and argument in such a way that the decision makers will want to find for its client. Imagine a summary judgment motion filed in a lawsuit involving an allegedly dangerous pharmaceutical, such as the MSD case described earlier in the chapter. By framing the issue as "whether the company should have marketed the drug when it knew that the drug would harm people," the plaintiff will put the defendant in the negative light of having knowingly caused a loss. Yet, the defendant in the same case can also try to emphasize a loss—specifically, that more people would have died without the drug.[61] This loss of life is likely to loom larger and be more persuasive than any health or economic gains offered by the drug.

Order of Arguments

Most legal writing texts counsel lawyers to lead with their best arguments.[62] While psychological studies support this recommendation in that information that is presented earlier (primacy) tends to be particularly memorable, psychological research has also found that information presented later (recency) can be more memorable than information that is buried in the middle. Luckily, this is an area in which good writers can have their cake and eat it, too, because writers can lead with strong arguments and then reiterate those arguments in an effective conclusion. As noted above, psychological studies also dictate leaving out weak arguments rather than throwing in the kitchen sink in the hope that something may stick (see chapter 6).

Psychology can also help a writer fit together a series of propositions in a particularly effective manner. *Chaining*, according to legal persuasion expert Kathryn

Stanchi, is a way to effectively move an argument forward by coaxing the reader up "the series of steps up to the high diving board: as the persuader gets the target up each step closer to the edge of the board, it becomes that much easier to decide to jump and that much harder to decide to go back down."[63] By carefully making the first link of the argument something that is compelling and easy to accept and stringing together the chain of the argument, the writer can get his foot in the door with the decision maker (see chapter 6). Once the decision maker joins the writer in making that first step, a psychological desire for consistency will work to push her to continue to accept the additional and more controversial links in the argument.

Stanchi notes how this tactic was used on behalf of the plaintiff in *Rosa v. Park West Bank & Trust Co.*[64] before the U.S. Court of Appeals for the First Circuit:

> [P]laintiff-appellant Rosa, a biological male, was denied a loan by the defendant bank because he appeared for his loan request dressed in "traditionally female" clothing. The audience might not have readily made the comparison between Rosa and *Price-Waterhouse v. Hopkins*,[65] in which a woman was denied partnership in part because of her abrasive, aggressive demeanor. The argument chain crafted by appellant Rosa, however, makes this non-obvious connection seem self-evident:
>
> > Actions based on sexual stereotypes are acts of impermissible sex discrimination (virtually indisputable, S. Ct. precedent).
> >
> > When a firm denies a woman partnership because the woman did not meet the firm's stereotype of femininity, the firm has impermissibly discriminated against her (virtually indisputable, S. Ct. precedent).
> >
> > When a woman is told that she should walk, talk and dress more femininely, she is the victim of impermissible sex stereotyping because she did not conform to notions of what a "real woman" should look like (virtually indisputable, S. Ct. precedent).
> >
> > When a man is told to dress in a more masculine fashion, he is the victim of sex stereotyping because he has not conformed to what a "real man" should look like (advocated premise).
> >
> > When a man is the victim of sex stereotyping, he has been subject to an act of impermissible sex discrimination (advocated premise).
>
> The chain . . . is constructed in such a way that the reader is led to believe that if she agrees with the prior premises, she must find for appellant Rosa. In other words, if the reader believes that sex stereotyping is illegal, she must agree that the bank's behavior was also illegal. A decision against appellant Rosa would be inconsistent and dissonant.[66]

Word Choice

A single word or phrase can sometimes evoke a story, emotion, or schema that will be highly persuasive. It is no coincidence that whereas environmentalists talk about "trees," logging companies talk about "harvestable timber."

In their book on legal writing, Supreme Court Justice Antonin Scalia and coauthor Bryan Garner explore the importance of word choice in depth. According to

Scalia and Garner, an attorney who challenged a speech regulation on college campuses referred to the case regularly in the media as the "speaker-ban" case, thereby successfully characterizing the case in a way geared to nudge decision makers to oppose the ban. In our generally pro–First Amendment culture, characterizing the issue as a ban on speech activates negative schema and is inherently unattractive. However, as Scalia and Garner point out, had the attorney's opponent been able to successfully frame the case as involving "peaceful neighborhood regulation," the result might have been different.[67]

Complaints

In contrast to documents such as briefs that are clearly intended to be persuasive, complaints are often viewed as formulaic documents whose only purpose is to ensure that all legal claims have been properly raised within the relevant statute of limitations.[68] Yet, complaints can do much more.

For example, although plaintiffs' lawyers do not always provide clients with a copy of the complaint, the client is worth considering as a potential audience for a complaint. Reading the complaint gives the client a glimpse into what the attorney is doing on the client's behalf and can help build trust. Thus, the complaint should be drafted, in part, with the client in mind. This means, in particular, drafting the complaint so that it is comprehensible to the client and will show the client that the lawyer is on the client's side.

The complaint will inevitably have other readers as well. It will certainly be read by the attorney for the defendant and quite possibly by the defendant as well. While a judge will not likely read the complaint when it is first filed with the court, a judge will likely read it later, for example, in connection with a motion for summary judgment or a discovery or status conference. In some cases, the complaint may also be read by members of the media or even members of the public as court documents are increasingly available to all through the wonders of modern technology.

In short, it is a mistake to treat the complaint as a mere mechanical document. Instead, attorneys should use the complaint as a potentially powerful persuasive tool. The complaint can, if properly written, demonstrate the lawyer's competence and help convince the adversary, the judge, and potentially the media and the public of the strength of the plaintiff's case. Impressing these readers early is worthwhile because their early impressions of the strength of the plaintiff's case will influence their views throughout the course of the litigation (see chapter 1).

Stories and Facts

Stories and facts can be as important to complaints as they are to briefs. The attorney can use the complaint to put the plaintiff in a favorable light and put the defendant in an unfavorable light. Detailed facts may aid perception and cognition, stimulate

> [P]ractitioners whose skills do not go beyond bare-bones form-book pleading risk disserving their clients, because legal readers, judges included, are as responsive to the call of stories as other readers.
> —Elizabeth Fajans & Mary R. Falk[71]

emotion, and enhance memory—evoking, for example, schemas such as "deadbeat dad" or "corporate greed."[69]

At the same time, it may not always be strategically wise for the plaintiff's attorney to tell the story in excruciating detail in the complaint. Some judges are not impressed by a "thick" style of pleading, and using too much detail may make the complaint less useful as a tool with which to secure admissions or may open too many lines of discovery.[70] Thus, the psychologically astute litigator will want to selectively use key facts.

Consider the use of facts in the complaint filed on behalf of Robert Bork, former judge and Supreme Court nominee, who was injured in a slip-and-fall accident:

2. Plaintiff Robert H. Bork is a resident and citizen of Virginia. He was injured while visiting the Yale Club in New York, New York, to give a speech at an event there on June 6, 2006. . . .

7. The New Criterion hosted the event in a banquet room at the Yale Club. As the host of the event, the Yale Club provided tables and chairs where guests could sit during the reception and the evening's speeches. At the front of the room, the Yale Club provided a dais, atop which stood a lectern for speakers to address the audience.

8. Because of the height of this dais, the Yale Club's normal practice is to provide a set of stairs between the floor and the dais. At the New Criterion event, however, the Yale club failed to provide any steps between the floor and the dais. Nor did the Yale Club provide a handrail or any other reasonable support feature to assist guests attempting to climb the dais.

9. . . . Because of the unreasonable height of the dais, without stairs or a handrail, Mr. Bork fell backwards as he attempted to mount the dais, striking his left leg on the side of the dais and striking his head on a heat register.

10. As a result of the fall, a large hematoma formed on Mr. Bork's lower left leg, which later burst. The injury required surgery, extended medical treatment, and months of physical therapy.[72]

Through the careful use of facts, the author of the complaint has impressed us with the plaintiff's importance (invitation to speak at Yale Club), personalized the plaintiff (repeated use of his name), shown us that the Yale Club did not take proper care (failure to provide stairs), given us a clear mental image of the accident ("fell backwards"), and stirred us with the severity of the injury (bursting hematoma that required surgery and extensive care). This careful factual presentation builds respect and sympathy for Bork and leads readers to believe that he was wronged and is not bringing a frivolous suit. Note that even factual omissions can be helpful. The drafter of the complaint chose not to say that Bork was an attorney, former judge, well-known conservative, and controversial Supreme Court nominee, presumably having decided that merely being a "resident and citizen of Virginia," or, for that matter, presumably any state, was more likely to elicit sympathy.

Word Choice

In complaints, as in briefs, the drafter's choice of words can be important. Lawyers should forsake legalese in favor of simple, evocative language that will build sympathy for the plaintiff and help persuade readers that the defendant acted wrongly. For example, in *Jones v. Clinton*, Paula Jones accused President Bill Clinton of sexually assaulting her when he was the governor of Arkansas and she was a state employee.[73] Her complaint employed language suggesting that Clinton took advantage of the imbalance of power between the two parties during their encounter:

> Words are the principal tools of lawyers and judges, whether we like it or not. They are to us what the scalpel and insulin are to the doctor.
> —*Zachariah Chafee Jr.*[74]

> 18. Clinton then took Jones' hand and pulled her toward him, so that their bodies were in close proximity.
>
> 19. Jones removed her hand from his and retreated several feet.
>
> 20. However, Clinton approached Jones again. He said: "I love the way your hair flows down your back" and "I love your curves." While saying these things, Clinton put his hand on Plaintiff's leg and started sliding it toward the hem of Plaintiff's culottes. Clinton also bent down to attempt to kiss Jones on the neck.
>
> 21. Jones exclaimed, "What are you doing?" and escaped from Clinton's physical proximity by walking away from him. Jones tried to distract Clinton by chatting with him about his wife. Jones later took a seat at the end of the sofa nearest the door. Clinton asked Jones: "Are you married?" She responded that she had a regular boyfriend. Clinton then approached the sofa and as he sat down he lowered his trousers and underwear exposing his erect penis and asked Jones to "kiss it."[75]

The graphic nature of the language also revealed that Jones would not hesitate to tell her story in all its gory detail.

Dead Rat Salad

Of course, sometimes stories are so colorful that no embellishment is necessary:

> This is a personal injury case brought by the Haleys (herein "Chrissy and Todd") and Ms. Kelley (herein "Katy"), Plaintiffs, against the owner-operator of the McDonald's fastfood [*sic*] restaurant at 2155 West Southlake Blvd., Southlake, Texas (herein "McDonald's"). They sue for injuries Chrissy and Katy suffered when a salad Chrissy purchased on June 5, 2006, at McDonald's contained a whole, dead rodent believed to be a juvenile roof rat. They ate some of the salad before their forks uncovered the rodent; they instantaneously gagged, heaved, and vomited. They have been ill, off and on, since that sickening afternoon.[76]

Credibility

Complaints must be credible in order to work well as persuasive documents. Thus, it is very important to tell stories in the complaint that are both true and believable. Exaggerating the scope of an injury or the extent of the defendant's liability can backfire, leading the reader of the complaint to discount not only that allegation but also other allegations in the complaint as well. Thus, although attorneys want to tell compelling stories, they must be careful to tell true and provable stories. Overly colorful language will often be less persuasive than a simple story that speaks for itself.[77]

Letters

Attorneys write lots of letters to their clients and others. They may, for example, write to opposing attorneys (or unrepresented clients) in litigation; insurance companies; companies or individuals with whom their client is collaborating (or hopes to collaborate) in a business deal; or government agencies from whom the client seeks a permit, license, or other type of permission. As with other documents, lawyers should make sure that all of their letters are clear and as jargon free as possible. They should craft letters with the relevant audience in mind, trying to imagine which statements and arguments will play best to a particular audience. Furthermore, attorneys should attempt to establish and maintain credibility—demonstrating their knowledge and trustworthiness—in all of their letters.

Letters to Clients

Retainer Letters

Attorneys use retainer letters to define their relationship with their clients. At minimum, such letters are a pro forma necessity and provide protection against possible future mishaps in the attorney-client relationship. There are, of course, a variety of subjects that lawyers need to cover in the retainer letter, such as the scope of representation, billing rates, possible termination of the relationship, and dispute resolution.

Retainer letters can also be used to further trust and maintain rapport with the client. Clients, especially those who are not frequent participants in the legal system, may read the initial retainer letter as an important document that sets the tone for their relationship with their attorney. Why not, therefore, include language that thanks the client for the opportunity to work on the case and reflects the attorney's eagerness to work hard on behalf of the client? It may be inevitable that language about such matters as fees and costs will make the client think that the lawyer is self-interested, but the lawyer can attempt to counterbalance these necessary parts of the letter with more positive sentiments as well.

Infusing Letters with Warmer Tones

Warmer Tone	Cooler Tone
• Beginning and ending the letter with content establishing a personal connection	• No content establishing a personal connection
• Word choices without connotations of blame, fault, criticism	• Word choices that are sharp, blunt, or biting . . .
• . . . Contractions (only when informality is appropriate)	• Liberal use of the pronoun "you" to underline the distinction between the writer and the reader
• Mutual references using the pronoun "we" to underline the relationship	• Discussing any uncomfortable subjects without any reassurances[78]
• Tempering any uncomfortable subjects with offsetting indirect assurances that the writer likes and respects the reader	

In addition to outlining the client's responsibilities (such as the obligations to pay the bill, cooperate with the attorney, and provide information), the letter can highlight the attorney's responsibilities. Consider the introductory language used in this sample retainer letter:

> It was a pleasure to meet with you in our office last Friday. We are very pleased to confirm our engagement by ABC Engineering Inc. (ABC) to represent it with respect to . . .
>
> Our services in this matter will be performed on behalf of ABC only. We will use our professional diligence to meet ABC's timing requirements and priorities. We will ensure that our office meets the highest ethical standards at all times, keeping ABC adequately informed of our progress and consulting with ABC as to all significant aspects of this matter. We expect that ABC will notify us if, at any time, ABC believes we are not performing adequately, and we will then do our best to allay any of ABC's concerns.

Some may be concerned that including attorney responsibilities in retainer letters will give clients grounds to complain that the attorney is not meeting her contractual obligations, but the letter above promises no more than is already required by the ethical rules. Including such language does, however, show the client that the attorney is committed to working with her in a cooperative manner. Including dispute resolution clauses that call for negotiation or mediation prior to arbitration or litigation if a dispute should arise can also be an effective means of using a letter or contract to build a more cooperative relationship.

Negotiation-Related Letters

Lawyers also often write letters to their clients as part of their discussion of possible negotiated outcomes. The attorney may, for example, write a letter before entering into negotiations. The purpose of such a letter is to make sure that the attorney has confirmed in writing her understanding of the client's negotiating position. Once negotiations have commenced, the attorney may also convey the other side's offers or demands to the client in writing.

Negotiation-related letters offer a number of opportunities to operationalize the kinds of suggestions we provided in chapter 11 on negotiation and mediation. For example, in writing a letter to the client regarding settlement of litigation, the attorney should always be conscious of the client's likely discomfort with loss (loss aversion) (see chapter 5). If the attorney were to write that "the proposed settlement requires you to drop your lawsuit in return for a lump sum payment of $20,000," the proposed settlement would likely be received less enthusiastically than had the attorney written that "the proposed settlement offers you a guaranteed lump sum payment of $20,000 and eliminates the risk of losing at trial." Similarly, the attorney should be conscious of additional judgment and decision-making biases, such as reactive devaluation, fixed pie bias, anchoring, overconfidence, and framing, in order to craft the most effective negotiation-related letters by not emphasizing to a client that the opponent was the source of an offer, by reminding the client that settlements can sometimes be mutually beneficial, and by being conscious of clients' strong aversion to certain losses.

In addition to being conscious of judgment shortcuts and decision-making biases, the attorney should also continue to focus on his relationship with the client in drafting negotiation-related letters. The transactional attorney will want to make sure that her client knows that the attorney understands the nature of the client's business and appreciates the client's goals. Litigators must remember that, at the time of potential settlement, it is quite possible that the client may feel insecure—worried that the attorney has lost faith in the case or the client or even sold out the client for other interests. Thus, the attorney should make a special effort to connect to the client in the letter, perhaps through personal references ("I hope you and your wife enjoyed your time at the beach") or by reminding the client of some things that are going well in the lawsuit ("I am pleased to report that Judge Jones ruled in our favor on the motion to compel.")

Advice or Opinion Letters

Attorneys may also write advice or "opinion" letters to their clients. Advice letters analyze the client's legal situation and opine about how the client should proceed. Opinion letters are formal statements as to whether, in the opinion of the attorney, a particular course of action is legal. In writing such letters, attorneys must focus on clarity and accuracy, as well as the substance of the advice. The attorney needs to ensure that she is providing information to the client in a form that the client can digest, using clear and straightforward language, a minimum of jargon, analogies that capitalize on the client's existing knowledge, and visual aids as necessary. The attorney should also continue to pay attention to the attorney-client relationship and ways in which the letter can further that relationship and serve to demonstrate the attorney's competence and trustworthiness (see chapter 7).

When asked to write advice or opinion letters, attorneys must try to break away from their own positive illusions by taking an outside perspective on the proposed deal or contract. Having taken this perspective, the attorney may realize that it is her responsibility to give the client some bad news. She may, for example, have to tell the client that the contract the client has submitted for review is not favorable or legally valid or that the transaction the client is contemplating is unwise. In these situations, the attorney must try to preserve the good lawyer-client relationship while using it to clearly convey the news that the client does not want to hear (see chapter 10).

When advice or opinion letters are designed to help the client choose among options, attorneys should remember that the way options are presented, grouped, and framed can make a big difference to how they are perceived (see chapter 5). Similarly, the attorney should recall that framing risks in different ways will affect the client's attitude toward those risks. Assuring a client that a particular course of action is quite likely to be successful or approved will please the client more than learning that there is even a small chance that the action will be unsuccessful or not be approved. The attorney's primary responsibility, however, is not to please the client but rather to represent the client competently.

Bills to Clients

Perhaps psychology should even influence the kinds of bills that attorneys send to their clients:

> Most associates know to pay close attention to the *amount* of time they spend on projects. They spend less time—often as little as possible—thinking about how they describe the services they provide. That can be a mistake. Bills are the one regular communication that clients get from your firm. Bills summarize all the work the firm did for the client in the preceding month. The cost of those services is always obvious on a bill. The value of those services needs to be just as obvious....
>
> Consider the following two hypothetical time entries:
>
> | | |
> |---|---|
> | Read documents; thought about case; called client | X hrs. $750 |
> | Reviewed opposing party's pleadings for deficiencies; developed litigation strategy; telephone conference to update client and receive additional direction | X hrs. $750[79] |

Which billing entry do you think will best establish the lawyer's credibility, build rapport with the client, and make the client feel that she is receiving value for her money?

Letters to Others

Letters in Negotiation

Demand letters and responses to such letters offer attorneys a chance to communicate directly with opposing counsel and likely with the opposing client as well. Earlier, in our discussion of complaints, we outlined the psychological benefits of telling a good story and conveying compelling facts to opposing counsel. However, we recognized that some judges and some court rules may limit attorneys' ability to tell a good story in a complaint. No such impediments curb an attorney's writing with respect to demand letters. Moreover, demand letters can be particularly influential in framing the issues and priming advantageous concepts because such letters are often sent early in the dispute, sometimes before suit is even filed. Thus, attorneys can and should artfully integrate fact and law to convince opposing counsel and opposing clients of the strength of their own client's position. A good demand letter or response can tell a compelling story, can prime ways of thinking about the case that benefit the attorney's own client, and can also include visual images designed to convince opponents of the merits of the position of the attorney's client. Thus, in the personal injury context, the plaintiff's counsel may want to include photos detailing the plaintiff's injuries or provide film clips demonstrating how the plaintiff's injuries cause her to suffer on a daily basis. In contrast, the defense counsel may want to include its own pictures to show that the plaintiff's injuries are not so limiting after all.

At the same time, attorneys should not be overly aggressive in crafting their demand letters or responses. As discussed in chapter 11, generating positive emotions can be very important to achieving the collaboration that is useful for resolving many kinds of disputes or for completing mutually beneficial transactions. Thus, demand letters should often be polite and avoid unduly nasty or accusatory assertions, particularly where collaborative solutions might be possible. A negative tone may simply provoke an opponent's anger and thereby delay or even prevent a mutually beneficial agreement. For example, rather than asserting that "XYZ Corporation willfully and intentionally caused serious harm to Ms. Jones," a plaintiff's attorney might simply assert that "we believe a jury in this jurisdiction is likely to conclude that XYZ Corporation is liable for the serious injuries suffered by Ms. Jones."

In crafting demand or offer letters, attorneys can also make use of their knowledge of the psychology of generating and presenting options we discussed in chapter 11. For example, demand or offer letters should take into account knowledge of what the client may want; explain how the proposed settlement will meet the other side's needs; and draw on the power of apology, knowledge of how people make judgments and decisions, and principles of persuasion.

Other Letters

In addition to negotiation-related letters, attorneys write a variety of other letters to opposing counsel, governmental or other entities, and opposing clients (if unrepresented). These letters may, for example, seek permits or licenses; relate to potential or pending transactions; or pertain to discovery, pretrial conferences, or logistical issues that come up in the course of litigation.

Although an attorney will have a very different relationship with her client than she does with opposing attorneys, opposing clients, or governmental or other entities, it turns out that many of the same psychological factors can be useful when crafting letters to these others as well. Attorneys will want to consider the nature of their audience, be clear and credible, and use facts and stories to be persuasive with all audiences. And, as we have learned, they can use tools such as likeability, social proof, scarcity, and commitment to increase their persuasiveness (see chapter 6).

It is also important to keep in mind the various cognitive biases and decisional frameworks that we have described (see chapters 4 and 5). For example, if the attorney is seeking a permit to allow his client to engage in conduct that might be deemed dangerous, such as selling fireworks, he may want to think about how to effectively help the reader get beyond the image of children being injured. For example, he might emphasize that permitting licensed fireworks decreases the risk that families will turn to illegal dangerous fireworks. Similarly, in representing a developer who seeks a permit to build residential housing in a protected park area, it will be more effective to focus on the positive results that the housing will have on the community than to say that the proposed housing development will "only" destroy 10% of the protected park area.

In addition, and perhaps less obviously, the attorney may want to build relationships with opposing attorneys or government officials so that they will hear the attorney's arguments more clearly and respond more positively. A government official tasked with supervising adoptions will likely respond more favorably to a request for expedited treatment if treated respectfully and asked for help than if she is sent a nasty letter demanding immediate action. Putting themselves in the shoes of the recipient of the letter can help lawyers see how the letter will be received.

Contracts

People do not necessarily think of contracts as providing an opportunity for good writing. Indeed, contracts are often based on preexisting forms and frequently contain extensive amounts of legalese that may be virtually gibberish, even to the attorney. (Check out your own cell phone and insurance contracts if you doubt this point.) When attorneys write contracts, they often base them on prior similar contracts. Indeed, "[o]ver time, many boilerplate contracts become larded with terms that no longer serve a useful function but that the drafters are reluctant to remove."[80] In addition, attorneys tend to focus on the legal impact of the clauses rather than on how these clauses may read or sound. Yet, as with other kinds of writing, there is more to effective contract drafting than merely getting the law right.

Framing, Status Quo Bias, and Anchoring

Contract drafters should pay attention to psychology when crafting the substance of their agreements. For example, the way in which a contract is framed can impact parties' future behavior. One study showed that contracts framed in terms of losses (for example, contracts that penalize parties that do not meet certain goals) encouraged greater effort than contracts framed in terms of gains (for example, contracts that provide a bonus for performance in excess of minimum expectations).[81]

Other research has found that the ways in which a contract is drafted can influence the perceptions of those subject to its terms. Consider the following example:

> In December of 2001, the Boston Fire Department changed its sick-leave policy to allow 15 sick days per year. The previous system had allowed unlimited sick time, and the new rule was part of an initiative to bring professional management tools to the department. In 2001, firefighters took a total of 6432 days. In 2002, the total number of sick days rose to 13,431—more than double the previous year.
>
> The new system was ostensibly more rigid, with a higher penalty for taking sick days—each sick day brought workers closer to the prospect of unpaid time off. The old system, by contrast, had no explicit penalty at all for sick time. The old system had something powerful in its favor, though: the firefighters had a tradition of "toughing it out" through illness, showing up for work even when it hurt. The new policy made sick leave into a contractual entitlement rather than a breach of protocol.[82]

Similar findings come from a study of the effects of fining parents for being late to pick up their children from day care. Researchers found that when fines were instituted, *more* parents started coming late to pick up their children. In part, the establishment of the fine changed what had previously been a matter of good manners into a cost-benefit analysis under the contract.[83] Contract drafters ought to take into account how the terms of the contract can influence willingness to breach and the consequences of such a possibility (positive or negative) for the client.

The party who takes the first crack at drafting a contract may also be able to use psychology to gain a significant advantage. Recall that people tend to prefer the status quo over switching to an alternative. When considering an alternative, the downsides tend to loom larger than the upsides (see chapter 5). And, of course, actions, like changing to an alternative contract term, that have undesirable results are judged more harshly and are expected to cause greater regret than inaction that results in similar consequences. Thus, because the first draft of a contract may be treated as the status quo or default rule, it may be difficult to move away from such provisions. Accordingly, even if the nondrafter does not like particular aspects of the proposed contract (say, a liquidated damages provision), she might not fight as hard against those provisions as she might have if those provisions had not been included in the proposed contract in the first place.[84] Along these same lines, a drafter may be able to use social proof to convince a reluctant counterpart to accept terms that "everyone else" is accepting (see chapter 6).⁸⁵

In addition, by writing the first draft of a contract, an attorney may secure the benefits of anchoring (see chapter 4). Just as making a high demand or low offer in a negotiation may anchor a negotiation counterpart to that position, taking an extreme (but not too extreme) position in drafting a contract can be beneficial. For example, an attorney who is drafting a dispute resolution clause that has not previously been discussed might want to insert provisions that are highly favorable to her client rather than starting with the compromise position that she speculates might ultimately be acceptable to the opposing party.

Promotion of Positive Relationships

Contracts can do more than merely protect legal rights. Particularly when contracts will govern a relationship between individuals or smaller entities controlled by individuals, it may be worthwhile trying to draft the contract in a way geared toward promoting positive relationships between the individuals or entities. For example, a marital separation agreement could highlight the shared values and goals of the parties: "In the interest of returning peace and tranquility to the household, the parties agree that . . ." Along the same lines, family law scholar Lenore Weitzman suggests that couples should create "intimate contracts" for psychological reasons: clarifying expectations, creating a blueprint for behavior, identifying potential problems in advance, and resolving conflict in an ongoing relationship. In many relationships, Weitzman argues, "[a] major complication arises when each spouse is aware of most of his or her own needs and wishes—of the terms of his or her own 'contract'—but neither is equally aware of the other's expectations; in this case important expectations on both sides go unfulfilled." Thus, creating a contract that explicitly articulates the couple's expectations helps each partner fulfill the other's needs. In addition, identifying expectations encourages the couple to act in ways that are consistent with the ideals set forth in the contract (see chapter 6).⁸⁶

Along similar lines, here is the introductory paragraph of a collaborative law agreement in which divorcing individuals and their attorneys commit to attempt to resolve their disputes in a nonadversarial manner:

> Collaborative Law is a cooperative, voluntary conflict resolution process. Both attorneys and both parties acknowledge that the essence of Collaborative Law is the shared belief that it is in the best interest of the parties and their families to avoid adversarial proceedings, to commit themselves to resolving their differences with minimum conflict and to work together to create shared solutions to the issues. This process relies on an atmosphere of honesty, cooperation, integrity and professionalism geared toward the future well-being of the parties and their children.⁸⁷

Such language is clearly designed to help clients and attorneys work together effectively.

Some estate planners are also very conscious of the language used in their documents. The Purposeful Planning Institute, founded by attorney John Warnick, advocates "purposeful planning collaboration" to both "empower clients to live the life they want" and "prepare[] heirs for the transition of the family's wealth. . . ."

> Instead of a traditional set of cold, brittle, and generic legal documents, devoid of love, appreciation, wisdom, and thoughtful counsel, Purposeful Planning leverages the client's life story and wisdom. It transforms the sterility of legal documents by capturing the client's voice, vision and purposes. The result is so powerful it often produces tears at the signing ceremony as the client realizes how positively their influence and legacy will be felt 20, 50 or 100 years into the future.[88]

A similar approach might be taken when creating partnership documents. In drafting a partnership agreement, attorneys are typically careful to include clauses covering a range of matters, such as who the partners are, the nature of the partners' duties and responsibilities, how profits will be divided, and how the partnership can be dissolved. The resulting partnership agreements are typically rather matter-of-fact, filled with definitions, and often rife with legalese. Yet, without omitting any key terms, attorneys might also add language describing the purpose of the partnership or the talents of the partners in positive ways:

> The parties are forming this partnership to fulfill their lifelong dream of joining together in a rock band. By bringing together Mack's awesome voice, Linda's fabulous guitar playing, and Junior's amazing drum-playing talents, they intend to bring the world some new great music and have a wonderful time together.

Including positive language in contracts is not aimed at gaining an advantage in a future court dispute. Indeed, such language does not necessarily define any duties; and even if it did, it might be found unenforceable by a court.[89] However, such language can help to establish a relationship that will work smoothly and minimize future disputes.

In drafting positive language in contracts, the drafter must pay careful attention to the possibility that the language could lead to ambiguous legal obligations. Thus, a contract that simply states that "the parties agree to use their best efforts to work together cooperatively" might lead to problems down the road. Ambiguous clauses can be construed differently by different parties and create room for self-interested interpretations and behavior.[90] Our naïve cynicism inclines us to expect others to act self-interestedly, and this may cause us to interpret ambiguities in our own favor, in part because we fear that the other side will do so to gain an advantage (see chapters 1 and 4). While there may be some tension between positive drafting and unambiguous drafting, we believe that the careful drafter can often meet both goals.

✦ ✦ ✦ ✦ ✦
Summing It Up

- Bear in mind the limits on readers' processing capacity and write clearly, accessibly, and as concisely as possible.

- Use concrete examples and stories to maximize persuasive power and make the work more memorable.
- Try to put yourself in the reader's shoes to ensure that you are connecting to the reader's concerns and prior assumptions.
- Recall that persuasiveness turns on credibility, as well as on more subtle approaches (such as priming, primacy, recency, and chaining).
- Take account of judgment and decision-making heuristics such as confirmation bias, biased assimilation, framing, loss aversion, and anchoring, as well as readers' perceptions of justice.
- Appreciate that legal documents need not be dry and impersonal but can attend to relationships in order to improve communication, enhance persuasion, and increase trust and rapport.

For Further Reading: Writing

Anthony G. Amsterdam & Jerome Bruner, Minding the Law (2000).
Linda Holdeman Edwards, Legal Writing and Analysis (3d ed. 2011).
Ronald T. Kellogg, The Psychology of Writing (1994).
Terrill Pollman et al., Legal Writing: Examples and Explanations (2011).
Antonin Scalia & Bryan A. Garner, Making Your Case: The Art of Persuading Judges (2008).
Michael R. Smith, Advanced Legal Writing: Theories and Strategies in Persuasive Writing (2d ed. 2008).

Ethics   14

> In civilized life, law floats in a sea of ethics.
>
> —*Earl Warren*[1]

Lawyers routinely face a range of ethical and moral issues. They make daily decisions about questions of confidentiality and attorney-client privilege, how to manage conflicts of interest, what constitutes material misrepresentation, how to bill for their services, how to allocate time and resources, and many other issues. While some ethical dilemmas loom large, many more situations implicate ethics or morality in ways that may not register as consciously. Either way, these situations can sometimes get lawyers into serious trouble. Lawyers have found themselves involved in ethical issues related to, for example, the collapse of Enron, the fallout of the Bernie Madoff case, and insider trading.

The psychology we present here helps explain how ethical lapses can occur more easily and less intentionally than we might imagine. Understanding this psychology can help us see how, even as we make what could be considered to be unethical decisions, we may still believe that we are ethical actors.

As an initial example, consider the downfall of prominent bankruptcy attorney John Gellene as described by Milton Regan in the book *Eat What You Kill*. Gellene, a "bankruptcy partner at the prestigious Wall Street law firm of Milbank, Tweed, Hadley & McCloy . . . was regarded as one of the best bankruptcy lawyers in the country, and had worked on some of the largest corporate reorganizations in the world." In the mid-1990s, Gellene and Milbank represented Bucyrus-Erie, a manufacturer of mining tools, as it reorganized in bankruptcy. Following the bankruptcy proceedings, Bucyrus-Erie was healthy enough to be purchased by "a large private investment partnership."[2] But the

Bucyrus-Erie bankruptcy did not turn out so successfully for Gellene—in fact, Gellene ended up in jail.

> [Gellene had originally] been asked by powerful Milbank partner Larry Lederman to provide his services to Bucyrus because of Gellene's experience in bankruptcy and financial restructuring. Lederman had advised Bucyrus off and on for five years. He also had provided legal guidance for several years to investment banker Mikael Salovaara. Salovaara had furnished financial advice to Bucyrus over the same five-year period. He was a former Goldman Sachs partner who had recently left the firm with a colleague to establish an investment fund known as South Street. In 1992, South Street had advanced several million dollars to Bucyrus in return for a lien on all the company's manufacturing equipment. As the company's major secured creditor, South Street would be first in line to be paid if Bucyrus filed for bankruptcy. . . .
>
> [In applying to be appointed as Bucyrus-Erie's counsel], Gellene was required under Bankruptcy Rule 2014 to list his and Milbank's connections with any party in interest in the bankruptcy. At the time, Milbank also was representing Mikael Salovaara on one matter and South Street on another. Gellene himself was the lead counsel in the South Street matter, although he had done very little work on the case. The work for Salovaara and South Street created a potential conflict of interest for the law firm. As counsel for Bucyrus in its bankruptcy, Milbank would represent a debtor that had a duty to treat fairly all parties with a claim on its assets. As counsel for Salovaara and South Street, Milbank might have an incentive to provide advice to Bucyrus that favored South Street over other creditors.
>
> [But] Gellene didn't disclose these Milbank ties to Salovaara when he submitted the affidavits that accompanied his application.³

When Milbank's ties to Salovaara and South Street were eventually uncovered, the firm was required to return the $1.86 million in fees that it had earned in the bankruptcy case and settled a professional malpractice suit for between $27 million and $50 million. For his part, Gellene was charged with and convicted of violating Bankruptcy Rule 2014 for "making false declarations in the affidavits he had submitted to [the judge and] for using a false affidavit under oath to claim that Milbank was eligible to receive payment for its work on the bankruptcy." He was sentenced to fifteen months in prison and a $15,000 fine.⁴ How did John Gellene fall so far and so hard?

It is tempting to see ethical lapses like those of Gellene and chalk them up to a few "bad apples" who engage in conduct that we ourselves would not. Instances of intentional unethical behavior surely do exist. But it is wishful thinking to assume that only bad apples—people who differ from us in important ways—will make unethical decisions:

> In our conventional way of thinking about ourselves, we are confident that we would know in advance that to do some set of actions would be morally wrong, and that this realization, occurring prior to the actions, would prevent us from taking them. These comforting thoughts turn out to be not true.⁶

> **Question:** How can you tell that a lawyer is lying?
> **Answer:** His lips are moving.⁵

Instead, we will see that many psychological phenomena contribute to decisions to act unethically and make it challenging to identify and appropriately respond to the ethical lapses of others, including colleagues and clients. Attorneys' ethical decision making is further complicated by the context in which they practice—a world defined by a jumble of ethical rules and norms in which attorneys act as agents on behalf of clients and in which adversarial norms and time pressures loom large. This context may be one reason why lawyers so often find themselves the butt of jokes and why movies so often portray lawyers in unflattering ways—whether it is as "Satans in suits (*The Devil's Advocate*), as amoral chiselers and con artists (*The Rainmaker*), as chronic liars (*Liar, Liar*), as apt appetizers for hungry dinosaurs (*Jurassic Park*), as elite narcissists (*A Civil Action*), or as myopic, feckless, unprincipled hacks (*Erin Brockovich*)."[7] Understanding the psychological phenomena involved can help lawyers take steps to effectively identify and respond to the ethical challenges they encounter.

Bounded Ethicality

Importantly, there are a range of "psychological processes that lead people to engage in ethically questionable behaviors that are inconsistent with their own preferred ethics."[8]

Ethical Blind Spots

> Moral people often fail to act morally.
> —C. Daniel Batson et al.[9]

One impediment to making ethical decisions is a lack of appreciation for the ethical tensions inherent in a particular decision or course of action. This can occur either because the decision maker does not see the decision at hand as involving ethical issues or because she believes that any potential ethical challenges can easily be overcome.

Recall that all of us believe that we see the world objectively (see chapter 1) and that we tend to see ourselves as more fair, unbiased, competent, and deserving than average (see chapter 4). The tendency to view the self in positive terms can be particularly pronounced when the characteristic at issue is socially desirable, as is the case with ethical behavior. Indeed, attorneys tend to believe that their own ethical standards are more stringent than those of other attorneys.[10]

These views of the self can lead to an *ethical blind spot* that gets in the way of our ability to perceive and thoughtfully consider the ethical tensions that we inevitably face.[11] If we are objective, fair, and unbiased, then we need not be concerned that we might take unfair advantage of another or unfairly privilege one person or position over another. If we are competent, then we need not question our ability to act or decide appropriately. If we are deserving, then any benefits we receive must be warranted. If we do not realize that our judgments of fairness are influenced by our own interests, then we do not need to be on guard against such conflicts.[12] And if we

> ✦ ✦ ✦ ✦ ✦
> ### Ethical Blind Spots and Judicial Recusal
>
> It is not just attorneys in practice who can have ethical blind spots. Consider this phenomenon in the context of two recent cases in which the possibility of judicial recusal was raised.
>
> In early 2004, Supreme Court Justice Antonin Scalia was asked to recuse himself from hearing a case involving then Vice President Dick Cheney's management of an energy task force because Scalia and Cheney had gone duck hunting together. Justice Scalia denied the motion, arguing that "[i]f it is reasonable to think that a Supreme Court Justice can be bought so cheap, the Nation is in deeper trouble than I had imagined."
>
> In June 2009, the U.S. Supreme Court decided *Caperton v. A.T. Massey Coal Co., Inc.*, finding that West Virginia Supreme Court of Appeals Judge Brent Benjamin should have recused himself from hearing A.T. Massey Coal Co.'s appeal of a $50 million verdict against it. While the case was pending, Don Blankenship, the CEO of Massey Coal, spent $3 million to support Benjamin's candidacy for a seat on the court. Considering "a realistic appraisal of psychological tendencies and human weakness," the Court found that the circumstances of the case—in particular the timing and "significant and disproportionate influence" of Blankenship's financial support—presented a risk of bias sufficient to interfere with due process.
>
> The illusion of objectivity presents difficulties for judges in trying to assess their own impartiality. As noted by Judge Richard A. Posner in his book *How Judges Think*, "[w]e use introspection to acquit ourselves of accusations of bias, while using realistic notions of human behavior to identify bias in others."[13]

are overconfident—in our own ethical judgment or in our ability to fix or otherwise manage ethical problems—then we are unlikely to stop and think carefully about a decision or to revisit that decision later.

Recall, too, that people commonly make inaccurate forecasts of their own future behavior, predicting that they will get projects done more quickly than they do (see chapter 4), that they will respond more vigorously to protest sexually harassing interview questions than they tend to do in practice, and that they will stand more firmly in competitive negotiation situations than they are often able to do (see chapter 5). Similarly, as we have seen, people tend to predict that they will act ethically.

However, it is clear that in the heat of the moment, we respond to a variety of incentives and practical

> " [T]he situations in which we find ourselves can often be decisive in determining the direction toward which our moral compass turns.
> —Karl Aquino et al.[14] "

pressures. Negotiators feel pressure to reach a settlement or to get a contract signed. We want to impress (or at least not disappoint) the client. We want to be seen (and to see ourselves) as competent.[15] Members of a firm don't want to act against the culture of the firm. Job candidates don't want to jeopardize their chance at a position. None of us wants to be seen as weak. Decision makers feel pressure to make decisions quickly and efficiently. Perhaps not surprisingly, research has found that the greater the incentives to act unethically, the more people are tempted to do so and the more likely they are to act on that temptation. Thus, for example, negotiators facing greater incentives to misrepresent a material fact in a negotiation turn out to be more likely to engage in such misrepresentation.[17]

There can be a lot of pressure to win. You don't want to embarrass yourself or your office. You know if you lose the case, the criticism will come in full force.
—Former Assistant U.S. Attorney Patrick Collins[16]

Why don't we anticipate the pull of such incentives? In part, it may not always be easy to anticipate what the relevant pressures will be.[18] However, psychologists Yifat Kivetz and Tom Tyler also explain this disconnect in terms of our focus when we are predicting our future behavior as compared to our actions in the moment. When we are considering our behavior from a distance, as when we are predicting future behavior, we focus on our *idealistic self*—the self that "places principles and values above practical considerations and seeks to express the person's sense of true self." With this ideal self in mind, abstract ethical considerations, rather than situational pressures, tend to be at the fore, and we anticipate that we will act ethically. However, when the time horizon shortens and we are in the moment, our focus shifts to our *pragmatic self*—the self that is "primarily guided by practical concerns" and is likely to seize opportunity, act impulsively, and focus on the pragmatics of the situation.[20] Thus, we can fail to anticipate the temptation to act in ways that are inconsistent with even our own ethical standards.

Most everyone is virtuous at the abstract level.
—Albert Bandura[19]

Slippery Slopes and Boiling Frogs

One factor in particular that can contribute to ethical blind spots is that the path to unethical conduct often runs along a *slippery slope*. To the extent that ethical conduct degrades gradually, it can be quite difficult to notice. Just as it is difficult for people to visually detect changes in their environment (see chapter 1), it is also difficult to perceive incremental changes in the ethicality of behavior.

Think back to the Milgram experiments that we described in chapter 6 in which people followed the instructions of an experimenter to administer increasingly severe shocks to another person. Participants were asked to gradually shift from administering only slight shocks to giving progressively more severe shocks.

> After the first lies, . . . others can come more easily. Psychological barriers wear down; lies seem more necessary, less reprehensible; the ability to make moral distinctions can coarsen; the liar's perception of his chances of being caught may warp.
> —Sissela Bok[21]

This gradual shift may be one reason why so many people were willing to give even the maximum shock. Gradually increasing the level of the shock made it difficult for participants to determine precisely when they were being asked to cross the line. It was likely difficult to distinguish how a particular level of shock was substantially different from the one that they had just administered. This ride down the slippery ethics slope turns out to be a bit like boiling frogs:

Folk wisdom says that if you throw a frog in boiling water, it will jump out. But if you put a frog in nice warm water and slowly raise the temperature, by the time the frog realizes the water has become too hot, it will already be cooked. Studies of ethical decision making confirm that people are more willing to accept ethical lapses when they occur in several small steps than when they occur in one large step.[22]

Other sorts of ethical decisions can also follow this same progression. Early decisions may be made in circumstances in which the ethical course of action is not clear. Small steps are easy to take and make it difficult to discern the point at which the conduct has become unethical. Wanting to believe that the decisions we have already made have been good ones and preferring to act in ways that are consistent with our previous behavior (see chapter 6), we find it difficult to shift course. Eventually, as a practice becomes routine, the points at which deliberation might have occurred disappear, as do the decision's ethical contours.[23] "Over time, people become more comfortable pushing the boundaries of professional propriety, and they also find themselves having to continue previous courses of action in order to avoid admitting that their earlier actions were improper."[24]

Ethical Fading

Ethical blind spots and the contours of the slippery slope contribute to a process of *ethical fading* or *moral disengagement* in which decision makers "do not 'see' the moral components of an ethical decision, not so much because they are morally uneducated, but because psychological processes *fade* the 'ethics' from an ethical dilemma."[25] A variety of additional psychological processes also play a role in fading ethical considerations from view, making unethical decisions more likely.

The scripts (see chapter 1) that govern a particular situation may determine whether or not ethical considerations are taken into account. A person "may approach a particular decision with a script that has moral content, triggering moral judgment processes, or with one that is devoid of moral content, triggering non-moral judgment processes."[26] For example, the relevant script may characterize a particular decision—such as whether a conflict is an obstacle to taking on

> ✦ ✦ ✦ ✦ ✦
> ### Kurzweil Applied Intelligence Company and the Slippery Slope
>
> The Kurzweil Applied Intelligence Company is just one example of a company that succumbed to the slippery slope:
>
>> [In 1996, the] former president and co-chief executive of Kurzweil Applied Intelligence Inc. was convicted ... of masterminding an astonishingly blatant accounting fraud.... [T]he company booked millions of dollars in phony sales in the two-year period straddling its August, 1993, initial public offering....
>>
>> Kurzweil's slow slide into fraud started in a fairly innocuous manner during 1991.... If a quarter was ending but a sales rep needed a few days to cement a sale, [the CEO] began allowing the company to book the revenue a bit early. Instead of being shipped to the customer, the goods were "temporarily" stored at a ... warehouse ... until the order was signed. Under generally accepted accounting principles, a sale can only be counted when goods leave the company's premises en route to the customer. But the maneuver was impossible to detect as long as the sale was consummated quickly.
>>
>> As sales proved harder to get during 1992, the company relaxed its policy to allow sales to be booked two weeks early. And by the following year ... the rules were stretched until "the whole policy basically went out the window and [we did] whatever was necessary to book the revenue [including forging customer signatures, altering logbooks and other documents, and moving merchandise to hide it from auditors]."[27]

representation of a new client—as a *business* decision as opposed to an ethical decision, thereby fading the ethical implications from view.[28] Alternatively, the relevant script may define how a particular problem is to be addressed. Take the Ford Pinto automobile, for example. The Pinto had design issues such that its gas tank was susceptible to rupture and burst into flames in slow-speed crashes. Consider how Ford's field recall coordinator described his reaction to early reports of fires involving the Pinto:

> My cue for labeling a case as a problem either required high frequencies of occurrence or directly-traceable causes. I had little time for speculative contemplation on potential problems that did not fit a pattern that suggested known courses of action leading to possible recall.... I remember no strong *ethical* overtones to the case whatsoever. It was a very straightforward decision, driven by dominant scripts for the time, place, and context.[29]

The early reports of Pintos "lighting up" did not fit the coordinator's schema for what a problem would look like: these reports "trickle[d] in" and "did not fit the pattern of recallable standards; the evidence was not overwhelming that the car was defective in some way." Accordingly, the ethical dimensions of the decision about whether to recall were not focal in the coordinator's mind.[30]

DILBERT © 2004 Scott Adams. Used by permission of UNIVERSAL UCLICK. All rights reserved.

So, too, can the language that we use to describe a particular act or decision make that decision seem more acceptable. For example, the use of language euphemisms—such as *friendly fire, collateral damage, downsizing, strategic misrepresentation, creative timekeeping, decedent*, a case with *bad facts*, or Ford Pintos *lighting up*—can strip the decision of much of its ethical content.[31]

The availability heuristic can also affect a whole range of perceptions that factor into ethical decision making. Ethical decisions can be influenced by the nature, magnitude, probability, and timing of any potential consequences. These kinds of factors influence what is known as the *moral intensity* of a decision. For example, when a harm is perceived as less likely to occur or more removed in time, the decision will feel less ethically fraught. As we saw in chapter 4, such judgments can be influenced by the ease with which examples can be drawn to mind.[32]

Similarly, decisions are seen as more unethical when they result in observable harm (the outcome bias—see chapter 4) and when they harm identifiable victims (see chapter 6).[33] In the absence of such harms, it can be easy to believe that "no one was hurt." Thus, to the extent that the impact of a particular course of unethical conduct—such as the failure to disclose a conflict—is not immediately observable, its ethical contours may not rise to the forefront.

Other aspects of the decision context can influence ethical decision making as well. For example, decision makers who have almost met their goals but are falling just short of reaching them are more likely to act unethically (such as by misrepresenting their performance).[34] Similarly, the way a decision is framed can influence willingness to engage in unethical conduct. As we learned in chapter 5, losses are particularly aversive and tend to loom larger than do gains of comparable magnitude. It turns out that the desire to avoid a loss can fuel unethical behavior. Studies have found that decision makers are more likely to engage in a range of unethical behaviors when facing a decision that is framed as a loss than when the same decision is framed as a gain.[35] Following a similar pattern, professional tax preparers have been found to be more likely to approve returns containing large deductions associated with ambiguous tax rules when they are faced with the possibility of losing an existing client (loss frame) than when they are in the position of trying to develop new clients.[36]

Consider how this might apply to a young associate trying to meet his firm's billable hour requirement. First, taking the billable hour requirement as the relevant reference point, the associate may be close to reaching the goal but find himself falling just short. In addition, falling short of the minimum number of hours is likely to be seen as a loss.[37] Both of these features of the situation tend to increase the likelihood of unethical behavior. Furthermore, imagine a client who is engaged in selling an unsuccessful business[38] or one who is in the middle of negotiating a deal that is starting to unravel. Both clients are likely to find themselves in a loss frame and at greater risk of unethical behavior. Similarly, once a person has stumbled into an unethical decision, considerations about what to do next are likely to be made in a loss frame. A person can own up to his unethical decision and face the negative consequences now or keep quiet and face a possible and uncertain loss sometime in the future. Such a posture can make risk-seeking behavior more likely.

Ethics in Law Practice

The psychological tendencies that may lead people to behave unethically can be compounded by the situation of legal practice. The rules governing professional conduct, the agency relationship between attorney and client, the attorney's role as advocate, the demands of practice, and the social environment of the firm or practice area can all influence the ways in which lawyers make decisions about issues that implicate ethics.

Ethical Rules and Standards

The regulation of lawyers' professional conduct has become increasingly complex, drawing on rules and norms from a variety of sources. Ethical constraints in particular contexts are sometimes set out in statutes or regulations. Similarly, statutory provisions against practices such as wiretapping and rules such as the Sarbanes-Oxley Act or the Foreign Corrupt Practices Act require particular disclosures, proscribe certain behavior, or seek to hold lawyers accountable in other ways. Court rules regarding evidence, discovery, and other matters provide additional regulation. Bankruptcy Rule 2014 tripped up John Gellene, the attorney in our opening example. Some situations—such as those implicating conflicts of interest, veracity, confidentiality, advertising, billing, and sex with clients—are covered by the *Model Rules of Professional Conduct*; others are not.

> Two lawyers were negotiating a case. "Look," said one to the other, "let's be honest with each other." "Okay, you first," replied the other. End of discussion.[39]

> ♦ ♦ ♦ ♦ ♦
> ### A Situationist Perspective
> In discussing ethics with a group of attorneys, Robert Nelson found that "[t]he answer to almost every question was that it 'depends.' Aggressiveness generally is inappropriate, unless the war was initiated by the other side. Hardball usually is inappropriate unless there is a specter of mischievous plaintiffs' lawyers waiting to use the information from discovery for other suits."[40]

Even when formal rules touch on an issue, these rules can be ambiguous and even conflicting. Many of the rules governing attorney conduct articulate a minimum standard of conduct that often needs to be supplemented with guidance from the attorney's own internal moral code. Some ethical questions have clear answers; many more implicate gray areas in which the rules and norms that apply to the situation are much more ambiguous. Indeed, "many legal-ethics standards, like other ethical principles, are formulated in broad abstract terms. How they apply in particular cases is often difficult to determine. What constitutes an 'incompetent' performance or 'unreasonable' fee are highly fact-specific questions."[41] The same is true for concepts like "zealous advocacy," whether information is "material," and whether an interpretation of the ethical rules is "reasonable." Ethical guidelines that make sense for litigators may not fit transactional work, and vice versa.[42]

Conflicting values, rules that are susceptible to interpretation, and routines that diverge from ethical standards can lead to the first missteps on the slippery slope. Initial decisions are often made when it is not clear whether and how the ethical rules apply. And, as we have seen, as small steps are taken down the path, it is difficult to recognize when ethical problems have begun to loom large and when conduct has crossed the line.

Consider how this pattern might play out within a law firm:

> Every litigation associate goes through a rite of passage: she finds a document that seemingly lies squarely within the scope of a legitimate discovery request, but her supervisor tells her to devise an argument for excluding it. As long as the argument isn't frivolous there is nothing improper about this, but it makes the first step onto the slippery slope. For better or for worse, a certain kind of innocence is lost. It is the moment when withholding information despite an adversary's legitimate request starts to feel like zealous advocacy rather than deception. It is the moment when the no-deception principle encoded in Model Rule 8.4(c) . . . gets gerrymandered away from its plain meaning. But, like any other piece of elastic, the no-deception principle loses its grip if it is stretched too often. Soon, if the lawyer isn't very careful,

every damaging request seems too broad or too narrow; every smoking-gun document is either work-product or privileged; no adversary ever has a right to "our" documents. At that point the fatal question is not far away: *Is lying really so bad when it is the only way to protect "our" documents from an adversary who has no right to them?*[43]

Consider how another chain of events might begin with a white lie:

> If, for example, a lawyer asks a secretary to tell a client that the lawyer is out so that the lawyer does not have to explain why the complaint has not yet been drafted, might that lawyer not take the next step and tell the client the complaint was finished when it was not? Once the lawyer has lied to the client about whether the work has been done, what is to prevent the lawyer from rounding up the hours recorded for the piece of work when it finally does get done?[44]

In similar ways, decisions about progress reports to clients, billing, discovery practices, and decisions in many other areas can lead down a slippery slope.[45]

The Agency Relationship

The fact that the attorney and the client are in an agency relationship—with the attorney representing the client's interests—can complicate ethical decision making in several important ways. First, an attorney as agent is expected to further the interests of the principal. But it is clear that attorneys have their own personal interests that may or may not be directly compatible with those of their client. Psychology teaches that these and other conflicts of interest that may arise in representing clients are not easily remedied. In particular, disclosing the conflict—a common remedy—can actually have pernicious effects. In addition, to the extent that clients act through their attorneys as agents, the clients may be willing to engage in conduct that they otherwise might not undertake. Similarly, a lawyer who might not have been disposed to undertake or to propose a particular course of unethical conduct directly may be more willing to accede to the client engaging in the same suggested course of action when it comes at the client's instigation.

The Role of the Lawyer's Interests

Often the interests of the lawyer and the client are aligned. Specifically, lawyers and clients will generally share an interest in winning a case or negotiating a favorable deal. But lawyers also routinely face situations in which their own interests come into conflict with the interests of their clients and with their professional responsibilities.

> " To nine out of ten of you the choice which could lead to scoundrelism will come, when it does come, in no very dramatic colours. Obviously bad men, obviously threatening or bribing, will almost certainly not appear.... [N]ext week, it will be something a little further from the rules, and next year something further still, but all in the jolliest, friendliest spirit. It may end in a crash, a scandal, and penal servitude; it may end in millions, a peerage and giving the prizes at your old school. But you will be a scoundrel.
> —C. S. Lewis[46] "

> [T]he temptation is to leave no stone unturned as long as lawyers can charge by the stone.
> —Deborah Rhode[48]

Take, for example, the lawyers advising Enron, who "agreed to review the propriety of Enron transactions in which [the lawyers'] own services had been used."[47] It would not be surprising if the lawyers were motivated (consciously or unconsciously) to find that the prior transactions—about which they had advised the company—had been proper. To find otherwise could have called into question the propriety of their advice.

Consider, too, how different billing arrangements might influence lawyer decision making.[49] A lawyer who is paid by the hour, for example, might be inclined to spend more time on a matter, while his client will want him to be efficient. Imagine Bill, an associate attorney who bills his time hourly and works at a firm with high billable hour requirements. Bill might be disinclined to stop and plan out an efficient case plan at the beginning of the representation, preferring instead to jump right into the work. He might not worry too much about spending time on additional (though maybe unnecessary) research, might not always avail himself of the firm's "on the shelf" research, and might sometimes be inclined to embark on a project before it is strictly necessary. He might tend to be aggressive rather than conservative in billing his time. And he might have a tendency to be slow in settling his clients' disputes.

In contrast, a lawyer who is paid on a flat-fee or other fixed-rate basis might be inclined to minimize the amount of time devoted to the matter, while her client might prefer that she devote more time. Consider Josie, a salaried legal aid lawyer; Marcus, a lawyer in private practice who charges a flat fee; and Anthony, a lawyer in private practice who has been appointed by the court to represent a criminal defendant for a fixed amount. These lawyers might be inclined to spend less time on a matter (for example, to do less discovery and file fewer motions) than had they been paid by the hour. Each of them might, therefore, spend less time on a case than might be ideal. For Josie and Marcus, spending more time on a client's case means either less time on other clients' cases or less personal time. For Anthony, "[t]horough preparation is a quick route to financial ruin"[50] if it takes him away from other, higher-paying work.

Finally, imagine Connie, who is a plaintiffs' lawyer working on a contingent fee. She may be motivated to devote time to the case in order to increase the amount of the verdict or settlement on which her fee will be based, but she will only want to do so to the extent that such an increase is greater than her investment. From her perspective, it may be better to spend a small amount of time on a large number of cases than to spend larger amounts of time on fewer cases. In addition, Connie may be more likely to focus on the financial aspects of settlement that will impact her fee rather than nonfinancial aspects that could benefit the client but may not directly benefit Connie. Connie's clients' interest is that Connie should spend as much time as possible on their cases and that she work hard on all kinds of options for settlement.

In each of these cases, the financial incentives of the lawyers may influence (consciously or unconsciously) their decision making.⁵¹

Moreover, consider that an attorney might feel the need to engage in puffing in order to land a particular client or how an attorney's view of the world might be influenced by the desire to obtain or keep a client:

> A businessman was trying to choose a lawyer, but was being very careful about it. He scheduled appointments to interview three lawyers.
>
> At the first lawyer's office, after an initial exchange of pleasantries, the businessman said, "Okay, let's get down to business. I have an important question for you, and I want you to think carefully before answering. How much is two plus two?" The lawyer raised his eyebrows. "Two plus two is four." The businessman thanked him for his time, and proceeded to his next appointment.
>
> The second lawyer, who was also a CPA, seemed a bit more particular than the first lawyer. After an initial discussion, the businessman again announced that he had a very important question, and asked, "How much is two plus two?" The second lawyer went over to a computer, and entered figures into a spreadsheet. "According to my calculations, two plus two is approximately four." The businessman thanked him for his time, and proceeded to his next appointment.
>
> The third lawyer sat behind a big mahogany desk, and smoked a cigar. He seemed rather self-important as compared to the other two, but at the same time appeared to be much more successful. The businessman again announced, "I would like you to answer a very important question for me, before I decide whether I should use your services. How much is two plus two?" The lawyer pulled the shades, locked the door to his office, and asked in a hushed voice, "How much do you want it to be?"⁵³

> " *A lawyer died and arrived at the pearly gates. To his dismay, there were thousands of people ahead of him in line to see St. Peter. But, to his surprise, St. Peter left his desk at the gate and came down the long line to where the lawyer was standing. St. Peter greeted him warmly. Then St. Peter and one of his assistants took the lawyer by the hands and guided him up to the front of the line into a comfortable chair by his desk.*
>
> *The lawyer said, "I don't mind all this attention, but what makes me so special?"*
>
> *St. Peter replied, "Well, I've added up all the hours for which you billed your clients, and by my calculation you must be about 193 years old!"*⁵² "

When we are motivated to see the world in a particular way or to reach a particular conclusion, the ways in which we seek out and interpret information and arguments can be influenced by our preferences and interests (see chapter 1). For lawyers, this can mean that their ethical judgments are influenced by a myriad of desires—the desire to satisfy the client, to make partner, to generate fees, to win a case, to achieve or maintain a particular reputation or status, to manage limited time, and so on. Such interests can affect how attorneys bill their time, the factual and legal conclusions they draw, how they behave in negotiation, and the advice they give to their clients.⁵⁴

Particularly when the situation is ambiguous, it is easy to interpret information in ways that favor our interests and to construe behavior so that it appears more ethically acceptable. Confirmation bias (see chapter 1) can lead us to interpret new information in ways that favor our existing beliefs and to ignore dissent or other indications of ethical challenges.[55] Recall, too, that we have a tendency to conflate what is fair or ethical with what is in our own interest. We learned in chapter 8, for example, that there are any number of different metrics by which we can judge fairness. And it can be easy to come up with justifications and rationalizations that make a particular course of action seem more ethically acceptable. All of this means that when an unethical course of action is otherwise compelling, it may not be difficult to latch onto the particular metric that validates that course of action or to interpret the facts or the law in ways that are consistent with a judgment that the desired course of action is appropriate. "The ethical failure is not in the commitment to fairness but in the biased interpretation of information."[56] And, of course, the illusion of objectivity makes it difficult for us to recognize these effects.

To see how this might happen, consider the case of lawyer Arthur Wisehart as described by Richard Abel in his book about disciplined attorneys, *Lawyers in the Dock*. Wisehart was representing Joan Lipin, the plaintiff in a sexual harassment and discrimination suit. During a break in a deposition, Lipin found a set of privileged documents belonging to the other side on a conference room table, read them, and removed them from the room. Upon learning of his client's action and unsure about how to respond, Wisehart began to interpret the facts in a favorable way (noting that the documents "were right in front of her" and were not marked *confidential*), to blame the other side (telling himself that "they certainly knew how to handle documents"), and to selectively read prior case law (relying on a case involving the inadvertent delivery of privileged documents). He obtained a second opinion, but from someone who also had an interest in the outcome of the case. In all of these ways, he convinced himself that the use of the documents was allowable.[57]

Conflicts and Disclosure

Conflicts can arise not only between attorney interests and those of their clients but also between the interests of multiple clients, between the interests of current and future clients, and so on. Although many believe that adequate disclosure of conflicts can help to address any potential problems, research has suggested that disclosure as a remedy is itself potentially problematic.

Ideally, the disclosure of a conflicting interest permits the affected party to discount the conflicted party's advice or opinion to account for the conflict. In practice, however, the affected party may not sufficiently discount the advice. Thus, for example, when the attorney for ABC Co. provides advice to ABC about doing a proposed deal with XYZ Inc., the ABC decision makers may have difficulty appropriately discounting that advice to account for the fact that the attorney's cousin is the CEO of XYZ. The client may have difficulty sufficiently adjusting away from the anchor provided by the advice (see chapter 4), may experience the curse of knowledge and find it difficult to ignore the advice (see chapter 7), and may underestimate the extent to which situational pressure—the attorney's relationship with the cousin—may have influenced the attorney's advice (the fundamental attribution error—see chapter 1). Even when trust in the recommendation is degraded, there may be increased pressure to act in accordance with the recommendation because the client does not want to signal her distrust of the adviser or does not want to deprive the adviser of the conflicted benefit, for example, a successful deal with the cousin's company. Disclosure may even *increase* trust in the conflicted adviser in some cases, particularly if the disclosure makes the adviser seem particularly forthright.[58]

But here is the most interesting part: not only might clients not sufficiently take account of the potentially biasing effect of a conflict, but disclosing the conflict might actually *increase* the influence of the conflict on attorney judgments. Why might this be the case? Research has found that behaving ethically at one point in time can result in less ethical behavior at a later point in time. In essence, the earlier ethical behavior is thought to establish the moral credentials of the actor in her own mind and licenses her to behave less ethically later.[59] Thus, the attorney who discloses a conflict may actually be more likely to give biased advice and have more rather than less influence on the client than the attorney who does not disclose, a process known as *disclosure distortion*.[60]

Indirect Unethical Actions

Another complication that flows from the agency relationship between the attorney and the client relates to the omission bias that we discussed in chapter 5. Because harms that are caused indirectly entail less moral intensity than do harms inflicted directly, people tend to be more willing to engage in unethical conduct when acting through an agent than they would be if acting themselves.[61] To take just one example, consider one variant of the Milgram shock experiments (see chapter 6) in which the participant relies on a confederate participant to actually administer the shock. In this version of the experiment, over 90% of participants continued to participate until the highest shock was administered.[62] In this way, then, a client who might not be prepared to engage in a particular unethical act herself may be willing for her attorney to so act on her behalf. Thus, to the extent that the attorney is the one directly engaged in negotiation or discovery rather than the client, the client may have a higher tolerance for questionable tactics.

❖ ❖ ❖ ❖ ❖
Turning Down Client Requests

"Sometimes the client says—I want an opinion letter that says this. The lawyer says 'But that's not true.' Then the client asks, 'How much will it cost me to get that letter?' You have to be willing to say no to a client."[63]

At the same time, because people tend to be more willing to endorse an unfair proposal that is suggested by someone else than they would be to originate such a suggestion themselves, lawyers may be more willing to approve a client's proposed unethical course of action than they would be to initiate such a course.[64] This psychological phenomenon is in step with norms that "assign ultimate responsibility for the moral content of a client's position to the client himself"[65] rather than to the attorney as agent. One study examined the extent to which attorneys would disclose against their client's wishes a material but damaging piece of information that had come to their attention on the eve of reaching a favorable settlement agreement. One of the primary justifications given by lawyers who chose not to disclose was that their client did not want them to divulge the information.[66]

Finally, psychologists have found that people are more willing to engage in unethical conduct when such conduct stands to benefit another person. Such conduct can be motivated by a sense of concern for the well-being or fair treatment of the other person and can make it easier to justify the behavior as prosocial.[67] Thus, lawyers may be more inclined, at least in the short term, to engage in unethical acts that benefit clients than they would be to engage in the same behavior to benefit themselves alone.

Benefits of Agency Relationship

While we have seen that agency relationships can create ethical difficulties for attorneys, it is also true that the attorney-client relationship can serve as a check on ethics. First, attorneys will not share all of their clients' interests, and attorneys have their own interests in avoiding censure. This different perspective on clients' decisions may allow the attorney to see the ethical contours of a decision that have faded for the client. Similarly, to the extent that an attorney has periodic involvement with a client, the attorney may be in a position to notice changes in practice that are not noticeable to a client who sees only the small day-to-day changes. That is, the attorney may be able to notice and stop the client's slide down the slippery slope. We have also seen that harmful behavior is less likely in the presence of a dissenter (see chapter 6). Thus, developing a relationship in which the attorney and the client are able to notice and express dissent can mean that each can serve as an ethical check on the other. Finally, to the extent that searching analysis is part of our schema for attorneys (see chapter 1), a client may be more receptive to the attorney questioning her plans or activities than to a similar critique from another source.

The Challenges of the Adversarial System

Much lawyering happens in the context of adversarial relationships. This is certainly true for litigators, but transactional attorneys also often represent parties with opposed positions. To advocate for a client's interests implies some level of partisanship.

Many ethical issues arise in this context. In the service of zealous advocacy, attorneys may, among other things, fail to ask important or probing questions of their client, fail to disclose material information, exaggerate claims, dissemble about alternative deals, coach rather than prepare witnesses, and aggressively cross-examine even candid witnesses. Indeed, the adversary system can incline lawyers to "treat[] behavior that would be ethically problematic in other contexts as not problematic."[68]

Consider how an adversarial mindset might have influenced John Gellene as he debated whether to disclose his ties to South Street and Salovaara in the Bucyrus bankruptcy:

> *"You are a cheat!" shouted the attorney to his opponent. "And you're a liar!" bellowed the opposition. Banging his gavel loudly, the judge interjected, "Now that both attorneys have been identified for the record, let's get on with the case."*[69]

> In the moral calculus that likely had emerged for Gellene during [the bankruptcy] negotiations, [disclosure] would mean that the party that had behaved so unreasonably during the past year [Jackson National Life Insurance Company (JNL), a large creditor who opposed the bankruptcy,] would gain the upper hand. The debtor would have to hire new counsel. That counsel would have to spend valuable time becoming familiar with Bucyrus, the other parties, and the plan. Furthermore, JNL undoubtedly would use this disruption as an opportunity to push for drastic changes in the plan. The more time passed, and the closer the deadline for obtaining tax benefits loomed, the more leverage JNL would have in pushing for concessions. Given the hostility of other parties to JNL, the result might be a bloody mess that would leave Bucyrus beyond repair.

> For these reasons, Gellene may have convinced himself that non-disclosure *not only was not morally blameworthy, but that it was morally justified*. . . . Disclosure would do little to add to the integrity of the bankruptcy process, but could seriously undermine the chance for a timely and successful reorganization.[70]

Acting in a way that would provide an advantage to an opponent may have been unthinkable.

Psychological research has also found that we tend to evaluate behavior as being more ethical when we believe that we are acting in response to unfair behavior by another.[71] Our belief is that the other side has acted inappropriately is used to justify reciprocal action on our part. Thus, one side may justify questionable behavior by pointing to the unjustness of the other side's alleged behavior. Consistent with this notion, attorneys who were asked to assess the propriety of a variety of questionable negotiation tactics found the maneuvers to be more acceptable when they were used to respond to a questionable tactic used by the other side.[72] This tendency can be particularly pernicious when combined with our tendency to attribute bias or unfairness to those with whom we simply disagree (see chapter 1).

> ✦ ✦ ✦ ✦ ✦
> ### They Started It!
>
> Consider how the tendency to evaluate behavior as more ethical when countering unfair behavior on the other side might play out in the context of discovery:
>
> > A question I have often asked lawyers is this: If the other side does it, can you retaliate? The legal answer is no. The federal rule against discovery abuse (Rule 26) does not have a "they started it!" exception. But many lawyers think that if the other side starts playing discovery games, they would be hurting their clients to turn the other cheek. The legal rules may be clear, but the moral rules are anything but.[73]

In addition, we may see particular acts as less unethical when we compare them to other real or hypothetical acts. We can usually imagine instances of behavior that are worse than the act at issue, and such *advantageous comparisons* can be used to cast a particular decision in a more positive light. Mild overbilling, for example, might be compared to more egregious problems in billing. Researcher Richard Abel finds that this sort of comparison is common among lawyers who have been disciplined for ethical breaches: "At least," one might argue, "I didn't dip into a client's trust account." Or, as another might say, "But, I wasn't about to bill the client for something I didn't do."[74]

Finally, lawyers may use their analytical skills, honed in an adversarial legal system, to excuse what others might see as unethical conduct. Lawyers are expert at closely parsing rules, paying attention to exceptions and loopholes, interpreting text, and making arguments on both sides of an issue. However, this approach can be problematic when it comes to ethical rules that specify only minimum standards, that raise conflicting standards and gray areas, and that must be supplemented by the attorney's own moral compass. As former Supreme Court Justice Potter Stewart said, "[e]thics is knowing the difference between what you have a right to do and what is right to do."

> ✦ ✦ ✦ ✦ ✦
> ### The Psychology of *Brady*
>
> Consider how the psychology discussed in chapters 1 and 2 might influence a prosecutor's application of *Brady v. Maryland*[75] in an adversarial context. The U.S. Supreme Court has held that *Brady* requires the prosecution to disclose evidence that is favorable to the defense when it "could reasonably be taken to

> put the whole case in such a different light as to undermine confidence in the verdict."[76] In making this assessment,
>
>> *Brady* requires a prosecutor who is determining whether to disclose a piece of evidence to the defense to speculate first about how the remaining evidence will come together against the defendant at trial, and then about whether a reasonable probability exists that the piece of evidence at issue would affect the result of the trial. During the first step, a risk exists that prosecutors will engage in biased recall, retrieving from memory only those facts that tend to confirm the hypothesis of guilt. Moreover, because of selective information processing, the prosecutor will accept at face value the evidence she views as inculpatory, without subjecting it to the scrutiny that a defense attorney would encourage jurors to apply.
>>
>> Cognitive bias would also appear to taint the second speculative step of the *Brady* analysis, requiring the prosecutor to determine the value of the potentially exculpatory evidence in the context of the entire record. Because of selective information processing, the prosecutor will look for weaknesses in evidence contradicting her existing belief in the defendant's guilt. In short, compared to a neutral decision maker, the prosecutor will overestimate the strength of the government's case against the defendant and underestimate the potential exculpatory value of the evidence whose disclosure is at issue. As a consequence, the prosecutor will fail to see materiality where it might in fact exist.[77]

The Tolls of Law Practice

Long hours, deadlines, and partnership pressures can combine to take a toll on lawyers. Indeed, many lawyers count time pressure and workload as among the most frustrating aspects of their job (see chapter 15).[78] As described in *Eat What You Kill*, John Gellene worked in an "environment of constant urgency," one in which getting five hours of sleep was thought to be a "luxury." In particular, Gellene did not sleep at all during the two days leading up to the filing of the bankruptcy petition and the application for appointment as Bucyrus's counsel, two days that were described as being "'a circus,' with people running around, papers flying, and a large group of lawyers, legal assistants, and financial advisors turning the Bucyrus board room into command central. The stress on everyone was palpable."[80]

> [I]f one is expected to bill more than two thousand hours per year, there are bound to be temptations to exaggerate the hours actually put in.
> —Chief Justice William Rehnquist[79]

Just as it is clear that the practice of law can be demanding, it is also clear that job stresses matter in terms of ethics. In particular, time pressures can influence ethical decision making. Consider a classic study in which seminary students were assigned the task of giving a three- to five-minute impromptu talk in an adjacent building. Some students were told that they were late for their turn to talk; others were led to believe that they had more time. On the way to the other building, each one encountered a person in need of help—a person planted by the researchers: "[T]he victim was sitting slumped in a doorway, head down, eyes closed, not moving. As the subject went by, the victim coughed twice and groaned, keeping his head down." Those participants who were in a hurry were significantly less likely to stop to help than were those who were less rushed. Interestingly, participants who were assigned to speak about the parable of the Good Samaritan—a story about helping someone in need—were no more likely to stop to help than those assigned to speak about another topic.[81]

Studies have also found that unethical decisions are more common when the decision maker suffers from a lack of sleep or is otherwise cognitively taxed. When decision makers' cognitive resources are in short supply (as may be the case for overworked and overtired attorneys), they are more likely to put themselves in temptation's way and then to succumb to that temptation. And, as we have seen with many other psychological effects, decision makers do not anticipate this pattern of decision making.[82]

Lawyers in Groups

> No dilemma causes [students] more anxiety than the prospect of being pressured by their boss to do something unethical. Not only do they worry about losing their jobs if they defy the boss to do the right thing, they also fear that the pressures of the situation might undermine their ability to know what the right thing is.[83]

These students are right to be worried. As we have seen, the pressures and ambiguities of the situation can change the nature of ethical judgments.

First, recall again the studies we described in chapter 6 in which people followed the instructions of an experimenter to administer increasingly severe shocks to another person. The Milgram studies make evident "that each of us ought to believe three things about ourselves: that we disapprove of destructive obedience, that we think we would never engage in it, and more likely than not, that we are wrong to think we would never engage in it."[84]

In the context of legal practice, the influence of authority can come in the form of a more senior lawyer, partner, or client.

> Consider the plight of a lawyer—fresh out of law school with crushing loan debt and few job offers—who accepts a position at the medium-sized firm. A partner asks the young lawyer to review a client's documents to determine what needs to be produced in discovery. In the stack, the associate finds a "smoking gun"

that is clearly within the scope of discovery and spells disaster for the client's case. The associate reports the document to the partner, who without explanation tells the associate not to produce it. The associate asks the partner a few questions and quickly drops the subject when the partner tells the associate to get back to work.[85]

While the rules of professional responsibility do not allow a lawyer who acts "at the direction of another person" to escape responsibility for ethical misconduct, the rules do provide that a "subordinate lawyer does not violate the Rules of Professional Conduct if that lawyer acts in accordance with a supervisory lawyer's reasonable resolution of an arguable question of professional duty."[86] But given all that we know about ethical blind spots, it would not be at all surprising if subordinate lawyers had difficulty making objective judgments about whether a question is arguable and about the reasonableness of the superior's resolution. And, as we have discussed, lawyers are skilled at making arguments on multiple sides of an issue. Thus, when a partner tells an associate to do something that the associate initially finds ethically questionable, the associate may well be able to craft an argument to convince himself that the particular behavior is acceptable.

Even in the absence of directions from an authority, ethical behavior can be influenced by the behavior of others. As we saw in chapter 6, we learn how to behave, in part, by watching the behavior of those around us—looking to see how others, particularly those with more experience or expertise, behave.[87] The more widespread an attorney believes a particular practice is, the more likely he is to indicate that he would engage in it;[88] and the more tempting the unethical behavior, the more widespread he will believe it to be.[89]

> When [lawyers] begin work at law firms, they watch the more experienced lawyers to see what the real standards of conduct are. Each firm quickly communicates its institutional norms to new associates; many associates are anxious to assimilate themselves into an institution and to be successful within it. Therefore, they are not critical of the norms they are asked to adopt. They redraw their lines to fit into the value systems of their firms. If the senior lawyers are not precise in their billing practices, the junior lawyers will not be. If the senior lawyers exaggerate their credentials or expertise when talking with new clients, the junior lawyers will do the same.[90]

We are particularly influenced by others whom we consider to be members of our group. Studies have found that observing an in-group peer acting unethically increases the likelihood that the observer will similarly act unethically.[91] And the Milgram studies also show the importance of social norms: recall that when participants worked together with a (confederate) peer who administered the shocks, compliance reached over 90%; but when peers refused to comply, compliance dropped to 10% (see chapter 6).[92]

> [We] learn from subtexts as well as texts, and silence is a powerful socializing force.
> —Deborah L. Rhode[93]

"Is it right? ... Is it fair?" Get a grip Carlton—we're a law firm!"

Leo Cullum/The New Yorker Collection/www.cartoonbank.com

When a lawyer is discomfited by what he sees, he may struggle to make sense of it. For example, David Luban describes a legal associate who observed a senior litigator lie to an opponent about a discovery matter and then watched the senior litigator compound that mistake by lying to a federal judge in an attempt to cover up the initial lie. The associate did not take any steps to correct the record and labored to make sense of what he was seeing—he "couldn't believe it . . . [and] kept thinking there must be a reason."[94]

Recall also the possibility of pluralistic ignorance, that is, mistakenly believing that others do not share our understanding or perception of the world (see chapter 6). When an attorney looks around the firm or other practice setting (or to other observers such as accountants or regulators) and does not see anyone else objecting to questionable behavior, he may conclude that nothing is amiss, judging others' failure to object as evidence that the behavior is not improper. But as we have seen, those others may be silent because they, too, are attempting to assess the situation.

> Rather than realize that the other silent individuals are being silent for exactly the same reasons that he is, the individual tends to conclude that these others think that the act is an acceptably moral one and are keeping silent for that reason. The individual then, is the deviant, and under this pressure, comes to think that the act is more normal and more ethical than he previously thought. It is now the standard for what is allowable in this organizational context.[95]

To make matters worse, the illusion of transparency (see chapters 3 and 7) can compound the difficulties that people have in assessing each other's reactions. In one set of studies, for example, observers' ratings of the extent to which people appeared outwardly concerned about another person's unethical behavior were significantly lower than their self-rated levels of actual concern. That is, people were more concerned than they looked. However, people overestimated the degree to which they manifested their concern to others. Thus, individuals may believe that their own concern is apparent to others when it is not.[96]

Finally, the presence of others can sometimes result in a diffusion of responsibility in which no one assumes responsibility for acting.

> A well-known example involves the failure of top Salomon Brothers officials to report or take prompt corrective action against a trader who submitted false auction bids to evade Treasury Department purchase limits. Four top executives knew

of the misconduct and failed to act for several months: the CEO, the president, the general counsel, and the vice chairman, who was the trader's supervisor. According to findings by the Securities and Exchange Commission, each of these officials "placed responsibility for investigating [and curbing the trader's] conduct ... on someone else." The result was a major financial crisis when the threat of a public investigation ultimately forced disclosure.⁹⁷

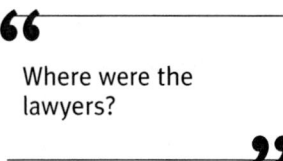

> Where were the lawyers?

Similar diffusion of responsibility can occur, for example, when an associate assumes that someone else will make a decision about how to bill her hours.

Responses to Others' Ethicality

Lawyers often find themselves in the position of dealing with the ethicality of others: clients, colleagues, and opponents. Interestingly, we can be much more judgmental of the ethical failings of others than we tend to be of our own. At the same time, though, many of the impediments to acting ethically that affect our own behavior also play a significant role in making it difficult to notice and respond to others' unethical behavior. This can be particularly true for lawyers operating in the context of law firms and the adversary system.

As we have discussed, we tend to see ourselves as more ethical, objective, and fair than other people. This means that we can be more willing to criticize others' ethics (or lack thereof) than our own, to doubt others' reasons for engaging in cooperative acts, and to assume that other people are motivated by self-interest.⁹⁸ Consistent with the fundamental attribution error, we attribute others' moral failings to flaws in their dispositions but attribute our own missteps to situational factors (see chapter 1). We have an *interpersonal ethics blind spot* in which others' unethical behaviors are more noticeable than their ethical ones.⁹⁹ We focus more on ethics when judging others but find competence more important than integrity when judging ourselves.¹⁰⁰ And we judge others based on faulty predictions about what we might have done under the same circumstances.¹⁰¹

> **Model Rule 8.3**
>
> A lawyer who knows that another lawyer has committed a violation of the Rules of Professional Conduct that raises a substantial question as to that lawyer's honesty, trustworthiness, or fitness as a lawyer in other respects, shall inform the appropriate appropriate authority.¹⁰²

Thus, we can be relatively harsh judges of others' ethical or unethical behavior in general. At the same time, however, it turns out that circumstances that are often present in the context of lawyering make it easy for us to look the other way and fail to ask hard questions.¹⁰³

First, as we saw in chapter 1, we have a tendency to miss things right in front of us when we are focused on other things. Just as we fail to see the gorilla in the basketball game, we can miss unethical behavior around us when we are paying attention to our own cases and deadlines. We've also seen that we have a tendency to identify with other people (colleagues or clients) whose interests are aligned with ours (see chapter 4), making it harder to notice and objectively assess the ethics of their behavior. In addition, it can be difficult to acknowledge the unethical behavior of others when doing so would harm our own interests. This *motivated blindness* can cause our judgments to be biased in favor of the client or colleague; we are inclined to view their actions favorably, disinclined to believe that they have acted wrongly, and able to recruit reasons to support their actions.[104] We may, therefore, not see or believe that our client or colleague has failed to produce required documents, lied in a proxy statement, or failed to disclose material information in a negotiation.

Second, as we saw above, it can be difficult to detect incremental changes in the ethicality of behavior. Just as it can be difficult to identify the point at which our own behavior has gradually crossed the line, detection of when others' behavior becomes unethical can be challenging.

> Imagine that you are . . . in charge of the audit of a large, well-respected corporation. After you have seen and approved of high-quality, highly ethical financial statements for one year, the corporation begins stretching the law in a few places, but commits no clearly unethical behaviors. The third year, the firm stretches the ethicality of its returns a bit further; some of the company's accounting decisions may in fact violate federal accounting standards. By the fourth year, the corporation is stretching the law in many areas and occasionally breaking laws. In this situation, do you ever notice the unethical aspects of the reporting? And, if so, at what point, if any, do you refuse to sign a statement affirming that the financial records are acceptable according to government regulations?[105]

To the extent that the changes in reporting have been gradual, we are much less likely to notice and object than if the client had abruptly shifted its practices.

Third, recall the outcome bias (see chapter 4), by which our evaluation of the quality of a decision is influenced by how the decision turns out. Outcome bias inclines us to base our judgments on the degree to which the decision caused harm rather than on the ethicality of the decision itself.[106] This can lead us to ignore others' unethical decisions unless and until something bad happens.

Finally, people tend to think that they "will take socially risky actions, when they, in fact, do not"—the *illusion of courage*.[107] In the abstract, we might think that we would call out the unethical behavior of a client or colleague; but when actually deciding whether to do so, it is easy to imagine the set of immediate negative consequences of confronting the other person (a difficult conversation, the loss of a client, the ire of a partner, the loss of a job, or difficulty procuring future employment). In the Supreme Court case *Garcetti v. Ceballos*,[108] for example, a deputy district attorney alleged that he was dismissed for having reported to his boss that the police used a false affidavit to support a search warrant. Attorneys may compare such anticipated losses to the less certain and more abstract future consequences of remaining silent. As we have seen, in the domain of losses, people are inclined to gamble, putting off the sure loss in the hope that any future loss will be smaller. This psychology may cause us to take risks that are not only unethical but also unwise because we may overweight the immediate risks of taking action and underweight the likelihood of getting caught in an ethical infraction.

Recall, too, another key lesson from the Milgram obedience studies (see chapter 6): The participants did, by and large, notice that what they were being asked to do was problematic. Indeed, many of them clearly expressed reservations. However, many participants were unable to turn their objections into a course of behavior that was effective in resisting the direction to continue. Lawyers, too, may have difficulty effectively raising objections to the unethical decisions of others.

Consider again the story of John Gellene and his false declarations about potential conflicts of interest in affidavits submitted to the court. At several points in the course of the representation, one of Gellene's partners, Toni Lichstein, asked questions about the potential conflict of interest raised by the firm's simultaneous representation of the company in bankruptcy (Bucyrus-Erie) and Mikael Salovaara, one of the company's chief creditors. However, Gellene and Lederman repeatedly told Lichstein that "it was not a problem . . . that Mr. Salovaara was not a creditor of Bucyrus-Erie, that Milbank had undertaken all of its disclosure obligations, and . . . that Milbank had fully disclosed all of its representations of Goldman, Sachs."[109]

Inability to Recognize and Learn from Ethical Failures

For many of the same reasons that we find it difficult to identify ethical challenges, we also find it difficult to see the ethical implications of our decisions after the fact. Indeed, in one study of lawyer discipline cases, most of the lawyers "were convinced that they had done nothing wrong."[110] Once we have engaged in unethical behavior, we feel the need to reconcile that behavior with our otherwise positive views of ourselves.[111] Thus, we may engage in a post hoc process of *moral disengagement* in which we recharacterize what happened so that questionable conduct becomes more permissible.[112] Conduct that is inconsistent with our image of ourselves as ethical people can be attributed to situational, rather than dispositional, factors (see chapter 1). An attorney can argue, for example, that a document was not produced because it was not precisely covered by the specifics of the discovery request. The consequences of the conduct can be distorted and minimized and the victim blamed. An attorney might blame a client for a billing dispute, for example, noting that the client received regular billing statements and should have raised any questions at an earlier stage. Alternatively, she might note that no one was really harmed. And the omission bias (see chapter 5) can be invoked to minimize blame when we do not engage in an affirmative act. For example, an attorney might tell herself that she would have disclosed particular information if the other side had specifically asked about it.

While many people think of ethical decision making as the product of deliberative ethical reasoning, psychologists have found that ethical decision making tends to be based on relatively intuitive judgments, with moral reasoning occurring after the fact.[113] We saw in chapter 5 that once we have made a choice, we are able to mobilize reasons to bolster that decision. Indeed, lawyers who face ethical complaints tend to recruit a range of justifications. For example, lawyers accused of billing problems argue that their big clients can afford to pay more, that generously billing big clients allows them to represent other clients who cannot afford them, and that they only billed what they were worth.[114] Similarly, unethical conduct is rationalized post hoc through appeals to different metrics of fairness (see chapter 8) or to other accepted values, such as notions of lawyers as zealous advocates or creative interpreters of legal rules, rules protecting client confidences, principles of reciprocity or self-defense, and the need to fight against injustice. Attempts may also be made to locate blame elsewhere: on adversaries, on the circumstances, on regulators, and on clients.[115]

> [A]ll the while that you're giving the Devil his due, a little bit more each day, you're also persuading yourself that the Devil is a misunderstood fellow whose hidden virtues are only now becoming transparent to you.
> —David Luban[116]

Confirmation bias (see chapter 1) also helps us remember aspects of the decision or situation that are consistent with an ethical self-image, rather than the details of any ethical lapse. "If mistakes were made, memory helps us remember that they were made by someone else. If we were there, we were just innocent bystanders."[117] Such memory effects can result in what ethicist Patricia Werhane calls *moral amnesia*, or "an inability to remember past mistakes and to transfer that knowledge when fresh challenges arise."[118]

All of this can conspire with the pressure to act consistently (see chapter 6), making it difficult to learn from or acknowledge any missteps. Consider again John Gellene, the bankruptcy attorney described in *Eat What You Kill*. Why didn't he, at some point, correct his misstatements to the court?

> It likely would have been psychologically stressful for Gellene to do so at this point, however. He had made a prior decision not to disclose the Salovaara and South Street connections. He had publicly proclaimed Milbank's fitness for the job in the face of an attack. He likely had rationalized his conduct in a way that permitted him to deny that he had done anything unethical. It would be hard at this point to disavow those representations and to reassess that rationalization.[119]

Finally, engaging in unethical behavior can even change our perspective on the relevant ethical standards. For example, engaging in unethical conduct leads to poorer memory for the relevant ethical rules.[120] And when our behavior and our beliefs conflict, one way to reduce the resulting discomfort is to change our beliefs to match our behavior. For example, those who engage in cheating behavior tend to become less harsh in their judgments of cheating, and those who resist cheating become even more intolerant of cheating.[121] Even considering the behavior from the perspective of the person who has acted unethically can affect judgments of ethicality. In one study, individuals were randomly assigned to consider a negotiation in which one party made an ethically ambiguous misrepresentation. Those who considered the negotiation from the perspective of the unethical actor rated the act as more ethically acceptable and the actor as more ethical than did those taking the other side's perspective.[123] Moreover, the effects of pluralistic ignorance (see chapter 6) can mean that as no one speaks up about particular unethical behavior, new norms of ethics will begin to emerge that alter attitudes about ethics.

> If you want people to soften their moral attitudes toward some misdeed, tempt them so that they perform that deed.
> —Eliot Aronson[122]

Solutions

The common prescriptions for ethical failures are to increase enforcement and applicable sanctions and to pay greater attention to ethics education. But while some ethical failures are the result of deliberate moral reasoning and cost-benefit analysis that leads to unethical decisions and some ethical failures are due to a lack of knowledge of the relevant rules, a range of evidence suggests that many ethical failures occur unconsciously and unintentionally. How can attorneys seek to avoid the pitfalls that we have described here?

Be Aware

As an initial matter, it is important for lawyers to recognize their susceptibility to ethical blind spots and to have an awareness of the factors that can influence ethical decision making. Attorneys who understand that their predictions about how they will act when faced with an ethical dilemma are not always accurate are in a better position to plan ahead. Attorneys who understand that unethical decisions are more likely when losses loom can exercise caution. Attorneys who understand the nature of the slippery ethics slope can seek to resist the pull of the next step. Attorneys who understand the dynamics of social norms and pluralistic ignorance will be equipped to reject the assumption that no one else is bothered. Attorneys who recognize the temptation of post hoc rationalization can question the reasons they generate for their behavior.[124]

Make Ethics Salient

"[I]f we are reminded of morality at the moment we are tempted, then we are much more likely to be honest."[125] Thus, it is important to find ways to include ethical considerations in the mix of considerations taken into account when determining how to act.[126]

> ✦ ✦ ✦ ✦ ✦
> **Bringing Ethics to the Fore**
>
> - Keep a reminder of core values front and center. A paperweight, wall hanging, or other memento can be a visual reminder of the standards that are important to uphold.
> - Avoid euphemisms.
> - Imagine and individualize the person on the other side or the person who will experience the consequences of a decision.
> - Work to make consideration of ethical consequences a part of each decision—not just those decisions for which ethics seem clearly central.

Making ethics salient by bringing those considerations to the forefront of our thinking can also help us to encourage others to behave ethically in their dealings with us. For example, negotiators are less likely to engage in deception when they have recently been reminded of ethical norms.[127] Similarly, negotiators who give reasons for their offers or demands that are in step with fairness norms are more likely to elicit ethical behavior from the other side.[128]

Within firms, it is important that individuals model ethical behavior and decision making. Lawyers who observe others within the firm engaging in ethical behavior are more likely to make ethical decisions themselves.

Be Critical

As we have seen throughout this book, it can be very helpful to develop a critical stance. We have seen how easy it can be to justify a desired course of action. Similarly, we have seen that attorneys can fall into the trap of telling the client what the client wants to hear. But attorneys should ask themselves whether their advice or ethical decisions would be the same if they were on the other side of the decision. Questioning our judgments, considering the opposite, and questioning "the justifications that we concoct to rationalize our actions" can help to temper ethical fading.[129]

Similarly, seeking an unbiased outside view—ideally before taking the first step but also when finding ourselves elsewhere on the slope—can help us take a broader perspective and consider a wider range of ethical implications.[130] Within firms, providing channels through which individuals can dissent and raise questions about ethics is key. Some large firms now have in-house ethics counsel or an ethics ombudsperson to formally serve this role.[131] While lawyers in such a role may share some incentives with others in the firm,[132] they may be more removed from the immediate pressures of the ethical situation. Finally, many lawyers find it helpful to consider how a trusted friend or family member might view a particular action—asking, for example, whether they could look their parents in the eyes and explain a particular choice.

> ✦ ✦ ✦ ✦ ✦
> **The Mirror Test**
>
> In describing decisions to act ethically, many people evoke the notion that they want to be able to "look at themselves in the mirror" afterward. This idea has been attributed to the following story:
>
>> [A] German ambassador in London . . . as part of a celebration he had to host in honor of Britain's King Edward VII, was asked to provide a bevy of prostitutes. The diplomat felt that he could not do this and instead resigned his position. Asked why, he responded, "I refused to see a pimp in the mirror in the morning when I shave."[133]
>
> Consistent with this instinct, psychological studies have found that increasing awareness of ourselves and our values—for example, actually looking at our own image in a mirror—reduces the incidence of unprincipled behavior (such as cheating, stealing, or littering).[134]

Plan Ahead

Critical thought takes time and cognitive resources. Thus, it can be important to take time to make thoughtful decisions when that is possible. Some of the effects we have described here, such as the effect of loss frames on ethical decision making, can be moderated when there is no time pressure.[135] But, of course, there is not always time for extended analysis. Thus, it can be helpful to cultivate a set of ethical habits so that making the right call becomes more automatic.[136] One way to alleviate the pressures attendant to deciding in the moment is to think ahead about how to respond to those pressures.

We have seen that it can be quite difficult to predict how we will handle ethical challenges. This suggests that we should not assume that we will always automatically act ethically. Instead, we should try to anticipate ethical dilemmas and to plan and rehearse our responses ahead of time, creating scripts for ourselves that we can follow when necessary (see chapter 1).[137] Taking the long view and thinking ahead can help to make ethical issues and ideals more salient.[138] Identifying the resources that might be available—for example, in-house ethics counsel, an ethics hotline, or a trusted confidant—can make them more likely to spring to mind when needed. Anticipating the pressures that are likely to be dominant at the time of the decision can minimize misprediction.[139] And establishing implementation intentions (see chapter 5), that is, anticipating concrete triggers and planning specific responses, can help us to act consistently with our ideals. Imagining and practicing, for example, how we will respond when a negotiation counterpart or discovery request asks for information that we would rather not disclose, what we will do when we are asked to do something with which we are uncomfortable, how we will bill time or deal with pressures to bill inappropriately, how we will proceed when we suspect that a client has not been candid, or how we will act when we observe a colleague behaving unethically can make it much easier to follow through with those plans.[140]

> ✦ ✦ ✦ ✦ ✦
> **Precommitment**
>
> Recall from chapter 6 that we feel inclined to act in ways that are consistent with our previous actions. This means that making a commitment to an ethical course of conduct, particularly an active or public commitment, can help us stay the course. Thus, we might "precommit to [an] intended ethical choice by sharing it with an unbiased individual whose opinion [we] respect and who [we] believe to be highly ethical,"[141] or we might write down a set of ethical commitments. These actions can increase the likelihood that we will act in keeping with our own ethical values.

We have seen how easy it can be to slide into problematic behavior without being clearly aware of it. Thus, as part of creating a set of implementation intentions, it can be helpful to identify concrete behaviors that can serve as warnings that a line may be crossed.

> Set yourself some telltale sign—something that you *know* is wrong. Write down on a piece of paper: "I will never backdate a document." Or "I will never let a co-worker get blamed for something that was my fault." Or "I will never paper a deal that I don't understand." Or "I will never do anything that I couldn't describe to my dad while looking him in the eye." Pick your telltale sign carefully—and, the moment the alarm rings, evacuate the building.[142]

This sort of advance planning can help attorneys keep their bearings and can serve as triggers for planned responses.

Finally, planning ahead can mean that potential problems, such as conflicts of interest, are eliminated in advance when that is possible. For example, an attorney might avoid a particular type of fee agreement in a particular case, or an attorney can decline to provide counsel when his judgment might be compromised. "No ethically sensitive (or even reasonably prudent) attorney should follow the example of Vinson & Elkins, which agreed to review the propriety of Enron transactions in which its own services had been used."[143] Similarly, planning ahead can mean that attorneys choose not to work in settings in which they believe that their ethics will be compromised.

Counsel Clients on Ethics

Many of these same strategies can make attorneys aware of potential ethical missteps by colleagues and clients. In chapter 10, we addressed the occasionally uncomfortable conversations that attorneys must have with clients when the attorney believes that the client is contemplating or has done something unwise, unethical, or illegal. At times, the

> [c]onduct that attorneys find ethically objectionable can be more diplomatically packaged [for the client] as unduly risky, as something that will not play well with jurors, government regulators, the media, or the general public. By the same token, the moral high road can also be portrayed as desirable for prudential reasons [important for the client's reputation or as a means of forestalling regulation].[144]

However, such characterizations are not always possible or sufficient, and in some instances attorneys will have to be even more blunt—serving the client by providing a reality check—or may even be required to withdraw from the representation.[145]

✦ ✦ ✦

"Attributing blame solely to flawed individuals or corrupt organizations . . . rarely captures the subtleties of how ethical misconduct occurs. Furthermore, it offers false reassurance that only moral deviants, not ordinary people, engage in such behavior."[146] Understanding how easy it can be to slide into misconduct and how difficult it can be to realize that it has happened should be cause for vigilance: "The point is that to understand all is *not* to forgive all. But . . . to understand all may well put us on guard against doing the unforgivable."[147]

✦ ✦ ✦ ✦ ✦
Summing It Up

- Recognize that ethical lapses can occur more easily and less intentionally than we might imagine. A variety of psychological phenomena contribute to decisions to act unethically and make it challenging to identify and appropriately respond to the ethical lapses of others.
- Keep in mind that the views we have of ourselves and the difficulty we have in predicting our own future reactions can lead to ethical blind spots.
- Watch out for the roots of ethical fading—the difficulty we have in detecting small changes in behavior, scripts, and euphemisms that fail to identify the implications of ethics in decisions—and factors that affect the moral intensity of a decision.
- Be aware of the ways in which certain aspects of legal practice—agency relationships with clients, the adversarial system, and the time pressures of practice—can heighten the potential for ethical failure.
- Subject decisions to searching analysis, plan ahead for how to handle difficult situations, and raise ethical issues with clients.

For Further Reading: Ethics

Richard L. Abel, Lawyers in the Dock: Learning from Attorney Discipline Proceedings (2008).

Max H. Bazerman & Maharzin R. Banaji, *The Social Psychology of Ordinary Ethical Failures*, 17 Soc. Just. Res. 111 (2004).

Max H. Bazerman & Ann E. Tenbrunsel, Blind Spots: Why We Fail to Do What's Right and What to Do About It (2011).

Codes of Conduct: Behavioral Research into Business Ethics (David M. Messick & Ann E. Tensbrunsel eds., 1996).

Conflicts of Interest: Challenges and Solutions in Business, Law, Medicine and Public Policy (Don A. Moore et al. eds., 2005).

Psychological Perspectives on Ethical Behavior and Decision Making (David de Cremer ed., 2009).

Social Decision Making: Social Dilemmas, Social Values, and Ethical Judgments (Roderick M. Kramer et al. eds., 2009).

Social Influences on Ethical Behavior in Organizations (John M. Darley et al. eds., 2001).

Special Issue, *Regulating Ethical Failures: Insights from Psychology*, 95 J. Bus. Ethics 1 (Supp. 1 2010).

Carol Tavris & Elliot Aronson, Mistakes Were Made (but Not by Me) (2007).

Ann E. Tenbrunsel & Kristin Smith-Crowe, *Ethical Decision Making: Where We've Been and Where We're Going*, 2 Acad. Mgmt. Annals 545 (2008).

Linda K. Treviño et al., *Behavioral Ethics in Organizations: A Review*, 32 J. Mgmt. 951 (2006).

On Being Productive, Successful, and Happy

15

> Success is getting what you want. Happiness is wanting what you get.
>
> —*Dale Carnegie*[1]

To this point, we have focused on how lawyers can draw on psychological insights to better represent their clients, examining a variety of discrete tasks that are central to such representation. In this chapter, we look more generally at how lawyers can use psychology to be productive, successful, and happy in their careers. We first discuss how psychology can help attorneys be more productive and successful in their work and then turn our attention to how psychology can help attorneys improve their overall well-being.

Attorney Productivity and Success

According to Colin Powell, "[t]here are no secrets to success. It is the result of preparation, hard work, and learning from failure."[2]

Time Management

The productive and successful attorney must be good at managing her time. She must be efficient; good at planning how long particular tasks will take; and, in most practices, good at recording her time. Unfortunately, these tasks are not as psychologically straightforward as they might seem.

Effective Use of Deadlines

Many of us procrastinate, particularly when we need to make a difficult decision or do something we regard as unpleasant. A lawyer may procrastinate writing a complaint or a brief, initiating settlement negotiations, informing her client that the court has rejected her motion to dismiss, or preparing a complex trust document.

One reason that lawyers may avoid working on something that they know they should work on is that contemplating the project triggers uncomfortable emotions, such as fear of failure.

> For example, a typical scenario might proceed as follows: You look at a file and say to yourself, "This is a difficult case." The underlying implication is that you are going to fail—and that triggers fear. Instead of confronting your original premise and all of its corollaries (e.g., "I'm not a good lawyer."), you get rid of the emotional pain by avoiding the task.[3]

Lawyers may also procrastinate due to their lack of interest in the particular project. Shocking as it may be, some lawyers are not excited by tasks such as drafting or responding to interrogatories.

> You say to yourself, "This is going to be boring!" In turn, this leads to thoughts about your whole identity and whether your life is fulfilling. Such thoughts may trigger a variety of negative emotions, including anger and guilt. Again, instead of confronting your thoughts and emotions in a constructive manner, you reduce the emotional pain by simply avoiding the boring task.[4]

Lawyers who like working close to the deadline may fear that more time will simply lead them to unduly tinker with the document or draw out the time spent on the task, perhaps even in ways that may make it worse. However, most of our written work products can benefit from a good edit, and delayed conversations may curtail options or lead to client anger.

The planning fallacy (see chapter 4) can exacerbate procrastination. We've seen that people tend to be overly optimistic regarding the time that will be needed to complete a particular task. If lawyers think that they can complete a summary judgment response in two days and, therefore, wait to start drafting until two days before the due date, they may find themselves in trouble when they are only a quarter of the way done after the first day of work. They will then be left with a series of unattractive options, such as working extremely late, doing a poor job on the brief, seeking an extension of the deadline (which they likely won't get), or recruiting help from others inside or outside the office. Unexpected illness, accidents, or new projects will also be particularly problematic for procrastinators. At the same time, failing to recognize that some tasks are quite easy and can be completed quickly (see chapter 4) can also lead people to procrastinate.

> "You may delay, but time will not.
> —Benjamin Franklin[5]

To deal with the planning fallacy, lawyers should remind themselves that because most tasks will take longer than they expect, they should start the task earlier in case extra time may be needed. They should also take the *outside view* on projects by considering how long it actually took them to complete similar projects. Rather than relying on possibly flawed memories, it is advisable to check actual time records when possible.

Whether we are managing our own work or the work of others on the team, strategically setting interim deadlines (see chapter 5) can help maximize productivity and avoid procrastination. With such a deadline looming, we often find ourselves better able to buckle down and be more efficient.

> Eat your peas first. If you tend to procrastinate, commit to spending the first fifteen minutes of each day working on a project that you have been putting off. After you start, you may find the project is not as horrible as you thought.
> —*Grover E. Cleveland*[6]

◆ ◆ ◆ ◆ ◆

Procrastination as an Adaptive Trait?

When we tell ourselves that we are increasing our efficiency by deliberately waiting until we are close to a due date, we may be engaging in a form of procrastination.

Procrastination is such a common habit that some people have actually come to consider it an adaptive trait. (A few lawyers I know think of it as an art form.) This faulty logic is expressed when some of us say, "I work better under pressure." In reality, it would be more accurate to say: "I work more efficiently when time runs out, and I have no choice but to stop procrastinating. I wish I could stop procrastinating before I find myself under pressure." Do you see the difference?

By definition you work more efficiently and think more clearly when you do not procrastinate. Time pressure does not improve your performance; it simply forces you to stop procrastinating. Your peak performance, however, is likely to occur when you do not procrastinate and are *not* under time pressure either. Not only is this preferable for health reasons, but it is also more likely to prevent mental errors and increase creativity.[7]

Senior lawyers who supervise junior lawyers or paralegals should set early deadlines by which the supervisees must complete their portion of projects. Such early deadlines can motivate the supervisees to complete their projects efficiently while still leaving the senior attorney time to edit the work and also leaving time in case projects take longer than expected or other events intervene. Deadlines set externally by an authority figure, for example, a senior attorney, can be even more effective than deadlines that we set for ourselves.[8]

> ✦ ✦ ✦ ✦ ✦
> ### External Deadlines
>
> In order to discipline himself, Tom Wolfe agreed to write the first version of *The Bonfire of the Vanities* in installments for *Rolling Stone* magazine. "I did get pretty stressed out meeting those deadlines," he later recalled. "By the end I was just sucking wind." When he asked for more time, however, *Rolling Stone* publisher Jann Wenner supplied only a shot of motivation. "Either you turn it in," he told Wolfe, "or I'm going to run blank pages!"[9]

It can also be helpful to break a larger project down into its components. Writing a brief with a deadline a week away may be daunting. However, if the attorney can break that brief down into its component parts—the research, the statement of facts, and each of several major sections—with interim deadlines for each, the daunting task becomes more doable, more concrete, and less likely to lead to procrastination.[10] It may also be helpful to look at some other similar documents as a means of concretizing the project.

In addition, implementation intentions can help lawyers to effectively operationalize their decisions (see chapter 5). Once the lawyer has decided to complete a particular task, it can be useful to identify a particular triggering event and a concrete plan for what to do. Thus, for example, the lawyer might commit that "at 2:00, I will start drafting the jurisdiction argument for the brief in the *Jimenez* case"; or the lawyer might decide that the first thing I will do "when I get to my office is pick up the phone and call Jane Kirkus about the *Billingsly* matter."[11]

It can also be helpful for attorneys to set explicit goals for what they will get done and then post clear reminders (such as notes on a whiteboard) of those goals, creating "cues that confirm goals and banish[ing] any sign that reminds them of temptation."[12] Writing down goals and deadlines takes advantage of the desire for consistency and commitment to generate movement toward those goals (see chapter 5).

> ✦ ✦ ✦ ✦ ✦
> ### Incentives for Completion
>
> Victor Hugo normally had little trouble producing such books as *The Hunchback of Notre Dame* and *Les Miserables*. But sometimes he did run into difficulties and was tempted to do things other than write. At such times he forced himself to work by having his servant take away all of his clothes, with instructions not to return them for several hours. Left with his own nude self and pen and paper, there was nothing to do but sit down and write.[13]

Similarly, minimizing distractions and the moments at which distractions have the most pull—for example, transitions and moments of choice about what to do next—can help lawyers move more seamlessly through a task or set of tasks without falling prey to procrastination.[14] Finally, providing incentives for the completion of tasks can also be effective. By rewarding themselves with a walk, a phone call, a chance to check Facebook, a meal, or a chocolate bar, lawyers can encourage themselves to complete particular tasks in a timely fashion.

The fact that lawyers must coordinate their time with colleagues, assistants, and clients adds additional challenges. Careful time management can enhance the lawyer's relationships with others, and poor time management can be detrimental to those relationships.

✦ ✦ ✦ ✦ ✦

Who Wants to Work Weekends?

Lawyers should consider the perspective of the senior lawyer for whom they are working:

If the brief is due on Monday, do not deliver a first draft to me at 7:00 on Friday night. What will I think? "This jerk has decided to blow up my weekend so that I can review this and put it in final form." Even worse, do not hand me a brief at 7:00 p.m. Tuesday and offer to come in early Wednesday to get my comments. Trust me: This is an offer I *can* refuse. What's the idea? *You* get to work during business hours, and *I'm* forced to work nights and weekends? If there is any chance that your draft will require substantial revisions—and I promise you, there is—deliver it early. That is the only way to ensure that you and I can perform our work on a mutually convenient schedule.

Finally, if you are *not* doing the work I asked you to do, warn me immediately. . . .

. . . I will find some other way to do the work. If you wait for the last minute to tell me that you have not done the work, we are out of luck. That is no way to run a law firm, and we do not run ours that way.[15]

Limitations of Multitasking

The modern electronic world has greatly increased the opportunities for and challenges of multitasking. It has become the norm for lawyers to check e-mails and texts or take phone calls as they work in their office or eat meals. It is also becoming more common for lawyers to use their smartphones in the courtroom. An ABA survey conducted in 2010 reported that 71% of attorneys used smartphones in court to check or send e-mail or to perform calendar functions.[16] Some judges are even said to check Facebook as they preside over trials. Such multitasking would have been unthinkable just a few years ago.

Yet, although opportunities for multitasking have multiplied, there is no evidence that our ability to multitask efficiently and effectively has improved. And, as we saw in chapter 1, although multitasking has negative effects on productivity, we tend to believe that we are much better at multitasking than we really are.[17] We continue to think that we are able to text while driving or check e-mails or Facebook while writing a brief—type the phrase *fountain while texting* into a search engine to find several amusing videos demonstrating the perils of walking while texting.

Structuring our environment to minimize the temptations to multitask can be helpful. For example, we may want to leave the iPod at home so that we are not tempted to listen to podcasts at work. Similarly, we should try to prohibit ourselves from checking Facebook or watching funny videos on YouTube, except perhaps as a reward for completing particular tasks. It is also generally wise to turn off chimes or visual notifications that announce the arrival of messages. Few can resist their siren call.

It is more difficult to figure out how to manage the distraction of text messages, e-mails, and phone calls that may be work related or involve an important family issue. Just a few years ago, we all somehow managed to live our personal and professional lives without these interruptions. We left phone messages and were satisfied when our calls were returned in a day or two. Today, however, clients, coworkers, bosses, and family expect us to be more readily available. The attorney keeps her phone accessible in court because her assistant may be sending her last-minute research or because a client in another case may expect immediate advice.

In the short term, we may not be able to significantly change others' expectations, but we still need to find ways to make ourselves as efficient as possible without unduly disappointing others. In particular, we might try to set aside big blocks of uninterrupted time to work on larger projects that will be demanding. Closing the door and requesting to be interrupted only for emergencies can be helpful. Assigning different ringtones to the various people in our lives can help us to assess which calls to answer immediately. Similarly, while it may be necessary for the lawyer to check e-mail or text messages in the midst of writing a major brief, it is surely not necessary to check every five minutes. Instead, it may be best to close the e-mail in-box or Internet connection while writing. The lawyer can still check messages at regular intervals by reopening the connection, but the lack of immediate accessibility will deter some waste of time.

Lawyers might also try to set the expectations of clients and colleagues regarding how and when the lawyers will respond to them. Lawyers should communicate to clients and colleagues regarding availability to

> If you need uninterrupted time to work, close your door, ask your assistant to tell people not to interrupt you, put a "do not disturb" note on your door, or leave and work from somewhere besides your office. Do whatever you need to get your work done; just make sure you can be reached in a crisis.
>
> —*Grover E. Cleveland*[18]

respond and act consistently with those expectations. In this way the attorney may reassure clients and colleagues that he is paying attention to them even though he is not immediately available at all times. One author suggests the following answering machine message:

> Hello, this is James. You've reached my voice mail, which means I'm probably with a [client] right now. I do check my messages frequently, usually at 10:00 a.m., 2:00 p.m., and 4:00 p.m. If you leave a message, I will be sure to get back to you before the day is over. Thank you![19]

Similar expectations can be set in initial client meetings, via receptionists or assistants, or with automatic e-mail responses. And, for our own part, we should not expect instant replies from others because by demanding such instantaneous responses, we reduce each other's efficiency and effectiveness. Thus, as bosses, coworkers, and family members, we should try to minimize the interruptions that we inflict on others.

Matching Mood to Task

As we saw in chapter 3, emotion affects productivity. Happy workers are generally more productive workers. Lawyers can also increase their productivity and success by capitalizing on the variations in their moods and better matching their mood to the task at hand. When people are feeling happier, they are well suited to efficiently engage in more creative brainstorming sessions, but they may need to double-check their detail work; and when feeling more neutral or even a bit down, they may want to focus on a task that requires great attention to detail, such as proofreading a brief or checking the numbers in a proposal. Remember, too, that people can take affirmative steps to affect their moods. Thus, it may make sense for lawyers to listen to a favorite song or take a quick walk before commencing a negotiation session or working on a brief that makes a creative argument.

Time Records

Having worked those well-planned and efficient hours, lawyers must, in most practices, account for their hours. Because billing is not a particularly pleasant part of the job, some lawyers procrastinate in actually recording the time they spent on particular tasks. Many lawyers may believe that they will easily be able to remember what they did and be able to write down all of their hours at the end of the day, after several days, or even later. Yet, as we know from chapter 2, memories are not that powerful. Particularly in a world of multitasking, it may be difficult for lawyers to keep track of how much time they spend on particular clients or tasks.

Second, as we saw in the last chapter, lawyers may find themselves tempted to bill a little bit more than they are sure that they worked, to double-bill certain tasks, or to bill ahead for work not yet performed. Recall the joke in which St. Peter let a lawyer go to the head of the line to enter Heaven because, according to the lawyer's billing records, the lawyer must have lived a very long life. To resist these temptations, lawyers should make a good effort not only to keep timely records but also to coach themselves in advance not to give in to unethical practices.[20]

Law Firms and Time Management

We all know that many law firms, particularly large private firms, are structured to require lawyers to work long hours and to give up vacations and weekends as needed. However, law firms should not necessarily require their attorneys to work these kinds of hours. There are, after all, productivity costs to imposing such arduous hours on attorneys. One study of attorneys found that 59.5% of surveyed attorneys agreed or strongly agreed that "working long hours adversely affects my ability to think critically and creatively."[21] Recall, too, from chapter 14 that people are more likely to take ethical missteps when they are tired. These findings are consistent with more general psychological research finding that fatigue and lack of sleep impair the ability to function well, creating problems for attention, memory, self-regulation, flexibility, creativity, critical thinking, decision making, ethics, and communication.[22]

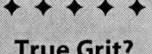

True Grit?

One factor that is associated with long-term success is grit. As defined by psychologists, *grit* involves "perseverance and passion for long term goals. Grit entails working strenuously toward challenges, maintaining effort and interest over years despite failure, adversity, and plateaus in progress. The gritty individual approaches achievement as a marathon; his or her advantage is stamina."[23] Importantly, grit is not associated with intelligence but is independently associated with success. Most of us have known individuals who seem to outperform their innate talent—and also those who underperform. The difference may be grit. In interviews with practitioners in a variety of fields, including law, the professionals were asked what characteristics set the top performers in their fields apart from the rest of the pack:

> [T]hese individuals cited grit or a close synonym as often as [they did] talent. In fact, many were awed by the achievements of peers who did not at first seem as gifted as others but whose sustained commitment to their ambitions was exceptional. Likewise, many noted with surprise that prodigiously gifted peers did not end up in the upper echelons of their field.[24]

Angela Duckworth, "a psychologist at the University of Pennsylvania who helped pioneer the study of grit," says, "I'd bet that there isn't a single highly successful person who hasn't depended on grit. Nobody is talented enough to not have to work hard, and that's what grit allows you to do."[25] Gritty lawyers set long-term goals and stick to them over the long haul.

Mistakes

As every practicing attorney knows, being a good attorney is incredibly difficult. Attorneys are challenged daily with difficult legal issues and even more difficult choices. It is impossible to predict with perfect accuracy how courts will respond to arguments, how opponents will view settlement proposals, how clients will react to recommendations, or how the economy will grow or shrink. Thus, lawyers are bound to make mistakes. Part of the measure of an attorney's success is how well she responds to the mistakes that she will inevitably make.

> Failure is success if we learn from it.
> —Malcolm S. Forbes[26]

> We are not going to achieve victory with every matter over a lifetime of practice. So many variables are outside of our individual control that it just won't happen. . . . [W]e need to develop strategies that enable us to learn from our mistakes and losses, to keep the negative aspects of disappointment and feelings of failure to a minimum, and to pick ourselves up, assess what went wrong, and move into the winning attitude sphere.[27]

> [E]xperience is that marvelous thing that enables you to recognize a mistake when you make it again.
> —Franklin P. Jones[28]

A variety of psychological phenomena can work together to make learning from mistakes difficult. First, it can be difficult to recognize that we have made a mistake from which lessons can be learned. Think back to the study of lawyer predictions of case outcomes described in chapter 4. Attorneys were overconfident in their predictions. But, importantly for present purposes, attorneys appeared not to realize that they had predicted better outcomes for their clients than had actually come to pass.

In many instances, lawyers do not have information about what might have been. "[B]ecause only one set of events occurs in our experience at a particular time," we do not find out what would have happened if a contract had been written differently, if a motion had not been filed, if a different discovery request had been made, if a different offer of settlement had been put forward, and so on.[29] The defense attorney who failed to file a winnable pretrial motion to dismiss may never realize that she could have settled the case for far less had she filed that motion. Similarly, a deal negotiator may never know that the deal could have been structured differently at great benefit to her client because that deal structure never occurred to her. In addition, even when colleagues or others provide feedback, they often hold back in order to spare others' feelings.[30]

These difficulties open the door for outcome bias (see chapter 4) to hinder improvement efforts. When we judge the quality of our decisions based on results, we can miss opportunities to improve bad decisions that just happened to turn out well and may take the wrong lessons from decisions that may have been good decisions but that turned out to have bad outcomes. A prosecutor who acted ethically

> We are forever being told that we should learn from our mistakes, but how can we learn unless we first admit that we made any?
> —Carol Tavris & Elliot Aronson[31]

in turning over exculpatory evidence to the defense and subsequently lost at trial may conclude that she made a poor decision and that honesty does not pay. Yet, the prosecutor might have lost the case even had she not turned over the exculpatory evidence and might have suffered other adverse consequences had she behaved unethically. In addition, confirmation bias (see chapter 1) may cause us to pay more attention to evidence that our decisions are good and to dismiss indications that our choices are less than stellar. And naïve realism (see chapter 1) can lead us to discount feedback from others who challenge our decisions.

Making a mistake can also lead to uncomfortable feelings of cognitive dissonance, that is, the tension that comes from trying to simultaneously hold opposing ideas in mind (see chapter 1). It is hard to maintain confidence in our competence and to simultaneously accept that we have made a mistake. This may be particularly true for attorneys. "Dissonance is bothersome under any circumstance, but it is most painful to people when an important element of their self-concept is threatened—typically when they do something that is inconsistent with their view of themselves."[32] For attorneys, who can be competitive and place a premium on achievement,[33] it can be difficult to admit mistakes.

As we have seen, it is fairly easy to come up with a range of justifications and rationalizations for poor outcomes, distorting reality to protect ourselves from having to admit mistakes. Lawyers may tell themselves that they were almost successful and would have been if it were not for that unexpected wrinkle: the alternate juror called in at the last minute, the judge who unexpectedly seemed to favor the other side, or the deposition that didn't go their way. They may come to believe that they were just off a bit on their timing or that inherently unpredictable circumstances were responsible for the error. They may convince themselves that the seeming mistake was actually a good decision, perhaps because they think it was "better to be safe than sorry."[34] They might even blame the other side. Indeed, lawyers on both sides of a case tend to attribute their inability to settle a case to the other side's unreasonableness.[35] These and other justifications can make it difficult for lawyers to turn a self-critical eye on their decisions and to learn from their mistakes.

> A great nation is like a great man:
> When he makes a mistake, he realizes it.
> Having realized it, he admits it.
> Having admitted it, he corrects it.
> He considers those who point out his faults as his most benevolent teachers.
> —Lao-Tzu[36]

Recall, too, that memories can change once a decision has been made and time has passed. For example, once we have made a decision, we tend to remember the attributes of the decision options in ways that bolster the decision we have made (see chapter 2). Our tendency to recall our decisions in a self-serving way (see chapters 2 and 4) can make them seem better than they were in fact. And hindsight bias (see chapter 4) makes us feel as if we "knew it all along." If our memory is that we had predicted what ended up happening, then we are unlikely to believe that there are mistaken predictions on which to improve.

> The greatest of faults, I should say, is to be conscious of none.
> —Thomas Carlyle[37]

In order to learn from mistakes and improve decision making, it is crucial to resist these barriers and systematically examine decisions, seeking out data and feedback about those decisions. As we saw in chapter 4, prompt feedback about the accuracy of judgments has been shown to improve future judgments. Examining the reasons for a success or failure can aid lawyers in replicating good decisions and avoiding bad ones. Similarly, it can be helpful to document decisions and expectations ahead of time and to refer back to them later to avoid the biasing influence of hindsight.

Psychological research also shows that the mindset with which we approach mistakes can make a tremendous difference in our ability to learn from them. Specifically, those with a *fixed mindset* see mistakes as an indication of incompetence or stupidity. But those with a *growth mindset* see mistakes as opportunities to learn how to do better.[39] Those with a fixed mindset may react more emotionally to mistakes, for example, feeling anger or depression, and can therefore miss out on occasions for learning and improving their skills. Consider attorney response to one judge's offer to provide feedback:

> I don't divide the world into the weak and the strong, or the successes and the failures. . . . I divide the world into the learners and nonlearners.
> —Benjamin Barber[38]

> Orange County Superior Court Judge Charles Margines[] . . . has presided over civil and criminal trials for more than 15 years. During the trials, he keeps copious notes of the attorneys' objections, questions, and arguments. At the end of the trial, he invites the attorneys into his chambers to evaluate their performance, telling them what questions they asked but should not have asked and, as one attorney said, "coaching me on some of the objections I did right and did wrong." . . . Given this singular opportunity to learn from an experienced and attentive judge who frequently has spent days watching their courtroom performance, many attorneys nevertheless decline Judge Margines' invitation to meet in his chambers and discuss their performance. "Very interestingly," Judge Margines muses, "I notice that a lot of the lawyers who really could use that don't take advantage of it."[40]

Good attorneys, in contrast, take an approach to growth that embraces, rather than avoids, such opportunities for critique.

When we do make a mistake or receive critical feedback, it is important to manage negative emotions by treating ourselves compassionately—talking to ourselves in the same way that we might counsel a good friend. This does not mean

> [I]f we can't do the emotional work of fully accepting our mistakes, we can't do the conceptual work of figuring out where, how, and why we made them.
> —Kathryn Schulz[41]

that we should give ourselves a free pass. Lawyers should strive to see their "problems, weaknesses, and shortcomings *accurately*, yet react[] with kindness and compassion rather than with self-criticism and harshness."[42] By doing so, self-compassionate lawyers are actually better able to identify their weaknesses, challenge themselves, and reach their goals.[43] And even when a mistake knocks them for a loop, it is still possible for lawyers to consider how that mistake can further their development: "You can feel miserable and still reach out for information that will help you improve. . . . It might be easier to mobilize for action if I felt better, but it doesn't matter. . . . The critical thing is to make a concrete, growth-oriented plan, and to stick to it."[44]

Explanatory Style: Lawyers and Pessimism

People differ in their typical *explanatory style*—the way in which they understand and explain the events in their lives. Those with a pessimistic explanatory style tend to gravitate toward explanations that are internal, stable or permanent, and generalizable or pervasive. Thus, someone with a pessimistic explanatory style would be more likely than someone with an optimistic explanatory style to blame himself, believe that the bad result will persist, and generalize the bad outcome to other domains. In contrast, those who tend toward a more optimistic explanatory style are more likely to make external attributions, to think of a bad outcome as a temporary setback, and to view such outcomes as isolated to the particular set of circumstances.[45]

In most domains, optimism is associated with positive effects: optimistic people have been found to be more motivated and to strive for more challenging goals, to persevere and be more productive, to feel more competent, to suffer less depression and anxiety and better physical health, and to be more liked. In contrast, pessimism is associated with a range of negative outcomes: less productivity, less persistence, more anxiety, and so on.[46]

However, the pattern may be slightly different for lawyers. A study of law students found that pessimistic law students outperformed optimistic students in law school, securing better grades and more positions on the boards of law reviews.[47] And it may be that pessimism—or prudence—is an adaptive explanatory style for some aspects of law practice. "A prudent perspective, which requires caution, skepticism and 'reality-appreciation,' may be an asset for law[yers]"[48] in that it helps lawyers to better predict and thus deal with problems that may occur in transactions or litigation.

> The ability to anticipate a [wide] range of problems that non-lawyers do not see is highly adaptive for the practicing lawyer. Indeed clients would be less effectively

served if lawyers did not so behave, even though this ability to question occasionally leads to lawyers being labeled as deal breakers or obstructionists.[49]

But the prudence that might be adaptive for some aspects of practice may not be adaptive for other aspects of practice or for lawyers in their lives more generally. "[P]essimists are more likely than optimists to believe that they will not make partner, that their profession is a racket, or that the economy is headed for disaster."[50] This style of thinking can be a recipe for unhappiness to the extent that it permeates the way that lawyers approach their own careers, their families, and their lives more generally.

The challenge for lawyers, then, is to adopt a sort of *flexible optimism* that capitalizes on their pessimistic explanatory style when it comes to anticipating problems for clients but adopts a more optimistic explanatory style when it comes to other aspects of lawyering or life. Using the techniques of *learned optimism*, lawyers can become skilled at identifying pessimistic thoughts and questioning their accuracy and utility. In critically examining the identified pessimistic thoughts, lawyers can begin to separate out those that are valid and should inspire corrective or forward-moving action and those that are not accurate or useful and should be replaced with a more optimistic style of thinking.[51]

Catherine Gage O'Grady, professor of law, gives the example of an associate who has appeared near the bottom of the firm's billable hours ranking. The pessimistic associate might make an internal attribution: "I'm not working as hard as the other associates." Furthermore, the pessimistic associate might suppose that this

✦ ✦ ✦ ✦ ✦

Conversations with Ourselves

One way to deal with pessimistic thoughts is by engaging in effective self-talk:

> [I]magine that one day you find yourself repeating the following prediction: "I am going to totally blow this case." The anxious emotions and behavior that such a thought is likely to create require you to at least evaluate its validity. Cross-examine yourself the same way that you would a witness. Say to yourself: "How do you know that you are going to blow this case even before it has begun? How many times has that happened to you in the past, even though you have said the same thing? Maybe what you really mean is that you need more time to prepare. Your original statement is not based on fact; it is your own insecurity jumping to negative conclusions. You are paying an emotional price for it, so get yourself together, and revise your original statement. The truth is that you just need more time to prepare."[52]

state of affairs will be permanent: "I'm going to be at the bottom of this ranking every month. . . . I'll never learn how to bill more hours and improve my performance." Finally, the pessimistic associate might conclude that the ranking speaks more generally about her functioning: "I'll probably fall flat on my face when I argue that motion to dismiss next week. . . . I can't seem to get anything right—I'm a poor attorney at work and a poor [parent] at home." Through learned optimism, however, the associate can make different (less internal, permanent, or global) attributions: "The partners did not give me enough work this month, even though I asked for it." "I cannot compare myself to these other associates—I'm raising two young children and working full time and they have more time to devote solely to work." "I just had a poor showing this month because I got the flu, but that's behind me now." "I may not be great at administrative timekeeping and office paperwork, but I'm going to nail the motion to dismiss next week."[53]

The Choke: Keeping Cool Under Pressure

Performing well under pressure—whether in a crucial negotiation, a pivotal client meeting, a decisive deposition, or a key closing argument—is an essential skill for attorneys. But stressful conditions can cause us to *choke*—to perform "worse than expected given what [we] are capable of doing, and worse than what [we] have in the past."[54]

Pressure can affect even the most experienced of performers. During the inauguration of Barack Obama in 2009, Chief Justice John Roberts changed the words in the presidential oath of office from ". . . that I will faithfully execute the office of President of the United States" to ". . . that I will execute the office of president to the United States faithfully." This little flub resulted in Obama having to retake the oath of office later that evening. In a similar public situation, Christina Aguilera forgot and then improvised the words to the national anthem during the 2011 Super Bowl. Both Chief Justice Roberts and Aguilera knew what they were supposed to be saying (or singing), but the pressure of the moment was enough to cause them to be unable to deliver in the moment.

When we are engaged in an activity that requires cognitive effort—say, legal analysis or negotiation—a high degree of stress can interfere with the ways in which the different parts of the brain communicate with each other, can make it difficult to inhibit unwanted emotions and behaviors, and can make us slip into less effortful shortcuts in our thinking. Worry and self-doubt can deplete the cognitive resources that would otherwise be available for deliberative and analytical thought.[55] Under stress, we may forget to say things that we intended to say, give in when we should stand our ground, fight when we should compromise, express things best left unsaid, use an inappropriate tone or decibel level, or rush through our statements.

To make matters worse, our interpretations of our stress reactions can compound the effects of stress on our performance. In particular, the fact that we are nervous may itself make us more nervous: "There is no way I can do well in this argument—I am just too nervous." Moreover, we are not always good at identifying the source of our feelings. Recall the study participants who were more likely to make a follow-up call to the attractive researcher when they met her on the anxiety-producing Capilano Suspension Bridge rather than when they met her after they were on solid ground with enough time passing for the thrill of the bridge to abate (see chapter 3). So, too, can people make different attributions about their reactions to stress. Those who focus on the pressure as a negative ("oh, shit, my heart is racing—I am really feeling the pressure now") rather than as something more positive ("my heart is racing—it must mean I am motivated") are more likely to succumb to the anxiety that makes deliberative thought more difficult.[56]

Ironically, it can be those who are the highest performers who are most adversely affected by stress. Interference with processing capacity makes a bigger difference for those who tend to engage in more complex patterns of thought and analysis.

> [I]ndividuals with the most cognitive horsepower tend to be bad at downplaying the importance of high-pressure testing situations when they find themselves under the gun, so they also have a hard time easing the pressure when the stress is on. High-performing people really feel the pressure, which hurts their ability to succeed.[57]

Thus, it can be important to do what psychologist Sian Beilock called *pausing the choke*—calling a temporary halt before, during, and after the task or decision. Pausing at the outset to think through the problem can help us focus on relevant aspects of the problem, help to avoid distraction, and allow time to think about the problem broadly. Pausing during the task can give us time to deliberate rather than falling back on heuristic thinking. And pausing after the task gives us time to regroup and recharge cognitively so that the pressure and cognitive strain of one situation does not bleed over into the next.[58] For example, an attorney who is going into an important deposition could pause prior to the deposition to carefully plan carefully strategy, take breaks during the deposition to consider whether she had covered all the issues she wanted to cover, and pause again afterward before starting her next task.

It can also be helpful to prepare for stressful conditions by practicing under some degree of pressure. For example, in one study, police officers who engaged in target practice under pressure—that is, with an antagonist who fired back (with colored pellets)—later performed better under pressure than did officers who had practiced without such pressure (shooting at cardboard targets).[59] Practicing under even moderate amounts of stress can improve performance in tasks that will occur under higher levels of stress.[60] Thus, lawyers who engage in mock arguments in front of an audience are not only gaining insights into the types of questions that judges might ask but also are learning to handle their own stress.

It is also the case that "people are often nervous about looking nervous.... This thought—that the audience is aware of just how nervous he or she feels—may ironically serve to make the speaker all the more nervous."[61] But people tend to overestimate the degree to which they appear nervous to others. Fortunately, remembering this illusion of transparency (see chapter 3) can help to alleviate this disconnect. Indeed, one study found that presenters who were told about the illusion of transparency still experienced nervousness about their presentations but thought that they appeared less nervous to others. Observers indicated that such presenters did in fact appear more composed and gave better presentations than those who did not know about the illusion of transparency.[62]

Sometimes falling apart under pressure is a problem caused by *too much* cognitive processing. When we overthink a highly practiced task, what Beilock called *paralysis by analysis* can cause us to flub even the most routine of tasks, particularly those that operate outside of our conscious awareness. While this problem is more likely to be seen with elite athletes (errant golf shots and missed free throws), it can also affect the routine or well-rehearsed tasks of nonathletes, such as Chief Justice Roberts improperly administering the oath of office to Barack Obama.[63] In these circumstances, thinking less is likely to improve performance under pressure.

Consider how these different types of choking might influence how lawyers plan for oral argument. When the lawyer is delivering a well-rehearsed opening statement or argument, it might be best not to overthink but simply allow the argument to flow. When it comes to fielding questions from judges, however, it is important to take the time to deliberate about the answers. As Beilock notes:

> Sometimes you may need several different pressure-fighting strategies at once—as when you find yourself delivering an important presentation that you've practiced to perfection while at the same time you have to field difficult questions on the fly. To succeed in this pressure-filled situation, you will not only have to combat worries, you will also have to make sure you don't exert too much control over your well-practiced speech routine.[64]

Collaboration

In the movies, lawyers are often portrayed as lone rangers. However, in real life, being a lawyer requires working with others. Most lawyers work in firms of varying sizes, government agencies, or corporate legal departments and need to collaborate with their peers, their bosses, and their subordinates. Attorneys in all settings need to collaborate with their secretaries and paralegals. And, of course, attorneys work with clients and need to pay attention to generating and managing those relationships.

Managing Impressions

It is often important for attorneys to make a good impression on others, such as colleagues, opposing counsel, regulators, and current and potential clients. Junior attorneys at law firms or government agencies particularly need to impress the bosses. To generate and retain business, attorneys need to impress clients. To a certain extent, of course, hard work and success will impress, and a lazy or incompetent attorney will have a hard time impressing others. But even attorneys who are hardworking and competent can fail to impress because they do not pay sufficient attention to other factors.

First Impressions
The old adage advises not to judge a book by its cover, and yet we all do. People take cues from attorneys' appearance and initial behavior. For example, many may assume that an attorney who dresses in a sloppy fashion will do sloppy work as well.

Similarly, the nature of people's interactions with others, especially their early interactions, can also make a substantial impression. In one study, researchers found that negotiators' speech patterns during the first five minutes of a negotiation predicted ultimate negotiation outcomes.[65] Interviews have shown that people who are less demanding in their initial salary negotiations are respected less. This finding may be double edged for women given studies finding that women who negotiated harder in salary negotiations are viewed less favorably than their male counterparts.[66] Along similar lines, it is important to remember that the effects of particular conversations can follow a person for a long time. Telling an off-color joke or appearing at a bond closing on October 31 in a Halloween costume may raise lasting questions about one's judgment. On a more positive note, making a key insightful comment or even asking an excellent question may have a lasting positive impact.

The Importance of Face Time
Young lawyers who believe that they will be judged solely or primarily on their work product may be tempted to simply work hard every day, keep their doors shut, and do excellent work. Such lawyers may be shocked to find that they are not necessarily perceived or treated as well as a colleague who, while producing less exceptional work product, spends more time networking and interacting with others.

"From the associate's perspective, . . . it is a potentially colossal mistake to assume that 'all I really need to do is to put in my time.' Most firms will view hard work (within reason) as a necessary, but not sufficient, condition for admission to partnership."[67]

In a work environment, it is often important to not only get the job done but also to spend time with coworkers and superiors.[68] Attention to the importance of face time can be particularly important for women: studies have shown that women tend to focus more than men do on getting the job done while ignoring the more social aspects of the workplace.[69] This face time may include schmoozing at meetings, eating or playing softball together, or chitchatting at the water cooler. Young lawyers should pay attention to their general level of interaction with senior lawyers in the firm:

- Do you spend all or most of your days in your own office?
- Have you shared a meal with any of the senior lawyers in your group?
- Do you have some basic understanding (from them) of what kinds of work and what kinds of clients occupy their time?
- Do these senior lawyers have a basic understanding (from you) of your talents and interests?
- Do you know something about their personal lives (and vice versa)?

Lawyers need not be social butterflies—and the quality of their work product certainly matters—but they should adopt a general goal of having at least enough contact with senior lawyers in the firm to avoid feeling isolated and out of step.[70]

Liking and Mimicry

People tend to like others to whom they are similar (see chapter 6). As we have seen, these similarities may include appearance, background, interests, or even features such as shared birthdays or names. While some aspects of appearance or background cannot be changed, it is certainly possible for lawyers to emphasize or even develop interests that they may share with influential members of the organization or with clients. If the leaders of the firm or agency are excited by biking or opera or NASCAR racing, it may be worthwhile to explore some of those same interests. But be careful—the novice who agrees to go on a twenty-mile mountain bike ride may hurt her body as well as her career.

Knowing that people tend to like those who agree with them, lawyers might be tempted to try to curry favor with bosses or clients by agreeing with their stated opinions. Of course, obvious brownnosing or ingratiation can easily backfire, so lawyers must do so with some degree of care. Moreover, to do good work and to act ethically, it will often be necessary to state a contrary position (see chapters 5 and 14).

We have seen (see chapter 7) that one means of developing rapport is to subtly mimic the mannerisms of another person in order to develop feelings of similarity, create a better impression, achieve greater cooperation, conduct more effective negotiations, and so on. Thus, subtly mirroring the speech patterns, postures, or facial expressions of a partner, colleague, or potential client may be useful. Yet, common sense is important—the associate who puts her feet on the partner's desk, or even on her own in the presence of the partner, is not likely to fare well.

Working in Groups

Communication

Communication is a key factor in working with others. However, recall the difficulties of perspective taking (see chapter 1) and the curse of knowledge (see chapter 7). These phenomena mean that attorneys will need to remember that things that are obvious to them will often not be clear to others. Thus, as attorneys give assignments to others, they must be very explicit regarding what kind of work product they are seeking and what format that work product should take. Similarly, when given an assignment, attorneys should be sure to clarify the expectations. *Draft a short memo* can have very different meanings to different attorneys in different contexts. It is also advisable for the work assigner and the work assignee to check back in with each other to make sure the work is proceeding appropriately. Listening to the concerns of the people to whom a project has been assigned rather than simply barking orders can not only ensure that assignments are understandable but also enhance the rapport that we have seen is key for good communication (see chapter 7). Good rapport among team members can help ensure that all are working hard to achieve a common end. When rapport is lacking, commitment to the common enterprise may be lacking as well.[71]

These days, much collaboration takes place using e-mail, instant messaging, and other forms of electronic communication. Electronic communication is marvelously convenient and allows communication that is nonsimultaneous and that occurs quickly across great distances. As we discussed in chapter 7, however, electronic communication also poses some risks. Because e-mail and text messaging are asynchronous and exclusively text-based, they create a greater risk of misunderstanding than face-to-face or even phone conversations. In addition, they foster anonymity and lack the nonverbal information present in other modes of communication. Thus, collaborators who rely on electronic communication may find it more difficult to trust one another than collaborators who use other forms of communication. Accordingly, attorneys who collaborate electronically should make special efforts to use good written etiquette, develop rapport, and take steps to ensure that both sides have an accurate understanding of all issues.[72] It can also be desirable to supplement the use of electronic communication with face-to-face meetings:

> Physical contact has a half-life. When people meet face to face, they can leverage that over a pretty lean communication medium for a while and the relationship will not degrade. But after a while, they need to get back together face to face to recharge the trust, the engagement, and the loyalty in the relationship.[73]

Sometimes face-to-face communication is impossible or economically infeasible. Attorneys who collaborate with colleagues in branch offices in different cities or whose clients are thousands of miles away face real hurdles. However, today's technology—including Skype, videoconferencing, and mobile robots—supports communication at a distance and contains many of the positive features of face-to-face communication.[74] Thus, even without significant face time, collaborators can use the schmoozing techniques that researchers have found facilitate online communications (see chapter 7).

Group Decision Making

Groups make decisions differently than do individuals. These differences offer opportunities for increased success and productivity but also reveal some potential pitfalls for collaborators. On the positive side, we learned, in chapter 4, about the wisdom of crowds. Because we all see the world from different perspectives, we are often well served by seeking and incorporating the opinions of others into our predictions and decisions. Thus, whether we are predicting how a jury will see a case, whether a merger will prove profitable, or the odds that a government agency will issue a particular set of regulations, we benefit from having full discussions with others on our team.

On the other hand, as we saw in chapter 5, the train of thought pursued by a group may inhibit other avenues of thought that its members might have independently pursued, and groups tend to discuss shared information to the neglect of distinctive information and perspectives. Pluralistic ignorance and the illusion of consensus may lead members of a group to ignore problems that have been noticed by individuals but not raised with the group. Recall, too, the experiment that we described in chapter 6 in which experimenters watched groups of people remain in a room becoming filled with smoke as they inferred from each other's lack of reaction that the situation must be safe. And in chapter 14, we saw how attorneys' adherence to group practices or norms can lead to ethical missteps. Members of groups may go along with the crowd both because they base their opinions on what others seem to believe and because they hesitate to publicly break with group norms.

However, encouraging lawyers to express their individuality can create opportunities for success. Behind most unique arguments is a lawyer who dared to try something different or to make an argument that others believed was doomed to fail. Consider just a few "innovative solutions to seemingly intractable legal problems" that have been developed by lawyers:

- Elimination of the privity requirement (that a manufacturer was only liable to the purchaser of a product) in product liability
- Recovery of compensatory damages for emotional distress
- The creation of a common law and later of a constitutional "right to privacy"
- Joint custody
- Same-sex marriage
- Condominiums, cooperatives, and the corporation
- Pornography as a violation of civil rights
- Sexual harassment as a violation of sex discrimination laws
- Truth and reconciliation commissions
- The joint venture
- The "poison pill" as a response to a threatened hostile takeover
- The political action committee (PAC) and its successors[75]

Note, similarly, that in 1908 when Louis Brandeis first prepared his highly fact-intensive brief in *Muller v. Oregon*, his co-counsel was so skeptical of the endeavor that they prepared an additional, backup brief. Eventually, of course, the innovative "Brandeis Brief" was not only accepted by the Court but also praised in the majority opinion.[76] Attorneys and firms should be careful not to allow group dynamics and processes to stifle such creativity.

The complications of group decision making go beyond the limits of information sharing. As we noted in chapter 5, psychological studies have shown that the process of group deliberation can lead a group to take positions that are more extreme than those of the individual members of the group. Thus, if members of the firm start to express the view that a plaintiff has a strong case, these expressed views may lead the members of the group to believe in that case even more strongly than they did before the meeting started. Jonathan Harr's book *A Civil Action* illustrates how this extremism can play out. Recall, as we described in chapter 11, that when Harvard law professor Charles Nesson urged plaintiffs' counsel to seek a punitive damage award of more than $500 million, plaintiffs' counsel adopted a negotiation position so extreme that it proved impossible for them to settle the case.[77]

To generate the full array of opinions in an organization, it may be necessary for the leaders to take specific steps to encourage all members of the group to state their views even if those views appear to depart from the norm. A partner at a law firm, for example, might want to specifically invite individual associates, paralegals, or secretaries to provide their sense of a case because those who are not expressly invited to opine may well remain silent. Recall our discussion in chapter 5 of how Supreme Court Justices state their views in order of seniority. We noted that reversing this sort of practice by encouraging junior members of the organization to speak first may better induce a full expression of views. Because junior team members may understandably be reticent about airing nonconformist views, it is critically important for senior attorneys to ensure that such junior team members are not harmed for stating such views. If a firm or agency were to ask its associates and paralegals to state their views and it later became known that senior attorneys in the firm or agency were using those views against the associates and paralegals, soon no junior members of the staff would be willing to offer frank commentary.

Group Cohesion

Modern law firms and government agencies face substantial threats to their group cohesion and morale. Considering the very real fear of layoffs, pay cuts, extreme billing and workload pressures, intrafirm squabbling over compensation, and the threat that key lawyers will leave, the modern law firm may more closely resemble a dysfunctional family than a cohesive environment.

> All that year, the animals worked like slaves. But they were happy in their work; they grudged no effort or sacrifice, well aware that everything that they did was for the benefit of themselves and those of their kind who would come after them.
> —George Orwell[78]

But group cohesion is important to quality work: cohesive groups add up to more than the sum of their parts. Examining groups such as military units, airplane crews, and factory work teams, psychologists have learned that a group's cohesion is related to its effectiveness. At a minimum, substantial interpersonal squabbling can be detrimental to a group's performance. And because differences of opinion can be useful for exploring all options and avoiding blind adherence to a single course of action, law organizations should try to take steps to build trust and manage conflicts when they do arise.[79] Similarly, expressing gratitude for a job well done, using good planning techniques to minimize work incursions into team members' personal time, communicating clearly, and soliciting suggestions so that all members of the team feel like they are a part of the enterprise can help build team cohesion.[80]

> ✦ ✦ ✦ ✦ ✦
> **Corporate Morale Boosting**
>
> Some high-tech companies, such as Microsoft, Google, and Pixar, have taken the project of morale boosting very seriously. Microsoft provides its employees with flexible schedules that cater to both night owls and early birds; access to an on-site gym; free health care, including free physician house calls; and unlimited free soda while at work. Google provides employees with similar perks and also generously funds savings and tuition plans, supports charitable giving, and encourages employees to spend a portion of their time on-the-clock on projects that interest them personally. Pixar provides opportunities for recreation (soccer, anyone?) as well as for education through Pixar University. Some law firms are introducing similar perks programs for their attorneys and (in some cases) their paralegals, clerks, and legal assistants, providing, for example, additional vacations or sabbaticals, flextime and telecommuting arrangements, gift cards, leadership development opportunities, child-care programs, and company-expensed cocktail hours to cut stress while increasing loyalty and productivity.[81]

Mentoring

Upon completing law school in 1933, Thurgood Marshall sought a job from Warner McGuinn, one of the best-known black lawyers in Maryland at the time. McGuinn promptly turned down the future Supreme Court Justice, stating that Marshall was unbelievably good and telling him, "You're going to practice by yourself and get your brains kicked out and then come back to me and we'll talk." Although upset at McGuinn's reaction, Marshall had a mentor from that point on who counseled him on the political scene in Baltimore, referred clients to him, and encouraged him to never give up.[82]

Given the importance of interpersonal relationships, it can be very beneficial for junior attorneys to obtain mentors and for senior attorneys to mentor those who are junior to them. Studies have shown that lawyers who have mentors tend to earn more, progress more rapidly in their careers, possess greater commitment to the organization, and be more satisfied with their careers.[83] Psychology suggests that mentors are important not only because they teach their protégés how to do the job more competently but also because they become internal advocates for those protégés. In a field like law, where many aspects of performance are difficult to measure objectively,[84] it can be particularly helpful to have an advocate who spreads the word that "Jack is a very bright, hardworking attorney." Indeed, mentors can provide "sponsorship, exposure and visibility, coaching, protection, and challenging assignments." In addition, mentors can provide assistance of a more interpersonal nature through "role modeling, acceptance and confirmation, counseling, and friendship."[85]

Given the range of functions that mentoring relationships can serve, it is often useful to have more than one mentor.[86] For example, an attorney might have mentors who have different levels of experience or who are of different races or genders. In this regard, one interesting study found that women at law firms who had male mentors earned substantially more than women at law firms who had female mentors but that women lawyers with female mentors received greater emotional or psychological benefits such as career satisfaction than did those with male mentors.[87]

> ✦ ✦ ✦ ✦ ✦
>
> **Mentoring and Lay Theories of Motivation**
>
> Mentors should take care to remember that there is a tendency to think that others are more motivated than we are by extrinsic incentives (for example, money) and less motivated than we are by intrinsic incentives (for example, learning something new, facing a new challenge, making a difference, and so on) (see chapter 1).
>
> Consider a study of 486 prospective lawyers, who were questioned by Kaplan Educational Centers during their preparation for the Law School Admissions Test. They were asked to describe their own motives for pursuing a legal career and to speculate about the motives of their peers. Sixty-four percent said that they were pursuing a legal career because it was intellectually appealing or because they had always been interested in the law, but only 12% thought so about their *peers*. Instead, 62% speculated that their peers were pursuing a legal career because of financial rewards. Thus, their lay theories stressed their peers' response to money and denied their peers' intellectual interest in the law.[88]
>
> Similarly, managers tend to focus on the external motives of employees to the neglect of more intrinsic motivators.[89] To the extent that the same lay theories of motivation influence lawyers in their mentoring roles, mentors might overlook particularly important aspects of the role, such as helping protégés to find challenging assignments, to find meaning in their work, and to find balance between work and the rest of their lives.

From the mentor's perspective, mentoring provides "the assistance on projects provided by proteges, reputational status for developing new talent within firms, and personal benefits of friendship, respect, and recognition for their senior status and expertise."[90] Mentors may be able to count on their protégé as a devoted helper even in last-minute situations and other grueling circumstances. Indeed, "[r]ainmakers are always looking to leverage their fortunes with talent, and sometimes the competition among partners for the top talent in the firm is fierce."[91] Furthermore, as we will see later in the chapter, assisting others is satisfying and associated with a greater sense of well-being.

While some firms or agencies may have formal mentoring programs in which they assign particular senior attorneys to mentor junior attorneys, junior attorneys can often benefit from finding mentors more informally. The prospective protégé might appeal to the mentor's self-interest, highlighting the benefits that a senior attorney would gain by spending time mentoring a junior attorney.[92] Capitalizing on the psychology of liking (see chapter 6), potential protégés can seek to highlight commonalities between themselves and the prospective mentor and use subtle flattery to their benefit. For their part, senior attorneys may look for associates who show promise. Interestingly, but perhaps not surprisingly, lawyers who show more commitment to their careers are more likely to have mentors.[93] Of course, to maintain a good relationship with the mentor, the protégé should remember to frequently thank the mentor for his help.

Rainmaking

As their careers mature, those lawyers who work at private firms must typically focus on generating business, or rainmaking. One author put it this way: "Economic strength in the private practice of law is found in one's ability to find and sign business. This is called 'rainmaking.'" The same author identified other, less senior members of the firm as *grinders* and *minders*:

> The grinder is the foot soldier, the infantryman who is getting the actual work completed. This is where most of us start—getting in early, staying late, working weekends, doing the traveling, and generally burning the midnight oil. . . .

> The "minder" is one step up from the "grinder." The minder, besides billing hours and completing work, may be given the opportunity to work directly with the client. This person has client contact, attends meetings, and often stands in the rainmaker's shoes by fielding phone calls and visiting the client when the rainmaker is unavailable. The minder is asked to sit in on meetings because of some attribute that has distinguished him or her from the grinder. It may be personality, special skills, legal talent, or, most likely, a combination of all of these that leads the rainmaker to select his minders.[94]

At many firms, the goal is to go from grinder to minder to rainmaker and then to retain a position as rainmaker. Sole practitioners or members of very small firms must become rainmakers right away in order for their firms to succeed.

Good business development involves a mix of salesmanship, persuasion, and good communication. The attorney must impress a potential client with both her expertise and her concern for the client, convincing the potential client that the attorney is highly capable, will provide the client with good value, will look out for the client's interests, and will be someone with whom the client will have an effective relationship. To be successful, the attorney must be a good communicator (see chapter 7), a good interviewer (see chapter 9), and a good persuader (see chapter 6). One of the greatest challenges for the attorney doing business development may be to use perspective taking (see chapter 1) to figure out how best to attract a particular client.

> ✦ ✦ ✦ ✦ ✦
> **Building Trust with a Potential Client**
>
> Think about how asking questions, considering the client's perspective, reciprocity, liking, rapport, and trust (see chapters 6 and 7) might work together to help generate business by considering one client's experience in seeking an attorney:
>
> David ... once had to hire a lawyer to probate a relative's will. The first few lawyers he spoke with tried to win his business by telling him when their firm was founded, how many offices they had, and how much they would charge. None of this inspired much confidence. In fact, the more they talked about themselves and their firms, the less interested they appeared to be in David and his problems.
>
> Finally, he encountered a lawyer who, in the initial phone call, asked how much David knew about probating a will. David's reply was "Nothing!" The lawyer then offered to fax to David a comprehensive outline of the steps involved, what he needed to do immediately, and what he should forget about for a while because it was not urgent. The fax also provided the phone numbers of all the governmental bodies David needed to notify, even though this had nothing to do with the legal work (or the lawyer's fees).
>
> All of this (immensely helpful) information was provided freely (and for free) before the lawyer had been retained. He had built confidence by demonstrating that he knew what information was most relevant to David, even though some of it had nothing to do with the practice of estate law. He had earned trust by being generous with his knowledge and proving that he was willing to earn the potential client's business.[95]

An attorney who seeks to attract a business client may want to use a broad range of skills. Imagine that Charles is a partner at a major firm who is seeking to convince Derrick, president of Widgets Inc., to retain Charles's firm to handle a bond deal. The deal is important to Widgets Inc., so Charles can be sure that Derrick and his company will process the arguments carefully. However, we know that more unconscious peripheral processing may also occur.

To establish credibility, Charles may want to convey his expertise by letting Derrick know that he and his firm have successfully handled similar representation for other clients in the past. Charles may want to highlight the credentials of attorneys in the firm. He will want to use a manner of speaking and delivery that comes across as fluent and powerful. Remember, also, that by admitting to weak points in their argument, people can establish their trustworthiness. Thus, Charles might state,

> I know that we are not the only firm in town and that XYZ firm has handled more of these types of matters than we have. But, frankly, I think we can do a better job. I believe the greater depth that we have in our bankruptcy department is exactly what you need for this matter.

We have seen that it is easier to sell a concept that is relatively concrete. Thus, rather than talk in vague abstractions, Charles might want to focus on a few specific benefits of retaining his firm:

> I believe that you will be happy with our services with regard to this bond issuance because we will cover all of your due diligence bases, pay attention to detail, get the work done in a timely fashion, and charge you a fair fee. It will be up to you to decide how you want to staff this matter. Unlike some firms, we won't insist on staffing the deal with junior attorneys who are still learning their way around a bond deal.

Such concrete arguments will also help Derrick justify his decision by giving him specific reasons that he can point to in support of his decision (see chapter 5).

Recall, too, the methods of influence that we discussed in chapter 6. Charles may use the reciprocity norm by offering Derrick a cold drink or taking him out to play golf. He could use the door-in-the-face technique by first asking Derrick if he would consider having Charles's firm handle all of Widgets Inc.'s business. Or, Charles might use the foot-in-the-door technique by trying to get a small piece of Derrick's business first. If Charles's firm already has some of Widgets Inc.'s business, Charles can note that the firm already represents the company with respect to its immigration needs and that the same level of talent would be marshaled to do a good job for the company on the bond deal. Charles might also use social proof by noting that several other sizable companies have already retained Charles's firm to handle bond deals. In this regard, it can be helpful for the potential client to talk with satisfied clients[96] (while respecting client confidences): "Derrick, you know that we have represented ABC Corp. for many years. If it would be helpful, I am sure that their president, Jeannette Price, would be happy to chat with you about how satisfied they have been with our work."

Finally, the lawyer must begin to develop rapport and build trust with the potential client so that the client feels that the lawyer understands his needs and would be looking out for the client's best interests. As we discussed in chapter 7, Charles can build trust by focusing on the client, listening effectively, using body language to communicate openness, and communicating concern for the needs of Derrick and Widgets Inc. As one commentator advises,

> I strongly advise that you begin every personal contact by spending a significant amount of time listening to your guest. You should ask questions to elicit information about the potential client's business or practice. Most people like to talk about themselves and will be turned off if you start talking about yourself right off the bat.[97]

> ✦ ✦ ✦ ✦ ✦
> **Building Relationships**
>
> Consider how Jim Copeland, the CEO of Deloitte & Touche, worked to build a relationship with a new corporate client following a merger:
>
> > [This client] leads with power, energy, wants to overwhelm you, to let you know who's in charge. And I didn't fight that. I just kept saying, "Tell me more about that problem. How did it happen, how did it come about, what's going on?" I wanted to know why he was upset and what it would take to fix things. Basically I was there for him and let him know that. You just start with an attitude that, by gosh, you are going to set things right, and to do that you have to totally focus on the client and the client's problems. . . .
> >
> > So, [the client] got the message that I cared about him, and wouldn't let things go by that weren't right for him. Years later, we had a chance to pitch a project to him, $5 million, a pretty big project in those days, and at the end of the pitch, he just looked at me and said, "Do *you* think I should do this?" meaning that if I could look him in the eye and say, "You bet," then he had me on the line to do the right thing for him. And he knew that if I didn't believe that, I wouldn't look him in the eye and say so, because he knew he could trust me. And I was able to say, in this case, "Absolutely you should do it; you need this, and we'll do great work for you."[98]

Maintaining Client Relationships

The effective rainmaker and her team must be successful not only at securing the client initially but also at maintaining good client relations throughout the representation. By serving clients well and making clients feel well represented, attorneys will increase the likelihood that satisfied clients will bring more of their business to the attorney and will refer other potential clients to the attorney.

In addition to doing good legal work, keeping the client informed about that work can help build trust and confidence. The attorney should send the client copies of central correspondence (including e-mails) and filings in the case so that the client is aware of all the work the attorney is doing on her behalf. Indeed, a large proportion of client complaints to attorney disciplinary bodies stem from attorneys' failure to communicate well with their clients.[99] Although it may not be appropriate to send copies of all filings and other communications, particularly in a large, paper-heavy case, the attorney can consult with the client to determine what documents the client would like to see.

It can also be helpful to generate and capitalize on opportunities to demonstrate reliability to clients. Setting interim deadlines and then meeting them or committing to specific tasks (for example, producing a report or making a phone call) and then completing them in a timely fashion can show clients that the attorney can be trusted to follow through.[100]

Similarly, it can be useful to provide a client with something tangible to reflect the work that was done on the client's behalf. One benefit of sending a client a lengthy deed of trust or summary judgment brief is that the client can see and feel the heft of the work that the attorney has done on behalf of the client. Sometimes the tangible reflection of the attorney's work may be more superficial. While the client may not completely understand the legal research or analysis reflected in the document, he may appreciate the professional look of the document with its polished text and custom-made folder. The minimal extra expense for the fancy folder may generate a positive feeling of reciprocity in the same way as the offer of a soda (see chapter 6), particularly if the client is not billed for that fancy folder.

Finally, it is important to recognize that billing statements to clients are not always a well-received form of communication. Indeed, bills that contain surprisingly high figures or that are not well explained may cause clients to lose faith in their attorneys. As we discussed in chapter 7, perceived betrayals of trust spark very strong negative reactions. Thus, it is essential that the attorney give the client a sense, in the beginning of the representation, of what kinds of bills to expect. The attorney can also draw on the framing literature discussed in chapter 5 to make bills more palatable. For example, an attorney can reframe a loss as a gain by preparing the client for a monthly bill that might be as high as $10,000 and then providing the client with a pleasant surprise when the bill is "only" $8,000. Similarly, the attorney might reframe a loss as a gain by telling the client that she discounted the bill from $10,000 to $8,000 in recognition of the client's long-standing relationship with the firm. Again, the client will likely appreciate the "gain" of $2,000 even though she still owes $8,000.

> [W]e all want happiness. And happiness, I am sure from having known many successful men, cannot be won simply by being counsel for great corporations and having an income of fifty thousand dollars. An intellect great enough to win the prize needs other food besides success.
>
> —Oliver Wendell Holmes Jr.[102]

Attorney Happiness and Well-Being

The familiar lilting song says, "Don't worry, be happy."[101] But lawyers do tend to worry, and lawyers vary in terms of their happiness. As we will see, many lawyers report being relatively satisfied with their lives and jobs, but at the same time there are varying sources of dissatisfaction. As we learned in chapter 3 it is possible to experience a mix of satisfaction and dissatisfaction. Most of us have good days and bad days and confront aspects of our jobs and lives that we love and other facets that frustrate us.

But what does it mean to be happy? Psychologists often talk in terms of *well-being*—having lots of (but not exclusively) positive emotions, being engaged and finding meaning in life activities and accomplishments, and participating in satisfying relationships with others. These components of well-being have implications for attorneys as they strive to be happy in their work and their broader life activities. Although attorneys who are unhappy or otherwise distressed can learn much from the psychology of happiness, even those attorneys who are relatively satisfied with their lives and jobs can benefit from paying attention to their own well-being.

> **"** What I love the most about being a lawyer is freedom. In 35 years, I have had three different careers in law, and even within those careers, I have been free to pursue my own professional desires.
> —Attorney Lee Nation[103] **"**

Lawyer Satisfaction

Are lawyers happy? A recent national survey conducted by the National Opinion Research Center (NORC) found that lawyers were more satisfied with their lives than not (scoring 2.37 on a scale of 1 ("very dissatisfied") to 4 ("very satisfied")), with 43% of lawyers reporting that they were very satisfied in general.[104] Similarly, in a 2007 study of lawyers who graduated from the University of Virginia in 1990, 85.5% reported that they were extremely or moderately satisfied with their lives generally, with only 14.5% reporting dissatisfaction.[105] This is quite similar to levels of satisfaction in the broader U.S. population: in a recent poll by the Pew Research Center, 84% of respondents reported that they were either "very" or "pretty" happy.[106]

Lawyers also report relatively high job satisfaction. The NORC survey found that although the legal profession was not among the twelve most satisfied professions surveyed, lawyers' reported job satisfaction was "above average" (scoring 3.33 on the 1-to-4 scale), with 52.4% of lawyers reporting that they were very satisfied with their jobs.[107] Similarly, data from the *After the JD* project, which surveyed a national sample representative of those who became lawyers in 2000, found that 79% of these lawyers reported being extremely or moderately satisfied with their decision to become a lawyer, while 13% expressed dissatisfaction with their choice.[108]

Recent studies examining lawyers who graduated from particular schools or who work in particular legal markets report similar findings. For example, a University of Virginia study found that 81.3% of respondents reported that they were extremely or moderately satisfied with their choice to become a lawyer.[109] Studies of lawyers who graduated from the University of Michigan across several decades have found that a relatively high proportion of them reported being satisfied with their careers.[110] And a study of Chicago lawyers conducted in the mid-1990s found that 84% expressed satisfaction with their jobs and 77% indicated that if they could do it over, they would still choose to be a lawyer.[111]

These broad outlines, however, can obscure variation in job satisfaction within the profession and across different aspects of the job. For example, attorneys tend to express relatively high satisfaction with aspects of their jobs such as their level of responsibility, the degree of control they have over how they engage in their work, the intellectual challenge and problem-solving aspects of the work, and their relationships with their colleagues. In contrast, attorneys tend to be less satisfied with other aspects of their jobs, including how they are evaluated, the opportunities they have to engage in pro bono work, their control over the amount of work that they have to do, and the value of their work to society.[112]

Practice setting also matters to job satisfaction. Lawyers in private practice tend to be more satisfied than lawyers in other settings with respect to the intellectual challenge and problem-solving aspects of the profession, but less satisfied with the social value of their work and the degree to which they are able to achieve work-life balance. Attorneys who work in large private firms tend to be more satisfied with their level of compensation, the opportunities they have for advancement, and the prestige of their jobs; but they tend to be less satisfied with the degree to which they control the amount of work they have to engage in and less satisfied overall. In contrast, government attorneys tend to be "more satisfied with the social value of their work and the balance of their work and professional lives than those in private practice."[113]

Attorneys who graduated from lower-tier law schools tend to be more satisfied with their decision to become a lawyer than those who graduated from elite schools. Attorneys who work in metropolitan areas tend to be less satisfied with their jobs than those in less populated areas. Those who are able to engage in more hours of pro bono work tend to be more satisfied overall, as do those who feel that they are able to achieve a suitable balance between work and family. Attorneys with higher incomes are more satisfied, and satisfaction increases the longer an attorney is in practice. Furthermore, partners tend to be more satisfied than associates.[114]

Thus, despite the fact that many lawyers are relatively satisfied with their jobs and their lives, there is variation across settings and aspects of the job, and a significant minority of lawyers expresses overall dissatisfaction. Moreover, it is possible to simultaneously express overall satisfaction while experiencing some distress: "the feelings of satisfaction [lawyers] often take in modern lawyering can obscure feelings of despondency and depression that also accompany legal careers."[115] Attorneys may experience relatively high levels of job satisfaction but concurrently feel some degree of either job or life distress. Indeed, the profession is well known for some of its less favorable aspects: high levels of stress, significant time demands and billable hour requirements, and the expectation of clients and colleagues that the lawyer will always be accessible. In addition, many lawyers feel the weight of the responsibility associated with helping clients with their deeply held problems and ambitions. These pressures and other sources of attorney dissatisfaction can be problematic.

In particular, depression, anxiety, feelings of inadequacy, loneliness, and other psychological problems; alcoholism and drug use; and heart disease and other physical ailments can be significant problems for attorneys. For example, one study found that approximately one-third of attorneys experienced either depression or problems with alcohol or cocaine. Twenty percent of attorneys in the study suffered from depression, a rate that is significantly higher than the 3%–9% that is found in the population more generally. And the attorneys were significantly more likely to have problems with alcohol—18% had problems with alcohol as compared to 10% of the general population—with the rate of problem drinking tending to increase with the length of practice.[116] Compared to the general population, lawyers have also exhibited elevated rates of anxiety, obsessive-compulsive disorder, problems with social alienation and isolation, feelings of inadequacy, difficulties in social interaction, and other psychological difficulties; and they experience more stress and less satisfaction with relationships.[117]

Dissatisfaction and its attendant problems can be detrimental to an attorney's practice. In particular, "[u]nhappiness and depression are intimately associated with passivity and poor productivity at work."[118] Dissatisfaction can make it difficult to muster the kind of engagement, creativity, and focus that will best serve clients. And a number of studies have shown that a high percentage of lawyers who become defendants in disciplinary cases suffer from psychological problems such as depression or are abusing drugs or alcohol.[119] Dissatisfaction at work can also wreak havoc on attorneys' private lives.[120] And, of course, even for an attorney who manages to effectively serve clients and stay out of ethical trouble, it is just not much fun to be unhappy.

In contrast, research has shown that happiness is not only its own reward but is also correlated with a variety of positive outcomes, both on the job and in life more generally (see chapter 3). Happy people are healthier, have more energy, and may even live longer than those who are not. Happy people tend to be more productive and to do higher quality work; be more creative; have jobs with more "autonomy, meaning, and variety"; get better performance evaluations; earn higher incomes; and be less susceptible to burnout. Happiness is associated with good citizenship and volunteerism. Happy people tend to be liked more; are seen as "more intelligent and competent, more friendly, warm, and assertive"; are better at building relationships; and are more likely to be perceived as worthy of trust. Happy people tend to set more ambitious goals, to feel more competent, and to be more resilient.[121] Thus, whether one is an unhappy attorney or one who feels relatively satisfied, paying attention to improving well-being has benefits.

Improving Well-Being

How much can people do to influence their level of satisfaction or well-being—in life or on the job? Psychologist Sonja Lyubomirsky and her colleagues estimate that approximately 50% of the variation in people's level of happiness can be attributed to genetics or a dispositional "set point," 10% to life circumstances, and the remaining

> ✦ ✦ ✦ ✦ ✦
> **A Surrogation Strategy**
>
> Recall the counterintuitive finding from chapter 5 that people make more accurate predictions about how an experience will make them feel by using information about how a similar experience made another person—even a stranger—feel. Thus, in trying to figure out what will make us happy, it can be quite helpful to find out what makes other lawyers happy.

> I fear that happiness isn't in my line, . . . blaming the disposition that was given to me at birth.
> —Benjamin N. Cardozo[123]

40% to personal actions and choices.[122] This means that a substantial proportion of a person's happiness is determined by factors that are not in his immediate control, but that well-being can still be influenced to a significant degree by personal choices, behaviors, and ways of thinking.

So, what can lawyers do to improve their well-being? It is tempting to get caught up in the notion that if we could just earn more money, we would be happier. "It's the most pernicious myth about lawyers: If you earn a high income, you will be happy."[124] However, as we noted in chapter 3, there is only a modest correlation between income and happiness, a relationship that diminishes as the level of wealth increases. Surely, money can put a roof over our heads, ensure that we are fed and clothed, and pay off those daunting student loans (relieving the associated stress). But we've also seen that the pursuit of money can lead to dissatisfaction by crowding out other activities that are associated with well-being, such as developing satisfying relationships, getting sufficient sleep and exercise, eating right, savoring life, and engaging in relaxing activities.

> ✦ ✦ ✦ ✦ ✦
> **There's an App for That**
>
> Psychologist Sonja Lyubomirsky has created an app—Live Happy—that is based on the psychological science of happiness.[125]
>
>

As we will see, well-being depends on a variety of factors. Chief among these are the psychological needs to be competent or effective in our undertakings, to act autonomously or in a way that we choose and that fits with our underlying values, and to be connected in relationships with other people. Indeed, autonomy and competence have been identified as among the most central human needs and are associated with higher positive affect and lower negative affect than other goals.[126]

> ✦ ✦ ✦ ✦ ✦
> **Self-Care**
>
> It can be challenging for busy attorneys to find time for themselves. One California attorney probably spoke for many attorneys when she said that she was "frustrated by the lack of time to develop my personal life—to make new friends, to find a romantic partner, and to be my best self physically."[127] But it is vitally important to well-being for attorneys to make time to take care of themselves. Importantly, physical health and well-being are interrelated. Time and effort spent on exercise, preventive health care, adequate sleep, and good nutrition can help improve well-being through improved physical health and the avoidance of serious health issues. Similarly, improvements in overall well-being can contribute to better physical health.[128]
>
> Engaging in some form of relaxation—such as meditation, yoga, or massage—can also be a form of self-care that is important to well-being. In particular, psychological studies have found that activities that promote mindfulness—heightened "attention to and awareness of current experience or present reality"—are associated with more positive emotion and less anxiety, depression, stress, negative emotions, and fatigue. Attorneys should try to find some form of relaxation that works for them.[129]

Job Tasks

The nature of a person's job impacts whether he feels competent and autonomous, experiences interest and variety in his work, and is appropriately challenged. On a related note, job stress is related to both the demands of the job (stress increases with the degree of challenge or time pressure) and the decision latitude available (workers who have greater control over how the job is done experience less stress).[130] Attorneys tend to be more satisfied with the degree of control that they have over *how* they work than they are with their control over the *amount* of work that they do.[131] Inevitably, legal practice involves "many things lawyers can't control, chief among them other lawyers, deadlines, and billing."[132] Predictably, high time pressure has

> Having to stay in the office all night to review and comment on an unexpected series of documents sent from lawyers on the other side of a transaction was certainly not ideal, but the nights when I left at 5 or 6 and spent the evening worrying that I had left too early because something unexpected might arise were probably even worse.
> —*New York City Lawyer*[135]

been found to be a notably important predictor of lack of well-being at work.[133]

In particular, junior associates in large private firms may "have little voice or control over their work, only limited contact with their superiors, and virtually no client contact."[134] Consider the following example of the lack of control experienced by one junior lawyer at a large New York firm:

Our corporate culture required the show of enthusiasm in all circumstances. A partner would come into your office and ask if you had any plans for the weekend. The correct answer was "no." And you would then be given an assignment to fill your empty Saturday and Sunday. The first time I was asked the question, I mumbled something about having hoped to go to Vermont. The young partner, who was nicknamed "Dave the Barracuda," looked at me with a combination of incredulity and sympathy, as if I had just confessed to a subnormal IQ. "It's a rhetorical question," he explained with an exasperated sigh.[136]

To try to gain control and a sense of competence within the constraints of their work environment, lawyers might capitalize on their ability to structure how they engage in the work. Even when they have little control over which project to work on or how much time to spend on it, they may have more freedom to choose how to structure an argument, which part of a brief to tackle first, or how to structure their physical work setting. More broadly, they can engage in *job crafting*. As lawyers "become the architects of their jobs," they can exercise control over what they do on the job, how they do it, their interpersonal interactions, and the way in which they conceptualize the meaning of their work. Attorneys in any setting can look for and take advantage of opportunities to work on projects that use and develop their strengths; cultivate relationships with others who can help them get experiences or training that will allow them to change the scope of their responsibilities; build the kind of trust that will convince others to accommodate their attempts to craft their jobs to their liking; and redefine how they think about a tedious task, like document review, so as to view it as an integral part of a larger whole.[137]

Similarly, lawyers might seek out opportunities to use what psychologist Martin Seligman called *signature strengths*—whether they be in the domain of leadership, social intelligence, creativity, or perspective—to increase their feelings of competence. Thus, lawyers might actively seek out experience on a particular committee or volunteer to research a particularly novel legal question.[138] Some firms or practice settings may be more receptive to these sorts of efforts than others. Thus, for some attorneys, finding satisfaction might mean finding new job settings in which they are more likely to feel engaged and autonomous.

Our engagement in our work can be reflected in the extent to which we experience what psychologist Mihaly Csikszentmihalyi calls a state of *flow*. When we have been so engaged in a project that we have lost track of time—have felt like we were *on a roll* or *in the zone*—we have probably experienced flow. When we are in a state of flow, we experience an

> intense and focused concentration on the here and now; a loss of self-consciousness as action and awareness merge; a sense that one will be able to handle the situation because one knows how to respond to whatever will happen next; a sense that time has passed more quickly or slowly than normal; and an experience of the activity as rewarding in and of itself, regardless of the outcome.[139]

Flow states tend to occur at times when we are able to work without interruption, in pursuit of one or more clear objectives, able to tell whether progress is being made, and faced with just the right degree of challenge. Growth and a sense of mastery come from fully using our abilities to tackle a challenge that is just difficult enough to stretch our capabilities. Insufficient challenge can result in boredom; too much challenge can result in frustration and anxiety. Because we are so engaged during flow, we do not necessarily experience positive emotions while in the state of flow. Instead, feelings of satisfaction and competence are likely to emerge later as we reflect on the experience.[140]

Values: Work as a Calling

It is also important for attorneys to find work that has meaning for them and is consistent with their own internal set of values. Positive well-being has been associated with the "successful pursuit of life goals that are intrinsic in content; concordant with a person's interests, motives, and values; and internally consistent."[141] In contrast, a sense of meaninglessness tends to be associated with distress.[142] Although individual attorneys will have different values and interests, the important thing is to be committed to a set of self-chosen goals and to find work that fits these goals and values.

>
> I'll tell you what the recipe is for a happy life. Work worth doing is the recipe for a happy life.
> —Sandra Day O'Connor[143]

Consider how one set of researchers explored the central value of meaning in work. Participants were paid to assemble Lego Bionicles (building blocks that construct a robot-like creature). The amount they were paid to assemble a Bionicle dropped with each successive completed Bionicle, and the researchers measured how many Bionicles each participant was willing to build. For one group of participants, the work was designed to be *meaningful*: the assembled Bionicles would accumulate on the table, providing a tangible display of their productivity. In another condition, however, the task was designed to be what the researchers described as *Sisyphean*: as the participant built each new Bionicle, the previous Bionicle was disassembled by a researcher to be offered back to the same participant as the next Bionicle to be built.

> I love being a lawyer because I can make a difference in someone's life. I help people live debt-free. I've had clients tell me it's changed their life for the better, that they can sleep at night and stop fighting with their spouse about money. How awesome is that?
> —Attorney Jeena Cho[145]

Although the mechanics of the building task were the same, participants in the meaningful condition were willing to build significantly more Bionicles (and therefore earned more money) than did those in the condition in which the work seemed less meaningful.[144]

Another research group asked participants to do two different activities of their choice: one that was *hedonistic*, or focused purely on pleasure (for example, enjoying a tasty dessert or meal), and a second that they found to be *meaningful*. When later asked to evaluate the two activities, the participants did indeed find the hedonistic activities to be enjoyable, but they were more likely to recommend that their friends engage in the meaningful activities. "Even though the meaningful activities weren't always fun, they tended to feel good later because they resonated with deeply held personal values."[146] Thus, not every pursuit must be pleasurable to contribute to well-being. For example, volunteer work such as picking up trash or helping to build a house or serving a meal to a homeless family may involve a measure of discomfort but may contribute to overall well-being. The question turns out to be "whether the person has internalized the non-enjoyable activity, that is, whether he or she is able to find meaning and value expression in it, even it is not pleasant to perform."[147]

Finally, consider the distinction that researchers have made among people who see their work as a *job*, a *career*, or a *calling*. Those who see their work as a job tend to see the work as instrumental—as simply a means for securing a paycheck. In contrast, those who see their work as a career are more focused on the opportunities for advancement that it provides—their work is a springboard to more responsibility, prestige, or money. On a

> Mattering makes us happy.
> —Daniel Gilbert[148]

different level, those who see their work as a calling find their work to be intrinsically meaningful, rewarding, and socially valuable. People who see their work as a calling "love their jobs. They feel like their work is important, and makes a contribution to the world. They are excited and challenged by their daily work."[149] Importantly, people who perform the same work as each other can differently conceptualize that work as a job, a career, or a calling. Regardless of whether a person is a lawyer or a custodian, she may regard her work in any one of these ways.

As noted above, attorneys tend to be relatively less satisfied with the value of their work to society than they are with other many other aspects of their jobs. Various aspects of the profession may conspire to threaten intrinsic meaning. Law professor Lawrence Krieger and psychologist Kennon Sheldon found that over the course of their first year of law school, law students tend to subscribe to more extrinsic values and motivations (money, social popularity, what others think they should do) and less intrinsic ones (intellectual growth, community involvement).[150] In addition, the structure of some sectors of the profession has implications for the meaning that lawyers find in their work:

> As firms grow bigger, the slices of work done on cases by individual lawyers get smaller. Attorneys work on minor pieces of huge cases and engage in endless review of documents with little human contact. When they do communicate with each other, they do so by e-mail and conference calls and through Fed Ex drops. Lawyers become alienated from the nature of their work, and they do not see how their work matters.[151]

However, there is potential to find meaning in each of the many aspects of lawyering, and individual attorneys are differentially attracted to the various goals embodied in these different roles.

The puzzle for attorneys, then, is to find a match between work and their own values and motivations that will give meaning to their work. "The larger issue for many attorneys comes down to a mismatch: The realities of their law practices simply don't fit their values, their temperament, or the expectations they had as law students."[152] According to law professors Nancy Levit and Doug Linder,

> [t]he perfect job is the one that lies at the intersection of our deeply held values, our personal strengths, and our pleasures. Rarely do people stumble into such jobs; to find these jobs requires a great deal of reflection about what truly matters to us, as well as what sorts of tasks test our strengths and give us the most pleasure.[153]

Those who see their work as a calling often engage in the kind of active job crafting we described above by structuring their jobs to "bring their work in line with their larger vision of what they value in life" and finding ways to make their jobs matter more.[154]

Even those attorneys whose regular practice is not perfectly in sync with their interests and values can find meaning in pro bono work or other forms of volunteerism. Helping other people turns out to be good for the individuals providing the help in addition to those who are helped, enhancing well-being, satisfaction, self-esteem, competence, a sense of contribution to society, and physical and psychological health—even resulting in a *helper's high*. Research has found that *generativity*—working toward "creating, giving of oneself to others, and having an influence on future generations"—is associated with increased well-being and positive emotion.[156] Unfortunately, we've seen that one aspect of their jobs with which lawyers are least satisfied is the degree to which they have opportunities to do pro bono work. Thus, to improve attorney well-being, firms should provide, and attorneys should seek out, opportunities to do pro bono work, particularly work that the individual attorney finds to be meaningful. Attorneys can also find opportunities to do meaningful service within their work setting, perhaps by mentoring others.

> " For it is in giving that we receive.
> —*St. Francis of Assisi*[155] "

Relationships

Social relationships are also central to well-being. Indeed, fulfilling relationships and well-being tend to interact in an upward spiral: positive well-being seems to lead to better relationships, and better relationships tend to lead to enhanced well-being. Studies have found that time spent in the company of other people—even bosses and clients—tends to be more enjoyable than time spent alone. Our relationships with other people often provide us with "encouragement, support, and mentorship"; sustain us emotionally; challenge and engage us; amuse us; and help us form our own identities.[157]

Interestingly, many of the techniques that psychologists have found to be effective at boosting happiness involve altering the ways in which we relate to and think about other people. For example, research has shown that engaging in acts of kindness, thinking about and expressing gratitude, and deepening our relationships can increase our own level of happiness.[158] Thus, doing a favor for a colleague, bringing coffee for an assistant, mentoring junior colleagues, thanking others for their contributions to joint projects, holding the door for a stranger, and similar acts can improve our own sense of well-being. Recent work has suggested that incorporating variety into these sorts of activities helps to avoid the risk that we will adapt to the new behavior, ceasing to find it as satisfying. Mixing up the nature and timing of our good deeds can help to sustain the rewards over the longer term.[159]

In the legal context, Levit and Linder concluded from their interviews with lawyers that "[l]awyers who regularly interact with colleagues and clients that they like and trust tend to report high levels of career satisfaction."[160] Other researchers have also found that having supportive colleagues and social support at work is associated with job satisfaction.[161] And the *After the JD* researchers concluded that "social networks play an important role in lawyers' satisfaction with their job setting, the substance of their work, and the social [contribution of their work], suggesting that relationships with more-senior lawyers result in better, or at least more interesting, work assignments."[162]

The good news is that lawyers report relatively high levels of satisfaction with their relationships with their colleagues.[163] Of course, the central importance of relationships to well-being means that lawyers should think about who they want to work with when choosing jobs and other activities. Moreover, attorneys can enhance their own well-being and the well-being of other attorneys by paying attention to the ways in which they can be supportive of other attorneys.

Work-Life Balance

Of course, attorneys should remember that relationships outside the office are also an important source of well-being and should seek to nurture relationships with family and friends. As they seek to lead happy and satisfactory lives, attorneys must necessarily pay attention to the balance between their work and other aspects of their lives. Time for hobbies, friendships, family, exercise and other forms of self-care, and other non-work activities are all important to well-being. The challenges of balancing work and other life activities given the demands of lawyering are much discussed within the profession, and attorneys tend to be less satisfied with their ability to achieve work-life balance than they are with other facets of their jobs. A recent study of attorney work-life balance found that most lawyers reported "needing more hours in a day (68%), too many demands being placed on their time (66%), overextending themselves (56%), and juggling different obligations that conflict with one another (69%)."[164]

Psychologists have found that work-life conflicts lead to a variety of negative outcomes: stress; dissatisfaction with one's job, relationships, and life in general; depression and substance abuse; and exhaustion, lack of exercise, poor nutrition, and poor health more generally. However, those who can achieve a high level of facilitation between their roles can reap large benefits such as stress reduction, better performance, and improved health and energy.[165]

> One of your biggest challenges as a lawyer will be finding time to not be a lawyer.
> —Stephen D. Easton[166]

Conflicts between work and other life responsibilities run in both directions, with the time demands, preoccupations, and stresses of work sometimes interfering with other aspects of life and with personal stressors and time demands sometimes interfering with work responsibilities.[167] This is consistent with the experiences of attorneys. In a recent study of attorney work-life balance, 59% of the lawyers studied reported feeling as though they had a "pretty balanced life," but approximately half (47%) reported that their work intruded on their family and one-quarter (23%) indicated that their home lives interfered with work responsibilities.[168] In particular, many attorneys reported that it is difficult to take time off of work to address personal matters; that work hours interfere with the time and energy they have for their families; that they have missed or had to reschedule family occasions or other activities because of work; that there have been occasions in which they have not been able to care for a sick family member; and that they do not have enough time to devote to themselves, their leisure activities, or their friends. With respect to family responsibilities interfering with work tasks, many attorneys reported having skipped "work-related social functions," been less available to clients, or turned down work because of their family responsibilities.[169]

While much of the discussion tends to center around the ways in which work and other aspects of life interfere with each other, it is also important to recognize the ways in which these different spheres can enhance or enrich each other. For example,

> satisfaction with work and satisfaction with family have been found to have additive effects on an individual's happiness, life satisfaction and perceived quality of life. . . . [R]esearch suggests that individuals who participate in—and are satisfied with—work *and* family roles experience greater well-being than those who participate in only one of these roles or who are dissatisfied with one or more of their roles.[170]

> I've tried the "total immersion" approach and find I cannot stay sane for very long. I must have another activity separate from "the law" where I can clear my mind of all the debris and frustrations of my job.
> —Michigan Graduate[172]

Recent research has found that those who are *dual-centric*—placing an equal degree of importance on work and other life activities—feel more successful at work and at home, are less stressed and more satisfied, and feel better able to manage their varied responsibilities. Satisfaction in both work and other life activities can also buffer individuals from the inevitable ups and downs that they will experience in the other domain.[171]

In addition, the skills, perspectives, moods, and energy developed in either work or nonwork life can transfer in a positive way to the other domain. For example, after an enjoyable evening spent with friends or family, a lawyer might be recharged for the next day at work. Lawyers might use skills developed in starting and sustaining friendships to improve their ability to engage in rainmaking, or they might think about the way they would counsel a friend or family member in considering how to handle their own work problems. Or, they might bounce ideas for how to handle work situations off of a partner or good friend. One study found that

> most married lawyers feel that when they talk about their work-related stresses, their spouses provide emotional support by showing concern (85%), offering support and encouragement (84%), listening to their problems (83%), and empathizing with their stresses (79%). Most also report receiving considerable instrumental support in terms of having spouses who share ideas or advice (73%) and offer suggestions or solutions (71%), and the majority report that their spouses share relevant experiences (67%) and help them to figure out the problem (58%).[173]

In addition, time management skills honed and motivated by combining work and familial roles can increase efficiency in the work context. Conversely, lawyers might use the listening strategies that they have developed in working with clients to better communicate with their teenage children.[174]

Because the number of hours that attorneys work is negatively associated with work-life satisfaction,[175] one possibility is to put in fewer hours at work. Indeed, one study of attorneys found that while those who reduced the number of hours that they worked experienced a reduction in income, they also tended to be more satisfied with their work-life balance.[176] In fact, many attorneys report that they would be willing to trade salary for the opportunity to put in fewer hours.[177] Some law students have recently called upon firms to rein in billable hour requirements.[178] Consistent with these impulses, psychologists have found that *time affluence* is associated with positive well-being.[179]

Even if we put significant time and effort into our work, satisfactory work-life balance is possible for those with good coping and time management skills.[180] Thus, as we noted above, attorneys need to be savvy about time management, working to be efficient but also setting good boundaries. Consider this advice from a veteran attorney:

> ✦ ✦ ✦ ✦ ✦
> ### Viewing Time as Money
>
> Remember that Time is Money. He that can earn Ten Shillings a day by his Labour, and goes abroad, or sits idle one half of that Day . . . has really spent or rather thrown away, Five Shillings.
>
> —*Benjamin Franklin*[181]
>
> While Frankin's advice may improve efficiency in one sense, it may decrease overall well-being. Researchers have found that people, like many lawyers, who bill their time by the hour begin to evaluate their time in economic terms and become "acutely aware that every hour they failed to work was lost compensation."[182] Yet, thinking about time in terms of hourly income has been found to decrease the savoring of leisure activities and the amount of happiness or satisfaction derived from them, to increase impatience, to decrease willingness to engage in volunteer or pro bono activities, to increase willingness to trade leisure time for more work, and to increase the degree to which economic factors are used to gauge life satisfaction.[183] Thus, lawyers who bill their time may need to pay particular attention to savoring non-economic uses of their time. Spending time engaged with others, leisure pursuits, and volunteer activities may turn out to be "time well wasted."[184]

> Train clients not to call you at the last minute or on your cell phone unless it is an emergency. Don't schedule conference calls at lunch time. Don't schedule plane flights at 6:00 a.m. Take time to go to your kid's events, but take turns with your spouse. Go home in time to have dinner with your family regardless of the looks you get from your partners. Be happy with your compensation, regardless of others who are making more because they have different priorities than you do.[185]

We recognize, of course, that some of this is easier said than done and may be more feasible in some practice settings than in others. But job demands can be considered when choosing a practice setting or a job. Work-life balance is more likely to be achieved when the lawyer has flexibility and control in scheduling and decision making, as well as supportive colleagues and workplace policies,[186] and these factors can be given substantial weight when making career decisions.

But Not Too Happy

While we all aspire to lead happy lives, it is not necessarily always wise to strive to experience positive emotions 100% of the time. Lawyers who experience only positive emotions might seem rather shallow, if not empty, and might not be as inclined to think deep thoughts or as able to effectively represent their clients. Indeed, as we saw in chapter 3, negative emotions can be functional. Negative emotions or a sense of dissatisfaction can provide useful information about our situation, assist in evaluating options, and provide motivation to change our circumstances for the better. Anxiety can stimulate us to exert more effort. Sadness or more neutral affect can result in more deliberative processing, more attention to detail, and more persuasive arguments, as well as more persistence. Guilt can lead to more ethical behavior. Our own difficult experiences can make us more understanding of others. These are all desirable effects that we should balance with the benefits of positive emotions. It might also be wise to remember, as we learned in chapter 5, that satisficers tend to be happier than maximizers.

Interestingly, psychologists have found that, depending on the nature of our goals, the optimal level of happiness is not necessarily at the top of the happiness scale. Psychologists Ed Diener and Robert Biswas-Diener refer to the *magic eights*, finding that "those scoring around an eight [on a happiness scale of one to ten] often tend to fare the best in achievement" and reasoning that "[i]t could be that eights benefit from the creativity and energy of happiness, but also maintain a touch of worry that helps to motivate them."[187] And, indeed, people with these moderately high levels of happiness or satisfaction tend to perform the best on facets of life that involve motivation (for example, educational attainment and income level), while people reporting the highest levels of happiness tend to be the most successful in their social relationships.[188]

Thus, achieving perfect happiness does not have to be the goal. Rather, lawyers should strive to improve the balances in their lives—seeking to increase the amount of positive emotions they experience but valuing the necessary negative emotions, working to gain control over a greater proportion of their lives and work while realizing that not everything will be under control, seeking a greater proportion of fulfilling work while understanding that not every task will exude meaning, and cultivating relationships while knowing that not every relationship will be perfectly satisfactory.

✦ ✦ ✦ ✦ ✦
Summing It Up

- Structure time effectively by using deadlines strategically, resisting the urge to multitask, matching mood to task when possible, and recognizing the negative effects of working long hours.
- Adopt a flexible approach to mistakes (a growth mindset) and with regard to explanatory style (optimism/pessimism). Seek out accurate feedback and opportunities to learn and capitalize on the lawyer's tendency toward pessimism when anticipating problems a client might face but take a more optimistic stance toward other aspects of life and career.

- Avoid choking under pressure by practicing and by pausing the choke: take time to think, focus, deliberate, and recharge.
- Pay attention to the importance of first impressions, the principle of liking, and the value of reliability when developing relationships with others; and develop systems for effective communication in groups, seeking out the opinions of others and adopting routines that encourage the sharing of diverse viewpoints.
- Improve life and career satisfaction by seeking work that provides an appropriate challenge, engages interests, has meaning, and provides opportunities for finding flow; developing satisfying relationships at work and elsewhere; and striving to find ways in which work and family can facilitate one another.

Final Thoughts

Many have noted that happiness is a process or a journey rather than a final destination. Indeed, people find happiness—in the form of satisfaction and a sense of purpose—in the process of actively working toward their intrinsic goals.[189]

We believe the same is true for success. As Lily Tomlin aptly put it, "[t]he road to success is always under construction."[190] Success is found in how we define our goals and in the activities that we undertake in striving to meet those goals.

Thus, both well-being and success come from an attitude of growth and an eye toward lifelong learning. Individuals with a growth mindset love what they do, focus on learning rather than proving themselves, and show their grit over the long haul.

In the end the great truth will have been learned: that the quest is greater than what is sought, the effort finer than the prize (or, rather, that the effort is the prize), the victory cheap and hollow were it not for the rigor of the game.
—Justice Benjamin Cardozo[191]

We hope that you will approach this book from a growth perspective as well and use it in your ongoing quest for improvement. We have done our best to describe a broad range of psychological findings and to help you apply them to the practice of law. However, we are confident that we have not tapped all the ways in which psychological science can help lawyers be more effective. Thus, we expect that you will continue to build on the insights developed here to discover new understandings of your own. We are confident that in doing so, you will continue to sharpen your awareness of psychology to better help yourselves, your clients, your colleagues, and the greater community.

For Further Reading: On Being Productive, Successful, and Happy

Sian Beilock, Choke: What the Secrets of the Brain Reveal About Getting It Right When You Have To (2010).

Susan Daicoff, Lawyer, Know Thyself (2004).

Ed Diener & Robert Biswas-Diener, Happiness: Unlocking the Mysteries of Psychological Wealth (2008).

Carol Dweck, Mindset: The New Psychology of Success (2006).

Amiram Elwork, Stress Management for Lawyers: How to Increase Personal & Professional Satisfaction in the Law (2007).

Nancy Levit & Douglas O. Linder, The Happy Lawyer: Making a Good Life in the Law (2010).

Sonja Lyubomirsky, The How of Happiness: A New Approach to Getting the Life You Want (2007).

Relationship-Centered Lawyering: Social Science Theory for Transforming Legal Practice (Susan L. Brooks & Robert G. Madden eds., 2010).

Martin Seligman et al., *Why Lawyers Are Unhappy*, 23 Cardozo L. Rev. 33 (2001).

Symposium, *Perspectives on Lawyer Happiness*, 58 Syracuse L. Rev. 217 (2008).

Endnotes

Introduction

1. Parke-Davis & Co. v. H. K. Mulford Co., 189 F. 95, 115 (1911).
2. Kevin W. Boyack et al., *Mapping the Backbone of Science*, 64 SCIENTOMETRICS 351 (2005); John T. Cacioppo, *Psychology Is a Hub Science*, OBSERVER, Sept. 2007, at 5, 42.
3. DAVID DUNNING, SELF-INSIGHT: ROADBLOCKS AND DETOURS ON THE PATH TO KNOWING THYSELF 57 (2005).
4. *See, e.g.*, ROBYN DAWES, RATIONAL CHOICE IN AN UNCERTAIN WORLD 100–20 (1988).
5. *See, e.g.*, THOMAS GILOVICH, HOW WE KNOW WHAT ISN'T SO (1991); DAVID G. MYERS, INTUITION: ITS POWERS AND PERILS (2002); LEE ROSS, *The Intuitive Psychologist and His Shortcomings: Distortions in the Attribution Process*, 10 ADVANCES EXPERIMENTAL SOC. PSYCHOL. 173 (1977).
6. CHRISTOPHER CHABRIS & DANIEL SIMONS, THE INVISIBLE GORILLA: AND OTHER WAYS OUR INTUITIONS DECEIVE US, at ix–x (2010).
7. Michael J. Saks, *Turning Practice into Progress: Better Lawyering Through Experimentation*, 66 NOTRE DAME L. REV. 801, 802–03 (1991).
8. ROBERT PIRSIG, ZEN AND THE ART OF MOTORCYCLE MAINTENANCE 94 (1974).
9. CHABRIS & SIMON, *supra* note 7, at 35.
10. Psychologists have, of course, done much research on particular populations. *See, e.g.*, JOHN MONAHAN ET AL., RETHINKING RISK ASSESSMENT: THE MACARTHUR STUDY OF MENTAL DISORDER AND VIOLENCE (2001); Maggie Bruck & Stephen J. Ceci, *The Suggestibility of Children's Memory*, 50 ANN. REV. PSYCHOL. 419 (1999); Gail G. Goodman & Annika Melinder, *Child Witness Research and Forensic Interviews of Young Children: A Review*, 12 LEGAL & CRIMINOLOGICAL PSYCHOL. 1 (2007); Allison M. Wright & Robyn E. Holliday, *Interviewing Cognitively Impaired Older Adults: How Useful Is a Cognitive Interview?*, 15 MEMORY 17 (2007).

11. *See, e.g.*, Dennis J. Devine, Jury Decision Making: The State of the Science (2012); Neal Feigenson, Legal Blame: How Jurors Think and Talk About Accidents (2000); Jessica D. Findley & Bruce D. Sales, The Science of Attorney Advocacy: How Courtroom Behavior Affects Jury Decision Making (2012); Edie Greene & Brian H. Bornstein, Determining Damages: The Psychology of Jury Awards (2003); Saul M. Kassin & Lawrence S. Wrightsman, The American Jury on Trial: Psychological Perspectives (1988); Joel D. Lieberman & Bruce D. Sales, Scientific Jury Selection (2007); Amy J. Posey & Lawrence S. Wrightsman, Trial Consulting (2005); The Psychology of the Courtroom (Norbert L. Kerr & Robert M. Bray eds., 1982); J. Alexander Tanford, The Trial Process: Law, Tactics, and Ethics (3d ed. 2002); Neil Vidmar & Valerie P. Hans, American Juries: The Verdict (2007); Richard C. Waites, Courtroom Psychology and Trial Advocacy (2003); Roger Park & Michael Saks, *Evidence Scholarship Reconsidered: Results of the Interdisciplinary Turn*, 47 B.C. L. Rev. 949 (2006).
12. *See, e.g.*, David Dunning, Self-Insight: Roadblocks and Detours on the Path to Knowing Thyself (2005); Emily Pronin, *The Introspection Illusion*, 41 Advances Experimental Soc. Psychol. 1 (2009); Emily Pronin et al., *Objectivity in the Eye of the Beholder: Divergent Perceptions of Bias in Self Versus Others*, 111 Psychol. Rev. 781 (2004).
13. Marjorie M. Schultz & Sheldon Zedeck, Final Report: Identification, Development, and Validation of Predictors for Successful Lawyering (2008).
14. Harris's Hints on Advocacy 310 (George W. Keeton ed., 18th ed. 1943).

Chapter 1

1. Benjamin N. Cardozo, The Nature of the Judicial Process 13 (1921).
2. Richard E. Nisbett & Lee Ross, Human Inference: Strategies and Shortcomings of Social Judgment 17 (1980).
3. Daniel J. Simons & Daniel T. Levin, *Failure to Detect Changes to People During a Real-World Interaction*, 5 Psychonomic Bull. & Rev. 644 (1998); Daniel J. Simons & Christopher F. Chabris, *Gorillas in Our Midst: Sustained Inattentional Blindness for Dynamic Events*, 28 Perception 1059 (1999). You can see a demonstration of this study at http://viscog.beckman.uiuc.edu/djs_lab/demos.html and view a regional Emmy award–winning description of the study at http://go.illinois.edu/invisiblegorilla. *See also* Ira E. Hyman Jr. et al., *Did You See the Unicycling Clown? Inattentional Blindness While Walking and Talking on a Cell Phone*, 24 Applied Cognitive Psychol. 597 (2010).
4. Deborah Davis et al., *"Unconscious Transference" Can Be an Instance of "Change Blindness,"* 22 App. Cognitive Psychol. 605 (2008); *see also* Graham Davies & Sarah Hine, *Change Blindness and Eyewitness Testimony*, 141 J. Psychol. 423 (2007); Kally J. Nelson et al., *Change Blindness Can Cause Mistaken Eyewitness Identification*, 16 Legal & Criminological Psychol. 62 (2011).
5. Christopher Chabris & Daniel Simons, The Invisible Gorilla: And Other Ways Our Intuitions Deceive Us 7 n.11 (2010). Similarly, most people endorse the notion that "[p]

eople generally notice when something unexpected enters their field of view, even when they're paying attention to something else." Daniel J. Simons & Christopher F. Chabris, *What People Believe About How Memory Works: A Representative Survey of the U.S. Population*, 6 PLoS ONE 1 (2011).
6. http://www.youtube.com/watch?v=UtKt8YF7dgQ (last visited March 25, 2012).
7. SCHACTER, *supra* note 7, at 35.
8. Christopher F. Chabris et al., *You Do Not Talk About Fight Club If You Do Not Notice Fight Club: Inattentional Blindness for a Simulated Real-World Assault*, 2 i-PERCEPTION 150 (2011); *see also* DICK LEHR, THE FENCE: A POLICE COVER-UP ALONG BOSTON'S RACIAL DIVIDE (2009).
9. CHABRIS & SIMON, *supra* note 7, at 35.
10. Anina N. Rich et al., *Why Do We Miss Rare Targets? Exploring the Boundaries of the Low Prevalence Effect*, 8 J. VISION 1 (2008); Jeremy M. Wolfe et al., *Rare Targets Are Often Missed in Visual Search*, 435 NATURE 439 (2005).
11. *Urbandictionary.com* (submitted by workinglate), cited in DAVE CRENSHAW, THE MYTH OF MULTITASKING 19 (2008).
12. Mathias S. Fleck et al., *Generalized "Satisfaction of Search": Adverse Influences on Dual-Target Search Accuracy*, 16 J. EXPERIMENTAL PSYCHOL.: APPLIED 60 (2010).
13. For research on interruptions, see Gloria Mark et al., *No Task Left Behind? Examining the Nature of Fragmented Work*, Proceedings of the SIGCHI Conference on Human Factors in Computing Systems (2005); J. Gregory Trafton & Christopher A. Monk, *Task Interruptions, in* 3 REVIEWS OF HUMAN FACTORS AND ERGONOMICS 111 (Deborah A. Boehm-Davis ed., 2007); Christopher A. Monk et al., *The Effect of Interruption Duration and Demand on Resuming Suspended Goals*, 14 J. EXPERIMENTAL PSYCHOL.: APPLIED 299 (2008).
14. Exercise adapted from DAVE CRENSHAW, THE MYTH OF MULTITASKING 35–48 (2008).
15. *See, e.g.*, Paul E. Dux et al., *Isolation of a Central Bottleneck of Information Processing with Time-Resolved fMRI*, 52 NEURON 1109 (2006); Harold Pashler, *Dual-Task Interference in Simple Tasks: Data and Theory*, 116 PSYCHOL. BULL. 220 (1994).
16. Catherine M. Arrington & Gordon D. Logan, *The Cost of a Voluntary Task Switch*, 15 PSYCHOL. SCI. 610 (2004); Sophie Leroy, *Why Is It So Hard to Do My Work? The Challenge of Attention Residue When Switching Between Work Tasks*, 109 ORGANIZATIONAL BEHAV. & HUM. DECISION PROCESSES 168 (2009); Stephen Monsell, *Task Switching*, 7 TRENDS COGNITIVE SCI. 134 (2003); Joshua S. Rubinstein et al., *Executive Control of Cognitive Processes in Task Switching*, 27 J. EXPERIMENTAL PSYCHOL.: HUM. PERCEPTION & PERFORMANCE 763 (2001).
17. Eyal Ophir et al., *Cognitive Control in Media Multitaskers*, 106 PNAS 15583 (2009).

18. Albert H. Hastorf & Hadley Cantril, *They Saw a Game: A Case Study*, 49 J. Abnormal & Soc. Psychol. 129 (1954).
19. Joseph Price & Justin Wolfers, *Racial Discrimination Among NBA Referees* (Nat'l Bureau of Econ. Research, Working Paper No. 13206, 2007), *available at* http://bpp.wharton.upenn.edu/jwolfers/Papers/NBARace(NBER).pdf.
20. *See, e.g.*, E. Tory Higgins, *Knowledge Activation: Accessibility, Applicability, and Salience*, in Social Psychology: Handbook of Basic Principles 133 (E. Tory Higgins & Arie W. Kruglanski eds., 1996) (reviewing studies); Varda Liberman et al., *The Name of the Game: Predictive Power of Reputations Versus Situational Labels in Determining Prisoner's Dilemma Game Moves*, 30 Personality & Soc. Psychol. Bull. 1175, 1177 (2004); Fritz Strack et al., *Priming and Communication: Social Determinants of Information Use in Judgments of Life Satisfaction*, 18 Eur. J. Soc. Psychol. 429 (1988); *see also* Barbara O'Brien & Daphna Oyserman, *It's Not Just What You Think, But Also How You Think About It: The Effect of Situationally Primed Mindsets on Legal Judgments and Decision Making*, 92 Marquette L. Rev. 149 (2008).
21. *See, e.g.*, John A. Bargh et al., *Automaticity of Social Behavior: Direct Effects of Trait Construct and Stereotype Activation on Action*, 71 J. Personality & Soc. Psychol. 230 (1996); Ap Dijksterhuis & Ad van Knippenberg, *The Relation Between Perception and Behavior, or How to Win a Game of Trivial Pursuit*, 74 J. Personality & Soc. Psychol. 865 (1998); Steven L. Neuberg, *Behavioral Implications of Information Presented Outside of Conscious Awareness: The Effect of Subliminal Presentation of Trait Information on Behavior in the Prisoner's Dilemma Game*, 6 Soc. Cognition 207 (1988); Kathleen D. Vohs et al., *Merely Activating the Concept of Money Changes Personal and Interpersonal Behavior*, 17 Current Directions in Psychol. Sci. 208 (2008); Kathleen D. Vohs et al., *The Psychological Consequences of Money*, 314 Science 1154 (2006).
22. Lee Ross & Richard E. Nisbett, The Person and the Situation: Perspectives of Social Psychology 11, 76 (1991).
23. Robert F. Cochran Jr., et al., The Counselor-at-Law: A Collaborative Approach to Client Interviewing and Counseling 39 (1999) (quoting Melvin S. Heller et al., An Introduction to Legal Interviewing and Counseling 11 (1960)).
24. *See, e.g.*, Michelene T. H. Chi, *Two Approaches to the Study of Experts' Characteristics*, in The Cambridge Handbook of Expertise and Expert Performance 21, 23 (K. Anders Ericsson et al. eds., 2006); Derek J. Koehler et al., *The Calibration of Expert Judgment*, in Heuristics and Biases: The Psychology of Intuitive Judgment 686, 692–93 (Thomas Gilovich et al. eds., 2002).
25. Robert P. Abelson, *Psychological Status of the Script Concept*, 36 Am. Psychologist 715, 715 (1981).
26. Susan T. Fiske, *Stereotyping, Prejudice, and Discrimination*, in 2 The Handbook of Social Psychology 357 (Daniel T. Gilbert et al. eds., 4th ed. 1998);

James L. Hilton & William von Hippel, *Stereotypes*, 47 Ann. Rev. Psychol. 237, 240 (1996).
27. Nisbett & Ross, *supra* note 2, at 67.
28. Solomon E. Asch, *Forming Impressions of Personality*, 41 J. Abnormal & Soc. Psychol. 258 (1946).
29. B. Keith Payne, *Prejudice and Perception: The Role of Automatic and Controlled Processes in Misperceiving a Weapon*, 81 J. Personality & Soc. Psychol. 181 (2001). Moreover, participants were more likely to misidentify tools as weapons when the tool was primed with a black face than they were when the tool was primed with a white face. *Id.* at 188.
30. Fiske, *supra* note 26; Mark Snyder & William B. Swann, *Hypothesis-Testing Processes in Social Interaction*, 36 J. Personality & Soc. Psychol. 1202 (1978).
31. *See, e.g.*, Patricia G. Devine, *Stereotypes and Prejudice: Their Automatic and Controlled Components*, 56 J. Personality & Soc. Psychol. 5, 15 (1989); Kerry Kawakami et al., *Just Say No (to Stereotyping): Effects of Training in the Negation of Stereotypic Associations on Stereotype Activation*, 78 J. Personality & Soc. Psychol. 871 (2000); C. Neil Macrae & Galen V. Bodenhausen, *Social Cognition: Thinking Categorically About Others*, 51 Ann. Rev. Psychol. 93, 96 (2000); Margo J. Monteith, *Self-Regulation of Prejudiced Responses: Implications for Progress in Prejudice-Reduction Efforts*, 65 J. Personality & Soc. Psychol. 469, 483 (1993); Gordon B. Moskowitz et al., *Preconscious Control of Stereotype Activation Through Chronic Egalitarian Goals*, 77 J. Personality & Soc. Psychol. 167, 182 (1999).
32. Chabris & Simon, *supra* note 6, at 76–77.
33. *See* Charles G. Lord, Lee Ross & Mark R. Lepper, *Biased Assimilation and Attitude Polarization: The Effects of Prior Theories on Subsequently Considered Evidence*, 37 J. Personality & Soc. Psychol. 2098 (1979).
34. Sir Arthur Conan Doyle *A Scandal in Bohemia*, in The Adventures of Sherlock Holmes 3, 7 (1891).
35. Max Bazerman & Don A. Moore, Judgment in Managerial Decision Making 95 (7th ed. 2008) (citing Erica Dawson et al., *Motivated Reasoning and Performance on the Watson Selection Task*, 28 Personality & Soc. Psychol. Bull. 1379 (2002)); *see* Lord, Ross & Lepper, *supra* note 33, at 2098; Raymond S. Nickerson, *Confirmation Bias: A Ubiquitous Phenomenon in Many Guises*, 2 Rev. Gen. Psychol. 175, 175 (1998).
36. Dan M. Kahan et al., *They Saw a Protest: Cognitive Illiberalism and the Speech-Conduct Distinction*, 64 Stan. L. Rev. (forthcoming 2012).
37. John Dewey, How We Think 13 (1910).
38. Barbara O'Brien, *Prime Suspect: An Examination of Factors That Aggravate and Counteract Confirmation Bias in Criminal Investigations*, 15 Psychol. Pub. Pol'y & L. 315 (2009); *see also* Craig A. Anderson, *Belief Perseverance*, in

ENCYCLOPEDIA OF SOCIAL PSYCHOLOGY (Roy F. Baumeister & Kathleen D. Vohs eds., 2007); Harold H. Kelley, *The Warm-Cold Variable in First Impressions of Persons*, 18 J. PERSONALITY 431 (1950); E. Tory Higgins et al., *Category Accessibility and Impression Formation*, 13 J. EXPERIMENTAL SOC. PSYCHOL. 141 (1977). Intelligence officers also grapple with the difficulties posed by confirmation bias. *See, e.g.*, S. SELECT COMM. ON INTELLIGENCE, 108TH CONG., REPORT ON THE U.S. INTELLIGENCE COMMUNITY'S PREWAR INTELLIGENCE ASSESSMENTS ON IRAQ 18–22 (2004) ("The Intelligence Community (IC) has long struggled with the need for analysts to overcome analytic biases, that is, to resist the tendency to see what they would expect to see in the intelligence reporting."). Nor are other experts immune. *See, e.g.*, Karl Ask & Pär Anders Granhag, *Motivational Bias in Criminal Investigators' Judgments of Witness Reliability*, 37 J. APPLIED SOC. PSYCHOL. 561 (2007) (police officers); Vicki R. Leblanc et al., *Believing Is Seeing: The Influence of a Diagnostic Hypothesis on the Interpretation of Clinical Features*, 77 ACAD. MED. S67 (2002) (medical residents); Stefan Schultz-Hardt et al., *Biased Information Search in Group Decision Making*, 78 J. PERSONALITY & SOC. PSYCHOL. 655 (2000) (bank and industrial managers).

39. Saul M. Kassin et al., *Behavioral Confirmation in the Interrogation Room: On the Dangers of Presuming Guilt*, 27 LAW & HUM. BEHAV. 187 (2003). Observers who were not privy to the interviewers' prior beliefs judged interviewers with a guilt presumption as having a higher belief in the interviewee's guilt and as exerting more pressure on the interviewee. *Id.*; *see also* Snyder & Swann, *supra* note 30, at 1205.

40. *See* Charles G. Lord et al., *Considering the Opposite: A Corrective Strategy for Social Judgment*, 47 J. PERSONALITY & SOC. PSYCHOL. 1231 (1984); *see also* Laura J. Kray & Adam D. Galinsky, *The Debiasing Effect of Counterfactual Mind-Sets: Increasing the Search for Disconfirmatory Information in Group Decisions*, 91 ORGANIZATIONAL BEHAV. & HUM. DECISION PROCESSES 69, 76 (2003).

41. KENNETH L. WOODWARD, MAKING SAINTS: HOW THE CATHOLIC CHURCH DETERMINES WHO BECOMES A SAINT, WHO DOESN'T, AND WHY (2006).

42. *See, e.g.*, Charlan Nemeth et al., *Devil's Advocate Versus Authentic Dissent: Stimulating Quantity and Quality*, 31 EUR. J. SOC. PSYCHOL. 707 (2001); David M. Schweiger et al., *Group Approaches for Improving Strategic Decision Making: A Comparative Analysis of Dialectic Inquiry, Devil's Advocacy, and Consensus*, 29 ACAD. MGMT. J. 51 (1986); Charles R. Schwenk, *Effects of Devil's Advocacy and Dialectical Inquiry on Decision Making: A Meta-Analysis*, 47 ORGANIZATIONAL BEHAV. & HUM. DECISION PROCESSES 161 (1990).

43. EDWARD E. JONES, INTERPERSONAL PERCEPTION 138–66 (1990); ROSS & NISBETT, *supra* note 22, at 76; BERNARD WEINER, JUDGMENTS OF RESPONSIBILITY: A FOUNDATION FOR A THEORY OF SOCIAL CONDUCT 5 (1995); Harold H. Kelley, *The Processes of Causal Attribution*, 28 AM. PSYCHOLOGIST 107 (1973).

44. Raymond S. Nickerson, *The Production and Perception of Randomness*, 109 PSYCHOL. REV. 330 (2002); Amnon Rapoport & David V. Budescu, *Randomization in Individual Choice Behavior*, 104 PSYCHOL. REV. 603 (1997); *see also* THOMAS GILOVICH, HOW WE KNOW WHAT ISN'T SO 15 (1991) (reviewing studies).
45. Thomas Gilovich et al., *The Hot Hand in Basketball: On the Misperception of Random Sequences*, 17 COGNITIVE PSYCHOL. 295 (1985); Jonathan J. Koehler & Caryn A. Conley, *The "Hot Hand" Myth in Professional Basketball*, 25 J. SPORT & EXERCISE PSYCHOL. 253 (2003).
46. JONAH LEHRER, HOW WE DECIDE 65–66 (2009).
47. *See* Edward E. Jones & Victor A. Harris, *The Attribution of Attitudes*, 3 J. EXPERIMENTAL SOC. PSYCHOL. 1 (1967).
48. Michael W. Morris et al., *Misperceiving Negotiation Counterparts: When Situationally Determined Bargaining Behaviors Are Attributed to Personality Traits*, 77 J. PERSONALITY & SOC. PSYCHOL. 52 (1999).
49. Incheol Choi et al., *Causal Attribution Across Cultures: Variation and Universality*, 125 PSYCHOL. BULL. 47 (1999); Michael W. Morris & Kaiping Peng, *Culture and Cause: American and Chinese Attributions and Social and Physical Events*, 67 J. PERSONALITY & SOC. PSYCHOL. 949 (1994). *See generally* RICHARD E. NISBETT, THE GEOGRAPHY OF THOUGHT (2003).
50. Morris & Peng, *supra* note 49, at 949.
51. Edward E. Jones & Richard E. Nisbett, *The Actor and the Observer: Divergent Perceptions of the Causes of Behavior*, *in* ATTRIBUTION: PERCEIVING THE CAUSES OF BEHAVIOR 82 (Edward E. Jones et al. eds., 1972); *see also* Michael D. Storms, *Videotape and the Attribution Process: Reversing Actors' and Observers' Points of View*, 27 J. PERSONALITY & SOC. PSYCHOL. 165, 171–72 (1973).
52. Robert J. MacCoun, *Blaming Others to a Fault?*, 6 CHANCE 31, 31 (1993).
53. *See* CAROL TAVRIS & ELLIOT ARONSON, MISTAKES WERE MADE (BUT NOT BY ME): WHY WE JUSTIFY FOOLISH BELIEFS, BAD DECISIONS, AND HURTFUL ACTS (2007) (review).
54. William B. Swann Jr. et al., *Causal Chunking: Memory and Inference in Ongoing Interaction*, 53 J. PERSONALITY & SOC. PSYCHOL. 858 (1987).
55. Daniel Gilbert, *He Who Cast the First Stone Probably Didn't*, N.Y. TIMES, July 24, 2006, at A17.
56. *See* Lee Ross, *The Intuitive Psychologist and His Shortcomings: Distortions in the Attribution Process*, *in* 10 ADVANCES IN EXPERIMENTAL SOC. PSYCHOL. 173 (Leonard Berkowitz ed., 1977); WEINER, *supra* note 43, at 5; Arie W. Kruglanski & Donna M. Webster, *Motivated Closing of the Mind: "Seizing" and "Freezing,"* 103 PSYCHOL. REV. 263, 265 (1996); Harriet Shaklee & Baruch Fischhoff, *Strategies of Information Search in Causal Analysis*, 10 MEMORY & COGNITION 520 (1982).
57. Emily Pronin et al., *Understanding Misunderstanding: Social Psychological Perspectives*, *in* HEURISTICS AND BIASES: THE PSYCHOLOGY OF INTUITIVE JUDGMENT 636 (Thomas Gilovich et al. eds., 2002).

58. Scott v. Harris, 550 U.S. 372 (2007).
59. *Id.*
60. *Id.* (Stephens, J., dissenting).
61. Dan M. Kahan et al., *Whose Eyes Are You Going to Believe? Scott v. Harris and the Perils of Cognitive Illiberalism*, 122 Harv. L. Rev. 837 (2009). For an excellent and detailed discussion of the footage in *Scott v. Harris* and the difficulties in interpretation presented by such evidence, see Neal Feigenson & Christina Spiesel, Law on Display: The Digital Transformation of Legal Persuasion and Judgment 35–49 (2009).
62. Pronin et al., *supra* note 57; Lee Ross & Andrew Ward, *Naïve Realism in Everyday Life: Implications for Social Conflict and Misunderstanding*, in Values and Knowledge 103, 110–11 (Edward S. Reed et al. eds., 1996).
63. Robert J. Robinson et al., *Actual Versus Assumed Differences in Construal: "Naïve Realism" in Intergroup Perception and Conflict*, 68 J. Personality & Soc. Psychol. 404 (1995).
64. Chip Heath, *On the Social Psychology of Agency Relationships: Lay Theories of Motivation Overemphasize Extrinsic Incentives*, 78 Organizational Behav. & Hum. Decision Processes 25 (1999); Dale T. Miller, *The Norm of Self-Interest*, 54 Am. Psychologist 1053 (1999); Rebecca K. Ratner & Dale T. Miller, *The Norm of Self-Interest and Its Effects on Social Behavior*, 81 J. Personality & Soc. Psychol. 5 (2001); *see also* Justin Kruger & Thomas Gilovich, *"Naïve Cynicism" in Everyday Theories of Responsibility Assessment: On Biased Assumptions of Bias*, 76 J. Personality & Soc. Psychol. 743 (1999).
65. Pronin et al., *supra* note 57 (listeners guessed right 2.5% of the time; tappers predicted that listeners would guess right 50% of the time); *see also* Justin Kruger et al., *Egocentrism over E-Mail: Can We Communicate as Well as We Think?*, 89 J. Personality & Soc. Psychol. 925 (2005).
66. *See* Ross & Ward, *supra* note 62, at 110–11; Emily Pronin et al., *Objectivity in the Eye of the Beholder: Divergent Perceptions of Bias in Self Versus Others*, 111 Psychol. Rev. 781, 793 (2004); Leigh Thompson & George Loewenstein, *Egocentric Interpretations of Fairness and Interpersonal Conflict*, 51 Orgizational Behav. & Hum. Decision Processes 176, 193 (1992).
67. Kathleen A. Kennedy & Emily Pronin, *When Disagreement Gets Ugly: Perceptions of Bias and the Escalation of Conflict*, 34 Personality & Soc. Psychol. Bull. 833 (2008).
68. Emily Pronin et al., *You Don't Know Me, But I Know You: The Illusion of Asymmetric Insight*, 81 J. Personality & Soc. Psychol. 639 (2001).
69. *Id.* (emphasis in original).
70. *See, e.g.*, Nancy Eisenberg et al., *The Development of Empathic Accuracy*, in Empathic Accuracy 73, 97–99 (William Ickes ed., 1997); William M. Bernstein & Mark H. Davis, *Perspective-Taking, Self-Consciousness, and Accuracy in Person Perception*, 3 Basic & Applied Soc. Psychol. 1, 5–9 (1982); Aimee Drolet et al.,

Thinking of Others: How Perspective Taking Changes Negotiators' Aspirations and Fairness Perceptions as a Function of Negotiator Relationships, 20 Basic & Applied Soc. Psychol. 23, 28 (1998); Adam D. Galinsky & Gordon B. Moskowitz, *Perspective-Taking: Decreasing Stereotype Expression, Stereotype Accessibility, and In-Group Favoritism*, 78 J. Personality & Soc. Psychol. 708, 721 (2000); Margaret A. Neale & Max H. Bazerman, *The Role of Perspective-Taking Ability in Negotiating Under Different Forms of Arbitration*, 36 Indus. & Lab. Rel. Rev. 378, 380 (1983); Dennis T. Regan & Judith Totten, *Empathy and Attribution: Turning Observers into Actors*, 32 J. Personality & Soc. Psychol. 850, 854 (1975).

71. Nicholas Epley et al., *Perspective Taking as Egocentric Anchoring and Adjustment*, 87 J. Personality & Soc. Psychol. 327 (2004).
72. Leaf Van Boven & George Loewenstein, *Social Projection of Transient Drive States*, 29 Personality & Soc. Psychol. Bull. 1159 (2003).
73. Harold H. Kelley & Anthony J. Stahelski, *Social Interaction Basis of Cooperators' and Competitors' Beliefs About Others*, 16 J. Personality & Soc. Psychol. 66 (1970).
74. Harper Lee, To Kill a Mockingbird 48 (1960).
75. Nicholas Epley & Eugene M. Caruso, *Perspective Taking: Misstepping into Others' Shoes*, in Handbook of Imagination and Mental Simulation 295 (Keith D. Markman et al. eds., 2009) (emphasis added).
76. Nicholas Epley et al., *When Perspective Taking Increases Taking: Reactive Egoism in Social Interaction*, 91 J. Personality & Soc. Psychol. 872 (2006).
77. Janet Malcolm, The Journalist and the Murderer 148 (1990).
78. Adam Galinsky et al., *Power and Perspectives Not Taken*, 17 Psychol. Sci. 1068, 1072 (2006).
79. *See, e.g.*, Williams Ickes et al., *Naturalistic Social Cognition: Empathic Accuracy in Mixed-Sex Dyads*, 59 J. Personality & Soc. Psychol. 730 (1990); Anu Realo et al., *Mind-Reading Ability: Beliefs and Performance*, 37 J. Res. Personality 420 (2003); William B. Swann & Michael J. Gill, *Confidence and Accuracy in Person Perception: Do We Know What We Think We Know About Our Relationship Partners?*, 73 J. Personality & Soc. Psychol. 747 (1997).
80. *See, e.g.*, Pronin et al., *supra* note 66.

Chapter 2

1. Barbara Kingsolver, Animal Dreams 48 (1990).
2. Rashomon (Daiei Motion Picture Co. Ltd. 1950).
3. Jim Dwyer, *Rashomon in Blue; Memories of the Louima Case: 1 Meeting 4 Trained Observers*, N.Y. Times, Aug. 19, 2001.

4. Daniel J. Simons & Christopher F. Chabris, *What People Believe about How Memory Works: A Representative Survey of the U.S. Population*, 6 PLoS ONE 1, 5 (2011).
5. Daniel L. Schacter, The Seven Sins of Memory: How the Mind Forgets and Remembers 28 (2001).
6. Christopher Chabris & Daniel Simons, The Invisible Gorilla: And Other Ways Our Intuitions Deceive Us 47 (2010).
7. Schacter, *supra* note 5.
8. Samuel Johnson, The Works of Samuel Johnson 173 (1818).
9. Karim S. Kassam et al., *Misconceptions of Memory: The Scooter Libby Effect*, 20 Psychol. Sci. 551, 551 (2009); *see also* Geoffrey R. Loftus & Thomas D. Wickens, *Effect of Incentive on Storage and Retrieval Processes*, 85 J. Experimental Psychol.: Gen. 1 (1970); Moshe Naveh-Benjamin et al., *Asymmetry Between Encoding and Retrieval Processes: Evidence from Divided Attention and a Calibration Analysis*, 28 Memory & Cognition 965 (2000).
10. Schacter, *supra* note 5, at 15-16.
11. Oliver Wendell Holmes, The Autocrat of the Breakfast-Table (1858).
12. H. Schmolck et al., *Memory Distortions Develop over Time: Recollections of the O.J. Simpson Trial After 15 and 32 Months*, 11 Psychol. Sci. 39 (2000).
13. Scott Plous, The Psychology of Judgment and Decision Making 37 (1993) (citing Ian Hunter, Memory (1964)).
14. Carol Tavris & Elliot Aronson, Mistakes Were Made (but Not by Me) 71–72 (2007).
15. Deborah Davis & Richard D. Friedman, *Memory for Conversation: The Orphan Child of Witness Memory Researchers*, in Memory for Events 3 (Michael P. Toglia et al. eds., 2007) (vol. 1 of Handbook of Eyewitness Psychology); Roger Buehler & Michael Ross, *How Do Individuals Remember Their Past Statements?*, 64 J. Personality & Soc. Psychol. 538 (1993).
16. *Albert Einstein Quotes*, ThinkExist.com, http://thinkexist.com/quotation/memory_is_deceptive_because_it_is_colored_by/222585.html (last visited, March 24, 2012).
17. George Loewenstein & Jennifer Lerner, *The Role of Affect in Decision Making*, in Handbook of Affective Sciences 619, 629 (Richard J. Davidson et al. eds., 2003).
18. William F. Brewer & James C. Treyens, *Role of Schemata in Memory for Places*, 13 Cognitive Psychol. 207 (1981).
19. Michelle Rae Tuckey & Neil Brewer, *The Influence of Schemas, Stimulus Ambiguity, and Interview Schedule on Eyewitness Memory over Time*, 9 J. Experimental Psychol.: Gen. 101 (2003).
20. Davis & Friedman, *supra* note 15, at 3 (citing N.Y. Times, Oct. 5, 1997).
21. David A. Pizaro et al., *Ripple Effects in Memory: Judgments of Moral Blame Can Distort Memory for Events*, 34 Memory & Cognition 550 (2006).

22. *See* Marcia K. Johnson, *Memory and Reality*, 61 Am. Psychologist 760, 761 (2006); Marcia K. Johnson et al., *Source Monitoring*, 114 Psychol. Bull. 3, 4 (1993); *see also* Ayanna K. Thomas et al., *How Self-Relevant Imagination Affects Memory for Behavior*, 21 Applied Cognitive Psychol. 69 (2007).
23. Paul Brest & Linda Hamilton Krieger, Problem Solving, Decision Making, and Professional Judgment: A Guide for Lawyers and Policymakers 250 (2010).
24. Elizabeth F. Loftus, *Leading Questions and the Eyewitness Report*, 7 Cognitive Psychol. 560, 566 (1975). In a similar study, participants were asked about an accident they had viewed, including a question about how fast the car was going either "when it ran the stop sign" or "when it turned right." When later asked if they had seen a stop sign in the video, 53% of those who had been asked the question referencing a stop sign indicated that they had seen a stop sign, compared to only 35% of those who had been asked the question referencing a right turn. *Id. See generally* Schacter, *supra* note 5, at 113.
25. Eric Jaffe, *Remember When?*, APS Observer 9, 9 (Mar. 2011) (describing William Saletan, *The Memory Doctor*, Slate, June 4, 2010).
26. Elizabeth F. Loftus, *Intelligence Gathering Post-9/11*, 66 Am. Psychologist 532, 536 (2011).
27. *See* Elizabeth F. Loftus, *Make-Believe Memories*, 58 Am. Psychologist 867 (2003).
28. Saul M. Kassin & Gisli H. Gudjonsson, *The Psychology of Confessions: A Review of the Literature and Issues*, 5 Psychol. Sci. Pub. Int. 33, 50 (2004).
29. *Id.*; *see also* Steven A. Drizin & Richard A. Leo, *The Problem of False Confessions in the Post-DNA World*, 82 N.C. L. Rev. 891 (2004); Saul M. Kassin et al., *Police-Induced Confessions: Risk Factors and Recommendations*, 34 Law & Hum. Behav. 3 (2010); Saul M. Kassin & Katherine L. Kiechel, *The Social Psychology of False Confessions: Compliance, Internalization, and Confabulation*, 7 Psychol. Sci. 125 (1996).
30. Simons & Chabris, *supra* note 4, at 5.
31. *See, e.g.*, Andrea Fagerlin et al., *The Use of Advance Directives in End-of-Life Decision Making*, 46 Am. Behav. Sci. 268 (2002); Stefanie J. Sharman et al., *False Memories for End-of-Life Decisions*, 27 Health Psychol. 291 (2008).
32. Chabris & Simon, *supra* note 6, at 76–77.
33. Kassam et al., *supra* note 9, at 552.
34. *See* Endel Tulving & Zena Pearlstone, *Availability Versus Accessibility of Information in Memory for Words*, 5 J. Verbal Learning & Verbal Behav. 381 (1966).
35. *See* Ronald P. Fisher, *Interviewing Victims and Witnesses of Crime*, 1 Psychol. Pub. Pol'y & L. 732 (1995); Martine B. Powell et al., *Investigating Interviewing*,

in PSYCHOLOGY AND LAW: AN EMPIRICAL PERSPECTIVE 11 (Neil Brewer & Kipling D. Williams eds., 2005).

36. *See* Morris Goldsmith et al., *Strategic Regulation of Grain Size in Memory Reporting*, 131 J. EXPERIMENTAL PSYCHOL.: GEN. 73, 88 (2002) (finding that people are "at least moderately successful in choosing a grain size that [will] enhance their accuracy with minimal loss of informativeness"); Asher Koriat & Morris Goldsmith, *Monitoring and Control Processes in the Strategic Regulation of Memory Accuracy*, 103 PSYCHOL. REV. 490, 498–503 (1996) (finding that free report resulted in an increase in accuracy but a decrease in the quantity of information provided); Ulrich Neisser, *Time Present and Time Past, in* PRACTICAL ASPECTS OF MEMORY: CURRENT RESEARCH AND ISSUES 553 (Michael M. Gruneberg et al. eds., 1988) (finding that in answering open-ended questions, people responded at "a level of generality at which they were not mistaken"); *see also* Ilan Yaniv & Dean P. Foster, *Precision and Accuracy of Judgmental Estimation*, 10 J. BEHAV. DECISION MAKING 21 (1997).

37. Rakefet Ackerman & Morris Goldsmith, *Control over Grain Size in Memory Reporting—With and Without Satisficing Knowledge*, 34 J. EXPERIMENTAL PSYCHOL.: LEARNING MEMORY & COGNITION 1224 (2008).

38. Asher Koriat & Morris Goldsmith, *Memory in Naturalistic and Laboratory Contexts: Distinguishing the Accuracy-Oriented and Quantity-Oriented Approaches to Memory Assessment*, 123 J. EXPERIMENTAL PSYCHOL.: GEN. 297, 307 (1994); *see also* Ackerman & Goldsmith, *supra* note 37.

39. *See* Reid Hastie et al., *Eyewitness Testimony: The Dangers of Guessing*, 19 JURIMETRICS J. 1 (1978); Kathy Pezdek et al., *Interviewing Witnesses: The Effect of Forced Confabulation on Event Memory*, 31 LAW & HUM. BEHAV. 463 (2007); Maria S. Zaragota et al., *Interviewing Witnesses: Forced Confabulation and Confirmatory Feedback Increase False Memories*, 12 PSYCHOL. SCI. 473 (2001).

40. Malcolm MacLeod, *Retrieval-Induced Forgetting in Eyewitness Memory: Forgetting as a Consequence of Remembering*, 16 APPLIED COGNITIVE PSYCHOL. 135 (2002); *see also* John S. Shaw III et al., *Retrieval-Induced Forgetting in an Eyewitness-Memory Paradigm*, 2 PSYCHONOMIC BULL. & REV. 249 (1995).

41. Elizabeth F. Loftus & John C. Palmer, *Reconstruction of Automobile Destruction: An Example of the Interaction Between Language and Memory*, 13 J. VERBAL LEARNING & VERBAL BEHAV. 585 (1974); Elizabeth F. Loftus & Guido Zanni, *Eyewitness Testimony: The Influence of the Wording of a Question*, 5 BULL. PSYCHONOMIC SOC'Y 86 (1975).

42. Loftus, *supra* note 24.

43. SCHACTER, *supra* note 5, at 102; Fisher, *supra* note 35, at 742; Elizabeth J. Marsh et al., *How Eyewitnesses Talk About Events: Implications for Memory*, 19 APPLIED COGNITIVE PSYCHOL. 531, 541 (2005); Timothy J. Perfect et al., *How Can We Help Witnesses to Remember More? It's an (Eyes) Open and Shut Case*, 32 LAW & HUM. BEHAV. 314 (2008); Henry L. Roediger III & David A.

Gallo, *Processes Affecting Accuracy and Distortion in Memory: An Overview*, in Memory and Suggestibility in the Forensic Interview 3, 8 (Mitchell L. Eisen et al. eds., 2002).

44. Mark R. Kebbell & David C. Giles, *Some Experimental Influences of Lawyers' Complicated Questions on Eyewitness Confidence and Accuracy*, 134 J. Psychol. 129 (2000); Mark R. Kebbell & Shane D. Johnson, *Lawyers' Questioning: The Effect of Confusing Questions on Witness Confidence and Accuracy*, 24 Law & Hum. Behav. 629 (2000).
45. Charles Darwin, The Descent of Man 4 (1871).
46. Research has demonstrated a generally weak correlation between confidence and accuracy, although the relationship can be stronger under some circumstances. *See* Steven Penrod & Brian Cutler, *Witness Confidence & Witness Accuracy: Assessing Their Forensic Relation*, 1 Psychol. Pub. Pol'y & L. 817 (1995); Siegfried Ludwig Sporer et al., *Choosing, Confidence, and Accuracy: A Meta-Analysis of the Confidence-Accuracy Relation in Eyewitness Identification Studies*, 118 Psychol. Bull. 315 (1995); Gary L. Wells et al., *Eyewitness Evidence: Improving Its Probative Value*, 7 Psychol. Sci. Pub. Int. 45 (2006).
47. *See* Neil Brewer et al., *Beliefs and Data on the Relationship Between Consistency and Accuracy of Eyewitness Testimony*, 13 Applied Cognitive Psychol. 297 (1999); Fisher, *supra* note 35 (reviewing studies); Ronald P. Fisher & Brian L. Cutler, *The Relation Between Consistency and Accuracy of Eyewitness Testimony*, in Psychology, Law, and Criminal Justice: International Developments in Research and Practice 21 (Graham Davies et al. eds., 1995).

Chapter 3

1. Susan A. Bandes, The Passions of Law 2 (1999).
2. Barbara S. Dohrenwend et al., *Exemplification of a Method for Scaling Life Events: The PERI Life Events Scale*, 19 J. Health & Soc. Behav. 205 (1978).
3. Dale Carnegie, How to Win Friends and Influence People 14 (1936).
4. Do Emotions Help or Hurt Decision Making? A Hedgefoxian Perspective 205 (Kathleen D. Vohs et al. eds., 2007); Shirli Kopelman et al., *The Three Faces of Eve: Strategic Displays of Positive, Negative, and Neutral Emotions in Negotiation*, 99 Organizational Behav. & Hum. Decision Processes 81 (2006); George Loewenstein & Jennifer Lerner, *The Role of Affect in Decision Making*, in Handbook of Affective Sciences 619 (Richard J. Davidson et al. eds., 2003).
5. James J. Gross & Ross A. Thompson, *Emotion Regulation: Conceptual Foundations*, in Handbook of Emotion Regulation 3, 4 (James J. Gross ed., 2007).
6. Sir Arthur Conan Doyle, The Sign of Four 31 (1890).

7. Jonah Lehrer, How We Decide 13–15 (2009) (citing Antonio R. Damasio, Descartes' Error 43–44 (2005)).
8. Walter R. Fisher, Human Communications as Narration: Toward a Philosophy of Reason, Value, and Action 37 (1987).
9. Donald G. Dutton & Arthur P. Aron, *Some Evidence for Heightened Sexual Attraction Under Conditions of High Anxiety*, 30 J. Personality & Soc. Psychol. 510 (1974); *Capilano Suspension Bridge*, Capbridge.com, http://www.capbridge.com/thebridge.php (last visited Oct. 2, 2011); Lyndsey Matthews, *World's Scariest Bridges*, Yahoo.com, http://travel.yahoo.com/p-interests-35868704 (last visited Oct. 2, 2011) (describing the bridge as one of the world's scariest); *see also* Tim Wilson, Strangers to Ourselves: Discovering the Adaptive Unconscious (2002).
10. Thomas Gilovich et al., *The Illusion of Transparency: Biased Assessments of Others' Ability to Read One's Emotional States*, 75 J. Personality & Soc. Psychol. 332 (1998).
11. *See* Adam D. Galinsky et al., *Power and Perspectives Not Taken*, 17 Psychol. Sci. 1068 (2006); Gian C. Gonzaga et al., *Power in Mixed-Sex Stranger Interactions*, 22 Cognition & Emotion 1555 (2008); *see also* Cameron Anderson et al., *Emotional Convergence Between People over Time*, 84 J. Personality & Soc. Psychol. 1054 (2003); Gerben A. van Kleef et al., *Power and Emotion in Negotiation: Power Moderates the Interpersonal Effects of Anger and Happiness on Concession Making*, 36 Eur. J. Soc. Psychol. 557 (2006).
12. *See, e.g.*, Paul Ekman, Emotions Revealed (2003). Ekman's book includes a collection of pictures showing the facial displays that are associated with a variety of emotions. *See also* Leonard L. Riskin, *Further Beyond Reason: Emotions, the Core Concerns, and Mindfulness in Negotiation*, 10 Nev. L.J. 289 (2010) (arguing that mindfulness mediation can increase a person's sensitivity to emotions).
13. David H. Maister et al., The Trusted Advisor 112–13 (2000).
14. Jeff T. Larsen et al., *The Agony of Victory and Thrill of Defeat: Mixed Emotional Reactions to Disappointing Wins and Relieving Losses*, 15 Psychol. Sci. 325 (2004). *See generally* Allan Filipowicz et al., *Understanding Emotional Transitions: The Interpersonal Consequences of Changing Emotions in Negotiations*, 101 J. Personality & Soc. Psychol. 541 (2011); Jeff T. Larsen et al., *Can People Feel Happy and Sad at the Same Time?*, 81 J. Personality & Soc. Psychol. 684 (2001); Jeff T. Larsen & A. Peter McGraw, *Further Evidence for Mixed Emotions*, 100 J. Personality & Soc. Psychol. 1095 (2011).
15. David R. Caruso & Peter Salovey, The Emotionally Intelligent Manager (2004); *see also* Lisa Feldman Barrett & Thyra Fossum, *Mental Representations of Affect Knowledge*, 15 Cognition & Emotion 333 (2001).
16. *See, e.g.*, Loewenstein & Lerner, *supra* note 4.

17. Caruso & Salovey, *supra* note 15; Do Emotions Help or Hurt Decision Making?, *supra* note 4, at 107; Barbara L. Fredrickson, *The Role of Positive Emotions in Positive Psychology: The Broaden-and-Build Theory of Positive Emotions*, 56 Am. Psychologist 218 (2001); Karuna Subramaniam et al., *A Brain Mechanism for Facilitation of Insight by Positive Affect*, 21 J. Cognitive Neuroscience 415 (2009).
18. Karl Duncker, *On Problem Solving*, 58 Psychol. Monographs (1945); *see* Alice M. Isen et al., *Positive Affect Facilitates Creative Problem Solving*, 32 J. Personality & Soc. Psychol. 1122 (1987); Carlos A. Estrada et al., *Positive Affect Influences Creative Problem Solving and Reported Source of Practice Satisfaction in Physicians*, 18 Motivation & Emotion 285 (1994); Teresa M. Amabile et al., *Affect and Creativity at Work*, 50 Admin. Sci. Q. 367 (2005).
19. *See* Herbert Bless, *The Interplay of Affect and Cognition: The Mediating Role of General Knowledge Structures*, *in* Feeling and Thinking: The Role of Affect in Social Cognition 201 (Joseph P. Forgas ed., 2000).
20. Caruso & Salovey, *supra* note 15; Do Emotions Help or Hurt Decision Making?, *supra* note 4, at 105–06; Karl Ask & Pär Anders Granhag, *Hot Cognition in Investigative Judgments: The Differential Influence of Anger and Sadness*, 31 Law & Hum. Behav. 537 (2007); Joseph P. Forgas, *When Sad Is Better Than Happy: Negative Affect Can Improve the Quality and Effectiveness of Persuasive Messages and Social Influence Strategies*, 43 J. Experimental Soc. Psychol. 513 (2007); Joseph P. Forgas, *Happy and Mistaken? Mood Effects on the Fundamental Attribution Error*, 75 J. Personality & Soc. Psychol. 318 (1998); Joseph P. Forgas & Rebekah East, *On Being Happy and Gullible: Mood Effects on Skepticism and the Detection of Deception*, 44 J. Experimental Soc. Psychol. 1362 (2008); Karen Gasper & Gerald L. Clore, *Attending to the Big Picture: Mood and Global Versus Local Processing of Visual Information*, 13 Psychol. Sci. 34 (2002).
21. Robert A. Baron, *Reducing Organizational Conflict: An Incompatible Response Approach*, 69 J. Applied Psychol. 272 (1984); Robert A. Baron et al., *Reducing Organizational Conflict: The Role of Socially Induced Positive Affect*, 1 Int'l J. Conflict Mgmt. 133 (1990); Bruce Barry et al., *Bargaining with Feeling: Emotionality in and Around Negotiation*, *in* Negotiation Theory & Research 99, 113 (Leigh L. Thompson ed., 2006); Peter J. Carnevale & Alice M. Isen, *The Influence of Positive Affect and Visual Access on the Discovery of Integrative Solutions in Bilateral Negotiations*, 37 Organizational Behav. & Hum. Decision Processes 1 (1986); Joseph P. Forgas, *On Feeling Good and Getting Your Way: Mood Effects on Negotiation Cognition and Behavior*, 74 J. Personality & Soc. Psychol. 565 (1998); Roderick M. Kramer et al., *Self-Enhancement Biases and Negotiator Judgment: Effects of Self-Esteem and Mood*, 56 Organizational Behav. & Hum. Decision Processes 110 (1993).

22. Keith G. Allred et al., *The Influence of Anger and Compassion on Negotiation Performance*, 70 Organizational Behav. & Hum. Decision Processes 175 (1997); Baron et al., *supra* note 21; Forgas, *supra* note 21.
23. W. Gerrod Parrott, *The Nature of Emotion*, in Emotion and Motivation 5, 12 (Marilynn B. Brewer & Miles Hewstone eds., 2004); *see also* Dacher Keltner et al., *Beyond Simple Pessimism: Effects of Sadness and Anger on Social Perception*, 64 J. Personality & Soc. Psychol. 740 (1993); Jennifer S. Lerner & Larissa Z. Tiedens, *Portrait of the Angry Decision Maker: How Appraisal Tendencies Shape Anger's Influence on Cognition*, 19 J. Behav. Decision Making 115, 118 (2006); Brian M. Quigley & James T. Tedeschi, *Mediating Effects of Blame Attributions on Feelings of Anger*, 22 Personality & Soc. Psychol. Bull. 1280 (1996); Larissa Z. Tiedens, *The Effect of Anger on the Hostile Inferences of Aggressive and Nonaggressive People: Specific Emotions, Cognitive Processing, and Chronic Accessibility*, 25 Motivation & Emotion 233 (2001).
24. Jennifer R. Dunn & Maurice E. Schweitzer, *Feeling and Believing: The Influence of Emotion on Trust*, 88 J. Personality & Soc. Psychol. 736 (2005); Phoebe C. Ellsworth & Klaus R. Scherer, *Appraisal Processes in Emotion*, in Handbook of Affective Sciences, *supra* note 4, at 572, 574; Keltner et al., *supra* note 23; Craig A. Smith & Phoebe C. Ellsworth, *Patterns of Cognitive Appraisal in Emotion*, 48 J. Personality & Soc. Psychol. 813 (1985).
25. Victoria Husted Medvec et al., *When Less Is More: Counterfactual Thinking and Satisfaction Among Olympic Medalists*, 69 J. Personality & Soc. Psychol. 603 (1995); *see also* A. Peter McGraw et al., *Expectations and Emotions of Olympic Athletes*, 41 J. Experimental Soc. Psychol. 438 (2005).
26. Parrott, *supra* note 23; Craig A. Smith & Leslie D. Kirby, *Consequences Require Antecedents: Toward a Process Model of Emotion Elicitation*, in Feeling and Thinking: The Role of Affect in Social Cognition, *supra* note 19, at 83.
27. Keltner et al., *supra* note 23, at 741.
28. Paul Rozin et al., *The CAD Triad Hypothesis: A Mapping Between Three Moral Emotions (Contempt, Anger, Disgust) and Three Moral Codes (Community, Autonomy, Divinity)*, 76 J. Personality & Soc. Psychol. 574 (1999) (finding connections between violations of autonomy and anger, community and contempt, and divinity and disgust); *see* Laurie J. Barclay et al., *Exploring the Role of Emotions in Injustice Perceptions and Retaliation*, 90 J. Applied Psychol. 629 (2005); Ellsworth & Scherer, *supra* note 24; Jennifer S. Lerner et al., *Sober Second Thought: The Effects of Accountability, Anger, and Authoritarianism on Attributions of Responsibility*, 24 Personality & Soc. Psychol. Bull. 563 (1998).
29. Mark D. Alicke, *Culpable Control and the Psychology of Blame*, 126 Psychol. Bull. 556 (2000); Allred et al., *supra* note 22; Dunn & Schweitzer, *supra* note 24; Keltner et al., *supra* note 23; Lerner et al., *supra* note 28; Lerner & Tiedens, *supra* note 23, at 123; *see also* Neal Feigenson & Jaihyun Park,

Emotions and Attributions of Legal Responsibility and Blame: A Research Review, 30 Law & Hum. Behav. 143 (2006).

30. Barclay et al., *supra* note 28; Lerner & Tiedens, *supra* note 23; *see* Lerner et al., *supra* note 28; Keith G. Allred, *Anger and Retaliation in Conflict: The Role of Attribution*, in The Handbook of Conflict Resolution: Theory and Practice 236 (Morton Deutsch & Peter T. Coleman eds., 2000).

31. Julie H. Goldberg et al., *Rage and Reason: The Psychology of the Intuitive Prosecutor*, 29 Eur. J. Soc. Psychol. 781 (1999); Lerner et al., *supra* note 28; Lerner & Tiedens, *supra* note 23.

32. Francesca Gino & Maurice E. Schweitzer, *Blinded by Anger or Feeling the Love: How Emotions Influence Advice Taking*, 93 J. Applied Psychol. 1165 (2008).

33. Galen V. Bodenhausen et al., *Negative Affect and Social Judgment: The Differential Impact of Anger and Sadness*, 24 Eur. J. Soc. Psychol. 45 (1994); David DeSteno et al., *Prejudice from Thin Air: The Effect of Emotion on Automatic Intergroup Attitudes*, 15 Psychol. Sci. 319 (2004); Lerner & Tiedens, *supra* note 23; Lerner et al., *supra* note 28. *But see* Wesley G. Moons & Diane M. Mackie, *Thinking Straight While Seeing Red: The Influence of Anger on Information Processing*, 33 Personality & Soc. Psychol. Bull. 706 (2007) (finding evidence of systematic thinking).

34. Ask & Granhag, *supra* note 20.

35. Alicke, *supra* note 29; Keltner et al., *supra* note 23; Lerner & Tiedens, *supra* note 23.

36. Dacher Keltner & Brenda N. Buswell, *Embarrassment: Its Distinct Form and Appeasement Functions*, 122 Psychol. Bull. 250 (1997); Mark R. Leary, *Motivation and Emotional Aspects of the Self*, 58 Ann. Rev. Psychol. 317 (2007).

37. Roy F. Baumeister et al., *Guilt: An Interpersonal Approach*, 115 Psychol. Bull. 243 (1994); Jonathan Haidt, *The Moral Emotions*, in Handbook of Affective Sciences, *supra* note 4; Dacher Keltner & Brenda N. Buswell, *Evidence for the Distinctness of Embarrassment, Shame, and Guilt: A Study of Recalled Antecedents and Facial Expressions of Emotion*, 10 Cognition & Emotion 155 (1996); *see also* Leary, *supra* note 36.

38. *See, e.g.*, Alison M. Wood & Maurice E. Schweitzer, *Can Nervous Nelly Negotiate? How Anxiety Causes Negotiators to Make Low First Offers, Exit Early, and Earn Less Profit*, 115 Organizational Behav. & Hum. Decision Processes 43 (2011) (finding that anxiety is one of the most common emotions reported when contemplating negotiation).

39. Keith Oatley et al., Understanding Emotions (2d ed. 2006); Gino & Schweitzer, *supra* note 32; Francesca Gino et al., *Anxiety, Advice, and the Ability to Discern: Feeling Anxious Motivates Individuals to Seek and Use Advice*, 102 J. Personality & Soc. Psychol. 497 (2012); Jon K. Maner & Mary A. Gerend, *Motivationally Selective Risk Judgments: Do Fear and Curiosity Boost the Boons*

or the Banes?, 103 ORGANIZATIONAL BEHAV. & HUM. DECISION PROCESSES 256 (2007); Rajagopal Raghunathan & Michel Tuan Pham, *All Negative Moods Are Not Equal: Motivational Influences of Anxiety and Sadness on Decision Making*, 79 ORGANIZATIONAL BEHAV. & HUM. DECISION PROCESSES 56 (1999); Ashleigh Shelby Rosette et al., *Good Grief! Feelings of Anxiety Sour the Economic Benefit of First Offers* (Duke University, Working Paper 2006); Kathleen D. Vohs et al., *Feeling Duped: Emotional, Motivational, and Cognitive Aspects of Being Exploited by Others*, 11 REV. GEN. PSYCHOL. 127 (2007); Tess Wilkinson-Ryan, *The Sucker Norm* (Univ. of Pa. Inst. for Law & Econ. Research, Working Paper No. 09-05, 2008); Wood & Schweitzer, *supra* note 38; *see also* Jennifer S. Lerner & Dacher Keltner, *Fear, Anger, & Risk*, 81 J. PERSONALITY & SOC. PSYCHOL. 146 (2001).

40. CARUSO & SALOVEY, *supra* note 15; DO EMOTIONS HELP OR HURT DECISION MAKING?, *supra* note 4, at 103 (confirmation bias); Ask & Granhag, *supra* note 20; Joseph P. Forgas, *Happy and Mistaken?*, *supra* note 20; Forgas, *When Sad Is Better Than Happy*, *supra* note 20; Forgas & East, *supra* note 20; Raghunathan & Pham, *supra* note 39.

41. On pride, see Jessica L. Tracy & Richard W. Robins, *The Psychological Structure of Pride: A Tale of Two Facets*, 92 J. PERSONALITY & SOC. PSYCHOL. 506 (2007); Lisa A. Williams & David DeSteno, *Pride: Adaptive Social Emotion or Seventh Sin?*, 20 PSYCHOL. SCI. 284 (2009); Lisa A. Williams & David DeSteno, *Pride and Perseverance: The Motivational Role of Pride*, 94 J. PERSONALITY & SOC. PSYCHOL. 1007 (2008).

42. Dacher Keltner & Jennifer S. Lerner, *Emotion*, *in* HANDBOOK OF SOCIAL PSYCHOLOGY 317 (Susan T. Fiske et al. eds., 2010); SONJA LYUBOMIRSKY, THE HOW OF HAPPINESS 25 (2007); Fredrickson, *supra* note 17.

43. ED DIENER & ROBERT DISWAS-DIENER, HAPPINESS: UNLOCKING THE MYSTERIES OF PSYCHOLOGICAL WEALTH (2008); LYUBOMIRSKY, *supra* note 42, at 22–23; *see also* Jordi Quoidbach et al., *Money Giveth, Money Taketh Away: The Dual Effect of Wealth on Happiness*, 21 PSYCHOL. SCI. 759 (2010) (finding that wealth is associated with a lower ability to savor).

44. Ed Diener et al., *Happiness of the Very Wealthy*, 16 SOC. INDICATORS RES. 263 (1985); Ed Diener & Robert Biswas-Diener, *Will Money Increase Subjective Well-Being? A Literature Review and Guide to Needed Research*, 57 SOC. INDICATORS RES. 119 (2002); Daniel Kahneman et al., *Would You Be Happier If You Were Richer? A Focusing Illusion*, 312 SCIENCE 1908 (2006).

45. DIENER & DISWAS-DIENER, *supra* note 43.

46. DIENER & DISWAS-DIENER, *supra* note 43, at 102–04 (2008); Russell W. Belk, *Materialism: Trait Aspects of Living in the Material World*, 14 J. CONSUMER RES. 113 (1985); Carol Nickerson et al., *Zeroing in on the Dark Side of the American Dream: A Closer Look at the Negative Consequences of the Goal for Financial Success*, 14 PSYCHOL. SCI. 531 (2003); Marsha L. Richins & Scott

Dawson, *A Consumer Values Orientation for Materialism and Its Measurement: Scale Development and Validation*, 19 J. CONSUMER RES. 303 (1992).

47. Leaf Van Boven, *Experientialism, Materialism, and the Pursuit of Happiness*, 9 REV. GEN. PSYCHOL. 132 (2005); Leaf Van Boven & Thomas Gilovich, *To Do or To Have? That Is the Question*, 85 J. PERSONALITY & SOC. PSYCHOL. 1193 (2005); Travis J. Carter & Thomas Gilovich, *The Relative Relativity of Material and Experiential Purchases*, 98 J. PERSONALITY & SOC. PSYCHOL. 146 (2010); Elizabeth W. Dunn et al., *If Money Doesn't Make You Happy Then You Probably Aren't Spending It Right*, 21 J. CONSUMER PSYCHOL. 115 (2011).

48. LYUBOMIRSKY, *supra* note 42, at 16–17 (quoting Dan Gilbert) (emphasis in original).

49. James J. Gross, *Emotion Regulation*, in HANDBOOK OF EMOTIONS 497 (Michael Lewis et al. eds., 3d ed. 2008); *see also* James J. Gross, *The Emerging Field of Emotion Regulation: An Integrative Review*, 2 REV. GEN. PSYCHOL. 271 (1998); Randy J. Larsen & Zvjezdana Prizmic, *Affect Regulation*, in HANDBOOK OF SELF-REGULATION: RESEARCH, THEORY, AND APPLICATIONS 40 (Roy F. Baumeister & Kathleen D. Vohs eds., 2004); Peter Salovey & Daisy Grewal, *The Science of Emotional Intelligence*, 14 CURRENT DIRECTIONS PSYCHOL. SCI. 281 (2005).

50. CARUSO & SALOVEY, *supra* note 15, at 62.

51. ARISTOTLE, THE NICOMACHEAN ETHICS 111 (H. Rackham trans., 1926).

52. CARUSO & SALOVEY, *supra* note 15, at 62.

53. Lawrence R. Richard, *Hiring Emotionally Intelligent Associates*, 56 BENCH & BAR MINN. 46, 46–47 (Oct. 1999).

54. ANALYZE THIS (Warner Bros. 1999). Also described in Brad J. Bushman, *Does Venting Anger Feed or Extinguish the Flame? Catharsis, Rumination, Distraction, Anger, and Aggressive Responding*, 28 PERSONALITY & SOC. PSYCHOL. BULL. 724 (2002).

55. Bushman, *supra* note 54; *see also* Allred et al., *supra* note 22; Jack E. Hokanson & Michael Burgess, *The Effects of Status, Type of Frustration, and Aggression on Vascular Processes*, 65 J. ABNORMAL & SOC. PSYCHOL. 232 (1962) (finding that aggression against source of frustration increases blood pressure).

56. Jonathan Rottenberg et al., *Is Crying Beneficial?*, 17 CURRENT DIRECTIONS PSYCHOL. SCI. 400 (2008).

57. *Id.*; *see also* Ad J. J. M. Vingerhoets et al., *Adult Crying: A Model and Review of the Literature*, 4 REV. GEN. PSYCHOL. 354 (2000).

58. Kenneth J. Kleppel, *Emotional Intelligence Is Key to Success*, OHIO LAW. 18, 20–21 (July/Aug. 2007).

59. James J. Gross, *Emotion Regulation in Adulthood: Timing Is Everything*, 10 CURRENT DIRECTIONS PSYCHOL. SCI. 214 (2001).

60. Daniel M. Wegner, *Ironic Processes of Mental Control*, 101 PSYCHOL. REV. 34 (1994).

61. Barry et al., *supra* note 21; Roy F. Baumeister et al., *Ego Depletion: A Resource Model of Volition, Self-Regulation, and Control Processing*, 18 Soc. Cognition 130 (2000); Gross, *supra* note 59; Iris B. Mauss et al., *How to Bite Your Tongue Without Blowing Your Top: Implicit Evaluation of Emotion Regulation Predicts Affective Responding to Anger Provocation*, 32 Personality & Soc. Psychol. Bull. 589 (2006); Jane M. Richards & James J. Gross, *Emotion Regulation and Memory: The Cognitive Costs of Keeping One's Cool*, 79 J. Personality & Soc. Psychol. 410 (2000); Leigh Thompson et al., *Poker Face, Smiley Face, and Rant 'n' Rave: Myths and Realities About Emotion in Negotiation*, in Emotion and Motivation, *supra* note 23, at 70.
62. Gross, *Emotion Regulation*, *supra* note 49; Gross & Thompson, *supra* note 5.
63. *See, e.g.*, Rebecca D. Ray et al., *All in the Mind's Eye? Anger Rumination and Reappraisal*, 94 J. Personality & Soc. Psychol. 133 (2008); Cheryl L. Rusting & Susan Nolen-Hoeksema, *Regulating Responses to Anger: Effects of Rumination on Angry Mood*, 74 J. Personality & Soc. Psychol. 790 (1998).
64. Gross & Thompson, *supra* note 5.
65. Mark Twain, The Tragedy of Pudd'nhead Wilson 121 (1894).
66. Ray et al., *supra* note 63.
67. Gross & Thompson, *supra* note 5, at 15.
68. Mark Muraven et al., *Self-Control as Limited Resource: Regulatory Depletion Patterns*, 74 J. Personality & Soc. Psychol. 774 (1998). *See generally* Roy F. Baumeister et al., *The Strength Model of Self-Control*, 16 Current Directions Psychol. Sci. 351 (2007).
69. *See* Peter M. Gollwitzer & Paschal Sheeran, *Implementation Intentions and Goal Achievement: A Meta-Analysis of Effects of Processes*, 38 Advances Experimental Soc. Psychol. 69 (2006); Inge Schweiger Gallo et al., *Strategic Automation of Emotion Regulation*, 96 J. Personality & Soc. Psychol. 11 (2009).
70. William Shakespeare, Measure for Measure, at act 2, scene 2.
71. Hillary Anger Elfenbein et al., *Reading Your Counterpart: The Benefit of Emotion Recognition Accuracy for Effectiveness in Negotiation*, 31 J. Nonverbal Behav. 205 (2007).
72. Loewenstein & Lerner, *supra* note 4, at 635.
73. Greg Mortenson & David Oliver Relin, Three Cups of Tea: One Man's Mission to Promote Peace . . . One School at a Time 333 (2006).
74. *See* Loewenstein & Lerner, *supra* note 4.
75. Martin E. P. Seligman, Authentic Happiness 39 (2004).
76. *See, e.g.*, Elaine Hatfield et al., *Emotional Contagion*, 2 Current Directions Psychol. Sci. 96 (1993).
77. Kopelman et al., *supra* note 4; Michael W. Morris & Dacher Keltner, *How Emotions Work: The Social Functions of Emotional Expression in Negotiations*, 22 Res. Organizational Behav. 1 (2000); Marwan Sinaceur & Larissa Z. Tiedens, *Get Mad and Get More Than Even: When and Why Anger Expression*

Is Effective in Negotiations, 42 J. Experimental Soc. Psychol. 314 (2006); Gerben A. van Kleef et al., *The Interpersonal Effects of Emotions in Negotiations: A Motivated Information Processing Approach*, 87 J. Personality & Soc. Psychol. 510 (2004); Gerben A. van Kleef et al., *Supplication and Appeasement in Conflict and Negotiation: The Interpersonal Effects of Disappointment, Worry, Guilt, and Regret*, 91 J. Personality & Soc. Psychol. 124 (2006); Maarten J. J. Wubben et al., *How Emotion Communication Guides Reciprocity: Establishing Cooperation Through Disappointment and Anger*, 45 J. Experimental Soc. Psychol. 987 (2009).

78. Dunn & Schweitzer, *supra* note 24; Morris & Keltner, *supra* note 77.
79. Gilovich et al., *supra* note 10 at 332.
80. *Id.*
81. Leigh Thompson et al., *supra* note 61, at 83.
82. *See* Carol L. Barr & Robert E. Kleck, *Self-Other Perception of the Intensity of Facial Expressions of Emotion: Do We Know What We Show?*, 68 J. Personality & Soc. Psychol. 608 (1995); Gilovich et al., *supra* note 10; Saul M. Kassin & Christina T. Fong, *"I'm Innocent!": Effects of Training on Judgments of Truth and Deception in the Interrogation Room*, 23 Law & Hum. Behav. 499 (1999); Saul M. Kassin & Gisli H. Gudjonsson, *The Psychology of Confessions: A Review of the Literature and Issues*, 5 Psychol. Sci. Pub. Int. 33 (2004); Leaf Van Boven et al., *The Illusion of Transparency in Negotiations*, 19 Negotiation J. 117 (2003); *see also* Stephen M. Garcia, *Power and the Illusion of Transparency in Negotiations*, 17 J. Bus. & Psychol. 133 (2002).

Chapter 4

1. Thomas Gilovich & Dale Griffin, *Introduction—Heuristics and Biases: Then and Now*, in Heuristics and Biases: The Psychology of Intuitive Judgment 1 (Thomas Gilovich et al. eds., 2002).
2. *ThinkExist.com Quotations*, ThinkExist.com, http://thinkexist.com/quotation/heuristics_are_bug_ridden_by_definition_if_they/338537.html (March 24, 2012).
3. *Niels Bohr Quotes*, ThinkExist.com, http://thinkexist.com/quotation/prediction-is-very-difficult-especially-about-the/1273367.html (March 24, 2012).
4. Jane Goodman-Delahunty et al., *Insightful or Wishful: Lawyers' Ability to Predict Case Outcomes*, 16 Psychol. Pub. Pol'y & L. 133 (2010); *see also* Elizabeth F. Loftus & Willem A. Wagenaar, *Lawyers' Predictions of Success*, 28 Jurimetrics J. 437 (1988); Zev J. Eigen & Yair Listokin, *Do Lawyers Really Believe Their Own Hype and Should They? A Natural Experiment* (Yale Law

& Econ. Research Paper No. 412, July 12, 2011), *available at* http://ssrn.com/abstract=1640062.
5. Roger Buehler et al., *The Planning Fallacy: Cognitive, Motivational, and Social Origins*, 43 ADVANCES EXPERIMENTAL SOC. PSYCHOL. 1 (2010).
6. *See, e.g.*, Lynn A. Baker & Robert E. Emery, *When Every Relationship Is Above Average: Perceptions and Expectations of Divorce at the Time of Marriage*, 17 LAW & HUM. BEHAV. 439 (1993); Zlatan Krizan & Paul D. Windschitl, *The Influence of Outcome Desirability on Optimism*, 133 PSYCHOL. BULL. 95 (2007); Terence R. Mitchell et al., *Temporal Adjustments in the Evaluation of Events: The "Rosy" View*, 33 J. EXPERIMENTAL SOC. PSYCHOL. 421 (1997); Don A. Moore & Paul J. Healy, *The Trouble with Overconfidence*, 115 PSYCHOL. REV. 502 (2008); Linda S. Perloff & Barbara K. Fetzer, *Self-Other Judgments and Perceived Vulnerability of Victimization*, 50 J. PERSONALITY & SOC. PSYCHOL. 502 (1986); Neil D. Weinstein, *Unrealistic Optimism About Susceptibility to Health Problems: Conclusions from a Community-Wide Sample*, 10 J. BEHAV. MED. 481 (1987); Neil D. Weinstein, *Unrealistic Optimism About Future Life Events*, 39 J. PERSONALITY & SOC. PSYCHOL. 806 (1980).
7. Daniel Kahneman & Amos Tversky, *Conflict Resolution: A Cognitive Perspective*, in BARRIERS TO CONFLICT RESOLUTION 44 (Kenneth Arrow et al. eds., 1995); *see also* Arnold C. Cooper et al., *Entrepreneurs' Perceived Chances for Success*, 3 J. BUS. VENTURING 97 (1988); Laurie Larwood & William Whittaker, *Managerial Myopia: Self-Serving Biases in Organizational Planning*, 62 J. APPLIED PSYCHOL. 194 (1977); Margaret A. Neale & Max H. Bazerman, *The Role of Perspective-Taking Ability in Negotiating Under Different Forms of Arbitration*, 36 INDUS. & LAB. REL. REV. 378 (1983); Terrance Odean, *Volume, Volatility, Price, and Profit When All Traders Are Above Average*, 53 J. FIN. 1887 (1998).
8. Max H. Bazerman & Margaret A. Neale, *Improving Negotiation Effectiveness Under Final Offer Arbitration: The Role of Selection and Training*, 67 J. APPLIED PSYCHOL. 543 (1982).
9. Daniel Kahneman & Amos Tversky, *Conflict Resolution: A Cognitive Perspective*, in CHOICES, VALUES, AND FRAMES 473, 476 (2000).
10. Lyle A. Brenner et al., *On the Evaluation of One-Sided Evidence*, 9 J. BEHAV. DECISION MAKING 59 (1996).
11. Ellen J. Langer, *The Illusion of Control*, 32 J. PERSONALITY & SOC. PSYCHOL. 311 (1975); Shelley E. Taylor & Jonathon D. Brown, *Illusion and Well-Being: A Social Psychological Perspective on Mental Health*, 103 PSYCHOL. BULL. 193 (1988); *see also* Paul K. Presson & Victor A. Benassi, *Illusion of Control: A Meta-Analytic Review*, 11 J. SOC. BEHAV. & PERSONALITY 493 (1996); Emily Pronin et al., *Everyday Magical Powers: The Role of Apparent Mental Causation in the Overestimation of Personal Influence*, 91 J. PERSONALITY & SOC. PSYCHOL. 218 (2006).

12. Russell Korobkin, *Aspirations and Settlement*, 88 CORNELL L. REV. 1 (2002).
13. *See* Colin Camerer & Dan Lovallo, *Overconfidence and Excess Entry: An Experimental Approach*, 89 AM. ECON. REV. 306 (1999) (overconfidence among entrepreneurs leads to excessive business entry into the market).
14. MARTHA NEIL, SURVEY: MOST PRE-LAW STUDENTS CONFIDENT RE OWN PROSPECTS, BUT DUBIOUS ABOUT OTHERS, http://www.abajournal.com/news/article/survey_most_pre-law_students_confident_re_own_prospects_but_dubious_about_o/.
15. *See generally* Moore & Healy, *supra* note 6.
16. *See, e.g.*, Scott T. Allison et al., *On Being Better but Not Smarter Than Others: The Muhammad Ali Effect,* 7 SOC. COGNITION 275 (1989); David Alain Armor, The Illusion of Objectivity: A Bias in the Perception of Freedom from Bias (1998) (dissertation abstract, University of California, Los Angeles), *available at* http://psycnet.apa.org/index.cfm?fa=search.displayRecord&uid=1999-95006-117; Nicholas Epley & David Dunning, *Feeling "Holier Than Thou": Are Self-Serving Assessments Produced by Errors in Self- or Social Prediction?*, 79 J. PERSONALITY & SOC. PSYCHOL. 861 (2000); Roderick M. Kramer et al., *Self-Enhancement Biases and Negotiator Judgment: Effects of Self-Esteem and Mood*, 56 ORGANIZATIONAL BEHAV. & HUM. DECISION PROCESSES 110 (1993); Wim B. G. Liebrand et al., *Why Are We Fairer Than Others: A Cross-Cultural Replication and Extension*, 22 J. EXPERIMENTAL SOC. PSYCHOL. 590 (1986); David M. Messick, *Why We Are Fairer Than Others*, 21 J. EXPERIMENTAL SOC. PSYCHOL. 480 (1985); Ola Svenson, *Are We All Less Risky and More Skillful Than Our Fellow Drivers?*, 47 ACTA PSYCHOLOGICA 143 (1981); Leigh Thompson & Reid Hastie, *Judgment Tasks and Biases in Negotiation*, *in* 2 RESEARCH ON NEGOTIATION IN ORGANIZATIONS 31 (Blair H. Sheppard et al. eds., 1986).
17. Richard Birke, *Settlement Psychology: When Decision-Making Processes Fail*, 18 ALTERNATIVES TO HIGH COST LITIG. 212, 214 (2000).
18. Chris Guthrie et al., *Inside the Judicial Mind*, 86 CORNELL L. REV. 777, 813–14 (2001).
19. *See, e.g.*, Allan Fenigstein, *Self-Consciousness and the Overperception of Self as a Target*, 47 J. PERSONALITY & SOC. PSYCHOL. 860 (1984); Thomas Gilovich et al., *The Spotlight Effect in Social Judgment: An Egocentric Bias in Estimates of the Salience of One's Own Actions and Appearance*, 78 J. PERSONALITY & SOC. PSYCHOL. 211 (2000); Raymond S. Nickerson, *How We Know—and Sometimes Misjudge—What Others Know: Imputing One's Own Knowledge to Others*, 125 PSYCHOL. BULL. 737 (1999); Kenneth Savitsky et al., *Do Others Judge Us as Harshly as We Think? Overestimating the Impact of Our Failures, Shortcomings, and Mishaps*, 81 J. PERSONALITY & SOC. PSYCHOL. 44 (2001).
20. *See, e.g.*, Don A. Moore, *Myopic Biases in Strategic Social Prediction: Why Deadlines Put Everyone Under More Pressure Than Everyone Else*, 31 PERSONALITY & SOC. PSYCHOL. BULL. 668 (2005).

21. *See, e.g.*, Michael Ross & Fiore Sicoly, *Egocentric Biases in Availability and Attribution*, 37 J. Personality & Soc. Psychol. 322 (1979).
22. Justin Kruger & Thomas Gilovich, *"Naive Cynicism" in Everyday Theories of Responsibility Assessment: On Biased Assumptions of Bias*, 76 J. Personality & Soc. Psychol. 743 (1999); *see also* Epley & Dunning, *supra* note 16; Nicholas Epley & David Dunning, *The Mixed Blessings of Self-Knowledge in Behavioral Prediction: Enhanced Discrimination but Exacerbated Bias*, 32 Personality & Soc. Psychol. Bull. 641 (2006).
23. *See* Carol Tavris & Elliot Aronson, Mistakes Were Made (but Not by Me): Why We Justify Foolish Beliefs, Bad Decisions, and Hurtful Acts (2007).
24. Kruger & Gilovich, *supra* note 22 (reviewing studies); Ross & Sicoly, *supra* note 21.
25. Stephen Budiansky et al., *How Lawyers Abuse the Law*, U.S. News & World Rep. at 50 (Jan. 30, 1995).
26. *See, e.g.*, Don A. Moore et al., *Conflict of Interest and the Intrusion of Bias*, 5 Judgment & Decision Making 37 (2010).
27. George Loewenstein et al., *Self-Serving Assessments of Fairness and Pretrial Bargaining*, 22 J. Legal Stud. 135 (1993); Leigh Thompson & George Loewenstein, *Egocentric Interpretations of Fairness and Interpersonal Conduct*, 51 Organizational Behav. & Hum. Decision Processes 176 (1992).
28. Leigh Thompson, *"They Saw a Negotiation": Partisanship and Involvement*, 68 J. Personality & Soc. Psychol. 839 (1995).
29. Scott Plous, The Psychology of Judgment and Decision Making 146 (1993); Amos Tversky & Daniel Kahneman, *Judgment Under Uncertainty: Heuristics and Biases*, in Judgment Under Uncertainty: Heuristics and Biases 3, 14 (Daniel Kahneman et al. eds., 1982).
30. Guthrie et al., *supra* note 18.
31. Max H. Bazerman & Don A. Moore, Judgment in Managerial Decision Making 33 (2009) (describing Edward J. Joyce & Gary C. Biddle, *Anchoring and Adjustment in Probabilistic Inference in Auditing*, 19 J. Acct. Res. 120 (1981)).
32. *See* Linda Babcock & Greg Pogarsky, *Damage Caps and Settlement: A Behavioral Approach*, 28 J. Legal Stud. 341 (1999); Gretchen B. Chapman & Brian H. Bornstein, *The More You Ask For, the More You Get: Anchoring in Personal Injury Verdicts*, 10 Applied Cognitive Psychol. 519 (1996); Adam D. Galinsky & Thomas Mussweiler, *First Offers as Anchors: The Role of Perspective-Taking and Negotiator Focus*, 81 J. Personality & Soc. Psychol. 657 (2001); Reid Hastie et al., *Juror Judgments in Civil Cases: Effects of Plaintiff's Requests and Plaintiff's Identity on Punitive Damage Awards*, 23 Law & Hum. Behav. 445 (1999); Verlin B. Hinsz & Kristin E. Indahl, *Assimilation to Anchors for Damage Awards in a Mock Civil Trial*, 25 J. Applied Soc. Psychol. 991 (1995); Russell Korobkin & Chris Guthrie, *Opening Offers and Out-of-Court Settlement: A Little Moderation May Not Go a Long Way*, 10 Ohio St. J. on Disp. Resol. 1 (1994); Korobkin, *supra* note 12; John Malouff & Nicola S. Schutte,

Shaping Juror Attitudes: Effects of Requesting Different Damage Amounts in Personal Injury Trials, 129 J. Soc. Psychol. 491 (1989); Jennifer K. Robbennolt & Christina A. Studebaker, *Anchoring in the Courtroom: The Effects of Caps on Punitive Damages*, 23 Law & Hum. Behav. 353 (1999); Michael J. Saks et al., *Reducing Variability in Civil Jury Awards*, 21 Law & Hum. Behav. 243 (1997).

33. Birte Englich & Thomas Mussweiler, *Sentencing Under Uncertainty: Anchoring Effects in the Courtroom*, 31 J. Applied Soc. Psychol. 1535 (2001); Birte Englich et al., *Playing Dice with Criminal Sentences: The Influence of Irrelevant Anchors on Experts' Judicial Decision Making*, 32 Personality & Soc. Psychol. Bull. 188 (2006).

34. Gregory B. Northcraft & Margaret A. Neale, *Experts, Amateurs, and Real Estate: An Anchoring-and-Adjustment Perspective on Property Pricing Decisions*, 39 Orgizational Behav. & Hum. Decision Processes 84 (1987).

35. Letter from Oliver Wendell Holmes to Frederick Pollock (July 9, 1912), *in* Holmes-Pollock Letters: The Correspondence of Mr. Justice Holmes and Sir Frederick Pollock, 1874–1932, at 194 (Mark Dewolfe Howe ed., 1961).

36. *See* Plous, *supra* note 29, at 121 (reporting that the chance of dying from falling airplane parts is thirty times greater than the chance of being killed in a shark attack); J. Edward Russo & Paul J. H. Schoemaker, Decision Traps: Ten Barriers to Brilliant Decision-making and How to Overcome Them 82–83 (1989) (reviewing two newspapers over a one-year period and finding 137 articles about deaths in motor vehicle accidents and only one story about a stomach cancer death).

37. *See, e.g.*, Harvard Medical Practice Study, Patients, Doctors, and Lawyers: Medical Injury, Malpractice Litigation, and Patient Compensation in New York: The Report of the Harvard Medical Practice Study to the State of New York (1990); Donald R. Songer, *Tort Reform in South Carolina: The Effect of Empirical Research on Elite Perceptions Concerning Jury Verdicts*, 39 S.C. L. Rev. 585 (1988). *See generally* Daniel S. Bailis & Robert J. MacCoun, *Estimating Liability Risks with the Media as Your Guide: A Content Analysis of Media Coverage of Tort Litigation*, 20 Law & Hum. Behav. 419 (1996); Jennifer K. Robbennolt & Christina A. Studebaker, *News Media Reporting on Civil Litigation and Its Influence on Civil Justice Decision Making*, 27 Law & Hum. Behav. 5 (2003).

38. Michael Lewis, Moneyball: The Art of Winning an Unfair Game 15–20 (2003). The A's were first or second in their division, the American League West, from 1999 to 2006.

39. Nancy Levit, *Confronting Conventional Thinking: The Heuristics Problem in Feminist Legal Theory*, 28 Cardozo L. Rev. 391, 397 (2006); *see also* Cass R. Sunstein, *Moral Heuristics and Moral Framing*, 88 Minn. L. Rev. 1556, 1562 (2004).

40. *See* Thomas Gilovich & Kenneth Savitsky, *Like Goes with Like: The Role of Representativeness in Erroneous and Pseudo-Scientific Beliefs*, *in* Heuristics and Biases: The Psychology of Intuitive Judgment, *supra* note 1, at 617.

41. David G. Meyers, Intuition 204–05 (2002).
42. Example adapted from Amos Tversky & Daniel Kahneman, *Judgment Under Uncertainty: Heuristics and Biases*, 185 Science 1124 (1974).
43. *Id.*; *see also* Thomas Gilovich et al., *The Hot Hand in Basketball: On the Misperception of Random Sequences*, 17 Cognitive Psychol. 295 (1985).
44. *See* Ali Siddiq Alhakami & Paul Slovic, *A Psychological Study of the Inverse Relationship Between Perceived Risk and Perceived Benefit*, 14 Risk Analysis 1085 (1994); Melissa L. Finucane et al., *The Affect Heuristic in Judgments of Risks and Benefits*, 13 J. Behav. Decision Making 1 (2000); Paul Slovic et al., *The Affect Heuristic, in* Heuristics and Biases: The Psychology of Intuitive Judgment, *supra* note 1, at 398.
45. Slovic et al., *supra* note 44, at 398.
46. Paul Slovic et al., *Rational Actors or Rational Fools: Implications of the Affect Heuristic for Behavioral Economics*, 31 J. Socio-Econ. 329, 339–40 (2002).
47. *See* Lawrence J. Sanna & Norbert Schwarz, *Metacognitive Experiences and Hindsight Bias: It's Not Just the Thought (Content) That Counts!*, 25 Soc. Cognition 185 (2007).
48. *See* Jeffrey J. Rachlinski, *A Positive Psychological Theory of Judging in Hindsight*, 65 U. Chi. L. Rev. 571 (1998). *See generally* Baruch Fischhoff, *Hindsight ≠ Foresight: The Effect of Outcome Knowledge on Judgment Under Uncertainty*, 1 J. Experimental Psychol.: Hum. Perception & Performance 288 (1975); Scott A. Hawkins & Reid Hastie, *Hindsight: Biased Judgments of Past Events After the Outcomes Are Known*, 107 Psychol. Bull. 311 (1990). *See also* Erin M. Harley, *Hindsight Bias in Legal Decision Making*, 25 Soc. Cognition 48 (2007); Kim A. Kamin & Jeffrey J. Rachlinski, *Ex Post ≠ Ex Ante: Determining Liability in Hindsight*, 19 Law & Hum. Behav. 89 (1995); Susan J. LaBine & Gary LaBine, *Determinations of Negligence and the Hindsight Bias*, 20 Law & Hum. Behav. 501 (1996).
49. *See generally* Rachlinski, *supra* note 48. *See also* Mitu Gulati et al., *Fraud by Hindsight*, 98 Nw. U. L. Rev. 773 (2004).
50. Randall Kiser, Beyond Right and Wrong: The Power of Effective Decision Making for Attorneys and Clients 133 (2010).
51. Jonathan Baron & John C. Hershey, *Outcome Bias in Decision Evaluation*, 54 J. Personality & Soc. Psychol. 569 (1988). While hindsight bias and outcome bias may produce similar results and may often work in tandem, outcome bias is a distinct bias that is distinguishable from hindsight bias. *Id.*
52. Kiser, *supra* note 50, at 306.
53. Edie Greene & Brian H. Bornstein, *Cloudy Forecasts*, 47 Trial 28 (Apr. 2011); *see also* Songer, *supra* note 37; Roselle L. Wissler et al., *Decisionmaking About General Damages: A Comparison of Jurors, Judges, and Lawyers*, 98 Mich. L. Rev. 751 (1999).

54. *See generally* Robbennolt & Studebaker, *supra* note 37.
55. Baruch Fischhoff, *Debiasing, in* Judgment Under Uncertainty: Heuristics and Biases, *supra* note 29, at 422; Asher Koriat et al., *Reasons for Confidence*, 6 J. Experimental Psychol.: Hum. Learning & Memory 107 (1980); Paul Slovic & Baruch Fischhoff, *On the Psychology of Experimental Surprises*, 3 J. Experimental Psychol.: Hum. Perception & Performance 544 (1977) (hindsight bias); Linda Babcock et al., *Creating Convergence: Debiasing Biased Litigants*, 22 Law & Soc. Inquiry 913 (1997) (self-serving bias); Thomas Mussweiler et al., *Overcoming the Inevitable Anchoring Effect: Considering the Opposite Compensates for Selective Accessibility*, 26 Personality & Soc. Psychol. Bull. 1142 (2000).
56. Russell Korobkin, *Psychological Impediments to Mediation Success: Theory and Practice*, 21 Ohio St. J. on Disp. Resol. 281, 296 (2006) (emphasis added).
57. *Id.*
58. *See* Craig A. Anderson et al., *Perseverance of Social Theories: The Role of Explanation in the Persistence of Discredited Information*, 39 J. Personality & Soc. Psychol. 1037 (1980); Adam D. Galinsky & Gordon B. Moskowitz, *Counterfactuals as Behavioral Primes: Priming the Simulation Heuristic and Consideration of Alternatives*, 36 J. Experimental Soc. Psychol. 384 (2000); Edward R. Hirt & Keith D. Markman, *Multiple Explanation: A Consider-an-Alternative Strategy for Debiasing Judgments*, 69 J. Personality & Soc. Psychol. 1069 (1995).
59. Antonin Scalia & Brian A. Garner, Making Your Case: The Art of Persuading Judges 11 (2008).
60. Daniel Kahneman & Dan Lovallo, *Timid Choices and Bold Forecasts: A Cognitive Perspective on Risk Taking*, 39 Mgmt. Sci. 17, 24–25 (1993).
61. *Id.*
62. J. Scott Armstrong, *Combining Forecasts, in* Principles of Forecasting: A Handbook for Researchers and Practitioners 417 (J. Scott Armstrong ed., 2001) (reviewing studies); James Surowiecki, Wisdom of Crowds (2004) (reviewing studies); *see also* Dan Ariely et al., *The Effects of Averaging Subjective Probability Estimates Between and Within Judges*, 6 J. Experimental Psychol.: Applied 130 (2000).
63. *See* Jack B. Soll & Richard P. Larrick, *Strategies for Revising Judgment: How (and How Well) People Use Others' Opinions*, 35 J. Experimental Psychol.: Learning Memory & Cognition 780 (2009); Richard P. Larrick & Jack B. Soll, *Intuitions About Combining Opinions: Misappreciation of the Averaging Principle*, 52 Mgmt. Sci. 111 (2006); Ilan Yaniv & Maxim Milyavsky, *Using Advice from Multiple Sources to Revise and Improve Judgments*, 103 Orgizational Behav. & Hum. Decision Processes 104 (2007).
64. Soll & Larrick, *supra* note 63.

65. Jonas Jacobson et al., *Predicting Civil Jury Verdicts: How Attorneys Use (and Misuse) a Second Opinion*, 8 J. EMPIRICAL LEGAL STUD. 99 (2011).
66. *Id.*
67. *Id.* (reporting that 82% of sampled attorneys reported "always" or "frequently" consulting with colleagues when predicting jury verdicts).
68. *Id.*; Soll & Larrick, *supra* note 63; Yaniv & Milyavsky, *supra* note 63.
69. Stefan M. Herzog & Ralph Hertwig, *The Wisdom of Many in One Mind: Improving Individual Judgments with Dialectical Bootstrapping*, 20 PSYCHOL. SCI. 231 (2009); Edward Vul & Harold Pashler, *Measuring the Crowd Within: Probabilistic Representations Within Individuals*, 19 PSYCHOL. SCI. 645 (2008).
70. *See* Chip Heath et al., *Cognitive Repairs: How Organizational Practices Can Compensate for Individual Shortcomings*, 20 RES. ORGANIZATIONAL BEHAV. 1 (1998).

Chapter 5

1. J.K. ROWLING, HARRY POTTER AND THE SORCERER'S STONE 217 (1997).
2. MODEL RULES OF PROF'L CONDUCT R. 1.2, 2.1 (2007).
3. MAX H. BAZERMAN, JUDGMENT IN MANAGERIAL DECISION MAKING 3–4 (4th ed. 1998).
4. HERBERT A. SIMON, MODELS OF MAN 204–06 (1957).
5. *See* Amos Tversky, *Elimination by Aspects: A Theory of Choice*, 79 PSYCHOL. REV. 281 (1972).
6. *See, e.g.*, Barry Schwartz et al., *Maximizing Versus Satisficing: Happiness Is a Matter of Choice*, 83 J. PERSONALITY & SOC. PSYCHOL. 1178, 1179 (2002); *see also* Sheena S. Iyengar et al., *Doing Better but Feeling Worse: Looking for the "Best" Job Undermines Satisfaction*, 17 PSYCHOL. SCI. 143, 147 (2006).
7. Amos Tversky & Eldar Shafir, *The Disjunction Effect in Choice Under Uncertainty*, 3 PSYCHOL. SCI. 305 (1992).
8. Anthony Bastardi & Eldar Shafir, *Nonconsequential Reasoning and Its Consequences*, 9 CURRENT DIRECTIONS PSYCHOL. SCI. 216 (2000); *see also* Anthony Bastardi & Eldar Shafir, *On the Pursuit and Misuse of Useless Information*, 75 J. PERSONALITY & SOC. PSYCHOL. 19, 28 (1998).
9. Donald A. Redelmeier et al., *The Beguiling Pursuit of More Information*, 21 MED. DECISION MAKING 374 (2001).
10. *See, e.g.*, Amos Tversky & Eldar Shafir, *Choice Under Conflict: The Dynamics of Deferred Decision*, 3 PSYCHOL. SCI. 358 (1992).
11. RANDALL KISER, BEYOND RIGHT AND WRONG: THE POWER OF EFFECTIVE DECISION MAKING FOR ATTORNEYS AND CLIENTS 336 (2010).
12. Daniel Kahneman & Amos Tversky, *Choices, Values, and Frames*, 39 AM. PSYCHOLOGIST 341, 343–44 (1984); Daniel Kahneman & Amos Tversky, *Prospect Theory: An Analysis of Decision Under Risk*, 47 ECONOMETRICA 263, 263

(1979); Amos Tversky & Daniel Kahneman, *The Framing of Decisions and the Psychology of Choice*, 211 SCIENCE 453, 453 (1981); *see also* Chris Guthrie, *Framing Frivolous Litigation: A Psychological Theory*, 67 U. CHI. L. REV. 163 (2000).
13. 900 F.2d 429 (1st Cir. 1990).
14. STEPHEN BREYER, BREAKING THE VICIOUS CIRCLE: TOWARD EFFECTIVE RISK REGULATION 12 (1995), *discussed in* PAUL BREST & LINDA HAMILTON KRIEGER, PROBLEM SOLVING, DECISION MAKING, AND PROFESSIONAL JUDGMENT: A GUIDE FOR LAWYERS AND POLICYMAKERS 484 (2010).
15. Tversky & Kahneman, *supra* note 12.
16. Sabrina M. Tom et al., *The Neural Basis of Loss Aversion in Decision-Making Under Risk*, 315 SCIENCE 515, 516 (2007).
17. Daniel Kahneman et al., *Experimental Tests of the Endowment Effect and the Coase Theorem*, 98 J. POL. ECON. 1325 (1990). *But see* Charles R. Plott & Kathryn Zeiler, *The Willingness to Pay-Willingness to Accept Gap, the "Endowment Effect," Subject Misperceptions, and Experimental Procedures for Eliciting Valuations*, 95 AM. ECON. REV. 530 (2005).
18. KISER, *supra* note 11, at 121.
19. Eric J. Johnson et al., *Framing, Probability Distortions, and Insurance Decisions*, 7 J. RISK & UNCERTAINTY 35, 48 (1993); *see also* Lyle Brenner et al., *Comparison, Grouping, and Preference*, 10 PSYCHOL. SCI. 225, 227 (1999); Itamar Simonson & Amos Tversky, *Choice in Context: Tradeoff Contrast and Extremeness Aversion*, 29 J. MARKETING RES. 281, 286–87 (1992).
20. KISER, *supra* note 11, at 123.
21. *See* Edward J. McCaffery & Jonathan Baron, *Framing and Taxation: Evaluation of Tax Policies Involving Household Consumption*, 25 J. ECON. PSYCHOL. 679 (2004).
22. *See* Brenner et al., *supra* note 19; Simonson & Tversky, *supra* note 19.
23. THE FRIAR'S CLUB BIBLE OF ROASTS, TOASTS, POKES AND JOKES 316 (Nina Colman et al. eds., 2001).
24. Hal R. Arkes & Catherine Blumer, *The Psychology of Sunk Cost*, 35 ORGANIZATIONAL BEHAV. & HUM. DECISION PROCESSES 124 (1985).
25. *See* KISER, *supra* note 11, at 138.
26. Chris Guthrie, *Panacea or Pandora's Box? The Costs of Options in Negotiation*, 88 IOWA L. REV. 601 (2003); *see* Joel Huber et al., *Adding Asymmetrically Dominated Alternatives: Violations of Regularity and the Similarity Hypothesis*, 9 J. CONSUMER RES. 90 (1982); Mark Kelman et al., *Context-Dependence in Legal Decision Making*, 25 J. LEGAL STUD. 287 (1996).
27. Jeffrey J. Rachlinski et al., *Context Effects in Judicial Decision Making* 1 (Empirical Legal Studies Paper, Aug. 3, 2009), *available at* http://papers.ssrn.com/sol3/papers.cfm?abstract_id=1443596.
28. *See* Simonson & Tversky, *supra* note 19.

29. Guthrie, *supra* note 26.
30. Kelman et al., *supra* note 26.
31. Guthrie, *supra* note 26.
32. Christopher J. Anderson, *The Psychology of Doing Nothing: Forms of Decision Avoidance Result from Reason and Emotion*, 129 Psychol. Bull. 139, 146 (2003).
33. *Id.* at 146. *See also* Orit E. Tykocinski & Thane S. Pittman, *The Consequences of Doing Nothing: Inaction Inertia as Avoidance of Anticipated Counterfactual Regret*, 75 J. Personality & Soc. Psychol. 607 (1998).
34. Anderson, *supra* note 32, at 147.
35. Niels van de Ven et al., *Delay, Doubt, and Decision: How Delaying a Choice Reduced the Appeal of (Descriptively) Normative Options*, 21 Psychol. Sci. 568 (2010).
36. Deal or No Deal, NBC.com, http://www.nbc.com/Deal_or_No_Deal/about/index.shtml; *see also* Thierry Post et al., *Deal or No Deal? Decision Making Under Risk in a Large-Payoff Game Show*, 98 Am. Econ. Rev. 38 (2008).
37. *See* Richard Thaler, *Some Empirical Evidence on Dynamic Inconsistency*, 8 Econ. Letters 201 (1981); *see also* George Ainslie & Varda Haendel, *The Motives of the Will*, in Etiologic Aspects of Alcohol and Drug Abuse 119 (Edward Gottheil et al. eds., 1983); Uri Benzion et al., *Discount Rates Inferred from Decisions: An Experimental Study*, 35 Mgmt. Sci. 270 (1989); Gretchen B. Chapman, *Temporal Discounting and Utility for Health and Money*, 22 J. Experimental Psychol.: Learning Memory & Cognition 771 (1996); Jerry A. Hausman, *Individual Discount Rates and the Purchase and Utilization of Energy-Using Durables*, 10 Bell J. Econ. 33 (1979).
38. *See, e.g.*, George Loewenstein, *Frames of Mind in Intertemporal Choice*, 34 Mgmt. Sci. 200 (1988).
39. *See* Thaler, *supra* note 37.
40. George Loewenstein & N. Sicherman, *Do Workers Prefer Increasing Wage Profiles?*, 9 J. Labor Econ. 67 (1991).
41. Lee Ross & Andrew Ward, *Psychological Barriers to Dispute Resolution*, 27 Advances Experimental Soc. Psychol. 255, 270 (1995).
42. *See* Russell Korobkin, *Psychological Impediments to Mediation Success: Theory and Practice*, 21 Ohio St. J. Disp. Resol. 281, 316–18 (2006); Russell Korobkin & Chris Guthrie, *Psychological Barriers to Litigation Settlement: An Experimental Approach*, 93 Mich. L. Rev. 107, 151–52 (1994).
43. Daniel T. Gilbert & Jane E. J. Ebert, *Decisions and Revisions: The Affective Forecasting of Changeable Outcomes*, 82 J. Personality & Soc. Psychol. 503, 503 (2002) (citing studies).

44. Daniel T. Gilbert et al., *Immune Neglect: A Source of Durability Bias in Affective Forecasting*, 75 J. PERSONALITY & SOC. PSYCHOL. 617, 622–24 (1998); Barbara A. Mellers & A. Peter McGraw, *Anticipated Emotions as Guides to Choice*, 10 CURRENT DIRECTIONS PSYCHOL. SCI. 210, 212 (2001).
45. Julie A. Woodzicka & Marianne LaFrance, *Real Versus Imagined Gender Harassment*, 57 J. SOC. ISSUES 15 (2001); *see also* Janet K. Swim & Lauri L. Hyers, *Excuse Me—What Did You Just Say?!: Women's Public and Private Responses to Sexist Remarks*, 35 J. EXPERIMENTAL SOC. PSYCHOL. 68 (1999).
46. Kristina A. Diekmann, *"She did what? There is no way I would do that!" The Potential Interpersonal Harm Caused by Mispredicting One's Behavior*, 80 J. BUS. ETHICS 5, 7 (2008). *See* Kristina A. Diekmann et al., *From Self-Prediction to Self-Defeat: Behavioral Forecasting, Self-Fulfilling Prophecies, and the Effect of Competitive Expectations*, 85 J. PERSONALITY & SOC. PSYCHOL. 672 (2003).
47. Daniel Kahneman, *What Were They Thinking?*, GALLUP MGMT. J. (Jan. 13, 2005), http://gmj.gallup.com/content/14503/what-were-they-thinking.aspx.
48. Daniel Kahneman & Amos Tversky, *Prospect Theory: An Analysis of Decision Under Risk*, 47 ECONOMETRICA 263, 271 (1979).
49. Daniel T. Gilbert & Timothy D. Wilson, *Prospection: Experiencing the Future*, 317 SCIENCE 1351 (2007); Allen R. McConnell et al., *Blind Spots in the Search for Happiness: Implicit Attitudes and Nonverbal Leakage Predict Affective Forecasting Errors*, 47 J. EXPERIMENTAL SOC. PSYCHOL. 628 (2011); Jordi Quoidbaqch & Elizabeth W. Dunn, *Personality Neglect: The Unforeseen Impact of Personality Dispositions on Emotional Life*, 21 PSYCHOL. SCI. 1783 (2010); David A. Schkade & Daniel Kahneman, *Does Living in California Make People Happy? A Focusing Illusion in Judgments of Life Satisfaction*, 9 PSYCHOL. SCI. 340, 340 (1998); Timothy D. Wilson et al., *Focalism: A Source of Durability Bias in Affective Forecasting*, 78 J. PERSONALITY & SOC. PSYCHOL. 821, 822 (2000); Timothy D. Wilson & Daniel T. Gilbert, *Affective Forecasting*, 35 ADVANCES EXPERIMENTAL SOC. PSYCHOL. 345 (2003).
50. Daniel T. Gilbert et al., *The Surprising Power of Neighborly Advice*, 323 SCIENCE 1617 (2009).
51. Chris Guthrie, *Better Settle Than Sorry: The Regret Aversion Theory of Litigation Behavior*, U. ILL. L. REV. 43, 65–66 (1999).
52. *Id.* at 69; *see* David E. Bell, *Regret in Decision Making Under Uncertainty*, 30 OPERATIONS RES. 961 (1982); Thomas Gilovich & Victoria H. Medvec, *The Experience of Regret: What, When, and Why*, 102 PSYCHOL. REV. 379, 380–81 (1995); Graham Loomes & Robert Sugden, *Regret Theory: An Alternative Theory of Rational Choice Under Uncertainty*, 92 ECON J. 805 (1982); Dale T. Miller et al., *Counterfactual Thinking and Social Perception: Thinking About What Might Have Been*, 23 ADVANCES EXPERIMENTAL SOC. PSYCHOL. 305

(1990); Ilana Ritov, *Probability of Regret: Anticipation of Uncertainty Resolution in Choice*, 66 Organizational Behav. & Hum. Decision Processes 228 (1996); Marcel Zeelenberg et al., *Consequences of Regret Aversion: Effects of Expected Feedback on Risky Decision Making*, 65 Organizational Behav. & Hum. Decision Processes 148 (1996).

53. Mara Mather et al., *Misremembrance of Options Past: Source Monitoring and Choice*, 11 Psychol. Sci. 132, 132 (2000).
54. *See, e.g.*, Jochen Reb, *Regret Aversion and Decision Process Quality: Effects of Regret Salience on Decision Process Carefulness*, 105 Organizational Behav. & Hum. Decision Processes 169 (2008).
55. Gilbert & Ebert, *supra* note 43.
56. Laurence J. Peter, Peter's Quotations: Ideas for our Time 297 (1977).
57. Piers Steel, *The Nature of Procrastination: A Meta-Analytic and Theoretical Review of Quintessential Self-Regulatory Failure*, 133 Psychol. Bull. 65, 66 (2007) (emphasis added).
58. Tversky & Shafir, *supra* note 10.
59. Anderson, *supra* note 32. *See generally* Jonathan Baron & Ilana Ritov, *Reference Points and Omission Bias*, 59 Organizational Behav. & Hum. Decision Processes 475 (1994); Mark Spranca et al., *Omission and Commission in Judgment and Choice*, 27 J. Experimental Soc. Psychol. 76 (1991).
60. Jiwoong Shin & Dan Ariely, *Keeping Doors Open: The Effect of Unavailability on Incentives to Keep Options Viable*, 50 Mgmt. Sci. 575, 576–77 (2004) (emphasis in original). These results held even when the players were given information about the payoff distributions of the doors (Study 2) and when an additional monetary cost was assessed for each "door-click" (Study 3). *Id.*
61. *See* Lottie Bullens et al., *Keeping One's Options Open: The Detrimental Consequences of Decision Reversability*, 47 J. Experimental Soc. Psychol. 800 (2011); Gilbert & Ebert, *supra* note 43.
62. Letter from Benjamin Franklin to Joseph Priestley (Sept. 19, 1772), *available at* http://www.nickols.us/Ben_Franklin_Decision_Making.pdf.
63. Benjamin Franklin, The Autobiography of Benjamin Franklin 27 (Stanley Appelbaum & Philip Smith eds., 1996).
64. *See, e.g.*, Carla M. Kmett et al., *The Influence of Decision Aids on High School Students' Satisfaction with Their College Choice Decision*, 25 Personality & Soc. Psychol. Bull. 1293 (1999).
65. Robyn LeBoeuf & Eldar Shafir, *Decision Making*, *in* The Cambridge Handbook of Thinking and Reasoning 301, 308 (Keith J. Holyoak & Robert G. Morrison eds., 2005); *see also* McConnell et al., *supra* note 49.
66. David A. Armor, *The Illusion of Objectivity: Bias in the Belief in Freedom from Bias* (1998) (dissertation abstract, University of California, Los Angeles), *available at* http://psycnet.apa.org/index.cfm?fa=search.displayRecord&uid=1999-95006-117.

67. Samuel R. Sommers & Michael I. Norton, *Race-Based Judgments, Race Neutral Justifications: Experimental Examination of Peremptory Use and the Batson Challenge Procedure*, 31 Law & Hum. Behav. 261 (2007). Similar results have been found when people are asked to make hiring or college admissions decisions: decision makers justify decisions that have been influenced by factors such as race or gender by recruiting reasons based on their valuing of particular candidate qualifications. *See* Michael I. Norton et al., *Casuistry and Social Category Bias*, 87 J. Personality & Soc. Psychol. 817 (2004). The more elastic or ambiguous the justifiable reasons for a decision are, the more likely it is that they will be recruited to mask the effects of less justifiable influences. Christopher K. Hsee, *Elastic Justification: How Unjustifiable Factors Influence Judgments*, 66 Organizational Behav. & Hum. Decision Processes 122 (1996); *see also* Richard Nisbett & Timothy Wilson, *Telling More Than We Can Know: Verbal Reports on Mental Processes*, 84 Psychol. Rev. 231 (1977).

68. Christopher K. Hsee et al., *Lay Rationalism and Inconsistency Between Predicted Experience and Decision*, 16 J. Behav. Decision Making 257, 265 (2003) (describing three manifestations of lay rationalism: lay economism, lay scientism, and lay functionalism). There can be differences in the sorts of reasons that people from different cultures offer and find socially acceptable to justify their choices. *See, e.g.*, Donnel A. Briley et al., *Reasons as Carriers of Culture: Dynamic Versus Dispositional Models of Cultural Influence on Decision Making*, 27 J. Consumer Res. 157 (2000).

69. *See* Timothy D. Wilson & Jonathan W. Schooler, *Thinking Too Much: Introspection Can Reduce the Quality of Preferences and Decisions*, 60 J. Personality & Soc. Psychol. 181 (1991); Timothy D. Wilson et al., *Introspecting About Reasons Can Reduce Post-Choice Satisfaction*, 19 Personality & Soc. Psychol. Bull. 331 (1993).

70. Robin M. Hogarth, Educating Intuition (2001); John McMackin & Paul Slovic, *When Does Explicit Justification Impair Decision Making?*, 14 Applied Cognitive Psychol. 527 (2000).

71. *See, e.g.*, Yoel Inbar et al., *Decision Speed and Choice Regret: When Haste Feels Like Waste*, 47 J. Experimental Soc. Psychol. 533 (2011).

72. *Lou Schwartz' Favorite Quotes*, Am. Sportscasters Online, http://www.americansportscastersonline.com/quotes.html (last visited Nov. 9, 2011).

73. E. Tory Higgins et al., *How Making the Same Decision in a "Proper Way" Creates Value*, 26 Soc. Cognition 496 (2008); *see also* E. Tory Higgins, *Making a Good Decision: Value from Fit*, 55 Am. Psychologist 1217 (2000); Daniel C. Molden & E. Tory Higgins, *Motivated Thinking*, in The Cambridge Handbook of Thinking and Reasoning, *supra* note 65, at 295.

74. Arie W. Kruglanski, The Psychology of Closed-Mindedness (2004); Arie W. Kruglanski & Donna M. Webster, *Motivated Closing of the Mind: "Seizing" and "Freezing,"* 103 Psychol. Rev. 263 (1996).

75. Eldar Shafir, *Choosing Versus Rejecting: Why Some Options Are Both Better and Worse Than Others*, 21 MEMORY & COGNITION 546 (1993).
76. This example was adapted from Christopher K. Hsee, *The Evaluability Hypothesis: An Explanation of Preference Reversals Between Joint and Separate Evaluations of Alternatives*, 46 ORGANIZATIONAL BEHAV. & HUM. DECISION PROCESSES 247 (1996).
77. Max H. Bazerman, et al., *Reversals of Preference in Allocation Decisions: Judging an Alternative Versus Choosing Among Alternatives*, 37 ADMIN. SCI. Q. 220 (1992).
78. Christopher K. Hsee et al., *Preference Reversals Between Joint and Separate Evaluations of Options: A Review and Theoretical Analysis*, 125 PSYCHOL. BULL. 576, 588 (1999).
79. Christopher K. Hsee & Jiao Zhang, *Distinction Bias: Misprediction and Mischoice Due to Joint Evaluation*, 86 J. PERSONALITY & SOC. PSYCHOL. 680 (2004).
80. *Id.*
81. Tversky & Shafir, *supra* note 10, at 361 (emphasis in original).
82. *Id.*; *see also* Tim Silk, *Getting Started Is Half the Battle: The Influence of Deadlines and Effort on Consumer Self-Regulation to Redeem Rewards* (Working Paper, 2005) (on file with the Sauder Sch. of Bus., Univ. of British Columbia), *described in* Andrew J. Wistrich, *Procrastination, Deadlines, and Statutes of Limitation*, 50 WM. & MARY L. REV. 607, 635–37 (2008).
83. Dan Ariely & Klaus Westenbroch, *Procrastination, Deadlines, and Performance: Self-Control by Precommitment*, 13 PSYCHOL. SCI. 219 (2002).
84. *See* Norbert L. Kerr et al., *Bias in Judgment: Comparing Individuals and Groups*, 103 Psychol. Rev. 687 (1996). *See generally* Special Issue, *Theoretical Perspectives on Groupthink: A Twenty-Fifth Anniversary Appraisal*, 73 ORGANIZATIONAL BEHAV. & HUM. DECISION PROCESSES 103 (1998); Robert S. Baron, *So Right It's Wrong: Groupthink and the Ubiquitous Nature of Polarized Group Decision-Making*, 37 ADVANCES EXPERIMENTAL SOC. PSYCHOL. 219 (2005); Norbert Kerr & R. Scott Tindale, *Group Performance and Group Decision Making*, 55 ANN. REV. PSYCHOL. 623, 628 (2004).
85. Kerr & Tindale, *supra* note 84, at 628.
86. *Id.* at 627.
87. *Id.*
88. Garold Stasser & W. Titus, *Pooling of Unshared Information in Group Decision Making: Biased Information Sampling During Discussion*, 48 PERSONALITY & SOC. PSYCHOL. 1467 (1985); *see also* Daniel Gigone & Reid Hastie, *The Common Knowledge Effect: Information Sharing and Group Judgment*, 65 J. PERSONALITY & SOC. PSYCHOL. 959 (1993); James R. Larson Jr., et al., *Diagnosing Groups: Charting the Flow of Information in Medical Decision Making Teams*, 71 J. PERSONALITY & SOC. PSYCHOL. 315 (1996); Garold Stasser et al., *Information*

Sampling in Structured and Unstructured Discussions of Three- and Six-Person Groups, 57 J. PERSONALITY & SOC. PSYCHOL. 67 (1989).

89. MAX. H. BAZERMAN & DON A. MOORE, JUDGMENT IN MANAGERIAL DECISION MAKING 51 (2009).

90. Kerr & Tindale, *supra* note 84, at 637; *see also* Garold Stasser & Sandra I. Vaughan, *Pooling Unshared Information: The Benefits of Knowing How Access to Information is Distributed Among Group Members*, 82 ORG. BEHAV. & HUM. DECISION PRECESSES 102 (2000).

91. Baron, *supra* note 84, at 236; *see* Dale T. Miller & Deborah A. Prentice, *Collective Errors and Errors About the Collective*, 20 PERSONALITY & SOC. PSYCHOL. BULL. 541 (1994); Deborah A. Prentice & Dale T. Miller, *Pluralistic Ignorance and the Perpetuation of Social Norms by Unwitting Actors*, 28 ADVANCES EXPERIMENTAL SOC. PSYCHOL. 161 (Mark P. Zanna ed., 1996).

92. Dale T. Miller, *The Norm of Self-Interest*, 54 AM. PSYCHOLOGIST 1053 (1999) (describing Rebecca K. Ratner's dissertation).

93. *See generally* Daniel J. Eisenberg, *Group Polarization: A Critical Review and Meta-Analysis*, 50 J. PERSONALITY & SOC. PSYCHOL. 1141 (1986).

94. *See generally* KISER, *supra* note 11, at 385–95; *see* Charles R. Schwenk, *Effects of Devil's Advocacy and Dialectical Inquiry on Decision Making: A Meta-Analysis*, 47 ORGANIZATIONAL BEHAV. & HUM. DECISION PROCESSES 161 (1990).

95. KISER, *supra* note 11, at 395.

96. *See* Peter M. Gollwitzer & Paschal Sheeran, *Implementation Intentions and Goal Achievement: A Meta-Analysis of Effects of Processes*, 38 ADVANCES EXPERIMENTAL SOC. PSYCHOL. 69 (2006).

97. *See* Roy F. Baumeister et al., *The Strength Model of Self-Control*, 16 CURRENT DIRECTIONS PSYCHOL. SCI. 351 (2007); Martin S. Hagger et al., *Ego Depletion and the Strength Model of Self-Control*, 136 PSYCHOL. BULL. 495 (2010). Recent research has suggested that a person's expectations about the degree to which self-control is a limited resource can moderate this effect. That is, those who believe that their willpower is an unlimited resource are less likely to show decreased performance following a demanding task. Veronika Job et al., *Ego Depletion—Is It All in Your Head? Implicit Theories About Willpower Affect Self-Regulation*, 21 PSYCHOL. SCI. 1686 (2010).

98. Baba Shiv & Alexander Fedorikhin, *Heart and Mind in Conflict: The Interplay of Affect and Cognition in Consumer Decision Making*, 26 J. CONSUMER RES. 278 (1999).

99. Kathleen D. Vohs et al., *Making Choices Impairs Subsequent Self-Control: A Limited-Resource Account of Decision Making, Self-Regulation, and Active Initiative*, 94 J. PERSONALITY & SOC. PSYCHOL. 883 (2008).

100. Attributed to St. Bernard of Clairvaux.

101. *See* Gollwitzer & Sheeran, *supra* note 96; Inge Schweiger Gallo et al., *Strategic Automation of Emotion Regulation*, 96 J. Personality & Soc. Psychol. 11 (2009).

Chapter 6

1. R. Gordon Hoxie, *Dwight David Eisenhower: Bicentennial Considerations*, 20 Presidential Stud. Q. 253, 257 (1990).
2. Erwin N. Griswold, *Law Schools and Human Relations*, 1955 Wash. U. L.Q. 217, 223 (1955).
3. The most prominent models include the *elaboration likelihood model* and the *heuristic-systematic model*. Richard E. Petty & John T. Cacioppo, Attitudes and Persuasion: Classic and Contemporary Approaches (1996) (elaboration likelihood model); Shelly Chaiken, *Heuristic Versus Systematic Information Processing and the Use of Source Versus Message Cues in Persuasion*, 39 J. Personality & Soc. Psychol. 752 (1980) (heuristic-systematic model); Richard E. Petty & John T. Cacioppo, *The Elaboration Likelihood Model of Persuasion*, 19 Advances Experimental Soc. Psychol. 123 (1986).
4. *See* Richard E. Petty et al., *Elaboration as a Determinant of Attitude Strength*, *in* Attitude Strength: Antecedents and Consequences 93 (Richard E. Petty & Jon A. Krosnick eds., 1995).
5. John T. Cacioppo et al., *Dispositional Differences in Cognitive Motivation: The Life and Times of Individuals Varying in Need for Cognition*, 119 Psychol. Bull. 197 (1996); John T. Cacioppo & Richard E. Petty, *The Need for Cognition*, 42 J. Personality & Soc. Psychol. 116 (1982); *see also* Donna Shestowsky et al., *Need for Cognition and Interpersonal Influence: Individual Differences in Impact on Dyadic Decisions*, 74 J. Personality & Soc. Psychol. 1317 (1998).
6. *See* Jennifer S. Lerner & Philip E. Tetlock, *Accounting for the Effects of Accountability*, 125 Psychol. Bull. 255 (1999); Richard E. Petty & John T. Cacioppo, *Involvement and Persuasion: Tradition Versus Integration*, 107 Psychol. Bull. 367 (1990); Richard E. Petty et al., *Personal Involvement as a Determinant of Argument-Based Persuasion*, 41 J. Personality & Soc. Psychol. 847 (1981).
7. Shelly Chaiken & Durairaj Maheswaran, *Heuristic Processing Can Bias Systematic Processing: Effects of Source Credibility, Argument Ambiguity, and Task Importance on Attitude Judgment*, 66 J. Personality & Soc. Psychol. 460 (1994) (heuristic cue establishes expectancy about message validity, which can influence systematic processing).
8. Gerd Bohner et al., *The Interplay of Heuristic and Systematic Processing of Social Information*, 6 Eur. Rev. Soc. Psychol. 33, 35 (1995); *see also* Hans-Peter Erb & Gerd Bohner, *Social Influence and Persuasion: Recent Theoretical*

Developments and Integrative Attempts, in SOCIAL COMMUNICATION 191 (Klaus Fiedler ed. 2007).

9. MICHAEL J. SAKS & REID HASTIE, SOCIAL PSYCHOLOGY IN COURT 104–05 (1978).
10. *Id.* (emphasis in original).
11. *See generally* Richard E. Petty & Pablo Briñol, *Persuasion: From Single to Multiple to Metacognitive Processes*, 3 PERSP. PSYCHOL. SCI. 137 (2008).
12. Pablo Briñol et al., *Happiness Versus Sadness as a Determinant of Thought Confidence in Persuasion: A Self-Validation Analysis*, 93 J. PERSONALITY & SOC. PSYCHOL. 711 (2007).
13. *See generally* Carl I. Hovland et al., *Communication and Persuasion: Psychological Studies of Opinion Change*, 45 J. EXPERIMENTAL PSYCHOL. 175 (1953); Carl I. Hovland & Walter Weiss, *The Influence of Source Credibility on Communication Effectiveness*, 15 PUB. OPINION Q. 635 (1952).
14. ISOCRATES, ANTIDOSIS, *reprinted in* READINGS FROM CLASSICAL RHETORIC 47, 56 (Patricia P. Matsen et al. eds., 1990).
15. *See, e.g.*, Ayn E. Crowley & Wayne D. Hoyer, *An Integrative Framework for Understanding Two-Sided Persuasion*, 20 J. CONSUMER RES. 561 (1994).
16. *See* Elaine Walster et al., *On Increasing the Persuasiveness of a Low Prestige Communicator*, 2 J. EXPERIMENTAL SOC. PSYCHOL. 325 (1966).
17. Petty & Cacioppo, *supra* note 3.
18. Joseph R. Priester & Richard E. Petty, *The Influence of Spokesperson Trustworthiness on Message Elaboration, Attitude Strength, and Advertising Effectiveness*, 13 J. CONSUMER PSYCHOL. 408 (2003).
19. ANTONIN SCALIA & BRYAN A. GARNER, MAKING YOUR CASE: THE ART OF PERSUADING JUDGES 205 (2008).
20. Steven D. Penrod & Brian L. Cutler, *Witness Confidence and Witness Accuracy: Assessing Their Forensic Relation*, 1 PSYCHOL. PUB. POL'Y & L. 817 (1995); Lynn M. van Swol & Janet A. Sniezek, *Factors Affecting the Acceptance of Expert Advice*, 44 BRIT. J. SOC. PSYCHOL. 443 (2005); Paul Zarnoth & Janet A. Sniezek, *The Social Influence of Confidence in Group Decision Making*, 33 J. EXPERIMENTAL SOC. PSYCHOL. 345 (1997).
21. *See, e.g.*, Garrett L. Berman & Brian L. Cutler, *Effects of Inconsistencies in Eyewitness Testimony on Mock-Juror Decision Making*, 81 J. APPLIED PSYCHOL. 170 (1996); Garrett L. Berman et al., *Effects of Inconsistent Eyewitness Statements on Mock-Jurors' Evaluations of the Eyewitness, Perceptions of Defendant Culpability, and Verdicts*, 19 LAW & HUM. BEHAV. 79 (1995); Jeffrey J. Borckardt et al., *Effects of the Inclusion and Refutation of Peripheral Details on Eyewitness Credibility*, 33 J. APPLIED SOC. PSYCHOL. 2187 (2003); Nina Hatvany & Fritz Strack, *The Impact of a Discredited Key Witness*, 10 J. APPLIED SOC. PSYCHOL. 490 (1980).
22. Elizabeth R. Tenney et al., *Calibration Trumps Confidence as a Basis for Witness Credibility*, 18 PSYCHOL. SCI. 46 (2007); Elizabeth R. Tenney et al., *The*

Benefits of Knowing What You Know (and What You Don't): How Calibration Affects Credibility, 44 J. EXPERIMENTAL SOC. PSYCHOL. 1368 (2008).

23. *Id.*

24. Sunita Sah et al., *Cheap Talk and Credibility: The Consequences of Confidence and Accuracy on Advisor Credibility and Persuasiveness* (Working Paper, June 9, 2011), *available at* http://ssrn.com/abstract=1861475.

25. Bonnie Erickson et al., *Speech Style and Impression Formation in a Court Setting: The Effects of "Powerful" and "Powerless" Speech*, 14 J. EXPERIMENTAL SOC. PSYCHOL. 266 (1978); E. Allan Lind & William M. O'Barr, *The Social Significance of Speech in the Court*, *in* LANGUAGE AND SOCIAL PSYCHOLOGY 66 (Howard Giles & Robert N. St. Clair eds., 1979); Christine L. Ruva & Judith Becker Bryant, *The Impact of Age, Speech Style, and Question Form on Perceptions of Witness Credibility and Trial Outcome*, 34 J. APPLIED SOC. PSYCHOL. 1919 (2004); *see also* Robert K. Bothwell & Mehri Jalil, *The Credibility of Nervous Witnesses*, 7 J. SOC. BEHAV. & PERSONALITY 581 (1992).

26. *See, e.g.*, Gerald R. Miller & Murray A. Hewgill, *The Effect of Variations in Nonfluency on Audience Ratings of Source Credibility*, 50 Q. J. SPEECH 36 (1964); Rolf Reber & Norbert Schwarz, *Effects of Perceptual Fluency on Judgments of Truth*, 8 CONSCIOUSNESS & COGNITION 338 (1999).

27. Joseph Cesario & E. Tory Higgins, *Making Message Recipients "Feel Right": How Nonverbal Cues Can Increase Persuasion*, 19 PSYCHOL. SCI. 415 (2008); *see also* Joseph Cesario et al., *Regulation Fit and Persuasion: Basic Principles and Remaining Questions*, 2 SOC. & PERSONALITY PSYCHOL. COMPASS 444 (2008); Joseph Cesario et al., *Regulatory Fit and Persuasion: Transfer from "Feeling Right,"* 86 J. PERSONALITY & SOC. PSYCHOL. 388 (2004).

28. Stephen G. Harkins & Richard E. Petty, *Effects of Source Magnification of Cognitive Efforts on Attitudes: An Information-Processing View*, 40 J. PERSONALITY & SOC. PSYCHOL. 401 (1981); Stephen G. Harkins & Richard E. Petty, *Information Utility and the Multiple Source Effect*, 52 J. PERSONALITY & SOC. PSYCHOL. 260 (1987); Stephen G. Harkins & Richard E. Petty, *The Multiple Source Effect in Persuasion: The Effects of Distraction*, 7 PERSONALITY & SOC. PSYCHOL. BULL. 627 (1981).

29. *See* Kate A. Ranganath et al., *Cognitive "Category-Based Induction" Research and Social "Persuasion" Research Are Each About What Makes Arguments Believable: A Tale of Two Literatures*, 5 PERSP. PSYCHOL. SCI. 115 (2010) (review).

30. *See, e.g.*, John T. Cacioppo et al., *The Effects of a Salient Self-Schema on the Evaluation of Proattitudinal Editorials: Top-Down Versus Bottom-Up Message Processing*, 18 J. EXPERIMENTAL SOC. PSYCHOL. 324 (1982).

31. Wendi Lyn Adair & Jeanne M. Brett, *Culture and Negotiation Processes*, *in* THE HANDBOOK OF NEGOTIATION AND CULTURE 158, 162 (Michele J. Gelfand & Jeanne M. Brett eds., 2004).

32. *See, e.g.*, Adam L. Alter et al., *Overcoming Intuition: Metacognitive Difficulty Activates Analytical Reasoning*, 136 J. EXPERIMENTAL PSYCHOL.: GEN. 569 (2007); Adam L. Alter & Daniel M. Oppenheimer, *Uniting the Tribes of Fluency to Form a Metacognitive Nation*, 13 PERSONALITY & SOC. PSYCHOL. REV. 219 (2009) (reviewing studies); Susan E. Brennan & Maurice Williams, *The Feeling of Another's Knowing: Prosody and Filled Pauses as Cues to Listeners About the Metacognitive States of Speakers*, 34 J. MEMORY & LANGUAGE 383 (1995); Alice H. Eagly, *Comprehensibility of Persuasive Arguments as a Determinant of Opinion Change*, 29 J. PERSONALITY & SOC. PSYCHOL. 758 (1974); Christopher Hertzog et al., *Encoding Fluency Is a Cue Used for Judgments About Learning*, 29 J. EXPERIMENTAL PSYCHOL.: LEARNING MEMORY & COGNITION 22 (2003); Ranganath et al., *supra* note 29 (reviewing studies); Reber & Schwarz, *supra* note 26; Joseph P. Simmons & Lief D. Nelson, *Intuitive Confidence: Choosing Between Intuitive and Nonintuitive Alternatives*, 135 J. EXPERIMENTAL PSYCHOL.: GEN. 409 (2006).
33. *See, e.g.*, Mark Sadoski et al., *Engaging Texts: Effects of Concreteness on Comprehensibility, Interest, and Recall in Four Text Types*, 92 J. EDUC. PSYCHOL. 85 (2000).
34. *See, e.g.*, Allan Paivio et al., *Concreteness Effects on Memory: When and Why?*, 20 J. EXPERIMENTAL PSYCHOL.: LEARNING MEMORY & COGNITION 1196 (1994); *see also* RICHARD E. MAYER, APPLYING THE SCIENCE OF LEARNING (2010).
35. CHIP HEATH & DAN HEATH, MADE TO STICK: WHY SOME IDEAS SURVIVE AND OTHERS DIE 142 (2008) (emphasis in original).
36. ANTON ANTONOV-OVSEYENKO, THE TIME OF STALIN 287 (1980) (translated into English by George Sanders, 1981).
37. Thomas Schelling, *The Life You Save May Be Your Own*, *in* PROBLEMS IN PUBLIC EXPENDITURE ANALYSIS 127, 129 (Samuel B. Chase ed., 1968).
38. Paul Slovic, *If I Look at the Mass I Will Never Act: Psychic Numbing and Genocide*, *in* EMOTIONS AND RISKY TECHNOLOGIES 37, 37 (Sabine Roeser ed., 2010).
39. *See, e.g.*, Karen E. Jenni & George Loewenstein, *Explaining the "Identifiable Victim Effect,"* 14 J. RISK & UNCERTAINTY 235 (1997); Deborah A. Small & George Loewenstein, *The Devil You Know: The Effects of Identifiability on Punishment*, 18 J. BEHAV. DECISION MAKING 311 (2005); Deborah A. Small & George Loewenstein, *Helping a Victim or Helping the Victim: Altruism and Identifibililty*, 26 J. RISK & UNCERTAINTY 5 (2003).
40. Ruth Hamill et al., *Insensitivity to Sample Bias: Generalizing from Atypical Cases*, 39 J. PERSONALITY & SOC. PSYCHOL. 578 (1980).
41. Jonathan Shedler & Melvin Manis, *Can the Availability Heuristic Explain Vividness Effects?*, 51 J. PERSONALITY & SOC. PSYCHOL. 26 (1986).
42. Richard E. Petty et al., *Effects of Rhetorical Questions on Persuasion: A Cognitive Response Analysis*, 40 J. PERSONALITY & SOC. PSYCHOL. 432 (1981); *see also* Kurt P. Frey & Alice H. Eagly, *Vividness Can Undermine the Persuasiveness*

of Messages, 65 J. PERSONALITY & SOC. PSYCHOL. 32 (1993); Shelley E. Taylor & Suzanne C. Thompson, *Stalking the Elusive "Vividness" Effect*, 89 PSYCHOL. REV. 155 (1982).

43. *See, e.g.*, S. E. Asch, *Forming Impressions of Personality*, 41 J. ABNORMAL & SOC. PSYCHOL. 258 (1946); Wiliam D. Crano, *Primacy Versus Recency in Retention of Information and Opinion Change*, 101 J. SOC. PSYCHOL. 87 (1977); Saul M. Kassin et al., *Juror Interpretations of Ambiguous Evidence: The Need for Cognition, Presentation Order, and Persuasion*, 14 LAW & HUM. BEHAV. 43 (1990); Norman Miller & Donald T. Campbell, *Recency and Primacy in Persuasion as a Function of the Timing of Speeches and Measurements*, 59 J. ABNORMAL SOC. PSYCHOL. 1 (1959); Richard E. Petty et al., *Motivation to Think and Order Effects in Persuasion: The Moderating Role of Chunking*, 27 PERSONALITY & SOC. PSYCHOL. BULL. 332 (2001).

44. *See* Crowley & Hoyer, *supra* note 15 (review).

45. William J. McGuire, *Inducing Resistance to Persuasion: Some Contemporary Approaches*, 1 ADVANCES EXPERIMENTAL SOC. PSYCHOL. 191 (1964); Wendy Wood & Jeffrey M. Quinn, *Forewarned and Forearmed? Two Meta-Analytic Syntheses of Forewarnings of Influence Appeals*, 129 PSYCHOL. BULL. 119 (2003).

46. Laura M. Arpan & David R. Roskos-Ewoldsen, *Stealing Thunder: Analysis of the Effects of Proactive Disclosure of Crisis Information*, 31 PUB. REL. REV. 425 (2005); Lara Dolnik et al., *Stealing Thunder as a Courtroom Tactic Revisited: Processes and Boundaries*, 27 LAW & HUM. BEHAV. 267 (2003); Mark V. A. Howard et al., *How Processing Resources Shape the Influence of Stealing Thunder on Mock-Juror Verdicts*, 13 PSYCHIATRY PSYCHOL. & L. 60 (2006); Kipling D. Williams et al., *The Effects of Stealing Thunder in Criminal and Civil Trials*, 17 LAW & HUM. BEHAV. 597 (1993); *see also* Ronen Perry & Dana Weimann-Saks, *Stealing Sunshine*, 74 LAW & CONTEMP. PROBS. 33 (2011).

47. Williams et al., *supra* note 46 (Experiment 2).

48. *See, e.g.*, Arpan & Roskos-Ewoldsen, *supra* note 46.

49. Gonzalez-Servin v. Ford Motor Co., 2011 WL 5924441 (7th Cir. Nov. 23, 2011).

50. ANTONIN SCALIA & BRYAN A. GARNER, MAKING YOUR CASE: THE ART OF PERSUADING JUDGES 21–22 (2008).

51. James Friedrich et al., *Argument Integration and Attitude Change: Suppression Effects in the Integration of One-Sided Arguments That Vary in Persuasiveness*, 22 PERSONALITY & SOC. PSYCHOL. BULL. 179 (1996); Richard E. Petty & John T. Cacioppo, *The Effects of Involvement on Responses to Argument Quantity and Quality: Central and Peripheral Routes to Persuasion*, 46 J. PERSONALITY & SOC. PSYCHOL. 69 (1984); Itamar Simonson et al., *The Effect of Irrelevant Preference Arguments on Consumer Choice*, 2 J. CONSUMER PSYCHOL. 287 (1993).

52. THE GODFATHER (Paramount Pictures 1972).

53. Deepak Malhotra & Max H. Bazerman, *Psychological Influence in Negotiation: An Introduction Long Overdue*, 34 J. MGMT. 509, 512 (2008) (emphasis added).
54. Francis J. Flynn & Vanessa K. B. Lake, *If You Need Help, Just Ask: Underestimating Compliance with Direct Requests for Help*, 95 J. PERSONALITY & SOC. PSYCHOL. 128 (2008).
55. LINDA BABCOCK & SARA LASCHEVER, WOMEN DON'T ASK: NEGOTIATION AND THE GENDER DIVIDE 1–7 (2003).
56. Lee Ross & Donna Shestowsky, *Contemporary Psychology's Challenges to Legal Theory and Practice*, 97 NW. U. L. REV. 1081, 1088 (2003).
57. Malhotra & Bazerman, *supra* note 53.
58. David B. Strohmetz et al., *Sweetening the Till: The Use of Candy to Increase Restaurant Tipping*, 32 J. APPLIED SOC. PSYCHOL. 300 (2002).
59. Letter from Samuel Johnson to James Boswell (1774), *in* JAMES BOSWELL, THE LIFE OF SAMUEL JOHNSON 473, 473 (1776).
60. *See* ROBERT B. CIALDINI, INFLUENCE: SCIENCE AND PRACTICE 19 (5th ed. 2009).
61. *See* Robert B. Cialdini & Noah J. Goldstein, *Social Influence: Compliance and Conformity*, 55 ANN. REV. PSYCHOL. 591, 599 (2004).
62. *See generally* Alan A. Benton et al., *Effects of Extremity of Offers and Concession Rate on the Outcomes of Bargaining*, 24 J. PERSONALITY & SOC. PSYCHOL. 73 (1972).
63. *See* Mark Bennett & Christopher Dewberry, *"I've Said I'm Sorry, Haven't I?" A Study of the Identity Implications and Constraints That Apologies Create for Their Recipients*, 13 CURRENT PSYCHOL. 10 (1994); Jane L. Risen & Thomas Gilovich, *Target and Observer Differences in the Acceptance of Questionable Apologies*, 92 J. PERSONALITY & SOC. PSYCHOL. 418 (2007).
64. CIALDINI, *supra* note 60, at 35–36 (emphasis in original).
65. Robert B. Cialdini et al., *Reciprocal Concessions Procedure for Inducing Compliance: The Door-in-the-Face Technique*, 31 J. PERSONALITY & SOC. PSYCHOL. 206 (1975); Daniel J. O'Keefe & Scott L. Hale, *An Odds-Ratio-Based Meta-Analysis of Research on the Door-in-the-Face Influence Strategy*, 14 COMM. REP. 31 (2001).
66. Tad Friend, *You Can't Say That*, NEW YORKER 44, 49 (Nov. 19, 2001).
67. Cialdini & Goldstein, *supra* note 61; *see* Jerry M. Burger et al., *The Effects of Initial Request Size on Compliance: More About the That's-Not-All Technique*, 21 BASIC & APPLIED SOC. PSYCHOL. 243 (1999); Jerry M. Burger, *Increasing Compliance by Improving the Deal: The That's-Not-All Technique*, 51 J. PERSONALITY & SOC. PSYCHOL. 277 (1986).
68. *See* Neil Vidmar, *Retribution and Revenge*, *in* HANDBOOK OF JUSTICE RESEARCH IN LAW 31 (Joseph Sanders & V. Lee Hamilton eds., 2000); Dale T. Miller, *Disrespect and the Experience of Injustice*, 52 ANN. REV. PSYCHOL. 527 (2001).

69. Boaz Keysar et al., *Reciprocity Is Not Give and Take: Asymmetric Reciprocity to Positive and Negative Acts*, 19 Psychol. Sci. 1280 (2008); *see also* Sukhwinder S. Shergill et al., *Two Eyes for an Eye: The Neuroscience of Force Escalation*, 301 Science 187 (2003).
70. Cialdini, *supra* note 60, at 199–200 (5th ed. 2009).
71. *Id.* at 52; Robert B. Cialdini & Melanie R. Trost, *Social Influence: Social Norms, Conformity, and Compliance*, in The Handbook of Social Psychology 151 (Daniel T. Gilbert et al. eds., 4th ed. 1998); *see also* Robert B. Cialdini et al., *Compliance with a Request in Two Cultures: The Differential Influence of Social Proof and Commitment/Consistency on Collectivists and Individualists*, 25 Personality & Soc. Psychol. Bull. 1242 (1999).
72. Norbert L. Kerr & Robert J. MacCoun, *The Effects of Jury Size and Polling Method on the Process and Product of Jury Deliberations*, 48 J. Personality & Soc. Psychol. 349 (1985).
73. Jonathan L. Freedman & Scott C. Fraser, *Compliance Without Pressure: The Foot-in-the-Door Technique*, 4 J. Personality & Soc. Psychol. 195 (1966).
74. *See* Michael J. Saks, *Social Psychological Contributions to a Legislative Subcommittee on Organ and Tissue Transplants*, 33 Am. Psychologist 680 (1978); Shalom H. Schwartz, *Elicitation of Moral Obligation and Self-Sacrificing Behavior: An Experimental Study of Volunteering to Be a Bone Marrow Donor*, 15 J. Personality & Soc. Psychol. 283 (1970).
75. Robert B. Cialdini et al., *Low-Ball Procedure for Producing Compliance: Commitment Then Cost*, 36 J. Personality & Soc. Psychol. 463 (1978).
76. Barry M. Staw, *Knee-Deep in the Big Muddy: A Study of Escalating Commitment to a Chosen Course of Action*, 16 Organizational Behav. & Hum. Performance 27 (1976).
77. Gillian Ku, *Before Escalation: Behavioral and Affective Forecasting in Escalation of Commitment*, 34 Personality & Soc. Psychol. Bull. 1477, 1485 (2008).
78. Itamar Simonson & Barry M. Staw, *Deescalation Strategies: A Comparison of Techniques for Reducing Commitment to Losing Courses of Action*, 77 J. Applied Psychol. 419 (1992).
79. Cialdini, *supra* note 60, at 142–44; *see also* Jerry M. Burger et al., *What a Coincidence! The Effects of Incidental Similarity on Compliance*, 30 Personality & Soc. Psychol. Bull. 35 (2004); Shelly Chaiken, *Communicator Physical Attractiveness and Persuasion*, 37 J. Personality & Soc. Psychol. 1387 (1979); Dariusz Dolinski et al., *Dialogue Involvement as a Social Influence Technique*, 27 Personality & Soc. Psychol. Bull. 1395 (2001); Daniel J. Howard et al., *The Name Remembrance Effect: A Test of Alternative Explanations*, 12 J. Soc. Behav. & Personality 801 (1997); Daniel J. Howard et al., *What's in a Name? A Complimentary Means of Persuasion*, 22 J. Consumer Res. 200 (1995); Michael Morris et al., *Schmooze or Lose: Social Friction and Lubrication in E-Mail Negotiations*, 6 Group Dynamics: Theory Res. & Prac. 89 (2002);

Paul J. Silvia, *Deflecting Reactance: The Role of Similarity in Increasing Compliance and Reducing Resistance*, 27 BASIC & APPLIED SOC. PSYCHOL. 277 (2005).
80. RONALD WAICUKAUSKI ET AL., THE 12 SECRETS OF PERSUASIVE ARGUMENT 3 (2009).
81. *See* Randall A. Gordon, *Impact of Ingratiation on Judgments and Evaluations: A Meta-Analytic Investigation*, 71 J. PERSONALITY & SOC. PSYCHOL. 54 (1996); Roos Vonk, *Self-Serving Interpretations of Flattery: Why Ingratiation Works*, 82 J. PERSONALITY & SOC. PSYCHOL. 515 (2002); *see also* EDWARD E. JONES, INGRATIATION: A SOCIAL PSYCHOLOGICAL ANALYSIS (1964); EDWARD E. JONES & CAMILLE B. WORTMAN, INGRATIATION: AN ATTRIBUTIONAL APPROACH (1973).
82. DALE CARNEGIE, HOW TO WIN FRIENDS AND INFLUENCE PEOPLE 88 (1936).
83. Jason Scott Johnson & Joel Waldfogel, *Does Repeat Play Elicit Cooperation? Evidence From Federal Civil Litigation*, 31 J. LEGAL STUD. 39 (2002).
84. Morris et al., *supra* note 79.
85. Bibb Latané & John M. Darley, *Group Inhibition of Bystander Intervention in Emergencies*, 10 J. PERSONALITY & SOC. PSYCHOL. 215, 216 (1968).
86. *See* John M. Darley & Bibb Latané, *Bystander Intervention in Emergencies: Diffusion of Responsibility*, 8 J. PERSONALITY & SOC. PSYCHOL. 377 (1968); A. M. ROSENTHAL, THIRTY-EIGHT WITNESSES: THE KITTY GENOVESE CASE (1964).
87. CIALDINI, *supra* note 60, at 99.
88. *See, e.g.*, Robert B. Cialdini, *Social Motivations to Comply: Norms, Values, and Principles*, in TAXPAYER COMPLIANCE 200 (Jeffrey A. Roth & John T. Scholz eds., 1989); Robert B. Cialdini, *Crafting Normative Messages to Protect the Environment*, 12 CURRENT DIRECTIONS PSYCHOL. SCI. 105 (2003) Yuval Feldman & Janice Nadler, *The Law and Norms of File Sharing*, 43 SAN DIEGO L. REV. 577 (2006); Art Hinshaw & Jess K. Alberts, *Doing the Right Thing: An Empirical Study of Attorney Negotiation Ethics*, 16 HARV. NEGOTIATION L. REV. 95 (2011); Latané & Darley, *supra* note 85; Stanley Milgram et al., *Note on the Drawing Power of Crowds of Different Size*, 13 J. PERSONALITY & SOC. PSYCHOL. 79 (1969); *see also* MUZAFER SHERIF, THE PSYCHOLOGY OF SOCIAL NORMS (1936).
89. *See* Chris Guthrie, *Courting Compliance*, in THE NEGOTIATOR'S FIELDBOOK 371 (Andrea Kupfer Schneider & Christopher Honeyman eds., 2006).
90. Deborah A. Prentice & Dale T. Miller, *Pluralistic Ignorance and the Perpetuation of Social Norms by Unwitting Actors*, 28 ADVANCES EXPERIMENTAL SOC. PSYCHOL. 161 (Mark P. Zanna ed., 1996); Dale T. Miller & Deborah A. Prentice, *Collective Errors and Errors About the Collective*, 20 PERSONALITY & SOC. PSYCHOL. BULL. 541 (1994).
91. Kimberlee Weaver et al., *Inferring the Popularity of an Opinion from Its Familiarity: A Repetitive Voice Can Sound Like a Chorus*, 92 J. PERSONALITY & SOC. PSYCHOL. 821 (2007); *see also* Ian Begg et al., *On Believing What We Remember*, 17 CANADIAN J. BEHAV. SCI. 199 (1985); Gerd Gigerenzer, *External Validity of Laboratory Experiments: The Frequency-Validity Relationship*, 97 AM. J. PSYCHOL. 185 (1984).

92. *See* Noah J. Goldstein et al., Yes! 50 Scientifically Proven Ways to Be Persuasive 10 (2008).
93. Solomon E. Asch, *Studies of Independence and Conformity: A Minority of One Against a Unanimous Majority*, 70 Psychol. Monographs: Gen. & Applied 1 (1956); *see also* Gregory S. Berns et al., *Neurobiological Correlates of Social Conformity and Independence During Mental Rotation*, 58 Biological Psychiatry 245 (2005) (examining the effects of conformity and independence on brain activity). For examination of conformity and culture, *see* Rod Bond & Peter B. Smith, *Culture and Conformity: A Meta-Analysis of Studies Using Asch's (1952b, 1956) Line Judgment Task*, 119 Psychol. Bull. 111 (1996); Cialdini et al., *supra* note 71; Heejung Kim & Hazel Rose Markus, *Deviance or Uniqueness, Harmony or Conformity? A Cultural Analysis*, 77 J. Personality & Soc. Psychol. 785 (1999). To see a video description of the Asch experiment, see *Group Influence*, Situationalist, (June 2, 2011, 7:44 p.m.), https://thesituationist.wordpress.com/2011/06/02/group-influence/.
94. *See, e.g.*, David Crump, *The Social Psychology of Evil: Can the Law Prevent Groups from Making Good People Go Bad?*, 2008 BYU L. Rev. 1441 (2008).
95. Cialdini, *supra* note 60, at 175–76.
96. Stanley Milgram, Obedience to Authority: An Experimental View (1974).
97. Peter Gabriel, *We Do What We're Told (Milgram's 37)*, *on* So (Virgin UK Music 2004).
98. Lee Ross & Richard Nisbett, The Person and the Situation: Perspectives of Social Psychology 57 (1991) (emphasis in original).
99. Milgram, *supra* note 96, at 30.
100. Kurt Lewin, *Group Decision and Social Change*, *in* Readings in Social Psychology 330 (Guy E. Swanson et al. eds., 1952).
101. *See, e.g.*, Howard Leventhal et al., *Effects of Fear and Specificity of Recommendation upon Attitudes and Behavior*, 2 J. Personality & Soc. Psychol. 20 (1965).
102. Kurt Lewin, Field Theory in Social Science (1951); Ross & Nisbett, *supra* note 98.
103. Chip Heath & Dan Heath, Switch: How to Change Things When Change Is Hard 184–85 (2010) (emphasis in original).
104. Brad J. Saragin et al., *Dispelling the Illusion of Invulnerability: The Motivations and Mechanisms of Resistance to Persuasion*, 83 J. Personality & Soc. Psychol. 526 (2002); *see also, e.g.*, Julie M. Duck & Barbara-Ann Mullin, *The Perceived Impact of the Mass Media: Reconsidering the Third Person Effect*, 25 Eur. J. Soc. Psychol. 77 (1995); Robert P. Vallone et al., *The Hostile Media Phenomenon: Biased Perception and Perceptions of Media Bias in Coverage of the Beirut Massacre*, 49 J. Personality & Soc. Psychol. 577 (1985).
105. Saragin et al., *supra* note 104, at 539.

106. For discussion of the sucker norm, see Tess Wilkinson-Ryan, *The Sucker Norm* (Univ. of Penn. Inst. of Law & Econ. Research Paper, Paper No. 09-05, July 17, 2008), *available at* http://papers.ssrn.com/sol3/papers.cfm?abstract_id=1162313.
107. Saragin et al., *supra* note 104, at 528; *see also* Brad J. Sagarin & Robert B. Cialdini, *Creating Critical Consumers: Motivating Receptivity by Teaching Resistance*, *in* Resistance and Persuasion 259 (Eric S. Knowles & Jay A. Linn eds., 2004).
108. David M. Hardesty et al., *Persuasion Knowledge and Consumer Reactions to Pricing Tactics*, 83 J. Retailing 199 (2007); Saragin et al., *supra* note 104 (false authorities); Lara Dolnik et al., *supra* note 46.
109. Robert B. Cialdini et al., *The Science of Influence: Using Six Principles of Persuasion to Negotiate and Mediate More Effectively*, Disp. Resol. Mag. 20–22 (Fall 2002).

Chapter 7

1. Bernard Kalb & Martin Kalb, *Along the Diplomatic Trail: Of Cannibals, Khruschev and Kissinger*, T.V. Guide, March 31, 1984, at 2, 6.
2. Kenneth R. Feinberg, What Is Life Worth? The Unprecedented Effort to Compensate the Victims of 9/11, at 53–54 (2005).
3. *See, e.g.*, Marcus T. Boccaccini & Stanley L. Brodsky, *Characteristics of the Ideal Criminal Defense Attorney from the Client's Perspective: Empirical Findings and Implications for Legal Practice*, 25 Law & Psychol. Rev. 81 (2001); Stephen Feldman & Kent Wilson, *The Value of Interpersonal Skills in Lawyering*, 5 Law & Hum. Behav. 311 (1981).
4. Klaus Fiedler, Social Communication 3 (2007).
5. David Greenberg, Calvin Coolidge 40–41 (2007).
6. Raymond S. Nickerson, *How We Know—and Sometimes Misjudge—What Others Know: Imputing One's Own Knowledge to Others*, 125 Psychol. Bull. 737 (1999); *see also* Dale J. Barr & Boaz Keysar, *Making Sense of How We Make Sense: The Paradox of Egocentrism in Language Use*, *in* Figurative Language Comprehension: Social and Cultural Influences 21 (Herbert L. Colston & Albert N. Katz eds., 2005); Nicholas Epley & Adam Waytz, *Mind Perception*, *in* Handbook of Social Psychology 14 (2010); Boaz Keysar et al., *Taking Perspective in Conversation: The Role of Mutual Knowledge in Comprehension*, 11 Psychol. Sci. 32 (2000); Edward Royzman et al., *"I Know, You Know": Epistemic Egocentrism in Children and Adults*, 7 Rev. Gen. Psychol. 38 (2003) (reviewing literature).
7. Boaz Keysar et al., *States of Affairs and States of Mind: The Effect of Knowledge of Beliefs*, 64 Organizational Behav. & Hum. Decision Processes 283 (1995);

see also Sheryl B. Ball et al., *An Evaluation of Learning in the Bilateral Winner's Curse*, 48 Organizational Behav. & Hum. Decision Processes 1 (1991); John S. Carroll et al., *Negotiator Cognitions: A Descriptive Approach to Negotiators' Understanding of Their Opponents*, 41 Organizational Behav. & Hum. Decision Processes 352 (1988).

8. Boaz Keysar & Anne S. Henly, *Speakers' Overestimation of Their Effectiveness*, 13 Psychol. Sci. 207 (2002); *see also* Nicholas Fay et al., *Listeners Influence Speakers' Perceived Communication Effectiveness*, 46 J. Experimental Soc. Psychol. 689 (2010); Nicholas Fay et al., *Speaker Overestimation of Communication Effectiveness and Fear of Negative Evaluation: Being Realistic Is Unrealistic*, 15 Psychonomic Bull. & Rev. 1160 (2008).

9. Norbert Schwartz, Cognition and Communication: Judgmental Biases, Research Methods, and the Logic of Conversation (1996).

10. *Id.* at 64.

11. Steven Lubet, Lawyers' Poker: 52 Lessons That Lawyers Can Learn from Card Players 113 (2006).

12. Henry Wadsworth Longfellow, *The Hanging of the Crane*, in The Poetical Works of Henry Wadsworth Longfellow 352, 352 (1878).

13. Francis Bacon, The Advancement of Learning 131 (William Aldis Wright ed., 1873).

14. *See* Randall A. Gordon et al., *Non-Verbal Behaviour as Communication: Approaches, Issues, and Research*, in The Handbook of Communication Skills 73 (Owen Hargie ed., 2006); Mark L. Knapp & Judith A. Hall, Nonverbal Communication in Human Interaction (6th ed. 2005).

15. Nalini Ambady et al., *Surgeons' Tone of Voice: A Clue to Malpractice History*, 132 Surgery 5 (2002).

16. Nalini Ambady & Robert Rosenthal, *Half a Minute: Predicting Teacher Evaluations from Thin Slices of Nonverbal Behavior and Physical Attractiveness*, 64 J. Personality & Soc. Psychol. 431 (1993); *see also* Nalini Ambady & Robert Rosenthal, *Thin Slices of Expressive Behavior as Predictors of Interpersonal Consequences: A Meta-Analysis*, 111 Psychol. Bull. 256 (1992).

17. Knapp & Hall, *supra* note 14, at 89.

18. *See, e.g.*, David Matsumoto, *Culture and Nonverbal Behavior*, in The Sage Handbook of Nonverbal Communication 219 (Valerie Manusov & Miles L. Patterson eds., 2006).

19. Bella M. DePaulo, *Nonverbal Behavior and Self-Presentation*, 111 Psychol. Bull. 203, 206 (1992).

20. Mark L. Knapp & Judith A. Hall, *supra* note 14, at 75; *see also* Ronald E. Riggio & Heidi R. Riggio, *Self-Report Measurement of Interpersonal Sensitivity*, in Interpersonal Sensitivity: Theory and Measurement 127 (Judith A. Hall & Frank J. Bernieri eds., 2001).

21. One might even imagine a world in which electronic communication has gone even further. *See, e.g.*, David Allen Larson, *Artificial Intelligence: Robots, Avatars, and the Demise of the Human Mediator*, 25 Ohio St. J. on Disp. Resol. 105 (2010).
22. Poll, *Do You Take Your Technology Everywhere?*, A.B.A. J. (Sept. 30, 2010), http://www.abajournal.com/polls/P16/.
23. Raymond A. Friedman & Steven C. Currall, *Conflict Escalation: Dispute Exacerbating Elements of E-Mail Communication*, 56 Hum. Rel. 1325 (2003); Jeffrey Loewenstein et al., *At a Loss for Words: Dominating the Conversation and the Outcome in Negotiation as a Function of Intricate Arguments and Communication Media*, 98 Organizational Behav. & Hum. Decision Processes 28 (2005).
24. Michael Morris et al., *Schmooze or Lose: Social Friction and Lubrication in E-Mail Negotiations*, 6 Group Dynamics: Theory Res. & Prac. 89 (2002).
25. Leigh Thompson & Janice Nadler, *Negotiating via Information Technology: Theory and Application*, 58 J. Soc. Issues 109 (2002).
26. Morris et al., *supra* note 24.
27. Loewenstein et al., *supra* note 23.
28. Morris et al., *supra* note 24; *see also* Aimee L. Drolet & Michael W. Morris, *Rapport in Conflict Resolution: Accounting for How Nonverbal Exchange Fosters Coordination on Mutually Beneficial Settlements to Mixed Motive Conflicts*, 36 J. Experimental Soc. Psychol. 26 (2000).
29. Nicholas Epley & Justin Kruger, *When What You Type Isn't What They Read: The Perseverance of Stereotypes and Expectancies over E-Mail*, 41 J. Experimental Soc. Psychol. 414 (2005).
30. Justin Kruger et al., *Egocentrism over E-mail: Can We Communicate as Well as We Think?*, 89 J. Personality & Soc. Psychol. 925 (2005).
31. *See, e.g.*, Guido Hertel et al., *Do Shy People Prefer to Send E-Mail? Personality Effects on Communication Media Preferences in Threatening and Nonthreatening Situations*, 39 Soc. Psychol. 231 (2008); Donna J. Reid & Fraser J. M. Reid, *Text or Talk? Social Anxiety, Loneliness, and Divergent Preferences for Cell Phone Use*, 10 CyberPsychol. & Behav. 424 (2007). *See generally* Katelyn Y. A. McKenna & John A. Bargh, *Plan 9 from Cyberspace: The Implications of the Internet for Personality and Social Psychology*, 4 Personality & Soc. Psychol. Rev. 57 (2000).
32. *See, e.g.*, Adam N. Joinson, *Self-Disclosure in Computer-Mediated Communication: The Role of Self-Awareness and Visual Anonymity*, 31 Eur. J. Soc. Psychol. 177 (2001).
33. Tresa Baldas, *Lawyers' Ethical Stumbles Increase Online*, Nat'l L.J., May 11, 2010, http://www.law.com/jsp/lawtechnologynews/PubArticleLTN.jsp?id=1202457938246 (quoting Michael Downey, past chairman of the American Bar Association's Ethics and Technology Committee).

34. Vitaly J. Dubrovsky et al., *The Equalization Phenomenon: Status Effects in Computer-Mediated and Face-to-Face Decision-Making Groups*, 6 Hum.-Computer Interaction 119 (1991); *see also* Charles E. Naquin et al., *The Finer Points of Lying Online: E-Mail Versus Pen and Paper*, 95 J. Applied Psychol. 387 (2010).
35. Maryalice Citera et al., *An Experimental Study of Credibility in E-Negotiations*, 22 Psychol. & Marketing 163 (2005); Charles E. Naquin et al., *E-Mail Communication and Group Cooperation in Mixed Motive Contexts*, 21 Soc. Just. Res. 470 (2008) (also finding that e-mail communicators feel more justified in being uncooperative); Charles E. Naquin & Gaylen D. Paulson, *Online Bargaining and Interpersonal Trust*, 88 J. Applied Psychol. 113 (2003); Paul W. Paese et al., *Caught Telling the Truth: Effects of Honesty and Communication Media in Distributive Negotiations*, 12 Group Decision & Negot. 537 (2003); Kevin W. Rockman & Gregory B. Northcraft, *To Be or Not to Be Trusted: The Influence of Media Richness on Defection and Deception*, 107 Organizational Behav. & Hum. Decision Processes 106 (2008).
36. Morris et al., *supra* note 24.
37. Tresa Baldas, *Lawyers' Ethical Stumbles Increase Online*, Nat'l L.J., May 11, 2010, *available at* http://www.law.com/jsp/article.jsp?id=1202457938246&rss=newswire/.
38. Morris et al., *supra* note 24; *see also* Don A. Moore et al., *Long and Short Routes to Success in Electronically Mediated Negotiations: Group Affiliations and Good Vibrations*, 77 Organizational Behav. & Hum. Decision Processes 22 (1999).
39. Derald Wing Sue & David Sue, Counseling the Culturally Diverse: Theory and Practice 143 (2003); Richard W. Brislin & Eugene S. Kim, *Cultural Diversity in People's Understanding and Uses of Time*, 52 Applied Psychol.: An Int'l Rev. 363 (2003); Tanya L. Chartrand & Rick van Baaren, *Human Mimicry*, 41 Advances Experimental Soc. Psychol. 219 (2009); Rosaleen Ow & Dafna Katz, *Family Secrets and the Disclosure of Distressful Information in Chinese Families*, 80 Fam. Soc'y 620 (1999); Harry C. Triandis, *Some Dimensions of Intercultural Variation and Their Implications for Community Psychology*, 11 J. Community Psychol. 285 (1983); Jeffrey Sanchez-Burks et al., *Performance in Intercultural Interactions at Work: Cross-Cultural Differences in Response to Behavioral Mirroring*, 94 J. Applied Psychol. 216 (2009); Shali Wu & Boaz Keysar, *The Effect of Culture on Perspective Taking*, 18 Psychol. Sci. 604 (2007).
40. Wendi Lyn Adair & Jeanne M. Brett, *Culture and Negotiation Processes*, *in* The Handbook of Negotiation and Culture 158, 162 (Michele J. Gelfand & Jeanne M. Brett eds., 2004); Jeanne M. Brett & Michele J. Gelfand, *A Cultural Analysis of the Underlying Assumptions of Negotiation Theory*, *in* Negotiation Theory and Research 173 (Leigh L. Thompson ed., 2006).
41. Brett & Gelfand, *supra* note 40, at 187–90.

42. Edward T. Hall & Mildred Reed Hall, Understanding Cultural Differences 9 (1990) (emphasis in original).
43. Charles Dickens, Works of Charles Dickens: Great Expectations 20 (1874).
44. *See generally* Charles F. Bond Jr. & Bella M. DePaulo, *Accuracy of Deception Judgments*, 10 Personality & Soc. Psychol. Rev. 214 (2006) (reporting a meta-analysis of such studies).
45. Bella M. DePaulo et al., *The Accuracy-Confidence Correlation in the Detection of Deception*, 1 Personality & Soc. Psychol. Rev. 346, 346 (1997).
46. Bella M. DePaulo & Roger L. Pfeifer, *On-the-Job Experience and Skill at Detecting Deception*, 16 J. Applied Soc. Psychol. 249 (1986); Saul M. Kassin et al., *"I'd Know a False Confession If I Saw One": A Comparative Study of College Students and Police Investigators*, 29 Law & Hum. Behav. 211 (2005).
47. Leif A. Strömwall et al., *Practitioners' Beliefs About Deception*, in The Detection of Deception in Forensic Contexts 229 (Pär Anders Granhag & Leif A. Strömwall eds., 2004) (reviewing studies); Bella M. DePaulo et al., *Cues to Deception*, 129 Psychol. Bull. 74 (2003) (reporting a meta-analysis of such studies). Laypeople and practitioners (e.g., police officers, customs officers) have similar beliefs. *See* Strömwall et al., *supra*. Interestingly, criminals actually tend to hold less stereotypical beliefs about cues to deception—and are somewhat better at detecting lies. *Id.*
48. *See* Leslie A. Zebrowitz et al., *"Wide-Eyed" and "Crooked-Faced": Determinants of Perceived and Real Honesty Across the Life Span*, 22 Personality & Soc. Psychol. Bull. 1258 (1996).
49. DePaulo et al., *supra* note 47, at 105.
50. *See generally* Ann E. Tenbrunsel & David M. Messick, *Ethical Fading: The Role of Self-Deception in Unethical Behavior*, 17 Soc. Just. Res. 223 (2004).
51. DePaulo et al., *supra* note 47.
52. Hee Sun Park et al., *How People Really Detect Lies*, 69 Comm. Monographs 144 (2002); *see also* J. Pete Blair et al., *Content in Context Improves Deception Detection Accuracy*, 36 Hum. Comm. Res. 423 (2010).
53. Maria Hartwig et al., *Detecting Deception via Strategic Disclosure of Evidence*, 29 Law & Hum. Behav. 469 (2005); Maria Hartwig et al., *Strategic Use of Evidence During Police Interviews: When Training to Detect Deception Works*, 30 Law & Hum. Behav. 603 (2006).
54. Aldert Vrij et al., *Outsmarting the Liars: The Benefit of Asking Unanticipated Questions*, 33 Law & Hum. Behav. 159 (2009).
55. Aldert Vrij et al., *Outsmarting the Liars: Toward a Cognitive Lie Detection Approach*, 20 Current Directions Psychol. Sci. 28 (2011); *see also* Drew Leins et al., *Using Sketch Drawing to Induce Inconsistency in Liars*, 16 Legal & Criminological Psychol. 253 (2010); Aldert Vrij et al., *Drawings as an Innovative and Successful Lie Detection Tool*, 24 Applied Cognitive Psychol. 587 (2010);

Aldert Vrij et al., *Is Anyone Out There? Drawings as a Tool to Detect Deception in Occupations Interviews*, PSYCHOL. CRIME & L. (forthcoming).
56. PAUL EKMAN, TELLING LIES: CLUES TO DECEIT IN THE MARKETPLACE, POLITICS, AND MARRIAGE (2001).
57. Steven Lubet, *Lawyers' Poker*, 57 U. MIAMI L. REV. 283, 307 (2003).
58. Aldert Vrij et al., *Increasing Cognitive Load to Facilitate Lie Detection: The Benefit of Recalling an Event in Reverse Order*, 32 LAW & HUM. BEHAV. 253 (2008).
59. Maurice E. Schweitzer & Rachel Croson, *Curtailing Deception: The Impact of Direct Questions on Lies and Omissions, in* WHAT'S FAIR: ETHICS FOR NEGOTIATORS 175 (Carrie Menkel-Meadow & Michael Wheeler eds., 2004); *see also* Timothy R. Levine et al., *Increasing Deception Detection Accuracy with Strategic Questioning*, 36 HUM. COMM. RES. 216 (2010).
60. Maureen O'Sullivan, *Emotional Intelligence and Deception Detection: Why Most People Can't "Read" Others, but a Few Can, in* APPLICATIONS OF NONVERBAL COMMUNICATION 215 (Ronald E. Riggio & Robert S. Feldman eds., 2005); Paul Ekman et al., *A Few Can Catch a Liar*, 10 PSYCHOL. SCI. 263 (1999).
61. GOVERNING BD. OF THE NAT'L RESEARCH COUNCIL, THE POLYGRAPH AND LIE DETECTION 11 (2003).
62. *Id.* at 2.
63. United States v. Scheffer, 523 U.S. 303, 303 (1998).
64. *See, e.g.*, Jeffrey Rosen, *The Brain on the Stand*, N.Y. TIMES, Mar. 11, 2007, § 6, at 49; Margaret Talbot, *Duped: Can Brain Scans Uncover Lies?*, NEW YORKER, July 2, 2007, at 52; *see also* David P. McCabe & Alan D. Castel, *Seeing Is Believing: The Effect of Brain Images on Judgments of Scientific Reasoning*, 107 Cognition 343 (2008) (finding that neuroimages are particularly persuasive).
65. *See generally* MICHAEL S. GAZZANIGA, THE ETHICAL BRAIN: THE SCIENCE OF OUR MORAL DILEMMAS (2005); Paul Root Wolpe et al., *Emerging Neurotechnologies for Lie-Detection: Promises and Perils*, 5 Am. J. Bioethics 39 (2005). *See also* Mark Hansen, *True Lies*, ABA J., Oct. 2009, at 56.
66. Denise M. Rousseau et al., *Not So Different After All: A Cross-Discipline View of Trust*, 23 ACAD. MGMT. REV. 393, 395 (1998). Distrust, which can exist simultaneously with trust, involves negative expectations about the behavior or intentions of the other. *Id.* at 398.
67. John K. Butler Jr., *Trust Expectations, Information Sharing, Climate of Trust, and Negotiation Effectiveness and Efficiency*, 24 GROUP & ORG. MGMT. 217, 227 (1999); Kevin J. Corcoran, *The Relationship of Interpersonal Trust to Self-Disclosure When Confidentiality Is Assured*, 122 J. PSYCHOL. 193 (1988).
68. Jonathan J. Koehler & Andrew D. Gershoff, *Betrayal Aversion: When Agents of Protection Become Agents of Harm*, 90 ORGANIZATIONAL BEHAV. & HUM. DECISION PROCESSES 244 (2003).

69. Michael Price, *A Mental Health Crisis Unfolds*, 41 MONITOR ON PSYCHOL. 16, 16 (2010).
70. *See* Janet A. Sniezek & Lyn M. van Swol, *Trust, Confidence, and Expertise in a Judge-Advisor System*, 84 ORGANIZATIONAL BEHAV. & HUM. DECISION PROCESSES 288 (2001); *see also* Marcus T. Boccaccini et al., *Development and Effects of Client Trust in Criminal Defense Attorneys: Preliminary Examination of the Congruence Model of Trust Development*, 22 BEHAV. SCI. & L. 197 (2004); David H. Thom et al., *Patient Trust in the Physician: Relationship to Patient Requests*, 19 FAM. PRAC. 476 (2002); Felicia Trachtenberg et al., *How Patients' Trust Relates to their Involvement in Medical Care*, 54 J. FAM. PRAC. 344 (2005).
71. *See, e.g.*, Carsten K. W. De Dreu et al., *Social Motives and Trust in Integrative Negotiation: The Disruptive Effects of Punitive Capability*, 83 J. APPLIED PSYCHOL. 408 (1998); Melvin J. Kimmel et al., *Effects of Trust, Aspiration, and Gender on Negotiation Tactics*, 38 J. PERSONALITY & SOC. PSYCHOL. 9 (1980); Naquin & Paulson, *supra* note 35; William Ross & Jessica LaCroix, *Multiple Meanings of Trust in Negotiation Theory and Research: A Literature Review and Integrative Model*, 7 INT'L J. CONFLICT MGMT. 314 (1996); Leigh L. Thompson et al., *Negotiation*, 61 ANN. REV. PSYCHOL. 491 (2010).
72. *See* Debra Meyerson et al., *Swift Trust and Temporary Groups*, in TRUST IN ORGANIZATIONS: FRONTIERS OF THEORY AND RESEARCH 166 (Roderick M. Kramer & Tom R. Tyler eds., 1996); Rousseau et al., *supra* note 66; Susan P. Shapiro, *The Social Control of Impersonal Trust*, 93 AM. J. SOC. 623 (1987); Ellen M. Whitener et al., *Managers as Initiators of Trust: An Exchange Relationship Framework for Understanding Managerial Trustworthy Behavior*, 23 ACAD. MGMT. REV. 513 (1998).
73. Feldman & Wilson, *supra* note 3; Morris et al., *supra* note 24 (citing Michael Morris & Dacher Keltner, *How Emotions Work: An Analysis of the Social Functions of Emotional Expression in Negotiations*, 22 REV. ORGANIZATIONAL BEHAV. 1 (2000)); Rousseau et al., *supra* note 66; Sniezek & van Swol, *supra* note 70; Whitener et al., *supra* note 72.
74. Boccaccini et al., *supra* note 70 (finding that those who did not desire to participate and those who both desired to and were allowed to participate had more trust in their attorneys than those who desired to but were not allowed to participate); Whitener et al., *supra* note 72.
75. Linda Tickle-Degnen & Robert Rosenthal, *The Nature of Rapport and Its Nonverbal Correlates*, 1 PSYCHOL. INQUIRY 285, 286 (1990).
76. *See, e.g.*, Martine B. Powell et al., *Investigative Interviewing*, in PSYCHOLOGY AND LAW: AN EMPIRICAL PERSPECTIVE 11, 13–14 (Neil Brewer & Kipling D. Williams eds., 2005); DEBRA L. ROTER & JUDITH A. HALL, DOCTORS TALKING WITH PATIENTS/PATIENTS TALKING WITH DOCTORS: IMPROVING COMMUNICATION IN MEDICAL VISITS (2d ed. 2006) (reviewing studies); Roger Collins et al., *The Effect of Rapport in Forensic Interviewing*, 9 PSYCHIATRY PSYCHOL. & L. 69 (2002); Drolet & Morris,

supra note 28; Thompson & Nadler, *supra* note 25, at 111 (describing Aimee L. Drolet & Michael W. Morris, Communication Media and Interpersonal Trust in Conflicts: The Role of Rapport and Synchrony on Nonverbal Behavior (1995) (unpublished manuscript)); Tickle-Degnen & Rosenthal, *supra* note 75, at 287 (1990); Jonathan P. Vallano & Nadja Schreiber Compo, *A Comfortable Witness Is a Good Witness: Rapport-Building and Susceptibility to Misinformation in an Investigative Mock-Crime Interview*, 6 APPLIED COGNITIVE PSYCHOL. 960 (2011).

77. Chartrand & Baaren, *supra* note 39; Amy N. Dalton et al., *The Schema-Driven Chameleon: How Mimicry Affects Executive and Self-Regulatory Resources*, 98 J. PERSONALITY & SOC. PSYCHOL. 605 (2010); Eli J. Finkel et al., *High-Maintenance Interaction: Inefficient Social Coordination Impairs Self-Regulation*, 91 J. PERSONALITY & SOC. PSYCHOL. 456 (2006).
78. *See generally* Moore et al., *supra* note 38; Morris et al., *supra* note 24.
79. Lawrence E. Williams & John A. Bargh, *Experiencing Physical Warmth Promotes Interpersonal Warmth*, 322 SCIENCE 606 (2008).
80. ROTER & HALL, *supra* note 76 (reviewing studies).
81. *See generally* Chartrand & Baaren, *supra* note 39.
82. Rick B. van Baaren et al., *Mimicry for Money: Behavioral Consequences of Imitation*, 39 J. EXPERIMENTAL SOC. PSYCHOL. 393 (2003).
83. Sanchez-Burks et al., *supra* note 39.
84. *See generally* Chartrand & Baaren, *supra* note 39; *see also* Jessica L. Lakin & Tanya L. Chartrand, *Using Nonconscious Behavioral Mimicry to Create Affiliation and Rapport*, 14 PSYCHOL. SCI. 334 (2003).
85. William W. Maddux et al., *Chameleons Bake Bigger Pies and Take Bigger Pieces: Strategic Behavioral Mimicry Facilitates Negotiation Outcomes*, 44 J. EXPERIMENTAL SOC. PSYCHOL. 461, 463 (2008) (emphasis in original).
86. *Id.*
87. http://thinkexist.com/quotation/it_is_the_province_of_knowledge_to_speak-and_it/146515.html
88. Marcus T. Boccaccini et al., *Client-Relations Skills in Effective Lawyering: Attitudes of Criminal Defense Attorneys and Experienced Clients*, 26 LAW & PSYCHOL. REV. 97 (2002).
89. Jay Sullivan, *Building a Reputation as a Listener*, N.Y. L.J., Sept. 7, 2007.
90. Jenny B. Davis, *What I Like About My Lawyer*, 89 ABA J. 33, 36 (2003) (quoting Dr. Stephen S. Wachtel).
91. OLIVER WENDELL HOLMES, THE WORKS OF OLIVER WENDELL HOLMES: THE POET AT THE BREAKFAST-TABLE 264 (1872).
92. Monisha Pasupathi et al., *How What We Tell Becomes What We Know: Listener Effects on Speakers' Long-Term Memory for Events*, 26 DISCOURSE PROCESSES 1 (1998); Rosemary P. Ramsey & Ravipreet S. Sohi, *Listening to Your Customers: The Impact of Perceived Salesperson Listening Behavior on*

Relationship Outcomes, 25 J. Acad. Marketing Sci. 127 (1997); E. Vermeire et al., *Patient Adherence to Treatment: Three Decades of Research; A Comprehensive Review*, 26 J. Clinical Pharmacy & Therapeutics 331 (2001).

93. David H. Maister et al., The Trusted Advisor 97 (2000) (quoting *Master of the M & A Universe*, Bus. Wk. (Mar. 1997)).
94. William B. Swann et al., *Causal Chunking: Memory and Inference in Ongoing Interaction*, 53 J. Personality & Soc. Psychol. 858 (1987).
95. Maister et al., *supra* note 93, at 100 (emphasis in original).
96. Bryna Bogoch & Brenda Danet, *Challenge and Control in Lawyer-Client Interaction: A Case Study in an Israeli Legal Aid Office*, 4 Text 249, 254 (1984).
97. Carl J. Hosticka, *We Don't Care About What Happened, We Only Care About What Is Going to Happen: Lawyer-Client Negotiations of Reality*, 26 Soc. Probs. 599, 605 (1979); *see also* Roter & Hall, *supra* note 76; Howard B. Beckman & Richard M. Frankel, *The Effect of Physician Behavior on the Collection of Data*, 101 Annals Internal Med. 692, 694 (1984); Ronald P. Fisher, *Interviewing Victims and Witnesses of Crime*, 1 Psychol. Pub. Pol'y & L. 732, 738 (1995).
98. Greg Mortenson, Stones Into Schools: Promoting Peace with Books, Not Bombs, in Afghanistan and Pakistan 191 (2010).
99. David Dickson, *Reflecting*, in The Handbook of Communication Skills, *supra* note 14, at 165 (reviewing studies).
100. Steven Keeva, Transforming Practices: Finding Joy and Satisfaction in the Legal Life 109 (10th anniv. Ed. 2009).
101. Peter M. Tiersma, Legal Language 55 (1999).
102. *See, e.g.*, Michael E. J. Masson & Mary Anne Waldron, *Comprehension of Legal Contracts by Non-Experts: Effectiveness of Plain Language Redrafting*, 8 Applied Cognitive Psychol. 67 (1994); Richard Rogers et al., *An Analysis of Miranda Warnings and Waivers: Comprehension and Coverage*, 31 Law & Hum. Behav. 177 (2007); Special Issue, *The Jury Instruction Process*, 6 Psychol. Pub. Pol'y & L. 587 (2000).
103. Bryan A. Garner, *Interviews with the United States Supreme Court Justices*, 13 Scribes J. Legal Writing 1, 156 (2010).
104. Brenda Danet, *Language and Law: An Overview of 15 Years of Research*, in Handbook of Language and Social Psychology 537 (Howard Giles & William Peter Robinson eds., 1990); Tiersma, *supra* note 101.
105. A. A. Milne, The House at Pooh Corner 58 (1928).
106. *See generally* Adam L. Alter & Daniel M. Oppenheimer, *Uniting the Tribes of Fluency to Form a Metacognitive Nation*, 13 Personality & Soc. Psychol. Rev. 219 (2009).
107. Daniel M. Oppenheimer, *Consequences of Erudite Vernacular Utilized Irrespective of Necessity: Problems with Using Long Words Needlessly*, 20 Applied Cognitive Psychol. 139 (2006).
108. Masson & Waldron, *supra* note 102.

109. Robert W. Benson & Joan B. Kessler, *Legalese v. Plain English: An Empirical Study of Persuasion and Credibility in Appellate Brief Writing*, 20 Loy. L.A. L. Rev. 301 (1987).
110. *See* Alan L. Chaikin & Valerian J. Derlega, *Variables Affecting the Appropriateness of Self-Disclosure*, 42 J. Consulting & Clinical Psychol. 588 (1974); *see also* Nancy L. Collins & Lynn Carol Miller, *Self-Disclosure and Liking: A Meta-Analytic Review*, 116 Psychol. Bull. 457 (1994).
111. *See* Emily Pronin et al., *Value Revelations: Disclosure Is in the Eye of the Beholder*, 95 J. Personality & Soc. Psychol. 795 (2008); Emily Pronin et al., *You Don't Know Me, but I Know You: The Illusion of Asymmetric Insight*, 81 J. Personality & Soc. Psychol. 639 (2001).
112. Butler Jr., *supra* note 67, at 227; Collins & Miller, *supra* note 110; Corcoran, *supra* note 67; Lynn C. Miller et al., *Openers: Individuals Who Elicit Intimate Self-Disclosure*, 44 J. Personality & Soc. Psychol. 1234 (1983); Linda J. Pegalis et al., *On the Ability to Elicit Self-Disclosure: Are There Gender-Based and Contextual Limitations on the Opener Effect?*, 20 Personality & Soc. Psychol. Bull. 412 (1994); James A. Purvis et al., *The "Opener": Skilled User of Facial Expression and Speech Pattern*, 10 Personality & Soc. Psychol. Bull. 61 (1984); David R. Shaffer et al., *The "Opener": Highly Skilled as Interviewer or Interviewee*, 16 Personality & Soc. Psychol. Bull. 511 (1990).
113. Adam L. Alter & Daniel M. Oppenheimer, *Suppressing Secrecy Through Metacognitive Ease: Cognitive Fluency Encourages Self-Disclosure*, 20 Psychol. Sci. 1414 (2009).
114. *See* Charles J. Holahan & Karl A. Slaikeu, *Effects of Contrasting Degrees of Privacy on Client Self-Disclosure in a Counseling Setting*, 24 J. Counseling Psychol. 55, 58 (1977).
115. *See* Adam N. Joinson & Carina B. Paine, *Self-Disclosure, Privacy, and the Internet*, *in* Oxford Handbook of Internet Psychology 237 (Adam N. Joinson et al. eds., 2007); Nancy E. Frye & Michele M. Dornisch, *When Is Trust Not Enough? The Role of Perceived Privacy of Communication Tools in Comfort with Self-Disclosure*, 26 Computers Hum. Behav. 1120 (2010); *see also* Leslie K. John et al., *Strangers on a Plane: Context-Dependent Willingness to Divulge Sensitive Information*, 37 J. Consumer Res. 858 (2011).
116. Leslie A. Hayduk, *Personal Space: Where We Now Stand*, 94 Psychol. Bull. 293, 293 (1983); *see also* Leslie A. Hayduk, *Personal Space: An Evaluative and Orienting Overview*, 85 Psychol. Bull. 117, 118 (1978).
117. *See* Edward T. Hall, The Hidden Dimension 121–23 (1969); Vincent P. Skoto & Daniel Langmeyer, *The Effects of Interaction Distance and Gender on Self-Disclosure in Dyads*, 40 Sociometry 178 (1977).
118. *See* Alan L. Chaiken et al., *Effects of Room Environment on Self-Disclosure in a Counseling Analogue*, 23 J. Counseling Psychol. 479 (1976); P. Paul Heppner & Steve Pew, *Effects of Diplomas, Awards, and Counselor Sex on Perceived*

Expertness, 24 J. COUNSELING PSYCHOL. 147 (1977); Yoshiko Miwa & Kazunori Hanyu, *The Effects of Interior Design on Communication and Impressions of a Counselor in a Counseling Room*, 38 ENV'T & BEHAV. 484 (2006); Page K. Pressly & Martin Heesacker, *The Physical Environment and Counseling: A Review of Theory and Research*, 79 J. COUNSELING & DEV. 148 (2001) (reviewing studies); Jeffrey C. Siegel, *Effects of Objective Evidence of Expertness, Nonverbal Behavior, and Subject Sex on Client-Perceived Expertness*, 27 J. COUNSELING PSYCHOL. 117 (1980).

119. *See generally* RICHARD E. MAYER, APPLYING THE SCIENCE OF LEARNING (2010).
120. Ellen Peters et al., *Numeracy Skill and the Communication, Comprehension, and Use of Risk-Benefit Information*, 26 HEALTH AFF. 741, 745 (2007).
121. Harold Pashler et al., *Learning Styles: Concepts and Evidence*, 9 PSYCHOL. SCI. PUB. INT. 105 (2008).
122. *See, e.g.*, Thomas H. Gallagher et al., *Patients' and Physicians' Attitudes Regarding the Disclosure of Medical Errors*, 289 JAMA 1001 (2003).
123. Letter from Louis Brandeis to William H. Dunbar (1893), *in* ALPHEUS T. MASON, BRANDEIS: A FREE MAN'S LIFE 80 (1946).
124. *Abraham Lincoln Quotes*, THINKEXIST.COM, http://thinkexist.com/quotation/a_lawyer-s_time_and_advice_are_his_stock_in/162359.html (last visited March 25, 2012)
125. Silvia Bonaccio & Reeshad S. Dalal, *Advice Taking and Decision-Making: An Integrative Literature Review, and Implications for the Organizational Sciences*, 101 ORGANIZATIONAL BEHAV. & HUM. DECISION PROCESSES 127 (2006); Francesca Gino, *Do We Listen to Advice Just Because We Paid for It? The Impact of Advice Cost on Its Use*, 107 ORGANIZATIONAL BEHAV. & HUM. DECISION PROCESSES 234 (2008).
126. Sniezek & van Swol, *supra* note 70.
127. Helmut Jungermann & Katrin Fischer, *Using Expertise and Experience for Giving and Taking Advice*, *in* THE ROUTINES OF DECISION MAKING 157 (Tilmann Betsch & Susanne Haberstroh eds., 2005); Silvia Bonaccio & Reeshad S. Dalal, *Evaluating Advisors: A Policy-Capturing Study Under Conditions of Complete and Missing Information*, 23 J. BEHAV. DECISION MAKING 227 (2010); Francesca Gino & Maurice E. Schweitzer, *Blinded by Anger or Feeling the Love: How Emotions Influence Advice Taking*, 93 J. APPLIED PSYCHOL. 1165 (2008); Francesca Gino & Don A. Moore, *Effects of Task Difficulty on Use of Advice*, 20 J. BEHAV. DECISION MAKING 21 (2007); Nigel Harvey & Ilan Fisher, *Taking Advice: Accepting Help, Improving Judgment, and Sharing Responsibility*, 70 ORGANIZATIONAL BEHAV. & HUM. DECISION PROCESSES 117 (1997); Eva Jonas et al., *Giving Advice or Making Decisions in Someone Else's Place: The Influence of Impression, Defense, and Accuracy Motivation on the Search for New Information*, 31 PERSONALITY & SOC. PSYCHOL. BULL. 977 (2005); Gunnar E. Schrah et al., *No Decision-Maker Is an Island: Integrating Expert Advice*

with Information Acquisition, 19 J. BEHAV. DECISION MAKING 43 (2006); Janet A. Sniezek et al., *Improving Judgement with Prepaid Expert Advice*, 17 J. BEHAV. DECISION MAKING 173 (2004); Sniezek & Swol, *supra* note 70; Lyn M. van Swol & Janet A. Sniezek, *Factors Affecting the Acceptance of Expert Advice*, 44 BRIT. J. SOC. PSYCHOL. 443 (2005); Ilan Yaniv, *Receiving Other People's Advice: Influence and Benefit*, 93 ORGANIZATIONAL BEHAV. & HUM. DECISION PROCESSES 1 (2004).

128. See Bonaccio & Dalal, *supra* note 125; Erina L. MacGeorge et al., *Understanding Advice in Supportive Interactions: Beyond the Facework and Message Evaluation Paradigm*, 30 HUM. COMM. RES. 42 (2004); Schrah et al., *supra* note 127.

129. Letter from Benjamin Franklin to Joseph Priestley (Sept. 19, 1772), *in* Robyn M. Dawes & Bernard Corrigan, *Linear Models in Decision Making*, 81 PSYCHOL. BULL. 95, 95 (1974).

130. Reeshad S. Dalal & Silvia Bonaccio, *What Types of Advice Do Decision-Makers Prefer?*, 112 ORGANIZATIONAL BEHAV. & HUM. DECISION PROCESSES 11 (2010).

131. Sniezek & van Swol, *supra* note 70.

Chapter 8

1. *Oliver Wendell Holmes Jr. Quotes*, THINKEXIST.COM, http://thinkexist.com/quotation/this_is_a_court_of_law-young_man-not_a_court_of/148879.html (last visited March 24, 2012).

2. JONATHAN HARR, A CIVIL ACTION 340 (1995); *see also* A CIVIL ACTION (Touchstone Pictures 1999).

3. *See, e.g.*, PAUL H. ROBINSON & JOHN M. DARLEY, JUSTICE, LIABILITY AND BLAME: COMMUNITY VIEWS AND CRIMINAL LAWS (1995); TOM R. TYLER, WHY PEOPLE OBEY THE LAW (2d ed. 2006); John M. Darley, *Citizens' Sense of Justice and the Legal System*, 10 CURRENT DIRECTIONS PSYCHOL. SCI. 10 (2001).

4. *See* Jean R. Sternlight, *ADR Is Here: Preliminary Reflections on Where It Fits in a System of Justice*, 3 NEV. L.J. 289 (2003).

5. *See* Morton Deutsch, *Equity, Equality, and Need: What Determines Which Value Will Be Used as the Basis of Distributive Justice?*, 31 J. SOC. ISSUES 137 (Summer 1975).

6. Tom Tyler & Steven L. Blader, *Justice and Negotiation*, *in* THE HANDBOOK OF NEGOTIATION AND CULTURE 295, 297 (Michele J. Gelfand & Jeanne M. Brett eds., 2004); *see* David M. Messick, *Equality, Fairness, & Social Conflict*, 8 SOC. JUST. RES. 153 (1995).

7. *See* David M. Messick, *Equality as a Decision Heuristic*, *in* PSYCHOLOGICAL PERSPECTIVES ON JUSTICE: THEORY AND APPLICATIONS 11 (Barbara A. Mellers & Jonathan Baron eds., 1993).

8. Max H. Bazerman & Don Moore, Judgment in Managerial Decision Making 121 (7th ed. 2009) (emphasis in original); *see* Messick, supra note 7.
9. Maya Bar-Hillel & Menahem Yaari, *Judgments of Distributive Justice, in* Psychological Perspectives on Justice: Theory and Applications, *supra* note 7, at 55, 56.
10. David M. Messick, *Equality as a Decision Heuristic, in* Psychological Perspectives on Justice: Theory and Applications 11, 29 (Barbara A. Mellers & Jonathan Baron eds., 1993).
11. *See* Deutsch, *supra* note 5, at 143–47.
12. *See* Harry C. Triandis, Culture and Social Behavior (1994).
13. Alan Page Fiske & Philip E. Tetlock, *Taboo Trade-Offs: Reactions to Transactions That Transgress the Spheres of Justice*, 18 Pol. Psychol. 255, 285–86 (1997); Philip E. Tetlock et al., *The Psychology of the Unthinkable: Taboo Trade-Offs, Forbidden Base Rates, and Heretical Counterfactuals*, 78 J. Personality & Soc. Psychol. 853 (2000); *see also* Alan Page Fiske, *The Four Elementary Forms of Sociality: Framework for a Unified Theory of Social Relations*, 99 Psychol. Rev. 689 (1992) (distinguishing relationships governed by norms of communal sharing, authority ranking, equality matching, and market pricing).
14. Lieff Cabraser Heimann & Bernstein, http://www.lieffcabraser.com/attorneys (last visited March 24, 2012)
15. David M. Messick et al., *Why We Are Fairer Than Others*, 21 J. Experimental Soc. Psychol. 480 (1985).
16. Emily M. Zitek et al., *Victim Entitlement to Behave Selfishly*, 98 J. Personality & Soc. Psychol. 245 (2010).
17. *See generally* Dominique J. F. de Quervain et al., *The Neural Basis of Altruistic Punishment*, 305 Science 1254 (2004).
18. Based on a scenario in Max H. Bazerman et al., *Perceptions of Fairness in Interpersonal and Individual Choice Situations*, 4 Current Directions Psychol. Sci. 39, 39 (1995).
19. *See, e.g.*, Colin Camerer & Richard H. Thaler, *Anomalies: Ultimatums, Dictators, and Manners*, 9 J. Econ. Persp. 209 (1995).
20. Max H. Bazerman et al., *Reversals of Preference in Allocation Decisions: Judging an Alternative Versus Choosing Among Alternatives*, 37 Admin. Sci. Q. 220 (1992).
21. *See, e.g.*, Sarah F. Brosnan & Frans B. M. de Waal, *Monkeys Reject Unequal Pay*, 425 Nature 297 (2003).
22. Alan G. Sanfey et al., *The Neural Basis of Economic Decision-Making in the Ultimatum Game*, 300 Science 1755 (2003).
23. Golnaz Tabibnia et al., *The Sunny Side of Fairness: Preference for Fairness Activates Reward Circuitry (and Disregarding Unfairness Activates Self-Control Circuitry)*, 19 Psychol. Sci. 339 (2008).

24. *See* Daniel Kahneman et al., *Fairness and the Assumptions of Economics*, 59 J. Bus. 285 (1986).
25. *See, e.g.*, Kelly Evans, *Consumers Vent on Overdraft Fees*, Wall St. J., Mar. 26, 2009, at D2, *available at* http://online.wsj.com/article/SB123803178615743761.html; David Leonhardt, *Why Variable Pricing Fails at the Vending Machine*, N.Y. Times, June 27, 2005, at C5, *available at* http://www.nytimes.com/2005/06/27/business/27consuming.html (noting consumer anger over Coca-Cola's plans for variable-priced vending machines); Douglas Neumetzger, Op-Ed, *Coke's New Pricing*, N.Y. Times, Nov. 1, 1999, at A22; Gloria Goodale, *Airlines: First It Was the Baggage Fees; What's Next? Pay Toilets?*, Christian Sci. Monitor (Apr. 26, 2010), http://www.csmonitor.com/USA/2010/0426/Airlines-First-it-was-the-baggage-fees.-What-s-next-Pay-toilets.
26. Tom R. Tyler, *Procedural Justice*, in Jury Psychology: Social Aspects of Trial Processes 25, 29 (Joel D. Lieberman & Daniel A. Krauss eds., 2009).
27. Tom R. Tyler, *Procedural Justice and the Courts*, 44 Court Rev. 26, 26 (2007–2008).
28. E. Allan Lind et al., *The Winding Road from Employee to Complainant: Situational and Psychological Determinants of Wrongful-Termination Claims*, 45 Admin. Sci. Q. 557 (2000); *see also* Karen Roberts & Karen S. Markel, *Claiming in the Name of Fairness: Organizational Justice and the Decision to File for Workplace Injury Compensation*, 6 J. Occupational Health Psychol. 332 (2001); Daniel Skarlicki & Robert Folger, *Retaliation in the Workplace: The Roles of Distributive, Procedural, and Interactional Justice*, 82 J. Applied Psychol. 434 (1997).
29. E. Allan Lind et al., *Individual and Corporate Dispute Resolution: Using Procedural Fairness as a Decision Heuristic*, 38 Admin. Sci. Q. 224 (1993); *see also* Robert J. MacCoun et al., Alternative Adjudication: An Evaluation of the New Jersey Automobile Arbitration Program (1988).
30. Tyler, *supra* note 27.
31. *See, e.g.*, Michele Cascardi et al., *Procedural Justice in the Context of Civil Commitment: An Analogue Study*, 18 Behav. Sci. & L. 731 (2000); Loretta Stalans & E. Allan Lind, *The Meaning of Procedural Fairness: A Comparison of Taxpayers' and Representatives' Views of Their Tax Audits*, 10 Soc. Just. Res. 311 (1997); Kristina Murphy, *Procedural Justice and Tax Compliance* 2 (Ctr. For Tax Sys. Integrity, Working Paper No. 56, 2004).
32. Steven L. Blader & Tom R. Tyler, *A Four-Component Model of Procedural Justice: Defining the Meaning of a "Fair" Process*, 29 Personality & Soc. Psychol. Bull. 747, 749 (2003).
33. Tom R. Tyler & E. Allan Lind, *Procedural Justice*, in Handbook of Justice Research in Law 65, 79 (Joseph Sanders & V. Lee Hamilton eds., 2001).
34. E-mail from Tom Tyler to Jennifer K. Robbennolt (Aug. 22, 2011).

35. STEVEN KEEVA, TRANSFORMING PRACTICES: FINDING JOY AND SATISFACTION IN THE LEGAL LIFE 99 (10th anniv. ed. 2009).
36. Tyler & Lind, *supra* note 33, at 80 (fairness heuristic).
37. Tom R. Tyler, *Procedural Strategies for Gaining Deference: Increasing Social Harmony or Creating False Consciousness?*, in SOCIAL INFLUENCES ON ETHICAL BEHAVIOR IN ORGANIZATIONS 69, 83 (John M. Darley et al. eds., 2001).
38. MACCOUN ET AL., *supra* note 29.
39. E. Allan Lind et al., *Procedural Context and Culture: Variation in the Antecedents of Procedural Justice Judgments*, 73 J. PERSONALITY & SOC. PSYCHOL. 767 (1997).
40. GEERT HOFSTEDE, CULTURE'S CONSEQUENCES: INTERNATIONAL DIFFERENCES IN WORK-RELATED VALUES (1989); Tom R. Tyler et al., *Cultural Values and Authority Relations: The Psychology of Conflict Resolution Across Cultures*, 6 PSYCHOL. PUB. POL'Y & L. 1138 (2000).
41. Rebecca Hollander-Blumoff & Tom R. Tyler, *Procedural Justice in Negotiation: Procedural Fairness, Outcome Acceptance, and Integrative Potential*, 33 LAW & SOC. INQUIRY 473 (2008); Kwok Leung et al., *Effects of Interactional Justice on Egocentric Bias in Resource Decisions*, 89 J. APPLIED PSYCHOL. 405 (2004); *see also* Tyler G. Okimoto & Tom R. Tyler, *Is Compensation Enough? Relational Concerns in Responding to Unintended Inequity*, 10 GROUP PROCESSES & INTERGROUP REL. 399 (2007).
42. Hollander-Blumoff & Tyler, *supra* note 41.
43. Tom R. Tyler, *Process Utility and Help Seeking: What Do People Want from Experts?*, 27 J. ECON. PSYCHOL. 360 (2006).
44. Howard B. Beckman et al., *The Doctor-Patient Relationship and Malpractice: Lessons from Plaintiff Depositions*, 154 ARCHIVES INTERNAL MED. 1365 (1994); Gerald B. Hickson et al., *Patient Complaints and Malpractice Risk*, 287 JAMA 2951 (2002); LaRae I. Huycke & Mark M. Huycke, *Characteristics of Potential Plaintiffs in Malpractice Litigation*, 120 ANNALS INTERNAL MED. 792 (1994); Gregory W. Lester & Susan G. Smith, *Listening and Talking to Patients: A Remedy For Malpractice Suits?*, 258 W. J. MED. 268 (1993); Wendy Levinson et al., *Physician-Patient Communication: The Relationship with Malpractice Claims Among Primary Care Physicians and Surgeons*, 177 JAMA 553 (1997); Robyn S. Shapiro et al., *A Survey of Sued and Nonsued Physicians and Suing Patients*, 149 ARCHIVES INTERNAL MED. 2190 (1989).
45. *See, e.g.*, ILL. ATTORNEY REGISTRATION & DISCIPLINARY COMM'N, ANNUAL REPORT (2009).
46. *See* William L. F. Felstiner & Ben Petitt, *Paternalism, Power, and Respect in Lawyer-Client Relations*, in HANDBOOK OF JUSTICE RESEARCH IN LAW, *supra* note 33, at 135, 136.
47. Tyler & Lind, *supra* note 33, at 68.

48. For reviews of the research on just world beliefs, see Melvin J. Lerner & Dale T. Miller, *Just World Research and the Attribution Process: Looking Back and Ahead*, 85 Psychol. Bull. 1030 (1978); Adrian Furnham, *Belief in a Just World: Research Progress over the Past Decade*, 34 Personality & Individual Differences 795 (2003); Melvin J. Lerner, *The Justice Motive: Where Social Psychologists Found It, How They Lost It, and Why They Might Not Find It Again*, 7 Personality & Soc. Psychol. Rev. 388 (2003).

49. *See* John T. Jost & Mahzarin R. Banaji, *The Role of Stereotyping in System Justification and the Production of False Consciousness*, 33 Brit. J. Soc. Psychol. 1 (1994); John T. Jost et al., *A Decade of System Justification Theory: Accumulated Evidence of Conscious and Unconscious Bolstering of the Status Quo*, 25 Pol. Psychol. 881 (2004).

50. Garriy Shteynberg et al., *Peering into the "Magnum Mysterium" of Culture*, 40 J. Cross-Cultural Psychol. 46 (2009); *see also* Kwok Leung & Michael W. Morris, *Justice Through the Lens of Culture and Ethnicity*, in Handbook of Justice Research in Law, *supra* note 33, at 343; Jonathan Haidt et al., *Affect, Culture, and Morality, or Is It Wrong to Eat Your Dog?*, 65 J. Personality & Soc. Psychol. 613 (2001); Philip E. Tetlock et al., *The Punitiveness Paradox: When Is External Pressure Exculpatory—and When a Signal Just to Spread Blame?*, 46 J. Experimental Soc. Psychol. 388 (2010).

51. Dale T. Miller & Neil Vidmar, *The Social Psychology of Punishment Reactions*, in The Justice Motive in Social Behavior: Adapting to Times of Scarcity and Change 145, 146 (Melvin J. Lerner & Sally C. Lerner eds., 1981); *see also* Jonathan Haidt, *The Emotional Dog and Its Rational Tail: A Social Intuitionist Approach to Moral Judgment*, 108 Psychol. Rev. 814 (2001); Daniel Kahneman et al., *Shared Outrage and Erratic Awards: The Psychology of Punitive Damages*, 16 J. Risk & Uncertainty 49 (1998).

52. *See, e.g.*, Mario Gollwitzer et al., *What Gives Victims Satisfaction When They Seek Revenge?*, 41 Eur. J. Soc. Psychol. 364 (2011); Mario Gollwitzer & Markus Denzler, *What Makes Revenge Sweet: Seeing the Offender Suffer or Delivering a Message?*, 45 J. Experimental Soc. Psychol. 840 (2009).

53. William Shakespeare, The Merchant of Venice, at act 3, scene 1.

54. Kevin M. Carlsmith, *The Roles of Retribution and Utility in Determining Punishment*, 42 J. Experimental Soc. Psychol. 437 (2006); *see also* Kevin M. Carlsmith et al., *Why Do We Punish? Deterrence and Just Deserts as Motives for Punishment*, 83 J. Personality & Soc. Psychol. 284 (2002); John M. Darley, *Incapacitation and Just Deserts as Motives for Punishment*, 24 Law & Hum. Behav. 659 (2000); Kevin M. Carlsmith, *On Justifying Punishment: The Discrepancy Between Words and Actions*, 21 Soc. Just. Res. 119 (2008). Similar patterns have been found with respect to torture—support for torture tends to be articulated in terms of utilitarian reasons (for example, to achieve deterrence or to obtain information), but choices tend to be influenced more

by the moral status of the target than by information about effectiveness. Kevin M. Carlsmith & Avani Mehta Sood, *The Fine Line Between Interrogation and Retribution*, 45 J. EXPERIMENTAL SOC. PSYCHOL. 191 (2009).

55. Bernard Weiner et al., *An Attributional Examination of Retributive Versus Utilitarian Philosophies of Punishment*, 10 SOC. JUST. RES. 431 (1997).

56. Arlene M. Stillwell et al., *We're All Victims Here: Toward a Psychology of Revenge*, 30 BASIC & APPLIED SOC. PSYCHOL. 253, 254 (2008).

57. *Alfred Hitchcock Quotes*, THINKEXIST.COM, http://thinkexist.com/quotation/revenge-is-sweet-and-not/348471.html (last visited March 24, 2012).

58. Brad J. Bushman et al., *Do People Aggress to Improve Their Mood? Catharsis Beliefs, Affect Regulation Opportunity, and Aggressive Responding*, 81 J. PERSONALITY & SOC. PSYCHOL. 17 (2001).

59. *See, e.g.*, Stillwell et al., *supra* note 56.

60. Letter to W. D. Howells (1886), *in* MARK TWAIN—HOWELLS LETTERS: THE CORRESPONDENCE OF SAMUEL L. CLEMENS AND WILLIAM D. HOWELLS 266 (1960).

61. *Francis Bacon Sr. Quotes*, THINKEXIST.COM, http://thinkexist.com/quotation/a_man_that_studieth_revenge_keeps_his_own_wounds/187998.html (last visited March 25, 2012).

62. Kevin M. Carlsmith et al., *The Paradoxical Consequences of Revenge*, 95 J. PERSONALITY & SOC. PSYCHOL. 1316 (2008).

63. Dena M. Gromet & John M. Darley, *Punishment and Beyond: Achieving Justice Through the Satisfaction of Multiple Goals*, 43 LAW & SOC'Y REV. 1 (2009); *see also* Jennifer K. Robbennolt, John M. Darley & Robert J. MacCoun, *Symbolism and Incommensurability in Civil Sanctioning: Decision Makers as Goal Managers*, 68 BROOK. L. REV. 1121 (2003). *See generally* Tyler G. Okimoto et al., *Beyond Retribution: Conceptualizing Restorative Justice and Exploring Its Determinants*, 22 SOC. JUST. RES. 156 (2009); Michael Wenzel et al., *Retributive and Restorative Justice*, 32 LAW & HUM. BEHAV. 375 (2008).

64. Jonathan R. Cohen, *Advising Clients to Apologize*, 72 S. CAL. L. REV. 1009, 1020 (1999).

65. John Hill, *Kent Hospital Settles Suit with Woods Family*, PROVIDENCE J. (Dec. 2, 2009, 12:56 p.m.), http://www.projo.com/health/content/woods_trial_new_2_12-02-09_KVGLE5A_v12.3cf5131.html; Russell J. Moore & John Howell, *"I'm Sorry" Paves Way to Woods' Suit Settlement*, WARWICK BEACON (Dec. 3, 2009); *see also Hospital's Apology Ends Contentious Litigation*, HEALTHCARE RISK MGMT. (Mar. 1, 2010), http://www.highbeam.com/doc/1G1-221753620.html.

66. *See generally* NICHOLAS TAVUCHIS, MEA CULPA: A SOCIOLOGY OF APOLOGY AND RECONCILIATION (1991).

67. Kathleen M. Mazor et al., *Disclosure of Medical Errors: What Factors Influence How Patients Respond?*, 21 J. GEN. INTERNAL MED. 704 (2006); Kathleen M. Mazor et al., *Health Plan Members' Views About Disclosure of Medical Errors*, 140 ANNALS INTERNAL MED. 409 (2004); Jennifer K. Robbennolt, *Apologies and*

Legal Settlement: An Empirical Examination, 102 MICH. L. REV. 460 (2003); Jennifer K. Robbennolt, *Apologies and Settlement Levers*, 3 J. EMPIRICAL LEGAL STUD. 333 (2006).
68. Jennifer K. Robbennolt, *Attorneys, Apologies, and Settlement Negotiation*, 13 HARV. NEGOT. L. REV. 349 (2008).
69. Jennifer K. Robbennolt, *Apologies and Settlement*, 45 COURT REV. 76, 81 (2010) (emphasis in original).

Chapter 9

1. NEIL POSTMAN & CHARLES WEINGARTNER, TEACHING AS A SUBVERSIVE ACTIVITY 81 (1971).
2. David M. Trubek et al., *The Costs of Ordinary Litigation*, 31 UCLA L. REV. 72, 91 (1983) (finding that the lawyers studied spent 16% of their time solely in conferring with clients—more time than they spent on research or conducting hearings or trials).
3. *See* Charles J. Holahan & Karl A. Slaikeu, *Effects of Contrasting Degrees of Privacy on Client Self-Disclosure in a Counseling Setting*, 24 J. COUNSELING PSYCHOL. 55, 58 (1977).
4. *See, e.g.*, Allison B. Arnell & Ann Sloan Devlin, *Perceived Quality of Care: The Influence of the Waiting Room Environment*, 22 J. ENVTL. PSYCHOL. 345, 355–56 (2002) (examining medical waiting rooms).
5. *See, e.g.*, Ann Sloan Devlin et al., *"Impressive?" Credentials, Family Photographs, and the Perception of Therapist Qualities*, 29 J. ENVTL. PSYCHOL. 503, 509 (2009); P. Paul Heppner & Steve Pew, *Effects of Diplomas, Awards, and Counselor Sex on Perceived Expertness*, 24 J. COUNSELING PSYCHOL. 147 (1977); William T. Hoyt, *Antecedents and Effects of Perceived Therapist Credibility: A Meta-Analysis*, 43 J. COUNSELING PSYCHOL. 430, 441 (1996); Page K. Pressly & Martin Heesacker, *The Physical Environment and Counseling: A Review of Theory and Research*, 79 J. COUNSELING & DEV. 148, 156 (2001) (reviewing studies); Jeffrey C. Siegel, *Effects of Objective Evidence of Expertness, Nonverbal Behavior, and Subject Sex on Client-Perceived Expertness*, 27 J. COUNSELING PSYCHOL. 117, 120 (1980).
6. *See, e.g.*, EDWARD T. HALL, THE HIDDEN DIMENSION 121–23 (1969); Leslie A. Hayduk, *Personal Space: Where We Now Stand*, 94 PSYCHOL. BULL. 293, 319 (1983); Leslie A. Hayduk, *Personal Space: An Evaluative and Orienting Overview*, 85 PSYCHOL. BULL. 117, 121 (1978); Pressly & Heesacker, *supra* note 5, at 153 (reviewing studies); Nan M. Sussman & Howard M. Rosenfeld, *Influence of Culture, Language, and Sex on Conversation Distance*, 42 J. PERSONALITY & SOC. PSYCHOL. 66, 71–72 (1982).
7. *See, e.g.*, Gary L. Brase, *The White-Coat Effect: Physician Attire and Perceived Authority, Friendliness, and Attractiveness*, 34 J. APPLIED SOC. PSYCHOL. 2469,

2478 (2004); Yoon-Hee Kwon & Julie Johnson-Hillery, *College Students' Perceptions of Occupational Attributes Based on Formality of Business Attire*, 87 PERCEPTUAL & MOTOR SKILLS 987, 992–93 (1998).
8. LEGALLY BLONDE (Metro-Goldwyn-Mayer 2001).
9. Michael Morris et al., *Schmooze or Lose: Social Friction and Lubrication in E-Mail Negotiations*, 6 GROUP DYNAMICS: THEORY RES. & PRAC. 89, 95–99 (2002).
10. DERALD WING SUE & DAVID SUE, COUNSELING THE CULTURALLY DIVERSE: THEORY AND PRACTICE (2003); Richard W. Brislin & Eugene S. Kim, *Cultural Diversity in People's Understanding and Uses of Time*, 52 APPLIED PSYCHOL.: INT'L REV. 363, 374 (2003); Tanya L. Chartrand & Rick van Baaren, *Human Mimicry*, 41 ADVANCES EXPERIMENTAL SOC. PSYCHOL. 219 (2009); Harry C. Triandis, *Some Dimensions of Intercultural Variation and Their Implications for Community Psychology*, 11 J. COMMUNITY PSYCHOL. 285, 297 (1983); Jeffrey Sanchez-Burks et al., *Performance in Intercultural Interactions at Work: Cross-Cultural Differences in Response to Behavioral Mirroring*, 94 J. APPLIED PSYCHOL. 216, 222 (2009); Shali Wu & Boaz Keysar, *The Effect of Culture on Perspective Taking*, 18 PSYCHOL. SCI. 600, 604–05 (2007); *see also* Rosaleen Ow & Dafna Katz, *Family Secrets and the Disclosure of Distressful Information in Chinese Families*, 80 FAM. SOC'Y 620, 620 (1999).
11. Jeanne M. Brett & Michele J. Gelfand, *A Cultural Analysis of the Underlying Assumptions of Negotiation Theory*, in NEGOTIATION THEORY AND RESEARCH 173, 180–183 (Leigh L. Thompson ed., 2006); Ken-Ichi Ohbuchi et al., *Cultural Values in Conflict Management: Goal Orientation, Goal Attainment, and Tactical Decision*, 30 J. CROSS-CULTURAL PSYCHOL. 51, 64 (1999).
12. NADYA A. FOUAD & PATRICIA ARREDONDO, BECOMING CULTURALLY ORIENTED: PRACTICAL ADVICE FOR PSYCHOLOGISTS AND EDUCATORS 58 (2007).
13. Paul R. Tremblay, *Interviewing and Counseling Across Cultures: Heuristics and Biases*, 9 CLINICAL L. REV. 373, 378 (2003).
14. *Id.* at 373.
15. Jeffrey Sanchez-Burks & Fiona Lee, *Cultural Psychology of Workways*, in HANDBOOK OF CULTURAL PSYCHOLOGY 346, 363 (Shinobu Kitayama & Dov Cohen eds., 2007); P. C. EARLEY & S. ANG, CULTURAL INTELLIGENCE: AN ANALYSIS OF INDIVIDUAL INTERACTIONS ACROSS CULTURES (2003).
16. Lawrence J. Vilardo, *Communicating with Clients*, 27:3 LITIGATION 45, 45 (2001).
17. Some suggest that the practice of mindfulness mediation is a good way for attorneys to become more aware of their own and others' words and body language. *See* Leonard L. Riskin, *The Contemplative Lawyer: On the Potential Contributions of Mindfulness Mediation to Law Students, Lawyers, and Their Clients*, 7 HARV. NEGOT. L. REV. 1, 45–46 (2002).

18. *See, e.g.*, Stefan H. Krieger & Richard K. Neumann Jr., Essential Lawyering Skills: Interviewing, Counseling, Negotiation, and Persuasive Fact Analysis 82–84 (2d ed. 2003).
19. Helaine Golann & Dwight Golann, *Why Is It Hard for Lawyers to Deal with Emotional Issues? A Dialogue Between a Lawyer-Mediator and a Therapist*, 9 Disp. Resol. Mag. 26, 26 (2003) (emphasis in original).
20. Steven Keeva, *Emotional Subtext*, 89 A.B.A. J. 85, 86 (Dec. 2008). The presenter at the conference was Sanford M. Portnoy, author of The Family Lawyer's Guide to Building Successful Client Relationships (2000).
21. *Meryl Streep Quotes*, Finest Quotes, http://www.finestquotes.com/author_quotes-author-Meryl%20Streep-page-0.htm (last visited March 24, 2012).
22. Keeva, *supra* note 20.
23. Mark R. Kebbell & David C. Giles, *Some Experimental Influences of Lawyers' Complicated Questions on Eyewitness Confidence and Accuracy*, J. Psychol. 129, 134, 137 (2000); Mark R. Kebbell & Shane D. Johnson, *Lawyers' Questioning: The Effect of Confusing Questions on Witness Confidence and Accuracy*, 24 Law & Hum. Behav. 629, 640 (2000).
24. Although some attorneys tend to believe that it is improper or perhaps even unethical to consider nonlegal interests, in fact the ethical rules make clear that it is permissible and even desirable for attorneys to counsel on nonlegal issues. Model Rules of Prof'l Conduct R. 2.1 (2007).
25. *See* David G. Payne, *Hyperamnesia and Reminiscence in Recall: A Historical and Empirical Review*, 101 Psychol. Bull. 5 (1987); *see also* Brian Bornstein et al., *Repeated Testing in Eyewitness Memory: A Means to Improve Recall of a Negative Emotional Event*, 12 Applied Cognitive Psychol. 119, 127 (1998).
26. Malcolm D. MacLeod & C. Neil Macrae, *Gone but Not Forgotten: The Transient Nature of Retrieval-Induced Forgetting*, 12 Psychol. Sci. 148, 151 (2001).
27. Karen J. Mitchell & Maria S. Zaragoza, *Repeated Exposure to Suggestion and False Memory: The Role of Contextual Variability*, 35 J. Memory & Language 246, 257 (1996); Henry L. Roediger III et al., *Misinformation Effects in Recall: Creating False Memories Through Repeated Retrieval*, 35 J. Memory & Language 300, 301, 315 (1996).
28. Leonard Riskin et al., Dispute Resolution and Lawyers 109 (4th ed. 2009).
29. Paul Ekman, Telling Lies: Clues to Deceit in the Marketplace 91–95 (3d ed. 2001).
30. Aldert Vrij et al., *Increasing Cognitive Load to Facilitate Lie Detection: The Benefit of Recalling an Event in Reverse Order*, 32 Law & Hum. Behav. 253, 262–63 (2008).
31. Maurice E. Schweitzer & Rachel Croson, *Curtailing Deception: The Impact of Direct Questions on Lies and Omissions*, in What's Fair: Ethics for Negotiators (Carrie Menkel-Meadow & Michael Wheeler eds., 2004).

32. Maria Hartwig et al., *Detecting Deception via Strategic Disclosure of Evidence*, 29 LAW & HUM. BEHAV. 469, 479–80 (2005); Maria Hartwig et al., *Strategic Use of Evidence During Police Interviews: When Training to Detect Deception Works*, 30 LAW & HUM. BEHAV. 603, 617 (2006).
33. For a discussion of the discoverability of witness statements, see ROGER S. HAYDOCK & DAVID F. HERR, DISCOVERY PRACTICE § 4.06(B) (2010).

Chapter 10

1. WILLIAM SHAKESPEARE, MEASURE FOR MEASURE, at act 1, scene 2.
2. Katherine R. Kruse, *Beyond Cardboard Clients in Legal Ethics*, 23 GEO. J. LEGAL ETHICS 103, 104 (2010).
3. Mathias S. Fleck et al., *Generalized "Satisfaction of Search": Adverse Influences on Dual-Target Search Accuracy*, 16 J. EXPERIMENTAL PSYCHOL.: APPLIED 60 (2010).
4. DAVID H. MAISTER ET AL., THE TRUSTED ADVISOR 41 (2000).
5. Chris Guthrie, *Be Curious*, 25 NEGOT. J. 401 (2009) (discussing ways to spark curiosity); *see also* George Loewenstein, *The Psychology of Curiosity: A Review and Reinterpretation*, 116 PSYCHOL. BULL. 75 (1994); Paul J. Silvia, *Interest—the Curious Emotion*, 17 CURRENT DIRECTIONS PSYCHOL. SCI. 57 (2008).
6. *See* Kelly L. Centofanti, *Sometimes, You Should Just Say No*, TRIAL, July 2011, at 18; Atul Gawande, *The Checklist: If Something So Simple Can Transform Intensive Care, What Else Can It Do?*, NEW YORKER, Dec. 10, 2007.
7. *See* Dennis P. Stolle et al., *Integrating Preventive Law and Therapeutic Jurisprudence: A Law and Psychology Based Approach to Lawyering*, in PRACTICING THERAPEUTIC JURISPRUDENCE: LAW AS A HELPING PROFESSION 5, 17–18, 23, 44 (Dennis P. Stolle et al. eds., 2000) (advocating the use of "legal checkups" and checklists to present structured opportunities for clients to reevaluate their life situations relative to their goals and to consider and plan for the immediate and distant future).
8. *See* Silvia Bonaccio & Reeshad S. Dalal, *Advice Taking and Decision-Making: An Integrative Literature Review, and Implications for the Organizational Sciences*, 101 ORGANIZATIONAL BEHAV. & HUM. DECISION PROCESSES 127 (2006).
9. Tamara Relis, *"It's Not About the Money!": A Theory on Misconceptions of Plaintiffs' Litigation Aims*, 68 U. PITT. L. REV. 701, 744–45 (2007) (finding that attorneys on all sides of medical malpractice cases tended to think that plaintiffs sued solely or mostly for money, and suggesting that this phenomenon is due in part to miscommunication and in part to the emphasis on litigation in legal education).

10. *See* Susan Daicoff, *Lawyer, Know Thyself: A Review of Empirical Research on Attorney Attributes Bearing on Professionalism*, 46 AM. U. L. REV. 1337 (1997); Chris Guthrie, *The Lawyers' Philosophical Map and the Disputant's Perceptual Map: Impediments to Facilitative Mediation and Lawyering*, 6 HARV. NEGOT. L. REV. 145 (2001); Leonard L. Riskin, *Mediation and Lawyers*, 43 OHIO ST. L.J. 29 (1982).
11. *See* Chip Heath, *On the Social Psychology of Agency Relationships: Lay Theories of Motivation Overemphasize Extrinsic Incentives*, 78 ORGANIZATIONAL BEHAV. & HUM. DECISION PROCESSES 25 (1999) (Studies show that when choosing between two jobs, one high in salary but low in personal satisfaction, the other low in salary but high on personal satisfaction, we choose the high-personal-satisfaction job for ourselves but the high salary job for others.); Laura J. Kray, *Contingent Weighting in Self-Other Decision Making*, 83 ORGANIZATIONAL BEHAV. & HUM. DECISION PROCESSES 82 (2000); *see also* Laura Kray & Richard Gonzalez, *Differential Weighting in Choice Versus Advice: I'll Do This, You Do That*, 12 J. BEHAV. DECISION MAKING 207 (1999).
12. OXFORD DICTIONARY OF HUMOROUS QUOTATIONS 220 (Ned Sherrin ed., 4th ed. 2008).
13. *Bo Derek Quotes*, THINKEXIST.COM, http://thinkexist.com/search/search Quotation.asp?search=whoever+said+money+can%27t+buy+happiness+si mply (last visited March 24, 2012).
14. Gillian K. Hadfield, *Framing the Choice Between Cash and the Courthouse: Experiences with the 9/11 Compensation Fund,* 42 LAW & SOC'Y REV. 645, 645, 649 (2008).
15. Gerald B. Hickson et al., *Factors That Prompted Families to File Medical Malpractice Claims Following Perinatal Injuries*, 267 JAMA 1359 (1992); Charles Vincent et al., *Why Do People Sue Doctors? A Study of Patients and Relatives Taking Legal Action*, 343 LANCET 1609 (1994); *see also* Hadfield, *supra* note 14 (discussing 9/11 victims' quest for information).
16. A FEW GOOD MEN, at 2:06:24–2:06:31 (Columbia Pictures 1992).
17. DICTIONARY OF CONTEMPORARY QUOTATIONS 242 (John Gordon Burke et al. eds., 1987).
18. Benjamin Weiser, *Among 9/11 Families, a Last Holdout Remains*, N.Y. TIMES, Sept. 10, 2010, at A13, *available at* http://www.nytimes.com/2010/09/11/nyregion/11family.html?pagewanted=1&_r=1&emc=eta1.
19. *Id.*; *see also* Hadfield, *supra* note 14.
20. Letter from Charles Vest, MIT President, MIT News (Sept. 8, 2000), http://web.mit.edu/newsoffice/2000/letter.html.
21. John McCormick, *At MIT, the Party's Over*, NEWSWEEK, Sept. 25, 2000.
22. *See* Relis, *supra* note 9.
23. WILLIAM HALTOM & MICHAEL MCCANN, DISTORTING THE LAW: POLITICS, MEDIA, AND THE LITIGATION CRISIS 186–87 (2004); Liebeck v. McDonald's Rests., P.T.S., Inc.,

CV-93-02419, 1995 WL 360309 (D.N.M. Aug. 18, 1994), *vacated sub nom.*, Liebeck v. McDonald's Rests., P.T.S., Inc., CV-93-02419, 1994 WL 16777704 (D.N.M. Nov. 28, 1994).

24. *See* Ethan Smith, *Apple Finally Snares Beatles*, WALL ST. J., Nov. 16, 2010; Heidi N. Moore, *Apple and the Beatles: A Long and Winding Road*, N.Y. TIMES, Nov. 16, 2010.

25. Jayson Clark, *Cliff Lee's Return Simply Stunning*, ESPN.com (Dec. 14, 2010), http://sports.espn.go.com/mlb/hotstove10/columns/story?columnist =stark_jayson&id=5918008.

26. Lea Winerman, *A Market for Market Psychology*, MONITOR ON PSYCHOL., Sept. 2011, at 52, 54 (quoting psychologist Frank Murtha).

27. Bruce J. Winick, *Overcoming Psychological Barriers to Settlement: Challenges for the TJ Lawyer*, in THE AFFECTIVE ASSISTANCE OF COUNSEL: PRACTICING LAW AS A HEALING PROFESSION 341, 346 (MARJORIE A. SILVER ED., 2007).

28. Centofanti, *supra* note 6.

29. PAUL BREST & LINDA HAMILTON KRIEGER, PROBLEM SOLVING, DECISION MAKING, AND PROFESSIONAL JUDGMENT: A GUIDE FOR LAWYERS AND POLICYMAKERS 37–38 (2010).

30. DISCLOSURE (Warner Bros. Pictures 1994).

31. BENJAMIN FRANKLIN, THE AUTOBIOGRAPHY OF BENJAMIN FRANKLIN 17 (Peter Conn ed., Penn Reading Project ed. 2005) (emphasis in original).

32. Eva Jonas et al., *Giving Advice or Making Decisions in Someone Else's Place: The Influence of Impression, Defense, and Accuracy Motivation on the Search for New Information*, 31 PERSONALITY & SOC. PSYCHOL. BULL. 977 (2005).

33. Jane Goodman-Delahunty et al., *Insightful or Wishful: Lawyers' Ability to Predict Case Outcomes*, 16 PSYCHOL. PUB. POL'Y & L. 133 (2010).

34. Randall Kiser et al., *Let's Not Make a Deal: An Empirical Study of Decision Making in Unsuccessful Settlement Negotiations*, 5 J. EMPIRICAL LEGAL STUD. 551, 566 (2008); *see also* Elizabeth F. Loftus & Willem A. Wagenaar, *Lawyers' Predictions of Success*, 28 JURIMETRICS 437, 437 (finding that "in general lawyers were overconfident in the chances of winning, especially so in cases in which they had been highly confident to begin with").

35. Loftus & Wagenaar, *supra* note 34, at 450 (speculating that lawyers' overconfidence may help them in court).

36. Ron L. Olson, *Yes Is Easy; No Is Important*, in A LIFE IN THE LAW: ADVICE FOR YOUNG LAWYERS 79, 80 (William S. Duffey Jr. & Richard A. Schneider eds., 2009).

37. ABBE SMITH, CASE OF A LIFETIME: A CRIMINAL DEFENSE LAWYER'S STORY 30 (2008) (emphasis in original).

38. Ian Weinstein, *Don't Believe Everything You Think: Cognitive Bias in Legal Decision Making*, 9 CLINICAL L. REV. 783, 813 (2003)

39. Lisa Lerman, *Lying to Clients*, 138 U. Pa. L. Rev. 661, 735 (1990) (quoting George Brenner, a former partner in a small law firm).

40. William Domnarski, *The Curse of Compassion for Clients—When Advocacy Sacrifices Objectivity*, S.F. DAILY J., Oct. 15, 2007, at 6; *see also* Randall Kiser, BEYOND RIGHT AND WRONG: THE POWER OF EFFECTIVE DECISION MAKING FOR ATTORNEYS AND CLIENTS 178 (2010) (quoting Erwin Chemerinsky, *Help Wanted*, S.F. DAILY J. 6, 6 (May 8, 2009) ("My sense, after over 30 years as a lawyer, is that a very large percentage of serious ethical violations come when lawyers go too far in their effort to please the client or get the results the client wants.").
41. Mark Wolfe, *Managing Expectations*, 47 TRIAL 16, 17 (July 2011).
42. *See generally* NANCY B. RAPOPORT ET AL., ENRON AND OTHER CORPORATE FIASCOS: THE CORPORATE SCANDAL READER (Foundation Press, 2d ed. 2009).
43. Early neutral evaluation (ENE) is a form of dispute resolution in which an experienced attorney provides a frank evaluation of the strengths and weaknesses of the claim or defense to both sides. While the evaluation is merely advisory, the hope is that the evaluation will help the disputants arrive at a settlement. ENE is popular in a few jurisdictions, such as the Northern District of California. U.S. DIST. COURT—N. DIST. CAL., EARLY NEUTRAL EVALUATION: GOVERNING RULE ADR LOCAL RULE 5, http://www.cand.uscourts.gov/ene (last visited Sept. 25, 2011).
44. Mark Wolfe, *Managing Expectations*, 47 TRIAL 16, 17 (July 2011).
45. Jeffrey Rachlinski, *A Positive Psychological Theory of Judging in Hindsight*, 65 U. CHI. L. REV. 571 (1998).
46. Of course a certain amount of deference to clients is required by the *Model Rules of Professional Conduct*, which, for example, say that the client must ultimately decide whether a settlement is acceptable and also make other major decisions in the course of litigation. MODEL RULES OF PROF'L CONDUCT R. 1.2 (2002) ("[A] lawyer shall abide by a client's decisions concerning the objectives of representation and, as required by Rule 1.4, shall consult with the client as to the means by which they are to be pursued. A lawyer may take such action on behalf of the client as is impliedly authorized to carry out the representation. A lawyer shall abide by a client's decision whether to settle a matter.").
47. DAVID H. MAISTER ET AL., THE TRUSTED ADVISOR 27 (2000).
48. For a good discussion of the range of views on lawyers' appropriate deference to their clients' expressed views, and also for a summary of relevant empirical studies, see Lynn Mather, *What Do Clients Want? What Do Lawyers Do?*, 52 EMORY L.J. (2003).
49. ROBERT MNOOKIN, BARGAINING WITH THE DEVIL: WHEN TO NEGOTIATE, WHEN TO FIGHT (2010) (explaining how someone who thinks like Mr. Spock, the highly rational half-human, half-Vulcan character from the *Star Trek* television series and films, might use a cost-benefit analysis to decide when it is and is not appropriate to negotiate with a distasteful or evil counterpart).

50. William H. Simon, *Lawyer Advice and Client Autonomy: Mrs. Jones's Case*, in Ethics in Practice: Lawyers' Roles, Responsibilities, and Regulation 165, 165–67 (Deborah L. Rhode ed., 2000).
51. 1 Philip C. Jessup, Elihu Root, 1845–1909, at 133 (1938).
52. David H. Maister et al., The Trusted Advisor 20–21 (2000).
53. At times it may be clear to the attorney that she is incapable of helping the client get beyond particular debilitating emotions. In such circumstances, the attorney should be prepared to suggest that the client may want to obtain help from a mental health counselor.
54. Diedre Combs, The Way of Conflict: Elemental Wisdom for Resolving Disputes and Transcending Differences 160 (2004).
55. For a good discussion of this literature, see Katherine R. Kruse, *Fortress in the Sand: The Plural Values of Client-Centered Representation*, 12 Clinical L. Rev. 369 (2006).
56. Erin Brockovich (Universal Pictures 2000).
57. Olson, *supra* note 36, at 81.
58. *Id.* at 80.

Chapter 11

1. 10 Adam Smith, An Inquiry into the Nature and Causes of the Wealth of Nations 19 (1909).
2. James J. White, *Machiavelli and the Bar: Ethical Limitations on Lying in Negotiation*, Am. B. Found. Res. J. 926, 927 (1980).
3. For discussion of these and other approaches to negotiation, see, e.g., Deepak Malhotra & Max H. Bazerman, Negotiation Genius: How to Overcome Obstacles and Achieve Brilliant Results at the Bargaining Table and Beyond (2008); Robert H. Mnookin et al., Beyond Winning: Negotiating to Create Value in Deals and Disputes (2000); G. Richard Shell, Bargaining for Advantage: Negotiation Strategies for Reasonable People (2d ed. 2006).
4. The term *BATNA*, best alternative to a negotiated agreement, was coined by Roger Fisher and William Ury in their pathbreaking book *Getting to Yes*.
5. Daniel Kahneman & Amos Tversky, *Conflict Resolution: A Cognitive Perspective*, in Barriers to Conflict Resolution 45, 45–46 (Kenneth J. Arrow et al. eds., 1995).
6. The Collected Works of Abraham Lincoln 81 (Roy P. Basler ed., 1953).
7. Don A. Moore et al., *Conflict of Interest and the Intrusion of Bias*, 5 Judgment & Decision Making 37 (2010).
8. Model Rules of Prof'l Conduct R. 1.2(a) (1983).
9. *See generally* Rachel Croson & Robert H. Mnookin, *Does Disputing Through Agents Enhance Cooperation? Experimental Evidence*, 26 J. Legal Stud. 331

(1997); Ronald J. Gilson & Robert H. Mnookin, *Disputing Through Agents: Cooperation and Conflict Between Lawyers in Litigation*, 94 COLUM. L. REV. 509 (1994).

10. Sandy Jap et al., *The Dark Side of Rapport: Agent Misbehavior Face-to-Face and Online*, 57 MGMT. SCI. 1610, 1612 (2011) (noting that "agent-negotiators can choose to sacrifice some of the interests of their clients in the name of successfully closing a deal").

11. Gerry Spence, *Persuading Yourself You Can Win*, 36:2 LITIGATION 14, 14 (2010).

12. No doubt for this reason, many popular books examine how people can better learn to make themselves happier. *See, e.g.*, SONJA LYUBORMIRSKY, THE HOW OF HAPPINESS: A NEW APPROACH TO GETTING THE LIFE YOU WANT (2007); MARTIN E. P. SELIGMAN, AUTHENTIC HAPPINESS: USING THE NEW POSITIVE PSYCHOLOGY TO REALIZE YOUR POTENTIAL FOR LASTING FULFILLMENT (2002). For additional discussion, see chapter 15.

13. MALHOTRA & BAZERMAN, *supra* note 3, at 112–13.

14. 347 U.S. 483 (1954).

15. Derrick A. Bell Jr., *Serving Two Masters: Integration Ideals and Client Interests in School Desegregation*, 85 YALE L.J. 470, 472, 482–92 (1976).

16. TAMARA RELIS, PERCEPTIONS IN LITIGATION AND MEDIATION: LAWYERS, DEFENDANTS, PLAINTIFFS, AND GENDERED PARTIES 34 (2009). Relis found that almost all of the physicians' attorneys believed that plaintiffs sue for solely monetary compensation; the hospitals' attorneys believed they sue mostly because of the money; and both plaintiffs' and defendants' attorneys believed that the claims are partly about money and partly about other issues, including "obtaining answers about what happened, acknowledgments of harm, apologies, defendants accepting responsibility, and retribution for insulting physician conduct." *Id.* at 36–39.

17. *Oscar Wilde Quotes*, THINKEXIST.COM, http://thinkexist.com/quotation/when_i_was_young-i_thought_that_money_was_the/196777.html (last visited Nov. 18, 2011).

18. WOODY ALLEN, THE INSANITY DEFENSE: THE COMPLETE PROSE 151 (2007).

19. THE BEATLES, CAN'T BUY ME LOVE (Parlophone 1964).

20. *CEO Quotes*, CEO LIBRARY, http://ceolibrary.org/quotes/ceoquotes.htm (last visited March 25, 2012).

21. ROBERT MNOOKIN, NEGOTIATING WITH THE DEVIL 124 (2010).

22. SHELL, *supra* note 3, at 87; *see also* Chris Guthrie, *Be Curious*, 25 NEGOTIATION J. 401 (2009).

23. Michael W. Morris et al., *Misperceiving Negotiation Counterparts: When Situationally Determined Bargaining Behaviors Are Attributed to Personality Traits*, 77 J. PERSONALITY & SOC. PSYCHOL. 52 (1999) (overcoming fixed pie assumptions); *see also* Adam D. Galinsky et al., *Why It Pays to Get Inside the*

Head of Your Opponent: The Differential Effects of Perspective Taking and Empathy in Negotiations, 19 Psychol. Sci. 378, 383 (2008).
24. Robert H. Mnookin et al., Beyond Winning: Negotiating to Create Value in Deals and Disputes 58 (2000).
25. Deepak Malhotra & Max Bazerman, *Investigative Negotiation*, Harv. Bus. Rev. 72, 73–74 (Sept. 2007).
26. Roger Fisher & Daniel Shapiro, Beyond Reason: Using Emotions as You Negotiate 18–21 (2005).
27. Leonard L. Riskin, *Further Beyond Reason: Emotion, the Core Concerns, and Mindfulness in Negotiation*, 10 Nev. L.J. 289, 301–02 (2010) (emphasis omitted).
28. Paul C. Cozby, *Self-Disclosure: A Literature Review*, 79 Psychol. Bull. 73 (1973); Valerian J. Derlega et al., *Self-Disclosure Reciprocity, Liking, and the Deviant*, 9 J. Experimental Soc. Psychol. 277 (1973).
29. Malhotra & Bazerman, *supra* note 25, at 77.
30. *See, e.g.*, Sally Blount White et al., *Alternative Models of Price Behavior in Dyadic Negotiations: Market Prices, Reservation Prices, and Negotiator Aspirations*, 57 Organizational Behav. & Hum. Decision Processes 430 (1994); Sally Blount White & Margaret Neale, *Role of Negotiator Aspirations and Settlement Expectancies in Bargaining Outcomes*, 57 Organizational Behav. & Hum. Decision Processes 303 (1994); W. Clay Hamner & Donald L. Harnett, *The Effects of Information and Aspiration Level on Bargaining Behavior*, 11 J. Experimental Soc. Psychol. 329 (1975); Vandra L. Huber & Margaret A. Neale, *Effects of Self and Competitor Goals on Performance in an Interdependent Bargaining Task*, 72 J. Applied Psychol. 197 (1987); Russell Korobkin, *Aspirations and Settlement*, 88 Cornell L. Rev. 1 (2002); Margaret A. Neale & Max H. Bazerman, *The Effect of Externally Set Goals on Reaching Integrative Agreements in Competitive Markets*, 6 J. Occupational Behav. 19 (1985). *See generally* Edwin A. Locke & Gary P. Latham, A Theory of Goal Setting & Task Performance (1990).
31. ThinkExist.com, http://thinkexist.com/quotation/always_aim_your_goals_and_aspiration_for_the_moon/165807.html (last visited March 12, 2012).
32. *See* Korobkin, *supra* note 30.
33. *See generally* Mollie W. Marti & Roselle Wissler, *Be Careful What You Ask For: The Effects of Anchors on Personal Injury Damage Awards*, 6 J. Experimental Psychol.: Applied 91 (2000).
34. Gretchen B. Chapman & Eric J. Johnson, *Anchoring, Activation, and the Construction of Values*, 79 Organizational Behav. & Hum. Decision Processes 1 (1999); Duane T. Wegener et al., *Implications of Attitude Change Theories for Numerical Anchoring: Anchor Plausibility and the Limits of Anchor Effectiveness*, 37 J. Experimental Soc. Psychol. 62 (2001); *see also* Kevin L. Blankenship et al., *Elaboration and Consequences of Anchored Estimates: An Attitudinal*

Perspective on Numerical Anchoring, 44 J. Experimental Soc. Psychol.1465 (2008).

35. Jonathan Harr, A Civil Action 249–50 (1998).
36. *See, e.g.*, Adam D. Galinsky et al., *Disconnecting Outcomes and Evaluations: The Role of Negotiator Focus*, 83 J. Personality & Soc. Psychol. 1131 (2002); Korobkin, *supra* note 30; Leigh Thompson, *The Impact of Minimum Goals and Aspirations on Judgments of Success in Negotiations*, 4 Group Decision & Negot. 513 (1995).
37. Galinsky et al., *supra* note 36.
38. Max Bazerman & Margaret Neale, *Heuristics in Negotiation: Limitations to Dispute Resolution Effectiveness*, in Negotiations in Organizations 51 (Max H. Bazerman & Roy Lewicki eds., 1983); Leigh Thompson & Reid Hastie, *Social Perception in Negotiation*, 47 Organizational Behav. & Hum. Decision Processes 98 (1990); *see also* Leigh Thompson & Dennis Hrebec, *Lose-Lose Agreements in Interdependent Decision Making*, 120 Psychol. Bull. 396 (1996).
39. Mitchell J. Callan et al., *The Effects of Priming Legal Concepts on Perceived Trust and Competitiveness, Self-Interested Attitudes, and Competitive Behavior*, 46 J. Experimental Soc. Psychol. 325 (2010). Similarly, objects common to legal settings such as business suits and briefcases, as well as notions of money (see chapter 1), can prime a competitive stance. Aaron C. Kay et al., *Material Priming: The Influence of Mundane Physical Objects on Situational Construal and Competitive Behavioral Choice*, 95 Organizational Behav. & Hum. Decision Processes 83 (2004).
40. Max H. Bazerman & Andrew J. Hoffman, *Applying the Insights of Walton and McKersie to the Environmental Context*, in Negotiations and Change: From the Workplace to Society 265 (Thomas A. Kochan & David B. Lipsky eds., 2003).
41. Malhotra & Bazerman, *supra* note 3, at 110 (citing Leigh Thompson, The Mind and Heart of the Negotiator (2001)).
42. Nira Liberman & Yaacov Trope, *The Role of Feasibility and Desirability Considerations in Near and Distant Future Decisions: A Test of Temporal Construal Theory*, 75 J. Personality & Soc. Psychol. 5 (1998); Gerardo A. Okhuysen et al., *Saving the Worst for Last: The Effect of Time Horizon on the Efficiency of Negotiating Benefits and Burdens*, 91 Organizational Behav. & Hum. Decision Processes 269 (2003); Todd Rogers & Max H. Bazerman, *Future Lock-Ins: Future Implementation Increases Selection of "Should" Choices*, 106 Organizational Behav. & Hum. Decision Processes 1 (2008); Yaacov Trope & Nira Liberman, *Temporal Construal*, 110 Psychol. Rev. 403 (2003).
43. *Unique Settlements Help the Poor: Time and Again, Settlement Negotiations in Civil Cases Reach an Impasse: The Plaintiff Wants Punitive Damages, but the Defendant Won't Budge*, 64 Tex. B.J. 230 (Mar. 2001).
44. Richard H. Thaler, *Mental Accounting Matters*, 12 J. Behav. Decision Making 183 (1999).

45. Chris Guthrie, *Panacea or Pandora's Box? The Costs of Options in Negotiation*, 88 Iowa L. Rev. 601, 605 (2003).
46. Avishalom Tor et al., *Fairness and the Willingness to Accept Plea Offers*, 7 J. Empirical Legal Stud. 97 (2010).
47. Peter Reilly, *Resistance is NOT Futile: Harnessing the Power of Counter-Offensive Tactics in Legal Persuasion*, 64 Hastings L.J. ___ (forthcoming 2012).
48. Model Rules of Prof'l Conduct R. 4.2 (1983).
49. Model Rules of Prof'l Conduct R. 1.4 (1983); *see also* Model Rules of Prof'l Conduct R. 1.4 cmt. 2 (1983) ("[A] lawyer who receives from opposing counsel an offer of settlement in a civil controversy or a proffered plea bargain in a criminal case must promptly inform the client of its substance unless the client has previously indicated that the proposal will be acceptable or unacceptable or has authorized the lawyer to accept or to reject the offer.").
50. Harr, *supra* note 35, at 230.
51. Adam D. Galinsky & Thomas Mussweiler, *First Offers as Anchors: The Role of Perspective-Taking and Negotiator Focus*, 81 J. Personality & Soc. Psychol. 657 (2001); Russell Korobkin & Chris Guthrie, *Opening Offers and Out-of-Court Settlement: A Little Moderation May Not Go a Long Way*, 10 Ohio St. J. on Disp. Resol. 1 (1994).
52. Richard Polsky, I Sold Andy Warhol (Too Soon) 1–5 (2009).
53. Ashleigh Shelby Rosette et al., *Good Grief! Feelings of Anxiety Sour the Economic Benefits of First Offers* (Duke University, Working Paper, 2008).
54. Chris Guthrie, *Better Settle Than Sorry: The Regret Aversion Theory of Litigation Behavior*, U. Ill. L. Rev. 43 (1999).
55. Groucho Marx, Groucho and Me 321 (1959) (telegram to the Friar's Club of Beverly Hills).
56. Howard Raiffa, Negotiation Analysis: The Science and Art of Collaborative Decision Making 281 (2002).
57. *See, e.g.*, John K. Butler, *Behaviors, Trust, and Goal Achievement in a Win-Win Negotiating Role Play*, 20 Group & Org. Mgmt. 486 (1995); Carsten K. W. de Dreu et al., *Social Motives and Trust in Integrative Negotiation: The Disruptive Effects of Punitive Capability*, 83 J. Applied Psychol. 408 (1998); Melvin J. Kimmel et al., *Effects of Trust, Aspiration, and Gender on Negotiation Tactics*, 38 J. Personality & Soc. Psychol. 9 (1980); Charles E. Naquin & Gaylen D. Paulson, *Online Bargaining and Interpersonal Trust*, 88 J. Applied Psychol. 113 (2003); William Ross & Jessica LaCroix, *Multiple Meanings of Trust in Negotiation Theory and Research: A Literature Review*, 7 Int'l J. Conflict Mgmt. 314 (1996); *see also* Leigh L. Thompson et al., *Negotiation*, 61 Ann. Rev. Psychol. 491 (2010).
58. David Ritz, Divided Soul: The Life of Marvin Gaye 35 (2003).

59. Sandy D. Jap et al., *The Dark Side of Rapport: Agent Misbehavior Face-to-Face and Online*, 57 Mgmt. Sci. 1610 (2011).
60. *The Chronicle Interview*, 37:3 UN Chron. 26, 27 (Fall 2000) (interview with Harri Holkeri, Finnish politician who helped negotiate the Good Friday Agreement in Northern Ireland).
61. Jeanne M. Brett & Michele J. Gelfand, *A Cultural Analysis of the Underlying Assumptions of Negotiation Theory*, in Negotiation Theory and Research 173, 184 (Leigh L. Thompson ed., 2006) (internal citation omitted).
62. Margaret A. Neale & Max H. Bazerman, *The Role of Perspective-Taking Ability in Negotiating Under Different Forms of Arbitration*, 36 Indus. & Lab. Rel. Rev. 378 (1983) (improved outcomes and ability to extract concessions).
63. Galinsky et al., *supra* note 23, at 383 (emphasis added).
64. For discussion of lying in negotiation, see generally Peter R. Reilly, *Lying in Negotiation and the Art of Defensive Self Help*, 24 Ohio St. J. on Disp. Resol. 481 (2009).
65. Leigh Thompson et al., *Some Like It Hot: The Case for the Emotional Negotiator*, in Shared Cognition in Organizations: The Management of Knowledge 139 (Leigh Thompson et al. eds., 1999).
66. Maarten J. J. Wubben et al., *How Emotion Communication Guides Reciprocity: Establishing Cooperation Through Disappointment and Anger*, 45 J. Experimental Soc. Psychol. 987 (2009). Disappointment directed at the offer is less likely to induce guilt or elicit concessions. Gert-Jan Lelieveld et al., *Disappointed in You, Angry About Your Offer: Distinct Negative Emotions Induce Concessions via Different Mechanisms*, 47 J. Experimental Soc. Psychol. 635 (2011).
67. Marwan Sinaceur & Larissa Z. Tiedens, *Get Mad and Get More Than Even: When and Why Anger Expression Is Effective in Negotiations*, 42 J. Experimental Soc. Psychol. 314 (2006) (finding that negotiators who expressed anger were perceived as tougher and claimed more value when their counterpart did not have good options but not when the counterpart's options were good); Gerben A. van Kleef & Stéphane Côté, *Expressing Anger in Conflict: When It Helps and When It Hurts*, 92 J. Applied Psychol. 1557 (2007); *see also* Robert S. Adler et al., *Emotions in Negotiation: How to Manage Fear and Anger*, 14 Negot. J. 161 (1998). Anger directed at the counterpart personally is less effective at eliciting concessions. Lelieveld et al., *supra* note 66.
68. Thomas Schelling, The Strategy of Conflict 37 (1960). Of course, the irrevocable commitment "gained" by ripping off the steering wheel adds a great deal to that negotiating position as well.
69. Eric van Dijk et al., *A Social Functional Approach to Emotions in Bargaining: When Communicating Anger Pays and When It Backfires*, 94 J. Personality & Soc. Psychol. 600 (2008); Sinaceur & Tiedens, *supra* note 67; Kleef & Côté, *supra* note 67.

70. John L. Graham, *The Influence of Culture on the Process of Business Negotiations: An Exploratory Study*, 16 J. INT'L BUS. STUD. 81 (1985).
71. Russell Korobkin, *Inertia and Preference in Contract Negotiation: The Psychological Power of Default Rules and Form Terms*, 51 VAND. L. REV. 1583 (1998).
72. Russell Korobkin, *Bounded Rationality, Standard Form Contracts, and Unconscionability*, 70 U. CHI. L. REV. 1203, 1203 (2003).
73. Robert J. Condlin, *"Cases on Both Sides": Patterns of Argument in Legal Dispute-Negotiation*, 44 MD. L. REV. 65, 68 (1985).
74. Studies have even found that gratuitous reasons can hold sway. In one experiment, researchers found that those who asked to cut in line to make copies "because I have to make some copies" were accommodated more often than those who did not provide such a reason. Ellen Langer et al., *The Mindlessness of Ostensibly Thoughtful Action: The Role of "Placebic" Information in Interpersonal Interaction*, 36 J. PERSONALITY & SOC. PSYCHOL. 635 (1978).
75. Deepak Malhotra & Max Bazerman, *Psychological Influence in Negotiation: An Introduction Long Overdue*, 34 J. MGMT. 509, 510 (2008).
76. Francesca Gino & Don Moore, *Using Final Deadlines Strategically in Negotiation*, 1 NEGOT. & CONFLICT MGMT. RES. 371, 375 (2008).
77. Gino & Moore, *supra* note 76; Don A. Moore, *Myopic Prediction, Self-Destructive Secrecy, and the Unexpected Benefits of Revealing Final Deadlines in Negotiation*, 94 ORGANIZATIONAL BEHAV. & HUM. DECISION PROCESSES 125 (2004).
78. Don A. Moore, *Myopic Biases in Strategic Social Prediction: Why Deadlines Put Everyone Under More Pressure Than Everyone Else*, 31 PERSONALITY & SOC. PSYCHOL. BULL. 668 (2005); Don A. Moore, *The Unexpected Benefits of Final Deadlines in Negotiation*, 40 J. EXPERIMENTAL SOC. PSYCHOL. 121 (2004).
79. THE BIG BOOK OF BUSINESS QUOTATIONS 190 (2003).
80. *See* Michael W. Morris & Dacher Keltner, *How Emotions Work: The Social Functions of Emotional Expression in Negotiations*, 22 RES. ORGANIZATIONAL BEHAV. 1 (2000).
81. *Howard Baker Quotes*, THINKEXIST.COM, http://thinkexist.com/quotes/howard_baker/.
82. Riskin, *supra* note 27, at 294.
83. Leigh Thompson et al., *Poker Face, Smiley Face, and Rant 'n' Rave: Myths and Realities About Emotion in Negotiation, in* EMOTION AND MOTIVATION (Marilynn B. Brewer & Miles Hewstone eds., 2004); Thompson et al., *supra* note 65, at 142. These studies have focused primarily on integrative negotiations where cooperation is particularly beneficial.
84. Delee Fromm, *Emotion in Negotiation*, NEG. MAG. (2008), *available at* http://www.negotiatormagazine.com/article404.html.
85. Alison M. Wood & Maurice E. Schweitzer, *Can Nervous Nelly Negotiate? How Anxiety Causes Negotiators to Exit Early and Make Steep Concessions*

(Russell Ackoff Fellowship of the Wharton Risk Ctr., Working Paper No. 2011-04, 2011).

86. *See, e.g.*, Keith G. Allred et al., *The Influence of Anger and Compassion on Negotiation Performance*, 70 ORGANIZATIONAL BEHAV. & HUM. DECISION Processes 175 (1997); Madan M. Pillutla & J. Keith Murnigham, *Unfairness, Anger, and Spite: Emotional Rejections of Ultimatum Offers*, 68 ORGANIZATIONAL BEHAV. & HUM. DECISION PROCESSES 208 (1996).

87. Riskin, *supra* note 27, at 290–91.

88. In his book *A Civil Action*, author Jonathan Harr describes how plaintiff's attorney Jan Schlictmann used an extreme version of this approach to try to settle his cases. He successfully settled a case regarding a hotel fire for $2.25 million after having hosted an elaborate three-day banquet at the Ritz-Carlton Hotel. However, when Schlictmann tried to use a fancy meal at the Four Seasons to settle the major environmental tort case that is the focus of the book, he was unsuccessful. The defense attorney was disgusted by the plaintiff's high demand and walked out with a croissant and a pen after thirty-seven minutes. Clearly, fancy atmosphere alone will not settle cases. HARR, *supra* note 35, at 123–24, 276–79.

89. Thompson et al., *supra* note 65, at 149.

90. Adler et al., *supra* note 67, at 170–71.

91. MODEL RULES OF PROF'L CONDUCT R. 1.4 (2008).

92. Galinsky & Mussweiler, *supra* note 51.

93. Liebeck v. McDonald's Rests., 1995 WL 360309 (D.N.M. 1994). However, note that the trial court subsequently reduced the jury award to $640,000 and that the case then settled for a confidential amount prior to being resolved on appeal. *See also* Boyle v. Christensen, 251 P.3d 810 (2011) (noting that "[a]lthough the public view of the [McDonald's] case is understandable when limited to a superficial view of its facts, a deeper look at the details and issues in the case may dramatically alter one's perspective" and finding that defense counsel's reference to the McDonald's case in closing argument was prejudicial error).

94. For a good discussion of decision trees, see http://www.settlementperspectives.com/2009/01/decision-tree-analysis-in-litigation-the-basics/.

95. Alafair Burke, *Improving Prosecutorial Decision Making: Some Lessons of Cognitive Science*, 47 WM. & MARY L. REV. 1587 (2006); *see also* Russell Covey, *Reconsidering the Relationship Between Cognitive Psychology and Plea Bargaining*, 91 MARQ. L. REV. 213 (2007).

96. *Id.*

97. Rebecca Hollander-Blumoff, *Psychology, Information Processing and Plea Bargaining*, 91 MARQ. L. REV. 163, 179–80 (2007).

98. *See generally* Joanna Gallant et al., The Science of Courtroom Litigation: Jury Research and Analytical Graphics (2008); Amy J. Posey & Lawrence S. Wrightsman, Trial Consulting (2005).
99. *See* Jennifer K. Robbennolt, *Attorneys, Apologies, and Settlement Negotiation*, 13 Harv. Negot. L. Rev. 349 (2008).
100. *The Plea: Interview; Abbe Smith*, Pub. Broad. Serv., http://www.pbs.org/wgbh/pages/frontline/shows/plea/ interviews/smith.html (last visited Nov. 10, 2010).
101. Abbe Smith, Case of a Lifetime: A Criminal Defense Lawyer's Story 40 (2008).
102. *Id.* at 42–44; *The Plea, supra* note 100.
103. For example, an attorney representing a claimant on a contingent fee basis may prefer to accept a lower percentage of an amount that the plaintiff might receive in the settlement rather than hold out for a higher percentage of an amount that the plaintiff might secure at trial. This could be true if the attorney saw the trial prospects as very risky or time consuming.
104. Leonard L. Riskin, *Mediation and Lawyers*, 43 Ohio St. L.J. 29, 43 (1982).
105. Carrie J. Menkel-Meadow et al., Dispute Resolution: Beyond the Adversarial Model 223 (2d ed. 2011).
106. *See* Robert A. Baruch Bush, *"What Do We Need a Mediator For?" Mediation's "Value-Added" for Negotiators*, 12 Ohio St. J. on Disp. Resol. 1 (1996).
107. Russell Korobkin, *Psychological Impediments to Mediation Success: Theory and Practice*, 21 Ohio St. J. on Disp. Resol. 281, 307 (2006) (emphasis in original).
108. *See generally, e.g.*, Robert I. Edelman & Roderick Snead, *Self-Disclosure in a Simulated Psychiatric Interview*, 38 J. Consulting & Clinical Psychol. 354 (1972) (finding that assurances of confidentiality increased disclosure); Carol A. Ford et al., *Influence of Physician Confidentiality Assurances on Adolescents' Willingness to Disclose Information and Seek Future Health Care: A Randomized Controlled Trial*, 278 JAMA 1029 (1997).
109. The description is taken from a presentation at a Harvard Faculty Seminar on April 13, 1982, and is summarized in Carrie Menkel-Meadow et al., Dispute Resolution: Beyond the Adversarial Model 289–92 (2005).
110. Korobkin, *supra* note 107, at 295–97.
111. Douglas Landau, *How I Learned to Relax and Love Mediation*, Trial 40, 40 (Dec. 2009); *see* Roselle L. Wissler, *Representation in Mediation: What We Know from Empirical Research*, 37 Fordham Urb. L.J. 419 (2010) (finding that the experience of voice was more closely related to procedural justice than was how much a party talked).
112. This anecdote is based closely on a mediation described in Eric Galton, *Mediation of Medical Negligence Claims*, 28 Cap. U. L. Rev. 321, 324–25 (2000).
113. *Id.* at 325.

114. Tamara Relis's study shows, however, that attorneys on both sides of medical negligence cases tend not to realize how important apologies and personal interaction may be to their clients. RELIS, *supra* note 16, at 34.
115. Landau, *supra* note 111.
116. *See* Richard Birke & Craig R. Fox, *Psychological Principles in Negotiating Civil Settlements*, 4 HARV. NEGOT. L. REV. 1 (1999); James R. Coben, *Gollum, Meet Smeagol: A Schizophrenic Ruination on Mediator Values Beyond Self-Determination and Neutrality*, 5 CARDOZO J. CONF. RES. 65, 75 (2004).
117. *See, e.g.*, Coben, *supra* note 116, at 74; James R. Coben, *Mediation's Dirty Little Secret: Straight Talk About Mediator Manipulation and Deception* 2 J. ALTERNATIVE DISP. RESOL. IN EMP. 4, 6 (2000); Barry Goldman, *The Psychology of Mediation*, 4 NAELA J. 115 (2008); James H. Stark & Douglas N. Frenkel, *Changing Minds: The Work of Mediators and Empirical Studies of Persuasion* (Univ. of Penn. Law Sch., Pub. Law Research Paper No. 11-07, 2011), *available at* http://ssrn.com/abstract=1769167; Nancy A. Welsh, *The Thinning Vision of Self-Determination in Court-Connected Mediation: The Inevitable Price of Institutionalization?*, 6 HARV. NEGOT. L. REV. 1 (2001).
118. Carrie Menkel-Meadow, *Ethics in Alternative Dispute Resolution: New Issues, No Answers from the Adversary Conception of Lawyers' Responsibilities*, 38 S. TEX. L. REV. 407, 411 (1997) (noting that "one of the most troubling of our ethical dilemmas in ADR [is determining] when . . . a solution suggested . . . by a third party neutral [is] too coercive on the parties").
119. James H. Stark & Douglas N. Frenkel, *Changing Minds: The Work of Mediators and Empirical Studies of Persuasion* 4 (Univ. of Penn. Law Sch., Pub. Law Research Paper No. 11-07, 2011) (emphasis in original), *available at* http://ssrn.com/abstract=1769167.
120. Welsh, *supra* note 117, at 12 (quoting Transcript of Proceedings Before the Honorable Davit Hittner, Settlement Hearing at 36–38 (Aug. 7, 1998), Allen v. Leal, 27 F. Supp. 2d 945 (S.D. Tex. 1998)).
121. Lawrence M. Watson, *Effective Legal Representation in Mediation*, 2 ALTERNATIVE DISP. RESOL. FLA. 17 (2d ed. 1995).
122. Nancy A. Welsh, *The Thinning Vision of Self-Determination in Court-Connected Mediation: The Inevitable Price of Institutionalization?*, 6 HARV. NEGOT. L. REV. 1, 5 (2001).
123. Patricia J. Dauser et al., *Effects of Disclosure of Comprehensive Pretherapy Information on Clients at a University Counseling Center*, 26 PROF. PSYCHOL.: RES. & PRAC. 190 (1995); Marc W. Haut & Thomas Muehleman, *Informed Consent: The Effects of Clarity and Specificity on Disclosure in a Clinical Interview*, 23 PSYCHOTHERAPY 93 (1986); Thomas G. Kremer & Ellis L. Gesten, *Confidentiality Limits of Managed Care and Clients' Willingness to Self-Disclose*, 29 PROF. PSYCHOL.: RES. & PRAC. 553 (1998); Thomas Muehleman et

al., *Informing Clients About the Limits to Confidentiality, Risks, and Their Rights: Is Self-Disclosure Limited?*, 16 Prof. Psychol.: Res. & Prac. 385 (1985).
124. *See generally* Welsh, *supra* note 117, at 86–92 (urging that a three-day cooling-off period be implemented before mediation agreements would become binding).
125. *See generally* Jean R. Sternlight, *Lawyers' Representation of Clients in Mediation: Using Economics and Psychology to Structure Advocacy in a Non-Adversarial Setting*, 14 Ohio St. J. Disp. Resol. 269–366 (1999).
126. Roderick Swaab & Jeanne Brett, Caucus with Care: The Impact of Pre-Mediation Caucuses on Conflict Resolution (2007), http://ssrn.com/abstract=1080622.
127. Harold I. Abramson, Mediation Representation: Advocating in a Problem-Solving Process 182 (2004).
128. *See* Wissler, *supra* note 111 (finding that the participation of lawyers helps to lessen settlement pressure).

Chapter 12

1. *Discovery*, 23:2 Litigation 5, 5 (1997) (calling discovery a "most essential part of our profession").
2. Stephen N. Subrin, *Discovery in Global Perspective: Are we Nuts?*, 52 DePaul L. Rev. 299, 300 (2002).
3. David I. C. Thomson, Skills and Values: Discovery Practice, at vii (2010).
4. Benjamin Franklin to the Federal Convention, 2 The Records of the Federal Convention of 1787, at 641–42 (Max Farrand ed., rev. ed. 1937).
5. Randall Kiser, Beyond Right and Wrong: The Power of Effective Decision Making for Attorneys and Clients 125 (2010).
6. Dwight Golann, *Dropped Medical Malpractice Claims: Their Surprising Frequency, Apparent Causes, and Potential Remedies*, 30 Health Aff. 1343 (July 2011); *see also* David M. Studdert et al., *Claims, Errors, and Compensation Payments in Medical Malpractice Litigation*, 354 New Eng. J. Med. 2024, 2030–31 (2006) (noting that "our findings underscore how difficult it may be for plaintiffs and their attorneys to discern what has happened before the initiation of a claim and the acquisition of knowledge that comes from the investigations, consultation with experts, and sharing of information that litigation triggers").
7. Kiser, *supra* note 5 at 125.
8. Stephen Lubet, Lawyers' Poker: 52 Lessons That Lawyers Can Learn from Card Players 35 (2006).
9. Jonathan Harr, A Civil Action 239 (1995).
10. Rebecca Hollander-Blumoff, *The Psychology of Procedural Justice in the Federal Courts*, 63 Hastings L.J. 127, 154–55 (Dec. 2011).

11. To see a number of the key documents pertaining to this lawsuit, see Nan D. Hunter, The Power of Procedure: The Litigation of Jones v. Clinton 81 (2002).
12. *Id.* at 102–04, 109–10.
13. John Markoff, *Armies of Expensive Lawyers, Replaced by Cheaper Software*, N.Y. Times, Mar. 5, 2011, at A1.
14. Qualcomm Inc. v. Broadcom Corp., 05CV1958-B (BLM), 2008 WL 66932, at *12 (S.D. Cal. Jan. 7, 2008). A similar cautionary tale could be told using the events described in two decisions regarding a major lawsuit brought against Morgan Stanley & Co. Coleman (Parent) Holdings, Inc. v. Morgan Stanley & Co., No. CA 03-5045 AI, 2005 WL 674885 (Fla. Cir. Ct. Mar. 23, 2005) (granting default judgment to plaintiff on ground that Morgan Stanley egregiously failed to comply with its discovery obligations, particularly by failing to produce requested documents).
15. *Id.* at *13.
16. Qualcomm Inc. v. Broadcom Corp., 2010 WL 1336937, at *2 (Apr. 2, 2010).
17. Walter Kiechel III, *The Strange Case of Kodak's Lawyers*, Fortune, May 8, 1978, at 188; *see also* James B. Stewart, The Partners 327–65 (1983) (discussing Donovan Leisure's representation of Kodak).
18. Robert L. Nelson, *The Discovery Process as a Circle of Blame: Institutional, Professional and Socio-Economic Factors That Contribute to Unreasonable, Inefficient and Amoral Behavior in Corporate Litigation*, 67 Fordham L. Rev 773, 777–78 (1999); see also Appendix, Problems Presented to Study Participants, 67 Fordham L. Rev. 885, 890 (1998).
19. Wash. State Physicians Ins. Exch. & Ass'n v. Fisons Corp., 858 P.2d 1054 (Wash. 1993).
20. *Id.* at 1074.
21. For example, studies have found that hospitals that adopt a checklist approach to treatment and anti-infection are more effective than hospitals that rely more on the knowledge and discretion of hospital personnel. Atul Gawande, The Checklist Manifesto: How to Get Things Right (2009).
22. Lubet, *supra* note 8, at 186.
23. Mark Wolfe, *The Purpose-Driven Interrogatory Response*, 44 Trial 48 (Dec. 2008).
24. *E.g.*, Fed. R. Civ. P. 26 (defining broad scope of discovery), 30(c)(2) (limiting defending attorney's ability to make "speaking" objections).
25. Mark Herrmann, The Curmudgeon's Guide to Practicing Law 54 (2006).
26. Rule 4.2 of the ABA *Model Rules of Professional Conduct* states that "[i]n representing a client, a lawyer shall not communicate about the subject of the representation with a person the lawyer knows to be represented by another lawyer in the matter, unless the lawyer has the consent of the other lawyer or is authorized to do so by law or a court order." Ambiguities

exist in some states as to whether an employee like Al Love would be considered to be an opposing client represented by another attorney.

27. HARR, *supra* note 9, at 160–71.
28. LUBET, *supra* note 8, at 113.
29. Jim McElhaney, *It's All About You: Use Cross-Examination to Get Their Witness to Agree to Your Version of the Case*, A.B.A J. 22, 23 (Sept. 2010).
30. Lance Morrow, *The Dance of Negotiation*, TIME MAG. at 113, 114 (Dec. 7, 1981).
31. *See* Barry R. Schlenker & Michael F. Weigold, *Interpersonal Processes Involving Impression Regulation and Management*, 43 ANN. REV. PSYCHOL. 133 (1992).
32. BRAINYQUOTE, http://www.brainyquote.com/quotes/authors/c/chris_matthews.html (last visited Nov. 29, 2011).
33. LUBET, *supra* note 8, at 159–61.
34. *See also* Douglas L. Keene, *Cross-Examination of a Narcissistic Witness*, 20 JURY EXPERT 30 (2008).
35. Neil J. Dilloff, *Deposition Tricks: The Dirty Dozen*, MD. B.J. 48, 49 (July 2009).
36. Deposition of Bill Gates, August 27, 1998, *available at* http://www.washingtonpast.com/wp-srv/business/longterm/microsoft/documents/gates0827p2.htm (last visited 11/28/11).
37. A DICTIONARY OF QUOTATIONS ABOUT COMMUNICATION 146 (Robert A. Nowlan & Gwendoly L. Nowlan eds., 2000).
38. JOEL BRINKLEY & STEVE LOHR, U.S. v. MICROSOFT 191–92 (2001).
39. FELIX FRANKFURTER, THE CASE OF SACCO AND VANZETTI 79 (Universal Library ed. 1962).
40. *Id.* at 73.
41. www.ahajokes.com
42. William M. McErlean et al., *The Evolution of Witness Preparation*, 37:1 LITIGATION 21, 23 (2010)).
43. Martha Neil, *Clutch Player, Book Cites David Boies as Exemplar of Success*, 97 A.B.A. J. 5 (Feb. 2011) (reviewing PAUL SULLIVAN, CLUTCH: WHY SOME PEOPLE EXCEL UNDER PRESSURE AND OTHERS DON'T (2011).
44. McErlean et al., *supra* note 42, at 25.
45. OSCAR WILDE, THE IMPORTANCE OF BEING EARNEST, at act 1, pt. 1 (1899).
46. BRINKLEY & LOHR, *supra* note 38, at 88–89; *see also* Elizabeth Wasserman, *Gates' Deposition Makes Judge Laugh in Court*, CNN.COM (Nov. 17, 1998), http://www.cnn.com/TECH/computing/9811/17/judgelaugh.ms.idg/index.html (discussing various of Gates's evasive answers).
47. *Libby Describes Forgetting, Relearning, CIA Operative's Identity*, USA TODAY (Feb. 6, 2007), *available at* http://www.usatoday.com/news/washington/2007-02-06-libby-trial_x.htm?csp=34 (last visited Nov. 29, 2011).
48. Dantube23, *Rudy Giuliani: I Do Not Recall*, YOUTUBE (Dec. 21, 2007), http://www.youtube.com/watch?v=eQ8rnhi1kqU.
49. THE MAMMOTH BOOK OF ZINGERS, QUIPS, AND ONE-LINERS: OVER 10,000 GEMS OF WIT, WISDOM, ONE-LINERS AND WISECRACKS 338 (Geoff Tibbalis ed., 2004).

50. Todd Rogers & Michael Norton, *Artful Dodging in the Courtroom*, 23 Jury Expert 1, 1 (2011) (emphasis omitted).
51. *Id.*
52. Todd Rogers & Michael Norton, *The Artful Dodger: Answering the Wrong Question the Right Way*, 17 J. Experimental Psychol.: Applied 139 (2011).
53. *See also* William Hirst & Gerald Echterhoff, *Remembering in Conversations: The Social Sharing and Reshaping of Memories*, 63 Ann. Rev. Psychol. 55 (2011); Elizabeth J. Marsh, *Retelling Is Not the Same as Recalling: Implications for Memory*, 16 Current Directions Psychol. Sci. 16 (2007).
54. David M. Malone et al., The Effective Deposition: Techniques and Strategies That Work 118 (rev. 3d ed. 2007).
55. One writer calls this being "Mr. Nasty." Dilloff, *supra* note 35, at 48.
56. Saul M. Kassin & Gisli H. Gudjonsson, *The Psychology of Confessions: A Review of the Literature and Issues*, 5 Psychol. Sci. Pub. Int. 33 (2004); Saul M. Kassin et al., *Police-Induced Confessions: Risk Factors and Recommendations*, 34 Law & Hum. Behav. 49 (2010); *see also* John Schwartz, *Confessing to Crime, but Innocent*, N.Y. Times, Sept. 14, 2010, at A14; Robert Kolker, *I Did It: Why Do People Confess to Crimes They Didn't Commit*, N.Y. Mag., Oct. 3, 2010.
57. Kassin & Gudjonsson, *supra* note 56, at 34.
58. *Id.*
59. *Id.* at 48. For a discussion of how a gentler psychology of interrogation was successfully used on terrorists in Iraq, see Matthew Alexander & John Bruning, How to Break a Terrorist: The U.S. Interrogators Who Used Brains, Not Brutality, to Take Down the Deadliest Man in Iraq (2008).
60. David M. Malone et al., The Effective Deposition: Techniques and Strategies that Work 225 (rev. ed. 2007).
61. *See, e.g.*, Davidlat, *How to Handle a Tough Deposition Question*, YouTube (Sept. 14, 2006), http://www.youtube.com/watch?v=RjtnRmy0H-U&feature=related.
62. Iowapublicdefender, *Texas Style Deposition*, YouTube (June 27, 2007), http://www.youtube.com/watch?v=ZlxmrvbMeKc.
63. *See generally* Mary R. Rose et al., *Appropriately Upset? Emotion Norms and Perceptions of Crime Victims*, 30 Law & Hum. Behav. 203 (2006). *But see, e.g.*, Larissa Z. Tiedens, *Anger and Advancement Versus Sadness and Subjugation: The Effect of Negative Emotion Expressions on Social Status Conferral*, 80 J. Personality & Soc. Psychol. 86 (2001).
64. *See, e.g.*, Karl Ask & Sara Landström, *Why Emotions Matter: Expectancy Violation and Affective Response Mediate the Emotional Victim Effect*, 34 Law & Hum. Behav. 392 (2010); Geir Kaufman et al., *The Importance of Being Earnest: Displayed Emotions and Witness Credibility*, 17 Applied Cognitive Psychol. 21 (2003); Rose et al., *supra* note 63.

65. HARR, *supra* note 9, at 231.
66. Iowapublicdefender, *supra* note 62; *see also* Paramount Commc'ns Inc. v. QVC Nat'l Inc., 637 A.2d 34, 53–54 (Del. 1994) (recounting another set of abusive remarks by Joe Jamail). For one discussion of attorney abuses in depositions, see Jean M. Cary, *Rambo Depositions: Controlling an Ethical Cancer in Civil Litigation*, 25 HOFSTRA L. REV. 561 (1996); *see also* Eric B. Miller, Note, *Lawyers Gone Wild: Are Depositions Still a "Civil" Procedure?*, 42 CONN. L. REV. 1527, 1530–31 (2010) (asserting that attorney misconduct in depositions is "commonplace," although such instances are often anecdotal and frequently go unreported). Psychologists may want to study what it is about depositions that tends to set off certain attorneys (perhaps exploring the effects of the defending attorneys' limited role, boredom, or the inclination to showboat for the client).
67. Fla. Bar v. Robert Joseph Ratiner, No. SC08-689, 46 So. 3d 35, 37 (2010).
68. McErlean et al., *supra* note 42, at 21.
69. *Id.* at 22.
70. DANIEL I. SMALL, PREPARING WITNESSES: A PRACTICAL GUIDE FOR LAWYERS AND THEIR CLIENTS 89–90 (3d ed. 2009).
71. David Illig, *Witness Preparation: Hidden False Assumptions, Real Truths, and Recommendations (Part Two)*, 20 JURY EXPERT 23, 24–25 (2008).
72. *Id.* at 24.
73. *Id.* at 26 (emphasis in original).
74. Janeen Kerper, *Preparing a Witness for Deposition*, 24:4 LITIGATION 11, 14 (1998) (quoting Frank Rothschild).
75. BRAD BRADSHAW, THE SCIENCE OF PERSUASION: A LITIGATOR'S GUIDE TO JUROR DECISION-MAKING 47 (2011).
76. *Id.* at 67–70.
77. JAMES W. MCELHANEY, MCELHANEY'S TRIAL NOTEBOOK 101 (2005).
78. Richard L. Berke & Kevin Sack, *The 2000 Campaign: The Debates; In Debate 2, Microscope Focuses on Gore*, N.Y. TIMES A1 (Oct. 11, 2000).
79. McErlean et al., *supra* note 35, at 22.
80. Diane R. Follingstad, *Preparing the Witness for Courtroom Testimony: Modifying Negative Behavior Through Employment of Psychological Principles*, 20 TRIAL 50 (Jan. 1984).
81. Stuart Rothenberg, *Gore, Bush Hope Third Debate Is the Charm*, CNNPOLITICS.COM (Oct. 16, 2000), http://articles.cnn.com/2000-10-16/politics/rothenberg.column_1_third-debate-second-debate-bush-and-gore?_s=PM:ALLPOLITICS.
82. Rebecca Leung, *Parting Shots from Fritz Hollings*, CBS NEWS (Dec. 12, 2004), http://www.cbsnews.com/stories/2004/12/10/60minutes/main660368.shtml.

83. McErlean et al., *supra* note 42, at 22.
84. BRADSHAW, *supra* note 75, at 47.
85. THE GREATEST QUOTATIONS OF ALL-TIME 422 (Anthony St. Peter ed., 2010).
86. Brad E. Bell & Elizabeth Loftus, *Trivial Persuasion in the Courtroom: The Power of (a Few) Minor Details*, 56 J. PERSONALITY & SOC. PSYCHOL. 669 (1989).
87. See Jeffrey J. Brockardt et al., *Effects of the Inclusion and Refutation of Peripheral Details on Eyewitness Credibility*, 33 J. APPLIED SOC. PSYCHOL. 2187 (2003); Elizabeth R. Tenney et al., *Calibration Trumps Confidence as a Basis for Witness Credibility*, 18 PSYCHOL. SCI. 46 (2007); Elizabeth R. Tenney et al., *The Benefits of Knowing What You Know (and What You Don't): How Calibration Affects Credibility*, 44 J. EXPERIMENTAL SOC. PSYCHOL. 1368 (2008).
88. GERALD M. STERN, THE BUFFALO CREEK DISASTER 148 (1976). Elsewhere in the book, Stern comments again about memory, noting that he doubted a witness was lying when he said he did not recall a conversation someone else did remember in detail. "I don't think he was lying. I believe he was too crushed by the disaster to lie. He may have completely forgotten about this conversation. I know that my sisters and I remember incidents from our childhood in different ways. Something that is important to me may have been completely unimportant to them and vice versa." *Id.* at 158. [The highlighted quote is more than 50 words. Do you want to set it as a block quotation?]
89. MARK TWAIN'S NOTEBOOK 240 (Albert Bigelow Paine ed., 1935).
90. David Johnston & Eric Lipton, *Gonzales Endures Harsh Session with Senate Panel*, N.Y. TIMES, Apr. 20, 2007, at A1.
91. ANATOMY OF A MURDER (Carlyle Productions 1959). For a nice analysis of the scene, see law professor Michael Asimow's discussion at http://usf.usfca.edu/pj//articles/anatomy.htm.
92. McErlean et al., *supra* note 42, at 25.
93. Robert K. Bothwell & Mehri Jalil, *The Credibility of Nervous Witnesses*, 7 J. SOC. BEHAV. & PERSONALITY 581 (1992); Barbara A. Spellman & Elizabeth R. Tenney, *Credible Testimony in and out of Court*, 17 PSYCHONOMIC BULL. & REV. 168 (2010).
94. SMALL, *supra* note 70, at 39 (emphasis in original).
95. Adapted from Roy Futterman, *Advanced Witness Preparation Using Psychological Techniques*, *in* THE SCIENCE OF COURTROOM LITIGATION: JURY RESEARCH AND ANALYTICAL GRAPHICS 93, 104–105 (Joanna Gallant et al. eds., 2008).
96. SMALL, *supra* note 70, at 6.
97. *See generally* Marcus T. Boccaccini et al., *Effects of Witness Preparation on Witness Confidence and Nervousness*, 3 J. FORENSIC PSYCHOL. PRAC. 39 (2003).
98. *E.g.*, FED. R. CIV. P. 30(c)(2) ("An objection must be stated concisely in a nonargumentative and nonsuggestive manner. A person may instruct a deponent not to answer only when necessary to preserve a privilege, to

enforce a limitation ordered by the court, or to present a motion under Rule 30(d)(3).").

99. Of course, if the deponent does not like attorneys, the attorney may not want to sit too close. Dennis P. Stolle & Mark D. Stuaan, *Defending Depositions in High-Stakes Civil and Quasi-Criminal Litigation: An Application of Therapeutic Jurisprudence*, 4 W. CRIM. REV. 134, 139 (2003).

100. MARK HERRMANN, THE CURMUDGEON'S GUIDE TO PRACTICING LAW 54 (2006).

101. Jean M. Cary, *supra* note 66, at 381 (summarizing disparate case law on this issue).

102. Erika Tyner Allen, *The Kennedy-Nixon Presidential Debates, 1960*, MUSEUM OF BROADCAST COMM., http://www.museum.tv/archives/etv/K/htmlK/kennedy-nixon/kennedy-nixon.htm (last visited Oct. 13, 2010).

103. Bob Secter, *The Kennedy-Nixon Debate: Presidential Politics Enter the Television Age*, CHI. TRIB., Sept. 26, 1960, http://www.chicagotribune.com/news/politics/chi-chicagodays-kennedynixon-story,0,4569752.story (last visited Oct. 13, 2010); *see also* James N. Druckman, *The Power of Television Images: The First Kennedy-Nixon Debate Revisited*, 65 J. POL. 559 (2003).

104. BRADSHAW, *supra* note 75, at 56.

105. PHILLIP G. CLAMPITT & ROBERT J. DEKOCH, EMBRACING UNCERTAINTY: THE ESSENCE OF LEADERSHIP 163 (2001).

106. 329 U.S. 495, 500–501 (1947).

107. George Loewenstein & Don A. Moore, *When Ignorance Is Bliss: Information Exchange and Inefficiency in Bargaining*, 33 J. LEGAL STUD. 37, 37 (2004).

108. MIGUEL DE CERVANTES, DON QUIXOTE, at pt. 2, bk. 4, ch. 43 (1615) (1605).

109. To the extent, however, that the outside companies' compensation is tied to the success of the transaction, their ability to offer a less biased perspective will be compromised.

Chapter 13

1. BARTLETT'S FAMILIAR QUOTATIONS: A COLLECTION OF PASSAGES, PHRASES, AND PROVERBS TRACED TO THEIR SOURCES IN ANCIENT AND MODERN LITERATURE 78 (John Bartlett & Justin Kaplan eds., 17th ed. 2002).

2. DICTIONARY OF QUOTATIONS IN COMMUNICATIONS 197 (Lilless McPherson Shilling & Linda K. Fuller eds., 1997).

3. RONALD T. KELLOGG, THE PSYCHOLOGY OF WRITING 16–18, 25–28 (1994).

4. John R. Hayes & Linda S. Flower, *Writing Research and the Writer*, 41 AM. PSYCHOLOGIST 1106, 1111 (1986).

5. 2,000 FAMOUS LEGAL QUOTATIONS 89 (M. Frances McNamara ed., 1967).

6. ANTONIN SCALIA & BRYAN A. GARNER, MAKING YOUR CASE: THE ART OF PERSUADING JUDGES 107 (2008) (quoting Hon. Irving R. Kaufman).

7. Ruth Anne Robbins, *Painting with Print: Incorporating Concepts of Typographic and Layout Design in the Text of Legal Writing Documents*, 2 J. Ass'n Legal Writing Directors 108 (2004).
8. Thomas R. Haggard & George W. Kuney, Legal Drafting in a Nutshell 422 (3d ed. 2007).
9. Stanard v. Nygren, 658 F.3d 792, 799 (7th Cir. 2011).
10. David Lewis, *Common Knowledge About Appellate Briefs: True or False?*, 6 J. App. Prac. & Process 331, 335 (2004); Susan Hanley Kosse & David T. ButleRitchie, *How Judges, Practitioners, and Legal Writing Teachers Assess the Writing Skills of New Law Graduates: A Comparative Study*, 53 J. Legal Educ. 80, 85 (2003); Kristen K. Robbins, *The Inside Scoop: What Federal Judges Really Think About the Way Lawyers Write*, 8 Legal Writing: Legal Writing Inst. 257, 279 (2002); *see also* Scalia & Garner, *supra* note 6, at 98 ("Judges often associate the brevity of the brief with the quality of the lawyer. Many judges we've spoken with say that good lawyers often come in far below the page limits—and that bad lawyers almost never do.").
11. Scalia & Garner, *supra* note 6, at 99 (quoting Hon. Alex Kozinski).
12. Debra Cassens Weiss, Appellate Lawyers Challenged to Write Twitter-Length Briefs, A.B.A. J. (Aug. 15, 2011), http://www.abajournal.com/news/article/appellate_lawyers_challenged_to_write_twitter-length_briefs/.
13. Scalia & Garner, *supra* note 6, at 61.
14. Bryan A. Garner, The Redbook: A Manual on Legal Style 183 (2d ed. 2006).
15. Scalia & Garner, *supra* note 6, at 87.
16. *Id.* at 88. Law students are often taught—and some courts may require—that they must cram the entire issue as to which review is sought into a single question. However, this practice is often unnecessary and can detract from clarity. For discussion of "traditional" and "alternative" formats, see Richard K. Neumann Jr. & Sheila Simon, Legal Writing 278–79 (2d ed. 2011).
17. *See, e.g.*, Robert W. Benson & Joan B. Kessler, *Legalese v. Plain English: An Empirical Study of Persuasion and Credibility in Appellate Brief Writing*, 20 Loy. L.A. L. Rev. 301 (1987) (finding, in an experiment, that judges and senior attorneys found briefs stronger and more persuasive when they were written in plain English rather than legalese).
18. Tina L. Stark, Drafting Contracts: How and Why Lawyers Do What They Do 201 (2007).
19. 329 U.S. 495, 511 (1947).
20. Amos Tversky & Derek J. Koehler, *Support Theory: A Nonextensional Representation of Subjective Probability*, *in* Preference, Belief and Similarity: Selected Writings by Amos Tversky 370 (Eldar Shafir ed., 2004).

21. Oliver Wendell Holmes, *The Profession of the Law, reprinted in* Collected Legal Papers 29, 29 (1920) ("Of course, the law is not the place for the artist or the poet.").
22. Stephen M. Kosslyn, Graph Design for the Eye and Mind 3 (2006).
23. Joanna Gallant & Lauren Shepherd, *Effective Visual Communication: Scientific Principles and Research Findings, in* The Science of Courtroom Litigation: Jury Research and Analytical Graphics 187, 190 (Joanna Gallant et al. eds., 2008).
24. David F. Herr et al., Motion Practice 5-1 (4th ed. 2008).
25. John W. Tukey, *Data-Based Graphics: Visual Display in the Decades to Come, in* Proceedings of the Meeting of the American Statistical Association: Sesquicentennial Invited Paper Sessions 367 (1990) (on file with the American Statistical Association, Washington, D.C.).
26. James Parry Eyster, *Lawyer as Artist: Using Significant Moments and Obtuse Objects to Enhance Advocacy*, 14 Legal Writing 87, 97 (2008); *see also* Elyse Pepper, *The Case for "Thinking Like a Filmmaker": Using Lars von Trier's Dogville as a Model for Writing a Statement of Facts*, 14 Legal Writing 171 (2008); Graham B. Strong, *The Lawyer's Left Hand: Nonanalytical Thought in the Practice of Law*, 69 U. Colo. L. Rev. 759 (1998).
27. Jerome Bruner, Making Stories: Law, Literature, Life 13 (2002).
28. Jennifer K. Robbennolt et al., *Multiple Constraint Satisfaction in Judging, in* The Psychology of Judicial Decision-Making 27 (David Klein & Gregory Mitchell eds., 2010); *see also* Jennifer K. Robbennolt et al., *Symbolism and Incommensurability in Civil Sanctioning: Decision Makers as Goal Managers*, 68 Brook. L. Rev. 1121 (2003).
29. John C. Shepherd & Jordan B. Cherrick, *Advocacy and Emotion*, 138 F.R.D. 619, 620 (1991) (citing Aristotle, The "Art" of Rhetoric (J. H. Freese trans., Loeb Classical Library ed. 1982); Quintilian, The Institutio Oratoria (H. E. Butler trans., Loeb Classical Library ed. 1980)).
30. Michael Frost, *Ethos, Pathos and Legal Audience*, 99 Dick. L. Rev. 85, 104 (1994).
31. Model Rules of Prof'l Conduct R. 3.3 (2006).
32. *See generally* Kathryn M. Stanchi, *Playing with Fire: The Science of Confronting Adverse Material in Legal Advocacy*, 60 Rutgers L. Rev. 381 (2008). Bringing up the opponent's arguments may not be wise (except when ethically required) when the attorney believes that the other side is not itself aware of the argument or when the attorney has no good counter to the argument.
33. 121 P.3d 1026 (Nev. 2005).
34. *See, e.g.*, Valerie P. Hans, Business on Trial 22–49 (2000).
35. Gerry Spence, Win Your Case: How to Present, Persuade, Prevail Every Place, Every Time 86 (2005); *see also* James McElhaney, *Story Line: Write Briefs*

That Use the Facts to Establish Your Theme of the Case, A.B.A. J., Apr. 22, 2006, *available at* http://www.abajournal.com/magazine/article/story_line/ (noting that "to really sing, a winning brief has to have a theme, a theory, a guiding idea that ties everything together into a simple package that satisfies both the head and the heart"); THOMAS A. MAUET, TRIALS: STRATEGY, SKILLS, AND THE NEW POWER OF PERSUASION 120 (2009).

36. JAMES W. MCELHANEY, MCELHANEY'S TRIAL NOTEBOOK 181 (4TH ED. 2005).
37. Nancy Pennington & Reid Hastie, *The Story Model for Juror Decision Making*, *in* INSIDE THE JUROR: THE PSYCHOLOGY OF JUROR DECISION MAKING 198–99, 210–13 (Reid Hastie ed., 1993).
38. Amos Tversky & Daniel Kahneman, *Extensional Versus Intuitive Reasoning: The Conjunction Fallacy in Probability Judgment*, 90 PSYCHOL. REV. 293, 307 (1983); *see also* PAUL BREST & LINDA HAMILTON KRIEGER, PROBLEM SOLVING, DECISION MAKING, AND PROFESSIONAL JUDGMENT 573–74 (2010).
39. STEVEN L. WINTER, A CLEARING IN THE FOREST: LAW, LIFE AND MIND 94 (2001).
40. Amos Tversky & Daniel Kahneman, *Judgments of and by Representativeness*, *in* JUDGMENT UNDER UNCERTAINTY: HEURISTICS AND BIASES 98 (Daniel Kahneman et al. eds., 1982).
41. GEORGE LAKOFF, WOMEN, FIRE AND DANGEROUS THINGS: WHAT CATEGORIES REVEAL ABOUT THE MIND (1987).
42. GEORGE LAKOFF & MARK JOHNSON, METAPHORS WE LIVE BY 117 (2003); *see also* J. S. COVINGTON JR., THE STRUCTURE OF LEGAL ARGUMENT AND PROOF 133 (1993) ("Human reasoning seems to have an imperative that says 'fill in the blanks to make the idea complete' when a few pieces of data are given."); Gerald P. Lopez, *Lay Lawyering*, 32 UCLA L. REV. 1, 3 (1984); Toni M. Massaro, *Empathy, Legal Story-Telling and the Rule of Law: New Words, Old Wounds*, 87 MICH. L. REV. 2099, 2105 (1989) (telling stories both brings law to life and also invokes empathy); Ruth Anne Robbins, *Harry Potter, Ruby Slippers and Merlin: Telling the Client's Story Using the Characters and Paradigm of the Archetypal Hero's Journey*, 29 SEATTLE U. L. REV. 767 (2005).
43. Gerald P. Lopez, *Lay Lawyering*, 32 UCLA L. REV. 1, 3 (1984).
44. Steven L. Winter, *The Cognitive Dimension of the Agon Between Legal Power and Narrative Meaning*, 87 MICH. L. REV. 2225, 2228 (1989).
45. Reid Hastie, *What's the Story? Explanations and Narratives in Civil Jury Decisions*, *in* CIVIL JURIES AND CIVIL JUSTICE: PSYCHOLOGICAL AND LEGAL PERSPECTIVES 23, 31 (Brian H. Bornstein et al. eds., 2008).
46. *Id.* at 32.
47. *See generally* Kurt A. Carlson & J. Edward Russo, *Biased Interpretation of Evidence by Mock Jurors*, 7 J. EXPERIMENTAL PSYCHOL.: APPLIED 91 (2001); Lorraine Hope et al., *Understanding Pretrial Publicity: Predecisional Distortion of Evidence by Mock Jurors*, 10 J. EXPERIMENTAL PSYCHOL.: APPLIED 111 (2004);

Gary W. McCullough, *Function of Text Structure in Jurors' Comprehension and Decision Making*, 101 PSYCHOL. REP. 723 (2007).
48. DANIEL KAHNEMAN, THINKING FAST AND SLOW 199 (2011).
49. *See, e.g.*, Terry A. Maroney, *Emotional Regulation and Judicial Behavior*, 99 CAL. L. REV. 1485 (2011).
50. LOUIS J. SIRICO JR. & NANCY L. SCHULTZ, PERSUASIVE WRITING FOR LAWYERS AND THE LEGAL PROFESSION 14 (2d ed. 2001) (emphasis in original).
51. Robert H. Jackson, *Advocacy Before the Supreme Court: Suggestions for Effective Case Presentations*, 37 A.B.A. J. 801, 803 (1951).
52. Kathryn M. Stanchi, *The Power of Priming in Legal Advocacy: Using the Science of First Impressions to Persuade the Reader*, 89 OR. L. REV. 305, 315 (2010).
53. Roper v. Simmons, 543 U.S. 551, 578–79 (2005).
54. Brief for Petitioner at 3–5, *Roper*, 543 U.S. 551 (No. 03-633), 2004 WL 903158.
55. Brief for Respondent at 1–2, *Roper*, 543 U.S. 551 (No. 03-633), 2004 WL 1947812 (emphasis in original).
56. Indeed, it is intriguing that although the Court found for respondent Simmons in a five-to-four decision, the majority's statement of facts was essentially taken from the Brief for Petitioner but adds the fact that Simmons was a junior in high school. 543 U.S. at 556–57.
57. *See* Stanchi, *supra* note 52, at 310.
58. McDonald v. City of Chi., 130 S. Ct. 3020 (2010).
59. Brief of Amicus Curiae Jews for the Preservation of Firearms Ownership in Support of Petitioners at 1, *McDonald*, 130 S. Ct. 3020 (No. 08-1521), 2009 WL 4099511.
60. Brief for Respondents City of Chicago and Village of Oak Park at 1–2, *McDonald*, 130 S. Ct. 3020 (No. 08-1521), 2009 WL 5190478.
61. Stanchi, *supra* note 52.
62. *E.g.*, LINDA H. EDWARDS, LEGAL WRITING AND ANALYSIS 321–22 (3d ed. 2011); MICHAEL D. MURRAY & CHRISTY H. DESANCTIS, ADVANCED LEGAL WRITING AND ORAL ADVOCACY: TRIALS, APPEALS, AND MOOT COURT 5 (2009).
63. Kathryn M. Stanchi, *The Science of Persuasion: An Initial Exploration*, MICH. ST. L. REV. 411, 416 (2006).
64. 214 F.3d 213 (1st Cir. 2000).
65. 490 U.S. 228 (1989).
66. Stanchi, *supra* note 63, at 425–26 (footnotes omitted).
67. SCALIA & GARNER, *supra* note 6, at 36.
68. *See* Elizabeth Fajans & Mary R. Falk, *Untold Stories: Restoring Narrative to Pleading Practice*, 15 J. LEGAL WRITING INST. 3, 3, 10–11 n.38 (2009) (stating that "[i]n mainstream modern pleading practice, storytelling tends to be seen either as inimical to effective pleading or as applied decoration,

rhetorical adornment to be reserved for compelling cases," and citing numerous legal writing books that focus primarily on tactical or instrumental aspects of pleading, albeit recognizing that many at least mention the rhetorical power of complaints).

69. *See id.* at 20–22.
70. In some cases, the tactical aim of a complaint may be to "focus discovery where you want it and elicit the maximum number of significant admissions from defendant." ELIZABETH FAJANS, MARY R. FALK & HELENE S. SHAPO, WRITING FOR LAW PRACTICE 56 (2004). These goals may counsel keeping the complaint quite simple and nonconclusory.
71. Fajans & Falk, *supra* note 68.
72. *Id.* at 49–51, 57–61. Fajans and Falk excerpt (mostly in the original wording) and analyze the entire Bork complaint.
73. Complaint, Jones v. Clinton, 858 F. Supp. 902 (E.D. Ark. 1994).
74. Zachariah Chafee Jr., *The Disorderly Conduct of Words*, 41 COLUM. L. REV. 381, 382 (1941).
75. NAN D. HUNTER, THE POWER OF PROCEDURE: THE LITIGATION OF JONES V. CLINTON 9 (2002).
76. Plaintiff's Original Petition for Personal Injury Damages, Haley v. Lobato, No. 34822091206, (Dist. Ct. Tarrant County, Tex. Oct. 26, 2006) (on file with authors).
77. *See generally* Kurt P. Frey & Alice H. Eagly, *Vividness Can Undermine the Persuasiveness of Messages*, 65 J. PERSONALITY & SOC. PSYCHOL. 32 (1993).
78. LINDA H. EDWARDS, LEGAL WRITING: PROCESS, ANALYSIS, AND ORGANIZATION 237 (2010).
79. GROVER E. CLEVELAND, SWIMMING LESSONS FOR BABY SHARKS: THE ESSENTIAL GUIDE TO THRIVING AS A NEW LAWYER 80 (2011) (emphasis in original).
80. Mark C. Weidemaier et al., *Origin Myths, Contracts, and the Hunt for Pari Passu*, LAW & SOC. INQUIRY (forthcoming 2011), *available at* http://papers.ssrn.com/sol3/papers.cfm?abstract_id=1633439 (noting that "[i]n the context of sovereign lending . . . it is fair to say that no one really knows what the *pari passu* clause means, something that even eminent practitioners in the field have long acknowledged" (emphasis in original)).
81. Richard R. W. Brooks et al., *Framing Contracts: Why Loss Framing Increases Effort* (John M. Olin Ctr. for Studies in Law, Econ., & Pub. Policy, Research Paper No. 438, 2011), *available at* http://ssrn.com/abstract=1884269.
82. Tess Wilkinson-Ryan, *Do Liquidated Damages Encourage Breach? A Psychological Experiment,* 108 MICH. L. REV. 633 (2010) (citing Douglas Belkin, *Boston Firefighters Sick—or Tired of Working 15-Day Allowance Seen Fueling Call-Ins,* BOSTON GLOBE, Jan. 18, 2002, at B1; Scott S. Greenberger, *Sick day abuses focus of fire talks,* BOSTON GLOBE, Sept. 17, 2003, at B7).
83. Uri Gneezy & Aldo Rustichini, *A Fine Is a Price*, 29 J. LEG. STUD. 1 (2000). *See also* Tess Wilkinson-Ryan, *Do Liquidated Damages Encourage Breach? A*

Psychological Experiment, 108 Mich. L. Rev. 633 (2010) (reporting additional studies about the effects of liquidated damages clauses).

84. *See generally* Russell Korobkin, *The Status Quo Bias and Contract Default Rules*, 83 Cornell L. Rev. 608 (1998).
85. Brest & Krieger, *supra* note 38, at 549.
86. Lenore Weitzman, The Marriage Contract 223, 228, 232–37 (1981).
87. *See* Maury Beaulier, *Collaborative Law: Sample Collaborative Law Agreement*, Divorce Source, http://www.divorcesource.com/info/collaborativelaw/agreement.shtml (last visited Oct. 30, 2011).
88. John A. Warnick, *Purposeful Planning Collaboration*, Purposeful Planning Institute, http://purposefulplanninginstitute.com/purposefulplanning_collaboration.html (last visited Oct. 29, 2011).
89. *Cf.* Ralph Underwager & Hollinda Wakefield, *Psychological Considerations in Negotiating Premarital Contracts*, *in* Premarital and Marital Contracts: A Lawyer's Guide to Drafting and Negotiating Enforceable Marital and Cohabitation Agreements 217, 222–24 (Edward L. Winer & Lewis Becker eds., 1993).
90. Yuval Feldman & Doron Teichman, *Are All Contractual Obligations Created Equal?*, 100:5 Geo. L.J. 5 (2011), *available at* http://papers.ssrn.com/sol3/papers.cfm?abstract_id=1633415.

Chapter 14

1. Earl Warren, Speech at the Louis Marshall Award Dinner of the Jewish Theological Seminary (Nov. 11, 1962), *quoted in* Robert V. Evanson, *Law and Ethics in Practice*, *in* Pharmacy Ethics 55, 55 (Mickey Smith et al. eds., 1991).
2. Milton C. Regan Jr., Eat What You Kill: The Fall of a Wall Street Lawyer 1 (2004); *see also* Nancy B. Rapoport, *The Curious Incident of the Law Firm That Did Nothing in the Night-Time*, 10 Legal Ethics 98 (2007) (reviewing Milton C. Regan Jr., Eat What You Kill: The Fall of a Wall Street Lawyer (2004)).
3. Regan, *supra* note 2, at 2.
4. *Id.* at 3, 287.
5. Peter Tiersma, Lawyer Jokes, http://www.languageandlaw.org/JOKES.HTM (last visited March 25, 2012).
6. John M. Darley, *The Cognitive and Social Psychology of Contagious Organizational Corruption*, 70 Brook. L. Rev. 1177, 1180 (2005).
7. William Haltom & Michael McCann, Distorting the Law: Politics, Media, and the Litigation Crisis 133 (2004).
8. Max H. Bazerman & Don A. Moore, Judgment in Managerial Decision Making 123 (7th ed. 2009).
9. C. Daniel Batson et al., *Moral Hypocrisy: Appearing Moral to Oneself Without Being So*, 77 J. Personality & Soc. Psychol. 525, 525 (1999).

10. Jonathan R. B. Halbesleben et al., *The Role of Pluralistic Ignorance in Perceptions of Unethical Behavior: An Investigation of Attorneys' and Students' Perceptions of Ethical Behavior*, 14 ETHICS & BEHAV. 17 (2004); *see also* Robert L. Nelson, *The Discovery Process as a Circle of Blame: Institutional, Professional, and Socio-Economic Factors That Contribute to Unreasonable, Inefficient, and Amoral Behavior in Corporate Litigation*, 67 FORDHAM L. REV. 773 (1998) (finding that lawyers tend to report that attorneys at their own firms are more ethical than attorneys at other firms).
11. Dolly Chugh et al., *Bounded Ethicality as a Psychological Barrier to Recognizing Conflicts of Interest*, *in* CONFLICTS OF INTEREST: CHALLENGES AND SOLUTIONS IN BUSINESS, LAW, MEDICINE, AND PUBLIC POLICY 74, 80 (Don A. Moore et al. eds., 2005).
12. Nicholas Epley & Eugene M. Caruso, *Egocentric Ethics*, 17 SOC. JUST. RES. 171 (2004).
13. RICHARD A. POSNER, HOW JUDGES THINK 121 (2008).
14. Karl Aquino et al., *Testing a Social-Cognitive Model of Moral Behavior: The Interactive Influence of Situations and Moral Identity Centrality*, 97 J. PERSONALITY & SOC. PSYCHOL. 123, 123 (2009).
15. Dennis J. Moberg, *Ethics Blind Spots in Organizations: How Systematic Errors in Person Perception Undermine Moral Agency*, 27 ORG. STUD. 413 (2006).
16. Anna Stolley Persky, *Aggressive Justice*, 96 A.B.A. J. 2, 2 (May 2010).
17. *See, e.g.*, Karl Aquino et al., *Testing a Social-Cognitive Model of Moral Behavior: The Interactive Infuence of Situations and Moral Identity Centrality*, 97 J. PERSONALITY & SOC. PSYCHOL. 123 (2009); Ann E. Tenbrunsel, *Misrepresentation and Expectations of Misrepresentation in an Ethical Dilemma: The Role of Incentives and Temptation*, 41 ACAD. MGMT. J. 330 (1998).
18. *See* Emily Balcetis & David A. Dunning, *A Mile in Moccasins: How Situational Experience Diminishes Dispositionism in Social Inference*, 34 PERSONALITY & SOC. PSYCHOL. BULL. 102 (2008).
19. Albert Bandura, *Moral Disengagement in the Perpetration of Inhumanities*, 3 PERSONALITY & SOC. PSYCHOL. REV. 193, 206 (1999).
20. Yifat Kivetz & Tom R. Tyler, *Tomorrow I'll Be Me: The Effect of Time Perspective on the Activation of Idealistic Versus Pragmatic Selves*, 102 ORGANIZATIONAL BEHAV. & HUM. DECISION PROCESSES 193, 193 (2007); *see also* Daniel Read et al., *Mixing Virtue and Vice: Combining the Immediacy Effect and the Diversification Heuristic*, 12 J. BEHAV. DECISION MAKING 257 (1999); Yaacov Trope & Nira Liberman, *Temporal Construal*, 110 PSYCHOL. REV. 403 (2003).
21. SISSELA BOK, LYING: MORAL CHOICE IN PUBLIC AND PRIVATE LIFE 27 (1979).
22. BAZERMAN & MOORE, *supra* note 8, at 48; *see also* Francesca Gino & Max H. Bazerman, *When Misconduct Goes Unnoticed: The Acceptability of Gradual Erosion in Others' Unethical Behavior*, 45 J. EXPERIMENTAL SOC. PSYCHOL. 708 (2009).

23. *See* Blake E. Ashforth & Vikas Anand, *The Normalization of Corruption in Organizations*, 25 Res. Organizational Behav. 1 (2003); Linda K. Treviño et al., *Behavioral Ethics in Organizations: A Review*, 32 J. Mgmt. 951 (2006); *see also* Herbert C. Kelman & V. Lee Hamilton, Crimes of Obedience (1990).
24. Don A. Moore & George Loewenstein, *Self-Interest, Automaticity, and the Psychology of Conflict of Interest*, 17 Soc. Just. Res. 189, 196 (2004); *see also* Michael Guttentag, *Stumbling into Crime: Stochastic Process Models of Accounting Fraud*, in Research Handbook on the Economics of Criminal Law (Alon Harel & Keith Hylton eds., forthcoming).
25. Ann E. Tenbrunsel & David M. Messick, *Ethical Fading: The Role of Self-Deception in Unethical Behavior*, 17 Soc. Just. Res. 223, 224 (2004) (emphasis in original); *see also* Albert Bandura, *Moral Disengagement in the Perpetration of Inhumanities*, 3 Personality & Soc. Psychol. Rev. 193 (1999); James R. Detert et al., *Moral Disengagement in Ethical Decision Making: A Study of Antecedents and Outcomes*, 93 J. Applied Psychol. 374 (2008).
26. Kenneth D. Butterfield et al., *Moral Awareness in Business Organizations: Influences of Issue-Related and Social Context Factors*, 53 Hum. Rel. 981, 989 (2000).
27. Mark Maremont, *Anatomy of the Kurzweil Fraud*, Bus. Wk. 90, 90–92 (Sept. 16, 1996).
28. Butterfield et al., *supra* note 26; Tenbrunsel & Messick, *supra* note 25; *see also* Aaron C. Kay et al., *Material Priming: The Influence of Mundane Physical Objects on Situational Construal and Competitive Behavioral Choice*, 95 Organizational Behav. & Hum. Decision Processes 83 (2004) (those primed with things associated with business tend to act less cooperatively); Kathleen D. Vohs et al., *The Psychological Consequences of Money*, 314 Science 1154 (2006) (when reminded of money, people tend to behave more selfishly); Francesca Gino & Lamar Pierce, *The Abundance Effect: Unethical Behavior in the Presence of Wealth*, 109 Organizational Behav. & Hum. Decision Processes 142 (2009). For evidence that clearing conflicts is often thought of as a business rather than an ethical decision, *see, e.g.*, Kimberly Kirkland, *Ethical Infrastructures and De Facto Ethical Norms at Work in Large US Law Firms: The Role of Ethics Counsel*, 11 Legal Ethics 181 (2008).
29. Dennis A. Gioia, *Pinto Fires and Personal Ethics: A Script Analysis of Missed Opportunities*, 11 J. Bus. Ethics 379, 381–88 (1992) (emphasis added).
30. *Id.*; *see also* Mark Dowie, *Pinto Madness*, Mother Jones, Sept./Oct. 1977.
31. Tenbrunsel & Messick, *supra* note 25; *see also* Bandura, *supra* note 19; William Safire, *The Fine Art of Euphemism*, S.F. Examiner & Chron., May 13, 1979, at 34.
32. Sefa Hayibor & David M. Wasieleski, *Effects of the Use of the Availability Heuristic on Ethical Decision-Making in Organizations*, 84 J. Bus. Ethics 151 (2009); *see also* Jennifer J. Kish-Gephart et al., *Bad Apples, Bad Cases, and*

Bad Barrels: Meta-Analytic Evidence About Sources of Unethical Decisions at Work, 95 J. APPLIED PSYCHOL. 1 (2010).

33. Francesca Gino et al., *Nameless + Harmless = Blameless: When Seemingly Irrelevant Factors Influence Judgment of (Un)ethical Behavior* (Harvard Bus. Sch., Working Paper No. 09-020, 2009); Francesca Gino et al., *No Harm, No Foul: The Outcome Bias in Ethical Judgments* (Harvard Bus. School, Working Paper NO. 08-080, 2009).

34. Maurice E. Schweitzer et al., *Goal Setting as a Motivator of Unethical Behavior*, 47 ACAD. MGMT. J. 422 (2004).

35. Mary C. Kern & Dolly Chugh, *Bounded Ethicality: The Perils of Loss Framing*, 20 PSYCHOL. SCI. 378 (2009) (examining willingness to hire consultant to dig up dirt, to be dishonest, to lie about client's intentions, to engage in misrepresentation tactics, and to make false promises); Jessica S. Cameron & Dale T. Miller, *Ethical Standards in Gain Versus Loss Frames*, in PSYCHOLOGICAL PERSPECTIVES ON ETHICAL BEHAVIOR AND DECISION MAKING 91 (David de Cremer ed., 2009); Jeffrey J. Rachlinski, *Gains, Losses, and the Psychology of Litigation*, 70 S. CAL. L. REV. 113 (1996) (Study 2); *see also* Francesca Gino & Joshua D. Margolis, *Bringing Ethics into Focus: How Regulatory Focus and Risk Preferences Influence (Un)Ethical Behavior*, 115 ORGANIZATIONAL BEHAV. & HUM. DECISION PROCESSES 145 (2011).

36. Kaye J. Newberry et al., *An Examination of Tax Practitioner Decisions: The Role of Preparer Sanctions and Framing Effects Associated with Client Condition*, 14 J. ECON. PSYCHOL. 439 (1993); *see also* Elizabeth F. Loftus, *To File, Perchance to Cheat*, PSYCHOL. TODAY 35, 37–38 (Apr. 1985) (A taxpayer anticipating a refund "is in a gain situation; she could gamble and cheat in hopes of achieving a larger return or file an honest return. Since she will get a refund either way, she will probably avoid the risk of cheating." In contrast, a taxpayer facing a tax bill "is in a loss situation. She owes the IRS money. She could choose to pay what she owes, or she could gamble and cheat, in hopes of reducing what she owes. Since she is in a loss situation, she is more likely . . . to risk filing a fraudulent return."); Henry S. J. Robben et al., *Decision Frame and Opportunity as Determinants of Tax Cheating: An International Experimental Study*, 11 J. ECON. PSYCHOL. 341 (1990).

37. Cameron & Miller, *supra* note 35, at 102–03.

38. *See* Richard W. Painter, *Lawyers' Rules, Auditors' Rules and the Psychology of Concealment*, 84 MINN. L. REV. 1399 (2000).

39. ALAN C. BAIRD, ATTORNEY JOKES FROM SNIFTER, FLUTE AND STEIN, http://www.9timezones.com/ia/lawethi.htm (last visited March 25, 2012).

40. Robert L. Nelson, *The Discovery Process as a Circle of Blame: Institutional, Professional, and Socio-Economic Factors That Contribute to Unreasonable, Inefficient, and Amoral Behavior in Corporate Litigation*, 67 FORDHAM L. REV. 773, 780 (1998) (emphasis added).

41. Deborah L. Rhode, *Ethics in Practice*, in Ethics in Practice: Lawyers' Roles, Responsibilities, and Regulation 3, 15 (Deborah L. Rhode ed., 2000); *see also* David Luban, *Making Sense of Moral Meltdowns*, in Lawyers' Ethics and the Pursuit of Social Justice: A Critical Reader 355, 360 (Susan D. Carle ed., 2005) ("[T]here are very few consensus moral rules for highly adversarial, competitive settings. That implies a lot of moral uncertainty and ambiguity in a culture as addicted to competition as ours is.").
42. Carrie Menkel-Meadow, *The Limits of Adversarial Ethics*, in Ethics in Practice: Lawyers' Roles, Responsibilities, and Regulation, *supra* note 31, at 123, 126 n.14; Regan, *supra* note 2 (describing how conflicts of interest differ in litigation and transactional work).
43. David J. Luban, *The Ethics of Wrongful Obedience*, in Ethics in Practice: Lawyers' Roles, Responsibilities, and Regulation, *supra* note 41, at 94, 106 (emphasis in original).
44. Lisa G. Lerman, *Lying to Clients*, 138 U. Pa. L. Rev. 659, 680 (1990).
45. *See also* Patrick J. Schiltz, *On Being a Happy, Healthy, and Ethical Member of an Unhappy, Unhealthy, and Unethical Profession*, 52 Vand. L. Rev. 871, 918 (1999).
46. C. S. Lewis, Professor, Cambridge Univ., Memorial Lecture at King's Coll., Univ. of London: *The Inner Ring* (1944), in The Weight of Glory 141, 153–54 (2001).
47. Deborah L. Rhode, *Moral Counseling*, 75 Fordham L. Rev. 1317, 1334 (2006).
48. Deborah Rhode, *Ethics in Practice*, in Ethics in Practice: Lawyers' Roles, Responsibilities, and Regulation 3, 6 (Deborah L. Rhode ed., 2000).
49. *See generally* Herbert M. Kritzer, *Lawyer Fees and Lawyer Behavior in Litigation: What Does the Empirical Literature Really Say?*, 80 Tex. L. Rev. 1943 (2002).
50. Rhode, *supra* note 41, at 7.
51. *See* Kritzer, *supra* note 49; *see also* Am. Bar Ass'n, ABA Commission on Billable Hours Report 2001–2002, *available at* http://www.legalbenchmarket.com/documents/bhcomplete.pdf; Geoffrey P. Miller, *Some Agency Problems in Settlement*, 16 J. Legal Stud. 189 (1987); Jean R. Sternlight, *Lawyers' Representation of Clients in Mediation: Using Economics and Psychology to Structure Advocacy in a Nonadversarial Setting*, 14 Ohio St. J. Disp. Resol. 269 (1999).
52. *Excess Billing Hours*, AhaJokes.com, http://www.ahajokes.com/law007.html (last visited March 25, 2012).
53. *Two Plus Two*, Law Laughs, http://www.lawlaughs.com/honesty/howmuch.html (last visited Oct. 24, 2011).
54. *See, e.g.*, Donald C. Langevoort & Robert K. Rasmussen, *Skewing the Results: The Role of Lawyers in Transmitting Legal Rules*, 5 S. Cal. Interdisc. L.J. 375 (1997) (discussing how attorney self-interest might affect advice about risk).

55. Scott Sonenshein, *The Role of Construction, Intuition, and Justification in Responding to Ethical Issues at Work: The Sensemaking-Intuition Model*, 32 ACAD. MGMT. REV. 1022 (2007).
56. Chugh et al., *supra* note 11, at 83; *see also* David M. Messick & Keith P. Sentis, *Fairness and Preference*, 15 J. EXPERIMENTAL SOC. PSYCHOL. 418 (1979).
57. RICHARD L. ABEL, LAWYERS IN THE DOCK: LEARNING FROM ATTORNEY DISCIPLINARY PROCEEDINGS 389 (2008) (chapter 7: "The Purloined Papers"); Leslie C. Levin, *Bad Apples, Bad Lawyers or Bad Decisionmaking: Lessons from Psychology and from Lawyers in the Dock*, 22 GEO. J. LEGAL ETHICS 1549 (2009) (reviewing ABEL, *supra*).
58. Daylian M. Cain et al., *The Dirt on Coming Clean: Perverse Effects of Disclosing Conflicts of Interest*, 34 J. LEGAL STUD. 1 (2005); Daylian Cain et al., *When Sunlight Fails to Disinfect: Understanding the Perverse Effects of Disclosing Conflicts of Interest*, 37 J. CONSUMER RES. 836 (2011); Sunita Sah et al., *The Burden of Disclosure: Increased Compliance with Distrusted Advice* (Working Paper 2011), *available at* http://www.econ.upf.edu/docs/seminars/sah.pdf. See reviews in Daylian M. Cain, George Loewenstein & Don A. Moore, *Coming Clean but Playing Dirtier: The Shortcomings of Disclosure as a Solution to Conflicts of Interest, in* CONFLICTS OF INTEREST: CHALLENGES AND SOLUTIONS IN BUSINESS, LAW, MEDICINE AND PUBLIC POLICY, *supra* note 9, at 104; George Loewenstein et al., *The Limits of Transparency: Pitfalls and Potential of Disclosing Conflicts of Interest*, 101 AM. ECON. REV.: PAPERS & PROC. 423 (2011); *see also* Colin Camerer et al., *The Curse of Knowledge in Economic Settings: An Experimental Analysis*, 97 J. POL. ECON. 1232 (1989); Fritz Strack & Thomas Mussweiler, *Explaining the Enigmatic Anchoring Effect: Mechanisms of Selective Accessibility*, 73 J. PERSONALITY & SOC. PSYCHOL. 437 (1997).
59. Benoît Monin & Dale T. Miller, *Moral Credentials and the Expression of Prejudice*, 81 J. PERSONALITY & SOC. PSYCHOL. 33 (2001).
60. Cain et al., *The Dirt on Coming Clean*, *supra* note 58.
61. Neeru Paharia et al., *Dirty Work, Clean Hands: The Moral Psychology of Indirect Agency*, 109 ORGANIZATIONAL BEHAV. & HUM. DECISION PROCESSES 134 (2009); *see also* Edward B. Royzman & Jonathan Baron, *The Preference for Indirect Harm*, 15 SOC. JUST. RES. 165 (2002).
62. STANLEY MILGRAM, OBEDIENCE TO AUTHORITY 119–22 (1974).
63. Kimberly Kirkland, *Ethical Infrastructures and De Facto Ethical Norms at Work in Large U.S. Law Firms: The Role of Ethics Counsel*, 11 LEGAL ETHICS 181, 195 (2008) (quoting firm ethics counsel).
64. Don A. Moore et al., *Conflicts of Interest and the Case of Auditor Independence: Moral Seduction and Strategic Issue Cycling*, 31 ACAD. MGMT. REV. 10 (2006) (describing Kristina A. Diekmann et al., *Self-Interest and Fairness in Problems of Resource Allocation: Allocators Versus Recipients*, 72 J. PERSONALITY & SOC. PSYCHOL. 1061 (1997)); Paharia et al., *supra* note 61.

65. Austin Sarat, *Ethics in Litigation: Rhetoric of Crisis, Realities of Practice*, in Ethics in Practice: Lawyers' Roles, Responsibilities, and Regulation, *supra* note 41, at 145, 149.
66. Art Hinshaw & Jess K. Alberts, *Doing the Right Thing: An Empirical Study of Attorney Negotiation Ethics*, 16 Harv. Negot. L. Rev. 95 (2011).
67. *See, e.g.*, Francesca Gino & Lamar Pierce, *Lying to Level the Playing Field: Why People May Dishonestly Help or Hurt Others to Create Equity*, 95 J. Bus. Ethics 89 (2011); Francesca Gino & Lamar Pierce, *Dishonesty in the Name of Equity*, 20 Psychol. Sci. 1153 (2009); Francesca Gino & Lamar Pierce, *Robin Hood Under the Hood: Wealth-Based Discrimination in Illicit Customer Help*, 21 Org. Sci. 1176 (2010); Scott S. Wiltermuth, *Cheating More When the Spoils Are Split*, 115 Organizational Behav. & Hum. Decision Processes 157 (2011).
68. Sarat, *supra* note 65, at 149.
69. *Introduce Lawyers*, AhaJokes.com, http://www.ahajokes.com/ (last visited March 25, 2012).
70. Regan, *supra* note 2, at 347–48 (emphasis added).
71. Maurice E. Schweitzer & Donald E. Gibson, *Fairness, Feelings, and Ethical Decision-Making: Consequences of Violating Community Standards of Fairness*, 77 J. Bus. Ethics 287 (2008).
72. Stephen M. Garcia et al., *Morally Questionable Tactics: Negotiations Between District Attorneys and Public Defenders*, 27 Personality & Soc. Psychol. Bull. 731 (2001).
73. Luban, *supra* note 41, at 360.
74. Abel, *supra* note 57, at 32, 200.
75. 373 U.S. 83 (1963).
76. Kyles v. Whitley, 514 U.S. 419, 435 (1995); *see also* United States v. Bagley, 473 U.S. 667 (1985).
77. Alafair S. Burke, *Improving Prosecutorial Decision Making: Some Lessons of Cognitive Science*, 47 Wm. & Mary L. Rev. 1587, 1611–12 (2006).
78. *See, e.g.*, Janine Robben, *Burnout: Cautionary Tales*, Or. St. B. Bull., Oct. 2008, *available at* http://www.osbar.org/publications/bulletin/08oct/burnout.html.
79. William Rehnquist, *The Legal Profession Today*, 62 Ind. L.J. 151, 155 (1987).
80. Regan, *supra* note 2, at 99, 134, 163.
81. John M. Darley & C. Daniel Batson, *From Jerusalem to Jericho: A Study of Situational and Dispositional Variables in Helping Behavior*, 27 J. Personality & Soc. Psychol. 100, 104 (1973).
82. Christopher M. Barnes et al., *Lack of Sleep and Unethical Conduct*, 115 Organizational Behav. & Hum. Decision Processes 169 (2011); Nicole L. Mead et al., *Too Tired to Tell the Truth: Self-Control Resource Depletion and Dishonesty*, 45 J. Experimental Soc. Psychol. 594 (2009).
83. Luban, *supra* note 43, at 94–95.

84. *Id.* at 97; *see also* Andrew M. Perlman, *Unethical Obedience by Subordinate Attorneys: Lessons from Social Psychology*, 36 HOFSTRA L. REV. 451 (2007); Sung Hui Kim, *The Banality of Fraud: Re-Situating the Inside Counsel as Gatekeeper*, 74 FORDHAM L. REV. 983 (2005); KELMAN & HAMILTON, *supra* note 23.
85. Perlman, *supra* note 84, at 451.
86. MODEL RULES OF PROF'L CONDUCT R. 5.2 (2010).
87. *See, e.g.*, ELLIOT ARONSON, THE SOCIAL ANIMAL (9th ed. 2004).
88. *See, e.g.*, Hinshaw & Alberts, *supra* note 66.
89. Tenbrunsel, *supra* note 17.
90. Lerman, *supra* note 44, at 681; *see* JEROME E. CARLIN, LAWYERS' ETHICS: A SURVEY OF THE NEW YORK CITY BAR (1966); *see also* LYNN MATHER ET AL., DIVORCE LAWYERS AT WORK: VARIETIES OF PROFESSIONALISM IN PRACTICE (2001); Kimberly Kirkland, *Ethics in Large Law Firms: The Principles of Pragmatism*, 35 U. MEM. L. REV. 631 (2005); Leslie C. Levin, *The Ethical World of Solo and Small Law Firm Practitioners*, 41 HOUS. L. REV. 309 (2005); Robert L. Nelson, *Ideology, Practice, and Professional Autonomy: Social Values and Client Relationships in the Large Law Firm*, 37 STAN. L. REV. 503 (1985); Mark C. Suchman, *Working Without a Net: The Sociology of Legal Ethics in Corporate Litigation*, 67 FORDHAM L. REV. 837 (1998).
91. Francesca Gino et al., *Contagion and Differentiation in Unethical Behavior: The Effect of One Bad Apple on the Barrel*, 20 PSYCHOL. SCI. 393 (2009). In contrast, "observing an *out*-group peer engaging in unethical behavior reduced participants' likelihood of acting unethically themselves." *Id.* at 397 (emphasis added).
92. MILGRAM, *supra* note 62.
93. DEBORAH L. RHODE, MORAL LEADERSHIP 48 (Deborah L. Rhode ed., 2006).
94. Luban, *supra* note 43, at 95.
95. Darley, *supra* note 6, at 1186.
96. Thomas Gilovich et al., *The Illusion of Transparency: Biased Assessments of Others' Ability to Read One's Emotional States*, 75 J. PERSONALITY & SOC. PSYCHOL. 332 (1998) (Studies 3a and 3b).
97. Deborah L. Rhode, Introduction, *Where Is the Leadership in Moral Leadership?*, *in* MORAL LEADERSHIP 1, 27–28 (Deborah L. Rhode ed., 2006).
98. Epley & Caruso, *supra* note 12; Nicholas Epley & David Dunning, *Feeling "Holier Than Thou": Are Self-Serving Assessments Produced by Errors in Self- or Social Prediction?*, 79 J. PERSONALITY & SOC. PSYCHOL. 861 (2000); Tal Eyal et al., *Judging Near and Distant Virtue and Vice*, 44 J. EXPERIMENTAL SOC. PSYCHOL. 1204 (2008); Clayton R. Critcher & David Dunning, *No Good Deed Goes Unquestioned: Cynical Reconstruals Maintain Belief in the Power of Self-Interest*, 47 J. EXPERIMENTAL SOC. PSYCHOL. 1207 (2011); Dale T. Miller & Rebecca K. Ratner, *The Disparity Between the Actual and Assumed Power of Self-Interest*, 74 J. PERSONALITY & SOC. PSYCHOL. 53 (1998).

99. Moberg, *supra* note 15.
100. *See, e.g.*, Bogdan Wojciszke, *Morality and Competence in Person- and Self-Perception*, 16 Eur. Rev. Soc. Psychol. 155 (2005).
101. *See* Mark D. Alicke, *Egocentric Standards of Conduct Evaluation*, 14 Basic & Applied Soc. Psychol. 171 (1993); Balcetis & Dunning, *supra* note 18; David A. Dunning, Self-Insight: Roadblocks and Detours on the path to Knowing Thyself 131 (2005); Kristina A. Diekmann, *"She Did What? There Is No Way I Would Do That!" The Potential Interpersonal Harm Caused by Mispredicting One's Behavior*, 80 J. Bus. Ethics 5 (2008); Julie A. Woodzicka & Marianne LaFrance, *Real Versus Imagined Gender Harassment*, 57 J. Soc. Issues 15 (2001).
102. Model Rules of Prof'l Conduct R. 8.3 (2008).
103. Francesca Gino et al., *See No Evil: When We Overlook Other People's Unethical Behavior*, in Social Decision Making: Social Dilemmas, Social Values, & Ethical Judgments 241 (Roderick M. Kramer et al. eds., 2010).
104. *Id.*; *see also* Donald C. Langevoort, *Where Were the Lawyers? A Behavioral Inquiry Into Lawyers' Responsibility for Clients' Frauds*, 46 Vand. L. Rev. 75 (1993).
105. Bazerman & Moore, *supra* note 8, at 48.
106. Francesca Gino et al., *No Harm, No Foul*, *supra* note 33.
107. Dunning, *supra* note 101, at 137.
108. 547 U.S. 410 (2006) (holding that the First Amendment provided no protection to the dismissed district attorney).
109. Regan, *supra* note 2, at 250.
110. Abel, *supra* note 57, at 491.
111. *See* Leon Festinger, A Theory of Cognitive Dissonance (1957).
112. Bandura, *supra* note 19; Lisa L. Shu et al., *Dishonest Deed, Clear Conscience: Self-Preservation Through Moral Disengagement and Motivated Forgetting*, 37 Personality & Soc. Psychol. Bull. 330 (2011).
113. Jonathan Haidt, *The Emotional Dog and Its Rational Tail: A Social Intuitionist Approach to Moral Judgment*, 108 Psychol. Rev. 814 (2001).
114. *See* Abel, *supra* note 57; Lisa G. Lerman, *Blue-Chip Bilking: Regulation of Billing and Expense Fraud by Lawyers*, 12 Geo. J. Legal Ethics 205 (1999); Lisa G. Lerman, *Scenes from a Law Firm*, 50 Rutgers L. Rev. 2153 (1998).
115. *See* Abel, *supra* note 57.
116. David Luban, *Integrity: Its Causes and Cures*, 72 Fordham L. Rev. 279, 286 (2003).
117. Carol Tavris & Elliot Aronson, Mistakes Were Made (but Not by Me): Why We Justify Foolish Beliefs, Bad Decisions, and Hurtful Acts 70 (2007).
118. Patricia Werhane, Moral Imagination and the Search for Ethical Decision-Making in Management 75 (1998).
119. Regan, *supra* note 2, at 343.
120. Shu et al., *supra* note 112.

121. *See, e.g.*, Judson Mills, *Changes in Moral Attitudes Following Temptation*, 26 J. PERSONALITY 517 (1958). *See generally* Leon Festinger & James M. Carlsmith, *Cognitive Consequences of Forced Compliance*, 58 J. ABNORMAL & SOC. PSYCHOL. 203 (1959).
122. ELIOT ARONSON, THE SOCIAL ANIMAL 162 (9th ed. 2003).
123. Shirit Kronzon & John Darley, *Is This Tactic Ethical? Biased Judgments of Ethics in Negotiation*, 21 BASIC & APPLIED SOC. PSYCHOL. 49 (1999).
124. Tenbrunsel & Messick, *supra* note 25. *See generally* HEROIC IMAGINATION PROJECT, http://heroicimagination.org/ (an effort to foster the ability to act with integrity by teaching about the situational forces that can influence behavior).
125. DAN ARIELY, PREDICTABLY IRRATIONAL: THE HIDDEN FORCES THAT SHAPE OUR DECISIONS 213 (2008); *see also* Nina Mazar et al., *The Dishonesty of Honest People: A Theory of Self-Concept Maintenance*, 45 J. MARKETING RES. 633 (2008).
126. Kish-Gephart et al., *supra* note 32; *see also* David F. Caldwell & Dennis Moberg, *An Exploratory Investigation of the Effect of Ethical Culture in Activating Moral Imagination*, 73 J. BUS. ETHICS 193 (2007).
127. *See, e.g.*, Karl Aquino, *The Effects of Ethical Climate and the Availability of Alternatives on the Use of Deception During Negotiation*, 9 INT'L J. CONFLICT MGMT. 195 (1998).
128. Schweitzer & Gibson, *supra* note 71.
129. Tenbrunsel & Messick, *supra* note 25.
130. Rhode, *supra* note 41; Tenbrunsel & Messick, *supra* note 25.
131. *See* Elizabeth Chambliss & David B. Wilkins, *The Emerging Role of Ethics Advisors, General Counsel, and Other Compliance Specialists in Large Law Firms*, 44 ARIZ. L. REV. 559 (2002); Elizabeth Chambliss, *The Professionalization of Law Firm In-House Counsel*, 84 N.C. L. REV. 1515 (2006); Jonathan D. Glater, *In a Complex World, Even Lawyers Need Lawyers*, N.Y. TIMES, Feb. 2, 2004.
132. Kirkland, *supra* note 28, at 188, 192 (finding that "ethics counsel see their jobs as finding ways to take on as much new work as they can without running afoul of the ethics rules" and that the following sentiment is common: "We like to say yes to new business—we struggle to find ways to say yes even when there is a conflict").
133. HOWARD GARDNER ET AL., GOOD WORK: WHEN EXCELLENCE AND ETHICS MEET 11 (2001).
134. *See, e.g.*, Arthur L. Beaman et al., *Self-Awareness and Transgression in Children: Two Field Studies*, 37 J. PERSONALITY & SOC. PSYCHOL. 1835 (1979); Edward Diener & Mark Wallbom, *Effects of Self-Awareness on Antinormative Behavior*, 10 J. RES. PERSONALITY 107 (1976); Karl A. Kallgren et al., *A Focus Theory of Normative Conduct: When Norms Do and Do Not Affect Behavior*, 26 PERSONALITY & SOC. PSYCHOL. BULL. 1002 (2000).
135. Kern & Chugh, *supra* note 35.
136. Moore & Loewenstein, *supra* note 24.

137. Ann E. Tenbrunsel et al., *The Ethical Mirage: A Temporal Explanation as to Why We Aren't as Ethical as We Think We Are* (Harvard Bus. Sch., Working Paper No. 08-012, 2009); *see also* Trope & Liberman, *supra* note 20.
138. Kivetz & Tyler, *supra* note 20.
139. MAX H. BAZERMAN & ANN E. TENBRUNSEL, BLIND SPOTS: WHY WE FAIL TO DO WHAT'S RIGHT AND WHAT TO DO ABOUT IT 154 (2011), (citing Kristina A. Diekmann et al., *An Examination of the Relationship Between Behavioral Forecasts and Interpersonal Condemnation in Two Organizational Conflict Situations* (Univ. of Utah, Working Paper)).
140. *See* G. Richard Shell, *Bargaining with the Devil Without Losing Your Soul*, *in* WHAT'S FAIR: ETHICS FOR NEGOTIATORS 57, 71–73 (Carrie Menkel-Meadow & Michael Wheeler eds., 2004) (discussing ways to respond to questions without lying). In similar ways, crafting a strategy in advance for how to disobey authority might serve to channel disobedience. Lee Ross and Richard Nisbett proposed the following "thought experiment":

> Suppose that the experimenter had announced at the beginning of the session that, if at any time the teacher wished to terminate his participation in the experiment, he could indicate his desire to do so by pressing a button on the table in front of him. We trust the reader agrees with us that if this channel factor had been opened up, the obedience rate would have been a fraction of what it was. The converse of this is that the absence of such a "disobedience channel" is precisely what condemned Milgram's subjects to their hapless behavior. In Lewinian terms, there was no well-defined, legitimate, channel that the teacher could use to escape from the situation and discontinue participation in the experiment; and any attempt to create such a channel was met with implacable opposition from an experimenter who, significantly, never even acknowledged the legitimacy of the teacher's concerns.

LEE ROSS & RICHARD E. NISBETT, THE PERSON AND THE SITUATION: PERSPECTIVES OF SOCIAL PSYCHOLOGY 57 (1991).
141. BAZERMAN & TENBRUNSEL, *supra* note 139, at 156.
142. Luban, *supra* note 41, at 369 (emphasis in original).
143. Rhode, *supra* note 47, at 1334.
144. *Id.* at 1318–19.
145. *See* MODEL RULES OF PROF'L CONDUCT R. 1.6 (2010).
146. REGAN, *supra* note 2, at 294.
147. Luban, *supra* note 43, at 116 (emphasis in original).

Chapter 15

1. *Dale Carnegie Quotes*, GOODREADS, http://www.goodreads.com/author/quotes/3317.Dale_Carnegie.
2. OWEN HARARI, THE LEADERSHIP SECRETS OF COLIN POWELL 164 (2003).
3. AMIRAM ELWORK, STRESS MANAGEMENT FOR LAWYERS: HOW TO INCREASE PERSONAL & PROFESSIONAL SATISFACTION IN THE LAW 200 (3d ed. 2007).
4. *Id.*
5. BENJAMIN FRANKLIN, POOR RICHARD'S ALMANAC 1758, *in* THE PAPERS OF BENJAMIN FRANKLIN VOLUME 7: OCTOBER 1, 1756 THROUGH MARCH 31, 1758 326 (Leonard W. Labaree et al. eds. 1963) (1748).
6. GROVER E. CLEVELAND, SWIMMING LESSONS FOR BABY SHARKS: THE ESSENTIAL GUIDE TO THRIVING AS A NEW LAWYER 60 (2010).
7. ELWORK, *supra* note 3, at 199 (emphasis in original).
8. Dan Ariely & Klaus Wertenbroch, *Procrastination, Deadlines, and Performance: Self-Control by Precommitment*, 13 PSYCHOL. SCI. 219 (2002); *see also* DAN ARIELY, PREDICTABLY IRRATIONAL: THE HIDDEN FORCES THAT SHAPE OUR DECISIONS (2008) (emphasizing that deadlines set by authoritative figures can be particularly effective).
9. *Wolfe's World*, NEW YORK TIMES MAG., Oct. 31, 2004, *available at* www.select.nytimes.com.
10. Sean M. McCrea et al., *Construal Level and Procrastination*, 19 PSYCHOL. SCI. 1308 (2008).
11. Frank Wieber & Peter M. Gollwitzer, *Overcoming Procrastination Through Planning*, *in* THE THIEF OF TIME: PHILOSOPHICAL ESSAYS ON PROCRASTINATION 185 (Chrisoula Andreou & Mark D. White eds., 2010).
12. Piers Steel, *The Nature of Procrastination: A Meta-Analytic and Theoretical Review of Quintessential Self-Regulatory Failure*, 133 PSYCHOL. BULL. 65, 82 (2007).
13. DAVID WALLENCHINSKY ET AL., THE PEOPLE'S ALMANAC PRESENTS: THE BOOK OF LISTS 466–67 (1977).
14. Steel, *supra* note 12, at 82.
15. MARK HERRMANN, THE CURMUDGEON'S GUIDE TO PRACTICING LAW 13 (2006) (emphasis in original).
16. Nicole Black, *Law Life: Confidentiality, Smart Phones and Lawyers, Oh My!*, LEGALNEWS.COM, Mar. 22, 2011, *available at* http://www.legalnews.com/detroit/904161 (citing ABA's 2010 Legal Technology Survey).
17. David Glenn, *Divided Attention: In an Age of Classroom Multitasking, Scholars Probe the Nature of Learning and Memory*, CHRON. HIGHER EDUC., Feb. 28, 2010, *available at* http://chronicle.com/article/Scholars-Turn-Their-Attention/63746/.
18. CLEVELAND, *supra* note 6, at 62.

19. Dave Crenshaw, The Myth of Multitasking: How "Doing it All" Gets Nothing Done 60 (2008); *see also* Daniel Gilbert, *What You Don't Know Makes You Nervous*, N.Y. Times, May 20, 2009, *available at* http://opinionator.blogs.nytimes.com/2009/05/20/what-you-dont-know-makes-you-nervous/ (noting the negative effects of uncertainty).
20. Cleveland, *supra* note 18, at 16.
21. Susan Saab Fortney et al., In Pursuit of Attorney Work-Life Balance: Best Practices in Management: A Report on a Cross-Profession National Study of Attorneys 27 (2005).
22. *See, e.g.*, Christopher M. Barnes, *I'll Sleep When I'm Dead: Managing Those Too Busy to Sleep*, 40 Organizational Dynamics 18 (2011); Christopher M. Barnes et al., *Lack of Sleep and Unethical Conduct*, 115 Organizational Behav. & Hum. Decision Processes 169 (2011); Yvonne Harrison & James A. Horne, *The Impact of Sleep Deprivation on Decision Making: A Review*, 6 J. Experimental Psychol.: Applied 236 (2000); Julian Lim & David F. Dinges, *A Meta-Analysis of the Impact of Short-Term Sleep Deprivation on Cognitive Variables*, 136 Psychol. Bull. 375 (2010); June J. Pilcher & Allen J. Huffcutt, *Effects of Sleep Deprivation on Performance: A Meta-Analysis*, 19 Sleep: J. Sleep Res. & Sleep Med. 318 (1996); Donna M. Webster et al., *On Leaping to Conclusions When Feeling Tired: Mental Fatigue Effects on Impressional Primacy*, 32 J. Experimental Soc. Psychol. 181 (1996).
23. Angela L. Duckworth et al., *Grit: Perseverance and Passion for Long-Term Goals*, 92 J. Personality & Soc. Psychol. 1087, 1088 (2007); *see also* Angela Lee Duckworth & Patrick D. Quinn, *Development and Validation of the Short Grit Scale (GRIT-S)*, 91 J. Personality Assessment 166 (2009).
24. Duckworth et al., *supra* note 23, at 1088.
25. *Id.* at 29.
26. Malcolm Forbes, *Thoughts on the Business of Life*, Forbes, March 30, 1992 at 158.
27. Gerald G. Goldberg, Practical Lawyering: The Skills You Did Not Learn in Law School 85–86 (2009).
28. David Dunning, Self-Insight: Roadblocks and Detours on the Path to Knowing Thyself 57 (2005).
29. Reid Hastie & Robyn M. Dawes, Rational Choice in an Uncertain World: The Psychology of Judgement and Decision Making 113 (2d ed. 2001).
30. Dunning, *supra* note 28.
31. Carol Tavris & Elliot Aronson, Mistakes Were Made (but Not by Me): Why We Justify Foolish Beliefs, Bad Decisions, and Hurtful Acts 10 (2007).
32. *Id.* at 29.
33. *See generally* Susan Swaim Daicoff, Lawyer, Know Thyself: A Psychological Analysis of Personality Strengths and Weaknesses 26–28 (2004).

34. Randall Kiser, Beyond Right and Wrong: The Power of Effective Decision Making for Attorneys and Clients (2010); Philip Tetlock, Expert Political Judgment: How Good Is It? How Can We Know? (2006).
35. Samuel Gross & Kent Syverud, *Don't Try: Civil Jury Verdicts in a System Geared to Settlement*, 44 UCLA L. Rev. 1 (1996); *see also* Ward Farnsworth, *Do Parties to Nuisance Cases Bargain After Judgment? A Glimpse Inside the Cathedral*, in 2 Behavioral Law and Economics 3 (Cass Sunstein ed., 2009).
36. Tavris & Aronson, *supra* note 31, at vii (quoting Lao-Tzu, Tao Te Ching (Stephen Mitchell trans., 2009)).
37. Thomas Carlyle, The Works of Thomas Carlyle: On Heroes, Hero Worship, and the Heroic in History 46 (1841).
38. Carol S. Dweck, Mindset: The New Psychology of Success 16 (2007) (quoting Benjamin Barber).
39. *Id.*
40. Kiser, *supra* note 34, at 288 (citing S.F. Daily J., Jan. 31, 2007, at 5).
41. Kathryn Schulz, Being Wrong 208 (2010).
42. Mark Leary et al., *Self-Compassion and Reactions to Unpleasant Self-Relevant Events: The Implications of Treating Oneself Kindly*, 92 J. Personality & Soc. Psychol. 887, 887 (2007) (emphasis added); *see also* Dean A. Shepard & Melissa S. Cardon, *Negative Emotional Reactions to Project Failure and the Self-Compassion to Learn from the Experience*, 46 J. Mgmt. Stud. 923 (2009).
43. *See, e.g.*, Kristin D. Neff et al., *An Examination of Self-Compassion in Relation to Positive Psychological Functioning and Personality Traits*, 41 J. Res. Personality 908 (2007); Neff et al., *Self-Compassion, Achievement Goals, and Coping with Academic Failure*, 4 Self & Identity 263 (2005).
44. Dweck, *supra* note 38, at 228–29.
45. Martin E. P. Seligman et al., *Why Lawyers Are Unhappy*, 23 Cardozo L. Rev. 33 (2001).
46. *See, e.g.*, Sonja Lyubomirsky, The How of Happiness: A New Approach to Getting the Life You Want 106–07 (2007) (reviewing studies); Seligman et al., *supra* note 45 (reviewing studies).
47. Jason M. Satterfield et al., *Law School Performance Predicted by Explanatory Style*, 15 Behav. Sci. & L. 95 (1997).
48. Seligman et al., *supra* note 45, at 41.
49. *Id.*
50. *Id.*
51. Elwork, *supra* note 3; *see also* Pamela Butler, Talking to Yourself: How Cognitive Behavior Therapy Can Change Your Life (2008). Seligman has several books on the topic of how to learn to be more optimistic: Martin E. P. Seligman, Learned Optimism: How to Change Your Mind and Your Life (2006); Martin E. P. Seligman, Authentic Happiness: Using the New Positive Psychology to Realize

Your Potential for Lasting Fulfillment (2002); *see also* Martin E. P. Seligman, Flourish: A Visionary New Understanding of Happiness and Well-Being (2011).

52. Elwork, *supra* note 3, at 114.
53. Catherine Gage O'Grady, *Cognitive Optimism and Professional Pessimism in the Large-Firm Practice of Law: The Optimistic Associate*, 30 Law & Psychol. Rev. 23, 45–47 (2006)
54. Sian Beilock, Choke: What the Secrets of the Brain Reveal About Getting It Right When You Have To 6 (2010).
55. *Id.*; *see also* Daniel M. Wegner, *How to Think, Say, or Do Precisely the Worst Thing for Any Occasion*, 325 Science 48 (2009).
56. Beilock, *supra* note 54, at 139; *see also* Sarra Hayes et al., *Restriction of Working Memory Capacity During Worry*, 117 J. Abnormal Psychol. 712 (2008); Kevin N. Ochsner & James J. Gross, *Cognitive Emotion Regulation: Insights from Social Cognitive and Affective Neuroscience*, 17 Current Directions Psychol. Sci. 153 (2008).
57. Beilock, *supra* note 54, at 137; *see also* David Gimming et al., *Choking Under Pressure and Working Memory Capacity: When Performance Pressure Reduces Fluid Intelligence*, 13 Psychonomic Bull. & Rev. 1005 (2006).
58. Beilock, supra note 54; *see also* Michelene Chi et al., *Categorization and Representation of Physics Problems by Experts and Novices*, 5 Cognitive Sci. 121 (1981); E. J. Masicampo & Roy F. Baumeister, *Unfulfilled Goals Interfere with Tasks That Require Executive Functions*, 47 J. Experimental Soc. Psychol. 300 (2011).
59. Raôul R. D. Oudejans, *Reality-Based Practice Under Pressure Improves Handgun Shooting Performance of Police Officers*, 51 Ergonomics 261 (2008); *see also* Raôul R. D. Oudejans & J. R. Pijpers, *Training with Anxiety has a Positive Effect on Expert Perceptual-Motor Performance Under Pressure*, 62 Q.J. Experimental Psychol. 1631 (2009).
60. Beilock, *supra* note 54; *see also* Oudejans & Pijpers, *supra* note 59.
61. Kenneth Savitsky & Thomas Gilovich, *The Illusion of Transparency and the Alleviation of Speech Anxiety*, 39 J. Experimental Soc. Psychol. 618, 619 (2003).
62. *Id.*
63. Beilock, *supra* note 54; *see also* Roy F. Baumeister, *Choking Under Pressure: Self-Consciousness and Paradoxical Effects of Incentives on Skillful Performance*, 46 J. Personality & Soc. Psychol. 610 (1984).
64. Beilock, *supra* note 54, at 256.
65. Jared R. Curhan & Alex Pentland, *Thin Slices of Negotiation: Predicting Outcomes from Conversational Dynamics Within the First 5 Minutes*, 92 J. Applied Psychol. 802 (2007).
66. Hanah Riley Bowles et al., *Social Incentives for Gender Differences in the Propensity to Initiate Negotiations: Sometimes It Does Hurt to Ask*, 103

ORGANIZATIONAL BEHAV. & HUM. DECISION PROCESSES 84 (2007) (finding that women who asked for more were seen as less "nice" than men who did the same).

67. STEVEN C. BENNETT, THE PATH TO PARTNERSHIP: A GUIDE FOR JUNIOR ASSOCIATES 186 (2004).
68. James M. Podolny & James N. Baron, *Resources and Relationships: Social Networks and Mobility in the Workplace*, 62 AM. SOC. REV. 673 (1997); Ajay Mehra et al., *The Social Networks of High and Low Self-Monitors: Implications for Workplace Performance*, 46 ADMIN. SCI. Q. 121 (2001).
69. VIRGINIA VALIAN, WHY SO SLOW?: THE ADVANCEMENT OF WOMEN (1999).
70. STEVEN C. BENNETT, *supra* note 67.
71. Gail Fann Thomas et al., *The Central Role of Communication in Developing Trust and Its Effect on Employee Involvement*, 46 J. BUS. COMM. 287 (2009); Patricia Pullin, *Small Talk, Rapport, and International Communicative Competence: Lessons to Learn from BELF*, 47 J. BUS. COMM. 455 (2010).
72. *See* JOHN R. SAPP, MAKING PARTNER: A GUIDE FOR LAW FIRM ASSOCIATES (3d ed. 2006); DAVID SHIPLEY & WILL SCHWALBE, SEND: WHY PEOPLE E-MAIL SO BADLY AND HOW TO DO IT BETTER (2d ed. 2008); Kevin W. Rockmann & Gregory B. Northcraft, *To Be or Not to Be Trusted: The Influence of Media Richness on Defection and Deception*, 107 ORGANIZATIONAL BEHAV. & HUM. DECISION PROCESSES 106 (2008).
73. Jan Dennis, *Relying Too Much on Email Bad for Business, Study Says*, 30:1 INSIDE ILL. (Jul. 1, 2010) (quoting Gregory Northcraft) *available at* http://news.illinois.edu/news/10/0616comm.html.
74. Min Kyung Lee & Leila Takayama, *"Now, I Have a Body": Uses and Social Norms for Mobile Remote Presence in the Workplace*, CHI 2011 33 (2011) (proceedings of the 2011 annual Conference on Human Factors in Computing Systems).
75. PAUL BREST & LINDA HAMILTON KRIEGER, PROBLEM SOLVING, DECISION MAKING, AND PROFESSIONAL JUDGMENT: A GUIDE FOR LAWYERS AND POLICYMAKERS 72 (2010); *see also* Carrie Menkel-Meadow, *Aha? Is Creativity Possible in Legal Problem Solving and Teachable in Legal Education?*, 6 HARV. NEGOT. L. REV. 97 (2001).
76. NANCY WOLOCH, MULLER V. OREGON: A BRIEF HISTORY WITH DOCUMENTS (1996).
77. JONATHAN HARR, A CIVIL ACTION 249–50 (1995).
78. GEORGE ORWELL, ANIMAL FARM 38–39 (Everyman's Library ed., Knopf 1993) (1946).
79. Steve W. J. Kozlowski & Daniel R. Ilgen, *Enhancing the Effectiveness of Work Groups and Teams*, 7 PSYCHOL. SCI. PUB. INT. 77 (2006); Charles R. Evans & Kenneth L. Dion, *Group Cohesion and Performance: A Meta-Analysis*, 22 SMALL GROUP RES. 175 (1991).
80. Nadine Heintz, *Building a Culture of Employee Appreciation: How Datotel Overhauled Its Employee-Appreciation, -Recognition, and -Incentive Programs*, INC., Sept. 1, 2009, *available at* http://www.inc.com/magazine/20090901/

building-a-culture-of-employee-appreciation.html. *See generally* Paul Sullivan, *How to Boost Office Morale Without Spending a Dime*, 89 Ill. B.J. 491 (2001).

81. *Benefits*, Google, http://www.google.com/intl/en/jobs/lifeatgoogle/benefits/index.html (last visited Jul. 14, 2011); Bharat Mediratta as told to Julie Bick, *The Google Way: Give Engineers Room*, N.Y. Times, Oct. 21, 2007, at 31; Margaret Graham Tebo, *Gifts That Keep on Giving*, 90 A.B.A. J. 30 (2004); Anthony Lane, *The Fun Factory: Life at Pixar*, New Yorker, May 16, 2011, at 74; *Perks and Benefits*, Microsoft Careers, http://careers.microsoft.com/careers/en/us/benefits-and-perks.aspx (last visited Jul. 14, 2011); Press Release, NAFE and Flex-Time Lawyers Salute 2011 Best Law Firms for Women (Sept. 13, 2011), *available at* http://www.flextimelawyers.com/best/release11.pdf.

82. Juan Williams, Thurgood Marshall: American Revolutionary 61 (1998); *see also* Atul Gawande, *Personal Best: Top Athletes and Singers Have Coaches; Should You?*, New Yorker, Oct. 3, 2011, at 44 (contemplating the utility of "coaching" for professionals).

83. Fiona M. Kay & Jean E. Wallace, *Mentors as Social Capital: Gender, Mentors, and Career Rewards in Law Practice*, 79 Soc. Inquiry 418 (2009); *see also* Tammy D. Allen et al., *Career Benefits Associated with Mentoring for Protégés: A Meta-Analysis*, 89 J. Applied Psychol. 127 (2004); Lillian T. Eby et al., *Does Mentoring Matter? A Multidisciplinary Meta-Analysis Comparing Mentored and Non-Mentored Individuals*, 72 J. Vocational Behav. 254 (2008).

84. *See* Marjorie Schultz & Sheldon Zedek, Final Report: Identification, Development, and Validation of Predictors for Successful Lawyering (Sept. 2008), *available at* http://www.law.berkeley.edu/files/LSACREPORTfinal-12.pdf.

85. Allen et al., *supra* note 83, at 128.

86. Fiona M. Kay & Jean E. Wallace, *Is More Truly Merrier?: Mentors and the Practice of Law*, 47 Canadian Rev. Soc. 1 (2010).

87. Jean E. Wallace, *The Benefits of Mentoring for Female Lawyers*, 58 J. Vocational Behav. 366 (2001) (finding that the average income of the female protégés studied was $82,650 and that the female protégés who had male mentors earned $14,020 more than the female protégés with female mentors).

88. Chip Heath, *On the Social Psychology of Agency Relationships: Lay Theories of Motivation Overemphasize Extrinsic Incentives*, 78 Organizational Behav. & Hum. Decision Processes 25, 28 (1999) (emphasis in original).

89. *Id.*

90. Kay & Wallace, *supra* note 83.

91. Goldberg, *supra* note 27, at 71.

92. *See generally* Tammy D. Allen et al., *The Mentor's Perspective: A Qualitative Inquiry and Agenda for Future Research*, 51 J. Vocational Behav. 70 (1997);

Tammy D. Allen et al., *Protégé Selection by Mentors: What Makes the Difference?*, 21 J. ORGANIZATIONAL BEHAV. 271 (2000).

93. Kay & Wallace, *supra* note 8 § 16. It is not clear whether this makes protégés more attractive to mentors or whether it makes them more likely to seek out mentorship. *Id.*
94. GOLDBERG, *supra* note 27, at 68–70.
95. DAVID H. MAISTER ET AL., THE TRUSTED ADVISOR 18 (2000).
96. Jeffrey Pfeffer et al., *Overcoming the Self-Promotion Dilemma: Interpersonal Attraction and Extra Help as a Consequence of Who Sings One's Praises*, 32 PERSONALITY & SOC. PSYCHOL. BULL. 1362 (2006).
97. GOLDBERG, *supra* note 27, at 110.
98. MAISTER ET AL., *supra* note 95, at 97–99 (emphasis in original).
99. Barbara Power, *Good Client Communications Can Help Lawyers Avoid Malpractice Claims*, LAW PRACTICE TODAY (Aug. 2009), *available at* http://apps.americanbar.org/lpm/lpt/articles/mgt08091.shtml ("Surprisingly, roughly 10% of malpractice claims stem from poor application of the law, while the overwhelming remainder of claims are a result of poor communications.").
100. *See* MAISTER ET AL., *supra* note 95, at 76, 174.
101. Bobby McFerrin's song was initially released in 1988.
102. Oliver Wendell Holmes Jr., *The Path of the Law*, 10 HARV. L. REV. 457, 478 (1897).
103. *Why I Love Being a Lawyer (Seriously)*, A.B.A. J. 34, 38 (Feb. 2011).
104. TOM W. SMITH, NAT'L OPINION RESEARCH CTR., JOB SATISFACTION IN THE UNITED STATES (Univ. of Chi. 2007), *available at* http://www-news.uchicago.edu/releases/07/pdf/070417.jobs.pdf.
105. John Monahan & Jeffrey Swanson, *Lawyers at Mid-Career: A 20-Year Longitudinal Study of Job and Life Satisfaction*, 6 J. EMPIRICAL LEGAL STUD. 451, 469–75 (2009). A study of lawyers in Alberta, Canada, reported similar findings: "Overall, most lawyers (75%) report that they are satisfied with their lives. Almost half (43%) report that they feel their lives are close to ideal and 52% feel the conditions of their lives are excellent." JEAN E. WALLACE, JUGGLING IT ALL: A STUDY OF LAWYERS' WORK, HOME, AND FAMILY DEMANDS AND COPING STRATEGIES: REPORT OF STAGE 2 FINDINGS 61 (Law Sch. Admission Council 2004).
106. Pelin Kesebir & Ed Diener, *In Pursuit of Happiness: Empirical Answers to Philosophical Questions*, 3 PERSPECTIVES ON PSYCHOL. SCI. 117 (2008) (describing PEW RESEARCH CENTER, ARE WE HAPPY YET? (2006)); *see also* Ed Diener, *Subjective Well-Being: The Science of Happiness and a Proposal for a National Index*, 55 AM. PSYCHOLOGIST 34, 37 (2000) (reporting that on a scale from 1 to 10, people in the United States report an average happiness level of 7.77); Ed Diener & Carol Diener, *Most People Are Happy*, 7 PSYCHOL. SCI. 181 (1996).
107. SMITH, *supra* note 104.
108. Ronit Dinovitzer & Bryant Garth, *Lawyer Satisfaction in the Process of Structuring Legal Careers*, 41 LAW & SOC'Y REV. 1 (2007) (35% extremely satisfied,

44% moderately satisfied, 8% neither satisfied nor dissatisfied, 11% moderately dissatisfied, and 2% extremely dissatisfied); *see also* Ronit Dinovitzer et al., After the JD II: Second Results from a National Study of Legal Careers 14 (Am. Bar Found. & NALP Found. for Law Career Research & Educ. 2009) (finding that 76% of respondents were satisfied with their choice of career).

109. Monahan & Swanson, *supra* note 105, at 469–75 (43.3% extremely satisfied, 38% moderately satisfied, 6.9% neither, 8.6% moderately dissatisfied, and 3.3% extremely dissatisfied).

110. *See, e.g.*, David L. Chambers, *Accommodation and Satisfaction: Women and Men Lawyers and the Balance of Work and Family*, 14 Law & Soc. Inquiry 251 (1989); Kenneth G. Dau-Schmidt & Kaushik Mukhopadhaya, *The Fruits of Our Labors: An Empirical Study of the Distribution of Income and Job Satisfaction Across the Legal Profession*, 49 J. Legal Educ. 342 (1999); Kenneth G. Dau-Schmidt et al., *Men and Women of the Bar: An Empirical Study of the Impact of Gender on Legal Careers*, 16 Mich. J. Gender & L. 49 (2009); Richard O. Lempert et al., *Michigan's Minority Graduates in Practice: The River Runs Through Law School*, 25 Law & Soc. Inquiry 395 (2000); *see also* Kenneth G. Dau-Schmidt et al., *"The Pride of Indiana": An Empirical Study of the Law School Experience and Careers of Indiana University School of Law-Bloomington Alumni*, 81 Ind. L.J. 1427 (2006); Paul W. Mattessich & Cheryl W. Heilman, *The Career Paths of Minnesota Law School Graduates: Does Gender Make a Difference?*, 9 Law & Inequality J. 59 (1990) (surveying graduates of the University of Minnesota Law School, Hamline University School of Law, and William Mitchell College of Law); Janet Taber et al., *Gender, Legal Education, and the Legal Profession: An Empirical Study of Stanford Law Students and Graduates*, 40 Stan. L. Rev. 1209 (1988); Lee E. Teitelbaum et al., *Gender, Legal Education, and Legal Careers*, 41 J. Legal Educ. 443 (1991) (surveying graduates of the University of New Mexico School of Law).

111. John P. Heinz et al., *Lawyers and Their Discontents: Findings from a Survey of the Chicago Bar*, 74 Ind. L.J. 735 (1999).

112. Dinovitzer & Garth, *supra* note 108, at 9. Other lower-rated aspects of their jobs include diversity (4.4), amount of travel (4.4), compensation (4.5), and opportunities for advancement (4.7). *Id.*; *see also* Dau-Schmidt et al., *Men and Women of the Bar*, *supra* note 108, at 120; Dinovitzer et al., *supra* note 95, at 14; Monahan & Swanson, *supra* note 105, at 473.

113. Lempert et al., *supra* note 110, at 446; *see* Dau-Schmidt & Mukhopadhaya, *supra* note 110, at 360–62; Dinovitzer & Garth, *supra* note 108, at 22; Kathleen E. Hull, *Cross-Examining the Myth of Lawyers' Misery*, 52 Vand. L. Rev. 971 (1999); Monahan & Swanson, *supra* note 105, at 477.

114. Dau-Schmidt & Mukhopadhaya, *supra* note 110, at 360–62; Dinovitzer & Garth, *supra* note 108, at 12; Heinz et al., *supra* note 111, at 748; Hull, *supra* note 112; Lempert et al., *supra* note 110, at 485–86.

115. John Hagan & Fiona Kay, *Even Lawyers Get the Blues: Gender, Depression, and Job Satisfaction in Legal Practice*, 41 LAW & SOC'Y REV. 51, 55 (2007).
116. G. Andrew H. Benjamin et al., *The Prevalence of Depression, Alcohol Abuse, and Cocaine Abuse Among United States Lawyers*, 13 INT'L J.L. & PSYCHIATRY 233 (1990); *see also* G. Andrew H. Benjamin et al., *The Role of Legal Education in Producing Psychological Distress Among Law Students and Lawyers*, 11 AM. B. FOUND. RES. J. 225 (1986); William W. Eaton et al., *Occupations and the Prevalence of Major Depressive Disorder*, 32 J. OCCUPATIONAL MED. 1079 (1990).
117. Connie J. A. Beck et al., *Lawyer Distress: Alcohol-Related Problems and Other Psychological Concerns Among a Sample of Practicing Lawyers*, 10 J.L. & HEALTH 1 (1995).
118. Seligman et al., *supra* note 45, at 38.
119. *See* ILLINOIS ATTORNEY REGISTRATION AND DISCIPLINARY COMMISSION ANNUAL REPORT 28–29 (2007) (finding that between 1998 and 2007, 28% of sanctioned attorneys were impaired by some form of psychological problem or substance abuse and finding high rates of impairment among attorneys who were disciplined or placed on probationary status); ELWORK, *supra* note 3, at 17; DAICOFF, *supra* note 33, at 13.
120. *See generally* ELWORK, *supra* note 3, at 17, 30–31; *see also* Monahan & Swanson, *supra* note 105, at 475–77 (finding negative correlation between hours worked and both life and work-life satisfaction).
121. Deborah D. Danner et al., *Positive Emotions in Early Life and Longevity: Findings from the Nun Study*, 80 J. PERSONALITY & SOC. PSYCHOL. 804 (2001); ED DIENER & ROBERT BISWAS-DIENER, HAPPINESS: UNLOCKING THE MYSTERIES OF PSYCHOLOGICAL WEALTH (2008); Sonja Lyubomirsky et al., *The Benefits of Frequent Positive Affect: Does Happiness Lead to Success?*, 131 PSYCHOL. BULL. 803 (2005) (reviewing studies); Edward Diener & Micaela Y. Chan, *Happy People Live Longer: Subjective Well-Being Contributes to Health and Longevity*, 3 APPLIED PSYCHOL.: HEALTH & WELL-BEING 1 (2011); Bruno S. Frey, *Happy People Live Longer*, 331 SCIENCE 542 (2011); Sonja Lyubomirsky et al., *Pursuing Happiness: The Architecture of Sustainable Change*, 9 REV. GEN. PSYCHOL. 111 (2005) (reviewing studies).
122. Lyubomirsky et al., *supra* note 121.
123. SELIGMAN, *supra* note 45 (quoting Letter from Benjamin N. Cardozo to Elvira Solis (Feb. 15, 1933)).
124. Becky Beaupre Gillespie & Hollee Schwartz Temple, *Hunting Happy: In Grim Times, a Search for Joy Gains Ground*, A.B.A. J. 41, 43 (Feb. 2011) (quoting Nancy Levit).
125. SIGNAL PATTERNS, http://www.signalpatterns.com/iphone/livehappy_std.html (last visited March 25, 2012); Elizabeth Leis-Newman, *Unhappy? There's an App for That*, MONITOR ON PYSCHOL. 30 (June 2011).
126. Edward L. Deci & Richard M. Ryan, *The "What" and "Why" of Goal Pursuits: Human Needs and the Self-Determination of Behavior*, 11 PSYCHOL. INQUIRY 227

(2000); Kennon M. Sheldon et al., *What Is Satisfying About Satisfying Events? Testing Ten Candidate Psychological Needs*, 80 J. Personality & Soc. Psychol. 325 (2001); Kennon M. Sheldon et al., *Variety Is the Spice of Happiness: The Hedonic Adaptation Prevention (HAP) Model*, in Oxford Handbook of Happiness (I. Boniwell & S. David eds., forthcoming); Kennon M. Sheldon & Vincent Filak, *Manipulating Autonomy, Competence, and Relatedness Support in a Game-Learning Context: New Evidence That All Three Needs Matter*, 47 Brit. J. Soc. Psychol. 267 (2008); *see also* Edward L. Deci, Why We Do What We Do: Understanding Self-Motivation (1995); Kennon M. Sheldon & Lawrence S. Krieger, *Understanding the Negative Effects of Legal Education on Law Students: A Longitudinal Test of Self-Determination Theory*, 33 Personality & Soc. Psychol. Bull. 883 (2007).

127. Nancy Levit & Douglas O. Linder, The Happy Lawyer: Making a Good Life in the Law 210 (2010).

128. *See generally* Ed Diener & Martin E.P. Seligman, *Toward an Economy of Well-Being*, 5 Psychol. Sci. In the Pub. Interest 1 (2004) (reviewing studies). *See e.g.*, Brent A. Scott & Timothy A. Judge, *Insomnia, Emotions, & Job Satisfaction: A Multilevel Study*, 32 J. Mgmt. 622 (2006).

129. *See, e.g.*, Kirk Warren Brown & Richard M. Ryan, *The Benefits of Being Present: Mindfulness and Its Role in Psychological Well-Being*, 84 J. Personality & Soc. Psychol. 822 (2003); *see also, e.g.*, James Carmody & Ruth A. Baer, *Relationships Between Mindfulness Practice and Levels of Mindfulness, Medical and Psychological Symptoms and Well-Being in a Mindfulness-Based Stress Reduction Program*, 31 J. Behav. Med. 23 (2008); Shauna Shapiro et al., *Mindfulness-Based Stress Reduction for Health Care Professionals: Results from a Randomized Trial*, 12 Int'l J. Stress Mgmt. 164 (2005); Shauna Shapiro, *Meditation and Positive Psychology*, in Oxford Handbook of Positive Psychology 601 (Shane J. Lopez & C. R. Snyder eds., 2d ed. 2009) (reviewing studies); Leonard L. Riskin, *The Contemplative Lawyer: On the Potential Contributions of Mindfulness Meditation to Law Students, Lawyers, and Their Clients*, 7 Harv. Negot. L. Rev. 1 (2002).

130. *See* Robert A. Karasek Jr., *Job Demands, Job Decision Latitude and Mental Strain: Implications for Job Redesign*, 24 Admin. Sci. Q. 285 (1979).

131. Dinovitzer & Garth, *supra* note 108, at 9 (control over amount of work (4.6), control over how they work (5.4)); *see also* Janine Robben, *Burnout: Cautionary Tales*, Or. St. B. Bull. 17, 18 (Oct. 2008) (Oregon State Bar survey: 54% indicated that time pressure/workload was a dissatisfying aspect of their jobs).

132. Levit & Linder, *supra* note 127, at 52–53.

133. Daniel Kahneman et al., *A Survey Method of Characterizing Daily Life Experience: The Day Reconstruction Method*, 306 Science 1776 (2004); *see also* Barbara S. McCann et al., *Hostility, Social Support, and Perceptions of Work*, 2 J. Occupational Health Psychol. 175, 179 (1997) (finding that time pressure was associated with job dissatisfaction in a sample that included attorneys).

134. Seligman et al., *supra* note 45, at 42.
135. Levit & Linder, *supra* note 127 at 210.
136. *Id.* at 53–54 (quoting Jonathan Foreman, *My Life as an Associate*, City J. (Winter 1997)).
137. Justin M. Berg et al., *Perceiving and Responding to Challenges in Job Crafting at Different Ranks: When Proactivity Requires Adaptivity*, 31 J. Organizational Behav. 158 (2010); Seligman et al., *supra* note 45, at 44 (suggesting that lawyers tailor their days to gain more control over their work); Amy Wrzeniewski & Jane E. Dutton, *Crafting a Job: Revisioning Employees as Active Crafters of Their Work*, 26 Acad. Mgmt. Rev. 179, 179–80 (2001).
138. *See* Christopher Peterson & Martin E. P. Seligman, Character Strengths and Virtues: A Handbook and Classification (2004); Martin E. P. Seligman et al., *Positive Psychology Progress: Empirical Validation of Interventions*, 60 Am. Psychologist 410 (2005) (finding that using signature strengths in a new way was associated with happiness and reduced depression).
139. Jeanne Nakamura & Mihaly Csikszentmihalyi, *The Construction of Meaning Through Vital Engagement*, in Flourishing: Positive Psychology and the Life Well-Lived 83, 88–89 (Corey L. M. Keyes & Jonathan Haidt eds., 2003).
140. Mihaly Csikszentmihalyi, Finding Flow 29–32 (1997); *see also* Nakamura & Csikszentmihalyi, *supra* note 139, at 88–89; Seligman, Flourish, *supra* note 53, at 24 ("You go into flow when your highest strengths are deployed to meet the highest challenges that come your way.").
141. Lyubomirsky et al., *supra* note 121, at 114.
142. *See, e.g.*, Kennon M. Sheldon & Linda Houser-Marko, *Self-Concordance, Goal-Attainment, and the Pursuit of Happiness: Can There Be an Upward Spiral?*, 80 J. Personality & Soc. Psychol. 152 (2001); Robert A. Emmons, *Personal Goals, Life Meaning, and Virtue: Wellsprings of a Positive Life*, in Flourishing: Positive Psychology and the Life Well-Lived, *supra* note 139, at 105, 113; Tim Kasser & Richard M. Ryan, *Further Examining the American Dream: Differential Correlates of Intrinsic and Extrinsic Goals*, 22 Personality & Soc. Psychol. Bull. 280 (1996); Kennon M. Sheldon et al., *The Independent Effects of Goal Contents and Motives on Well-Being: It's Both What You Pursue and Why You Pursue It*, 30 Personality & Soc. Psychol. Bull. 475 (2004); *see also* Lawrence S. Krieger, *The Inseparability of Professionalism and Personal Satisfaction: Perspectives on Values, Integrity and Happiness*, 11 Clinical L. Rev. 425 (2005); Seligman, *supra* note 41, at 17 (meaning is "belonging to and serving something that you believe is bigger than the self").
143. Becky Beaupre Gillespie & Hollee Schwartz Temple, *Hunting Happy*, A.B.A. J. 41, 46 (Feb. 2011) (quoted by Gretchen Rubin, author of The Happiness Project).
144. Dan Ariely, *Man's Search for Meaning: The Case of Legos*, 67 J. Econ. Behav. & Org. 671 (2008).

145. *Why I Love Being a Lawyer (Seriously)*, A.B.A. J. 34, 36 (Feb. 2011).
146. Diener & Biswas-Diener, *supra* note 121, at 225.
147. Lyubomirsky et al., *supra* note 121, at 123.
148. Daniel Gilbert, Stumbling on Happiness 24 (2007).
149. Diener & Biswas-Diener, *supra* note 121, at 70. See generally Amy Wrzesniewski et al., *Jobs, Careers, and Callings: People's Relations to their Work*, 31 J. Res. Personality 21 (1997).
150. Kennon M. Sheldon & Lawrence S. Krieger, *Does Legal Education Have Undermining Effects on Law Students? Evaluating Changes in Motivation, Values, and Well-Being*, 22 Behav. Sci. & L. 261 (2004).
151. Levit & Linder, *supra* note 127, at 63.
152. Gillespie & Temple, *supra* note 124, at 43.
153. Levit & Linder, *supra* note 127, at 108.
154. Diener & Biswas-Diener, *supra* note 121, at 72; Wrzeniewski & Dutton, *supra* note 137.
155. Jane Allyn Piliavin, *Doing Well by Doing Good: Benefits for the Benefactor*, in Flourishing: Positive Psychology and the Life Well Lived 227, 235–36 (Corey L. M. Keyes & Jonathan Haidt eds., 2003).
156. Emmons, *supra* note 142, at 111; Lyubomirsky et al., *supra* note 121 (reviewing studies); Piliavin, *supra* note 155, at 227, 235–36 (reviewing studies); Peggy A. Thoits & Lyndi N. Hewitt, *Volunteer Work and Well-Being*, 42 J. Health & Soc. Behav. 115 (2001).
157. Diener & Biswas-Diener, *supra* note 121, at 54 (see generally chapter 4); Kahneman et al., *supra* note 133; *see also* Sheldon et al., *What Is Satisfying About Satisfying Events?*, *supra* note 129.
158. *See, e.g.*, Robert A. Emmons & Michael E. McCullough, *Counting Blessings Versus Burdens: An Experimental Investigation of Gratitude and Subjective Well-Being in Daily Life*, 84 J. Personality & Soc. Psychol. 377 (2003) (gratitude); Lyubomirsky et al., *supra* note 121 (gratitude and acts of kindness); Kennon M. Sheldon & Sonja Lyubomirsky, *How to Increase and Sustain Positive Emotion: The Effects of Expressing Gratitude and Visualizing Best Possible Selves*, 1 J. Positive Psychol. 73 (2006) (gratitude). See generally Diener & Biswas-Diener, *supra* note 121, at 65; Seligman, *supra* note 53, at 17; Lyubomirsky, *supra* note 37, at 22; Elizabeth W. Dunn et al., *Spending Money on Others Promotes Happiness*, 319 Science 1687 (2008); Robert A. Emmons & Michael E. McCullough, The Psychology of Gratitude (2004); Keiko Otake et al., *Happy People Become Happier Through Kindness: A Counting Kindnesses Intervention*, 7 J. Happiness Stud. 361 (2006); Nancy L. Sin & Sonja Lyubomirsky, *Enhancing Well-Being and Alleviating Depressive Symptoms with Positive Psychology Interventions: A Practice-Friendly Meta-Analysis*, 65 J. Clinical Psychol.: In Session 467 (2009).
159. Sheldon et al., *Variety Is the Spice of Happiness*, *supra* note 129

160. Levit & Linder, *supra* note 127, at 213.
161. McCann et al., *supra* note 133, at 180.
162. Dinovitzer & Garth, *supra* note 108, at 20 (statistics omitted); Wallace, *supra* note 105, at 51.
163. Dinovitzer & Garth, *supra* note 108; Monahan & Swanson, *supra* note 105.
164. Wallace, *supra* note 105, at 46; *see also* Chambers, *supra* note 110, at 273–74.
165. Tammy D. Allen et al., *Consequences Associated with Work-to-Family Conflict: A Review and Agenda for Future Research*, 5 J. Occupational Health Psychol. 278 (2000); Tammy D. Allen & Jeremy Armstrong, *Further Examination of the Link Between Work-Family Conflict and Physical Health: The Role of Health-Related Behaviors*, 49 Am. Behav. Sci. 1204 (2006); David L. Chambers, *supra* note 96, at 253–54; Michael R. Frone et al., *Relation of Work-Family Conflict to Health Outcomes: A Four-Year Longitudinal Study of Employed Parents*, 70 J. Occupational & Organizational Psychol. 325 (1997); Joseph G. Grzywacz et al., *Work, Family, and Health: Work-Family Balance as a Protective Factor Against Stresses of Daily Life*, in The Changing Realities of Work and Family 194, 205 (Amy Marcus-Newhall et al. eds., 2008); Ellen Ernst Kossek & Cynthia Ozeki, *Work-Family Conflict, Policies, and the Job-Life Satisfaction Relationship: A Review and Directions for Organizational Behavior–Human Resources Research*, 83 J. Applied Psychol. 139 (1998); Elianne F. van Steenbergen & Naomi Ellemers, *Is Managing the Work-Family Interface Worthwhile? Benefits for Employee Health and Performance*, 30 J. Organizational Behav. 617 (2009).
166. Stephen D. Easton, *My Last Lecture: Unsolicited Advice for Future and Current Lawyers*, 56 S.C. L. Rev. 229, 269 (2005).
167. *See generally* Kristin Byron, *A Meta-Analytic Review of Work-Family Conflict and Its Antecedents*, 67 J. Vocational Behav. 169 (2005); Michael T. Ford et al., *Work and Family Satisfaction and Conflict: A Meta-Analysis of Cross-Domain Relations*, 92 J. Applied Psychol. 57 (2007); Jeffrey H. Greenhaus & Nicholas J. Beutell, *Sources of Conflict Between Work and Family Roles*, 10 Acad. Mgmt. Rev. 76 (1985).
168. Wallace, *supra* note 105, at 46, 62. This asymmetry is consistent with other work in psychology. *See* Ford et al., *supra* note 167; *see also* Dau-Schmidt et al., *Men and Women of the Bar*, *supra* note 110, at 69–70 (Michigan grads reported positive satisfaction with work-family balance); Dinovitzer et al., *supra* note 95, at 14, 31 (finding that satisfaction with work-life balance was 5.13 on a 1-to-7 scale where 7 indicated highly satisfied and that between 46% and 60% of lawyers have a "good balance" between work and personal life).
169. Wallace, *supra* note 105; *see also* Chambers, *supra* note 110, at 271; Fortney et al., *supra* note 21, at 25–27.
170. Jeffrey H. Greenhaus & Gary N. Powell, *When Work and Family Are Allies: A Theory of Work-Family Enrichment*, 31 Acad. Mgmt. Rev. 72, 73 (2006) (emphasis in original); *see also* Samuel Aryee et al., *Rhythms of Life: Antecedents*

and Outcomes of Work-Family Balance in Employed Parents, 90 J. APPLIED PSYCHOL. 132 (2005); Fanny M. Cheung & Diane F. Halpern, *Women at the Top: Powerful Leaders Define Success as Work + Family in a Culture of Gender*, 65 AM. PSYCHOLOGIST 182 (2010); Karen C. Gareis et al., *Work-Family Enrichment and Conflict: Additive Effects, Buffering, or Balance?*, 71 J. MARRIAGE & FAM. 696 (2009); Joseph G. Grzywacz & Nadine F. Marks, *Reconceptualizing the Work-Family Interface: An Ecological Perspective on the Correlates of Positive and Negative Spillover Between Work and Family*, 5 J. OCCUPATIONAL HEALTH PSYCHOL. 111 (2000); Steenbergen & Ellemers, *supra* note 165. The enhancement of work *by* family tends to be stronger than the enhancement of work *on* family. Greenhaus & Powell, *supra*.

171. Kristina A. Bourne et al., *Embracing the Whole Individual: Advantages of a Dual-Centric Perspective of Work and Life*, 52 BUS. HORIZONS 387 (2009); ELLEN GALINSKY, DUAL-CENTRIC: A NEW CONCEPT OF WORK-LIFE (2003), *available at* http://www.familiesandwork.org/site/research/reports/dual-centric.pdf; Grzywacz et al., *supra* note 144, at 205.

172. David L. Chambers, *Accommodation and Satisfaction: Women and Men Lawyers and the Balance of Work and Family*, 14 LAW & SOC. INQUIRY 251, 266 (1989).

173. WALLACE, *supra* note 105, at 52.

174. Greenhaus & Powell, *supra* note 170; Steenbergen & Ellemers, *supra* note 165.

175. Monahan & Swanson, *supra* note 105; Chambers, *supra* note 110, at 270.

176. Dau-Schmidt et al., *Men and Women of the Bar*, *supra* note 110, at 72.

177. *See, e.g.*, Stephanie Francis Ward, *The Ultimate Time-Money Tradeoff*, 93 A.B.A. J. 24 (Feb. 2007); *see also* JEAN E. WALLACE, *supra* note 92, at 33 ("Overall, 39% of the lawyers reported that they would prefer to work fewer hours. . . .").

178. *See* BUILDING A BETTER LEGAL PROFESSION, http://www.betterlegalprofession.org/; *see also* Mary Flood, *Pay Us Less, They Request, and Don't Work Us So Hard: Professors, Lawyers Have Seen a Change*, HOUS. CHRON. (2007), *available at* http://www.chron.com/business/article/New-lawyers-say-pay-us-less-don-t-work-us-so-1532672.php; Marisa McQuilken, *Students Seek a More Reasonable Law Firm Life*, NAT'L L.J. (2007), *available at* http://www.law.com/jsp/nlj/PubArticleNLJ.jsp?id=900005491755&slreturn=1.

179. Tim Kasser & Kennon M. Sheldon, *Time Affluence as a Path Toward P1 July 17ersonal Happiness and Ethical Business Practice: Empirical Evidence from Four Studies*, 84 J. BUS. ETHICS 243 (2009).

180. *See* Byron, *supra* note 167.

181. Benjamin Franklin, *Advice to a Young Tradesman, Written by an Old One* (21 July 1748), in FRANKLIN: THE AUTOBIOGRAPHY AND OTHER WRITING ON POLITICS, ECONOMICS, AND VIRTUE 200 (Alan Houston ed., 2004).

182. James A. Evans et al., *Beach Time, Bridge Time, and Billable Hours: The Temporal Structure of Technical Contracting*, 49 ADMIN. SCI. Q. 1 (2004). *See also* Dilip Soman, *The Mental Accounting of Sunk Time Costs: Why Time is Not Like Money*, 14 J. BEHAV. DECISION MAKING 169 (2001).
183. Sanford E. DeVoe & Julian House, *Time, Money, and Happiness: How Does Putting a Price on Time Affect Our Ability to Smell the Roses?*, 48 J. EXPERIMENTAL SOC. PSYCHOL. 466 (2012); Sanford DeVoe & Jeffrey Pfeffer, *When is Happiness About How Much You Earn? The Effect of Hourly Payment on the Money-Happiness Connection*, 35 PERSONALITY & SOC. PSYCHOL. BULL. 1602 (2009); Sanford E. DeVoe & Jeffrey Pfeffer, *Hourly Payment and Volunteering: The Effect of Organizational Practices on Decisions About Time Use*, 50 ACAD. MGMT J. 783 (2007); Sanford E. DeVoe & Jeffrey Pfeffer, *When Time is Money: The Effect of Hourly Payment on the Evaluation of Time*, 104 ORGANIZATIONAL BEHAV. & HUM. DECISION PROCESSES 1 (2007).
184. BRAD PAISLEY, *Time Well Wasted, on* TIME WELL WASTED (Arista Nashville 2005). *See also* ATP, *Time Wasted is Time Well Spent, on* ATP & The Undersound VR013 (Vibration Records Ltd. 2011).
185. LEVIT & LINDER, *supra* note 126, at 212.
186. *See* Bryon, *supra* note 167; Grzywacz & Marks, *supra* note 170.
187. DIENER & BISWAS-DIENER, *supra* note 121, at 214 (see generally chapter 12).
188. Shigehiro Oishi et al., *The Optimum Level of Well-Being: Can People Be Too Happy?*, 2 PERSP. PSYCHOL. SCI. 346 (2007); *see also* Manju Puri & David T. Robinson, *Optimism and Economic Choice*, 86 J. FIN. ECON. 71 (2007).
189. LYUBOMIRSKY, *supra* note 46, at 205–06 ("It turns out that the process of working toward a goal, participating in a valued and challenging activity, is as important to well-being as its attainment."); *see also* Kennon M. Sheldon et al., *Persistent Pursuit of Need-Satisfying Goals Leads to Increased Happiness: A 6-Month Experimental Longitudinal Study*, 34 MOTIVATION & EMOTION 39, 45 (2010).
190. *Lily Tomlin Quotes*, THINKEXIST.COM, http://thinkexist.com/quotation/the_road_to_success_is_always_under/191354.html (last visited Nov. 30, 2011).
191. DIENER & BISWAS-DIENER, *supra* note 121 at 18.

Index

A
ABA *Model Rules of Professional Conduct*, 287, 393, 407
Abel, Richard, 398
Abstract words, 121–122
Accessibility, 354–358
Accuracy, confirming, 207–209
Accurate memories, 42
Actor-observer effect, 19–20
Adversarial system, 400–403
Advice, 168
Advice letters, 376–377
Affect-congruent recall, 50
Affect heuristic, 75, 289
Affect-state dependent recall, 50
Affective forecasting, 97–99
African Americans
 effect of race on peremptory challenges, 103
 stereotypes of, 14
After the JD project, 445
Agency relationship
 benefits of, 400
 conflicts and disclosure, 398–399
 indirect unethical actions, 399–400
 role of the lawyer's interests, 395–398
 turning down client requests, 399
Alternatives, description of, 368–369
Ambady, Nalini, 146
Anatomy of a Murder (Preminger), 341
Anchoring, 71–72, 229–230, 273, 380–381
Anger, 52–53, 58, 63, 197, 279, 331–333
Anticipated regrets, 100, 241
Anxiety, 55, 59, 100, 343–344
Apologies, 182–183, 217–218, 268, 293
Apple Corps Ltd., 220
Apple Inc., 220
Appraisal, emotions and, 52–57, 60

Arguments
 number of, 125
 order of, 123, 369–370
 two-sided, 124
Aristotle, 57, 364
Aronson, Eliot, 411, 426
Asch compliance experiment, 133–134
Asch, Solomon, 133
Assumptions
 making, 324
 testing, 203
Asymmetric insight, illusion of, 21–24, 165
Asynchrony, 149
Attention
 focusing, 13
 limits of, 8–10
 rumination and, 60
Attorney self-interest, 255–256
Attribution
 of bias, 23–24
 causal, 17–20
 culture and, 19
 theory in psychology, 17
Audience perspective, 358–359
Authority, 284
 obedience to, 134–136
 trustworthiness of, 177
Availability, 72–73, 229–231, 297, 392
Averaging principle, 80–81
Awareness, 411

B
Bacon, Francis, 146, 182
Bad news, 278, 228–229
Baker, Howard, 285
Bandura, Albert, 389
Bankruptcy Rule 2014, 386, 394

BATNA. *See* Best alternative to a negotiated agreement
Batson, C. Daniel, 387
Bazerman, Max, 282
Beane, Billy, 73–74
Beatles, 220
Behavior, nonverbal, 147
Beilock, Sian, 431, 432
Bell, Derrick, Jr., 258
Best alternative to a negotiated agreement (BATNA), 246, 288
Bias
  attributions of, 23–24
  biased assimilation, 14–17, 350
  confirmation bias, 14–17, 205, 223–224, 276–277, 291, 308, 350, 398, 410
  correspondence bias, 18
  distinction bias, 107
  egocentrically biased judgments, 70
  fixed pie bias, 267
  hindsight bias, 76, 203, 231–232, 277, 427
  omission bias, 101, 409
  outcome bias, 76, 425
  self-serving bias, 71, 225, 427
  status quo bias, 91, 101, 380–381
  temporal synchrony bias, 149
  truth bias, 156
Bias blind spot, 4
Biased assimilation, 14–17, 350
Bills, 377–378
Biswas-Diener, Robert, 458
Blame, 53–54
Blind spots
  bias, 4
  ethical, 390–393
Body language, emotions and, 64
Boiling frogs, 389–390
Bok, Sissela, 390
Bork, Robert, 372
Brady v. Maryland, 402–403
Brain activity, losses, gains and, 90
Brain drain phenomenon, 31
Brevity, 355
Breyer, Stephen G., 22, 89, 164
Briefs
  credibility of, 360–361
  decision making and, 97–100
  description of alternatives, 368–369
  early sections of, 367–368
  order of arguments, 369–370
  storytelling, 361
  word choice, 370–371
  writing, 359–371

Brown v. Board of Education, 258
Bruner, Jerome, 359
Buffalo Creek Disaster, The (Stern), 339
Bush, George W., 36, 337, 338
Business development, 440–442
Bystander behavior, 132

C
Calling, work as a 451–453
Cambridge Psychological Society, 32
Caperton v. A.T. Massey Coal Co., Inc., 388
Capilano Suspension Bridge, 48, 431
Cardozo, Benjamin N., 7, 448
Career, work as a 452
Carlyle, Thomas, 427
Carnegie, Dale, 46, 417
Case of a Lifetime (Smith), 294
Causal attribution, 17–20
Centers for Disease Control and Prevention (CDC), 90
Central Park Jogger case, 330–331
Certainty effect, 89, 308
Chabris, Christopher, 30
Chafee, Zachariah, Jr., 373
Chaining, 369–370
Challenger (space shuttle), 31
Chameleon effect, 159
Change blindness, 8
Change blindness blindness, 8
Channel factors, 136–138, 248
Charitable contributions, 268
Child custody decisions, 105–106
Choice, time and, 95–96
Choke, 430–432
Churchill, Winston, 350
Cialdini, Robert, 127, 128, 299
Civil Action, A (Harr/Zallian), 171, 265, 272, 309, 317, 331, 387, 436
Clarity, 354–358
Clemens, Roger, 36
Client-centered attorneys, 232
Client(s)
  anger, 197
  assessing wants of, 256–260
  bad news, 227
  bills to, 377–378
  building trust, 441
  building trust with, 158–159
  communication with, 422–423
  conflicting emotions of, 197
  counseling, 211–252
  debriefing, 347–348
  desire for justice, 217–218

desire for procedural justice, 200
emotions of, 194–198
ethics in counseling, 414–415
feelings of guilt, 198
frame of, 224
giving advice to, 168
hindsight bias, 231
interviewing, 188–209
lawyer-client interaction in negotiation, 254–255
letters from attorneys, 374–378
listening to, 161–163
maintaining relationships, 443–444
mediation as benefit for, 301–303
preparing for interview, 188–209
rapport, 159–161, 191, 210
realistic expectations, 232–233
recall, 202
taking depositions from, 315–333
turning down requests, 399
weighing benefits and risks, 227–288
Clinton, Bill, 36, 286, 311, 319, 326, 373
Closed questions, 199
Closure, 105
Cognitive dissonance, 20, 426
Cognitive heuristics, 67
Coherence, 361
Collaboration, 432–444
   corporate morale boosting, 438
   managing impressions, 432–434
   mentoring, 438–440
   rainmaking, 440–442
   working in groups, 434–437
Commitment, 129–130, 283, 414
Communication. *See also* Writing
   building trust, 158–159
   complexities of, 142–157
   conversational norms, 144–145
   conveying information, 166
   culture and, 151–152
   development of effective, 157–169
   eliciting/facilitating disclosure, 165–166
   establishing rapport, 159–161
   fluency of, 164
   giving advice, 168
   lean forms of, 149
   legal, 163–165
   listening, 161–163
   lying, 153–157
   mediums, 148–151
   multitasking and, 421–423
   nonverbal communication, 145–148
   perspective taking in, 143–144
   in rainmaking, 440
   shared understanding in, 143
   in taking depositions, 317–326
   teaching and learning, 166–168
   working in groups and, 434–435
Compassion, 227
Complaints
   stories and facts, 371–372
   writing, 371–374
Compromise, contrast and, 92–94
Compromise effects, 93–94
Concept accessibility, 11
Concessions
   as losses and gains, 282
   persuading and eliciting, 281–285
Concrete words, 121–122, 167, 356
Condlin, Robert J., 281
Confessions, false, 37–38
Confidence, 69–70
Confirmation bias
   in agency relationship, 398
   countering effects of, 16
   counseling clients and, 223–224
   defined, 14–17
   in discovery and due diligence, 308, 350
   ethical decision making and, 410
   in interviews, 205
   in negotiation, 276–277, 291
Conflicts, 398–399
Conley, Kenny, 8–9
Consensus, 109
Consensus, illusion of, 109–110, 436
Consistency, 129–130, 283
Consultants, 334
Context reinstatement, 42
Contracts
   anchoring, 380–381
   framing, 380–381
   promotion of positive relationships, 381–382
   status quo bias, 380–381
   writing, 380–382
Contrast, compromise and, 92–94
Contrast effect, 92
Control, illusion of, 69
Conversational norms, 144–145, 318, 334–336
Conversations, with ourselves, 429
Copeland, Jim, 443
Corporate morale boosting, 438
Correspondence bias, 18
Counterarguments, 79

Courage, 408
Courage, illusion of, 408
Counseling clients
  advice, 223
  assessing likelihood of success,
    224–232
  broadening focus of consultation,
    211–222
  challenging preconceptions, 222–224
  choosing among alternatives, 232–244
  comparison of options, 240–241
  conveying bad news, 227
  dealing with availability and anchoring,
    229–231
  dealing with hindsight bias, 231
  dealing with positive illusions, 224–229
  dealing with representativeness
    heuristic, 231–232
  dealing with strong emotions, 244–246
  decision-making process, 232–233
  decisions for future, 241–244
  desired information, 233–235
  irrelevant information, 233
  keeping client expectations realistic,
    230–231
  for other nonmonetary outcomes,
    219–221
  presentation of options, 235–238
  quest for information, 213–215
  quest for justice, 215–217
  quest for litigation, 221–222
  quest for reform, 217–219
  rapport as persuasion, 247
  sunk costs, 238–240
  using persuasion effectively, 247–251
  using third parties to convey bad news,
    228–229
  weighing benefits and risks, 227–328
Coverage, 361
Credibility
  of briefs, 360–361
  in complaints, 373–374
  in negotiation, 275
  source, 118–120
  of witness, 336
Critical stance, 412
Csikszentmihalyi, Mihaly, 451
Culture
  attribution and, 19
  communication and, 151–152
  counseling clients and, 249
  distributive justice in, 173
  gestures, 147

  objectives in negotiation and,
    258–259
  procedural justice in, 179
  recognizing differences, 191–193
Curse of compassion, 227
Curse of knowledge, 143

D

Daniel Kahneman, 68
Darley, John, 131
Darrow, Clarence, 117, 131
Dead rat salad, 373–374
Deadlines, 108, 283–284, 418–421
Deal or No Deal (TV Game Show), 95
Debiasing, 77–83
Debriefing, 347–348
Deceit, 276, 278
Decision making, 85–113
  anchoring in, 72
  approaches, 104–105
  deadlines, 108
  emotions and, 47, 97–100
  ethical, 392, 409
  evaluation of options, 88–97
  group, 108–111, 435–436
  implementation of decisions,
    111–112
  influence of financial incentives, 397
  information gathering, 87–88
  joint vs. separate evaluation, 106–108
  in negotiation, 288, 291–292
  nondecisions, 100–102
  procedural justice and, 178
  process in counseling clients,
    232–233
  reason giving, 103–104
  schemas in, 13
  selection vs. rejection, 105–106
  strategies, 85–87
  structure of, 102–108
  use of schemas in, 13–14
  in writing of briefs, 369
Decision regret, 99–100
Decision tree, 291
Delay-speedup asymmetry, 96
Demand letters, 378–379
Depositions
  asking questions in, 317–326
  conducting, 315–333
  debriefing client, 347–348
  defending, 346–347
  differences between conversations
    and, 334–336

disorder, 332–333
eliciting/facilitating disclosure, 165
emotions in, 331–333
introducing, 315–317
lying and evasion, 326–328
normalizing faulty memory, 340
preparing witness for, 333–346
scaring deponents, 329–331
storytelling, 325
trust-building introduction for neutral witness, 316
undermining detrimental deponent testimony, 328–329
video recordings, 348–349
Descriptive norms, 133
Devil's advocate, 17, 111, 225
Dewey, John, 16
Diener, Ed, 458
Dignity, 177, 179
Direct questioning, 208
Directive attorneys, 232
Disagreeable adjudicator, 79, 351
Disclosure
conflicts and, 398–399
eliciting/facilitating, 165–166, 189
Disclosure distortion, 399
Discovery and due diligence, 307–352
conducting and defending depositions, 314–349
deciding what information to seek for, 308–310
interviews in due diligence reviews, 349
planning for, 308
reviewing information obtained through, 349–351
written requests for information, 310–314
Dispositional attributions, 18
Dissonance, 20, 426
Distinction bias, 107
Distraction, 60
Distributive justice, 172–176, 216, 265
Distributive negotiation techniques, 253
Document requests
preparing, 310–311
responding to, 311–314
Documents, 201, 248, 342
Door-in-the-face technique, 128, 282
Dual-centric, 456
Duckworth, Angela, 424
Due diligence reviews, 349
Duncker task, 50–51

E
Eastman Kodak Company, 312
Eat What You Kill (Regan), 385, 403
Egocentric bias. *See* Self-serving bias
Egocentrically biased judgments, 70, 71
Elaboration likelihood model, 116
Electronic communication, 148–151, 435
Elimination by aspects, 86
Embarrassment, 54–55
Emotional contagion, 64
Emotional what-if analyses, 50, 241
Emotions, 45–66
addressing client, 194–198
affective forecasting, 97–99
appraisal and, 52–57
clues, 196
decision making and, 47
decision regret, 99–100
display of, 63–65
as facilitator of thought, 63
failure to regulate, 58
general effects of mood, 50–52
ignoring client, 195
illusion of transparency, 65
listening for, 162
managing, 57–61
in negotiation, 278–280, 285–287
noticing, 49
perceiving and understanding, 48–57
persuasion and, 117–118, 126
productivity and, 425
as source of information, 62
as source of motivation, 62
types of, 53–57
using, 62–65
of witness, 343–346
Endowment effect, 90–91
Equality, 172
Equity, 172
Erin Brockovich (Soderbergh), 247, 387
Ethics, 385–416
agency relationship, 395–400
bounded ethicality, 387–393
challenges of adversarial system and, 400–403
counseling clients and, 414–415
decision making and, 392, 409
ethical blind spots, 387–389
ethical fading, 391–393
group decision making and, 436
impressions and, 434
judicial recusal and, 387–389
in law practice, 393–409

Ethics, *continued*
   lawyers in groups and, 404–406
   learning from failures, 409–410
   making salient, 411–412
   responses to others' ethicality, 407–409
   rules and standards, 393–395
   situationist perspective, 394
   slippery slope and boiling frogs, 389–391
   solutions, 411–415
   tolls of law practice and, 403–404
Evasion, 326–328
Exclusion, 177–178
Expertise, 118
Explanatory style, 428–430
Exploitation, 177–178
External deadlines, 420
Extremeness aversion, 93

F
Face time, 433–434
Face-to-face communication, 149, 435
Facebook, 421, 422
Facher, Jerry, 171, 272, 331–332
Facts, 78, 364, 371–372
Fairness
   distributive justice and, 172–173, 176
   judgments of, 71
   memory and, 33–34, 42–43
   in negotiation, 269–270, 273
   perspective taking, 24
False confessions, 37–38
False consensus effect, 23
Fear, 55, 59
Fee negotiation, 294–295
Feedback, 50, 82, 427–428
Feinberg, Kenneth, 141, 142
First impressions, 433
First offers, 274
Fischhoff, Baruch, 158
Fisher, Roger, 263
Fixed mindset, 427
Fixed pie bias, 267
Fluency
   of communication, 164, 165
   eliciting/facilitating disclosure and, 165–166, 198–199
   in processing, 116–118
   in writing, 354
fMRI. *See* functional magnetic resonance imaging
Focalism, 98–99
Focusing illusion, 98–99

Forbes, Malcolm S., 425
Framing, 88–92, 268, 280, 379, 380–381
Franklin, Benjamin, 102, 103, 168, 223, 308, 418
Frenkel, Douglas, N., 300
Functional magnetic resonance imaging (fMRI), 157
Fundamental attribution error, 18
Future, decisions for, 241–244

G
Galton, Eric, 299
Gambler's fallacy, 75, 231–232
Garcetti v. Ceballos, 408
Garner, Bryan, 79, 357, 372–373
Gates, Bill, 321, 325, 326
Gellene, John, 385–386, 394, 401, 403, 409
Gender bias, 33
General Electric Company, 161
Genovese, Kitty, 132
Gestures, 147
Gilbert, Dan, 20, 452
Gingrich, Newt, 286
Giuliani, Rudolph, 326–327
Goals
   client quest for reform, 217–219
   grit and, 424
   implementation of decisions and, 111–112
   in negotiation, 264–270
   of punishment, 181–182
   recognizing differences, 191–193
   regulating emotions and, 58
   restoration of justice and, 182–184
   schemas and, 13
Godfather, The (Coppola), 126
Golann, Dwight, 195
Good Samaritan, 404
Gore, Albert, Jr. "Al", 337, 338
Griffin, Dale, 67
Grinders, 440
Griswold, Erwin, 115
Grit, 424
Group cohesion, 437
Group decision making, 108–111, 435–436
Groups, lawyers in, 404–407
Growth mindset, 427
Guidance for writers, 354–359
Guilt, 54–55, 198
Guilt-presumptive questions, 16
Guthrie, Chris, 72

H

Hand, Learned, 1
Happiness
  lawyer satisfaction and, 445–447
  magic eights, 457
  positive emotions and, 457–458
  social relationships, 454
  well-being and, 444–457
  work as calling, 451–453
  work-life balance, 454–457
Harr, Jonathan, 265, 272, 309, 317, 331, 436
Harris, Victor, 21–22
Hedonistic activities, 452
Helper's high, 453
Heuristic-systematic model, 116
Hickman v. Taylor, 350, 356
High-context communication, 152
High-context culture, 249
Hindsight, 33, 297
Hindsight bias, 75–77, 203, 231, 277, 427
Hindsight debiasing, 231
Hitchcock, Alfred, 182
Hollander-Blumoff, Rebecca, 291, 310
Holmes, Oliver Wendell, Jr., 171, 444
Holmes, Oliver Wendell, Sr., 31, 73, 161
Hot-hand phenomenon, 17
Houck, Steve, 321
How Judges Think (Posner), 388

I

Illusion of asymmetric insight, 24, 165
Illusion of consensus, 109–110, 436
Illusion of control, 69
Illusion of courage, 408
Illusion of objectivity, 103
Illusion of transparency, 65, 148, 406, 432
Illusory correlations, 18
Immune neglect, 99
Implementation intentions, 61, 111–112, 293, 420
Impressions
  first impressions, 433
  importance of face time, 433–434
  liking and mimicry, 434
  managing, 432–434
Inaccurate memories, 42–43
Inaction inertia, 94–95
Inattentional blindness, 8–9
Inattentional blindness blindness, 8
Incidental affect, 46
Indirect unethical actions, 399–400

Influence
  resistance, 138–139
  through identifying inconsistency, 249
Influence tactics
  bystander behavior, 132
  channel factors, 136–138
  consistency and commitment, 129–130
  liking, 130–131
  obedience to authority, 134–136
  reciprocity, 127–128
  scarcity, 129
  social proof, 131–132
  tension systems, 136–138
Information
  confirming accuracy of, 207–209
  conveying, 166–168
  desired, 233–235
  for discovery and due diligence, 308–310
  emotions as source of, 62
  gathering for decision making, 87–88
  gathering pre-interview, 188–189
  general effects of mood and, 50
  influence of stereotypes in processing, 13
  irrelevant, 233
  multiple channels, 357–358
  nonverbal communication as source of, 146
  order of arguments and, 123
  quest for, 213–215
  reviewing, 349–351
  use in group decision making, 109
  written requests for, 310–314
Ingratiation, 131
Inoculation, 124
Insight, illusion of asymmetric, 21–24
Integrative negotiation methods, 254
Internalized false confessions, 37–38
Internet, 150–151
Interpersonal communication, 141–170. *See also* Communication
Interpersonal ethics blind spot, 407
Interpersonal relationships, 438
Interpretation
  observation and, 11–17
  perception and, 7
Interrogatories
  preparing, 310–311
  responding to, 311–314

Interviews
    addressing emotions, 194–198
    assisting client recall, 202
    building trust, 158–159
    conducting, 190–191
    confirming accuracy, 207–209
    considering confirmation bias, 205
    conversational norms, 144–145
    due diligence reviews, 349
    establishing rapport, 159–161, 191
    gathering pre-interview information, 188–189
    introducing deposition, 315–317
    listening, 161–163
    perspective taking, 203–204
    preparing for client interview, 188–209
    procedure, 193
    questioning, 198–207
    questioning and listening, 193–194
    in rainmaking, 440
    recognizing differences, 191–193
    recordings of, 208
    remembering, 207–208
    setting stage for, 189–190
    setting the problem, 206
    in taking depositions, 323
    testing assumptions, 206
iPod, 422
Isab, 62
Isocrates, 118
Isolation effect, 99
iTunes, 220

J
Jamail, Joe, 333
Johnson, Lyndon B., 161
Johnson, Samuel, 31, 127
Joint evaluation, 106–108
Jones, Franklin P., 427
Jones, Paula, 313
Jones v. Clinton, 313, 375
Judgments
    accuracy of, 80–83, 427
    affect heuristic, 75
    anchoring, 71–72
    availability, 72–73
    averaging principle, 80–81
    debiasing, 77–83
    heuristics, 77
    hindsight bias, 76
    joint vs. separate evaluation, 106–108, 176
    multiple opinions, 81–82
    positive illusions, 68–71
    representativeness, 73–75
    of responsibility, 17–20
    shortcuts, 67–84
    source credibility and, 119
    using facts in, 78
Judicial recusal, 388
Justice, 171–185
    distributive, 172–176
    objectives in negotiation and, 258, 269–270
    procedural, 176–180
    quest for, 215–218
    reestablishment of, 180–184
    restoration of, 182–184
    retribution, 181–182

K
Kahneman, Daniel, 68, 79, 88, 99, 254, 362, 364
Korobkin, Russell, 79, 296
Krieger, Lawrence, 452
Kurosawa, Akira, 29

L
Language. *See also* Writing
    euphemisms, 392
    legal, 163–165, 250, 355–356, 370–371, 373
    positive, 382
Lao-Tzu, 426
Last ten percent, 89–90
Latané, Bibb, 131
Lawyer-client relationship
    conducting depositions and, 315–333
    counseling clients, 211–252
    giving advice, 168
    interviewing clients, 188–209
    listening, 161–163
    in negotiation, 254–260
    rapport, 159–161, 191, 210
Lawyer satisfaction, 445–447
Lawyers
    attorney self-interest, 255
    avoiding talking like, 163–165
    communication technology and, 148
Internet and, 150–151
Lawyers in the Dock (Abel), 398
Lawyer's interests, 395–298
Lay rationalism, 104
Leading questions, 41
Lean forms of communication, 149
Learning, 166–168, 250, 338–339

Legal communication
  briefs, 359–371
  complaints, 371–374
  contracts, 380–382
  counseling clients and, 250
  fluency of communication and, 163–165
  letters, 374–380
  taking depositions and, 317–326
Legally Blonde (Luketic), 190
Letters
  advice or opinion letters, 376–377
  to clients, 374–378
  negotiation-related letters, 376
  to others, 378–380
  retainer letters, 374–376
  writing, 374–380
Levit, Nancy, 453, 454
Lewin, Kurt, 136, 137
Libby, I. Lewis "Scooter," 326
Lies of omission, 154
Liking, 130–131, 434
Lincoln, Abraham, 168, 255
Linder, Doug, 453, 454
Listening, 161–163, 179, 323
Litigation, 216, 218, 221–222, 314
Live Happy, 448
Loftus, Elizabeth F., 36
Long-term memory, 31
Lopez, Gerald, P., 362
Loss averse, 89
Louima, Abner, 29
Low-balling approach, 283
Low-context communication, 152
Low-context culture, 249
Luban, David, 406, 411
Lubet, Steven, 155, 314
Lying, 153–157, 207–209, 326–328
Lyubomirsky, Sonja, 57, 447

M
Magic eights, 458
Magnitude gap, 181
Maister, David H., 214
Malhotra, Deepak, 284
Malpractice, 146
Mandela, Nelson, 263
Manner of speaking, 119–120
Margines, Charles, 429
Marshall, John, 249
Marshall, Thurgood, 440
McCartney, Paul, 261
McDonald's Corporation, 221, 375–376
McVeigh, Timothy, 34
Meaningful activities, 452
Mediation
  as benefit for clients, 301–304
  nature of, 300
  in negotiation, 276
  preparing for, 303
  procedural justice and, 298
  psychological challenges posed by, 300–304
  psychological opportunities offered by, 295–300
Memory, 29–43
  accurate vs. inaccurate, 42–43, 326
  elicitation of, 39–42
  fallibility of, 35–36
  influence of, 323
  internalized false confessions, 37–38
  interview questioning and, 200–201
  lapses, 321–322
  memorable information and, 39
  misperceptions of, 38–39
  naïve realism and, 38
  negotiation and, 260, 278
  normalizing faulty, 340
  preconceptions of, 226
  source memory and Oklahoma City Bombing, 34
  vagaries of, 32
  of witness, 339–342
  workings of, 30–38
Menkel-Meadow, Carrie J., 295
Mentoring, 438–440
Message characteristics, 120–125
Microsoft Corporation, 321, 325
Milbank, Tweed, Hadley & McCloy, 385–386
Milgram shock experiments, 135–136, 389, 399, 404, 408
Milgram, Stanley, 135
Mimicry, 159–161, 434
Minders, 440
Mindset, 427
Mirror test, 413
Mistakes, 425–428
Mnookin, Robert, 261
Money
  fee negotiation, 294–295
  objectives in negotiation and, 259
  time value of, 95–96
Moneyball: The Art of Winning an Unfair Game (Lewis), 73
Mood congruency effect, 50

Moods. *See also* Emotions
　defined, 48
　general effects of, 50–52
　in negotiation, 285–287
Moral amnesia, 410
Moral disengagement, 390–393
Motivated blindness, 408
Motivation
　emotions as source of, 62
　influence and, 138
　mentoring and lay theories of, 439
Muller v. Oregon, 436
Multiple channels, 167, 357–358
Multitasking, 10, 421–423

N
Naïve cynicism, 71
Naïve realism, 21, 38, 212
Need, 172
Negative emotions/moods, 51–52, 457
Negotiation
　apologies in, 268, 293
　approaches to, 254
　assessing wants of client, 256–260
　assessing wants of other side, 260–264
　building relationships, 275–276
　charitable contribution in lieu of punitive damages, 268
　construction of initial proposals, 256–275
　conveying information, 278–280
　conveying offer to client, 287–288
　counterpart, 260–261
　dealing with emotion, 285–287
　devising proposal, 264–270
　dynamics of, 275–287
　evaluation of offer, 288–295
　fee, 294–295
　impediments to settlement, 262
　interpreting counterparts' behavior, 276–278
　lawyers, liking, and, 131
　letters in, 378–379
　perspective taking, 261
　persuading and eliciting concessions, 281–285
　presentation of options, 280–281
　presenting proposal, 270–275
　process, 266
　psychologically expanded model of, 254–256
　reciprocity aspect of persuasion and, 127–128
　requests for information as form of, 309
　response to a counterpart's proposal, 287–295
　underlying concerns, 263–264
Negotiation-related letters, 376
Neuroimaging, 156–157
Neutrality, 177
Nondecisions, 100–102
Nonleading questions, 201
Nonmonetary outcomes, 219–221, 259–260
Nonverbal behavior, 148
Nonverbal communication, 49, 145–148, 149–150, 260
Norms
　conversational, 144–145, 317, 334–336
　descriptive, 133
　reciprocity, 127

O
Obama, Barack, 35, 430, 432
Obedience to authority, 134–136
Objectivity, illusion of, 103
Observation
　biased assimilation, 14–16
　concept accessibility, 11
　confirmation bias, 14–16
　interpretation and, 11–17
　priming, 11
　schemas, scripts, and stereotypes, 12–14
O'Connor, Sandra Day, 33, 451
Offer letters, 378–379
Omission bias, 101, 409
One-sided arguments, 124
Open-ended questions, 39, 199, 318
Opinion letters, 376–377
Opinions, 80–83
Optimistic explanatory style, 428–430
Options
　client, 235–238, 240–241
　evaluation of, 88–97
Organization, 355
Outcome bias, 20, 76, 392, 425
Outside perspective, 79
Overall satisfaction, 254

P
Paralysis by analysis, 432
Partnership documents, 382
Pausing the choke, 431
Penalty aversion, 91
Peppet, Scott R., 261

Perception
    causal attribution and, 17–20
    of distributive justice, 172–176
    effects of persuasion, 126
    false consensus effect of, 23
    interpretation and, 7
    judgments of responsibility and, 17–20
    limits of attention, 8–10
    naïve realism and, 21–24
    observation and interpretation, 11–17
    perspective taking, 24–26
    preconceptions of, 224
Peripheral processing, 116, 117, 139
Personal space, 166
Perspective taking
    in communication, 143–144
    defined, 24–26
    in discovery and due diligence, 311
    in interviews, 203–204
    in negotiation, 261, 278
    in rainmaking, 441
Persuasion
    effective use of, 247–251
    effects of emotion on, 117–118
    elaboration likelihood model, 116
    heuristic-systematic model, 116
    influence tactics, 126–138
    mediation and, 299
    message characteristics, 120–125
    in negotiation, 281–285
    paths to, 116–125
    peripheral processing and, 139
    in rainmaking, 440
    rapport as, 247
    resistance, 138–139
    source credibility, 118–120
    of witness, 336
Pessimistic explanatory style, 428–430
Planning, 413–414
Planning fallacy, 68, 308, 389, 418–419
Pluralistic ignorance, 109–110, 133, 406, 410, 436
Polygraph testing, 156–157
Positive emotions/moods, 56–57, 457–458
Positive illusions, 68–71, 224–229
Positive language, 382
Positive moods, 50, 285
Posner, Richard A., 388
Postdeposition debriefing, 347–348
Pragmatic self, 389
Precommitment, 414
Predictions, 97–99, 425
Preference reversals, 106

Preferences, 104
Pre-interview information gathering, 188–189
Pressure, 430–432
Prevention focus, 105, 120
Price-Waterhouse v. Hopkins, 370
Primacy effect, 123
Priming, 11
Procrastination, 101, 418–419
Production blocking, 109
Productivity
    collaboration, 432–444
    deadlines and, 418–421
    emotions and, 423
    explanatory style, 428–430
    law firms and time management, 424
    mistakes, 425–428
    multitasking and, 421–423
    under pressure, 430–432
    success and, 417–444
    time management, 417–424
    time records, 423–424
Promotion focus, 105, 120
Prospect theory, 88, 89
Psychological influence, 126
Psychological science, trial and error vs., 2
Punishment, 181–182
Punitive damages, 268
Purposeful Planning Institute, 381–382

Q
Qualcomm Inc., 312
Questions
    closed, 199
    direct, 208
    guilt-presumptive, 16
    leading, 41
    nonleading, 201
    open-ended, 39–41, 199

R
Race, 33, 103
Rachlinski, Jeff, 72
Rapport
    in client interview, 191, 209
    deceit and, 276
    in deposition, 316
    establishing, 159–161
    impressions and, 434
    with negotiation counterpart, 260–261, 276
    with potential client, 441

Reactive devaluation, 96–97, 274–275, 284
Reagan, Ronald, 208, 285
Reason giving, 103–104
Recall, 31, 202
Recency effect, 123
Reciprocity, 127–128, 255
Reciprocity norm, 127, 442
Reform, 218–219
Regan, Milton, 385
Regret, 99–100, 241
Reilly, Peter, 37
Rejection, 105–106
Rejection-then-retreat technique, 128
Relationships. *See also* Lawyer-client relationship
 building, 443
 interpersonal, 438
 maintaining client, 443–444
 social, 453–454
Reminiscence, 203
Representativeness, 73–75, 289
Representativeness heuristic, 74–75, 231–232
Respect, 177, 179
Responsibility, judgments of, 17–20
Retainer letters, 374–376
Retribution, 181–182
Retributive justice, 181, 216
Retrieval-induced forgetting phenomenon, 40
Rhode, Deborah, 396, 406
Rich forms of communication, 149
Risk averse, 88
Risk seeking, 88
Risk tolerance, 269
Riskin, Leonard L., 285, 295
Roberts, John, 430, 432
Rogers, Will, 92, 326
Root, Elihu, 238
Roper v. Simmons, 365–366
Rosa v. Park West Bank & Trust Co., 370
Rumination, 60

S

Sacco, Nicola, 323–324
Sadness, 55–56
Saks, Michael, 117
Sarbanes-Oxley Act, 393
Satisfaction
 first offers and, 274
 lawyer, 445–447
 overall, 254
Satisficing, 86, 457

Scalia, Antonin G., 21, 79, 125, 370–371, 388
Scarcity, 129, 283
Schelling, Thomas, 279
Schemas, 12–14, 33, 203, 362, 363
Schultz, Marjorie, 5
Schulz, Kathryn, 428
Scott v. Harris, 21–22
Scripts, 12–14, 203, 363, 391
Second-chance meetings, 111
Selection, 105–106
Self-care, 449
Self-control, 111,
Self-critical thoughts, countering, 429
Self-interest, 255–256
Self-monitoring, 144
Self-regulation, 57–58, 324
Self-serving bias, 71, 225, 427
Seligman, Martin, 450
Separate evaluation, 106–108
September 11th Victim Compensation Fund, 141, 171, 213
Setting the problem, 206
Settlement offers
 conveying to client, 287–288
 evaluation of, 288–295
Shame, 54–55
Shapiro, Daniel, 263
Sign effect, 96
Signature strengths, 450
Silence, 279, 318
Simons, Daniel, 2, 8, 30
Simpson, O.J., 31
Sisyphean tasks, 451
Situational attribution, 19
Situationist perspective, 394
Slippery slope, 389–391
Smith, Abbe, 226, 294
Social norms, 284
Social proof, 131–132
Social relationships, 454
Source credibility, 118–120
Source monitoring, 34
Speaking, manner of, 119–120
Spence, Gerry, 255, 361
Stanchi, Kathryn, 369–370
Standards, 393–395
Status quo bias, 91, 101, 380–381
Stereotypes
 of African Americans, 14
 client assumptions, 203
 countering, 14
 defined, 12–14

lying, 153–154
memory and, 33
of women, 14, 370
Stern, Gerald, 339, 340
Stevens, John P., 21
Stories, 371–372
Storytelling, 325, 342, 361
Streep, Meryl, 195
Stress, 430–431
Strong emotions, 59
Suggestible, 34
Sunk costs, 92, 238–240, 284, 297, 308
Suppression, 59–60
Surrogation strategy, 99, 448
Systematic processing, 116, 138

T

Taboo trade-off, 173
Tavris, Carol, 426
Teaching, 166–168, 249–250
Television writing, reciprocity and, 128
Temporal synchrony bias, 149
Tension systems, 136–138
Tessmer, John, 365–366
That's-not-all technique, 128
Thompson, Leigh, 267, 287
Thomson, David I. C., 307
Thought, emotions as a facilitator of, 62–63
Thurber, James, 32
TIAA-CREF, 179
Time affluence, 457
Time, choice and, 95–96
Time management, 417–424
  deadlines, 418–421
  law firms and, 424
  planning fallacy, 418–419
  procrastination, 418–419
Time records, 423–424
"Tip of the tongue" phenomenon, 39
Transparency, illusion of, 65, 148, 406, 432
Trial and error, psychological science vs., 2
Trial consultants, 333–334
Trust
  building, 158–159
  deposition, 316
  display of anger and, 64
  maintaining client relationships, 443–444
  with potential client, 441
Trusted Advisor, The (Maister, Green & Galford), 245

Trustworthiness, 177
Truth bias, 156
Tuning, 278
Tversky, Amos, 68, 88, 254, 357, 362
Twain, Mark, 61, 182, 341
Tweets, 355
Twitter, 355
Two-sided arguments, 124
Tyler, Tom, 178, 389

U

United States v. Ottati & Goss Inc., 89

V

Values, 275–277, 451–454. *See also* Ethics
Video recordings, 209, 337, 348–349
Vilardo, Lawrence J., 194
Visual aids, 249–250
Vocal quality, emotions and, 65
Voice, 177–178

W

WalMart Stores, Inc., 277
Warhol, Andy, 273
Warm drinks, 159, 191
Warren, Earl, 387
Washington State Physicians Insurance Exchange & Ass'n v. Fisons Corp., 313
Webster, Daniel, 354
Weinstein, Ian, 226
Weitzman, Lenore, 381
Welch, Jack, 161
Well-being
  defined, 444–445
  happiness and, 448–459
  job tasks and, 451–454
  positive emotions and, 457–458
  social relationships, 454
  work as calling, 451–454
  work-life balance, 454–457
Welsh, Nancy A., 301
Winick, Bruce, 221
Winter, Steven L., 363
Wisdom of crowds, 80
Witnesses
  communication and, 338
  emotions of, 343–346
  good impressions of, 336–339
  memory of, 338–340
  preparation, 338–339
  preparing for depositions, 333–346
  storytelling, 342

Witnesses, *continued*
  trust-building deposition introduction for neutral, 316
  videotaping, 337
Wolfe, Mark, 229
Wolfe, Tom, 420
Women, stereotypes of, 13, 370
Wonderful O, The (Thurber), 32
Wood, James, 183
Word choice
  in briefs, 370–371
  in complaints, 373
  in writing, 357–356
Work product doctrine, 356

Writing, 353–383
  audience perspective, 358–359
  briefs, 359–371
  clarity, 353–358
  complaints, 371–374
  contracts, 302–382
  guidance for writers, 354–359
  letters, 374–380

Z

Zedek, Sheldon, 5